Historians
Sallust
Tacitus & Pliny
Livy
Pollio – history, civil war—
ones extract.

Poets:
Martial
Juvenal
Persius –

$3.50

Cato – Early Roman Empire – 43–172
Cq's & Customers 1–49
Abbott – Roman Political Institutions 37–45

ALLYN AND BACON'S COLLEGE LATIN SERIES

UNDER THE GENERAL EDITORSHIP OF

CHARLES E. BENNETT AND JOHN C. ROLFE

Q. HORATI FLACCI

SERMONES ET EPISTULAE

WITH INTRODUCTION AND NOTES BY

JOHN CAREW ROLFE

PROFESSOR OF LATIN IN THE UNIVERSITY OF PENNSYLVANIA

PITTSBURGH
LATIN MASS
COMMUNITY

ALLYN AND BACON

BOSTON   NEW YORK   CHICAGO
ATLANTA   SAN FRANCISCO   DALLAS

TAP

Norwood Press
J. S. Cushing & Co. — Berwick & Smith
Norwood Mass. U.S.A.

PREFACE.

In the preparation of this edition the needs of college students have steadily been kept in view, and I have endeavored not to lose sight of the fact that Horace is usually read in the earlier years of the college course. Therefore, while I have made full use of the available critical and epexegetical material, the commentary is usually brief and somewhat dogmatic, rarely offering more than one interpretation of the many disputed passages. The discussion of variant readings is also excluded.

I have consulted no American edition, for obvious reasons; but as I am more or less familiar with all of them, it is difficult to say how much I may be indebted to them indirectly. The same statement applies to the English editions, except that I have occasionally consulted Palmer and Wilkins. I have freely used the standard German commentaries, especially that of Kiessling.

I am under obligation to my friend, Professor Charles E. Bennett, for permission to use a part of his Introduction (§§ 1–14, and the greater part of his " General Character of Latin Poetry "), as well as for many helpful suggestions. Dr. Clarence L. Meader, of the University of Michigan, has read all the proofs, and my father has given me the benefit of his criticism of the Outlines and the Introduction.

JOHN CAREW ROLFE.

Ann Arbor, Michigan,
August, 1901.

v

INTRODUCTION TO THE SATIRES.

I.

HORACE'S LIFE.

1. Birth and Early Life. — Quintus Horatius Flaccus was born at the little town of Venusia, on the borders of Apulia and Lucania, December 8, 65 B.C. His father was a freedman, who seems to have been a collector of taxes. In this business he saved some money, and, dissatisfied with the advantages offered by the school at Venusia, took the young Horace to Rome for his early education. This plan evidently involved no little personal and financial sacrifice on the father's part — a sacrifice appreciated to the full by Horace, if not at the time, at least in his later life. In a touching passage almost unique in ancient literature (*Sat.* i. 6. 70 ff.), the poet tells us of the father's devotion at this period. Ambitious only for his son's mental and moral improvement, without a thought of the larger material prizes of life, he not only provided Horace with the best instruction the capital afforded, but watched with anxious care over the boy's moral training as well, even accompanying him to school and back again to his lodgings. One of Horace's teachers at this period was Orbilius, who is referred to in *Epist.* ii. 1. 70 as a severe disciplinarian (*plagosum*). Under Orbilius, Horace apparently pursued the grammatical studies which formed the staple of the literary training of the day. Later, he probably devoted attention to the more advanced rhetorical training; under what teacher is unknown.

2. Athens. — In his nineteenth year or thereabouts (*i.e.* about 46 B.C.), Horace went to Athens to add the finishing touches to his education by the study of philosophy, which still enjoyed a flourishing existence and was represented by several schools, — the Stoic, Epicurean, Peripatetic, and Academic. The Greek poets also engaged his attention largely. Among his friends at this time may be mentioned the young Cicero, son of the orator, and M. Valerius Messalla, who, with many other young Romans, were residing at Athens for the purpose of study.

3. Brutus and Philippi. — After some two years, the ' still air of delightful studies' was rudely agitated for Horace by political events. Caesar had been assassinated in March of 44 B.C., and, in September of that year, Brutus arrived in Athens, burning with the spirit of republicanism. Horace was easily induced to join his standard, and, though without previous military training or experience, received the important position of *tribunus militum* in Brutus's army. The battle of Philippi (November, 42 B.C.) sounded the death-knell of republican hopes, and left Horace in bad case. His excellent father had died, and the scant patrimony which would have descended to the poet had been confiscated by Octavian in consequence of the son's support of Brutus and Cassius.

4. Return to Rome. Beginning of Career as Man of Letters. Maecenas. The Sabine Farm. — Taking advantage of the general amnesty granted by Octavian, Horace returned to Rome in 41 B.C. and there secured a position as quaestor's clerk (*scriba*), devoting his intervals of leisure to composition in verse. He soon formed a warm friendship with Virgil, then just beginning his career as poet, and with

Varius; through their influence he was admitted (39 B.C.) to the intimacy and friendship of Maecenas, the confidential adviser of Octavian, and a generous patron of literature. About six years later (probably 33 B.C.), he received from Maecenas the Sabine Farm, situated some thirty miles to the northeast of Rome, in the valley of the Digentia, a small stream flowing into the Anio. This estate was not merely adequate for his support, enabling him to devote his entire energy to study and poetry, but was an unfailing source of happiness as well; Horace never wearies of singing its praises.

5. **Horace's Other Friendships.** — Horace's friendship with Maecenas, together with his own admirable social qualities and poetic gifts, won him an easy entrance into the best Roman society. His *Odes* bear eloquent testimony to his friendship with nearly all the eminent Romans of his time. Among these were: Agrippa, Octavian's trusted general, and later his son-in-law; Messalla, the friend of Horace's Athenian student days, and later one of the foremost orators of the age; Pollio, distinguished alike in the fields of letters, oratory, and arms. The poets Virgil and Varius have already been mentioned. Other literary friends were: Quintilius Varus, Valgius, Plotius, Aristius Fuscus, and Tibullus.

6. **Relations with Augustus.** — With the Emperor, Horace's relations were intimate and cordial. Though he had fought with conviction under Brutus and Cassius at Philippi, yet he possessed too much sense and patriotism to be capable of ignoring the splendid promises of stability and good government held out by the new régime inaugurated by Augustus. In sincere and loyal devotion to his sovereign, he not merely accepted the new order, but lent the best efforts of his verse to glorifying and strengthening it.

In the life of Horace attributed to Suetonius, we learn
that Augustus offered the poet the position of private secretary. Horace, with dignified independence, declined the
offer, a step that seems to have made no difference, however, in the cordial friendship with which Augustus continued to honor him.

He remained true to the Muse till his death, November
27, 8 B.C., a few days before the completion of his fifty-
seventh year, and but a few weeks after the death of his
patron and friend, Maecenas.

II.

HORACE'S WORKS.

7. The Satires. — Horace's first published work was Book I.
of the *Satires*, which appeared in 35 B.C. Five years later,
Book II. was published. Though conventionally called
'Satires,' and alluded to by Horace himself as *satirae*, these
were entitled by him *Sermones*, as being talks, so to speak,
couched in the familiar language of everyday life. They
represent a type of literature whose early beginnings are
obscure, but which is clearly an indigenous Roman product
and not an imitation of Greek models, as is the case with
almost every other type of Latin poetry. Horace was not
the first representative of this kind of writing among the
Romans. Ennius, Lucilius, and Varro had been his predecessors in the same field. Of these three, Lucilius beyond
question exercised the greatest influence upon the poet. In
Horace's hands, satire consists in the main of urbane comment upon the vices and foibles of the day, coupled with
amusing incidents of personal experience and good-natured
raillery at the defects of the prevailing philosophical systems,
of which he was always an earnest and intelligent student.
Besides this we have several pieces dealing directly with

the scope and function of satire as a species of literary composition.

8. The Epodes. — These were published in 29 B.C. and mark the transition from the *Satires* to the *Odes*. They resemble the *Satires* in their frequent polemic character, the *Odes* in the lyric form in which they are cast. Though published after the two books of the *Satires*, several of them apparently represent the earliest of Horace's efforts in verse that have been preserved.

9. The Odes and Carmen Saeculare. — Books I.–III. of the *Odes* were published in 23 B.C., when Horace was forty-two years old. Many of them had unquestionably been written several years before, some apparently as early as 32 B.C. These *Odes* at once raised Horace to the front rank of Roman poets, and assured his permanent fame. Six years later (17 B.C.), he was the natural choice of Augustus for the composition of the *Carmen Saeculare* to be sung at the saecular celebration held in that year. In 13 B.C. appeared Book IV. of the *Odes*. Though containing some of the poet's best work, this last book nevertheless bears certain traces of perfunctoriness. The Suetonian life of Horace records that it was written at the express request of the Emperor — a statement borne out by the lack of spontaneity characteristic of some of the poems.

10. The Epistles and Ars Poetica. — There are two books of *Epistles*. Book I. was published in 20 B.C., Book II. probably in 14 B.C. Of the epistles contained in Book I., some are genuine letters such as friend might write to friend; others are simply disquisitions in verse form on questions of life, letters, or philosophy. Book II. consists of but two epistles, one to Julius Florus, the other to Augustus. Both these pieces deal with questions of literary criticism and poetic composition.

The *Ars Poetica*, as it is conventionally designated, is an essay on the art of poetic composition — chiefly the drama. It is addressed to a certain Piso and his two sons, and Horace probably entitled it simply *Epistula ad Pisones*. The date of this composition is uncertain; but as it is one of the ripest, so it is probably one of the latest, if not the very latest, of all his extant writings. It is often printed as the third epistle of Book II.

11. Chronological Table of Horace's Works: —

35 B.C.	Satires, Book I.
30 B.C.	Satires, Book II.
29 B.C.	The Epodes.
23 B.C.	The Odes, Books I.–III.
20 B.C.	The Epistles, Book I.
17 B.C.	The Carmen Saeculare.
14 B.C.	The Epistles, Book II.
13 B.C.	The Odes, Book IV.
9 B.C. (?)	The Ars Poetica.

III.

MANUSCRIPTS, SCHOLIA, EDITIONS.

12. Manuscripts. — There are some two hundred and fifty manuscripts of Horace's works. No one of these is older than the eighth century, and most belong to the eleventh century and later. Among the most important manuscripts may be mentioned: —

V. Blandinius Vetustissimus. This manuscript, which once belonged to the Abbaye de St. Pierre on Mont Blandin (the modern Blankenberg), is now lost. It was destroyed by fire, together with the abbey, in 1566. But Cruquius (Jacques de Crusque), professor at Bruges, had previously examined it with care, and cites its readings with great frequency in his edition of 1577. Some critics have challenged the very existence of this manuscript, and have charged that Cruquius's citations of its alleged readings are forgeries. But while Cruquius is often guilty of carelessness and gross blunders, it is improbable that he was guilty of dishonesty, and most Horatian critics to-day recognize that *V* was a real manuscript, and that its readings as noted by Cruquius are of value.

B. Bernensis, 363, in the municipal library at Berne, Switzerland. This belongs to the ninth century, and has recently been published in an admirable photographic facsimile.

R. Sueco-Vaticanus, No. 1703, formerly the property of Queen Christina of Sweden, and now in the Vatican. This was written in the eighth century and, according to Keller, is the oldest of our extant manuscripts of Horace.

Keller attaches the greatest weight to these last two manuscripts, *B* and *R,* and holds that in nine cases out of ten their agreement points to the reading of the archetype of all our extant manuscripts.

No convincing classification of Horatian manuscripts has yet been made, and the great difficulties of the problem render extremely doubtful the eventual success of any such attempt.

13. Scholia. — Scholia are explanatory notes on the ancient writers. Sometimes these form separate works of elaborate scope; at other times they consist simply of additions made by copyists to the manuscripts themselves. Our Horatian scholia comprise the following: —

PORPHYRIO, a scholiast who lived probably in the early part of the third century A.D. and has left us an extensive commentary on all of Horace's writings.

PSEUDO-ACRON. This collection bears the name of Helenius Acron, who belonged perhaps in the third century of our era; but these scholia are not the work of Acron. His name apparently became attached to them only in late mediaeval times, as a result of the tradition that Acron was the author of certain scholia on Horace. These scholia of the pseudo-Acron are not even the work of a single hand, but are manifestly gathered from several sources.

COMMENTATOR CRUQUIANUS. This is a collective name given to the scholia gathered by the Cruquius already mentioned, from several manuscripts. They are relatively unimportant.

14. Editions. — Only a few of the most important editions are here given.

TEXTUAL.

Richard Bentley, 1711, and often reprinted.

Keller and Holder. Editio major. Leipzig. 1864–1870.

Keller and Holder. Editio minor. Leipzig. 1878.

Keller and Holder. Iterum recensuit Otto Keller. Vol. I.
    (*Odes, Epodes,* and *Carmen Saeculare*). Leipzig. 1899.
    Vol. II. (*Satires* and *Epistles*) has not yet appeared.

Otto Keller, *Epilegomena zu Horaz,* Leipzig. 1879–1880.
    An exhaustive presentation of variant readings, with discussion.

EXPLANATORY.

COMPLETE EDITIONS.

Orelli, Editio Quarta Major, Curaverunt Hirschfelder et
    Mewes. Berlin. 1886, 1892. With complete word index.

A. Kiessling. Berlin. 2d edition. 1890–1898. Vol. I.
    (*Odes* and *Epodes*) is now in 3d edition. 1898.

H. Schütz. Berlin. 1880–1883. Vol. I. (*Odes* and *Epodes*)
    is now in 3d edition. 1889.

Wickham. Oxford. Clarendon Press. *Odes* and *Epodes*, 3d edition. 1896. *Satires* and *Epistles*, 1891.

Page, Palmer, and Wilkins. London and New York. **1896.**

EDITIONS OF ODES AND EPODES.

K. K. Küster. Paderborn. 1890.

L. Müller. Leipzig. 1900.

EDITIONS OF SATIRES AND EPISTLES.

G. T. A. Krüger. Leipzig. 14th edition. **1898, 1901.**

L. Müller. Leipzig. 1891, 1893.

P. Lejoy. Paris. 1911.

IV.

THE DEVELOPMENT OF ROMAN SATIRE.

A. THE DRAMATIC SATURA.

15. The derivation of the adjective *satur* has not been satisfactorily explained. It is the only adjective in *-ur* in the Latin language which belongs to the *o*-declension, a fact which was observed and commented on by the native grammarians.[1] Its early occurrence in the sense of 'full' makes it improbable that it is a borrowed word, from the Greek σάτυροι. It is used with that meaning, for instance, by Plautus, *Men.* 927, *ubi satur sum, nulla crepitant: quando esurio, tum crepant; cf.* Horace, *Serm.* i. 1. 119, *cedat uti conviva satur.* In a metaphorical sense, as applied to the mind, the word is early and frequent, occurring, for example, in Plaut. *Poen.* prol. 8, *qui non edistis, saturi fite fabulis.* In post-classical Latin the adjective gradually went out of use, doubtless on account of its isolated grammatical form. *Satiatus* (It. *sazio*) and *satullus* (It. *estollo;* Fr. *soûl*) seem to have taken its place.

---

[1] *E.g.* Charisius in Keil's *Gramm. Lat.* I. 183. 7.

The original, and classical, orthography was *satura*. Besides this we find *satira* and *satyra*. The former was very
likely due to false analogy with words like *maxumus : maximus; optumus : optimus;* the latter to a fancied connection
with the Greek σάτυροι.

The transition to the meaning 'mixed' is found in the
expression *per saturam*, found, for example, in Sallust, *Jug.*
29. 5, *dein postero die quasi per saturam sententiis exquisitis,
in deditionem accipitur*.   Here we perhaps have ellipsis of
legem, although the often quoted *lex satura* and *lanx satura*
are not found in the literature, but rest only on the authority
of the grammarians.

16. The noun *satura (sc. fabula)* is applied by Livy, vii.
2. 4 ff. to an early form of the native Italian drama.   According to his very unsatisfactory account, the dramatic
satura formed a transition from the rude Fescennine verses
to the Graeco-Roman comedy of Livius Andronicus.   The
aetiological character of Livy's narrative is generally recognized, and some scholars [1] have gone so far as to deny the
existence of a dramatic *satura*, believing that it was invented
as a parallel to the Greek satyr-drama or to the Old Comedy.
This view has not been generally accepted, and the non-
existence of a dramatic *satura* cannot be regarded as proved.[2]

Concerning the meaning of *satura*, as applied to the drama,
opinions differ widely.   Mommsen [3] regards it as signifying
'the mask of the full men,' while Ribbeck [4] assumes that

---

[1] See Hendrickson, *The Dramatic Satura and the Old Comedy at
Rome*, and *A pre-Varronian Chapter of Roman Literary History,
Amer. Jour. of Phil.* xv. (1895), pp. 4 ff., and xix. (1898), 285 ff.

[2] See especially Schanz, *Geschichte der römischen Litteratur*, I²,
p. 19 ; Pease, article *Satira* in Harper's *Dict. of Class. Lit. and
Antiquities.*

[3] *Röm. Geschichte*, I⁶, p. 28.

[4] *Geschichte der römischen Dichtung*, I², p. 9.

the word has the sense of the Greek σάτυροι and refers to the dress of the actors, who he believes were clad in goat-skins. It seems simplest to regard the word as meaning 'a medley.' This view establishes a connection between the dramatic and the literary *satura,* and has a parallel in French *farce* (= *farsa*) and in Juvenal's lines,[1] —

> Quidquid agunt homines, votum, timor, ira, voluptas,
> Gaudia, discursus, nostri *farrago* libelli est.

B. The Literary Satura.

1. *The School of Ennius.*

17. When the dramatic *satura* gave place to the Graeco-Roman comedy, it seems to have survived as a literary form. The same thing was true of the *versus Fescennini,* which appear in the classical period in the *epithalamia,* in the songs of the soldiers during the triumphal processions, and the like. In its earliest form it seems to have been a medley of prose and of verse in various metres, in which a variety of subjects were briefly treated. The earliest representative of this form of composition is said to have been **Cn. Naevius** (269–204 B.C.) of Campania, the well-known dramatic and epic poet. It is, however, very probable that the *satura* of Naevius, to which Festus refers, was dramatic.

18. The first writer who is known to have published *saturae* is **Quintus Ennius** (239–169 B.C.) of Rudiae in Calabria,[2] 'the father of Roman poetry,' from whose work a number of fragments have been preserved. Quintilian, ix. 2. 26, tells us that they consisted, in part at least, of dialogue: *ut Mortem ac Vitam, quas contendentes in satura tradit Ennius.* They seem to have been wholly in verse and

---

[1] I. 86.

[2] Porphyrio, on Hor. *Serm.* i. 10. 46, *Ennius qui quattuor libros saturarum reliquit.*

to have been composed in various metres.   No prose frag·
ments can with certainty be attributed to the elder Ennius.

To what extent Ennius was indebted to Greek originals
is a matter of dispute.   If we take into account the well-
known statement of Quintilian[1] and the case of Varro,[2] it
seems probable that the form was original with Ennius,
and that it was adapted from the dramatic *satura*, although
in his subject-matter he undoubtedly followed Greek sources.
It is perhaps noteworthy that the early writers of satire, as
well as those to whom such works are attributed, were also
dramatic poets.

The satires of Ennius also resembled those of Horace, in
that he recorded his personal experiences and feelings,
and made free use of the Aesopian fables.[3]

Saturae are attributed by Diomedes[4] and by Porphyrio[5]
to the nephew of Ennius, the tragic poet and painter,
M. Pacuvius (220–132 B.C.) of Brundisium, but it is possible that his *saturae*, like those of Naevius, were dramatic.[6]

19. The Menippean satires of **M. Terentius Varro** (116–
28 B.C.) of Reate belong to the school of Ennius, so far as
their form is concerned.   In a medley of prose and verse, the
latter representing many different metres, he describes and
comments on familiar events of everyday life.   The collection consisted of one hundred and fifty books, and its nature
is indicated by some of the titles of the various topics which
have come down to us : *Cave canem; Nescis quid vesper serus
vehat; Cras credo, hodie nihil; Bimarcus; Marcopolis, etc.*

The titles, as well as the statement of Cicero in *Acad.
Post.* ii. 8, lead to the inference that, while Varro modelled
his work in general on the Σπουδογέλοιον of Menippus of

---

[1] *Satura quidem tota nostra est*, x. 1. 93.

[2] See below.   [4] *Gramm. Lat.* i. 485. 33. K.

[3] See Gellius, ii. 29. 20.   [5] On Hor. *Serm.* i. 10. 46.

[6] See, however, Hopkins, *Proc. Amer. Phil. Assoc.* xxxi. (1900) p. l.

Gadara (about 250 B.C.), he inserted much original matter, and that he chose as his literary form the native Roman *satura*.

Although the existing fragments belong to a work of superior finish and interest to that of Lucilius, it seems never to have become popular. Horace does not mention it at all, and in fact ignores the entire school of Ennius.[1]

2. *The School of Lucilius.*

20. At the hands of **C. Lucilius** the *satura* received a form which, through Horace's recognition of it as a standard, became the conventional one. After experimenting with various metres, he finally adopted the dactylic hexameter, and in that measure the greater part of his thirty books are composed. To the subject-matter also Lucilius gave a conventional form, which, though variously modified by his successors, continued to be regarded as characteristic of that class of writing.

Lucilius was born in Suessa Aurunca, in Campania, in 180 B.C.,[2] and died in 103. He was of equestrian rank, and is said by Porphyrio to have been a grand-uncle of Pompey the Great. He served with the younger Scipio in the Numantine War, and was afterwards on terms of familiar intimacy with his commander and with the latter's friend, Laelius.[3]

21. Lucilius composed thirty books of satires, which appear to have been published in three instalments, xxvi.–xxx.,

---

[1] See note on *Serm.* i. 10. 47.

[2] Hieronymus gives the date of his birth as 147 B.C., but Haupt suggested that Hieronymus confused the consuls of the year 180, A. Postumius Albinus and C. Calpurnius Piso, with those of 147, Sp. Postumius Albinus and L. Calpurnius Piso. Cichorius thought that LXIV was misread as XLIV, and that he was born in 167.

[3] See *Serm.* ii. 1. 71 ff.

xxii.–xxv., and i.–xxi. The first collection was composed in various metres, the last two in hexameters.

Of the work of Lucilius only a comparatively small number of fragments survive, and the longest continuous passage consists of but fourteen lines. Nevertheless, from these and from the scattered notices of the grammarians, some idea of its contents may be derived, and the extent of Horace's indebtedness to his predecessor may be inferred.

. Book xxvi., which was the first in order of publication, contained a justification of Satire, an account of the Numantine War, and an erotic satire. Book xxx. also treated of the nature and the object of Satire, and literary criticism seems to have been a feature of this, as well as of some of the other books. In Book ii. a suit is described, which was brought by T. Albucius against Q. Mucius Scaevola, on account of the latter's extortions in Asia. Book iii. contained an account of a journey from Rome to the Straits of Messana, on which Horace modelled the fifth *Sermo* of his first book. Book iv. included a discourse on gluttony, followed by Persius in his third satire. Book ix. dealt with literary criticism and with grammatical questions, in particular with orthography. Book x. inspired Persius to write Satire, and Book xiii. seems to have had the same theme as Horace's *Serm.* ii. 4. Of Book xvi. Porphyrio[1] says : *liber Lucilii sextus decimus Collyra inscribitur, eo quod de Collyra amica in eo scriptum sit.*

22. An examination of the existing fragments of Lucilius confirms Horace's judgment of his work, as given in *Serm.* i. 4 and 10, and in ii. 1. His language and versification are rude and unpolished, not only when judged by classical standards, but also as compared with the earlier writings of Terence. Munro[2] regards Horace's estimate of him as far

---

[1] On Hor. *Odes*, i. 22. 10.   [2] *Jour. of Phil.* vii. p. 294.

too high, 'raised designedly, not to excite the ill-will of his contemporaries.' His popularity was, however, unquestionably great in ancient times, and is testified to by Cicero, Quintilian, and Tacitus.

23. Horace seems to have written at first along the lines followed by Lucilius, to judge from *Serm.* i. 2. This style of writing did not, however, accord with his personal disposition, and in *Serm.* i. 4 and 10 [1] he criticises the work of his predecessor and defines his own ideal. At the same time, he regarded Lucilius as having established the outward form of this species of composition, and he follows him in using the dactylic hexameter, ignoring Varro's return to the old-fashioned medley. While deprecating Lucilius's severity in invective, he follows the general lines of his predecessor, giving us experiences from his own life,[2] treating ethical problems,[3] and defining his literary aims and ideals.[4]

24. The first collection, consisting of *Serm.* i., was published between 37 and 33 B.C., probably in the year 35. The title appears to have been *Sermones*,[5] or 'Talks,' while *Satura* seems to be a general designation for this species of composition and includes the *Epistulae* as well.[6] The book

---

[1] See the 'Outlines.'   [2] i. 5, 6, 7, 9.   [3] i. 1, 2, 3.   [4] i. 4, 10.

[5] See Porph. on *Serm.* i. 1, *Quamvis saturam esse opus hoc suum Horatius ipse confiteatur, cum ait: Sunt quibus in satura videar nimis acer, et ultra Legem tendere opus (Serm.* ii. 1. 1–2), *tamen proprios titulos voluit ei accommodare. Nam hos priores duos libros ' Sermonum,' posteriores ' Epistularum ' inscribens, in sermonum nomine vult intellegi quasi apud praesentem se loqui, epistulas vero quasi ad absentes missas.* In this book the terms Satires and Satire are used of the *Sermones* and *Epistulae* together or of the literary satire in general. The two divisions are referred to separately either by their Latin names, or as *Sermones* and *Epistles.*

[6] See below, p. xxii.

begins in due form with a dedication to Maecenas, and the arrangement of the separate satires is a natural, though not a chronological one, and may well be the one chosen by Horace himself. In most cases the poet himself appears as the speaker,[1] although considerable dialogue is introduced.

That the reception given to this work was not altogether favorable, is shown by Horace's own words in the introductory satire of the second Book of *Sermones*, which seems to have been published in 30 B.C. This book has no formal dedication and no epilogue, and is cast for the most part in dialogue form. Horace himself plays usually a very subordinate part, and in one satire he does not appear at all.[2] The first and sixth satires are of a personal nature; the former is a dialogue between Horace and Trebatius, the latter practically a monologue, although it is assimilated to the other works of the collection by the introduction of Cervius and his fable of the town and the country mouse.

25. The *Epistulae* belong to the general class of *Saturae*,[3] but they are distinguished from the *Sermones* not only by their form, but by their contents as well. Hexameter verse is not well suited to dialogue, and Horace evidently preferred to adopt a new literary form, the poetic epistle, for his *saturae*, rather than to abandon the conventional metre.

The first book of *Epistulae* seems to have been issued in 20 B.C. During the ten years which had elapsed since his last venture in the field of satire, Horace had published three books of *Odes*, and had reached the age of forty-five. The practical philosophy of life now seems to him the thing most worthy of his attention, and it is to the teaching of this that his first book of Epistles is in the main devoted.

---

[1] The only real exception is i. 8.   [2] ii. 5.

[3] See above, p. xxi., and Hendrickson's *Are the Letters of Horace Satires? Amer. Jour. of Phil.* xviii. (1897), pp. 313 ff.

It is dedicated to Maecenas and closes with an epilogue. It consists of actual letters and of fictitious ones.[1]

The second book of Epistles is devoted wholly to literary criticism. Horace has renounced the writing of lyrics, he tells us, and will hereafter teach the art of poetry instead of practising it. The chronology of this book offers not a few difficulties. The second Epistle is evidently the earliest and may be placed between 20 and 17 B.C.

The recognition of Horace as the poet laureate of Rome, by the invitation to write the *Carmen Saeculare*, gave him a very different position before the public, and is responsible for the assured tone of the *De Arte Poetica*, originally the third letter of the collection, although the second in chronological order. It is assigned with most probability to the year 16 B.C. These two letters, with an introductory epistle in which the collection is dedicated to Augustus, appear to have been published in 14 B.C.

26. The school of Lucilius is further represented by the six satires of **A. Persius Flaccus** (34–62 A.D.) of Volaterrae in Etruria. He was a diligent reader and ardent admirer of Horace, whose language he frequently paraphrases in his own peculiar style. Also by the sixteen satires of **D. Iunius Iuvenalis** (circ. 46–130 A.D.) of Aquinum.

27. Of other writers of satire, evidently of the school of Lucilius, Horace expressly mentions[2] **P. Terentius Varro** (82–37 B.C.) of Atax in Gallia Narbonensis, called *Atacinus* to distinguish him from the author of the *Saturae Menippeae*. No fragments of his satires have been preserved, although we have scanty remains of an epic, the *Bellum Sequanum*, of a *Chorographia*, and of an *Ephemeris*.

The *quibusdam aliis* of the same passage may refer to

---

[1] *E.g.* 13 and 14.   [2] *Serm.* i. 10. 46.

Sevius Nicanor[1] and L. Albucius,[2] and perhaps to others whose very names have been lost.

28. A decided satiric vein is found in many Roman writers whose works properly belong to other fields of literature. This is strikingly the case with Martial and with Tacitus. The latter's *Germania* has often erroneously been supposed to have been designed as a satire on Roman corruption and degeneracy.[3]

The work of Petronius Arbiter, of the time of Nero, is pervaded by this satiric vein, and has some resemblance to the satire of the school of Ennius in its literary form; but, like the *Metamorphoses* of Apuleius, it belongs properly to the field of the Romance.

V.

GENERAL CHARACTERISTICS OF THE SATIRES.

29. Horace expressly states that the model of his Satires is Lucilius, and, as has already been said, this is confirmed by a comparison of the two works, so far as this is possible. For reminiscences of Lucilius, see the *Notes, passim.* Horace's wide reading, both in the Greek literature and that of his native land, is shown by numerous passages. His acquaintance with, and admiration for, the Homeric poems are directly stated in *Epist.* i. 2, and are shown besides by frequent allusions to the heroes and events of the *Iliad* and the *Odyssey*, as well as by the occurrence of phrases and expressions which are reminiscent of both poems. He must have been a diligent reader of the dramatic writers both of Greece[4] and of Rome, and a frequent attendant at

---

[1] Suet. *de Gramm.* 5.   [2] Varro, *De Re Rust.* iii. 2. 7.

[3] See Gudeman's *Germania*, Introd. p. xi.

[4] See *Serm.* ii. 3. 11 f.

the theatre, to judge from his numerous references to the stage, and the abundance of metaphors derived from the drama. Although he does not anywhere mention Lucretius, the number of passages which show a parallelism with the *De Rerum Natura* is very striking. See the *Notes, passim.*

30. As Lucilius had evidently done,[1] Horace gives us in his Satires an intimate acquaintance with his life and habits. He sketches his early life and training, and pays a well-deserved tribute to his father. He tells us of his friendships and his enmities, his successes and disappointments. As a rule he is contented with his lot, although it is clear that the envious gossip which he pretends to despise and the unfavorable criticism of his literary work were not without a sting. He was evidently on most friendly terms with Virgil and Tibullus, and with Varius and other less well-known poets of the day. Propertius he never mentions by name, and while there is no evidence at all that the 'bore' of *Serm.* i. 9 is Propertius, there is an evident allusion to him in *Epist.* ii. 2. 95 ff., of such a nature as to show that he and Horace were rivals rather than friends.

31. One of the most striking features of the *Satires* is the keen observation of the daily life of the Romans by which they are characterized. It was Horace's custom, he tells us, to wander about the city and to observe the various occupations and amusements of the people. This he turned to account by drawing from them lessons for his own guidance and that of his friends, as well as by enlivening his literary work with many realistic pictures of daily life, — not only that of the higher classes, but also that of the humbler artisans and the slaves. Quite striking is the impression which the vast commercial and business interests of Rome

---

[1] See *Serm.* ii. 1. 32.

made upon him, and the number of allusions to them which are found in his works.[1]

32. The *Satires* are characterized by a genial and good-natured humor. This appears in Horace's choice of names for the objects of his comment, such as *Novius*, the parvenue; *Balbinus*, the doting lover; *Porcius*, the glutton; *Opimius*, the rich man; and the like. That these names occur in inscriptions and were many of them in common use is no proof that they were not selected (not invented) with reference to their appropriateness. Other phases of his humor are his parody of the epic, and higher poetic, style, and language under ludicrously inappropriate circumstances, his plays upon words, and his coinage of new terms, his irony and sarcasm, and in general a quizzical way of looking at things and an eye for the comical side of life.

VI.

THE SATIRES IN MEDIEVAL AND MODERN TIMES.[2]

33. Horace's works, as he himself had foreseen, became school text-books at an early period, and Suetonius speaks of elegies and a letter in prose which were falsely attributed to him. The number of commentators on his works is a further testimony to his popularity. He was evidently extensively read in medieval times as well, and his works were used for purposes of instruction. Numerous imitators of the Satires are found in this period. Of the *Ecbasis Captivi*, a 'beast-epic' of the tenth century, a fifth part consists of centos from Horace. The satirist Amarcius, of the eleventh century, made extensive use of Horace. Al-

---

[1] See Knapp, *Business Life in Horace*, P. A. P. A., xxix., p. xliv.

[2] See Showermann, *Horace and His Influence*, in "Our Debt to Greece and Rome" (Longmans, Green & Co.).

though Horace's fame in the Middle Ages was much less than that of Virgil, he too was regarded as a magician, and his grave was held in honor. These were, however, purely local manifestations and were confined to Palestrina and Venusia.

34. To speak here fully of Horace's popularity and influence in modern times is out of the question. He has been probably the most widely read and admired of all the Roman poets, and has appealed to men of the most widely different tastes.

Together with Juvenal, his influence upon French satire, which culminated in Boileau, was very great, while the English satirists, Dryden, Butler, Pope, Swift, Prior, Gay, Congreve, and others, show many evidences of the influence of Horace or Juvenal, or of both.

VII.

THE LANGUAGE AND STYLE OF THE SATIRES.[1]

1. FORMS AND VOCABULARY.

35. *a.* Archaisms are frequent: *e.g. ausim,* i. 10. 48;[2] *faxis,* ii. 3. 38; ii. 6. 5; *ast,* i. 6. 125; i. 8. 6; *duello,* E. i. 2. 7; ii. 2. 98; *autumat,* ii. 3. 45; *sodes,* i. 9. 41; E. i. 1. 62; E. 1. 7. 15; *licebit,* ii. 2. 59; and the archaic infinitive in *-ier,* which occurs five times in the *Sermones* and three times in the *Epistulae.*

---

[1] The examples are not intended to be exhaustive, and the *Introduction* as a whole is intended to be suggestive rather than complete. In his own teaching of Horace the editor is in the habit of assigning topics, such as are briefly touched on in the *Introduction*, to different members of the class for special study, being guided, of course, in his selection by the degree of advancement and capacity of the students.

[2] References like this are to the *Sermones;* those to the *Epistulae* are in the form E. i. 2. 7.

b. Horace frequently, in common with other Roman poets, uses the simple verb in place of a compound: *e.g. temnens = contemnens,* i. 1. 116; *solvas = dissolvas,* i. 4. 60; *poni = apponi,* ii. 3. 148; ii. 4. 14; *ruam = eruam,* ii. 5. 22.

c. Some borrowed words are found: *e.g.* from the Greek, *obsonia,* i. 2. 9; *hybrida,* i. 7. 2; *apotheca,* ii. 5. 7. Celtic or Germanic, *raeda,* i. 5. 86; *mannus,* E. i. 7. 77. Syrian, *ambubaia,* i. 2. 1; *etc.* In i. 10. 21, *seri studiorum,* he translates a Greek word; and, like many other Roman writers, he avoids *philosophus* and *philosophia,* using instead *sapiens* and *sapientia.*

d. Horace coins many new words: *e.g. abnormis,* ii. 2. 3; *ingustata,* ii. 8. 30; *inamarescere,* ii. 7. 107; *prodocere,* E. i. 1. 55.

e. Short forms of the verb, contractions, or formations of the aorist type, occur in i. 9. 48, *summosses;* i. 9. 62, *nosset;* i. 9. 73, *surrexe;* ii. 3. 169, *divisse.*

36. In the spelling, the *Sermones* and *Epistles,* which reflect the language of everyday life, were probably less conservative than the *Odes,* and the editor has made the orthography conform, in the main, to the standard of the Augustan age. For forms and spellings especially characteristic of the colloquial language, see below, § 55.

2. Syntax.

a. The Cases.

37. The vocative is used in place of a direct object in: *Matutine pater, seu 'Iane' libentius audis,* ii. 6. 20; '*rexque paterque' audisti coram,* E. i. 7. 37. The nominative is used for the vocative in *Ars Poet.* 292, *o Pompilius sanguis, carmen reprehendite.*

38. *a*. The accusative is found with some verbs which do not ordinarily govern a direct object: *e.g. ut aprum* cenem *ego*, ii. 3. 234; *si* pranderet *holus*, E. i. 17. 13; census *equestrem summam*, *Ars Poet.* 384; *neu quid medios* intercinat *actus*, *Ars Poet.* 194.

b. The accusative of the inner object (sometimes called 'cognate accusative') is frequent: *e.g. reges atque tetrarchas, omnia magna loquens*, i. 3. 12; *Pythia cantat, Ars Poet.* 414. With the neuter of the adjective: *cernis acutum*, i. 3. 26; *serviet aeternum*, E. i. 10. 41; *insanire sollemnia*, E. i. i. 101. Some bold uses of the construction occur: *e.g. pastorem saltaret uti Cyclopa*, i. 5. 63; *agrestem Cyclopa movetur*, E. ii. 2. 125; *cum Ilionam edormit*, ii. 3. 61; *magna coronari Olympia*, E. i. 1. 50.

c. The accusative of specification, or Greek accusative, occurs in *mentem concussa*, ii. 3. 295; *curatus capillos*, E. i. 1. 94. Many so-called examples of this construction are better explained in other ways. Thus we have appositives in *nugas* hoc genus, ii. 6. 44; *tremis* ossa *pavore* (partitive apposition), ii. 7. 57; the accusative of the inner object in *distat* nil, ii. 2. 29.

Passive verbs are often used with the force of the middle, and govern a direct object: *e.g.* nasum *nidore supinor*, ii. 7. 38; *purgor* bilem, *Ars Poet.* 302. Here we may put *fractus* membra *labore*, i. 1. 5 although *membra* may be taken as a Greek accusative, and *fractus* as passive.

39. *a*. The dative is used with verbs meaning 'contend,' 'differ from,' and the like: *e.g. certans semper melioribus*, ii. 5. 19; *Sidonio contendere ostro vellera*, E. i. 10. 26; *altercante libidinibus pavore*, ii. 7. 57.

b. The so-called dative of the agent is used not only with the future passive participle, but with the perfect participle: *Graecis intacti carminis*, i. 10. 66; *bella tibi pugnata*,

E. i. 16. 25 ; and with the uncompounded tenses : *carmina
quae scribuntur aquae potoribus*, E. i. 19. 3.

c. The dative of the goal occurs in *si quis casus puerum
egerit Orco*, ii. 5. 49.

d. Constructions influenced by the analogy of the Greek
are : *idem facit occidenti, Ars Poet.* 467 ; *dignis paratus*,
E. i. 7. 22 ; *Graecia Barbariae lento collisa duello*, E. i. 2. 7.
See also § 55. *g* below.

e. The passive of verbs governing the dative is used with a
subject in the nominative (instead of the impersonal construction) in *imperor*, i. 5. 21 ; *invideor, Ars Poet.* 56.

40. *a.* The genitive is used with adjectives much more
freely than in classical prose.   The extension of this construction is doubtless due to the analogy of the Greek genitive of specification : *e.g. pauperrimus bonorum*, i. 1. 79 ;
cerebri felicem, i. 9. 11 ; *pravi docilis*, ii. 2. 52 ; *donandi parca*,
ii. 5. 79.

b. The genitive with verbs and adjectives denoting separation is due to the analogy of the Greek : *e.g. morbi purgatum illius*, ii. 3. 27 ; *in medio positorum abstemius*, E. i. 12. 7.

c. Noteworthy also are : the free use of the genitive of
the whole, *num qua vitiorum*, i. 3. 35 ; *fictis rerum*, ii. 8. 83 ;
gladiatorum centum, ii. 3. 85 ; and in the predicate, *operum
hoc tuorum est*, i. 7. 35 ; *scribe tui gregis hunc*, E. i. 9. 13 ; of
the appositive genitive, *patrimoni mille talenta*, ii. 5. 226 ;
pueri pulchri munere, E. i. 18. 74 ; and *neque . . . ciceris nec
invidit avenae*, ii. 6. 84, after the analogy of verbs of plenty.

41. *a.* The ablative of instrument is used freely : *e.g.
teneas tuis te*, ii. 3. 324 ; *ire mulo*, i. 6. 105 ; *postico falle
clientem*, E. i. 5. 31 ; with adjectives, *laeva stomachosus
habena*, E. i. 15. 12 ; *sermo lingua concinnus utraque*, i. 10. 23 ;
in place of the ablative of agency with *ab : curatus inaequali*

tonsore capillos, E. i. 1. 94, and probably *cena ministratur pueris tribus,* i. 6. 116.

b. The ablative of association occurs with verbs of *joining, changing, mixing,* and the like: *e.g. verbis Graeca Latinis miscuit,* i. 10. 20; *stipare Platona Menandro,* ii. 3. 11; *forti miscebat mella Falerno,* ii. 4. 24.

c. The participle alone is used in the ablative absolute: *e.g. parto quod avebas,* i. 1. 94; *lecto aut scripto quod me iuvet,* i. 6. 122; *neglectis flagitium ingens,* ii. 4. 82; *vadato,* i. 9. 36.

42. Not infrequently a case may be taken in a different sense with two words in the same sentence, and may be said to be governed by both — the ἀπὸ κοινοῦ construction: *e.g. quid causae est merito quin illis Juppiter ambas iratus buccas inflet,* i. 1. 20; *male laxus in pede calceus haeret,* i. 3. 31; *tempestivum pueris concedere ludum,* E. ii. 2. 142; *data Romanis venia est indigna poetis, Ars Poet.* 264. See *Notes.*

b. The Verb.

1. Agreement.

43. *a.* A singular verb is used with a compound subject whose members are singular: *dum ficus prima calorque dissignatorem decorat,* E. i. 7. 5; *si quaestor avus pater atque meus patruusque fuisset,* i. 6. 131.

b. The neuter is used referring to a person in *nil fuit umquam sic impar sibi,* i. 3. 18; *quod eram narro,* i. 6. 60; *nisi quae terris semota suisque temporibus defuncta videt, fastidit et odit,* E. ii. 1. 21.

2. The Tenses.

44. *a.* The present is often used with the force of the future, a common usage in the language of everyday life: *e.g. nemon oleum fert ocius?* ii. 7. 34; *ut te ipsum serves, non* *expergisceris?* E. ii. 2. 33; and in a future condition, *nisi damnose bibimus, moriemur inulti*, ii. 8. 34. It has almost an aoristic force in *divinare magnus mihi donat Apollo*, ii. 5. 60.

b. The imperfect is used with nearly the force of the present in *non tu corpus eras sine pectore*, E. i. 4. 6; *poteras dixisse*, *Ars Poet.* 328. See *Notes* on these two passages. The epistolary imperfect occurs in *haec tibi dictabam*, E. i. 10. 49.

c. The future is frequently used with the force of an imperative: *e.g. hoc mihi iuris cum venia dabis*, i. 4. 105; *ferramenta Teanum tolletis, fabri*, E. i. 1. 87; *Augusto reddes volumina*, E. i. 13. 2. It has a gnomic force in *sordidus a tenui victu distabit*, ii. 2. 53, and a somewhat similar force in *ut tu semper eris derisor*, ii. 6. 54.

d. The gnomic perfect is frequent: *e.g. non domus et fundus aegroto domini deduxit corpore febres*, E. i. 2. 48; *sedit qui timuit ne non succederet*, E. i. 17. 37; and combined with the future: *haec seges ingratos tulit et feret omnibus annis*, E. i. 7. 21.

e. The potential perfect subjunctive is often used with practically the same force as the present: *e.g. dederim*, i. 4. 39; *contulerim*, i. 5. 44; *dixeris*, i. 4. 41.

f. The perfect infinitive is used with the force of the present in ii. 3. 187, *ne quis humasse velit Aiacem*. Usually, however, while approaching the force of the present, it represents instantaneous or completed action: *e.g. amet scripsisse ducentos ante cibum versus*, i. 10. 60; *sapientia prima stultitia caruisse*, E. i. 1. 42; *quod cures proprium fecisse*, E. i. 17. 5.

3. THE MOODS.

45. *a.* The indicative is used for vividness in the apodosis of conditions contrary to fact: *dedisses . . . erat*, i. 3. 17; *peream male si non optimum erat*, ii. 1. 7.

b. The indicative is sometimes used with *quamvis*: *e.g.*

quamvis tacet, i. 3. 129; *quamvis distat nil,* ii. 2. 29; *quam-vis periurus erit,* ii. 5. 15.

c. The indicative is sometimes used after *est qui* and similar expressions, though usually with a slightly different force from that of the subjunctive; *cf.* E. ii. 2. 182, *sunt qui non habeant, est qui non curat habere.*

d. The relatively rare 'can' and 'could' potential, confined to the second person singular of verbs of seeing, perceiving, thinking, knowing, and believing, is found in i. 4. 86, *saepe tribus lectis videas cenare quaternos;* and transposed to past time in i. 5. 76, *videres;* ii. 8. 77, *videres.* See Bennett, 'Critique of Some Recent Subjunctive Theories,' *Cornell Studies in Class. Phil.* ix. pp. 41 ff.

e. The stipulative subjunctive is found in i. 8. 12, *mille pedes in fronte, trecentos cippus in agrum, hic dabat, heredes monumentum ne sequeretur; Ars Poet.* 12, *hanc veniam damus, sed non ut placidis coeant immitia, non ut serpentes avibus geminentur, tigribus agni;* E. i. 18. 107, *sit mihi quod nunc est, etiam minus, ut mihi vivam, quod superest aevi.* See Bennett, *Trans. Amer. Phil. Assoc.* xxxi. pp. 223 ff.

f. The iterative subjunctive occurs in *Ars Poet.* 438, *Quintilio si quid recitares,* 'corrige, sodes,' *aiebat.*

46. a. The infinitive occurs freely with adjectives where other constructions would be used in classical prose: *e.g. dignus notari,* i. 3. 24; *durus componere versus,* i. 4. 8; *piger ferre laborem,* i. 4. 12; *doctus cantare,* i. 10. 19; *cereus in vitium flecti, Ars Poet.* 163.

b. The infinitive is used in exclamations: *huncine solem tam nigrum surrexe mihi !* i. 9. 73; *te petere !* ii. 2. 30; *tene ut ego accipiar torquerier !* ii. 8. 67.

c. The historical infinitive is occasionally used: *e.g. pueris convicia nautae ingerere,* i. 5. 12; *ire modo ocius, inter dum consistere . . . dicere,* i. 9. 9.

d. The infinitive is used freely as the subject and object of verbs, and governed by the preposition *praeter: e.g. quo tibi, Tilli, sumere clavum,* i. 6. 24; *inquiram, quid sit furere,* ii. 3. 41; *res gerere et captos ostendere civibus hostes attingit solium Iovis,* E. i. 17. 33; *dum tantundem haurire relinquas,* i. 1. 52; *adimam cantare severis,* E. i. 19. 9; *nihil sibi legatum praeter plorare,* ii. 5. 69.

47. The future participle is very freely used to denote intention, destiny, and similar ideas. It is usually best translated by a relative clause or by an independent clause: *e.g. quattuor hinc rapimur milia, mansuri oppidulo* (intention), i. 5. 86; *redis mutatae frontis, ut arte emendaturus fortunam,* ii. 8. 85; *his me consolor, victurum suavius ac si* (destiny), i. 6. 130; *i pede fausto, grandia laturus praemia (and you will receive),* E. ii. 2. 37; *arma Caesaris Augusti non responsura lacertis (which were fated not to respond),* E. ii. 2. 48; *segetes mox frumenta daturas (which will presently give),* E. ii. 2. 161.

c. Other Parts of Speech.

48. *a.* The usage, *hic . . . hic* for *hic . . . ille,* found chiefly in poetry, is frequent: *e.g. hunc atque hunc superare laborat,* i. 1. 112; *hoc amet, hoc spernat, Ars Poet.* 45; *haec amat obscurum, volet haec sub luce videri, Ars Poet.* 363. Horace, like most of the other poets, seldom uses *is,* either omitting it entirely or using a demonstrative pronoun as a substitute for it. A very rare poetic use of the pronominal adverb occurs in ii. 2. 75, *hac rabiosa fugit canis, hac lutulenta ruit sus.*

Hic has about the force of *talis, a man like that,* in E. i. 6. 40, *ne fueris hic tu;* E. i. 15. 42, *nimirum hic ego sum.* Similarly, *ille* in i. 1. 63, *quid facias illi.*[1]

---

[1] See Meader, *The Latin Pronouns is: hic: iste: ipse.* The Macmillan Company, 1901.

b. The relative and interrogative forms from the *i*-stem
are sometimes used in the ablative singular, and those from
the *o*-stem in the dative-ablative plural : *e.g. qui,* i. 1. 1 ;
quis, i. 3. 96, *etc. Cum* always precedes the ablative of the
relative pronoun, instead of being used as an enclitic : *e.g.
eorum vixi cum quibus,* i. 4. 81.

c. The plural *utrique* is used in i. 8. 25 of a closely connected pair of individuals. *Unus* is used for *quidam* in i.
5. 21. See also § 55. *f,* below.

49. *a.* Adjectives are frequently used to denote the effect
produced : *e.g. tarda podagra,* i. 9. 32 ; *plumbeus Auster,* ii.
6. 18 ; *exsangue cuminum,* E. i. 19. 18.

b. Adjectives are frequently used as substantives : —

1. Without an ellipsis, the meaning of the substantive
being determined by the gender of the adjective : *e.g. diversa
sequentis,* i. i. 3 ; *iocularia,* i. 1. 23 ; *avidos aegros,* i. 4. 126.
Contrary to the usage of the best prose, both pronouns and
adjectives are used as substantives in oblique cases where
the gender, and consequently the meaning, is ambiguous :
e.g. his ego quae nunc, olim quae scripsit Lucilius, eripias si
(= *his rebus*), i. 4. 56; *turpi secernis honestum,* i. 6. 63 ; *maiore
reprensis,* i. 10. 55. In the first case there is no question as
to the interpretation, but in the last two some editors see
masculine substantives, others neuters.

2. With ellipsis of a substantive. Here the meaning of
the new substantive is determined by the omitted word,
although there is not always a consciousness of the ellipsis :
e.g. venalis (sc. servos), i. 1. 47 ; *Appia (via),* i. 5. 6 ; *recta
(via),* i. 5. 71 ; *Atabulus (ventus),* i. 5. 78 ; *ferae (bestiae),*
i. 8. 17 ; *secundas (partes),* i. 9. 46 ; *impenso (pretio),* ii. 3.
245 ; *limis (oculis),* ii. 5. 53 ; *agninae (carnis),* E. i. 15. 35.

50. Numerals are frequently used, not in their literal
sense, but of indefinite large or small numbers, as in Eng·

lish we say 'hundreds' or 'thousands of,' 'half a dozen,' and the like. For an indefinite large number *mille* is most frequent: *e.g. mille versus*, ii. 1. 4; *quot capitum vivunt, totidem studiorum milia*, ii. 1. 27; *cf.* ii. 3. 116. Examples of other numerals used in this way are: *saepe ducentos, saepe decem servos*, i. 3. 11; *plostra ducenta*, i. 6. 42; *trecentos inseris*, i. 5. 12; and combined with *mille*: *Catienis mille ducentis clamantibus*, ii. 3. 61; *ter centum milibus*, ii. 3. 16. Of indefinite small numbers we have: *decem vitiis*, E. i. 18. 25; *decem servos*, i. 3. 12; *quinque dies*, E. i. 7. 1; *tribus Anticyris, Ars Poet.* 300. See *Notes*.

51. *a.* The adverb is frequently used to modify *esse: e.g. recte tibi semper erunt res*, ii. 2. 106; *bene erat non piscibus urbe petitis*, ii. 2. 120; *recte est*, ii. 3. 162; *pulchre fuerit tibi*, ii. 8. 19.

b. The following uses are also noteworthy: *fautor inepte est*, i. 10. 2; *male laxus*, i. 3. 31 (see above, § 42); *turpiter hirtum*, E. i. 3. 22; *turpiter atrum, Ars Poet.* 3.

3. WORD ORDER.

52. In spite of the trammels of metre, abundant scope is allowed in poetry for effective word order, and of this Horace takes the fullest advantage. Words are emphasized by being put out of their normal position; for most words the beginning or the end of lines and of clauses are emphatic positions. Anaphora, chiasmus, antithesis, and hyperbaton serve the same purpose. Considerations of space make it impossible to go into details. See the *Notes, passim*.

4. FIGURES OF RHETORIC AND GRAMMAR.

53. The following may be mentioned: *a.* Asyndeton: *e.g. contentus vivat, laudet diversa sequentis*, i. 1. 3.

b. Anaphora: *non ego me claro natum patre, non ego cir·*

cum . . . i. 6. 58; *aeque pauperibus prodest, locupletibus aeque* (combined with chiasmus), E. i. 1. 25.

c. Anacoluthon: *nam ut ferula caedas . . . non vereor,* i. 3. 122 (see the *Notes*). Closely allied are combinations of two constructions: *e.g. esse pares res furta latrociniis,* i. 3. 122; *saepe velut qui currebat fugiens hostem,* i. 3. 9; *animae quales neque candidiores terra tulit,* i. 5. 41. See the *Notes* on these passages. *Cf.* also the loose appositives, *garrulus,* i. 4. 12; *sermo merus,* i. 4. 48.

d. Brachylogy: *magnis parva mineris falce recisurum simili,* i. 3. 122; *cui non conveniet sua res, ut calceus olim, si pede maior erit, subvertet, si minor, uret,* E. i. 10. 42. See *Notes.*

e. Chiasmus: *stultus honores dat indignis et famae servit ineptus,* i. 6. 16; *hinc vos, vos hinc,* i. 1. 17; *numquam inducant animum cantare rogati, iniussi numquam desistunt* (combined with anaphora), i. 3. 2.

f. Hendiadys: *operum primos vitaeque labores,* ii. 6. 21; *dolor quod suaserit et mens,* E. i. 2. 60; *veniam somnumque,* E. i. 5. 10.

g. Hyperbaton: *di bene fecerunt inopis me quodque pusilli finxerunt animi,* i. 4. 17; *quattuor hinc rapimur viginti et milia raedis,* i. 5. 86; *incertus scamnum faceretne Priapum,* i. 8. 2; *Aiax immeritos cum occidit desipit agnos,* ii. 3. 211.

h. Hypallage: *non me Satureiano vectari rura caballo,* i. 6. 59.

i. Litotes: *non inultus,* i. 8. 44; *nec non verniliter ipsis fungitur officiis,* ii. 6. 108; *haud ignobilis,* E. ii. 2. 128.

k. Metonymy: *Volcano,* i. 5. 73; *Venerem,* E. ii. 2. 56.

l. Oxymoron: *strenua inertia,* E. i. 11. 28; *concordia discors,* E. i. 12. 19; *Stertinium deliret acumen,* E. i. 12. 20; *symphonia discors, Ars Poet.* 374.

m. Pleonasm: *verbum non amplius addam,* i. 1. 121; *nimio plura,* E. ii. 1. 198.

n. Prolepsis: *quid premat obscurum lunae orbem,* E. i. 12. 18.

o. Tmesis: *argento post omnia ponas,* i. 1. 86; *quando-cumque,* i. 9. 33; *unde-octoginta,* ii. 3. 117; *quo-circa,* ii. 6. 95.

p. Zeugma: *dum terras hominumque colunt genus,* E. ii. 1. 7.

q. Metaphors and similes are very numerous. It is characteristic of Horace's style that in the latter he *identifies* the person or thing with that with which it is compared. See note on *Tantalus,* i. 1. 68.

r. Of other rhetorical devices may be mentioned: *quid rides,* i. 1. 69; *horum pauperrimus esse* bonorum, i. 1. 79; *immo alia et fortasse* minora, i. 3. 20: *donent* tonsore, ii. 3. 17; *nocturno certare mero,* putere *diurno,* E. i. 19. 11.

VIII.

THE COLLOQUIAL LANGUAGE IN THE SATIRES.

54. Beside the literary language in the classical period, we find also the *sermo familiaris* or *sermo cotidianus,* the language used by educated Romans in the ordinary conversation of every-day life, and the *sermo plebeius* or *sermo rusticus,* the language of the common people.[1] Of the former we have representatives in the classical literature in the *Letters* of Cicero, and in the *Sermones,* and, to a less marked degree, in the *Epistles* of Horace. In early Latin, the plays of Terence belong to the same class, while in those of Plautus we have a combination of the *sermo cotidianus* and the *sermo plebeius.* It is not always easy to distinguish between the *sermo cotidianus* and the *sermo plebeius,* or to distinguish what is colloquial from what is merely archaic;

---

[1] See Cooper's *Word Formation in the Roman Sermo Plebeius,* Introd.

but the following features may safely be said to be **charac-**
teristic of the language of every-day life : —

55. *a.* Vocabulary. We find in the Satires a goodly number of words which were current in every-day conversation,
but not in the literary language. In many cases these words
eventually displaced the literary words and took their place
in the Romance languages : *e.g. caballus,* French *cheval,* Italian *cavallo.* Such words as French *équitation,* and the like,
are so-called 'learned words,' *i.e.* they did not come into the
language by direct descent, but were formed from classical
Latin words in the same way that our 'telephone,' 'phono-
graph,' etc., are formed from Greek. As examples of colloquial words may be cited: *bucca,* i. 1. 21 ; *caballus,* i. 6. 59 ;
i. 6. 103 ; E. i. 7. 88 ; E. i. 18. 36 ; *elutius,* ii. 4. 16 ; *ocreatus,* ii.
3. 234 ; *autumare,* ii. 3. 45 ; *scabere,* i. 10. 71 ; *largiter,* i. 4. 132.

Many words which are not in themselves colloquial are
used in colloquial senses: *e.g. latraverit,* ii. 1. 85 ; *extuderit,*
ii. 2. 14 ; *eripiam,* ii. 2. 23 ; *radere,* ii. 4. 83.

b. Certain forms are also colloquial : *e.g.* the archaisms
faxis, ausim, sodes, etc. (see above, § 35. *a.*) ; the full forms,
exclusus fuero, i. 9. 58 ; *iniecta fuerit,* i. 4. 95 ; the iteratives
and intensives, *captat,* i. 1. 68 ; *imperitarent,* i. 6. 4 ; *grassare,*
ii. 5. 93 ; the syncopated forms, *caldior,* i. 3. 53 ; *valdius,* E.
i. 9. 6 ; the contracted verb forms (see § 35. *e,* above) ; and
perhaps also in some cases the use of the simple verb for
the compound (see § 35. *b,* above).

c. Many colloquial phrases occur : *e.g. si me amas,* i. 9.
38 ; *unde et quo Catius,* ii. 4. 1 ; *quid agis, dulcissime rerum,*
i. 9. 4 ; *numquid vis,* i. 9. 6 ; *cf.* the use of the adverb with
esse, § 51. *a,* above.

d. Ellipsis. While the grammatical construction requires
us to supply something, as a rule no ellipsis is consciously
present to the speaker's mind : *e.g. unde mihi lapidem?* ii. 7

116; *unde et quo Catius*, ii. 4. 1.   Especially characteristic is the ellipsis of a subjunctive copula: *e.g.* i. 8. 32.

See also § 49. *b*, above.

e. The free use of diminutives. In many cases these have supplanted, in the Romance languages, the word from which they were derived: *e.g. auricula*, French *oreille*.   Horace uses many diminutives; in some cases they have actual diminutive force, as *parvola*, i. 1. 33; *villula*, i. 5. 45; *plostello*, ii. 3. 247. In some cases they denote possession or the like, as *lectulus*, i. 4. 133; *pelliculam*, ii. 5. 38; often affection, as *catelle*, ii. 3. 259; *matercula*, E. i. 7. 7; *nutricula*, E. i. 4. 8; frequently contempt or depreciation, as *popello*, E. i. 7. 65; *litterulis graecis*, E. ii. 2. 7; *asellus*, i. 1. 90. In other cases they appear to have no force which is ordinarily associated with diminutives, although the choice of the word produces a certain comic effect: *e.g. auriculas,* i. 9. 20; *auriculis*, E. i. 8 1.6; *gemelli*, E. i. 10. 3.

f. The frequent expression of the first and second personal pronouns: *e.g. cum tu argento post omnia ponas*, i. 1. 86; *post hanc vagor, aut ego lecto . . . unguor*, i. 6. 122 (the position of *ego, etc.*, with the second verb is a favorite use of Horace's): and such redundant expressions as *utrumne*, ii. 3. 251; ii. 6. 73; and the like. See also § 53. *m*, above. Paraphrases for the first personal pronoun: *hunc hominem*, i. 9. 47; *noster*, ii. 6. 48. The use of the so-called ethical dative: *quid mihi Celsus agit*, E. i. 3. 15.

g. The frequent use of the paratactic construction: *e.g. milia frumenti tua triverit area centum, non tuus hoc capiet venter plus ac meus*, i. 1. 45; *deciens centena dedisses: quinque diebus nil erat in loculis*, i. 3. 15; *scribe decem a Nerio; non est satis; adde Cicuti nodosi tabulas decem; effugiet tamen*, ii. 3. 69; *non es avarus; abi*, E. ii. 2. 205.

h. Pleonasm, anacoluthon, and alliteration.   See § 53. *c*, *m*, above, and § 58 below.

i. Proverbs and proverbial expressions: *stans pede in uno,*
i. 4. 10; *in silvam ligna feras,* i. 10. 34; *hac urget lupus, hac
canis,* ii. 2. 64; *ignem gladio scrutare,* ii. 3. 276; *etc.* And the
frequent allusions to fables.

k. Plays upon words: *saccis . . . sacris,* i. 1. 70–71;
libellos, i. 4. 66 and 71; mordacem *Cynicum,* E. i. 17. 18;
ventoso *curru,* E. ii. 1. 177.

IX.

METRES.

INTRODUCTORY.

GENERAL CHARACTER OF LATIN POETRY.

English poetry, as a rule, is based on *stress, i.e.* on a
regular succession of accented and unaccented syllables.
The versification of —

This is the forest primeval, the murmuring pines and the hemlocks,

depends entirely upon this alternation of accented and unaccented syllables, and the same thing is true of all ordinary English verse. This basis of English poetry, moreover,
is a result of the very nature of the English language.
Like all languages of the Teutonic group, our English
speech is characterized by a strong word-accent.

Latin verse, on the other hand, was based on *quantity;*
a line of Latin poetry consisted of a regular succession of
long and short syllables, *i.e.* of syllables which it took a
long or short time to pronounce. This basis of Latin
poetry, as in the case of English poetry, is strictly in con-
formity with the character of the spoken language; for
classical Latin was not a language in which there was a
strong word-accent. The word-accent, in fact, must have
been extremely weak. Different languages differ very
greatly in this respect, and we ought to bear this fact in

mind in thinking of Latin. In Latin, word-accent was so weak that it could not be made the basis of versification as it is in English, while, on the other hand, quantity was a strongly marked feature of the spoken language. Thus we see how it came about that quantity was made the basis of Latin verse, and why accent was not.

We are, then, to conceive of a line of Latin poetry as consisting simply of a regular arrangement of long and short syllables — nothing else.   To read Latin poetry, therefore, it is necessary simply to pronounce the words with the proper quantity. This takes some patience and practice, but it is easily within the power of every pupil of Latin who can read Latin prose with quantitative accuracy. It is in Latin as in English: any one who can read prose with accuracy and fluency has no difficulty in reading poetry. The poet arranges the words in such wise that they make poetry of themselves, if they are only properly pronounced. No other kind of poetry was ever known in any language. No other is easily conceivable.

Of course it necessarily takes time for the student's ear to become sensitive to quantitative differences and to acquire a feeling for the quantitative swing of Latin verse. Yet, with patience and abundant practice in careful pronunciation, the quantitative sense is bound to develop.

ICTUS.

Two views of ictus are held. According to one view, ictus is a stress accent. This makes Latin verse accentual, precisely like English poetry. According to the other view, ictus is merely the quantitative prominence inherent in the long syllable of every fundamental foot, — the iambus, trochee, dactyl, and anapaest.[1]

---

[1] The full discussion of this view of ictus may be found in the *American Journal of Philology*, vol. xix. No. 76.

WORD-ACCENT.

In reading Latin poetry, the ordinary accent of the words should not be neglected. But, as we have already seen above (p. xxv), the word-accent in Latin was exceedingly slight. We almost invariably accent Latin words altogether too strongly. As a result we destroy the quantity of the remaining syllables of a word. Thus, in a word like *ēvī-tābātur*, we are inclined to stress the penultimate syllable with such energy as to reduce the quantity of the vowel in each of the three preceding syllables. In this way the pupil says *ĕ-vi-tă-bā-tur*. Such a pronunciation is a fatal defect in reading. What we ought to do is to make the quantity prominent and the accent very slight. Where this is done, the accent will be felt to be subordinate to the quantity, as it ought to be, and as it must be if one is ever to acquire a feeling for the quantitative character of Latin poetry. If the quantity is not made more prominent than the accent, the accent is bound to be more prominent than the quantity, which will be fatal to the acquisition of a quantitative sense for the verse.

SPECIAL CAUTIONS TO BE OBSERVED IN ORDER TO SECURE CORRECT SYLLABIC QUANTITY IN READING.

Inasmuch as Latin poetry was based on the quantity of syllables, it is obvious that the greatest care must be taken in the pronunciation of the words with a view to securing an absolutely correct syllabic quantity. Otherwise the metrical (*i.e.* quantitative) character of the verse is violated, and the effect intended by the poet is lost. To ignore the proper quantity of the syllables is as disastrous in a line of Latin poetry as it would be in English poetry to misplace the word-accent. If one were to read the opening line of Longfellow's *Evangeline*, for example, as follows : —

This ís the forést prímeval

the result would be no more fatal than to read a line of
Latin poetry with neglect of the quantity.

In reading Latin verse, there are two classes of errors to
which the student is particularly liable, either one of which
results in giving a wrong syllabic quantity.

Class First.

In ' Open ' [1] Syllables

Here the quantity of the syllable is always the same as
the quantity of the vowel. Thus, in *mā-ter*, the first syllable
is long; in *pă-ter*, the first syllable is short.

This being so, it is imperative that the pupil should in
'open' syllables scrupulously observe the quantity of the
vowel. If he pronounces a short vowel long, or a long
vowel short, he thereby gives a false quantity to the syllable, and thus wrecks the line completely. The pupil,
therefore, must know the quantity of every vowel, and
must pronounce in the light of his knowledge. He must
not say *gērō, tērō, sērō* (for *gĕrō, tĕrō, sĕrō*); nor must he
say *pāter, āger, nīsī, quōd, quībus, ingēnium, ēs* ('thou art'),
etc. One such error in a verse is fatal to its metrical struc-
ture, and the pupil who habitually commits such errors in
reading is simply wasting valuable time.

Class Second.

In ' Closed ' [2] Syllables.

It is a fundamental fact that a 'closed' syllable is long.
But in order to be long it must *be actually closed in pro-*

---

[1] An ' open ' syllable is one whose vowel is followed by a single consonant (or by a mute with *l* or *r*). This single consonant (or the mute
with *l* or *r*) is joined with the vowel of the following syllable, thus
leaving the previous syllable ' open.'

[2] A ' closed ' syllable is one whose vowel is followed by two or more
consonants (except a mute with *l* or *r*). The first of the two (or more)

nunciation. Right here is where the pupil is apt to err. He fails to make the syllable 'closed,' *i.e.* he does not join the first of the two or more consonants to the *preceding* vowel, but joins all of the consonants with the *following* vowel. He thus leaves the preceding syllable 'open.' Hence, if the vowel itself is short, the syllable by this incorrect pronunciation is made short, where it ought to be made long. Thus the student is apt to say *tem-pe-stā-ti-bus* where he ought to say *tem-pes-tā-ti-bus, i.e.* he joins both the *s* and the *t* with the following vowel, where he ought to join the *s* with the preceding vowel (thus making a 'closed' syllable), and only the *t* with the following vowel.[1]

Errors of the kind referred to are so liable to occur that it seems best to classify them by groups : —

a. The commonest group consists of those words which contain a *short* vowel followed by doubled consonants (*pp, cc, tt,* etc.), — words of the type of *ap-parābat, ac-cipiēbam, at-tigerant, ges-sērunt, ter-rā-rum, an-nōrum, ad-diderat, flam-mārum, excel-lentia, ag-gerimus,* etc. In Latin, both of the doubled consonants were pronounced, one being combined with the previous vowel (thus closing the syllable and making it long), one with the following vowel. But in English we practically never have doubled consonants. We write them and print them, but we *do not pronounce* them. Thus, we write and print *kit-ty, fer-ry,* etc., but we do not pronounce two *t*'s or two *r*'s in these words any more than in *pity,* which we write with one *t,* or in *very,*

---

consonants is regularly joined in pronunciation with the preceding vowel, thus *closing* the preceding syllable. This is the real significance of the common rule that a syllable is long when a short vowel is followed by two consonants. It is because one of the consonants is joined to the preceding vowel, thus closing the syllable.

[1] This doctrine, to be sure, contradicts the rules given in grammars for division of words into syllables ; but those rules apply only to writing, not actual utterance. See Bennett, *Appendix to Latin Grammar,* § 35.

which we write with one *r*. Now, in pronouncing Latin
the pupil is very apt to pronounce the doubled consonants
of that language as single consonants, just as he does in
English. Thus he naturally pronounces the words above
given, not *ap-pa-rā-bat*, etc., but *ă-pa-rābat*, *ă-cipiēbam*, *ă-tige-*
rant, *gĕ-sērunt*, *tĕ-rārum*, *a-nōrum*, *ă-diderat*, *flă-mārum*, *excĕ-*
lentia, *ă-gerimus*. In other words, the pupil pronounces only
one consonant, where he ought to pronounce two, and that
one consonant he joins with the following vowel. He thus
leaves the preceding syllable 'open,' *i.e.* he makes it short
when it ought to be long.

The effects of this pronunciation are disastrous in reading Latin poetry, for these doubled consonants occur on an
average in every other line of Latin poetry.

b. The second group consists of words in which a short
vowel is followed by *sp, sc, st*; also by *scl, scr, str*. In
English, when the vowel following these combinations is
accented, we usually combine the consonants with the following vowel. Thus we say *a-scríbe, a-stoúnding*, etc. Now,
the Latin pupil is almost certain to do the same thing in
pronouncing Latin, unless he is on his guard, *i.e.* he is likely
to say *a-spérsus, i-stórum, tempe-stívus, coru-scábat, mi-scúerat,*
magi-strórum, a-scrípsit, etc. What he ought to do is to join
the *s* with the preceding vowel (thus making the syllable
closed, and long), pronouncing *as-persus, is-tōrum, tempes-*
tivus, corus-cābat, mis-cuerat, magis-trōrum, as-cripsit, etc. By
joining all the consonants to the following vowel he leaves
the preceding syllable open. Hence, when the preceding
vowel is short, the syllable also becomes short. This
destroys the metre of the line.

c. The third group consists of words containing a short
vowel followed by *r* and some consonant. In our common
English utterance we are very apt to neglect the *r*. This
tendency is all but universal in New England, and is widely

prevalent in the Middle states. As a result, the pupil is apt to pronounce Latin with the same neglect of the *r* that he habitually practises in the vernacular. This omission occurs particularly where the preceding vowel is unaccented, *e.g.* in *portărum, terminŏrum, etc.* The pupil is likely to say *po(r)-tārum, te(r)-minorum, i.e.* he makes the preceding syllable 'open' and short, where it ought to be 'closed' and long. In order to close the syllable, a distinct articulation of the *r* is necessary. When this is overlooked, the quantity of the syllable is lost and the metrical character of the line is destroyed.

d. The fourth group of words consists of those ending in *s*, preceded by a short vowel and followed by words beginning with *c, p, t, v, m, n, f.* In English we are very apt to join the final *s* to the initial consonant of the following word. Thus we habitually say *grievou stale* for *grievous tale; Lewi sTaylor* for *Lewis Taylor, etc.* There is great danger of doing the same thing in Latin. Experience teaches that pupils often say *urbĭ sportās* for *urbis portās; capĭ scanem* for *capis canem;* even *urbĭ svīcī* for *urbis vīcī, etc.* Care must be taken to join the final *s* clearly with the preceding vowel. Otherwise the preceding syllable will be left 'open' and short where it ought to be 'closed' and long.

The foregoing cautions are not mere theoretical inventions. They are vital, and are based on experience of the errors which we as English-speaking people naturally commit when we pronounce Latin. It is only by a conscientious observance of the principles above laid down that any one can read Latin poetry quantitatively; and unless we do so read it, we necessarily fail to reproduce its true character.

Common Syllables.

As is well known, when a *short* vowel is followed by a mute with *l* or *r* (*pl, cl, tl; pr, cr, tr; etc.*), the syllable is

common, *i.e.* it may be either long or short in verse at the
option of the poet. The explanation of this peculiarity is
as follows: —

In a word like *pătrem*, for example, it was recognized
as legitimate to pronounce in two ways: either to combine
the *tr* with the following vowel (*pa-trem*), thus leaving the
preceding syllable 'open' and short, or to join the *t* with
the preceding vowel (*pat-rem*), thus closing the preceding
syllable and making it long. Hence, in the case of common
syllables, the quantity in each individual instance depends
upon the mode of pronunciation, *i.e.* the mode in which we
divide the syllable. In reading Latin poetry, therefore, it
will be necessary for the pupil to observe how the poet
treats each common syllable, and to pronounce accordingly.

ELISION.

The rule for Elision, as stated in our Latin grammars, is
in substance as follows: "A final vowel, a final diphthong,
or *m* with a preceding vowel,[1] is regularly elided before a
word beginning with a vowel or *h*."

The exact nature of Elision, as observed by the ancients
in reading Latin verse, is still very uncertain. The Romans
may have slurred the words together in some way, or they
may have omitted the elided part entirely.

RULES FOR READING.

1. Observe the quantity of each syllable scrupulously,
taking care to observe the division of the syllables as indicated by the hyphens, joining the consonant before the hyphen
with the preceding vowel, and so closing the syllable.

2. Make the word-accent light; subordinate it carefully
to quantity.

---

[1] The elision of final *m* with a preceding vowel is sometimes called
Ecthlipsis.

3. Endeavor to cultivate the quantitative sense, *i.e.* to feel the verse as consisting of a succession of long and short intervals.

4. Do not attempt to give special expression to the *ictus* in any way. The *ictus* will care for itself if the syllables are properly pronounced.

The Metre of the Satires.

56. The metre of the *Sermones* and *Epistulae* is the dactylic hexameter, consisting of six dactyls ($-\cup\cup$), of which the last is catalectic, *i.e.* $-\cup(\cup)$. In any foot, including the last, a spondee ($--$) may be substituted for the dactyl. The last syllable is therefore long or short at the option of the poet. The fifth foot is always a dactyl, except for a single spondaic line in *Ars Poet.* 467, *invitum qui servat, idem facit occidenti.* We thus have the following scheme: —

$$
\left. \begin{matrix} -\cup\cup \\ -- \end{matrix} \right| \left. \begin{matrix} -\cup\cup \\ -- \end{matrix} \right| \left. \begin{matrix} -\cup\cup \\ -- \end{matrix} \right| \left. \begin{matrix} -\cup\cup \\ -- \end{matrix} \right| \left. -\cup\cup \right| -\underset{\smile}{\cup}
$$

The most common caesura, as in classical Roman poetry generally, is the so-called penthemimeral in the middle of the third foot: *e.g.* i. 1. 1, —

> *qui fit, Maecenas,* ‖ *ut nemo quam sibi sortem*

Next in frequency is the so-called hepthemimeral, in the fourth foot, which is usually accompanied by another caesura in the second foot: *e.g.* i. 1. 30, —

> *audaces* ‖ *mare qui currunt* ‖ *hac mente laborem*

Sometimes the caesura in the second foot is omitted: *e.g.* ii. 3. 142, —

> *pauper Opimius argenti* ‖ *positi intus et auri*

The so-called feminine caesura, after a short syllable, is not uncommon: *e.g.* i. 3. 51, —

> *postulat ut videatur.* ‖ *At est truculentior atque*

The bucolic diaeresis, after the fourth foot, is comparatively frequent: *e.g.* i. 8. 25,—

> *cum Sagana maiore ululantem.* ‖ *Pallor utrasque*

A verse without a caesura, written purposely to illustrate faulty metre, occurs in *Ars Poet.* 263, —

> *non quivis videt immodulata poemata iudex.*

In the *Sermones*, as in Comedy, and less so in the *Epistulae*, so-called elision, probably a blending of two vowels, is frequent. It is found in the first syllable of lines, *e.g.* i. 1. 52, *dum ex parvo nobis tantundem haurire relinquas;* before the caesura, *e.g.* i. 4. 58, *tempora certa modosque,* ‖ *et quod prius ordine verbum est;* and with long vowels: *e.g.* i. 1. 59, *at qui tantuli eget quanto est opus, is neque limo;* i. 9. 30, *quod puero cecinit divina motā anus urna.*

Hypermetric verses, the final vowels of which are elided before a vowel at the beginning of the next line, occur in i. 4. 96 and i. 6. 102. Four lines (i. 2. 62; ii. 3. 117; E. ii. 2. 93; *Ars Poet.* 424) are united to the following lines by a compound word, which is divided between the two lines by tmesis.

57. Metrical licenses are numerous.

a. Hiatus occurs with the interjection *O* in ii. 3. 265; E. i. 19. 19; *Ars Poet.* 301; and with *num* in ii. 2. 28. Semihiatus (with shortening of the first vowel) occurs in i. 9. 38, *si me amas*, and *Ars Poet.* 65, *diu aptaque*.

b. We have synezesis of two vowels in i. 5. 37, *in Mamurrarum lassi deinde urbe manemus;* i. 6. 39, *deicere;* i. 8. 43, *cerea;* ii. 3. 91, *quoad;* ii. 6. 67, *prout;* ii. 1. 222, *reprehendere.*

c. Semivowels are treated as vowels and vowels as semivowels: *e.g.* i. 7. 30, *vindemiator et invictus, cui saepe viator;*

ii. 2. 76 and E. i. 1. 108, *pituita;* ii. 8. 1, *Nasidieni;* i. 8. 17, *suëtae.*

d. The original long quantity of vowels which had in the classical period become short is retained in i. 5. 90, *callidus ut soleāt umeris portare viator;* i. 9. 21, *subiit;* E. i. 6. 40, *fuerīs.* After the analogy of such cases, originally short vowels are lengthened in i. 4. 82, *defendīt;* ii. 2. 74, *miscuerīs;* ii. 3. 260, *agīt;* ii. 3. 1, *scribīs.*

e. The original short quantity of a vowel which had become long is retained in i. 10. 45, *annuĕrunt;* E. i. 4. 7, *dedĕrunt.*

58. Alliteration is frequent, and onomatopoeia may often be observed: *e.g.* i. 3. 136, *magnorum maxime regum;* i. 6. 57, *pudor prohibebat plura profari* (alliteration and onomatopoeia); i. 9. 24, *membra movere mollius;* ii. 8. 78, *stridere secreta divisos aure susurros* (alliteration and onomatopoeia); E. i. 2. 43, *labitur et labetur in omne volubilis aevum* (of a flowing stream; note the abundance of dactyls, the alliteration, and the onomatopoeia); *Ars Poet.* 260, *in scaenam missos cum magno pondere versus* (parodying the heavy spondaic verses of Ennius). We have rhyme in E. i. 12. 25, *ne tamen* ignores, *quo sit Romana* loco res; *Ars Poet.* 176–177, *seniles . . . viriles.*

In some cases the choice of words is determined by the requirements of the metre: *e.g.* i. 5. 37, *in Mamurrarum urbe* (instead of *Fōrmiae); ii. 1. 17, *Scipiadam* (instead of *Scīpiōnem); cf.* i. 5. 87, *mansuri oppiàulo quod versu dicere non est.*

Q. HORATI FLACCI
SERMONUM
LIBER PRIMUS.

———◆———

I.

ON AVARICE.

A DEDICATION OF THE FIRST BOOK OF THE SERMONES TO MAECENAS.

1. Outline: Nearly all men are discontented and unhappy: the cause is avarice :

  1. All men are dissatisfied with their own callings, and envy the lot of others, 1–3 ;

  They say that their life is full of hardship, 4–14 ;

  Yet they would not change places with any one else, if they had the opportunity, 14–22.

  2. The real cause of their discontent is their desire for wealth :

    a) They say that they are toiling to secure a provision for old age ;

    But if this were so, they would cease when they had enough to live on, 23–40 ;

    b) They assert that if they retire and use their store, it will soon melt away ;

    But if they do not use it, it has no real value, 41–51 ;

    c) There is more satisfaction, they declare, in drawing on a great hoard ;

    But if a man has enough, greater possessions are only a burden and a source of danger, 51–60 ;

    d) They allege that men are esteemed in proportion to their wealth ;

    Such a perverted view can be treated only with contempt, 61–67.

1

3. The avaricious man is always wretched:
    a) He does not know how to enjoy his wealth, 68–75;
    b) He is in constant fear and apprehension, 76–79;
    c) He cannot buy affection, 80–91;
    d) And sooner or later some dreadful fate overtakes him, 92–100.
4. Yet a man should not go to the other extreme. He should aim
        at a mean between stinginess and prodigality, 101–107:
    a) He will thus be free from discontent and envy, 108–116;
    b) He will live happily and die contented, 117–119.
5. Horace ends abruptly, to avoid the charge of garrulousness, 120–121.

2. **Time:** 35 B.C.

Qui fit, Maecenas, ut nemo, quam sibi sortem
Seu ratio dederit seu fors obiecerit, illa
Contentus vivat, laudet diversa sequentis?
   'O fortunati mercatores!' gravis annis
Miles ait, multo iam fractus membra labore.   5
Contra mercator, navem iactantibus Austris:
'Militia est potior. Quid enim? Concurritur; horae
Momento cita mors venit aut victoria laeta.'
Agricolam laudat iuris legumque peritus,
Sub galli cantum consultor ubi ostia pulsat.   10
Ille datis vadibus qui rure extractus in urbem est,
Solos felices viventis clamat in urbe.
Cetera de genere hoc — adeo sunt multa — loquacem
Delassare valent Fabium. Ne te morer, audi
Quo rem deducam. Si quis deus 'En ego' dicat   15
'Iam faciam quod voltis; eris tu, qui modo miles,
Mercator; tu consultus modo, rusticus: hinc vos,
Vos hinc mutatis discedite partibus. Heia!
Quid statis?'— nolint. Atqui licet esse beatis.
Quid causae est, merito quin illis Iuppiter ambas   20
Iratus buccas inflet neque se fore posthac
Tam facilem dicat, votis ut praebeat aurem?
   Praeterea ne sic, ut qui iocularia, ridens
Percurram — quamquam ridentem dicere verum

Quid vetat? ut pueris olim dant crustula blandi   25
Doctores, elementa velint ut discere prima;
Sed tamen amoto quaeramus seria ludo —
Ille gravem duro terram qui vertit aratro,
Perfidus hic caupo, miles, nautaeque per omne
Audaces mare qui currunt, hac mente laborem   30
Sese ferre, senes ut in otia tuta recedant,
Aiunt, cum sibi sint congesta cibaria; sicut
Parvola — nam exemplo est — magni formica laboris
Ore trahit quodcumque potest atque addit acervo,
Quem struit, haud ignara ac non incauta futuri.   35
Quae, simul inversum contristat Aquarius annum,
Non usquam prorepit et illis utitur ante
Quaesitis sapiens, cum te neque fervidus aestus
Demoveat lucro, neque hiems, ignis, mare, ferrum,
Nil obstet tibi, dum ne sit te ditior alter.   40

   Quid iuvat immensum te argenti pondus et auri
Furtim defossa timidum deponere terra?
'Quod si comminuas, vilem redigatur ad assem.'
At ni id fit, quid habet pulchri constructus acervus?
Milia frumenti tua triverit area centum;   45
Non tuus hoc capiet venter plus ac meus; ut si
Reticulum panis venalis inter onusto
Forte vehas umero, nihilo plus accipias quam
Qui nil portarit. Vel dic, quid referat intra
Naturae finis viventi iugera centum an   50
Mille aret?
                     'At suave est ex magno tollere acervo.'
Dum ex parvo nobis tantundem haurire relinquas,
Cur tua plus laudes cumeris granaria nostris?
Ut tibi si sit opus liquidi non amplius urna
Vel cyatho, et dicas 'magno de flumine mallem,   55
Quam ex hoc fonticulo tantundem sumere.' Eo fit,
Plenior ut si quos delectet copia iusto,

Cum ripa simul avolsos ferat Aufidus acer.
At qui tantuli eget, quanto est opus, is neque limo
Turbatam haurit aquam neque vitam amittit in undis.　60
　At bona pars hominum decepta cupidine falso
'Nil satis est' inquit 'quia tanti quantum habeas sis.'
Quid facias illi? Iubeas miserum esse, libenter
Quatenus id facit; ut quidam memoratur Athenis
Sordidus ac dives, populi contemnere voces　65
Sic solitus: 'Populus me sibilat, at mihi plaudo
Ipse domi, simul ac nummos contemplor in arca.'
　Tantalus a labris sitiens fugientia captat
Flumina — Quid rides? Mutato nomine de te
Fabula narratur; congestis undique saccis　70
Indormis inhians et tamquam parcere sacris
Cogeris aut pictis tamquam gaudere tabellis.
Nescis quo valeat nummus? quem praebeat usum?
Panis ematur, holus, vini sextarius, adde
Quis humana sibi doleat natura negatis.　75
An vigilare metu exanimem, noctesque diesque
Formidare malos fures, incendia, servos,
Ne te compilent fugientes, hoc iuvat? Horum
Semper ego optarim pauperrimus esse bonorum.
　[At si condoluit temptatum frigore corpus　80
Aut alius casus lecto te adfixit, habes qui
Adsideat, fomenta paret, medicum roget ut te
Suscitet ac reddat gnatis carisque propinquis?
Non uxor salvum te volt, non filius; omnes
Vicini oderunt, noti, pueri atque puellae.　85
Miraris, cum tu argento post omnia ponas,
Si nemo praestet, quem non merearis, amorem?
An si cognatos, nullo natura labore
Quos tibi dat, retinere velis servareque amicos,
Infelix operam perdas, ut si quis asellum　90
In Campo doceat parentem currere frenis?

Denique sit finis quaerendi, cumque habeas plus,
Pauperiem metuas minus et finire laborem
Incipias, parto quod avebas, ne facias quod
Ummidius quidam.   Non longa est fabula: dives,   95
Ut metiretur nummos, ita sordidus, ut se
Non umquam servo melius vestiret, ad usque
Supremum tempus, ne se penuria victus
Opprimeret, metuebat.   At hunc liberta securi
Divisit medium, fortissima Tyndaridarum.   100
    'Quid mi igitur suades? Ut vivam Naevius, aut sic
Ut Nomentanus?'   Pergis pugnantia secum
Frontibus adversis componere; non ego, avarum
Cum veto te fieri, vappam iubeo ac nebulonem.
Est inter Tanain quiddam socerumque Viselli.   105
Est modus in rebus, sunt certi denique fines,
Quos ultra citraque nequit consistere rectum.
    Illuc, unde abii, redeo, qui nemo, ut avarus,
Se probet ac potius laudet diversa sequentis,
Quodque aliena capella gerat distentius uber,   110
Tabescat, neque se maiori pauperiorum
Turbae comparet, hunc atque hunc superare laboret.
Sic festinanti semper locupletior obstat,
Ut, cum carceribus missos rapit ungula currus,
Instat equis auriga suos vincentibus, illum   115
Praeteritum temnens extremos inter euntem.
    Inde fit, ut raro, qui se vixisse beatum
Dicat et exacto contentus tempore vita
Cedat uti conviva satur, reperire queamus.
    Iam satis est; ne me Crispini scrinia lippi   120
Compilasse putes, verbum non amplius addam.

II.

The coarseness of this satire leads to omission of an outline.

Ambubaiarum collegia, pharmacopolae,
Mendici, mimae, balatrones, hoc genus omne
Maestum ac sollicitum est cantoris morte Tigelli.
Quippe benignus erat.   Contra hic, ne prodigus esse
Dicatur metuens, inopi dare nolit amico,   5
Frigus quo duramque famem propellere possit.
Hunc si perconteris, avi cur atque parentis
Praeclaram ingrata stringat malus ingluvie rem,
Omnia conductis coemens obsonia nummis;
Sordidus atque animi quod parvi nolit haberi,   10
Respondet.   Laudatur ab his, culpatur ab illis.
Fufidius vappae famam timet ac nebulonis,
Dives agris, dives positis in faenore nummis;
Quinas hic capiti mercedes exsecat, atque
Quanto perditior quisque est, tanto acrius urguet;   15
Nomina sectatur modo sumpta veste virili
Sub patribus duris tironum. 'Maxime' quis non
'Iuppiter!' exclamat, simul atque audivit? 'At in se
Pro quaestu sumptum facit.' Hic? Vix credere possis,
Quam sibi non sit amicus, ita ut pater ille, Terenti   20
Fabula quem miserum gnato vixisse fugato
Inducit, non se peius cruciaverit atque hic.
    Si quis nunc quaerat 'Quo res haec pertinet?'   Illuc:
Dum vitant stulti vitia, in contraria currunt.
    Maltinus tunicis demissis ambulat; est qui   25
Inguen ad obscenum subductis usque facetus.
Pastillos Rufillus olet, Gargonius hircum.
Nil medium est.   Sunt qui nolint tetigisse nisi illas,
Quarum subsuta talos tegat instita veste;
Contra alius nullam nisi olenti in fornice stantem.   30
    Quidam notus homo cum exiret fornice, 'Macte
Virtute esto' inquit sententia dia Catonis:

' Nam simul ac venas inflavit taetra libido,
Huc iuvenes aequum est descendere, non alienas
Permolere uxores.'   'Nolim laudarier' inquit   35
' Sic me' mirator cunni Cupiennius albi.

   Audire est operae pretium, procedere recte
Qui moechos non voltis, ut omni parte laborent,
Utque illis multo corrupta dolore voluptas,
Atque haec rara, cadat dura inter saepe pericla.   40
Hic se praecipitem tecto dedit, ille flagellis
Ad mortem caesus, fugiens hic decidit acrem
Praedonum in turbam, dedit hic pro corpore nummos,
Hunc perminxerunt calones; quin etiam illud
Accidit, ut cuidam testis caudamque salacem   45
Demeterent ferro.   'Iure' omnes; Galba negabat.

   Tutior at quanto merx est in classe secunda,
Libertinarum dico, Sallustius in quas
Non minus insanit quam qui moechatur.   At hic si,
Qua res, qua ratio suaderet, quaque modeste   50
Munifico esse licet, vellet bonus atque benignus
Esse, daret quantum satis esset, nec sibi damno
Dedecorique foret.   Verum hoc se amplectitur uno,
Hoc amat et laudat, 'Matronam nullam ego tango.'
Ut quondam Marsaeus, amator Originis ille,   55
Qui patrium mimae donat fundumque Laremque
' Nil fuerit mi' inquit 'cum uxoribus umquam alienis.'
Verum est cum mimis, est cum meretricibus, unde
Fama malum gravius quam res trahit.   An tibi abunde
Personam satis est, non illud, quicquid ubique   60
Officit, evitare?   Bonam deperdere famam,
Rem patris oblimare, malum est ubicumque.   Quid inter
Est in matrona, ancilla peccesne togata?
Villius in Fausta Sullae gener, hoc miser uno
Nomine deceptus, poenas dedit usque superque   65
Quam satis est, pugnis caesus ferroque petitus,

Exclusus fore, cum Longarenus foret intus.
Huic si mutonis verbis mala tanta videnti
Diceret haec animus 'Quid vis tibi? numquid ego a te
Magno prognatum deposco consule cunnum   70
Velatumque stola, mea cum conferbuit ira?'
Quid responderet? 'Magno patre nata puella est.'
At quanto meliora monet pugnantiaque istis
Dives opis natura suae, tu si modo recte
Dispensare velis ac non fugienda petendis   75
Immiscere. Tuo vitio rerumne labores,
Nil referre putas? Quare, ne paeniteat te,
Desine matronas sectarier, unde laboris
Plus haurire mali est quam ex re decerpere fructus.
Nec magis huic, inter niveos viridesque lapillos —   80
Sit licet, hoc, Cerinthe, tuum — tenerum est femur aut crus
Rectius, atque etiam melius persaepe togatae est.
   Adde huc quod mercem sine fucis gestat, aperte
Quod venale habet ostendit, nec, si quid honesti est,
Iactat habetque palam, quaerit quo turpia celet.   85
Regibus hic mos est, ubi equos mercantur; opertos
Inspiciunt, ne si facies, ut saepe, decora
Molli fulta pede est, emptorem inducat hiantem,
Quod pulchrae clunes, breve quod caput, ardua cervix.
Hoc illi recte; ne corporis optima Lyncei   90
Contemplere oculis, Hypsaea caecior illa
Quae mala sunt spectes. 'O crus, o bracchia!' Verum
Depugis, nasuta, brevi latere ac pede longo est.
Matronae praeter faciem nil cernere possis,
Cetera, ni Catia est, demissa veste tegentis.   95
   Si interdicta petes, vallo circumdata — nam te
Hoc facit insanum — multae tibi tum officient res,
Custodes, lectica, ciniflones, parasitae,
Ad talos stola demissa et circumdata palla,
Plurima, quae invideant pure apparere tibi rem.   100

Altera, nil obstat; Cois tibi paene videre est
Ut nudam, ne crure malo, ne sit pede turpi;
Metiri possis oculo latus. An tibi mavis
Insidias fieri pretiumque avellier ante
Quam mercem ostendi? ' Leporem venator ut alta   105
In nive sectetur, positum sic tangere nolit,'
Cantat et adponit 'Meus est amor huic similis; nam
Transvolat in medio posita et fugientia captat.'
Hiscine versiculis speras tibi posse dolores
Atque aestus curasque gravis e pectore tolli?   110
Nonne, cupidinibus statuat natura modum quem,
Quid latura sibi, quid sit dolitura negatum,
Quaerere plus prodest et inane abscindere soldo?
   Num, tibi cum fauces urit sitis, aurea quaeris
Pocula? Num esuriens fastidis omnia praeter   115
Pavonem rhombumque? Tument tibi cum inguina, num, si
Ancilla aut verna est praesto puer, impetus in quem
Continuo fiat, malis tentigine rumpi?
Non ego: namque parabilem amo Venerem facilemque.
Illam 'Post paullo'; 'Sed pluris'; 'Si exierit vir'   120
Gallis, hanc Philodemus ait sibi, quae neque magno
Stet pretio neque cunctetur, cum est iussa venire.
Candida rectaque sit, munda hactenus, ut neque longa
Nec magis alba velit quam dat natura videri.
Haec, ubi supposuit dextro corpus mihi laevum,   125
Ilia et Egeria est; do nomen quodlibet illi,
Nec vereor ne, dum futuo, vir rure recurrat,
Ianua frangatur, latret canis, undique magno
Pulsa domus strepitu resonet, vepallida lecto
Desiliat mulier, miseram se conscia clamet,   130
Cruribus haec metuat, doti deprensa, egomet mi.
Discincta tunica fugiendum est ac pede nudo,
Ne nummi pereant aut puga aut denique fama.
Deprendi miserum est: Fabio vel iudice vincam.

III.

ON INTOLERANT JUDGMENT.

1. Outline :

1. Men have no patience with the faults of others, but are lenient toward their own :

   a) They see many inconsistencies in the conduct of their neighbors, 1–19 ;

   b) They plead guilty to a certain degree of fallibility, but their silly self-love makes them pardon themselves, 19–28 ;

   c) They will not see the good qualities of their fellows, even though these far outweigh their defects, 29–37 ;

   d) They would do well to cultivate love's blindness, and regard their friends' failings as virtues, 38–54 ;

   e) As a matter of fact, they exaggerate these failings into serious faults, 55–66 ;

   f) As they judge, so will they be judged, 66–75.

2. Intolerant judgment is fostered by the doctrine of the Stoics, that all faults are equal.   This doctrine is false :

   a) It is the height of folly to make no distinction between trivial offences and crimes, 76–95 ;

   b) To regard all faults as equal is contrary to common sense and to the interests of society, 96–98 ;

   c) It is founded on a false conception of the nature of law :

      1) As man emerged from a state of barbarism, he made laws for his own protection, 99–112 ;

      2) They were not based on a simple division of all acts into right and wrong, but on a gradation of offences according to their effect on the welfare of the community, 113–124 ;

   d) We might infer its falsity from that of another absurd doctrine of the Stoics, that the philosopher, as such, is skilled in every kind of work and is a king among men, 124–136.

3. Horace prefers to be a private citizen, and to live on terms of mutual tolerance with his fellowmen, 136–142.

2. Time : The exact date is uncertain ; not after 35 B.C.

Omnibus hoc vitium est cantoribus, inter amicos
Ut numquam inducant animum cantare rogati,
Iniussi numquam desistant. Sardus habebat
Ille Tigellius hoc. Caesar, qui cogere posset,

Si peteret per amicitiam patris atque suam, non   5
Quicquam proficeret; si collibuisset, ab ovo
Usque ad mala citaret 'io Bacchae' modo summa
Voce, modo hac, resonat quae chordis quattuor ima.
Nil aequale homini fuit illi: saepe velut qui
Currebat fugiens hostem, persaepe velut qui   10
Iunonis sacra ferret; habebat saepe ducentos,
Saepe decem servos; modo reges atque tetrarchas,
Omnia magna loquens, modo 'Sit mihi mensa tripes et
Concha salis puri et toga, quae defendere frigus,
Quamvis crassa, queat.' Deciens centena dedisses   15
Huic parco, paucis contento: quinque diebus
Nil erat in loculis. Noctes vigilabat ad ipsum
Mane, diem totum stertebat. Nil fuit umquam
Sic impar sibi.

         *Nunc aliquis dicat mihi 'quid tu?
·Nullane habes vitia?' Immo alia, et fortasse minora.   20
Maenius absentem Novium cum carperet, 'heus tu'
Quidam ait 'ignoras te, an ut ignotum dare nobis
Verba putas?' 'Egomet mi ignosco' Maenius inquit.
Stultus et improbus hic amor est dignusque notari.
Cum tua pervideas oculis mala lippus inunctis,   25
Cur in amicorum vitiis tam cernis acutum,
Quam aut aquila aut serpens Epidaurius? At tibi contra
Evenit, inquirant vitia ut tua rursus et illi.

    Iracundior est paullo, minus aptus acutis
Naribus horum hominum; rideri possit eo, quod   30
Rusticius tonso toga defluit et male laxus
In pede calceus haeret; at est bonus, ut melior vir
Non alius quisquam, at tibi amicus, at ingenium ingens
Inculto latet hoc sub corpore. Denique te ipsum
Concute, num qua tibi vitiorum inseverit olim   35
Natura aut etiam consuetudo mala; namque
Neglectis urenda filix innascitur agris.

Illuc praevertamur: amatorem quod amicae
Turpia decipiunt caecum, vitia aut etiam ipsa haec
Delectant, veluti Balbinum polypus Hagnae.   40
Vellem in amicitia sic erraremus et isti
Errori nomen virtus posuisset honestum.
Ac pater ut gnati, sic nos debemus amici
Si quod sit vitium, non fastidire.   Strabonem
Appellat paetum pater, et pullum, male parvus   45
Si cui filius est, ut abortivus fuit olim
Sisyphus; hunc varum distortis cruribus, illum
Balbutit scaurum, pravis fultum male talis.
Parcius hic vivit: frugi dicatur.   Ineptus
Et iactantior hic paullo est: concinnus amicis   50
Postulat ut videatur.   At est truculentior atque
Plus aequo liber: simplex fortisque habeatur.
Caldior est: acris inter numeretur.   Opinor,
Haec res et iungit, iunctos et servat amicos.

   At nos virtutes ipsas invertimus atque   55
Sincerum cupimus vas incrustare.   Probus quis
Nobiscum vivit, multum demissus homo; illi
Tardo cognomen pingui damus.   Hic fugit omnis
Insidias nullique malo latus obdit apertum;
Cum genus hoc inter vitae versetur, ubi acris   60
Invidia atque vigent ubi crimina, pro bene sano
Ac non incauto fictum astutumque vocamus.
Simplicior quis et est, qualem me saepe libenter
Obtulerim tibi, Maecenas, ut forte legentem
Aut tacitum impellat quovis sermone: 'Molestus!   65
Communi sensu plane caret' inquimus.
                                        Eheu,
Quam temere in nosmet legem sancimus iniquam!
Nam vitiis nemo sine nascitur; optimus ille est,
Qui minimis urgetur.   Amicus dulcis, ut aequum est,
Cum mea compenset vitiis bona, pluribus hisce,   70

Si modo plura mihi bona sunt, inclinet, amari
Si volet.   Hac lege in trutina ponetur eadem.
Qui ne tuberibus propriis offendat amicum
Postulat, ignoscet verrucis illius: aequum est
Peccatis veniam poscentem reddere rursus.   75
Denique, quatenus excidi penitus vitium irae,
Cetera item nequeunt stultis haerentia, cur non
Ponderibus modulisque suis ratio utitur, ac res
Ut quaeque est, ita suppliciis delicta coercet?
Si quis eum servum, patinam qui tollere iussus   80
Semesos piscis tepidumque ligurrierit ius,
In cruce suffigat, Labeone insanior inter
Sanos dicatur.   Quanto hoc furiosius atque
Maius peccatum est: paullum deliquit amicus,
Quod nisi concedas, habeare insuavis, acerbus: 85
Odisti et fugis ut Rusonem debitor aeris,
Qui nisi, cum tristes misero venere Kalendae,
Mercedem aut nummos unde unde extricat, amaras
Porrecto iugulo historias captivus ut audit.
Comminxit lectum potus mensave catillum   90
Evandri manibus tritum deiecit; ob hanc rem,
Aut positum ante mea quia pullum in parte catini
Sustulit esuriens, minus hoc iucundus amicus
Sit mihi?   Quid faciam si furtum fecerit, aut si
Prodiderit commissa fide sponsumve negarit?   95
   Quis paria esse fere placuit peccata, laborant
Cum ventum ad verum est: sensus moresque repugnant
Atque ipsa utilitas, iusti prope mater et aequi.
   Cum prorepserunt primis animalia terris,
Mutum et turpe pecus, glandem atque cubilia propter   100
Unguibus et pugnis, dein fustibus, atque ita porro
Pugnabant armis, quae post fabricaverat usus,
Donec verba, quibus voces sensusque notarent,
Nominaque invenere; dehinc absistere bello,

Oppida coeperunt munire et ponere leges,   105
Ne quis fur esset, neu latro, neu quis adulter;
Iura inventa metu iniusti fateare necesse est,   111
Tempora si fastosque velis evolvere mundi.

  Nec natura potest iusto secernere iniquum,
Dividit ut bona diversis, fugienda petendis;
Nec vincet ratio hoc, tantundem ut peccet idemque,   115
Qui teneros caules alieni fregerit horti
Et qui nocturnus sacra divum legerit.   Adsit
Regula, peccatis quae poenas inroget aequas,
Ne scutica dignum horribili sectere flagello.
Nam ut ferula caedas meritum maiora subire   120
Verbera, non vereor, cum dicas esse pares res
Furta latrociniis et magnis parva mineris
Falce recisurum simili te, si tibi regnum
Permittant homines.

                    Si dives, qui sapiens est,
Et sutor bonus et solus formosus et est rex,   125
Cur optas quod habes? 'Non nosti, quid pater' inquit
'Chrysippus dicat: sapiens crepidas sibi numquam
Nec soleas fecit, sutor tamen est sapiens'. Qui?
'Ut quamvis tacet Hermogenes, cantor tamen atque
Optimus est modulator; ut Alfenus vafer omni   130
Abiecto instrumento artis clausaque taberna
Tonsor erat; sapiens operis sic optimus omnis
Est opifex, solus sic rex.' ❡ Vellunt tibi barbam
Lascivi pueri, quos tu nisi fuste coerces,
Urgueris turba circum te stante miserque   135
Rumperis et latras, magnorum maxime regum.

  Ne longum faciam, dum tu quadrante lavatum
Rex ibis neque te quisquam stipator ineptum
Praeter Crispinum sectabitur, et mihi dulces
Ignoscent si quid peccaro stultus, amici,   140
Inque vicem illorum patiar delicta libenter,
Privatusque magis vivam te rege beatus.

IV.

THE OLD AND THE NEW SATIRE.

1. Outline:

   1. The earlier satire attacked all men who were vulnerable, and held them up to public ridicule. It was therefore generally feared and detested :

     a) Its prototype was the Old Comedy of the Greeks, 1–5 ;

     b) Its greatest Roman representative was Lucilius, who had two serious faults, 6–7 :

       1) He was too diffuse, 8–12 ;

       2) He was careless in composition, 12–13 ;

     c) Horace proposes to improve on Lucilius in two ways :

       1) By not writing voluminously and carelessly, 13–21 ;

       2) By not forcing his works on a public to which they might be distasteful, 21–38.

   2. Horace's conception of satire, and his reasons for choosing that field of writing :

     a) He does not claim the title of poet. He merely describes the events of everyday life in verse, 38–62 ;

     b) It is unreasonable to fear him, for no blameless man is attacked. Moreover, he writes merely for the entertainment and instruction of a small circle of friends, 63–78 ;

     c) He does not take pleasure in hurting people's feelings. He finds amusement in the weaknesses and eccentricities of others, but without malice, 78–103 ;

     d) It is natural for him to observe the conduct of others. He was trained to do so in his youth by his father, as a means of self-improvement, 103–126 ;

     e) He endeavors not merely to note the good and the bad qualities of others, but to profit by his observation. His readers may draw their own moral, 126–137 ;

     f) To jot down his thoughts is doubtless a weakness, but it should be forgiven. If not, he will call all his fellow-poets to his aid and compel his critics to join the craft, 137–143.

2. Time: The exact date is uncertain ; not after 35 B.C.

Eupolis atque Cratinus Aristophanesque poetae
Atque alii, quorum comoedia prisca virorum est,
Si quis erat dignus describi, quod malus ac fur,

Quod moechus foret aut sicarius aut alioqui
Famosus, multa cum libertate notabant.   5
  Hinc omnis pendet Lucilius, hosce secutus
Mutatis tantum pedibus numerisque, facetus,
Emunctae naris, durus componere versus.
Nam fuit hoc vitiosus: in hora saepe ducentos,
Ut magnum, versus dictabat stans pede in uno.   10
Cum flueret lutulentus, erat quod tollere velles;
Garrulus atque piger scribendi ferre laborem,
Scribendi recte; nam ut multum, nil moror.
                                    Ecce,
Crispinus minimo me provocat: 'accipe, si vis,
Accipe iam tabulas; detur nobis locus, hora,   15
Custodes; videamus uter plus scribere possit.'
Di bene fecerunt, inopis me quodque pusilli
Finxerunt animi, raro et perpauca loquentis;
At tu conclusas hirquinis follibus auras
Usque laborantis, dum ferrum molliat ignis,   20
Ut mavis, imitare.
              Beatus Fannius ultro
Delatis capsis et imagine; cum mea nemo
Scripta legat, volgo recitare timentis ob hanc rem,
Quod sunt quos genus hoc minime iuvat, utpote pluris
Culpari dignos.   Quemvis media elige turba;   25
Aut ab avaritia aut misera ambitione laborat.
Hunc capit argenti splendor; stupet Albius aere;
Hic mutat merces surgente a sole ad eum quo
Vespertina tepet regio; quin per mala praeceps   30
Fertur, uti pulvis collectus turbine, ne quid
Summa deperdat metuens aut ampliet ut rem.
Omnes hi metuunt versus, odere poetas.
'Faenum habet in cornu, longe fuge; dummodo risum
Excutiat sibi, non hic cuiquam parcet amico;   35
Et quodcumque semel chartis inleverit, omnis

Gestiet a furno redeuntis scire lacuque
Et pueros et anus.'
     Agedum, pauca accipe contra.
Primum ego me illorum, dederim quibus esse poetas,
Excerpam numero; neque enim concludere versum 40
Dixeris esse satis; neque, si qui scribat uti nos
Sermoni propiora, putes hunc esse poetam.
Ingenium cui sit, cui mens divinior atque os
Magna sonaturum, des nominis huius honorem.
Idcirco quidam comoedia necne poema 45
Esset quaesivere, quod acer spiritus ac vis
Nec verbis nec rebus inest, nisi quod pede certo
Differt sermoni, sermo merus. ' At pater ardens
Saevit, quod meretrice nepos insanus amica
Filius uxorem grandi cum dote recuset, 50
Ebrius et, magnum quod dedecus, ambulet ante
Noctem cum facibus.' Numquid Pomponius istis
Audiret leviora, pater si viveret ? Ergo
Non satis est puris versum perscribere verbis,
Quem si dissolvas, quivis stomachetur eodem 55
Quo personatus pacto pater. His, ego quae nunc,
Olim quae scripsit Lucilius, eripias si
Tempora certa modosque, et quod prius ordine verbum est
Posterius facias, praeponens ultima primis,
Non, ut si solvas ' postquam Discordia taetra 60
Belli ferratos postis portasque refregit,'
Invenias etiam disiecti membra poetae.
 Hactenus haec: alias iustum sit necne poema;
Nunc illud tantum quaeram, meritone tibi sit
Suspectum genus hoc scribendi. Sulcius acer 65
Ambulat et Caprius, rauci male cumque libellis,
Magnus uterque timor latronibus; at bene si quis
Et vivat puris manibus, contemnat utrumque.
Ut sis tu similis Caeli Birrique latronum,

Non ego sim Capri neque Sulci; cur metuas me ?　　　70
Nulla taberna meos habeat neque pila libellos,
Quis manus insudet volgi Hermogenisque Tigelli;
Nec recito cuiquam nisi amicis, idque coactus,
Non ubivis coramve quibuslibet.　In medio qui
Scripta foro recitent sunt multi, quique lavantes;　　75
Suave locus voci resonat conclusus.　Inanis
Hoc iuvat, haud illud quaerentis, num sine sensu,
Tempore num faciant alieno.
　　　　　　　　　　　　' Laedere gaudes,'
Inquit ' et hoc studio pravus facis.'　Unde petitum
Hoc in me iacis ?　Est auctor quis denique eorum　　80
Vixi cum quibus ?　Absentem qui rodit amicum,
Qui non defendit alio culpante, solutos
Qui captat risus hominum famamque dicacis,
Fingere qui non visa potest, commissa tacere
Qui nequit; hic niger est, hunc tu, Romane, caveto.　85
Saepe tribus lectis videas cenare quaternos,
E quibus unus amet quavis aspergere cunctos
Praeter eum qui praebet aquam; post hunc quoque potus,
Condita cum verax aperit praecordia Liber.
Hic tibi comis et urbanus liberque videtur,　　　　90
Infesto nigris; ego si risi, quod ineptus
Pastillos Rufillus olet, Gargonius hircum,
Lividus et mordax videor tibi ?　Mentio si quae
De Capitolini furtis iniecta Petilli
Te coram fuerit, defendas ut tuus est mos :　　　　95
' Me Capitolinus convictore usus amicoque
A puero est, causaque mea permulta rogatus
Fecit, et incolumis laetor quod vivit in urbe;
Sed tamen admiror quo pacto iudicium illud
Fugerit.'　Hic nigrae sucus lolliginis, haec est　　100
Aerugo mera; quod vitium procul afore chartis
Atque animo prius, ut si quid promittere de me

Possum aliud vere, promitto.
     Liberius si
Dixero quid, si forte iocosius, hoc mihi iuris
Cum venia dabis; insuevit pater optimus hoc me,   105
Ut fugerem exemplis vitiorum quaeque notando.
Cum me hortaretur, parce frugaliter atque
Viverem uti contentus eo quod mi ipse parasset:
'Nonne vides, Albi ut male vivat filius utque
Baius inops ? Magnum documentum, ne patriam rem   110
Perdere quis velit.' A turpi meretricis amore
Cum deterreret: 'Scetani dissimilis sis.'
Ne sequerer moechas, concessa cum venere uti
Possem: 'Deprensi non bella est fama Treboni'
Aiebat. 'Sapiens, vitatu quidque petitu   115
Sit melius, causas reddet tibi; mi satis est, si
Traditum ab antiquis morem servare tuamque,
Dum custodis eges, vitam famamque tueri
Incolumem possum; simul ac duraverit aetas
Membra animumque tuum, nabis sine cortice.' Sic me   120
Formabat puerum dictis, et sive iubebat,
Ut facerem quid, 'habes auctorem, quo facias hoc,'
Unum ex iudicibus selectis obiciebat;
Sive vetabat, 'an hoc inhonestum et inutile factu
Necne sit addubites, flagret rumore malo cum   125
Hic atque ille ?'
     Avidos vicinum funus ut aegros
Exanimat mortisque metu sibi parcere cogit,
Sic teneros animos aliena opprobria saepe
Absterrent vitiis. Ex hoc ego sanus ab illis,
Perniciem quaecumque ferunt, mediocribus et quis   130
Ignoscas vitiis teneor. Fortassis et istinc
Largiter abstulerit longa aetas, liber amicus,
Consilium proprium; neque enim, cum lectulus aut me
Porticus excepit, desum mihi. 'Rectius hoc est.

Hoc faciens vivam melius.   Sic dulcis amicis   135
Occurram.   Hoc quidam non belle; numquid ego illi
Imprudens olim faciam simile?'
                                    Haec ego mecum
Compressis agito labris; ubi quid datur oti,
Inludo chartis.   Hoc est mediocribus illis
Ex vitiis unum; cui si concedere nolis,   140
Multa poetarum veniet manus, auxilio quae
Sit mihi — nam multo plures sumus, — ac veluti te
Iudaei cogemus in hanc concedere turbam.

V.

A JOURNEY TO BRUNDISIUM.

1. Occasion of the Satire : In the year 40 B.C. Antony and Octavian became reconciled, and struck a treaty at Brundisium. Two years later Octavian was defeated in a naval engagement by Sextus Pompeius, and despatched Maecenas to Athens, to ask Antony for help.   In the spring of 37 the latter appeared off Brundisium with a fleet of three hundred ships, and Octavian, who had meanwhile repented of his call for aid, sent Maecenas, with Cocceius and Fonteius Capito, to come to terms with his rival.   It is the journey of Maecenas to Brundisium on this occasion which the satire describes.   Maecenas was evidently in no haste, since the trip, which might have been made in from six to nine days, occupied fifteen.

Antony was not allowed to land at Brundisium, and a treaty was finally made, with some difficulty, at Tarentum.

Lucilius had described a journey from Rome to Capua and thence along the coast to the Straits of Messana.   It is not impossible that Horace placed this satire immediately after his criticism of Lucilius with the purpose of challenging comparison.   An examination of the few extant fragments of the narrative of Lucilius fully supports Horace's claim of superiority in versification and general finish.

2. The Itinerary : The distances are for the most part known from inscriptions.   Uncertainty is caused in three cases by doubt as to the exact location of the villa near Trivicum and the *oppidulum quod versu dicere non est*.   Desjardins assumes that the travellers did not spend the night at Capua or at Beneventum, while Gibbon does not allow a night at Terracina.

Imitation of Sucillius — satirist who had
far bitter tongue than Horace.

Day.	Stopping place.	Distance in Roman miles (=1854 ft.).	Verses.
1.	Aricia	16	1-3
2.	Forum Appi	27	3-9
3.	Night journey by canal-boat, through the Pomptine marshes, to Lucus Feroniae	16 } 19	9-23
	Terracina	3	23-33
4.	Fundi	13 } 26	34-38
	Formiae	13	
5.	Sinuessa	18 } 27	39-46
	Villa near Fons Campanus	9	
6.	Capua	17	47-49
7.	Villa of Cocceius near Caudium	21	50-70
8.	Beneventum	11	71-76
9.	Villa near Trivicum	24 ?	77-81
10.	Oppidulum quod versu dicere non est	24 ?	86-90
11.	Canusium	35 ?	91-93
12.	Rubi	23	94-95
13.	Barium	23	96-97
14.	Gnatia	37	97-103
15.	Brundisium	39	104

3. Time: About 37 B.C.

Egressum magna me accepit Aricia Roma
Hospitio modico; rhetor comes Heliodorus,
Graecorum longe doctissimus; inde Forum Appi,
Differtum nautis, cauponibus atque malignis.
Hoc iter ignavi divisimus, altius ac nos   5
Praecinctis unum; minus est gravis Appia tardis.
Hic ego propter aquam, quod erat deterrima, ventri
Indico bellum, cenantis haud animo aequo
Exspectans comites.
                    Iam nox inducere terris
Umbras et caelo diffundere signa parabat;   10
Tum pueri nautis, pueris convicia nautae
Ingerere: 'huc appelle! trecentos inseris; ohe
Iam satis est!' Dum aes exigitur, dum mula ligatur,
Tota abit hora. Mali culices ranaeque palustres

Avertunt somnos, absentem ut cantat amicam   15
Multa prolutus vappa nauta atque viator
Certatim.   Tandem fessus dormire viator
Incipit, ac missae pastum retinacula mulae
Nauta piger saxo religat stertitque supinus.
Iamque dies aderat, nil cum procedere lintrem   20
Sentimus; donec cerebrosus prosilit unus
Ac mulae nautaeque caput lumbosque saligno
Fuste dolat; quarta vix demum exponimur hora.
    Ora manusque tua lavimus, Feronia, lympha;
Milia tum pransi tria repimus atque subimus   25
Impositum saxis late candentibus Anxur.
Huc venturus erat Maecenas optimus atque
Cocceius, missi magnis de rebus uterque
Legati, aversos soliti componere amicos.
Hic oculis ego nigra meis collyria lippus   30
Inlinere.   Interea Maecenas advenit atque
Cocceius, Capitoque simul Fonteius, ad unguem
Factus homo, Antoni non ut magis alter amicus.
    Fundos Aufidio Lusco praetore libenter
Linquimus, insani ridentes praemia scribae,   35
Praetextam et latum clavum prunaeque vatillum.
In Mamurrarum lassi deinde urbe manemus,
Murena praebente domum, Capitone culinam.
    Postera lux oritur multo gratissima; namque
Plotius et Varius Sinuessae Vergiliusque   40
Occurrunt, animae, qualis neque candidiores
Terra tulit, neque quis me sit devinctior alter.
O qui complexus et gaudia quanta fuerunt!
Nil ego contulerim iucundo sanus amico.
Proxima Campano ponti quae villula, tectum   45
Praebuit, et parochi quae debent ligna salemque.
    Hinc muli Capuae clitellas tempore ponunt.
Lusum it Maecenas, dormitum ego Vergiliusque:

Namque pila lippis inimicum et ludere crudis.

    Hinc nos Coccei recipit plenissima villa,   50
Quae super est Caudi cauponas.   Nunc mihi paucis
Sarmenti scurrae pugnam Messique Cicirri,
Musa, velim memores, et quo patre natus uterque
Contulerit litis.   Messi clarum genus Osci;
Sarmenti domina exstat; ab his maioribus orti   55
Ad pugnam venere.   Prior Sarmentus 'Equi te
Esse feri similem dico.' Ridemus, et ipse
Messius 'Accipio,' caput et movet.   'O, tua cornu
Ni foret exsecto frons,' inquit, 'quid faceres, cum
Sic mutilus minitaris?'   At illi foeda cicatrix   60
Setosam laevi frontem turpaverat oris.
Campanum in morbum, in faciem permulta iocatus,
Pastorem saltaret uti Cyclopa rogabat;
Nil illi larva aut tragicis opus esse coturnis.
Multa Cicirrus ad haec: donasset iamne catenam   65
Ex voto Laribus, quaerebat; scriba quod esset,
Nilo deterius dominae ius esse.   Rogabat
Denique cur umquam fugisset, cui satis una
Farris libra foret, gracili sic tamque pusillo.
Prorsus iucunde cenam producimus illam.   70

    Tendimus hinc recta Beneventum, ubi sedulus hospes
Paene macros arsit dum turdos versat in igni;
Nam vaga per veterem dilapso flamma culinam
Volcano summum properabat lambere tectum.
Convivas avidos cenam servosque timentis   75
Tum rapere atque omnis restinguere velle videres.

    Incipit ex illo montis Apulia notos
Ostentare mihi, quos torret Atabulus et quos
Numquam erepsemus, nisi nos vicina Trivici
Villa recepisset, lacrimoso non sine fumo,   80
Udos cum foliis ramos urente camino.

    Quattuor hinc rapimur viginti et milia raedis,

Mansuri oppidulo, quod versu dicere non est,
Signis perfacile est: venit vilissima rerum
Hic aqua, sed panis longe pulcherrimus, ultra
Callidus ut soleat umeris portare viator.　　　　　　90
Nam Canusi lapidosus, aquae non ditior urna
Qui locus a forti Diomede est conditus olim.
Flentibus hic Varius discedit maestus amicis.
Inde Rubos fessi pervenimus, utpote longum
Carpentes iter et factum corruptius imbri.　　　　　　95
Postera tempestas melior, via peior ad usque
Bari moenia piscosi; dein Gnatia lymphis
Iratis exstructa dedit risusque iocosque,
Dum flamma sine tura liquescere limine sacro
Persuadere cupit.　Credat Iudaeus Apella,　　　　100
Non ego; namque deos didici securum agere aevum,
Nec, si quid miri faciat natura, deos id
Tristis ex alto caeli demittere tecto.
Brundisium longae finis chartaeque viaeque est.

VI.

ON AMBITION.

Addressed to Maecenas.

1. Occasion of the Satire: Horace's friendship with Maecenas had
evidently led to unkind and unfair criticism, to which he replies in detail.

2. Outline: Worth, not station, makes the man.　Therefore one
should not aspire to positions for which one is not fitted.　Horace
has never done so.　He owes his intimacy with Maecenas to his early
training and his consequent good character.

　　1. The truly great estimate a man not by his social position, but
　　　　by his personal character:
　　　　a) Thus Maecenas, though of royal lineage, does not despise
　　　　　　the lowly born, 1-6:
　　　　　　1) For such men have often shown themselves worthy
　　　　　　　　of high positions, 7-11;

        2) While men of noble birth have been despised even
           by the common herd, 12–17 ;

    b) Since the judgment of the common people is notoriously
      bad, a truly superior man of humble origin ought not to
      aspire to office :

        1) For he will be accused with justice of being out of
           his sphere, 17–39 ;

        2) And it is often some insignificant trait which catches
           the popular fancy, 40–44.

2. Horace's position as a friend of Maecenas is not due to ambi-
    tion :

    a) He is criticised because, though the son of a freedman, he
      was tribune under Brutus and is now intimate with Mae-
      cenas, 45–48 :

        1) The first reproach is perhaps justified ;

        2) The second is not, because he did not force himself
           on Maecenas, 49–62 ;

    b) He is proud of the distinction because it is a proof of high
      character, 62–64 ;

    c) But the real credit belongs to his father :

        1) For he gave his son the best possible educational
           advantages, 65–80 ;

        2) And the benefit of his personal supervision, 81–84 ;

        3) Not that Horace might fit himself for a high position,
           but that he might be a cultured gentleman, 85–88 ;

    d) Horace honors his father, and is not ashamed of his parent-
      age. Besides, he would not, if he could, change places
      with any man of noble ancestry, 89–99 :

        1) For a high position demands social duties and a dis-
           play for which he has no inclination, 100–109 ;

        2) And he would be forced to give up his present sim-
           ple and independent life, 110–131.

   3. Time : Before the gift of the Sabine farm ; between 37 and
35 B.C.

    Non quia, Maecenas, Lydorum quidquid Etruscos
    Incoluit finis, nemo generosior est te,
    Nec quod avus tibi maternus fuit atque paternus,
    Olim qui magnis legionibus imperitarent,
    Ut plerique solent, naso suspendis adunco   5
    Ignotos, ut me libertino patre natum.

Cum referre negas quali sit quisque parente
Natus, dum ingenuus, persuades hoc tibi vere,
Ante potestatem Tulli atque ignobile regnum
Multos saepe viros nullis maioribus ortos   10
Et vixisse probos, amplis et honoribus auctos;
Contra Laevinum, Valeri genus, unde Superbus
Tarquinius regno pulsus fugit, unius assis
Non umquam pretio pluris licuisse, notante
Iudice quo nosti, populo, qui stultus honores   15
Saepe dat indignis et famae servit ineptus,
Qui stupet in titulis et imaginibus.
                              Quid oportet
Nos facere a volgo longe longeque remotos?
Namque esto, populus Laevino mallet honorem
Quam Decio mandare novo, censorque moveret   20
Appius, ingenuo si non essem patre natus:
Vel merito, quoniam in propria non pelle quiessem.
Sed fulgente trahit constrictos Gloria curru
Non minus ignotos generosis.   Quo tibi, Tilli,
Sumere depositum clavum fierique tribuno?   25
Invidia adcrevit, privato quae minor esset.
Nam ut quisque insanus nigris medium impediit crus
Pellibus et latum demisit pectore clavum,
Audit continuo 'quis homo hic et quo patre natus?'
Ut si qui aegrotet quo morbo Barrus, haberi   30
Ut cupiat formosus, eat quacumque, puellis
Iniciat curam quaerendi singula, quali
Sit facie, sura, quali pede, dente, capillo:
Sic qui promittit, civis, urbem sibi curae,
Imperium fore et Italiam, delubra deorum,   35
Quo patre sit natus, num ignota matre inhonestus,
Omnis mortalis curare et quaerere cogit.
'Tune, Syri, Damae aut Dionysi filius, audes
Deicere de saxo civis aut tradere Cadmo?'

'At Novius collega gradu post me sedet uno;   40
Namque est ille, pater quod erat meus.' 'Hoc tibi Paulus
Et Messalla videris?   At hic, si plostra ducenta
Concurrantque foro tria funera magna, sonabit
Cornua quod vincatque tubas; saltem tenet hoc nos.'

    Nunc ad me redeo libertino patre natum,   45
Quem rodunt omnes libertino patre natum,
Nunc, quia sim tibi, Maecenas, convictor, at olim,
Quod mihi pareret legio Romana tribuno.
    Dissimile hoc illi est, quia non, ut forsit honorem
Iure mihi invideat quivis, ita te quoque amicum,   50
Praesertim cautum dignos adsumere, prava
Ambitione procul.   Felicem dicere non hoc
Me possim, casu quod te sortitus amicum;
Nulla etenim mihi te fors obtulit; optimus olim
Vergilius, post hunc Varius dixere quid essem.   55
Ut veni coram, singultim pauca locutus —
Infans namque pudor prohibebat plura profari —
Non ego me claro natum patre, non ego circum
Me Satureiano vectari rura caballo,
Sed quod eram narro.   Respondes, ut tuus est mos,   60
Pauca; abeo, et revocas nono post mense iubesque
Esse in amicorum numero.
                        Magnum hoc ego duco, —
Quod placui tibi, qui turpi secernis honestum
Non patre praeclaro sed vita et pectore puro.
    Atqui si vitiis mediocribus ac mea paucis   65
Mendosa est natura, alioqui recta, velut si
Egregio insparsos reprehendas corpore naevos,
Si neque avaritiam neque sordis ac mala lustra
Obiciet vere quisquam mihi, purus et insons,
Ut me conlaudem, si et vivo carus amicis,   70
Causa fuit pater his, qui macro pauper agello
Noluit in Flavi ludum me mittere, magni

Quo pueri magnis e centurionibus orti,
Laevo suspensi loculos tabulamque lacerto,
Ibant octonos referentes Idibus aeris,   75
Sed puerum est ausus Romam portare docendum
Artis, quas doceat quivis eques atque senator
Semet prognatos.   Vestem servosque sequentis,
In magno ut populo, si qui vidisset, avita
Ex re praeberi sumptus mihi crederet illos.   80
Ipse mihi custos incorruptissimus omnis
Circum doctores aderat.   Quid multa?   Pudicum,
Qui primus virtutis honos, servavit ab omni
Non solum facto, verum opprobrio quoque turpi;
Nec timuit, sibi ne vitio quis verteret, olim   85
Si praeco parvas aut, ut fuit ipse, coactor
Mercedes sequerer; neque ego essem questus.   At hoc nunc
Laus illi debetur et a me gratia maior.

   Nil me paeniteat sanum patris huius; eoque
Non, ut magna dolo factum negat esse suo pars,   90
Quod non ingenuos habeat clarosque parentis,
Sic me defendam.   Longe mea discrepat istis
Et vox et ratio; nam si natura iuberet
A certis annis aevum remeare peractum
Atque alios legere ad fastum quoscumque parentis   95
Optaret sibi quisque, meis contentus honestos
Fascibus et sellis nollem mihi sumere, demens
Iudicio volgi, sanus fortasse tuo, quod
Nollem onus haud umquam solitus portare molestum.

   Nam mihi continuo maior quaerenda foret res   100
Atque salutandi plures, ducendus et unus
Et comes alter, uti ne solus rusve peregreve
Exirem, plures calones atque caballi
Pascendi, ducenda petorrita.   Nunc mihi curto
Ire licet mulo vel si libet usque Tarentum,   105
Mantica cui lumbos onere ulceret atque eques armos;

Obiciet nemo sordis mihi, quas tibi, Tilli,
Cum Tiburte via praetorem quinque sequuntur
Te pueri, lasanum portantes oenophorumque.
　Hoc ego commodius quam tu, praeclare senator,　　110
Milibus atque aliis vivo.　Quacumque libido est,
Incedo solus, percontor quanti holus ac far,
Fallacem circum vespertinumque pererro
Saepe forum, adsisto divinis, inde domum me
Ad porri et ciceris refero laganique catinum;　　　115
Cena ministratur pueris tribus, et lapis albus
Pocula cum cyatho duo sustinet, astat echinus
Vilis, cum patera guttus, Campana supellex.
Deinde eo dormitum, non sollicitus, mihi quod cras
Surgendum sit mane, obeundus Marsya, qui se　　120
Voltum ferre negat Noviorum posse minoris.
Ad quartam iaceo; post hanc vagor aut ego lecto
Aut scripto quod me tacitum iuvet, unguor olivo,
Non quo fraudatis immundus Natta lucernis.
Ast ubi me fessum sol acrior ire lavatum　　　　　125
Admonuit, fugio campum lusumque trigonem.
Pransus non avide, quantum interpellet inani
Ventre diem durare, domesticus otior.　Haec est
Vita solutorum misera ambitione gravique.
His me consolor victurum suavius, ac si　　　　　130
Quaestor avus pater atque meus patruusque fuisset.

VII.

A CLEVER PUN.

1. Occasion of the Satire: The main point of this brief but finished satire is the pun of Persius, which had evidently become the talk of the town. The incident occurred during Horace's service as tribune in the army of Brutus. In 43 B.C. the latter went from Macedonia into Asia, to raise troops and money, and to confer with Cassius. At Clazomenae one of his followers, P. Rupilius Rex, became involved in a lawsuit, which was tried before Brutus.

2. Outline:

1. The characteristics of the litigants, 1–8 ;
2. Their bitter animosity, 9–21 ;
3. The speech of Persius. He lauds Brutus and his staff, with the exception of Rex, whom he roundly abuses, 22–27 ;
4. Rex overwhelms him with a torrent of invective, 28–31.
5. But Persius turns the tables by his wit, 32–35.

3. Time: Opinions differ widely. Some assert that the story could have no point unless it were told soon after the event, and regard this as Horace's earliest satire. Others think that his attitude towards Brutus, and the finished style, point to a much later date. The latter view seems the more probable.

Proscripti Regis Rupili pus atque venenum
Hybrida quo pacto sit Persius ultus, opinor
Omnibus et lippis notum et tonsoribus esse.

Persius hic permagna negotia dives habebat
Clazomenis, etiam litis cum Rege molestas,   5
Durus homo atque odio qui posset vincere Regem,
Confidens tumidusque, adeo sermonis amari,
Sisennas, Barros ut equis praecurreret albis.

Ad Regem redeo. Postquam nihil inter utrumque
Convenit (hoc etenim sunt omnes iure molesti,   10
Quo fortes, quibus adversum bellum incidit: inter
Hectora Priamiden animosum atque inter Achillem
Ira fuit capitalis, ut ultima divideret mors,

Non aliam ob causam, nisi quod virtus in utroque
Summa fuit; duo si discordia vexet inertis   15
Aut si disparibus bellum incidat, ut Diomedi
Cum Lycio Glauco, discedat pigrior, ultro
Muneribus missis): Bruto praetore tenente
Ditem Asiam, Rupili et Persi par pugnat, uti non
Compositum melius cum Bitho Bacchius. In ius   20
Acres procurrunt, magnum spectaculum uterque.

   Persius exponit causam; ridetur ab omni
Conventu; laudat Brutum laudatque cohortem,
Solem Asiae Brutum appellat stellasque salubris
Appellat comites, excepto Rege; canem illum   25
Invisum agricolis sidus, venisse. Ruebat
Flumen ut hibernum, fertur quo rara securis.

   Tum Praenestinus salso multoque fluenti
Expressa arbusto regerit convicia, durus
Vindemiator et invictus, cui saepe viator   30
Cessisset magna compellans voce cuculum.

   At Graecus, postquam est Italo perfusus aceto,
Persius exclamat: 'Per magnos, Brute, deos te
Oro, qui reges consueris tollere, cur non
Hunc Regem iugulas? Operum hoc, mihi crede, tuorum
        est.'   35

VIII.

PRIAPUS AND THE WITCHES.

   1. Occasion of the Satire : The god Priapus, warder of the gardens of Maecenas, tells of the gruesome rites of two witches, and how
he frightened them away.
   The part of the Esquiline Hill which lay outside the wall of Servius Tullius was used until the time of Augustus as a burial place for
slaves, criminals, and paupers, who were cast indiscriminately into
pits, together with the carcasses of animals and general refuse. Close
by were the tombs and columbaria in which the ashes of those who

were not wealthy, but could yet afford to belong to a Burial Society, were deposited. This region was the resort of those who practised magic rites, since such ceremonies were associated with the under-world and with the dead.

At some time which is not exactly known, Maecenas purchased the place, and had it filled in and laid out with gardens. Here also stood his palace with a high tower (*cf. Odes* iii. 29. 10).

The tombs and columbaria seem to have been left undisturbed (*cf.* line 36), and on this account, or on account of the old associations of the place, the gardens were still sought by dealers in magic. Possibly the events described in the satire belong to a time when the gardens had been laid out, but the building of the palace had not been completed.

2. Outline:

1. Description of the god and his domain, 1–13 ;
2. He is annoyed by sorcerers, 14–22 ;
3. He describes the obscene rites of Canidia and Sagana, 23–36 ;
4. He drives them away in terror, 40–50.

3. Time : The exact date is uncertain ; not after 35 B.C.

Olim truncus eram ficulnus, inutile lignum,
Cum faber, incertus scamnum faceretne Priapum,
Maluit esse deum.   Deus inde ego, furum aviumque
Maxima formido ; nam fures dextra coercet ;
Ast importunas volucres in vertice harundo   5
Terret fixa vetatque novis considere in hortis.
Huc prius angustis eiecta cadavera cellis
Conservus vili portanda locabat in arca ;
Hoc miserae plebi stabat commune sepulcrum ;   10
Pantolabo scurrae Nomentanoque nepoti.
Mille pedes in fronte, trecentos cippus in agrum
Hic dabat, heredes monumentum ne sequeretur.
Nunc licet Esquiliis habitare salubribus atque
Aggere in aprico spatiari, qua modo tristes   15
Albis informem spectabant ossibus agrum ;
Cum mihi non tantum furesque feraeque suëtae
Hunc vexare locum curae sunt atque labori,

Quantum carminibus quae versant atque venenis
Humanos animos.   Has nullo perdere possum   20
Nec prohibere modo, simul ac vaga luna decorum
Protulit os, quin ossa legant herbasque nocentis.
  Vidi egomet nigra succinctam vadere palla
Canidiam pedibus nudis passoque capillo,
Cum Sagana maiore ululantem; pallor utrasque   25
Fecerat horrendas adspectu.   Scalpere terram
Unguibus et pullam divellere mordicus agnam
Coeperunt; cruor in fossam confusus, ut inde
Manis elicerent, animas responsa daturas.
Lanea et effigies erat, altera cerea; maior   30
Lanea, quae poenis compesceret inferiorem ;
Cerea suppliciter stabat, servilibus ut quae
Iam peritura modis.   Hecaten vocat altera, saevam
Altera Tisiphonen; serpentis atque videres
Infernas errare canes, lunamque rubentem,   35
Ne foret his testis, post magna latere sepulcra.
  Singula quid memorem, quo pacto alterna loquentes   40
Umbrae cum Sagana resonarint triste et acutum,
Utque lupi barbam variae cum dente colubrae
Abdiderint furtim terris, et imagine cerea
Largior arserit ignis, et ut non testis inultus
Horruerim voces Furiarum et facta duarum.   45
*   *   *   *   *   *
                    At illae currere in urbem;
Canidiae dentes, altum Saganae caliendrum
Excidere atque herbas atque incantata lacertis
Vincula cum magno risuque iocoque videres.   50

IX.

A PUSHING FELLOW.

1. Outline: Horace describes his sufferings at the hands of a determined fellow, who forced himself upon him in the hope of being presented to Maecenas. The poet freely reveals his lack of the moral courage necessary for snubbing his tormentor. The man very likely had no real existence, but merely represents a type ; at any rate, all attempts to identify him have failed.

1. The bore succeeds in attaching himself to Horace :
   a) Horace is accosted, and makes the fatal mistake of replying politely, 1–8 ;
   b) He tries to rid himself of the fellow, but though the latter sees that his company is unwelcome, he refuses to be shaken off, 8–19 ;
   c) The man tries to recommend himself by enumerating his doubtful accomplishments, 20–25 ;
   d) Horace interrupts him but cannot speak his mind, 26–34 ;
   e) An engagement which the man has in court promises relief, but he prefers to let it go, 35–43.
2. After wearing out Horace's rather feeble resistance, the man reveals his purpose :
   a) He assumes that Horace's intimacy with Maecenas is prompted by self-interest, and offers to help him push his fortunes, 43–48 ;
   b) Horace assures him that he is mistaken. His sense of humor leads him to encourage the fellow, 48–60.
3. A meeting with Aristius Fuscus gives Horace a ray of hope, but the former, who knows his friend's fatal weakness, amuses himself at his expense :
   a) He pretends not to see the situation, 60–66 ;
   b) He admits an appointment which Horace claims to have with him, but puts it off to a more favorable time, 66–74 ;
   c) The plaintiff in the lawsuit plays the part of a *deus ex machina*, 74–78.

2. Time : The exact date is uncertain ; not after 35 B.C.

Ibam forte Via Sacra, sicut meus est mos
Nescio quid meditans nugarum ; totus in illis.

Accurrit quidam notus mihi nomine tantum,
Arreptaque manu 'Quid agis, dulcissime rerum?'
'Suaviter, ut nunc est,' inquam 'et cupio omnia, quae vis.'   5
Cum adsectaretur, 'Numquid vis?' occupo.   At ille
'Noris nos' inquit, 'docti sumus.'   Hic ego 'Pluris
Hoc' inquam 'mihi eris.'
                              Misere discedere quaerens,
Ire modo ocius, interdum consistere, in aurem
Dicere nescio quid puero, cum sudor ad imos   10
Manaret talos.   'O te, Bolane, cerebri
Felicem' aiebam tacitus, cum quidlibet ille
Garriret, vicos, urbem laudaret.   Ut illi
Nil respondebam, 'Misere cupis' inquit 'abire;
Iamdudum video; sed nil agis; usque tenebo;   15
Persequar.   Hinc quo nunc iter est tibi?'   'Nil opus est te
Circumagi; quendam volo visere non tibi notum.
Trans Tiberim longe cubat is prope Caesaris hortos.'
'Nil habeo quod agam et non sum piger; usque sequar te.'
    Demitto auriculas, ut iniquae mentis asellus,   20
Cum gravius dorso subiit onus.   Incipit ille:
'Si bene me novi, non Viscum pluris amicum,
Non Varium facies; nam quis me scribere pluris
Aut citius possit versus?   Quis membra movere
Mollius?   Invideat quod et Hermogenes ego canto.'   25
    Interpellandi locus hic erat: 'est tibi mater,
Cognati, quis te salvo est opus?'   'Haud mihi quisquam.
Omnis composui.'   'Felices!   Nunc ego resto.
Confice; namque instat fatum mihi triste, Sabella
Quod puero cecinit divina mota anus urna: 30
"Hunc neque dira venena nec hosticus auferet ensis,
Nec laterum dolor aut tussis, nec tarda podagra;
Garrulus hunc quando consumet cumque; loquaces,
Si sapiat, vitet, simul atque adoleverit aetas."'
    Ventum erat ad Vestae, quarta iam parte diei   35

Praeterita, et casu tunc respondere vadato
Debebat; quod ni fecisset, perdere litem.
'Si me amas,' inquit 'paullum hic ades.' 'Inteream, si
Aut valeo stare aut novi civilia iura;
Et propero quo scis.' 'Dubius sum quid faciam' inquit,   40
'Tene relinquam an rem.' 'Me, sodes.' 'Non faciam' ille,
Et praecedere coepit; ego, ut contendere durum
Cum victore, sequor.
                'Maecenas quomodo tecum?'
Hinc repetit; 'Paucorum hominum et mentis bene sanae;
Nemo dexterius fortuna est usus. Haberes   45
Magnum adiutorem, posset qui ferre secundas,
Hunc hominem velles si tradere; dispeream, ni
Summosses omnis.' 'Non isto vivimus illic
Quo tu rere modo; domus hac nec purior ulla est
Nec magis his aliena malis; nil mi officit, inquam,   50
Ditior hic aut est quia doctior; est locus uni
Cuique suus.' 'Magnum narras, vix credibile.' 'Atqui
Sic habet.' 'Accendis, quare cupiam magis illi
Proxumus esse.' 'Velis tantummodo; quae tua virtus,
Expugnabis; et est qui vinci possit, eoque   55
Difficilis aditus primos habet.' 'Haud mihi dero.
Muneribus servos corrumpam; non, hodie si
Exclusus fuero, desistam; tempora quaeram,
Occurram in triviis, deducam. Nil sine magno
Vita labore dedit mortalibus.'
                  Haec dum agit, ecce   60
Fuscus Aristius occurrit, mihi carus, et illum
Qui pulchre nosset. Consistimus. 'Unde venis?' et
'Quo tendis?' rogat et respondet. Vellere coepi
Et pressare manu lentissima bracchia, nutans,
Distorquens oculos, ut me eriperet. Male salsus   65
Ridens dissimulare; meum iecur urere bilis.
'Certe nescio quid secreto velle loqui te

Aiebas mecum.' 'Memini bene, sed meliore
Tempore dicam; hodie tricesima sabbata; vin tu
Curtis Iudaeis oppedere?' 'Nulla mihi' inquam   70
'Religio est.' 'At mi; sum paullo infirmior, unus
Multorum. Ignosces; alias loquar.' Huncine solem
Tam nigrum surrexe mihi! Fugit improbus ac me
Sub cultro linquit.

    Casu venit obvius illi
Adversarius et 'Quo tu turpissime?' magna   75
Inclamat voce, et 'licet antestari?' Ego vero
Oppono auriculam. Rapit in ius; clamor utrimque,
Undique concursus. Sic me servavit Apollo.

X.

ON SATIRE.

1. Occasion of the Satire : Horace's criticism of Lucilius (*cf.* iv.) had doubtless awakened a great deal of opposition. In this satire, which forms the epilogue to his first collection, he justifies his opinion of his predecessor, and more fully defines his own position.

2. Outline :

 1. Horace not only found faults in Lucilius, but good points as well. He repeats his previous statement.

  a) The versification of Lucilius is careless and rude, although his wit is keen, 1–6 ;

  b) His style lacks brevity and variety, 7–14 ;

  c) He is too caustic. Good-natured raillery is often more effective, 14–19;

  d) His admirers praise his free use of Greek words and phrases. This is really a defect, 20–35.

 2 Horace defines his own ideal. He would found a new school of satire :

  a) He leaves epic and dramatic poetry to others. He finds himself best adapted to satire (*cf.* iv., *Outline*, 2, *c*, ff.), 36–45 ;

  b) He does not claim to equal Lucilius, but this does not prevent him from recognizing, and trying to avoid, the latter's faults, 46–64 ;

c) Lucilius may mark an advance on his predecessors. He is
   faulty, however, when judged by the higher standard of
   Horace's own day, 64–71 ;

d) Horace writes to please a small and critical circle of cultivated men. He despises the verdict of the general
   public, 72–91 ;

e) After thus defining his ideal, he launches his book, 92.

3. Time : 35 B.C.

> *Lucili, quam sis mendosus, teste Catone*
> *Defensore tuo pervincam, qui male factos*
> *Emendare parat versus, hoc lenius ille,*
> *Quo melior vir et est longe subtilior illo,*
> *Qui multum puer et loris et funibus udis*   5
> *Exoratus, ut esset opem qui ferre poetis*
> *Antiquis posset contra fastidia nostra,*
> *Grammaticorum equitum doctissimus.   Ut redeam illuc :*

Nempe incomposito dixi pede currere versus
Lucili.   Quis tam Lucili fautor inepte est
Ut non hoc fateatur ?   At idem, quod sale multo
Urbem defricuit, charta laudatur eadem.
Nec tamen, hoc tribuens, dederim quoque cetera ; nam sic   5
Et Laberi mimos, ut pulchra poemata, mirer.
  Ergo non satis est risu diducere rictum
Auditoris ; et est quaedam tamen hic quoque virtus.
Est brevitate opus, ut currat sententia neu se
Impediat verbis lassas onerantibus auris,   10
Et sermone opus est modo tristi, saepe iocoso,
Defendente vicem modo rhetoris atque poetae,
Interdum urbani parcentis viribus atque
Extenuantis eas consulto.
                            Ridiculum acri
Fortius et melius magnas plerumque secat res.   15
Illi, scripta quibus comoedia prisca viris est,
Hoc stabant, hoc sunt imitandi ; quos neque pulcher

Hermogenes umquam legit, neque simius iste
Nil praeter Calvum et doctus cantare Catullum.
   'At magnum fecit, quod verbis Graeca Latinis   20
Miscuit.'   O seri studiorum, quine putetis
Difficile et mirum, Rhodio quod Pitholeonti
Contigit?   'At sermo lingua concinnus utraque
Suavior, ut Chio nota si commixta Falerni est.'
Cum versus facias, te ipsum percontor, an et cum   25
Dura tibi peragenda rei sit causa Petilli?
Scilicet oblitus patriaeque patrisque Latini,
Cum Pedius causas exsudet Publicola atque
Corvinus, patriis intermiscere petita
Verba foris malis, Canusini more bilinguis?   30
Atque ego cum Graecos facerem, natus mare citra,
Versiculos, vetuit me tali voce Quirinus,
Post mediam noctem visus, cum somnia vera:
'In silvam non ligna feras insanius, ac si
Magnas Graecorum malis implere catervas.'   35
   Turgidus Alpinus iugulat dum Memnona dumque
Defingit Rheni luteum caput, haec ego ludo,
Quae neque in aede sonent certantia iudice Tarpa,
Nec redeant iterum atque iterum spectanda theatris.
Arguta meretrice potes Davoque Chremeta   40
Eludente senem comis garrire libellos
Unus vivorum, Fundani; Pollio regum
Facta canit pede ter percusso; forte epos acer
Ut nemo Varius ducit; molle atque facetum
Vergilio adnuerunt gaudentes rure Camenae.   45
   Hoc erat, experto frustra Varrone Atacino
Atque quibusdam aliis, melius quod scribere possem,
Inventore minor; neque ego illi detrahere ausim
Haerentem capiti cum multa laude coronam.
At dixi fluere hunc lutulentum, saepe ferentem   50
Plura quidem tollenda relinquendis. Age, quaeso,

Tu nihil in magno doctus reprehendis **Homero**?
Nil comis tragici mutat Lucilius Acci,
Non ridet versus Enni gravitate minores,
Cum de se loquitur non ut maiore reprensis?   55
Quid vetat et nosmet Lucili scripta legentis
Quaerere, num illius, num rerum dura negarit
Versiculos natura magis factos et euntis
Mollius, ac si quis pedibus quid claudere senis,
Hoc tantum contentus, amet scripsisse ducentos   60
Ante cibum versus, totidem cenatus?   Etrusci
Quale fuit Cassi rapido ferventius amni
Ingenium, capsis quem fama est esse librisque
Ambustum propriis.
                        Fuerit Lucilius, inquam,
Comis et urbanus, fuerit limatior idem,   65
Quam rudis et Graecis intacti carminis auctor
Quamque poetarum seniorum turba; sed ille,
Si foret hoc nostrum fato dilatus in aevum,
Detereret sibi multa, recideret omne quod ultra
Perfectum traheretur, et in versu faciendo   70
Saepe caput scaberet, vivos et roderet unguis.
    Saepe stilum vertas, iterum quae digna legi sint
Scripturus, neque te ut miretur turba labores,
Contentus paucis lectoribus.   An tua demens
Vilibus in ludis dictari carmina malis?   75
Non ego; nam satis est equitem mihi plaudere, ut **audax**,
Contemptis aliis, explosa Arbuscula dixit.
Men moveat cimex Pantilius, aut cruciet quod
Vellicet absentem Demetrius, aut quod ineptus
Fannius Hermogenis laedat conviva Tigelli?   80
Plotius et Varius, Maecenas Vergiliusque,
Valgius et probet haec Octavius optimus atque
Fuscus et haec utinam Viscorum laudet uterque!
Ambitione relegata te dicere possum,

Pollio, te, Messalla, tuo cum fratre, simulque   85
Vos, Bibule et Servi, simul his te, candide Furni,
Compluris alios, doctos ego quos et amicos
Prudens praetereo; quibus haec, sint qualiacumque,
Arridere velim, doliturus, si placeant spe
Deterius nostra.   Demetri, teque, Tigelli,   90
Discipularum inter iubeo plorare cathedras.

   I, puer, atque meo citus haec subscribe libello.

SERMONUM

LIBER SECUNDUS.

———◆———

I.

THE POET'S REPLY TO HIS CRITICS.

A DIALOGUE WITH C. TREBATIUS TESTA.

1. Occasion of the Satire : The first collection of *Sermones* had been severely criticized.   In the introduction to his second book Horace justifies his choice of a field for his literary work, and announces his determination to continue writing in the same line.

2. Outline :

1. Trebatius advises Horace to give up literary work, or, since he insists that he cannot do that, to turn to epic poetry, 1–12 ;
2. Horace replies that he has no gift for such work, and that the time is not favorable, 12–20 ;
3. He pleads an uncontrollable impulse to write satire, and refuses to be frightened from his purpose of following his bent :
   a) To the threat that he will incur general detestation he replies that :
      1) It is his nature to write satire, 21–28 ;
      2) He has a good precedent in Lucilius, 28–39 ;
      3) It is his natural defensive weapon.   He does not use it, unless he is attacked, 39–56 ;
      4) And he positively refuses to give it up, 57–60 ;
   b) To the warning that he will lose his powerful friends he replies that :
      1) Laelius and Scipio remained on terms of the closest intimacy with Lucilius, in spite of his attacks on all classes of society, 60–74 ;

42

   2) He has enjoyed the same good fortune, in spite of
      his humbler origin and ability, 74–79 ;
   c) When warned that there is a law against lampooning any
      one with bad (*i.e.* abusive) verses, Horace refuses to take
      the matter seriously. He writes only *good* verses, and
      the law does not apply to him, 79–86.

3. Time : 30 B.C.

Hor. Sunt quibus in satura videar nimis acer et ultra
Legem tendere opus ; sine nervis altera quicquid
Composui pars esse putat similisque meorum
Mille die versus deduci posse.   Trebati,
Quid faciam, praescribe. *Treb.* Quiescas. *H.* Ne
      faciam, inquis,   5
Omnino versus ? *T.* Aio. *H.* Peream male, si non
Optimum erat ; verum nequeo dormire.   *T.* Ter uncti
Transnanto Tiberim, somno quibus est opus alto,
Irriguumque mero sub noctem corpus habento.
Aut si tantus amor scribendi te rapit, aude   10
Caesaris invicti res dicere, multa laborum
Praemia laturus. *H.* Cupidum, pater optime, vires
Deficiunt ; neque enim quivis horrentia pilis
Agmina nec fracta pereuntis cuspide Gallos
Aut labentis equo describat vulnera Parthi.   15
T. Attamen et iustum poteras et scribere fortem,
Scipiadam ut sapiens Lucilius. *H.* Haud mihi dero,
Cum res ipsa feret ; nisi dextro tempore, Flacci
Verba per attentam non ibunt Caesaris aurem,
Cui male si palpere, recalcitrat undique tutus.   2C
   T. Quanto rectius hoc, quam tristi laedere versu
Pantolabum scurram Nomentanumque nepotem,
Cum sibi quisque timet, quamquam est intactus, et odit.
H. Quid faciam ? Saltat Milonius, ut semel icto
Accessit fervor capiti numerusque lucernis ;   2J
Castor gaudet equis, ovo prognatus eodem

Pugnis; quot capitum vivunt, totidem studiorum
Milia.
       Me pedibus delectat claudere verba
Lucili ritu, nostrum melioris utroque.
Ille velut fidis arcana sodalibus olim   30
Credebat libris, neque si male cesserat usquam
Decurrens alio, neque si bene; quo fit, ut omnis
Votiva pateat veluti descripta tabella
Vita senis.   Sequor hunc, Lucanus an Apulus, anceps;
Nam Venusinus arat finem sub utrumque colonus,   35
Missus ad hoc pulsis, vetus est ut fama, Sabellis,
Quo ne per vacuum Romano incurreret hostis,
Sive quod Apula gens seu quod Lucania bellum
Incuteret violenta.
           Sed hic stilus haud petet ultro
Quemquam animantem, et me veluti custodiet ensis   40
Vagina tectus; quem cur destringere coner
Tutus ab infestis latronibus?   O pater et rex
Iuppiter, ut pereat positum robigine telum,
Nec quisquam noceat cupido mihi pacis!   At ille,
Qui me commorit — melius non tangere! clamo —   45
Flebit et insignis tota cantabitur urbe.
Cervius iratus leges minitatur et urnam,
Canidia Albuci quibus est inimica venenum,
Grande malum Turius, si quid se iudice certes.
Ut quo quisque valet suspectos terreat, utque   50
Imperet hoc natura potens, sic collige mecum.
Dente lupus, cornu taurus petit; unde, nisi intus
Monstratum?   Scaevae vivacem crede nepoti
Matrem; nil faciet sceleris pia dextera — mirum,
Ut neque calce lupus quemquam neque dente petit bos; — 55
Sed mala tollet anum vitiato melle cicuta.
   Ne longum faciam, seu me tranquilla senectus
Exspectat seu mors atris circumvolat alis,

Dives, inops, Romae, seu fors ita iusserit exsul,
Quisquis erit vitae scribam color.

                          T. O puer, ut sis   60
Vitalis metuo, et maiorum ne quis amicus
Frigore te feriat. *H.* Quid ? cum est Lucilius ausus
Primus in hunc operis componere carmina morem,
Detrahere et pellem, nitidus qua quisque per ora
Cederet, introrsum turpis, num Laelius et qui   65
Duxit ab oppressa meritum Carthagine nomen
Ingenio offensi aut laeso doluere Metello
Famosisque Lupo cooperto versibus ?   Atqui
Primores populi arripuit populumque tributim,
Scilicet uni aequus virtuti atque eius amicis.   70
Quin ubi se a volgo et scaena in secreta remorant
Virtus Scipiadae et mitis sapientia Laeli,
Nugari cum illo et discincti ludere, donec
Decoqueretur holus, soliti.

                          Quicquid sum ego, quamvis
Infra Lucili censum ingeniumque, tamen me   75
Cum magnis vixisse invita fatebitur usque
Invidia, et fragili quaerens inlidere dentem,
Offendet solido, nisi quid tu, docte Trebati,
Dissentis.

            T. Equidem nihil hinc diffindere possum ;
Sed tamen ut monitus caveas, ne forte negoti   80
Incutiat tibi quid sanctarum inscitia legum ;
Si mala condiderit in quem quis carmina, ius est
Iudiciumque.   *H.* Esto, si quis mala ; sed bona si quis
Iudice condiderit laudatus Caesare ? si quis
Opprobriis dignum latraverit, integer ipse ?   85
T. Solventur risu tabulae, tu missus abibis.

II.

A PLEA FOR RATIONAL LIVING.

1. Outline : Horace tells his friends how an old neighbor of his, in his boyhood days at Venusia, advocated a frugal life, avoiding the extremes of extravagance and parsimony ; and how he lived happily by practising what he preached.

    1. Gluttony and extravagance in diet are the results of a perverted taste :

        a) Correct ideas on the subject can be gained only from an active life amid simple surroundings, 1–16 ;

        b) Men's tastes are corrupted by over-eating and by lack of exercise, 16–22 ;

        c) Their diet is regulated by fashion and by the relative costliness of viands, 23–52 ;

    2. Stinginess and sordid living are equally reprehensible, 53–69 ;

    3. A rational mode of life, avoiding both extremes, has many advantages :

        a) It gives bodily health, 70–77 ;

        b) Vigor and elasticity of mind, 77–81 ;

        c) Room for greater indulgence on festal days, when one's strength must be recruited, and in old age, 82–93 ;

        d) It keeps one from moral and financial ruin, 94–101 ;

        e) Enables one to exercise charity and philanthropy, 101–105 ;

        f) And better to endure a change of fortune, 106–111 ;

    4. These views of Ofellus are shown to be true by his own life, and by his happiness and contentment in prosperity and in adversity :

        a) Horace testifies to the frugality of his neighbor before, as well as after, his change of fortune, 112–115 ;

        b) He quotes his account of his simple life in the days of his prosperity, 116–125 ;

        c) And tells of his courage and contentment in adversity, 126–136.

2. Time : The exact date is uncertain ; not after 30 B.C.

Quae virtus et quanta, boni, sit vivere parvo —
Nec meus hic sermo est, sed quae praecepit Ofellus
Rusticus, abnormis sapiens crassaque Minerva —
Discite non inter lances mensasque nitentis,

Cum stupet insanis acies fulgoribus et cum   5
Adclinis falsis animus meliora recusat,
Verum hic impransi mecum disquirite.   Cur hoc?
Dicam, si potero.   Male verum examinat omnis
Corruptus iudex.   Leporem sectatus equove
Lassus ab indomito vel, si Romana fatigat   10
Militia adsuetum graecari, seu pila velox
Molliter austerum studio fallente laborem
Seu te discus agit, pete cedentem aëra disco;
Cum labor extuderit fastidia, siccus, inanis
Sperne cibum vilem; nisi Hymettia mella Falerno   15
Ne biberis diluta.
        Foris est promus, et atrum
Defendens piscis hiemat mare; cum sale panis
Latrantem stomachum bene leniet.   Unde putas aut
Qui partum?   Non in caro nidore voluptas
Summa, sed in te ipso est.   Tu pulmentaria quaere   20
Sudando; pinguem vitiis albumque neque ostrea
Nec scarus aut poterit peregrina iuvare lagois.
  Vix tamen eripiam, posito pavone velis quin
Hoc potius quam gallina tergere palatum,
Corruptus vanis rerum, quia veneat auro   25
Rara avis et picta pandat spectacula cauda;
Tamquam ad rem attineat quicquam.   Num vesceris ista,
Quam laudas, pluma?   Cocto num adest honor idem?
Carne tamen quamvis distat nil, hac magis illam
Imparibus formis deceptum te petere!   Esto: 30
Unde datum sentis, lupus hic Tiberinus an alto
Captus hiet?   Pontisne inter iactatus an amnis
Ostia sub Tusci?   Laudas, insane, trilibrem
Mullum, in singula quem minuas pulmenta necesse est.
Ducit te species, video: quo pertinet ergo   35
Proceros odisse lupos?   Quia scilicet illis
Maiorem natura modum dedit, his breve pondus.

Ieiunus raro stomachus volgaria temnit.
' Porrectum magno magnum spectare catino
Vellem' ait Harpyiis gula digna rapacibus.　At vos,　40
Praesentes Austri, coquite horum obsonia.　Quamquam
Putet aper rhombusque recens, mala copia quando
Aegrum sollicitat stomachum, cum rapula plenus
Atque acidas mavolt inulas.　Necdum omnis abacta
Pauperies epulis regum ; nam vilibus ovis　45
Nigrisque est oleis hodie locus.　Haud ita pridem
Galloni praeconis erat acipensere mensa
Infamis.　Quid ? tunc rhombos minus aequora alebant ?
Tutus erat rhombus tutoque ciconia nido,
Donec vos auctor docuit praetorius.　Ergo　50
Si quis nunc mergos suavis edixerit assos,
Parebit pravi docilis Romana iuventus.

Sordidus a tenui victu distabit, Ofello
Iudice ; nam frustra vitium vitaveris illud,
Si te alio pravum detorseris.　Avidienus,　55
Cui Canis ex vero dictum cognomen adhaeret,
Quinquennis oleas est et silvestria corna,
Ac nisi mutatum parcit defundere vinum, et
Cuius odorem olei nequeas perferre, licebit
Ille repotia, natalis aliosve dierum　60
Festos albatus celebret, cornu ipse bilibri
Caulibus instillat, veteris non parcus aceti.
Quali igitur victu sapiens utetur, et horum
Utrum imitabitur ?　Hac urget lupus, hac canis, aiunt.
Mundus erit, qua non offendat sordibus, atque　65
In neutram partem cultus miser.　Hic neque servis,
Albuci senis exemplo, dum munia didit,
Saevus erit ; nec sic ut simplex Naevius unctam
Convivis praebebit aquam : vitium hoc quoque magnum.

Accipe nunc, victus tenuis quae quantaque secum　70
Adferat.　In primis valeas bene ; nam variae res

(margin note: notorious)

Ut noceant homini, credas, memor illius escae,
Quae simplex olim tibi sederit; at simul assis
Miscueris elixa, simul conchylia turdis,
Dulcia se in bilem vertent stomachoque tumultum   75
Lenta feret pituita.   Vides, ut pallidus omnis
Cena desurgat dubia?

                 Quin corpus onustum
Hesternis vitiis animum quoque praegravat una,
Atque adfigit humo divinae particulam aurae.
Alter, ubi dicto citius curata sopori   80
Membra dedit, vegetus praescripta ad munia surgit.

  Hic tamen ad melius poterit transcurrere quondam;
Sive diem festum rediens advexerit annus,
Seu recreare volet tenuatum corpus, ubique
Accedent anni, et tractari mollius aetas   85
Imbecilla volet; tibi quidnam accedet ad istam,
Quam puer et validus praesumis mollitiem, seu
Dura valetudo inciderit seu tarda senectus?
Rancidum aprum antiqui laudabant, non quia nasus
Illis nullus erat, sed, credo, hac mente, quod hospes   90
Tardius adveniens vitiatum commodius quam
Integrum edax dominus consumeret.   Hos utinam inter
Heroas natum tellus me prima tulisset!

  Das aliquid famae, quae carmine gratior aurem
Occupat humanam?   Grandes rhombi patinaeque   95
Grande ferunt una cum damno dedecus.   Adde
Iratum patruum, vicinos, te tibi iniquum
Et frustra mortis cupidum, cum derit egenti
As, laquei pretium.   'Iure' inquit 'Trausius istis
Iurgatur verbis; ego vectigalia magna   100
Divitiasque habeo tribus amplas regibus.'

                      Ergo
Quod superat non est melius quo insumere possis?
Cur eget indignus quisquam te divite?   Quare

Templa ruunt antiqua deum ?   Cur, improbe, carae
Non aliquid patriae tanto emetiris acervo ?   105
    Uni nimirum tibi recte semper erunt res,
O magnus posthac inimicis risus !   Uterne
Ad casus dubios fidet sibi certius ?   Hic qui
Pluribus adsuerit mentem corpusque superbum,
An qui contentus parvo metuensque futuri   110
In pace, ut sapiens, aptarit idonea bello ?
    Quo magis his credas, puer hunc ego parvus Ofellum
Integris opibus novi non latius usum,
Quam nunc accisis.   Videas metato in agello
Cum pecore et gnatis fortem mercede colonum,   115
' Non ego' narrantem ' temere edi luce profesta
Quicquam praeter holus fumosae cum pede pernae.
Ac mihi seu longum post tempus venerat hospes
Sive operum vacuo gratus conviva per imbrem
Vicinus, bene erat non piscibus urbe petitis,   120
Sed pullo atque haedo ; tunc pensilis uva secundas
Et nux ornabat mensas cum duplice ficu.
Post hoc ludus erat culpa potare magistra ;
Ac venerata Ceres, ita culmo surgeret alto,
Explicuit vino contractae seria frontis.   125
Saeviat atque novos moveat fortuna tumultus :
Quantum hinc imminuit ?   Quanto aut ego parcius aut vos,
O pueri, nituistis, ut huc novus incola venit ?
Nam propriae telluris erum natura nec illum
Nec me nec quemquam statuit ; nos expulit ille ;   130
Illum aut nequities aut vafri inscitia iuris,
Postremum expellet certe vivacior heres.
Nunc ager Umbreni sub nomine, nuper Ofelli
Dictus, erit nulli proprius, sed cedet in usum
Nunc mihi, nunc alii.   Quocirca vivite fortes   135
Fortiaque adversis opponite pectora rebus.'

Carefully worked out from literary viewpoint.

Insanio: amens
demens
insanire
amentia versatio *insanio*
cerritus *furere*
commotus
commotae mentis III.
mentem concussus

ON THE MADNESS OF MANKIND.

A DIALOGUE WITH DAMASIPPUS.

1. Outline:

1. Horace has gone to his Sabine farm for the holidays. Damasippus appears and reproaches him for not writing more, 1–18.

2. He explains himself by saying that, since his business career ended in bankruptcy, he has busied himself with the affairs of others, 18–26.

3. Horace says that that is only another kind of folly ; whereupon his visitor retorts that Horace himself, in common with all the rest of the world, is mad, 26–36.

4. When Damasippus would drown himself, Stertinius saved his life by convincing him that all men, except the philosopher, are equally mad and foolish, 37–46.

5. He quotes the arguments of the Stoic:

   a) Everyone who is foolish and ignorant of the truth is a madman. This insanity manifests itself in various ways, 46–81 ;

   b) The avaricious are mad :

      1) Because they believe that poverty is a disgrace, and that wealth confers every blessing — even wisdom, 82–103 ;

      2) Because they hoard up riches which they are too stingy to use, 104–119 ;

      3) They may not seem mad, because avarice is so common, but they really are, 120–141 ;

      4) Think of Opimius, who would not spend a few pence in nourishing food, even to save his life, 142–157 ;

   c) The ambitious are mad :

      1) For they sacrifice their fortunes for office and empty glory, 158–186 ;

      2) Agamemnon, who sacrificed his daughter to his ambition, was as mad as Ajax when he slew the sheep. We should not question the madness of a man who treated a lamb like a favorite daughter. How about one who led his daughter like a lamb to the slaughter ? 187–223.

   d) The prodigal is mad :

      1) If a young heir should distribute his patrimony among the purveyors of luxuries, we should call

       him mad.   This is what the prodigal really does,
       224–238 ;

   2) A man who squanders money on costly dainties
       might as well throw it into a sewer, 239–246 ;

e) The amorous are all crazy :

   1) For a young man to indulge in child's play is a sign
       of madness.   It is equally so to sigh for love, 247–
       257 ;

   2) The petulant lover can learn wisdom even from a
       slave, 258–271 ;

   3) What of the silly superstitions and the childish bab-
       ble of old men, and the crimes committed by jeal-
       ous lovers ? 272–280 ;

f) The superstitious are insane :

   1) For instance, the man who prayed that he might live
       forever, 281–287 ;

   2) And the mother who sacrificed her child's life to a
       mad vow, 288–295.

6. Damasippus says that Horace is no exception to the general
     rule, 296–307 :

   a) For he is building a house, in imitation of the great and the
       wealthy, 308–320 ;

   b) He writes satire, is hot-tempered, extravagant, and amor-
       ous, 321–325.

7. Horace begs for mercy from his superior — in madness, 326.

2. Time : 33–32 B.C.

Dam.   Sic raro scribis, ut toto non quater anno
Membranam poscas, scriptorum quaeque retexens,
Iratus tibi, quod vini somnique benignus
Nil dignum sermone canas ; quid fiet ?   At ipsis
Saturnalibus huc fugisti sobrius.   Ergo   5
Dic aliquid dignum promissis.   Incipe.   Nil est.
Culpantur frustra calami, immeritusque laborat
Iratis natus paries dis atque poetis.
Atqui voltus erat multa et praeclara minantis,
Si vacuum tepido cepisset villula tecto.   10
Quorsum pertinuit stipare Platona Menandro ?
Eupolin, Archilochum, comites educere tantos ?

Invidiam placare paras virtute relicta?
Contemnere miser! Vitanda est improba Siren
Desidia, aut quicquid vita meliore parasti   15
Ponendum aequo animo. *Hor.* Di te, Damasippe, deaeque
Verum ob consilium donent tonsore. Sed unde
Tam bene me nosti?

               D. Postquam omnis res mea Ianum
Ad medium fracta est, aliena negotia curo
Excussus propriis. Olim nam quaerere amabam,   20
Quo vafer ille pedes lavisset Sisyphus aere,
Quid sculptum infabre, quid fusum durius esset.
Callidus huic signo ponebam milia centum;
Hortos egregiasque domos mercarier unus
Cum lucro noram; unde frequentia Mercuriale   25
Imposuere mihi cognomen compita. *H.* Novi,
Et miror morbi purgatum te illius.   Atqui
Emovit veterem mire novus, ut solet, in cor
Traiecto lateris miseri capitisve dolore,
Ut lethargicus hic cum fit pugil et medicum urget.   30
Dum ne quid simile huic, esto ut libet. *D.* O bone, ne te
Frustrere, insanis et tu stultique prope omnes,
Si quid Stertinius veri crepat, unde ego mira
Descripsi docilis praecepta haec, tempore quo me
Solatus iussit sapientem pascere barbam   35
Atque a Fabricio non tristem ponte reverti.

   Nam male re gesta cum vellem mittere operto
Me capite in flumen, dexter stetit et "Cave faxis
Te quicquam indignum; pudor" inquit "te malus angit,
Insanos qui inter vereare insanus haberi.   40
Primum nam inquiram, quid sit furere; hoc si erit in te
Solo, nil verbi, pereas quin fortiter, addam.
Quem mala stultitia et quemcumque inscitia veri
Caecum agit, insanum Chrysippi porticus et grex
Autumat. Haec populos, haec magnos formula reges,   45

Excepto sapiente, tenet.
                   Nunc accipe, quare
Desipiant omnes aeque ac tu, qui tibi nomen
Insano posuere. Velut silvis, ubi passim
Palantis error certo de tramite pellit,
Ille sinistrorsum, hic dextrorsum abit, unus utrique   50
Error, sed variis inludit partibus; hoc te
Crede modo insanum, nihilo ut sapientior ille,
Qui te derridet, caudam trahat. Est genus unum
Stultitiae nihilum metuenda timentis, ut ignis,
Ut rupes fluviosque in campo obstare queratur.   55
Alterum et huic varum et nihilo sapientius ignis
Per medios fluviosque ruentis: clamet amica
Mater, honesta soror cum cognatis, pater, uxor
'Hic fossa est ingens, hic rupes maxima: serva!'
Non magis audierit, quam Fufius ebrius olim,   60
Cum Ilionam edormit, Catienis mille ducentis
'Mater, te appello' clamantibus. Huic ego volgus
Errori similem cunctum insanire docebo.
Insanit veteres statuas Damasippus emendo;
Integer est mentis Damasippi creditor? Esto.   65
'Accipe quod numquam reddas mihi' si tibi dicam,
Tune insanus eris si acceperis? an magis excors,
Reiecta praeda quam praesens Mercurius fert?
Scribe decem a Nerio; non est satis: adde Cicutae
Nodosi tabulas centum, mille adde catenas;   70
Effugiet tamen haec sceleratus vincula Proteus.
Cum rapies in ius malis ridentem alienis,
Fiet aper, modo avis, modo saxum et, cum volet, arbor.
Si male rem gerere insani est, contra bene sani,
Putidius multo cerebrum est, mihi crede, Perelli   75
Dictantis, quod tu numquam rescribere possis.
    Audire atque togam iubeo componere, quisquis
Ambitione mala aut argenti pallet amore,

Quisquis luxuria tristive superstitione
Aut alio mentis morbo calet; huc propius me,   80
Dum doceo insanire omnis, vos ordine adite.

   Danda est ellebori multo pars maxima avaris;
Nescio an Anticyram ratio illis destinet omnem.
Heredes Staberi summam incidere sepulcro,
Ni sic fecissent, gladiatorum dare centum   85
Damnati populo paria atque epulum arbitrio Arri,
Frumenti quantum metit Africa. 'Sive ego prave
Seu recte hoc volui, ne sis patruus mihi.' Credo,
Hoc Staberi prudentem animum vidisse. 'Quid ergo
Sensit, cum summam patrimoni insculpere saxo   90
Heredes voluit?' Quoad vixit, credidit ingens
Pauperiem vitium et cavit nihil acrius, ut, si
Forte minus locuples uno quadrante perisset,
Ipse videretur sibi nequior; omnis enim res,
Virtus, fama, decus, divina humanaque pulchris   95
Divitiis parent; quas qui construxerit, ille
Clarus erit, fortis, iustus. 'Sapiensne?' Etiam, et rex
Et quicquid volet. Hoc, veluti virtute paratum,
Speravit magnae laudi fore. Quid simile isti
Graecus Aristippus, qui servos proicere aurum   100
In media iussit Libya, quia tardius irent
Propter onus segnes? Uter est insanior horum?
Nil agit exemplum, litem quod lite resolvit.

   Si quis emat citharas, emptas comportet in unum,
Nec studio citharae nec musae deditus ulli,   105
Si scalpra et formas non sutor, nautica vela
Aversus mercaturis, delirus et amens
Undique dicatur merito. Qui discrepat istis,
Qui nummos aurumque recondit, nescius uti
Compositis metuensque velut contingere sacrum?   110
Si quis ad ingentem frumenti semper acervum
Porrectus vigilet cum longo fuste, neque illinc

Audeat esuriens dominus contingere granum;
Ac potius foliis parcus vescatur amaris;
Si positis intus Chii veterisque Falerni   115
Mille cadis, nihil est, ter centum milibus, acre
Potet acetum; age, si et stramentis incubet unde-
Octoginta annos natus, cui stragula vestis,
Blattarum ac tinearum epulae, putrescat in arca;
Nimirum insanus paucis videatur, eo quod   120
Maxima pars hominum morbo iactatur eodem.
Filius aut etiam haec libertus ut ebibat heres,
Dis inimice senex, custodis? Ne tibi desit?
Quantulum enim summae curtabit quisque dierum,
Unguere si caules oleo meliore caputque   125
Coeperis impexa foedum porrigine? Quare,
Si quidvis satis est, periuras, surripis, aufers
Undique? Tun sanus? Populum si caedere saxis
Incipias servosve tuos, quos aere pararis,
Insanum te omnes pueri clamentque puellae;   130
Cum laqueo uxorem interimis matremque veneno,
Incolumi capite es? Quid enim? Neque tu hoc facis Argis,
Nec ferro ut demens genetricem occidis Orestes.
An tu reris eum occisa insanisse parente,
Ac non ante malis dementem actum Furiis quam   135
In matris iugulo ferrum tepefecit acutum?
Quin, ex quo est habitus male tutae mentis Orestes,
Nil sane fecit quod tu reprehendere possis;
Non Pyladen ferro violare aususve sororem
Electran, tantum maledicit utrique vocando   140
Hanc Furiam, hunc aliud, iussit quod splendida bilis.
    Pauper Opimius argenti positi intus et auri,
Qui Veientanum festis potare diebus
Campana solitus trulla vappamque profestis,
Quondam lethargo grandi est oppressus, ut heres   145
Iam circum loculos et clavis laetus ovansque

Curreret.   Hunc medicus multum celer atque fidelis
Excitat hoc pacto : mensam poni iubet atque
Effundi saccos nummorum, accedere pluris
Ad numerandum : hominem sic erigit, addit et illud :   150
'Ni tua custodis, avidus iam haec auferet heres.'
'Men vivo ?' 'Ut vivas igitur, vigila. Hoc age !' 'Quid vis?'
'Deficient inopem venae te, ni cibus atque
Ingens accedit stomacho fultura ruenti.
Tu cessas ?   Agedum, sume hoc tisanarium oryzae.'   155
'Quanti emptae ?' 'Parvo.' 'Quanti ergo ?' 'Octussibus.'
           'Eheu,
Quid refert morbo an furtis pereamque rapinis ?'
       'Quisnam igitur sanus ?' Qui non stultus. 'Quid avarus?'
Stultus et insanus.   'Quid, si quis non sit avarus,
Continuo sanus ?'   Minime.   'Cur, Stoice ?'   Dicam.   160
Non est cardiacus — Craterum dixisse putato —
Hic aeger ; recte est igitur, surgetque ?   Negabit,
Quod latus aut renes morbo temptentur acuto.
Non est periurus neque sordidus, immolet aequis
Hic porcum Laribus : verum ambitiosus et audax ;   165
Naviget Anticyram.   Quid enim differt barathrone
Dones quicquid habes, an numquam utare paratis ?
Servius Oppidius Canusi duo praedia, dives
Antiquo censu, gnatis divisse duobus
Fertur et haec moriens pueris dixisse vocatis   170
Ad lectum : 'Postquam te talos, Aule, nucesque
Ferre sinu laxo, donare et ludere vidi,
Te, Tiberi, numerare, cavis abscondere tristem ;
Extimui, ne vos ageret vesania discors,
Tu Nomentanum, tu ne sequerere Cicutam.   175
Quare per divos oratus uterque Penatis,
Tu cave ne minuas, tu ne maius facias id,
Quod satis esse putat pater et natura coercet.
Praeterea ne vos titillet gloria, iure

Iurando obstringam ambo: uter aedilis fueritve   180
Vestrum praetor, is intestabilis et sacer esto.
In cicere atque faba bona tu perdasque lupinis,
Latus ut in circo spatiere et aeneus ut stes,
Nudus agris, nudus nummis, insane, paternis;
Scilicet ut plausus, quos fert Agrippa, feras tu,   185
Astuta ingenuum volpes imitata leonem?'
    'Ne quis humasse velit Aiacem, Atrida, vetas cur?'
'Rex sum.' 'Nil ultra quaero plebeius.' 'Et aequam
Rem imperito; ac si cui videor non iustus, inulto
Dicere quod sentit permitto.' 'Maxime regum,   190
Di tibi dent capta classem redducere Troia.
Ergo consulere et mox respondere licebit?'
'Consule.' 'Cur Aiax heros ab Achille secundus
Putescit, totiens servatis clarus Achivis,
Gaudeat ut populus Priami Priamusque inhumato,   195
Per quem tot iuvenes patrio caruere sepulcro?'
'Mille ovium insanus morti dedit, inclitum Ulixen
Et Menelaum una mecum se occidere clamans.'
'Tu cum pro vitula statuis dulcem Aulide gnatam
Ante aras spargisque mola caput, improbe, salsa,   200
Rectum animi servas cursum?' Insanus quid enim Aiax
Fecit, cum stravit ferro pecus? Abstinuit vim
Uxore et gnato; mala multa precatus Atridis,
Non ille aut Teucrum aut ipsum violavit Ulixen.'
'Verum ego, ut haerentis adverso litore navis   205
Eriperem, prudens placavi sanguine divos.'
'Nempe tuo, furiose.' 'Meo, sed non furiosus.'
'Qui species alias veris scelerisque tumultu
Permixtas capiet, commotus habebitur, atque
Stultitiane erret, nihilum distabit, an ira.   210
Aiax immeritos cum occidit, desipit, agnos;
Cum prudens scelus ob titulos admittis inanis,
Stas animo et purum est vitio tibi, cum tumidum est cor?'

Si quis lectica nitidam gestare amet agnam,
Huic vestem ut gnatae paret, ancillas paret, aurum,   215
Rufam aut Pusillam appellet fortique marito
Destinet uxorem; interdicto huic omne adimat ius
Praetor et ad sanos abeat tutela propinquos.
Quid? si quis gnatam pro muta devovet agna,
Integer est animi?   Ne dixeris.   Ergo ubi prava   220
Stultitia, hic summa est insania; qui sceleratus
Et furiosus erit; quem cepit vitrea fama,
Hunc circumtonuit gaudens Bellona cruentis.

  Nunc age, luxuriam et Nomentanum arripe mecum:
Vincet enim stultos ratio insanire nepotes.   225
Hic simul accepit patrimoni mille talenta,
Edicit, piscator uti, pomarius, auceps,
Unguentarius ac Tusci turba impia vici,
Cum scurris fartor, cum Velabro omne macellum
Mane domum veniant. Quid tum? Venere frequentes;   230
Verba facit leno: 'Quicquid mihi, quicquid et horum
Cuique domi est, id crede tuum et vel nunc pete vel cras.'
Accipe quid contra iuvenis responderit aequus.
'In nive Lucana dormis ocreatus, ut aprum
Cenem ego; tu piscis hiberno ex aequore verris.   235
Segnis ego, indignus qui tantum possideam; aufer!
Sume tibi deciens.   Tibi tantundem.   Tibi triplex,
Unde uxor media currit de nocte vocata.'

  Filius Aesopi detractam ex aure Metellae,
Scilicet ut deciens solidum absorberet, aceto   240
Diluit insignem bacam: qui sanior, ac si
Illud idem in rapidum flumen iaceretve cloacam?
Quinti progenies Arri, par nobile fratrum,
Nequitia et nugis, pravorum et amore gemellum,
Luscinias soliti impenso prandere coemptas,   245
Quorsum abeant?   Sani ut creta an carbone notati?
  Aedificare casas, plostello adiungere mures,

Ludere par impar, equitare in arundine longa
Si quem delectet barbatum, amentia verset.
Si puerilius his ratio esse evincet amare,   250
Nec quicquam differre, utrumne in pulvere, trimus
Quale prius, ludas opus, an meretricis amore
Sollicitus plores: quaero, faciasne quod olim
Mutatus Polemon? ponas insignia morbi,
Fasciolas, cubital, focalia, potus ut ille   255
Dicitur ex collo furtim carpsisse coronas,
Postquam est impransi correptus voce magistri?
    Porrigis irato puero cum poma, recusat;
'Sume, catelle!' negat; si non des, optet.   Amator
Exclusus qui distat, agit ubi secum, eat an non,   260
Quo rediturus erat non arcessitus, et haeret
Invisis foribus?   'Nec nunc, cum me vocet ultro,
Accedam?   An potius mediter finire dolores?
Exclusit; revocat.   Redeam?   Non, si obsecret.' Ecce
Servus, non paulo sapientior: 'O ere, quae res   265
Nec modum habet neque consilium, ratione modoque
Tractari non volt.   In amore haec sunt mala, bellum,
Pax rursum; haec si quis tempestatis prope ritu
Mobilia et caeca fluitantia sorte laboret
Reddere certa sibi, nihilo plus explicet ac si   270
Insanire paret certa ratione modoque.'
Quid? cum Picenis excerpens semina pomis
Gaudes, si cameram percusti forte, penes te es?
Quid? cum balba feris annoso verba palato,
Aedificante casas qui sanior?   Adde cruorem   275
Stultitiae, atque ignem gladio scrutare.   Modo, inquam,
Hellade percussa Marius cum praecipitat se,
Cerritus fuit? an commotae crimine mentis
Absolves hominem, et sceleris damnabis eundem,
Ex more imponens cognata vocabula rebus?   280
    Libertinus erat, qui circum compita siccus

Lautis mane senex manibus currebat et 'unum —
Quid tam magnum ?' addens — 'unum me surpite morti;
Dis etenim facile est' orabat; sanus utrisque
Auribus atque oculis; mentem, nisi litigiosus,   285
Exciperet dominus, cum venderet. Hoc quoque volgus
Chrysippus ponit fecunda in gente Meneni.

       'Iuppiter, ingentis qui das adimisque dolores,'
Mater ait pueri menses iam quinque cubantis,
'Frigida si puerum quartana reliquerit, illo   290
Mane die, quo tu indicis ieiunia, nudus
In Tiberi stabit.' Casus medicusve levarit
Aegrum ex praecipiti; mater delira necabit
In gelida fixum ripa febrimque reducet.
Quone malo mentem concussa ? Timore deorum."   295
    Haec mihi Stertinius, sapientum octavus, amico
Arma dedit, posthac ne compellarer inultus.
Dixerit insanum qui me, totidem audiet atque
Respicere ignoto discet pendentia tergo.

    H. Stoice, post damnum sic vendas omnia pluris,   300
Qua me stultitia, quoniam non est genus unum,
Insanire putas ? ego nam videor mihi sanus.
D. Quid? caput abscisum demens cum portat Agave
Gnati infelicis, sibi tunc furiosa videtur ?
H. Stultum me fateor — liceat concedere veris —   305
Atque etiam insanum; tantum hoc edissere, quo me
Aegrotare putes animi vitio. *D.* Accipe: primum
Aedificas, hoc est, longos imitaris, ab imo
Ad summum totus moduli bipedalis, et idem
Corpore maiorem rides Turbonis in armis   310
Spiritum et incessum: qui ridiculus minus illo ?
An quodcumque facit Maecenas, te quoque verum est
Tantum dissimilem et tanto certare minorem ?
Absentis ranae pullis vituli pede pressis,
Unus ubi effugit, matri denarrat, ut ingens   315

Belua cognatos eliserit.   Illa rogare
Quantane? num tantum, sufflans se, magna fuisset?
'Maior dimidio.'   'Num tanto?'   Cum magis atque
Se magis inflaret, 'Non, si te ruperis' inquit,
'Par eris.'   Haec a te non multum abludit imago.   320
Adde poemata nunc, hoc est, oleum adde camino;
Quae si quis sanus fecit, sanus facis et tu.
Non dico horrendam rabiem. . . .   *H.* Iam desine.   *D.* Cultum
Maiorem censu . . .   *H.* Teneas, Damasippe, tuis te.
D. Mille puellarum, puerorum mille furores. . . .   325
H. O maior tandem parcas insane minori!

IV.

ON DINING AS A FINE ART.

A Dialogue with M. Catius.

1. Outline:

 1. Horace accosts Catius, who is rushing off to commit to writing
    a discourse on the subject of good-living, 1–3.
 2. He apologizes for his untimely interruption, but begs Catius to
    give him an outline of the discourse, which he finally
    consents to do, 4–11:

    a) Rules for the appetizers (*gustatio*):
       1) For selecting eggs and cabbages, 12–16;
       2) For making a fowl tender, 17–20;
       3) For selecting mushrooms and berries, 20–23;
       4) For the preparation of *mulsum*, 24–29;
       5) For selecting shell-fish, 30–34.

    b) Rules for the dinner (*mensa prima*):
       1) The cooking and seasoning of fish is as important as
          their selection, 35–39;
       2) The meats should be carefully chosen, 40–47;
       3) The preparation and mixing of the wines is equally
          important, 48–57;
       4) How to stimulate a jaded appetite, 58–62;
       5) How to make good sauce, 63–69.

    c) Rules for the dessert (*mensa secunda*):
       1) The selection of fruits and raisins, 70–72;
       2) Original work of the lecturer, 73–75.

    d) Proper service is essential :
        1) The servants should be neat and the dishes clean, 76–80 ;
        2) All the accessories should be tasteful and neat, 81–87.
  3. Horace pretends to be greatly impressed.　His sarcastic words
      show his real opinion of such trifling, and reveal the pur-
      pose of the satire, 88–95.
  2. Time: The exact date is uncertain ; not after 30 B.C.

Hor. Unde et quo Catius ?　*Cat.* Non est mihi tempus aventi
Ponere signa novis praeceptis, qualia vincunt
Pythagoran Anytique reum doctumque Platona.
H. Peccatum fateor, cum te sic tempore laevo
Interpellarim ; sed des veniam bonus, oro.　　　　　　　　　5
Quod si interciderit tibi nunc aliquid, repetes mox,
Sive est naturae hoc sive artis, mirus utroque.
C. Quin id erat curae, quo pacto cuncta tenerem,
Utpote res tenuis, tenui sermone peractas.
H. Ede hominis nomen, simul et, Romanus an hospes.　　10
  C. Ipsa memor praecepta canam, celabitur auctor.
Longa quibus facies ovis erit, illa memento,
Ut suci melioris et ut magis alba rotundis,
Ponere ; namque marem cohibent callosa vitellum.
Cole suburbano qui siccis crevit in agris　　　　　　　　15
Dulcior ; irriguo nihil est elutius horto.
Si vespertinus subito te oppresserit hospes,
Ne gallina malum responset dura palato,
Doctus eris vivam musto mersare Falerno ;
Hoc teneram faciet.　Pratensibus optima fungis　　　20
Natura est ; aliis male creditur.　Ille salubris
Aestates peraget, qui nigris prandia moris
Finiet, ante gravem quae legerit arbore solem.
Aufidius forti miscebat mella Falerno ;
Mendose, quoniam vacuis committere venis　　　　　25
Nil nisi lene decet ; leni praecordia mulso
Prolueris melius.　Si dura morabitur alvus,
Mitulus et viles pellent obstantia conchae

Et lapathi brevis herba, sed albo non sine Coo.
Lubrica nascentes implent conchylia lunae;   30
Sed non omne mare est generosae fertile testae:
Murice Baiano melior Lucrina peloris,
Ostrea Circeis, Miseno oriuntur echini,
Pectinibus patulis iactat se molle Tarentum.
  Nec sibi cenarum quivis temere arroget artem,   35
Non prius exacta tenui ratione saporum.
Nec satis est cara piscis averrere mensa,
Ignarum quibus est ius aptius et quibus assis
Languidus in cubitum iam se conviva reponet.
Umber et iligna nutritus glande rotundas   40
Curvat aper lances carnem vitantis inertem;
Nam Laurens malus est, ulvis et arundine pinguis.
Vinea submittit capreas non semper edulis.
Fecundi leporis sapiens sectabitur armos.
Piscibus atque avibus quae natura et foret aetas,   45
Ante meum nulli patuit quaesita palatum.
Sunt quorum ingenium nova tantum crustula promit.
Nequaquam satis in re una consumere curam;
Ut si quis solum hoc, mala ne sint vina, laboret,
Quali perfundat piscis securus olivo.   50
Massica si caelo suppones vina sereno,
Nocturna, si quid crassi est, tenuabitur aura
Et decedet odor nervis inimicus; at illa
Integrum perdunt lino vitiata saporem.
Surrentina vafer qui miscet faece Falerna   55
Vina, columbino limum bene colligit ovo,
Quatenus ima petit volvens aliena vitellus.
  Tostis marcentem squillis recreabis et Afra
Potorem coclea; nam lactuca innatat acri
Post vinum stomacho; perna magis et magis hillis   ·   60
Flagitat immorsus refici, quin omnia malit,
Quaecumque immundis fervent adlata popinis.

Est operae pretium duplicis pernoscere iuris
Naturam.   Simplex e dulci constat olivo,
Quod pingui miscere mero muriaque decebit   65
Non alia quam qua Byzantia putuit orca.
Hoc ubi confusum sectis inferbuit herbis
Corycioque croco sparsum stetit, insuper addes
Pressa Venafranae quod baca remisit olivae.

   Picenis cedunt pomis Tiburtia suco ;   70
Nam facie praestant.   Vennuncula convenit ollis ;
Rectius Albanam fumo duraveris uvam.
Hanc ego cum malis, ego faecem primus et allec,
Primus et invenior piper album cum sale nigro
Incretum puris circumposuisse catillis.   75

   Immane est vitium, dare milia terna macello
Angustoque vagos piscis urgere catino.
Magna movet stomacho fastidia, seu puer unctis
Tractavit calicem manibus, dum furta ligurrit,
Sive gravis veteri craterae limus adhaesit.   80
Vilibus in scopis, in mappis, in scobe quantus
Consistit sumptus?   Neglectis, flagitium ingens.
Ten lapides varios lutulenta radere palma,
Et Tyrias dare circum inlota toralia vestis,
Oblitum, quanto curam sumptumque minorem   85
Haec habeant, tanto reprehendi iustius illis,
Quae nisi divitibus nequeunt contingere mensis?

   H. Docte Cati, per amicitiam divosque rogatus,
Ducere me auditum, perges quocumque, memento.
Nam quamvis memori referas mihi pectore cuncta,   90
Non tamen interpres tantundem iuveris.   Adde
Voltum habitumque hominis, quem tu vidisse beatus
Non magni pendis, quia contigit; at mihi cura
Non mediocris inest, fontis ut adire remotos
Atque haurire queam vitae praecepta beatae.   95

V.

ON WILL HUNTING.

A DIALOGUE BETWEEN ODYSSEUS (ULIXES) AND TIRESIAS.

1. Outline :

1. Ulixes asks Tiresias how he can enrich himself, since a man
   must have wealth to be respected, 1–8 ;

2. The seer advises him to pay court to the rich and childless, in
   order to be remembered in their wills, 9–17 ;

3. Ulixes objects, but yields when Tiresias tells him it is his only
   hope, 18–22.

4. The latter then describes the details of the art:

   a) The will-hunter must not shrink from any service, and he
      must not be discouraged by failure, 23–44 ;

   b) It is well to pay court also to a rich man who has one sickly
      son, in order to be named second heir, 45–50 ;

   c) If offered the will to read he must put it aside, not, how-
      ever, without a hasty glance at its provisions, 51–69 ;

   d) He must not neglect the man's favorites, though he should
      pay special attention to the testator himself.   The story
      of the old woman of Thebes, 70–88 ;

   e) He must study his victim's peculiarities and adapt himself
      to them, 88–98 ;

   f) When his goal is reached, he must make a proper show of
      grief, and at once lay his toils for another prize, 99–110.

2. Time : 30 B.C.

Ulixes. Hoc quoque, Tiresia, praeter narrata petenti
Responde, quibus amissas reparare queam res
Artibus atque modis.   Quid rides?   *Tiresias.* Iamne doloso
Non satis est Ithacam revehi patriosque penatis
Aspicere?   *U.* O nulli quicquam mentite, vides ut   5
Nudus inopsque domum redeam te vate, neque illic
Aut apotheca procis intacta est aut pecus : atqui
Et genus et virtus, nisi cum re, vilior alga est.

   T. Quando pauperiem missis ambagibus horres,
Accipe qua ratione queas ditescere.   Turdus   10
Sive aliud privum dabitur tibi, devolet illuc,
Res ubi magna nitet domino sene ; dulcia poma

Et quoscumque feret cultus tibi fundus honores,
Ante Larem gustet venerabilior Lare dives;
Qui quamvis periurus erit, sine gente, cruentus   15
Sanguine fraterno, fugitivus, ne tamen illi
Tu comes exterior, si postulet, ire recuses.
U. Utne tegam spurco Damae latus?   Haud ita Troiae
Me gessi, certans semper melioribus.   *T.* Ergo
Pauper eris.   *U.* Fortem hoc animum tolerare iubebo;   20
Et quondam maiora tuli.   Tu protinus, unde
Divitias aerisque ruam, dic augur, acervos.
    T. Dixi equidem et dico.   Captes astutus ubique
Testamenta senum, neu, si vafer unus et alter
Insidiatorem praeroso fugerit hamo,   25
Aut spem deponas aut artem inlusus omittas.
Magna minorve foro si res certabitur olim,
Vivet uter locuples sine gnatis, improbus, ultro
Qui meliorem audax vocet in ius, illius esto
Defensor; fama civem causaque priorem   30
Sperne, domi si gnatus erit fecundave coniunx.
'Quinte' puta aut 'Publi' — gaudent praenomine molles
Auriculae — 'tibi me virtus tua fecit amicum;
Ius anceps novi, causas defendere possum;
Eripiet quivis oculos citius mihi quam te   35
Contemptum cassa nuce pauperet; haec mea cura est,
Ne quid tu perdas, neu sis iocus.'   Ire domum atque
Pelliculam curare iube; fi cognitor ipse;
Persta atque obdura, seu rubra Canicula findet
Infantis statuas seu pingui tentus omaso   40
Furius hibernas cana nive conspuet Alpis.
'Nonne vides' aliquis cubito stantem prope tangens
Inquiet, 'ut patiens, ut amicis aptus, ut acer?'
Plures adnabunt thunni et cetaria crescent.
    Si cui praeterea validus male filius in re   45
Praeclara sublatus aletur, ne manifestum

Caelibis obsequium nudet te, leniter in spem
Arrepe officiosus, uti scribare secundus
Heres et, si quis casus puerum egerit Orco,
In vacuum venias; perraro haec alea fallit.   50

    Qui testamentum tradet tibi cumque legendum,
Abnuere et tabulas a te removere memento,
Sic tamen, ut limis rapias quid prima secundo
Cera velit versu; solus multisne coheres,
Veloci percurre oculo. Plerumque recoctus   55
Scriba ex quinqueviro corvum deludet hiantem,
Captatorque dabit risus Nasica Corano.
U. Num furis? An prudens ludis me obscura canendo?
T. O Laertiade, quicquid dicam, aut erit aut non;
Divinare etenim magnus mihi donat Apollo.   60
U. Quid tamen ista velit sibi fabula, si licet, ede.
T. Tempore quo iuvenis Parthis horrendus, ab alto
Demissum genus Aenea, tellure marique
Magnus erit, forti nubet procera Corano
Filia Nasicae, metuentis reddere soldum.   65
Tum gener hoc faciet: tabulas socero dabit atque
Ut legat orabit; multum Nasica negatas
Accipiet tandem et tacitus leget, invenietque
Nil sibi legatum praeter plorare suisque.

    Illud ad haec iubeo; mulier si forte dolosa   70
Libertusve senem delirum temperet, illis
Accedas socius; laudes, lauderis ut absens:
Adiuvat hoc quoque, sed vincit longe prius ipsum
Expugnare caput.   Scribet mala carmina vecors;
Laudato.   Scortator erit; cave te roget; ultro   75
Penelopam facilis potiori trade.   *U.* Putasne,
Perduci poterit tam frugi tamque pudica,
Quam nequiere proci recto depellere cursu?
T. Venit enim magnum donandi parca iuventus,
Nec tantum Veneris quantum studiosa culinae;   80

Sic tibi Penelope frugi est; quae si semel uno
De sene gustarit tecum partita lucellum,
Ut canis a corio numquam absterrebitur uncto.
Me sene, quod dicam factum est : anus improba Thebis
Ex testamento sic est elata: cadaver   85
Unctum oleo largo nudis umeris tulit heres,
Scilicet elabi si posset mortua; credo,
Quod nimium institerat viventi.

                      Cautus adito,
Neu desis operae, neve immoderatus abundes.
Difficilem et morosum offendet garrulus; ultra   90
'Non, etiam' sileas. Davus sis comicus atque
Stes capite obstipo, multum similis metuenti.
Obsequio grassare; mone, si increbruit aura,
Cautus uti velet carum caput; extrahe turba
Oppositis umeris; aurem substringe loquaci.   95
Inportunus amat laudari; donec 'Ohe iam!'
Ad caelum manibus sublatis dixerit, urge et
Crescentem tumidis infla sermonibus utrem.
   Cum te servitio longo curaque levarit,
Et certum vigilans, 'Quartae esto partis Ulixes,   100
Audieris, 'heres;' 'Ergo nunc Dama sodalis
Nusquam est? Unde mihi tam fortem tamque fidelem?'
Sparge subinde et, si paullum potes, inlacrimare; est
Gaudia prodentem voltum celare. Sepulcrum
Permissum arbitrio sine sordibus exstrue; funus   105
Egregie factum laudet vicinia. Si quis
Forte coheredum senior male tussiet, huic tu
Dic, ex parte tua seu fundi sive domus sit
Emptor, gaudentem nummo te addicere. Sed me
Imperiosa trahit Proserpina; vive valeque.   110

VI.

THE DELIGHTS OF COUNTRY LIFE.

1. Outline: Horace finds life on his Sabine Farm more agreeable than the distractions of the metropolis.

    1. He has his heart's desire and envies no man. He prays only for a continuance of his present blessings and for intellectual activity, 1–15 ;

    2. He can find no better subject for his muse than the praises of country life, 16–23 :

       a) Life in Rome is full of care and annoyance :

          1) A thousand and one duties call him forth in all weathers, and keep him in a constant turmoil, 23–39 ;

          2) Even his friendship with Maecenas is a cause of envy and of constant demands for information on political matters, 40–58.

       b) Life in the country abounds in simple pleasures and in opportunities for self-improvement :

          1) He is able to read and to devote himself to literary work, 59–62 ;

          2) At table there is simple fare and improving conversation, 63–76 ;

          3) A rural neighbor points morals by means of fables. For example, to teach contentment with one's lot, he tells the fable of the Town and the Country Mouse, 77–79 :

             (*a*) The Country Mouse entertains his friend from the city, 79–89 ;

             (*b*) The latter induces him to go to town, 90–100 ;

             (*c*) But the luxurious surroundings do not make up for the dangers which accompany them, and the rustic prefers his quiet country life, 100–117.

2. Time: 31–30 B.C.

Hoc erat in votis : modus agri non ita magnus,
Hortus ubi et tecto vicinus iugis aquae fons
Et paullum silvae super his foret. Auctius atque

Di melius fecere.   Bene est.   Nil amplius oro,
Maia nate, nisi ut propria haec mihi munera faxis.   5
Si neque maiorem feci ratione mala rem,
Nec sum facturus vitio culpave minorem ;
Si veneror stultus nihil horum : 'O si angulus ille
Proximus accedat, qui nunc denormat agellum !
O si urnam argenti fors quae mihi monstret, ut illi   10
Thesauro invento qui mercennarius agrum
Illum ipsum mercatus aravit, dives amico
Hercule !' Si, quod adest, gratum iuvat, hac prece te oro :
Pingue pecus domino facias et cetera praeter
Ingenium, utque soles, custos mihi maximus adsis !   15
    Ergo ubi me in montis et in arcem ex urbe removi,
Quid prius inlustrem saturis Musaque pedestri ?
Nec mala me ambitio perdit nec plumbeus Auster
Autumnusque gravis, Libitinae quaestus acerbae.
Matutine pater, seu 'Iane' libentius audis,   20
Unde homines operum primos vitaeque labores
Instituunt — sic dis placitum, — tu carminis esto
Principium.   Romae sponsorem me rapis.   'Heia,
Ne prior officio quisquam respondeat, urge.'
Sive Aquilo radit terras seu bruma nivalem   25
Interiore diem gyro trahit, ire necesse est.
Postmodo, quod mi obsit clare certumque locuto
Luctandum in turba et facienda iniuria tardis.
'Quid vis, insane, et quas res agis ?' improbus urget
Iratis precibus : 'Tu pulses omne quod obstat,   30
Ad Maecenatem memori si mente recurras.'
Hoc iuvat et melli est, non mentiar.   At simul atras
Ventum est Esquilias, aliena negotia centum
Per caput et circa saliunt latus.   'Ante secundam
Roscius orabat sibi adesses ad Puteal cras.   35
De re communi scribae magna atque nova te
Orabant hodie meminisses, Quinte, reverti.

Imprimat his, cura, Maecenas signa tabellis.'
Dixeris, 'Experiar'; 'Si vis, potes,' addit et instat.

    Septimus octavo propior iam fugerit annus,   40
Ex quo Maecenas me coepit habere suorum
In numero, dumtaxat ad hoc, quem tollere raeda
Vellet iter faciens, et cui concredere nugas
Hoc genus: 'Hora quota est? Thraex est Gallina Syro par?
Matutina parum cautos iam frigora mordent;'   45
Et quae rimosa bene deponuntur in aure.
Per totum hoc tempus subiectior in diem et horam
Invidiae noster.   Ludos spectaverat una,
Luserat in campo; 'Fortunae filius!' omnes.
Frigidus a rostris manat per compita rumor;   50
Quicumque obvius est, me consulit: 'O bone, nam te
Scire, deos quoniam propius contingis, oportet,
Numquid de Dacis audisti?' 'Nil equidem.' 'Ut tu
Semper eris derisor.' 'At omnes di exagitent me,
Si quicquam.' 'Quid? militibus promissa Triquetra   55
Praedia Caesar an est Itala tellure daturus?'
Iurantem me scire nihil mirantur, ut unum
Scilicet egregii mortalem altique silenti.
   Perditur haec inter misero lux non sine votis.
O rus, quando ego te aspiciam, quandoque licebit   60
Nunc veterum libris nunc somno et inertibus horis
Ducere sollicitae iucunda oblivia vitae?
O quando faba Pythagorae cognata simulque
Uncta satis pingui ponentur holuscula lardo?
O noctes cenaeque deum! quibus ipse meique   65
Ante Larem proprium vescor vernasque procacis
Pasco libatis dapibus.   Prout cuique libido est,
Siccat inaequalis calices conviva solutus
Legibus insanis, seu quis capit acria fortis
Pocula seu modicis uvescit laetius.   Ergo   70
Sermo oritur, non de villis domibusve alienis,

Nec male necne Lepos saltet; sed quod magis ad nos
Pertinet et nescire malum est, agitamus : utrumne
Divitiis homines an sint virtute beati ;
Quidve ad amicitias, usus rectumne, trahat nos ;   75
Et quae sit natura boni summumque quid eius.
  Cervius haec inter vicinus garrit anilis
Ex re fabellas. Si quis nam laudat Arelli
Sollicitas ignarus opes, sic incipit : ' Olim
Rusticus urbanum murem mus paupere fertur   80
Accepisse cavo, veterem vetus hospes amicum,
Asper et attentus quaesitis, ut tamen artum
Solveret hospitiis animum. Quid multa ? neque ille
Sepositi ciceris nec longae invidit avenae,
Aridum et ore ferens acinum semesaque lardi   85
Frusta dedit, cupiens varia fastidia cena
Vincere tangentis male singula dente superbo ;
Cum pater ipse domus palea porrectus in horna
Esset ador loliumque, dapis meliora relinquens.
Tandem urbanus ad hunc ' Quid te iuvat,' inquit, ' amice,   90
Praerupti nemoris patientem vivere dorso ?
Vis tu homines urbemque feris praeponere silvis ?
Carpe viam, mihi crede, comes ; terrestria quando
Mortalis animas vivunt sortita, neque ulla est
Aut magno aut parvo leti fuga : quo, bone, circa,   95
Dum licet, in rebus iucundis vive beatus,
Vive memor, quam sis aevi brevis.'   Haec ubi dicta
Agrestem pepulere, domo levis exsilit; inde
Ambo propositum peragunt iter, urbis aventes
Moenia nocturni subrepere.
                        Iamque tenebat   100
Nox medium caeli spatium, cum ponit uterque
In locuplete domo vestigia, rubro ubi cocco
Tincta super lectos canderet vestis eburnos,
Multaque de magna superessent fercula cena,

Quae procul exstructis inerant hesterna canistris.　　105
Ergo ubi purpurea porrectum in veste locavit
Agrestem, veluti succinctus cursitat hospes
Continuatque dapes, nec non verniliter ipsis
Fungitur officiis, praelambens omne quod adfert.
Ille cubans gaudet mutata sorte bonisque　　　110
Rebus agit laetum convivam, cum subito ingens
Valvarum strepitus lectis excussit utrumque.
Currere per totum pavidi conclave, magisque
Exanimes trepidare, simul domus alta Molossis
Personuit canibus.　Tum rusticus 'Haud mihi vita　115
Est opus hac,' ait, 'et valeas; me silva cavusque
Tutus ab insidiis tenui solabitur ervo.'

VII.

A SLAVE'S LECTURE ON VIRTUE.

1. Outline : Horace's slave Davus retails the views of Crispinus,
the Stoic.

1. Davus obtains, as a privilege of the Saturnalia, permission to
speak his mind, 1–5 ;
2. He begins by general remarks on the inconsistency of mankind, 6–20 ;
3. On being asked to explain himself, he directly accuses his
master :
   a) Of longing for Rome when he is in the country, and *vice
   versa*, 21–29 ;
   b) Of pretending to be glad when he is not invited out, and
   joyfully accepting a summons from Maecenas at the
   eleventh hour, 29–37 ;
4. He proposes to prove that Horace is more foolish than his
slave, and is in fact himself a slave, by the arguments
of Crispinus, 37–45 ;
   a) A man who is again and again led into danger by his
   amorous passions is a slave to them, 46–82 ;
   b) Only the philosopher, who masters himself, is truly free,
   88–89.　Horace is not, for :
   1) He yields to his passions, 89–94 ;

2) He moons over pictures, like a slave staring at the
    posters of a gladiatorial show, 95–101 ;
3) He is a slave to his appetite, 102–111 ;
4) And after all he cannot live contentedly or drive
    away care, 111–115 ;
5. Horace loses his temper and silences his tormentor by threat-
    ening to send him to work on the farm, 116–118.

2. Time : 31–30 B.C.

Davus. Iamdudum ausculto et cupiens tibi dicere servus
Pauca reformido. *Hor.* Davusne ? *D.* Ita, Davus, amicum
Mancipium domino et frugi quod sit satis, hoc est,
Ut vitale putes. *H.* Age, libertate Decembri,
Quando ita maiores voluerunt, utere ; narra.   5

   D. Pars hominum vitiis gaudet constanter et urget
Propositum ; pars multa natat, modo recta capessens,
Interdum pravis obnoxia.   Saepe notatus
Cum tribus anellis, modo laeva Priscus inani,
Vixit inaequalis, clavum ut mutaret in horas,   10
Aedibus ex magnis subito se conderet, unde
Mundior exiret vix libertinus honeste ;
Iam moechus Romae, iam mallet doctus Athenis
Vivere Vertumnis, quotquot sunt, natus iniquis.
Scurra Volanerius, postquam illi iusta cheragra   15
Contudit articulos, qui pro se tolleret atque
Mitteret in phimum talos, mercede diurna
Conductum pavit ; quanto constantior isdem
In vitiis, tanto levius miser ac prior illo,
Qui iam contento, iam laxo fune laborat.   20

   H. Non dices hodie quorsum haec tam putida tendant,
Furcifer ? *D.* Ad te, inquam. *H.* Quo pacto, pessime?
   D. Laudas
Fortunam et mores antiquae plebis, et idem,
Si quis ad illa deus subito te agat, usque recuses,
Aut quia non sentis quod clamas rectius esse,   25

Aut quia non firmus rectum defendis, et haeres
Nequiquam caeno cupiens evellere plantam.
Romae rus optas; absentem rusticus urbem
Tollis ad astra levis. Si nusquam es forte vocatus
Ad cenam, laudas securum holus ac, velut usquam   30
Vinctus eas, ita te felicem dicis amasque,
Quod nusquam tibi sit potandum. Iusserit ad se
Maecenas serum sub lumina prima venire
Convivam: 'Nemon oleum fert ocius? ecquis
Audit?' cum magno blateras clamore fugisque.   35
Mulvius et scurrae, tibi non referenda precati,
Discedunt. 'Etenim fateor me' dixerit ille,
'Duci ventre levem, nasum nidore supinor,
Imbecillus, iners, si quid vis, adde, popino.
Tu cum sis quod ego et fortassis nequior, ultro   40
Insectere velut melior, verbisque decoris
Obvolvas vitium?' Quid, si me stultior ipso
Quingentis empto drachmis deprenderis? Aufer
Me voltu terrere; manum stomachumque teneto,
Dum quae Crispini docuit me ianitor edo.   45
    Te coniunx aliena capit, meretricula Davum:
Evasti; credo, metues doctusque cavebis.
Quaeres, quando iterum paveas iterumque perire
Possis, o totiens servus! Quae belua, ruptis   70
Cum semel effugit, reddit se prava catenis?
'Non sum moechus' ais. Neque ego, hercule, fur, ubi vasa
Praetereo sapiens argentea. Tolle periclum;
Iam vaga prosiliet frenis natura remotis.
Tune mihi dominus, rerum imperiis hominumque   75
Tot tantisque minor, quem ter vindicta quaterque
Imposita haud umquam misera formidine privet?
Adde super dictis quod non levius valeat; nam
Sive vicarius est, qui servo paret, uti mos
Vester ait, seu conservus; tibi quid sum ego? Nempe   80

Tu, mihi qui imperitas, alii servis miser atque
Duceris ut nervis alienis mobile lignum.
  Quisnam igitur liber ?   Sapiens, sibi qui imperiosus,
Quem neque pauperies neque mors neque vincula terrent,
Responsare cupidinibus, contemnere honores   85
Fortis, et in se ipso totus teres atque rotundus,
Externi ne quid valeat per leve morari,
In quem manca ruit semper fortuna.   Potesne
Ex his ut proprium quid noscere ?   Quinque talenta
Poscit te mulier, vexat foribusque repulsum   90
Perfundit gelida, rursus vocat.   Eripe turpi
Colla iugo, ' Liber, liber sum,' dic age !   Non quis ;
Urget enim dominus mentem non lenis et acris
Subiectat lasso stimulos versatque negantem.
Vel cum Pausiaca torpes, insane, tabella,   95
Qui peccas minus atque ego, cum Fulvi Rutubaeque
Aut Pacideiani contento poplite miror
Proelia rubrica picta aut carbone, velut si
Re vera pugnent, feriant vitentque moventes
Arma viri ?   Nequam et cessator Davus ; at ipse   100
Subtilis veterum iudex et callidus audis.
  Nil ego, si ducor libo fumante : tibi ingens
Virtus atque animus cenis responsat opimis ?
Obsequium ventris mihi perniciosius est cur ?
Tergo plector enim.   Qui tu impunitior illa,   105
Quae parvo sumi nequeunt, obsonia captas ?
Nempe inamarescunt epulae sine fine petitae,
Inlusique pedes vitiosum ferre recusant
Corpus.   An hic peccat, sub noctem qui puer uvam
Furtiva mutat strigili ; qui praedia vendit,   110
Nil servile gulae parens habet ?   Adde, quod idem
Non horam tecum esse potes, non otia recte
Ponere, teque ipsum vitas fugitivus et erro,
Iam vino quaerens, iam somno fallere curam ;

Frustra; nam comes atra premit sequiturque fugacem.   115
H. Unde mihi lapidem ?   D. Quorsum est opus ?   H. Unde
    sagittas ?

D. Aut insanit homo aut versus facit.   H. Ocius hinc te
Ni rapis, accedes opera agro nona Sabino.

VIII.

A COMICAL DINNER PARTY.

1. Outline: Fundanius tells Horace about the dinner party of an
ostentatious millionnaire, who prided himself on his novelties in the
gastronomic art.

  1. Horace begs for an account of the affair, 1–5.

  2. His friend describes the meal, which was elaborate and costly,
       but spoiled by the tiresome explanations of the host and
       his friend Nomentanus:

     a) The appetizers (*gustatio*), 6–9 ;

     b) The wines.   The host's ostentatious display, 10–17 ;

     c) The arrangement of the guests at table (see **2** below), 18–41 ;

     d) The *mensa prima*.   Nomentanus points out the costly fea-
         tures, 42–53 ;

     e) An untimely accident, which reveals the host's lack of
         neatness and care.   He loses his presence of mind, but
         Nomentanus comes to the rescue, 54–78 ;

     f) Balatro and Vibidius divert the attention of the guests, and
         the dinner proceeds with many luxuries, the enjoyment
         of which is spoiled by the host's wearisome talk, 79–95.

2. The Arrangement of the Guests: In accordance with the usual
arrangement, couches were placed on three sides of the table, and the
fourth was left open to allow access to the servants.   The couches had
arms only on one end, at *a*, *b*, and *c* ; in the other places the guests
rested their elbows on cushions.   The places on each couch next to the
arms were called *summus locus* (1, 4, 7), the next *medius locus* (2, 5,
8), and the next *imus locus* (3, 6, 9).

Maecenas, the guest of honor, occupied the *imus locus* on the *medius
lectus*, and the other two places on that couch were assigned to his
umbrae, Balatro and Vibidius, who distinguished themselves by their
bibulous feats.   Fundanius, Viscus, and Varius, friends of Maecenas
and men of letters, occupied the *summus lectus* in the order named.

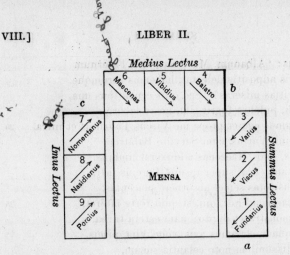

The usual place for the host would have been the *summus locus* on the *imus lectus*, next to Maecenas; but he had placed Nomentanus there to entertain (?) his distinguished guest, and himself occupied the *medius locus*. Beside him was the appropriately named buffoon, Porcius.

3. Time: The exact date cannot be determined.

Hor. Ut Nasidieni iuvit te cena beati?
Nam mihi quaerenti convivam dictus here illic
De medio potare die. *Fund.* Sic, ut mihi numquam
In vita fuerit melius. *H.* Da, si grave non est,
Quae prima iratum ventrem placaverit esca. **5**
F. In primis Lucanus aper leni fuit Austro
Captus, ut aiebat cenae pater; acria circum
Rapula, lactucae, radices, qualia lassum
Pervellunt stomachum, siser, allec, faecula Coa.

His ubi sublatis puer alte cinctus acernam **10**
Gausape purpureo mensam pertersit, et alter
Sublegit quodcumque iaceret inutile quodque
Posset cenantis offendere; ut Attica virgo
Cum sacris Cereris procedit fuscus Hydaspes,
Caecuba vina ferens, Alcon Chium maris expers. **15**

Hic erus: 'Albanum, Maecenas, sive Falernum
Te magis adpositis delectat, habemus utrumque.
H. Divitias miseras! Sed quis cenantibus una,
Fundani, pulchre fuerit tibi, nosse laboro.
F. Summus ego et prope me Viscus Thurinus et infra,   20
Si memini, Varius, cum Servilio Balatrone
Vibidius, quos Maecenas adduxerat umbras.
Nomentanus erat super ipsum, Porcius infra,
Ridiculus totas semel absorbere placentas.
Nomentanus ad hoc, qui, si quid forte lateret,   25
Indice monstraret digito: nam cetera turba,
Nos, inquam, cenamus avis, conchylia, piscis,
Longe dissimilem noto celantia sucum,
Ut vel continuo patuit, cum passeris atque
Ingustata mihi porrexerat ilia rhombi.   30
Post hoc me docuit melimela rubere minorem
Ad lunam delecta. Quid hoc intersit, ab ipso
Audieris melius. Tum Vibidius Balatroni:
'Nos nisi damnose bibimus, moriemur inulti,'
Et calices poscit maiores. Vertere pallor   35
Tum parochi faciem, nil sic metuentis ut acris
Potores, vel quod maledicunt liberius vel
Fervida quod subtile exsurdant vina palatum.
Invertunt Allifanis vinaria tota
Vibidius Balatroque, secutis omnibus; imi   40
Convivae lecti nihilum nocuere lagoenis.
    Adfertur squillas inter murena natantis
In patina porrecta. Sub hoc erus, 'Haec gravida' inquit
'Capta est, deterior post partum carne futura.
His mixtum ius est; oleo, quod prima Venafri   45
Pressit cella; garo de sucis piscis Hiberi;
Vino quinquenni, verum citra mare nato,
Dum coquitur — cocto Chium sic convenit, ut non
Hoc magis ullum aliud — pipere albo, non sine aceto,

Quod Methymnaeam vitio mutaverit uvam.   50
Erucas viridis, inulas ego primus amaras
Monstravi incoquere; inlutos Curtillus echinos,
Ut melius muria, quod testa marina remittat.'
    Interea suspensa gravis aulaea ruinas
In patinam fecere, trahentia pulveris atri   55
Quantum non Aquilo Campanis excitat agris.
Nos maius veriti, postquam nihil esse pericli
Sensimus, erigimur.   Rufus posito capite, ut si
Filius immaturus obisset, flere.   Quis esset
Finis, ni sapiens sic Nomentanus amicum   60
Tolleret: 'Heu, Fortuna, quis est crudelior in nos
Te deus?   Ut semper gaudes inludere rebus
Humanis!'   Varius mappa compescere risum
Vix poterat.   Balatro suspendens omnia naso,
'Haec est condicio vivendi,' aiebat, 'eoque   65
Responsura tuo numquam est par fama labori.
Tene, ut ego accipiar laute, torquerier omni
Sollicitudine districtum, ne panis adustus,
Ne male conditum ius adponatur, ut omnes
Praecincti recte pueri comptique ministrent?   70
Adde hos praeterea casus, aulaea ruant si,
Ut modo; si patinam pede lapsus frangat agaso.
Sed convivatoris, uti ducis, ingenium res
Adversae nudare solent, celare secundae.'
Nasidienus ad haec: 'Tibi di, quaecumque preceris,   75
Commoda dent! ita vir bonus es convivaque comis';
Et soleas poscit.   Tum in lecto quoque videres
Stridere secreta divisos aure susurros.
    H. Nullos his mallem ludos spectasse; sed illa
Redde, age, quae deinceps risisti.   *F.* Vibidius dum   80
Quaerit de pueris num sit quoque fracta lagoena,
Quod sibi poscenti non dantur pocula, dumque
Ridetur fictis rerum Balatrone secundo.

Nasidiene, redis mutatae frontis, ut arte
Emendaturus fortunam; deinde secuti   85
Mazonomo pueri magno discerpta ferentes
Membra gruis sparsi sale multo, non sine farre,
Pinguibus et ficis pastum iecur anseris albae,
Et leporum avolsos, ut multo suavius, armos,
Quam si cum lumbis quis edit.   Tum pectore adusto   90
Vidimus et merulas poni et sine clune palumbes;
Suaves res, si non causas narraret earum et
Naturas dominus, quem nos sic fugimus ulti,
Ut nihil omnino gustaremus, velut illis
Canidia adflasset peior serpentibus Afris.   95

EPISTULARUM

LIBER PRIMUS.

———◆———

I.

ON THE IMPORTANCE OF PHILOSOPHY.

1. Occasion of the Poem : Maecenas had probably urged upon Horace the publication of a second collection of lyrics (line 5), although he may have called for an epic in praise of Augustus (*cf. Serm.* ii. 1. 10 ff.). In dedicating the first book of Epistles to his patron, Horace states his plans for the future.

2. Outline :

1. Horace proposes to give up lyric poetry, in which line he thinks he has served his time, and to devote his spare moments to philosophy, 1–12.

2. He will not follow any particular school. He regrets that he cannot give more time to the subject, 13–26.

3. However, a slight knowledge is better than none, and serves to alleviate many evils, even if it cannot cure them, 27–40.

4. The philosophers, and not the general public, are the safe guides for the conduct of life :

   a) For it is better to learn not to desire wealth and honors than to toil to gain them, 41–51 ;

   b) But the masses care for nothing but money and the position which it secures, 52–69 ;

   c) Then, too, each man has a different idea of happiness, 70–80 ;

   d) And even the same individual changes his opinion from hour to hour, 80–93 ;

   e) So universal is this mad inconsistency that it attracts less attention than carelessness in dress or in personal neatness, 94–105.

5. Horace closes with a parting thrust at the exaggerated claims
       of the Stoics, 106-108.

3. Time : 20 B.C.

Prima dicte mihi, summa dicende Camena,
Spectatum satis et donatum iam rude quaeris,
Maecenas, iterum antiquo me includere ludo.
Non eadem est aetas, non mens.   Veianius, armis
Herculis ad postem fixis, latet abditus agro,   5
Ne populum extrema totiens exoret harena.
Est mihi purgatam crebro qui personet aurem :
' Solve senescentem mature sanus equum, ne
Peccet ad extremum ridendus et ilia ducat.'
Nunc itaque et versus et cetera ludicra pono ;   10
Quid verum atque decens curo et rogo, et omnis in hoc sum ;
Condo et compono quae mox depromere possim.

Ac ne forte roges quo me duce, quo Lare tuter,
Nullius addictus iurare in verba magistri,
Quo me cumque rapit tempestas, deferor hospes.   15
Nunc agilis fio et mersor civilibus undis,
Virtutis verae custos rigidusque satelles ;
Nunc in Aristippi furtim praecepta relabor,
Et mihi res, non me rebus, subiungere conor.
Ut nox longa quibus mentitur amica, diesque   20
Longa videtur opus debentibus, ut piger annus
Pupillis, quos dura premit custodia matrum ;
Sic mihi tarda fluunt ingrataque tempora, quae spem
Consiliumque morantur agendi naviter id quod
Aeque pauperibus prodest, locupletibus aeque,   25
Aeque neglectum pueris senibusque nocebit.
Restat ut his ego me ipse regam solerque elementis.
Non possis oculo quantum contendere Lynceus ;
Non tamen idcirco contemnas lippus inungui :
Nec, quia desperes invicti membra Glyconis,   30
Nodosa corpus nolis prohibere cheragra.

Est quadam prodire tenus, si non datur ultra.
Fervet avaritia miseroque cupidine pectus;
Sunt verba et voces quibus hunc lenire dolorem
Possis et magnam morbi deponere partem.   35
Laudis amore tumes; sunt certa piacula quae te
Ter pure lecto poterunt recreare libello.
Invidus, iracundus, iners, vinosus, amator,
Nemo adeo ferus est, ut non mitescere possit,
Si modo culturae patientem commodet aurem.   40
    Virtus est vitiùm fugere et sapientia prima
Stultitia caruisse.   Vides, quae maxima credis
Esse mala, exiguum censum turpemque repulsam,
Quanto devites animi capitisque labore;
Impiger extremos curris mercator ad Indos,   45
Per mare pauperiem fugiens, per saxa, per ignis;
Ne cures ea quae stulte miraris et optas,
Discere et audire et meliori credere non vis?
Quis circum pagos et circum compita pugnax
Magna coronari contemnat Olympia, cui spes,   50
Cui sit condicio dulcis sine pulvere palmae?
    Vilius argentum est auro, virtutibus aurum.
'O cives, cives, quaerenda pecunia primum est;
Virtus post nummos;' haec Ianus summus ab imo
Prodocet, haec recinunt iuvenes dictata senesque,   55
Laevo suspensi loculos tabulamque lacerto.
Est animus tibi, sunt mores, est lingua fidesque,
Sed quadringentis sex septem milia desunt;
Plebs eris.   At pueri ludentes 'Rex eris,' aiunt,
'Si recte facies.'   Hic murus aeneus esto: 60
Nil conscire sibi, nulla pallescere culpa.
Roscia, dic sodes, melior lex an puerorum est
Nenia, quae regnum recte facientibus offert,
Et maribus Curiis et decantata Camillis?
Isne tibi melius suadet, qui 'rem facias, rem,   65

Si possis, recte, si non, quocumque modo rem,'
Ut propius spectes lacrimosa poemata Pupi;
An qui Fortunae te responsare superbae
Liberum et erectum praesens hortatur et aptat?

   Quod si me populus Romanus forte roget cur   70
Non ut porticibus sic iudiciis fruar isdem,
Nec sequar aut fugiam quae diligit ipse vel odit,
Olim quod vulpes aegroto cauta leoni
Respondit, referam: ' Quia me vestigia terrent,
Omnia te adversum spectantia, nulla retrorsum.'   75
Belua multorum es capitum.   Nam quid sequar aut quem?
Pars hominum gestit conducere publica; sunt qui
Crustis et pomis viduas venentur avaras,
Excipiantque senes, quos in vivaria mittant;
Multis occulto crescit res faenore.

                          Verum   80
Esto aliis alios rebus studiisque teneri;
Idem eadem possunt horam durare probantes?
' Nullus in orbe sinus Bais praelucet amoenis'
Si dixit dives, lacus et mare sentit amorem
Festinantis eri; cui si vitiosa libido   85
Fecerit auspicium, ' Cras ferramenta Teanum
Tolletis, fabri.' Lectus genialis in aula est:
Nil ait esse prius, melius nil caelibe vita;
Si non est, iurat bene solis esse maritis.
Quo teneam voltus mutantem Protea nodo?   90
Quid pauper?   Ride: mutat cenacula, lectos,
Balnea, tonsores, conducto navigio aeque
Nauseat ac locuples, quem ducit priva triremis.

   Si curatus inaequali tonsore capillos
Occurri, rides, si forte subucula pexae   95
Trita subest tunicae, vel si toga dissidet impar,
Rides; quid, mea cum pugnat sententia secum,
Quod petiit spernit, repetit quod nuper omisit.

Aestuat et vitae disconvenit ordine toto,
Diruit, aedificat, mutat quadrata rotundis?   100
Insanire putas sollemnia me neque rides,
Nec medici credis nec curatoris egere
A praetore dati, rerum tutela mearum
Cum sis et prave sectum stomacheris ob unguem
De te pendentis, te respicientis amici.   105

    Ad summam : sapiens uno minor est Iove, dives,
Liber, honoratus, pulcher, rex denique regum,
Praecipue sanus, nisi cum pituita molesta est.

II.

HOMER THE TEACHER OF TRUE PHILOSOPHY.

ADDRESSED TO LOLLIUS MAXIMUS.

1. **Outline** :

  1. Horace has been re-reading Homer and believes him a better
     guide for the conduct of life than many a philosopher, 1–5 :

    a) The *Iliad* serves as a warning, by showing the folly of the
      conduct of Paris and the chiefs of the Greeks, 6–16 ;

    b) The *Odyssey* sets before us a model, by showing what cour-
      age and self-control can accomplish, 17–26 ;

    c) The majority of men are like the Suitors and the Phaeacians,
      sunk in sloth and caring only for pleasure, 27–31.

  2. The lessons that we should learn are these :

    a) It is better to exert oneself to live aright than in trying to
      remedy the evil results of negligence and sloth, 32–43 ;

    b) Not wealth, but a contented mind, brings true happiness,
      44–54 ;

    c) One who cannot govern himself becomes a slave to his pas-
      sions, 55–63.

  3. One can learn wisdom only when young. Now is the time for
     Lollius to begin, 64–71.

2. **Time** : About 22 B.C.

Troiani belli scriptorem, Maxime Lolli,
Dum tu declamas Romae, Praeneste relegi,
Qui quid sit pulchrum, quid turpe, quid utile, quid non,

Planius ac melius Chrysippo et Crantore dicit.
Cur ita crediderim, nisi quid te distinet, audi.   5

   Fabula, qua Paridis propter narratur amorem
Graecia barbariae lento conlisa duello,
Stultorum regum et populorum continet aestus.
Antenor censet belli praecidere causam :
Quid Paris ? ut salvus regnet vivatque beatus   10
Cogi posse negat.   Nestor componere litis
Inter Peliden festinat et inter Atriden.
Hunc amor, ira quidem communiter urit utrumque.
Quicquid delirant reges, plectuntur Achivi.
Seditione, dolis, scelere atque libidine et ira   15
Iliacos intra muros peccatur et extra.

   Rursus, quid virtus et quid sapientia possit,
Utile proposuit nobis exemplar Ulixen,
Qui domitor Troiae multorum providus urbes
Et mores hominum inspexit, latumque per aequor,   20
Dum sibi, dum sociis reditum parat, aspera multa
Pertulit, adversis rerum immersabilis undis.
Sirenum voces et Circae pocula nosti ;
Quae si cum sociis stultus cupidusque bibisset,
Sub domina meretrice fuisset turpis et excors,   25
Vixisset canis immundus vel amica luto sus.

   Nos numerus sumus et fruges consumere nati,
Sponsi Penelopae nebulones Alcinoique
In cute curanda plus aequo operata iuventus,
Cui pulchrum fuit in medios dormire dies et   30
Ad strepitum citharae cessatum ducere curam.

   Ut iugulent hominem, surgunt de nocte latrones ;
Ut te ipsum serves, non expergisceris ?   Atqui
Si noles sanus, curres hydropicus ; et ni
Posces ante diem librum cum lumine, si non   35
Intendes animum studiis et rebus honestis,
Invidia vel amore vigil torquebere.   Nam cur

Quae laedunt oculum festinas demere; si quid
Est animum, differs curandi tempus in annum?
Dimidium facti qui coepit habet; sapere aude;   40
Incipe! Qui recte vivendi prorogat horam,
Rusticus exspectat dum defluat amnis; at ille
Labitur et labetur in omne volubilis aevum.

    Quaeritur argentum puerisque beata creandis
Uxor, et incultae pacantur vomere silvae;   45
Quod satis est cui contingit, nihil amplius optet.
Non domus et fundus, non aeris acervus et auri
Aegroto domini deduxit corpore febris,
Non animo curas; valeat possessor oportet,
Si comportatis rebus bene cogitat uti.   50
Qui cupit aut metuit, iuvat illum sic domus et res,
Ut lippum pictae tabulae, fomenta podagram,
Auriculas citharae collecta sorde dolentis.
Sincerum est nisi vas, quodcumque infundis acescit.

    Sperne voluptates; nocet empta dolore voluptas.   55
Semper avarus eget; certum voto pete finem.
Invidus alterius macrescit rebus opimis;
Invidia Siculi non invenere tyranni
Maius tormentum. Qui non moderabitur irae,
Infectum volet esse, dolor quod suaserit et mens,   60
Dum poenas odio per vim festinat inulto.
Ira furor brevis est; animum rege; qui nisi paret,
Imperat: hunc frenis, hunc tu compesce catena.

    Fingit equum tenera docilem cervice magister
Ire viam qua monstret eques; venaticus, ex quo   65
Tempore cervinam pellem latravit in aula,
Militat in silvis catulus. Nunc adbibe puro
Pectore verba, puer, nunc te melioribus offer.
Quo semel est imbuta recens servabit odorem
Testa diu. Quodsi cessas aut strenuus anteis,   70
Nec tardum opperior nec praecedentibus insto.

III.

A LITERARY STAFF.

1. Occasion of the Epistle : When Augustus made his journey to the East in 21 B.C., he went by way of Samos. At the same time he sent an army by the land route through Macedonia and Thrace, under the command of Tiberius, who was at that time twenty-one years old. Tiberius, who was himself an admirer of the Hellenistic Greek poetry, had surrounded himself with a staff of young literary men. The letter is addressed to one of their number, Julius Florus, while the army was on the march.

2. Outline :
1. Horace asks where the army is at present, 1–5 ;
2. He inquires what literary work the staff is engaged in, and asks after several personal friends, 6–20 ;
3. He wishes to know what work Florus is doing and whether he has become reconciled with Munatius. He prays for their safe return, 20–36.

3. Time : The autumn of 21 B.C.

Iuli Flore, quibus terrarum militet oris
Claudius Augusti privignus, scire laboro.
Thracane vos Hebrusque nivali compede vinctus,
An freta vicinas inter currentia turris,
An pingues Asiae campi collesque morantur?   5
    Quid studiosa cohors operum struit?   Hoc quoque curo.
Quis sibi res gestas Augusti scribere sumit?
Bella quis et paces longum diffundit in aevum?
Quid Titius Romana brevi venturus in ora?
Pindarici fontis qui non expalluit haustus,   10
Fastidire lacus et rivos ausus apertos.
Ut valet?   Ut meminit nostri?   Fidibusne Latinis
Thebanos aptare modos studet auspice Musa,
An tragica desaevit et ampullatur in arte?
Quid mihi Celsus agit?   Monitus multumque monendus,   15
Privatas ut quaerat opes et tangere vitet

Scripta Palatinus quaecumque recepit Apollo,
Ne, si forte suas repetitum venerit olim
Grex avium plumas, moveat cornicula risum
Furtivis nudata coloribus.

                              Ipse quid audes ?   20
Quae circumvolitas agilis thyma ?   Non tibi parvum
Ingenium, non incultum est et turpiter hirtum :
Seu linguam causis acuis seu civica iura
Respondere paras seu condis amabile carmen,
Prima feres hederae victricis praemia.   Quod si   25
Frigida curarum fomenta relinquere posses,
Quo te caelestis sapientia duceret, ires.
Hoc opus, hoc studium parvi properemus et ampli,
Si patriae volumus, si nobis vivere cari.
Debes hoc etiam rescribere, sit tibi curae,   30
Quantae conveniat, Munatius ; an male sarta
Gratia nequiquam coit et rescinditur, ac vos
Seu calidus sanguis seu rerum inscitia vexat
Indomita cervice feros ?   Ubicumque locorum
Vivitis, indigni fraternum rumpere foedus,   35
Pascitur in vestrum reditum votiva iuvenca.

IV.

AN EXHORTATION TO CONTENTMENT.

ADDRESSED TO ALBIUS TIBULLUS.

1. Outline :

   1. Horace inquires how Tibullus is spending his time in the
       country, 1–5 ;

   2. He reminds his friend, who he had heard is suffering from
       melancholy, of the blessings which the gods have show-
       ered upon him, 6–11 ;

   3. And urges him to enjoy each passing hour.   He suggests that
       a visit to the Sabine Farm may divert him, 12–16.

2. Time : The exact date cannot be determined.   Not after 20 B.C.

Satires his early period of writing — allusion to his works *Meditates Roman nature* *Characteristics* *Probably to a Roman friend* *Me...abella Amici*

Albi, nostrorum sermonum candide iudex,
Quid nunc te dicam facere in regione Pedana?
Scribere quod Cassi Parmensis opuscula vincat,
An tacitum silvas inter reptare salubris,
Curantem quicquid dignum sapiente bonoque est?   5
  Non tu corpus eras sine pectore. Di tibi formam,
Di tibi divitias dederunt artemque fruendi.
Quid voveat dulci nutricula maius alumno,
Qui sapere et fari possit quae sentiat, et cui
Gratia, fama, valetudo contingat abunde,   10
Et mundus victus non deficiente crumena?
  Inter spem curamque, timores inter et iras
Omnem crede diem tibi diluxisse supremum;
Grata superveniet, quae non sperabitur hora.
Me pinguem et nitidum bene curata cute vises,   15
Cum ridere voles Epicuri de grege porcum.

V.

AN INVITATION.

ADDRESSED TO MANLIUS TORQUATUS.

1. Outline:

1. Horace invites Torquatus to spend the emperor's birthday with
   him in Rome, and to celebrate the event by a simple
   dinner, 1–11;
2. One should enjoy life and drive away care. The beneficent
   effects of wine, 12–20;
3. He promises neat and suitable accessories, and opportunities
   for confidential talk. He asks Torquatus to help select
   the guests, 21–31.

2. Time: Sept. 23, B.C. 21 or 20.

Si potes Archiacis conviva recumbere lectis
Nec modica cenare times holus omne patella,
Supremo te sole domi, Torquate, manebo.

Vina bibes iterum Tauro diffusa palustris
Inter Minturnas Sinuessanumque Petrinum.   5
Si melius quid habes, arcesse vel imperium fer.
Iamdudum splendet focus et tibi munda supellex.
Mitte levis spes et certamina divitiarum
Et Moschi causam: cras nato Caesare festus
Dat veniam somnumque dies; impune licebit   10
Aestivam sermone benigno tendere noctem.

　　Quo mihi fortunam, si non conceditur uti?
Parcus ob heredis curam nimiumque severus
Adsidet insano: potare et spargere flores
Incipiam patiarque vel inconsultus haberi.   15
Quid non ebrietas dissignat? Operta recludit,
Spes iubet esse ratas, ad proelia trudit inertem,
Sollicitis animis onus eximit, addocet artis.
Fecundi calices quem non fecere disertum,
Contracta quem non in paupertate solutum?   20

　　Haec ego procurare et idoneus imperor et non
Invitus, ne turpe toral, ne sordida mappa
Conruget naris, ne non et cantharus et lanx
Ostendat tibi te, ne fidos inter amicos
Sit qui dicta foras eliminet, ut coeat par   25
Iungaturque pari. Butram tibi Septiciumque
Et nisi cena prior potiorque puella Sabinum
Detinet adsumam. Locus est et pluribus umbris,
Sed nimis arta premunt olidae convivia caprae.
Tu quotus esse velis rescribe et rebus omissis   30
Atria servantem postico falle clientem.

VI.

ON PHILOSOPHIC INDIFFERENCE.

ADDRESSED TO NUMICIUS.

1. Outline :

1. The only way to be happy is to cultivate a spirit of indifference
to the possession or the loss of material blessings. Even
the pursuit of virtue may be carried to excess, 1–16 ;

2. It is folly to strive for wealth and position, which cannot affect
one's ultimate destiny, 17–27 ;

3. One must either cultivate indifference or spend one's life in a
constant struggle :

   a) By sacrificing everything to the pursuit of virtue, with a
   selfish purpose, 28–31 ;

   b) Or to acquiring wealth, in the belief that it confers all the
   blessings of life, 31–48 ;

   c) Or to winning the favor of the people and political preferment, 49–55 ;

   d) To luxurious living, 56–64 ;

   e) Or to love and pleasure, 65–66 ;

4. Since it is well known that such pursuits cannot confer happiness, Numicius should follow Horace's precept, unless he
can suggest a better one, 67–68.

2. Time : The exact date cannot be determined ; between 25 (line
26) and 20 B.C.

Nil admirari prope res est una, Numici,
Solaque quae possit facere et servare beatum.
Hunc solem et stellas et decedentia certis
Tempora momentis sunt qui formidine nulla
Imbuti spectent : quid censes munera terrae,   5
Quid maris extremos Arabas ditantis et Indos,
Ludicra quid plausus et amici dona Quiritis,
Quo spectanda modo, quo sensu credis et ore ?
Qui timet his adversa, fere miratur eodem
Quo cupiens pacto ; pavor est utrobique molestus,   10
Improvisa simul species exterret utrumque.
Gaudeat an doleat, cupiat metuatne, quid ad rem,

Si, quicquid vidit melius peiusve sua spe,
Defixis oculis animoque et corpore torpet?
Insani sapiens nomen ferat, aequus iniqui, 15
Ultra quam satis est virtutem si petat ipsam.

I nunc, argentum et marmor vetus aeraque et artis
Suspice, cum gemmis Tyrios mirare colores;
Gaude quod spectant oculi te mille loquentem;
Navus mane forum et vespertinus pete tectum, 20
Ne plus frumenti dotalibus emetat agris
Mutus et — indignum, quod sit peioribus ortus —
Hic tibi sit potius quam tu mirabilis illi.
Quicquid sub terra est, in apricum proferet aetas;
Defodiet condetque nitentia. Cum bene notum 25
Porticus Agrippae et via te conspexerit Appi,
Ire tamen restat Numa quo devenit et Ancus.

Si latus aut renes morbo temptantur acuto,
Quaere fugam morbi. Vis recte vivere; — quis non? —
Si virtus hoc una potest dare, fortis omissis 30
Hoc age deliciis.
                 Virtutem verba putas et
Lucum ligna; cave ne portus occupet alter,
Ne Cibyratica, ne Bithyna negotia perdas;
Mille talenta rotundentur, totidem altera, porro et
Tertia succedant, et quae pars quadret acervum. 35
Scilicet uxorem cum dote fidemque et amicos
Et genus et formam regina Pecunia donat,
Ac bene nummatum decorat Suadela Venusque.
Mancupiis locuples eget aeris Cappadocum rex;
Ne fueris hic tu. Chlamydes Lucullus, ut aiunt, 40
Si posset centum scaenae praebere rogatus,
'Qui possum tot?' ait; 'tamen et quaeram, et quot habebo
Mittam.' Post paulo scribit, sibi milia quinque
Esse domi chlamydum; partem vel tolleret omnis.
Exilis domus est, ubi non et multa supersunt 45

Et dominum fallunt et prosunt furibus.   Ergo
Si res sola potest facere et servare beatum,
Hoc primus repetas opus, hoc postremus omittas.—

   Si fortunatum species et gratia praestat,
Mercemur servum, qui dictet nomina, laevum   50
Qui fodicet latus et cogat trans pondera dextram
Porrigere :   'Hic multum in Fabia valet, ille Velina ;
Cui libet hic fascis dabit, eripietque curule
Cui volet importunus ebur.'   'Frater' 'pater' adde ;
Ut cuique est aetas, ita quemque facetus adopta.   55

   Si bene qui cenat bene vivit, lucet, eamus
Quo ducit gula ; piscemur, venemur, ut olim
Gargilius, qui mane plagas, venabula, servos,
Differtum transire forum populumque iubebat,
Unus ut e multis populo spectante referret   60
Emptum mulus aprum.   Crudi tumidique lavemur,
Quid deceat, quid non, obliti, Caerite cera
Digni, remigium vitiosum Ithacensis Ulixi,
Cui potior patria fuit interdicta voluptas.

   Si, Mimnermus uti censet, sine amore iocisque   65
Nil est iucundum, vivas in amore iocisque.

   Vive, vale.   Si quid novisti rectius istis,
Candidus imperti ; si nil, his utere mecum.

VII.

AN INDEPENDENT SPIRIT.

Addressed to Maecenas.

1. Occasion of the Epistle : Horace had left Rome in the month of
August and gone to his Sabine Farm on account of his health.   Maecenas had evidently taken him to task for remaining longer than he
had promised, and had perhaps hinted at Horace's obligations to him.
The frank independence of the poet's reply is creditable alike to himself and to his patron.

2. Outline :

1. Horace explains his reasons for prolonging his absence from Rome. He announces his intention of spending the winter by the sea, and of remaining away from the city until springtime, 1-13 ;
2. He is duly grateful for his patron's favors and for the spirit in which they are conferred ; but he must consider his health and his time of life, 14-28 ;
3. He would rather give up all that he has received than sacrifice his personal independence, 29-39 ;
4. One should lead the life for which nature has designed him. Horace finds Tibur and Tarentum more congenial than the capital, 40-45 ;
5. He illustrates his meaning by the story of Volteius Mena :
   a) The humble but contented auctioneer attracts the attention of Philippus, 46-59 ;
   b) The latter invites him to dinner, and then takes him to his estate in the country, 60-76 ;
   c) Volteius becomes enamored of the country, and his patron helps him to buy a farm, 77-82 ;
   d) But the denizen of the city does not make a success of his new life, and begs Philippus to restore him to his former condition, 82-98.

3. Time : The summer of 21 B.C.

Quinque dies tibi pollicitus me rure futurum,
Sextilem totum mendax desideror.   Atqui
Si me vivere vis sanum recteque valentem,
Quam mihi das aegro, dabis aegrotare timenti,
Maecenas, veniam, dum ficus prima calorque   5
Dissignatorem decorat lictoribus atris,
Dum pueris omnis pater et matercula pallet,
Officiosaque sedulitas et opella forensis
Adducit febris et testamenta resignat.
Quod si bruma nives Albanis inlinet agris,   10
Ad mare descendet vates tuus et sibi parcet
Contractusque leget ; te, dulcis amice, reviset
Cum Zephyris, si concedes, et hirundine prima.

Non quo more piris vesci Calaber iubet hospes
Tu me fecisti locupletem. 'Vescere, sodes.'   15
'Iam satis est.' 'At tu quantum vis tolle.' 'Benigne.'
'Non invisa feres pueris munuscula parvis.'
'Tam teneor dono, quam si dimittar onustus.'
'Ut libet; haec porcis hodie comedenda relinques.'
Prodigus et stultus donat quae spernit et odit;   20
Haec seges ingratos tulit et feret omnibus annis.
Vir bonus et sapiens dignis ait esse paratus,
Nec tamen ignorat quid distent aera lupinis.
Dignum praestabo me etiam pro laude merentis.
Quod si me noles usquam discedere, reddes   25
Forte latus, nigros angusta fronte capillos,
Reddes dulce loqui, reddes ridere decorum et
Inter vina fugam Cinarae maerere protervae.

Forte per angustam tenuis volpecula rimam
Repserat in cumeram frumenti, pastaque rursus   30
Ire foras pleno tendebat corpore frustra.
Cui mustela procul 'Si vis,' ait, 'effugere istinc,
Macra cavum repetes artum, quem macra subisti.' —
Hac ego si compellor imagine, cuncta resigno;
Nec somnum plebis laudo satur altilium nec   35
Otia divitiis Arabum liberrima muto.
Saepe verecundum laudasti, 'rexque paterque'
Audisti coram, nec verbo parcius absens;
Inspice si possum donata reponere laetus.

Haud male Telemachus, proles patientis Ulixi: 40
'Non est aptus equis Ithace locus, ut neque planis
Porrectus spatiis nec multae prodigus herbae;
Atride, magis apta tibi tua dona relinquam.'
Parvum parva decent; mihi iam non regia Roma,
Sed vacuum Tibur placet aut imbelle Tarentum.   45

Strenuus et fortis causisque Philippus agendis
Clarus, ab officiis octavam circiter horam

Dum redit atque Foro nimium distare Carinas
Iam grandis natu queritur, conspexit, ut aiunt,
Adrasum quendam vacua tonsoris in umbra   50
Cultello proprios purgantem leniter unguis.
'Demetri,' — puer hic non laeve iussa Philippi
Accipiebat — 'abi, quaere et refer, unde domo, quis,
Cuius fortunae, quo sit patre quove patrono.'
It, redit et narrat, Volteium nomine Menam,   55
Praeconem, tenui censu, sine crimine, notum
Et properare loco et cessare et quaerere et uti,
Gaudentem parvisque sodalibus et lare certo
Et ludis et post decisa negotia Campo.
'Scitari libet ex ipso quodcumque refers; dic,   60
Ad cenam veniat.' Non sane credere Mena,
Mirari secum tacitus. Quid multa? 'Benigne'
Respondet. 'Neget ille mihi?' 'Negat improbus et te
Neglegit aut horret.' Volteium mane Philippus
Vilia vendentem tunicato scruta popello   65
Occupat et salvere iubet prior; ille Philippo
Excusare laborem et mercennaria vincla,
Quod non mane domum venisset, denique quod non
Providisset eum. 'Sic ignovisse putato
Me tibi, si cenas hodie mecum.' 'Ut libet.' 'Ergo   70
Post nonam venies; nunc i, rem strenuus auge.'
Ut ventum ad cenam est, dicenda tacenda locutus
Tandem dormitum dimittitur. Hic ubi saepe
Occultum visus decurrere piscis ad hamum,
Mane cliens et iam certus conviva, iubetur   75
Rura suburbana indictis comes ire Latinis.
   Impositus mannis arvum caelumque Sabinum
Non cessat laudare. Videt ridetque Philippus,
Et sibi dum requiem, dum risus undique quaerit,
Dum septem donat sestertia, mutua septem   80
Promittit, persuadet uti mercetur agellum.

Mercatur.

    Ne te longis ambagibus ultra
Quam satis est morer, ex nitido fit rusticus atque
Sulcos et vineta crepat mera, praeparat ulmos,
Immoritur studiis et amore senescit habendi.   85
Verum ubi oves furto, morbo periere capellae,
Spem mentita seges, bos est enectus arando;
Offensus damnis media de nocte caballum
Arripit iratusque Philippi tendit ad aedis.
Quem simul aspexit scabrum intonsumque Philippus, 90
'Durus,' ait, 'Voltei, nimis attentusque videris
Esse mihi.' 'Pol, me miserum, patrone, vocares,
Si velles' inquit 'verum mihi ponere nomen.
Quod te per Genium dextramque deosque Penatis
Obsecro et obtestor, vitae me redde priori!'   95
Qui semel aspexit quantum dimissa petitis
Praestent, mature redeat repetatque relicta.
Metiri se quemque suo modulo ac pede verum est.

VIII.

A WORD OF WARNING.

1. Occasion of the Epistle : Albinovanus Celsus was a member of
the staff of Tiberius referred to in i. 3.   He had so far won the
approval of his commander as to be made his private secretary.
Horace warns his young friend not to be too much elated by his good
fortune.   The thought is the same as in *Odes*, ii. 3. 2-4.

2. Outline :

    1. Horace addresses his muse, and bids her report him as out of
        health, out of temper, and dissatisfied with himself, 1-12 ;

    2. And to warn Celsus against undue elation, 13-17.

3. Time : The autumn of 21 B.C.

Celso gaudere et bene rem gerere Albinovano
Musa rogata refer, comiti scribaeque Neronis.

Si quaeret quid agam, dic multa et pulchra minantem
Vivere nec recte nec suaviter; haud quia grando
Contuderit vitis oleamque momorderit aestus,   5
Nec quia longinquis armentum aegrotet in agris;
Sed quia mente minus validus quam corpore toto
Nil audire velim, nil discere, quod levet aegrum;
Fidis offendar medicis, irascar amicis,
Cur me funesto properent arcere veterno;   10
Quae nocuere sequar, fugiam quae profore credam;
Romae Tibur amem ventosus, Tibure Romam.

Post haec, ut valeat, quo pacto rem gerat et se,
Ut placeat iuveni percontare, utque cohorti.
Si dicet 'Recte,' primum gaudere, subinde   15
Praeceptum auriculis hoc instillare memento:
'Ut tu fortunam, sic nos te, Celse, feremus.'

IX.

A LETTER OF RECOMMENDATION.

ADDRESSED TO TIBERIUS.

1. Occasion of the Epistle: Septimius, to whom *Odes*, ii. 6 is
addressed, had asked Horace to recommend him for a position on the
staff of Tiberius. The fact that the letter was published indicates that
the recommendation was successful.

2. Outline:
  1. Horace tells Tiberius how reluctantly he granted his friend's
     request, 1–9;
  2. He recommends Septimius in a few words, 10–13.

3. Time: B.C. 21.

Septimius, Claudi, nimirum intellegit unus,
Quanti me facias; nam cum rogat et prece cogit,
Scilicet ut tibi se laudare et tradere coner,
Dignum mente domoque legentis honesta Neronis,

Munere cum fungi propioris censet amici,   5
Quid possim videt ac novit me valdius ipso.
Multa quidem dixi, cur excusatus abirem;
Sed timui mea ne finxisse minora putarer,
Dissimulator opis propriae, mihi commodus uni.

Sic ego, maioris fugiens opprobria culpae,   10
Frontis ad urbanae descendi praemia. Quod si
Depositum laudas ob amici iussa pudorem,
Scribe tui gregis hunc, et fortem crede bonumque.

X.

THE ADVANTAGES OF COUNTRY LIFE.

1. Occasion of the Epistle: Not only had Maecenas missed Horace during his sojourn in the country, but his friend Aristius Fuscus (see *Serm.* i. 9. 59 ff.) had evidently urged him to return to Rome, pointing out the attractions of city life.

2. Outline:

1. Horace agrees with his friend on every subject except that of the relative attractions of the city and of the country, 1–11;
2. He prefers the country:
    a) Because there one can live a natural life, 12–25;
    b) While the city creates artificial tastes, which make men slaves to money-making, 26–41;
3. But every one should be at liberty to follow his own inclinations. Horace is perfectly contented except for the absence of his friend Fuscus, 42–50.

3. Time: Apparently the same year as i. 7; *i.e.* 21 B.C.

Urbis amatorem Fuscum salvere iubemus
Ruris amatores; hac in re scilicet una
Multum dissimiles, at cetera paene gemelli
Fraternis animis — quidquid negat alter, et alter —
Adnuimus pariter, vetuli notique columbi.
Tu nidum servas, ego laudo ruris amoeni
Rivos et musco circumlita saxa nemusque.

Quid quaeris ?   Vivo et regno, simul ista reliqui
Quae vos ad caelum effertis rumore secundo,
Utque sacerdotis fugitivus liba recuso ;   10
Pane egeo iam mellitis potiore placentis.

  Vivere naturae si convenienter oportet,
Ponendaeque domo quaerenda est area primum,
Novistine locum potiorem rure beato ?
Est ubi plus tepeant hiemes, ubi gratior aura   15
Leniat et rabiem Canis et momenta Leonis,
Cum semel accepit Solem furibundus acutum ?
Est ubi divellat somnos minus invida cura ?
Deterius Libycis olet aut nitet herba lapillis ?
Purior in vicis aqua tendit rumpere plumbum,   20
Quam quae per pronum trepidat cum murmure rivum ?
Nempe inter varias nutritur silva columnas,
Laudaturque domus longos quae prospicit agros.
Naturam expelles furca, tamen usque recurret,
Et mala perrumpet furtim fastidia victrix.   25
  Non qui Sidonio contendere callidus ostro
Nescit Aquinatem potantia vellera fucum
Certius accipiet damnum propiusve medullis,
Quam qui non poterit vero distinguere falsum.
Quem res plus nimio delectavere secundae,   30
Mutatae quatient.   Si quid mirabere, pones
Invitus.   Fuge magna ; licet sub paupere tecto
Reges et regum vita praecurrere amicos.
Cervus equum pugna melior communibus herbis
Pellebat, donec minor in certamine longo   35
Imploravit opes hominis frenumque recepit.
Sed postquam victor violens discessit ab hoste,
Non equitem dorso, non frenum depulit ore.
Sic qui pauperiem veritus potiore metallis
Libertate caret, dominum vehet improbus atque   40
Serviet aeternum, quia parvo nesciet uti.

Cui non conveniet sua res, ut calceus olim,
Si pede maior erit, subvertet, si minor, uret.
Laetus sorte tua vives sapienter, Aristi,
Nec me dimittes incastigatum, ubi plura   45
Cogere quam satis est ac non cessare videbor.
Imperat aut servit collecta pecunia cuique,
Tortum digna sequi potius quam ducere funem.

Haec tibi dictabam post fanum putre Vacunae,
Excepto quod non simul esses, cetera laetus.   50

XI.

ON CONTENTMENT.

ADDRESSED TO BULLATIUS.

1. Outline :
   1. Horace asks for his friend's impression of the places he has
       visited, 1–10 ;
   2. He reminds him that happiness does not depend on one's place
       of abode, but on oneself, 11–21 ;
   3. The wise course is to enjoy each hour as it passes. Content-
       ment with one's lot will bring happiness amid the most
       unattractive surroundings, 22–30.
     With the sentiment of the Epistle, *cf. Odes*, ii. 16. 17–20.

2. Time : The exact date cannot be determined. Not after 20 B.C.

Quid tibi visa Chios, Bullati, notaque Lesbos,
Quid concinna Samos, quid Croesi regia Sardis,
Zmyrna quid et Colophon ? maiora minorave fama ?
Cunctane prae Campo et Tiberino flumine sordent,
An venit in votum Attalicis ex urbibus una,   5
An Lebedum laudas odio maris atque viarum ?
' Scis, Lebedus quid sit : Gabiis desertior atque
Fidenis vicus ; tamen illic vivere vellem,
Oblitusque meorum obliviscendus et illis
Neptunum procul e terra spectare furentem.'   10
Sed neque, qui Capua Romam petit, imbre lutoque

Aspersus volet in caupona vivere; nec qui
Frigus collegit, furnos et balnea laudat
Ut fortunatam plene praestantia vitam;
Nec, si te validus iactaverit Auster in alto,   **15**
Idcirco navem trans Aegaeum mare vendas.
Incolumi Rhodos et Mytilene pulchra facit, quod
Paenula solstitio, campestre nivalibus auris,
Per brumam Tiberis, Sextili mense caminus.
Dum licet ac voltum servat Fortuna benignum,   **20**
Romae laudetur Samos et Chios et Rhodos absens.
  Tu quamcumque deus tibi fortunaverit horam
Grata sume manu neu dulcia differ in annum,
Ut quocumque loco fueris, vixisse libenter
Te dicas; nam si ratio et prudentia curas,   **25**
Non locus effusi late maris arbiter aufert,
Caelum, non animum mutant, qui trans mare currunt.
Strenua nos exercet inertia; navibus atque
Quadrigis petimus bene vivere. Quod petis hic est,
Est Ulubris, animus si te non deficit aequus.   **30**

XII.

CONSOLATION.

1. Occasion of the Epistle: Iccius is represented in *Odes*, i. 29, as
on the point of abandoning the study of philosophy, in order to go to
Arabia in search of wealth. He is now *procurator* of Agrippa's estates
in Sicily. He seems to have complained to Horace of his failure in
attempting to make a fortune, and perhaps also of the small amount
of time which he could devote to his studies. The tone of the reply is
one of good-natured raillery.

  2. Outline:

    1. Iccius has no cause to complain. Wealth could add nothing
        to his bodily health, and such a true philosopher would
        of course live simply under any circumstances, 1–11;

    2. He deserves great credit for keeping up his interest in his stud-
        ies in spite of his business cares, 12–20;

3. He will do well to cultivate the acquaintance of Grosphus
         (*cf. Odes*, ii. 16), 21–24 ;
4. Horace gives his friend the latest news from Rome, 25–29.

3. Time : 20 B.C.

Fructibus Agrippae Siculis, quos colligis, Icci,
Si recte frueris, non est ut copia maior
Ab Iove donari possit tibi.   Tolle querellas ;
Pauper enim non est, cui rerum suppetit usus.
Si ventri bene, si lateri est pedibusque tuis, nil   5
Divitiae poterunt regales addere maius.
Si forte in medio positorum abstemius herbis
Vivis et urtica, sic vives protinus, ut te
Confestim liquidus Fortunae rivus inauret,
Vel quia naturam mutare pecunia nescit,   10
Vel quia cuncta putas una virtute minora.
   Miramur, si Democriti pecus edit agellos
Cultaque, dum peregre est animus sine corpore velox ;
Cum tu inter scabiem tantam et contagia lucri
Nil parvum sapias et adhuc sublimia cures :   15
Quae mare compescant causae, quid temperet annum,
Stellae sponte sua iussaene vagentur et errent,
Quid premat obscurum Lunae, quid proferat orbem,
Quid velit et possit rerum concordia discors,
Empedocles an Stertinium deliret acumen.   20
   Verum seu piscis seu porrum et caepe trucidas,
Utere Pompeio Grospho et si quid petet, ultro
Defer ; nil Grosphus nisi verum orabit et aequum.
Vilis amicorum est annona, bonis ubi quid deest.
   Ne tamen ignores, quo sit Romana loco res,   25
Cantaber Agrippae, Claudi virtute Neronis
Armenius cecidit ; ius imperiumque Phraates
Caesaris accepit genibus minor ; aurea fruges
Italiae pleno defundit Copia cornu.

XIII.

INSTRUCTIONS TO A MESSENGER.

1. Occasion of the Epistle : Horace has sent a copy of his *Odes* (Books I. to III.) to Augustus by a friend of his in court circles, one Vinius Asina. Instead of addressing himself directly to Augustus, the poet writes a playful note of instruction to the messenger, whom he likens, on account of his cognomen, to a beast of burden. Its purpose is to amuse the emperor, and at the same time to express Horace's unwillingness to force his works on him at an unfavorable time.

2. Outline :

　1. Vinius is to perform his mission with tact and discretion or not at all, 1-9 ;
　2. He is to use all haste, and to carry and deliver the book gracefully, 10-15 ;
　3. He is not to boast of the value of his burden, though he must guard it with all care, 16-19.

3. Time : 23 or 22 B.C.

Ut proficiscentem docui te saepe diuque,
Augusto reddes signata volumina, Vini,
Si validus, si laetus erit, si denique poscet;
Ne studio nostri pecces odiumque libellis
Sedulus importes opera vehemente minister.　　　　**5**
Si te forte meae gravis uret sarcina chartae,
Abicito potius, quam quo perferre iuberis
Clitellas ferus impingas, Asinaeque paternum
Cognomen vertas in risum et fabula fias.

Viribus uteris per clivos, flumina, lamas.　　　　**10**
Victor propositi simul ac perveneris illuc,
Sic positum servabis onus, ne forte sub ala
Fasciculum portes librorum ut rusticus agnum,
Ut vinosa glomus furtivae Pyrria lanae,
Ut cum pilleolo soleas conviva tribulis.　　　　**15**
Ne volgo narres te sudavisse ferendo

Carmina quae possint oculos aurisque morari
Caesaris. Oratus multa prece, nitere porro.
Vade! vale; cave ne titubes mandataque frangas.

XIV.

MASTER AND SLAVE.

1. Occasion of the Epistle : Horace has been obliged to remain in
town longer than usual owing to the bereavement of his friend L.
Aelius Lamia. The letter is addressed to his steward, who had been
discontented when in Rome, but is now longing for the city.

2. Outline :

1. Horace asks which is the more successful, the steward in up-
   rooting weeds from the soil, or his master in clearing his
   mind of the weeds of discontent, 1-5 ;
2. Although a pious duty detains Horace, his mind will turn
   towards the country. In this respect he is no wiser than
   his slave, 6-13 ;
3. But the steward longed for the country when he was in Rome:
   Horace is at least consistent. Moreover, the slave is attracted by the low pleasures of the city and by the desire
   to escape the hard work on the farm, 14-30 ;
4. The master has learned to despise degrading amusements ; the
   slave has not, and is therefore discontented, like the
   majority of mankind, 31-44.

3. Time : The exact date cannot be determined. Not after 20 B.C.

Vilice silvarum et mihi me reddentis agelli,
Quem tu fastidis, habitatum quinque focis et
Quinque bonos solitum Variam dimittere patres,
Certemus, spinas animone ego fortius an tu
Evellas agro, et melior sit Horatius an res.   5
   Me quamvis Lamiae pietas et cura moratur,
Fratrem maerentis, rapto de fratre dolentis
Insolabiliter ; tamen istuc mens animusque
Fert et amat spatiis obstantia rumpere claustra.
Rure ego viventem, tu dicis in urbe beatum :   10

Cui placet alterius, sua nimirum est odio sors.
Stultus uterque locum immeritum causatur inique:
In culpa est animus, qui se non effugit umquam.

Tu mediastinus tacita prece rura petebas,
Nunc urbem et ludos et balnea vilicus optas. 15
Me constare mihi scis et discedere tristem,
Quandocumque trahunt invisa negotia Romam.
Non eadem miramur; eo disconvenit inter
Meque et te; nam quae deserta et inhospita tesqua
Credis, amoena vocat mecum qui sentit, et odit 20
Quae tu pulchra putas.　Fornix tibi et uncta popina
Incutiunt urbis desiderium, video, et quod
Angulus iste feret piper et tus ocius uva,
Nec vicina subest vinum praebere taberna
Quae possit tibi, nec meretrix tibicina, cuius 25
Ad strepitum salias terrae gravis; et tamen urges
Iampridem non tacta ligonibus arva bovemque
Disiunctum curas et strictis frondibus exples;
Addit opus pigro rivus, si decidit imber,
Multa mole docendus aprico parcere prato. 30
　Nunc age, quid nostrum concentum dividat audi.
Quem tenues decuere togae nitidique capilli,
Quem scis immunem Cinarae placuisse rapaci,
Quem bibulum liquidi media de luce Falerni,
Cena brevis iuvat et prope rivum somnus in herba. 35
Nec lusisse pudet, sed non incidere ludum.
Non istic obliquo oculo mea commoda quisquam
Limat, non odio obscuro morsuque venenat;
Rident vicini glaebas et saxa moventem.
Cum servis urbana diaria rodere mavis; 40
Horum tu in numerum voto ruis; invidet usum
Lignorum et pecoris tibi calo argutus et horti.
Optat ephippia bos piger, optat arare caballus.
Quam scit uterque, libens, censebo, exerceat artem.

XV.

A REQUEST FOR INFORMATION.

1. Occasion of the Epistle: Horace has now decided to spend the winter at the seashore (see *Epist.* i. 7. 11), and writes to a friend of his, Numonius Vala, for information about the climate and resources of Velia and Salernum. Numonius was evidently a native of southern Italy (*cf.* line 25) ; the family is known from inscriptions of Paestum, Vibo, and Regium.

Horace represents himself as false to his ideals of life (*cf.* i. 1. 18, *nunc in Aristippi furtim praecepta relabor*), a state of mind doubtless due to his ill-health (*cf.* i. 8. 3–12), although we are hardly justified in taking him quite seriously.

2. Outline:

1. Horace inquires particularly about the climate, the people, the streets, the drinking-water, and the meats and fish, 1–25 ;
2. He explains his interest in matters which might well be matters of indifference to one of his views of life by telling the story of Maenius, 26–41 ;
3. He admits that he is like Maenius in being fond of good living, but praising simple fare when he can get nothing better, 42–46.

3. Time: The Epistle belongs to the same year as 7, 8, and 10, *i.e.* 21 B.C.

Quae sit hiems Veliae, quod caelum, Vala, Salerni,
Quorum hominum regio et qualis via — nam mihi Baias
Musa supervacuas Antonius, et tamen illis
Me facit invisum, gelida cum perluor unda
Per medium frigus. Sane murteta relinqui　　　　　　5
Dictaque cessantem nervis elidere morbum
Sulpura contemni vicus gemit, invidus aegris,
Qui caput et stomachum supponere fontibus audent
Clusinis, Gabiosque petunt et frigida rura.
Mutandus locus est et deversoria nota　　　　　　　10
Praeteragendus equus. 'Quo tendis ? Non mihi Cumas
Est iter aut Baias' laeva stomachosus habena

Dicet eques; sed equi frenato est auris in ore —
Maior utrum populum frumenti copia pascat,
Collectosne bibant imbres puteosne perennis　　　　15
Iugis aquae — nam vina nihil moror illius orae.
Rure meo possum quidvis perferre patique;
Ad mare cum veni, generosum et lene requiro,
Quod curas abigat, quod cum spe divite manet
In venas animumque meum, quod verba ministret,　　　20
Quod me Lucanae iuvenem commendet amicae —
Tractus uter pluris lepores, uter educet apros;
Utra magis piscis et echinos aequora celent,
Pinguis ut inde domum possim Phaeaxque reverti,
Scribere te nobis, tibi nos accredere par est.　　　25
　　Maenius, ut rebus maternis atque paternis
Fortiter absumptis urbanus coepit haberi
Scurra, vagus, non qui certum praesepe teneret,
Impransus non qui civem dinosceret hoste,
Quaelibet in quemvis opprobria fingere saevus,　　　30
Pernicies et tempestas barathrumque macelli,
Quicquid quaesierat, ventri donabat avaro.
Hic ubi nequitiae fautoribus et timidis nil
Aut paullum abstulerat, patinas cenabat omasi
Vilis et agninae, tribus ursis quod satis esset;　　　35
Scilicet ut ventres lamna candente nepotum
Diceret urendos correctus Bestius.　Idem,
Quicquid erat nanctus praedae maioris, ubi omne
Verterat in fumum et cinerem, 'Non hercule miror,'
Aiebat, 'si qui comedunt bona, cum sit obeso　　　40
Nil melius turdo, nil volva pulchrius ampla.'
　Nimirum hic ego sum; nam tuta et parvola laudo,
Cum res deficiunt, satis inter vilia fortis:
Verum ubi quid melius contingit et unctius, idem
Vos sapere et solos aio bene vivere, quorum　　　45
Conspicitur nitidis fundata pecunia villis.

XVI.

HAPPINESS DEPENDS UPON VIRTUE.

1. Occasion of the Epistle: Horace fears that his friend Quinctius Hirpinus, to whom he addressed *Odes*, ii. 11, cares too much for office and for political favor.   He reminds him in what true virtue consists, and that it alone can confer lasting happiness.

2. Outline:

1. Horace describes the simple attractions of his Sabine Farm, 1–16 ;
2. Hirpinus is generally regarded as a happy man ; he can be truly so, only by having right ideals of life, 17–20 :
   a) He must not rate too highly the verdict of the masses, and think himself a good man because they call him so, 21–32 ;
   b) A wise man will not value their honors, which they can take away as well as give, or fear their criticism, 33–40 ;
   c) Appearances are deceitful.   A man may be outwardly good, because he fears the law, while his heart is filled with evil desires ; such a one is really no better than a slave, 40–72 ;
   d) The truly virtuous man will fear nothing ; no threats, even of death, can make him guilty of an unworthy act, 73–79.

3. Time: The exact date cannot be determined.   Not after 20 B.C.

Ne perconteris, fundus meus, optime Quincti,
Arvo pascat erum an bacis opulentet olivae
Pomisne et pratis an amicta vitibus ulmo,
Scribetur tibi forma loquaciter et situs agri.
Continui montes, ni dissocientur opaca   5
Valle, sed ut veniens dextrum latus adspiciat sol,
Laevum discedens curru fugiente vaporet.
Temperiem laudes.   Quid si rubicunda benigni
Corna vepres et pruna ferant, si quercus et ilex
Multa fruge pecus, multa dominum iuvet umbra ?   10
Dicas adductum propius frondere Tarentum.
Fons etiam rivo dare nomen idoneus, ut nec
Frigidior Thracam nec purior ambiat Hebrus,
Infirmo capiti fluit utilis, utilis alvo.

Hae latebrae dulces etiam, si credis, amoenae,   15
Incolumem tibi me praestant Septembribus horis.
  Tu recte vivis, si curas esse quod audis.
Iactamus iam pridem omnis te Roma beatum ;
Sed vereor ne cui de te plus quam tibi credas,
Neve putes alium sapiente bonoque beatum,   20
Neu, si te populus sanum recteque valentem
Dictitet, occultam febrem sub tempus edendi
Dissimules, donec manibus tremor incidat unctis.
Stultorum incurata pudor malus ulcera celat.
Si quis bella tibi terra pugnata marique   25
Dicat, et his verbis vacuas permulceat auris,
'Tene magis salvum populus velit, an populum tu,
Servet in ambiguo, qui consulit et tibi et urbi,
Iuppiter,' Augusti laudes adgnoscere possis ;
Cum pateris sapiens emendatusque vocari,   30
Respondesne tuo, dic, sodes, nomine ?   'Nempe
Vir bonus et prudens dici delector ego ac tu.'
  Qui dedit hoc hodie, cras si volet auferet, ut si
Detulerit fasces indigno, detrahet idem.
'Pone, meum est,' inquit; pono tristisque recedo.   35
Idem si clamet furem, neget esse pudicum,
Contendat laqueo collum pressisse paternum,
Mordear opprobriis falsis mutemque colores ?
Falsus honor iuvat et mendax infamia terret
Quem nisi mendosum et medicandum ?
                              Vir bonus est quis ?   40
'Qui consulta patrum, qui leges iuraque servat,
Quo multae magnaeque secantur iudice lites,
Quo res sponsore et quo causae teste tenentur.'
Sed videt hunc omnis domus et vicinia tota
Introrsum turpem, speciosum pelle decora.   45
'Nec furtum feci nec fugi,' si mihi dicat
Servus, 'Habes pretium, loris non ureris,' aio.

'Non hominem occidi.' 'Non pasces in cruce corvos.'
'Sum bonus et frugi.' Renuit negitatque Sabellus.
Cautus enim metuit foveam lupus accipiterque 50
Suspectos laqueos et opertum miluus hamum.
Oderunt peccare boni virtutis amore.
Tu nihil admittes in te formidine poenae.
Sit spes fallendi, miscebis sacra profanis.
Nam de mille fabae modiis cum surripis unum, 55
Damnum est, non facinus, mihi pacto lenius isto.
Vir bonus, omne forum quem spectat et omne tribunal,
Quandocumque deos vel porco vel bove placat,
'Iane pater!' clare, clare cum dixit 'Apollo!'
Labra movet metuens audiri: 'Pulchra Laverna, 60
Da mihi fallere, da iusto sanctoque videri,
Noctem peccatis et fraudibus obice nubem.'
Qui melior servo, qui liberior sit avarus,
In triviis fixum cum se demittit ob assem,
Non video: nam qui cupiet, metuet quoque; porro 65
Qui metuens vivet, liber mihi non erit umquam.
Perdidit arma, locum virtutis deseruit, qui
Semper in augenda festinat et obruitur re.
Vendere cum possis captivum, occidere noli.
Serviet utiliter; sine pascat durus aretque, 70
Naviget ac mediis hiemet mercator in undis,
Annonae prosit, portet frumenta penusque.

    Vir bonus et sapiens audebit dicere: 'Pentheu,
Rector Thebarum, quid me perferre patique
Indignum coges?' 'Adimam bona.' 'Nempe pecus,
    rem, 75
Lectos, argentum. Tollas licet.' 'In manicis et
Compedibus saevo te sub custode tenebo.'
'Ipse deus, simul atque volam, me solvet.' Opinor,
Hoc sentit 'Moriar.' Mors ultima linea rerum est.

XVII.

ON TRUE INDEPENDENCE.

1. Occasion of the Epistle : In this letter addressed to Scaeva, who is otherwise unknown, Horace shows that one may observe proper deference towards a patron without sacrificing one's self-respect. He gives some humorous directions for gaining the favor of great men.

2. Outline :

1. Horace modestly asks to be allowed to express his views on the subject, 1–5 ;
2. If one is really indifferent to riches and honors, one must act accordingly, 6–12 ;
3. But such an attitude is not essential to a proper independence :
   a) This is shown by the conduct of Aristippus. The excessive asceticism of Diogenes was due to the fact that he did not know how to act in good company, and to a desire to win the approbation of the vulgar, 13–32 ;
   b) There is no disgrace in being great. Consequently to win the friendship of the great is not of necessity degrading, 33–42 ;
4. How to behave toward a patron :
   a) One must make one's requests with good judgment, and know how to preserve a discreet silence, 43–51 ;
   b) The client must not clamor for help in all his little troubles, or he will not be taken seriously when he is really in difficulty, 52–62.

3. Time : The exact date cannot be determined. Not after 20 B.C.

Quamvis, Scaeva, satis per te tibi consulis et scis
Quo tandem pacto deceat maioribus uti,
Disce, docendus adhuc quae censet amiculus, ut si
Caecus iter monstrare velit; tamen adspice, si quid
Et nos, quod cures proprium fecisse, loquamur.　　　　5
　　Si te grata quies et primam somnus in horam
Delectat, si te pulvis strepitusque rotarum,
Si laedit caupona, Ferentinum ire iubebo.

Nam neque divitibus contingunt gaudia solis,
Nec vixit male, qui natus moriensque fefellit.   10
Si prodesse tuis paulloque benignius ipsum
Te tractare voles, accedes siccus ad unctum.
  'Si pranderet holus patienter, regibus uti
Nollet Aristippus.' 'Si sciret regibus uti,
Fastidiret holus qui me notat.'   Utrius horum   15
Verba probes et facta doce, vel iunior audi
Cur sit Aristippi potior sententia.   Namque
Mordacem Cynicum sic eludebat, ut aiunt:
'Scurror ego ipse mihi, populo tu; rectius hoc et
Splendidius multo est.   Equus ut me portet, alat rex,   20
Officium facio; tu poscis vilia, verum
Dante minor, quamvis fers te nullius egentem.'
Omnis Aristippum decuit color et status et res,
Temptantem maiora fere, praesentibus aequum.
Contra, quem duplici panno patientia velat,   25
Mirabor, vitae via si conversa decebit.
Alter purpureum non exspectabit amictum,
Quidlibet indutus celeberrima per loca vadet,
Personamque feret non inconcinnus utramque;
Alter Mileti textam cane peius et angue   30
Vitabit chlamydem; morietur frigore, si non
Rettuleris pannum.   Refer et sine vivat ineptus.
  Res gerere et captos ostendere civibus hostis,
Attingit solium Iovis et caelestia temptat.
Principibus placuisse viris non ultima laus est.   35
Non cuivis homini contingit adire Corinthum.
Sedit qui timuit, ne non succederet: esto.
Quid? qui pervenit, fecitne viriliter?   Atqui
Hic est aut nusquam quod quaerimus.   Hic onus horret,
Ut parvis animis et parvo corpore maius;   40
Hic subit et perfert.   Aut virtus nomen inane est,
Aut decus et pretium recte petit experiens vir.

  Coram rege suo de paupertate tacentes
Plus poscente ferent.   Distat, sumasne pudenter
An rapias; atqui rerum caput hoc erat, hic fons.   45
'Indotata mihi soror est, paupercula mater,
Et fundus nec vendibilis nec pascere firmus'
Qui dicit, clamat 'Victum date.'   Succinit alter
'Et mihi!' dividuo findetur munere quadra.
Sed tacitus pasci si posset corvus, haberet   50
Plus dapis, et rixae multo minus invidiaeque.

  Brundisium comes aut Surrentum ductus amoenum,
Qui queritur salebras et acerbum frigus et imbres,
Aut cistam effractam et subducta viatica plorat,
Nota refert meretricis acumina, saepe catellam,   55
Saepe periscelidem raptam sibi flentis, uti mox
Nulla fides damnis verisque doloribus adsit.
Nec semel inrisus triviis attollere curat
Fracto crure planum.   Licet illi plurima manet
Lacrima, per sanctum iuratus dicat Osirim,   60
'Credite, non ludo; crudeles, tollite, claudum;'
'Quaere peregrinum' vicinia rauca reclamat.

XVIII.

ON THE PROPER DEMEANOR TOWARDS A PATRON.

1. Occasion of the Epistle : Horace's friend Lollius Maximus (see
i. 2) had evidently found a powerful and distinguished patron who
is unknown to us.   The high-spirited and well-connected young man
seems to have found the relation somewhat trying, and Horace assures
him that he can show a proper deference without laying himself open
to the charge of obsequiousness.

2. Outline :

  1. An excessive display of independence is ill-judged and un-
      necessary.   The true gentleman does not need to vindi-
      cate his claim to the title, 1-20,

2. Certain marks of consideration are due a man from whom one
    is willing to accept patronage :
    a) A life of high ideals. The great man can allow himself
        some indulgences which would ruin his protégé. One
        must regulate one's conduct according to one's position
        in life, 21–36 ;
    b) Respect for the patron's confidences, 37–38 ;
    c) An effort to take part cheerfully in his amusements, re-
        gardless of one's own inclinations, 39–66 ;
    d) Discretion in criticising others, 66–71 ;
    e) And in his relations with the patron's household, 72–75 ;
    f) Extreme care in recommending men to the patron's favor,
        but unfailing loyalty to those whom he has once judged
        worthy of it, 76–85 ;
3. To maintain a proper attitude is not easy.   It requires :
    a) Constant watchfulness of one's conduct and no little self-
        denial, 86–95 ;
    b) A constant study of the true philosophy of life and of the
        real causes of happiness, 96–103 ;
    c) Horace's own ideas of happiness, 104–112.

3. Time : 20 B.C.

Si bene te novi, metues, liberrime Lolli,
Scurrantis speciem praebere, professus amicum.
Ut matrona meretrici dispar erit atque
Discolor, infido scurrae distabit amicus.
Est huic diversum vitio vitium prope maius,   5
Asperitas agrestis et inconcinna gravisque,
Quae se commendat tonsa cute, dentibus atris,
Dum volt libertas dici mera veraque virtus.
Virtus est medium vitiorum et utrimque reductum.
Alter in obsequium plus aequo pronus et imi   10
Derisor lecti sic nutum divitis horret,
Sic iterat voces et verba cadentia tollit,
Ut puerum saevo credas dictata magistro
Reddere vel partis mimum tractare secundas ;
Alter rixatur de lana saepe caprina,   15
Propugnat nugis armatus : ' Scilicet, ut non

Sit mihi prima fides et vere quod placet ut non
Acriter elatrem ! pretium aetas altera sordet.'
Ambigitur quid enim ?　Castor sciat an Docilis plus;
Brundisium Minuci melius via ducat an Appi.　　　　20
　　Quem damnosa Venus, quem praeceps alea nudat,
Gloria quem supra vires et vestit et unguit,
Quem tenet argenti sitis importuna famesque,
Quem paupertatis pudor et fuga, dives amicus,
Saepe decem vitiis instructior, odit et horret,　　　　25
Aut, si non odit, regit ac veluti pia mater
Plus quam se sapere et virtutibus esse priorem
Volt et ait prope vera: ' Meae — contendere noli —
Stultitiam patiuntur opes; tibi parvola res est.
Arta decet sanum comitem toga; desine mecum　　　　30
Certare.'　Eutrapelus cuicumque nocere volebat
Vestimenta dabat pretiosa: ' Beatus enim iam
Cum pulchris tunicis sumet nova consilia et spes,
Dormiet in lucem, scorto postponet honestum
Officium, nummos alienos pascet, ad imum　　　　35
Thraex erit aut holitoris aget mercede caballum.'
　　Arcanum neque tu scrutaberis illius umquam,
Commissumque teges et vino tortus et ira.
Nec tua laudabis studia aut aliena reprendes,
Nec, cum venari volet ille, poemata panges.　　　　40
Gratia sic fratrum geminorum, Amphionis atque
Zethi, dissiluit, donec suspecta severo
Conticuit lyra.　Fraternis cessisse putatur
Moribus Amphion: tu cede potentis amici
Lenibus imperiis, quotiensque educet in agros　　　　45
Aetolis onerata plagis iumenta canesque,
Surge et inhumanae senium depone Camenae,
Cenes ut pariter pulmenta laboribus empta;
Romanis sollemne viris opus, utile famae
Vitaeque et membris, praesertim cum valeas et　　　　50

Vel cursu superare canem vel viribus aprum
Possis. Adde virilia quod speciosius arma
Non est qui tractet; scis, quo clamore coronae
Proelia sustineas campestria; denique saevam
Militiam puer et Cantabrica bella tulisti   55
Sub duce qui templis Parthorum signa refigit
Nunc et, si quid abest, Italis adiudicat armis.
Ac ne te retrahas et inexcusabilis absis,
Quamvis nil extra numerum fecisse modumque
Curas, interdum nugaris rure paterno: 60
Partitur lintres exercitus, Actia pugna
Te duce per pueros hostili more refertur;
Adversarius est frater, lacus Hadria, donec
Alterutrum velox victoria fronde coronet.
Consentire suis studiis qui crediderit te,   65
Fautor utroque tuum laudabit pollice ludum.

Protinus ut moneam — siquid monitoris eges tu, —
Quid de quoque viro et cui dicas, saepe videto.
Percontatorem fugito; nam garrulus idem est,
Nec retinent patulae commissa fideliter aures,   70
Et semel emissum volat inrevocabile verbum.

Non ancilla tuum iecur ulceret ulla puerve
Intra marmoreum venerandi limen amici,
Ne dominus pueri pulchri caraeve puellae
Munere te parvo beet aut incommodus angat.   75

Qualem commendes, etiam atque etiam aspice, ne mox
Incutiant aliena tibi peccata pudorem.
Fallimur et quondam non dignum tradimus: ergo
Quem sua culpa premet, deceptus omitte tueri,
Ut penitus notum, si temptent crimina, serves   80
Tuterisque tuo fidentem praesidio: qui
Dente Theonino cum circumroditur, ecquid
Ad te post paullo ventura pericula sentis?
Nam tua res agitur, paries cum proximus ardet,

Et neglecta solent incendia sumere vires.   85
    Dulcis inexpertis cultura potentis amici;
Expertus metuet.   Tu, dum tua navis in alto est,
Hoc age, ne mutata retrorsum te ferat aura.
Oderunt hilarem tristes tristemque iocosi,
Sedatum celeres, agilem navumque remissi;   90
Potores bibuli media de nocte Falerni
Oderunt porrecta negantem pocula, quamvis
Nocturnos iures te formidare tepores.
Deme supercilio nubem : plerumque modestus
Occupat obscuri speciem, taciturnus acerbi.   95
    Inter cuncta leges et percontabere doctos,
Qua ratione queas traducere leniter aevum,
Num te semper inops agitet vexetque cupido,
Num pavor et rerum mediocriter utilium spes,
Virtutem doctrina paret naturane donet,   100
Quid minuat curas, quid te tibi reddat amicum,
Quid pure tranquillet, honos an dulce lucellum,
An secretum iter et fallentis semita vitae.
    Me quotiens reficit gelidus Digentia rivus,
Quem Mandela bibit, rugosus frigore pagus,   105
Quid sentire putas ?   Quid credis, amice, precari ?
'Sit mihi, quod nunc est, etiam minus, ut mihi vivam
Quod superest aevi, si quid superesse volunt di;
Sit bona librorum et provisae frugis in annum
Copia, neu fluitem dubiae spe pendulus horae.'   11C
    Sed satis est orare Iovem, quae ponit et aufert;
Det vitam, det opes; aequum mi animum ipse parabo.

XIX.

THE POET ON HIS CRITICS.

1. Occasion of the Epistle : The *Odes* (Books I.-III.) had evidently met with unfavorable criticism outside of the small circle of the poet's friends.   He points out to Maecenas the injustice of the charges which have been made against him, and expresses contempt for his detractors.

2. Outline :

   1. It is one thing to follow a model, quite another to stoop to slavish and ignorant imitation :

     a) Because Homer, Cratinus, and Ennius have written in praise of wine, obscure poets hope to become great by hard drinking, 1-11 ;

     b) Just as if the virtue of a Cato depended on his stern face and careless dress, or a poet's success on his complexion, 12-18 ;

   2. Horace is a pioneer and no imitator. He followed Greek originals, but not with servile imitation. Alcaeus and Sappho also had their models, 19-34;

   3. The real reason for his unpopularity is that he has not tried to please the masses, or deigned to court the favor of the critics. If he is therefore accused of arrogance, he prefers not to argue the matter, 35-49.

3. Time : From its position in the collection the letter would seem to belong to the year 20 B.C.

Prisco si credis, Maecenas docte, Cratino,
Nulla placere diu nec vivere carmina possunt,
Quae scribuntur aquae potoribus.   Ut male sanos
Adscripsit Liber Satyris Faunisque poetas,
Vina fere dulces oluerunt mane Camenae.   5
Laudibus arguitur vini vinosus Homerus ;
Ennius ipse pater numquam nisi potus ad arma
Prosiluit dicenda.   'Forum putealque Libonis
Mandabo siccis, adimam cantare severis :'
Hoc simul edixi, non cessavere poetae   10

Nocturno certare mero, putere diurno.
Quid? Si quis voltu torvo ferus et pede nudo
Exiguaeque togae simulet textore Catonem,
Virtutemne repraesentet moresque Catonis?
Rupit Iarbitam Timagenis aemula lingua,   15
Dum studet urbanus tenditque disertus haberi.
Decipit exemplar vitiis imitabile. Quod si
Pallerem casu, biberent exsangue cuminum.

O imitatores, servum pecus, ut mihi saepe
Bilem, saepe iocum vestri movere tumultus!   20
Libera per vacuum posui vestigia princeps,
Non aliena meo pressi pede. Qui sibi fidet,
Dux reget examen. Parios ego primus iambos
Ostendi Latio, numeros animosque secutus
Archilochi, non res et agentia verba Lycamben.   25
Ac ne me foliis ideo brevioribus ornes,
Quod timui mutare modos et carminis artem,
Temperat Archilochi musam pede mascula Sappho,
Temperat Alcaeus, sed rebus et ordine dispar,
Nec socerum quaerit, quem versibus oblinat atris,   30
Nec sponsae laqueum famoso carmine nectit.
Hunc ego, non alio dictum prius ore, Latinus
Volgavi fidicen. Iuvat immemorata ferentem
Ingenuis oculisque legi manibusque teneri.

Scire velis, mea cur ingratus opuscula lector   35
Laudet ametque domi, premat extra limen iniquus:
Non ego ventosae plebis suffragia venor
Impensis cenarum et tritae munere vestis;
Non ego, nobilium scriptorum auditor et ultor,
Grammaticas ambire tribus et pulpita dignor.   40
Hinc illae lacrimae. 'Spissis indigna theatris
Scripta pudet recitare et nugis addere pondus'
Si dixi, 'Rides' ait, 'et Iovis auribus ista
Servas; fidis enim, manare poetica mella

Te solum, tibi pulcher.' Ad haec ego naribus uti 45
Formido et, luctantis acuto ne secer ungui,
' Displicet iste locus' clamo et diludia posco.
Ludus enim genuit trepidum certamen et iram,
Ira trucis inimicitias et funebre bellum.

XX.

EPILOGUE.

1. Subject of the Epistle : Horace addresses his book, which is represented as anxious to try its fate with the public. He compares it to a young and beautiful slave, and foretells its destiny.

2. Outline :

 1. The poet warns his book that, once issued, it cannot return, 1–8 ;
 2. He predicts its career :
  a) Success until it falls into the hands of the vulgar ;
  b) Banishment to the provinces ;
  c) An old age spent in the schools, 9–18 ;
 3. He charges it in the days of its prosperity to make known the parentage, career, and personal characteristics of its author, 19–28.

3. Time : Between December 8, 21 B.C., and December 8, 20 B.C.

Vertumnum Ianumque, liber, spectare videris,
Scilicet ut prostes Sosiorum pumice mundus.
Odisti clavis et grata sigilla pudico,
Paucis ostendi gemis et communia laudas,
Non ita nutritus. Fuge quo descendere gestis : 5
Non erit emisso reditus tibi. ' Quid miser egi ?
Quid volui ?' dices, ubi quid te laeserit, et scis
In breve te cogi, cum plenus anguet amator.
 Quodsi non odio peccantis desipit augur,
Carus eris Romae, donec te deserat aetas ; 10
Contrectatus ubi manibus sordescere volgi

Coeperis, aut tineas pasces taciturnus inertis
Aut fugies Uticam aut vinctus mitteris Ilerdam.
Ridebit monitor non exauditus, ut ille
Qui male parentem in rupes protrusit asellum   15
Iratus; quis enim invitum servare laboret?
Hoc quoque te manet, ut pueros elementa docentem
Occupet extremis in vicis balba senectus.

    Cum tibi sol tepidus pluris admoverit auris,
Me libertino natum patre et in tenui re
Maiores pinnas nido extendisse loqueris,   20
Ut quantum generi demas, virtutibus addas;
Me primis urbis belli placuisse domique,
Corporis exigui, praecanum, solibus aptum,
Irasci celerem, tamen ut placabilis essem.   25
Forte meum si quis te percontabitur aevum,
Me quater undenos sciat implevisse Decembris,
Collegam Lepidum quo dixit Lollius anno.

EPISTULARUM

LIBER SECUNDUS.

———◆———

I.

ON THE POPULAR TASTE AND JUDGMENT.

1. Occasion of the Epistle : Horace dedicates his second collection
of Letters to Augustus, who had apparently urged him to undertake
something in the line of dramatic or of epic poetry. He complains of
the poor taste shown by the general public, especially in regard to the
drama, and says that he is unwilling to make an attempt in that line.
For epic poetry he has no ability.

2. Outline :

1. Horace will be brief and not make great demands on the time
   of a busy man, 1–4 ;
2. Augustus is more fortunate than Romulus, Castor and Pollux,
   and Hercules, in having his services to his country recognized during his lifetime, 5–17 ;
3. In this the people have shown excellent judgment ; but in
   literary criticism they fail to use the same discrimination :
   a) They admire only what is ancient, justifying themselves by
   the plea that the earliest works of the Greeks were their
   best, 18–33 ;
   b) If their view is correct, what limits would they set ? Antiquity is a relative term, 34–49 ;
   c) They blindly follow the critics and admire everything from
   Livius down to their own day, 50–62 ;
   d) Horace is ready to agree with them in praising the earlier
   writers, if only they will be reasonable, 63–68 ;
   e) He has no patience with admiration of ancient poetry as
   such, and with wilful blindness to its obvious defects,
   69–85 ;

f) The real motive of the critics is envy of their contemporaries. That the Greeks had had no such spirit is shown by the development of their literature, which would otherwise have ended, as it began, with Homer, 86–102 ;

4. As a matter of fact, Roman literature, like the Greek, developed gradually :

    a) The people were for a long time devoted to practical life and to money-making, 103–107 ;

    b) Nowadays every one writes, regardless of his fitness for such work. Even Horace cannot keep his resolve to compose no more poetry, 108–117 ;

    c) This state of things has its advantages :

        1) It cultivates an indifference to material things, 118–125 ;

        2) It fosters general education and refinement by presenting worthy models for imitation, 126–131 ;

        3) It furnishes a means by which men may address the gods, 132–138 ;

5. This gradual development is clearly seen in the history of dramatic poetry :

    a) Out of the harvest festivals grew a rude Italic drama, whose freedom of speech had finally to be regulated by law, 139–155 ;

    b) But our conquest of Greece led to the introduction of Greek art, though the native uncouthness was only gradually eliminated, 156–160 ;

    c) First came tragedy, well suited to Roman tastes, but marred by careless composition, 161–167 ;

    d) Then comedy, which suffers even more from careless writing, in which Plautus made but an indifferent success, 168–176 ;

6. To-day dramatic poetry has passed its zenith, and Horace has no desire to write in that line, 177–181 :

    a) For success depends largely on the judgment of the masses, who care only for spectacular effects, 182–186 ;

    b) While the better class have similar tastes in a slightly higher form, 187–200 ;

    c) The audience is noisy and cares not what the actor says, provided he makes an imposing appearance, 200–207.

7. Still Horace has no prejudice against dramatic writing as such, provided it be done with due care, 208–213 ;

8. But he believes that Augustus ought especially to **favor epic and lyric verse** :

a) They are worthy of his patronage, although some poets run
the risk of losing it :
1) By presenting their works at an unfavorable time ;
2) By oversensitiveness to criticism ;
3) By a lack of originality ;
4) And by too great a desire for recognition, 214–228 ;
b) He should be careful in selecting those who are to sing his
praises :
1) It would be bad to fall into the hands of a Choerilus,
whom Alexander, in spite of his good taste in
painting and sculpture, judged so falsely, 229–244 ;
2) But Augustus has better taste, and has honored
himself by honoring Varius and Virgil, 245–250 ;
3) Horace himself would gladly write an epic if he had
the ability, 250–257 ;
4) But Augustus is worthy of a greater poet.   Horace
does not wish to undertake a task beyond his
powers, and thus do more harm than good, 257–
263 ;
5) His reluctance is due less to consideration for
Augustus, than to regard for his own reputation,
264–270.

3. **Time :** 14 B.C.

Cum tot sustineas et tanta negotia solus,
Res Italas armis tuteris, moribus ornes,
Legibus emendes ; in publica commoda peccem,
Si longo sermone morer tua tempora, Caesar.

Romulus et Liber pater et cum Castore Pollux,   5
Post ingentia facta deorum in templa recepti,
Dum terras hominumque colunt genus, aspera bella
Componunt, agros adsignant, oppida condunt,
Ploravere suis non respondere favorem
Speratum meritis.   Diram qui contudit hydram   10
Notaque fatali portenta labore subegit,
Comperit invidiam supremo fine domari.
Urit enim fulgore suo, qui praegravat artis
Infra se positas ; exstinctus amabitur idem.
Praesenti tibi maturos largimur honores,   15

Iurandasque tuum per numen ponimus aras,
Nil oriturum alias, nil ortum tale fatentes.

   Sed tuus hic populus, sapiens et iustus in uno,
Te nostris ducibus, te Grais anteferendo,
Cetera nequaquam simili ratione modoque   20
Aestimat et, nisi quae terris semota suisque
Temporibus defuncta videt, fastidit et odit,
Sic fautor veterum, ut tabulas peccare vetantis
Quas bis quinque viri sanxerunt, foedera regum
Vel Gabiis vel cum rigidis aequata Sabinis,   25
Pontificum libros, annosa volumina vatum
Dictitet Albano Musas in monte locutas.
Si, quia Graecorum sunt antiquissima quaeque
Scripta vel optima, Romani pensantur eadem
Scriptores trutina, non est quod multa loquamur: 30
Nil intra est olea, nil extra est in nuce duri;
Venimus ad summum fortunae, pingimus atque
Psallimus et luctamur Achivis doctius unctis.

   Si meliora dies, ut vina, poemata reddit,
Scire velim, chartis pretium quotus adroget annus.   35
Scriptor abhinc annos centum qui decidit, inter
Perfectos veteresque referri debet an inter
Vilis atque novos?   Excludat iurgia finis!
'Est vetus atque probus, centum qui perficit annos.'
Quid? qui deperiit minor uno mense vel anno,   40
Inter quos referendus erit?   Veteresne poëtas,
An quos et praesens et postera respuat aetas?
'Iste quidem veteres inter ponetur honeste,
Qui vel mense brevi vel toto est iunior anno.'
Utor permisso, caudaeque pilos ut equinae   45
Paullatim vello, et demo unum, demo etiam unum
Dum cadat elusus ratione ruentis acervi,
Qui redit in fastos et virtutem aestimat annis
Miraturque nihil nisi quod Libitina sacravit.

Ennius, et sapiens et fortis et alter Homerus,   50
Ut critici dicunt, leviter curare videtur,
Quo promissa cadant et somnia Pythagorea.
Naevius in manibus non est et mentibus haeret
Paene recens ?   Adeo sanctum est vetus omne poema.
Ambigitur quotiens uter utro sit prior, aufert   55
Pacuvius docti famam senis, Accius alti;
Dicitur Afrani toga convenisse Menandro,
Plautus ad exemplar Siculi properare Epicharmi,
Vincere Caecilius gravitate, Terentius arte.
Hos ediscit et hos arto stipata theatro   60
Spectat Roma potens, habet hos numeratque poetas
Ad nostrum tempus Livi scriptoris ab aevo.
     Interdum volgus rectum videt; est ubi peccat.
Si veteres ita miratur laudatque poetas,
Ut nihil anteferat, nihil illis comparet, errat;   65
Si quaedam nimis antique, si pleraque dure
Dicere credit eos, ignave multa fatetur,
Et sapit et mecum facit et Iove iudicat aequo.
     Non equidem insector delendave carmina Livi
Esse reor, memini quae plagosum mihi parvo   70
Orbilium dictare ; sed emendata videri
Pulchraque et exactis minimum distantia miror.
Inter quae verbum emicuit si forte decorum,
Si versus paullo concinnior unus et alter,
Iniuste totum ducit venditque poema.   75
Indignor quicquam reprehendi, non quia crasse
Compositum inlepideve putetur, sed quia nuper,
Nec veniam antiquis, sed honorem et praemia posci.
Recte necne crocum floresque perambulet Attae
Fabula si dubitem, clament periisse pudorem   80
Cuncti paene patres, ea cum reprehendere coner,
Quae gravis Aesopus, quae doctus Roscius egit;
Vel quia nil rectum, nisi quod placuit sibi, ducunt,

Vel quia turpe putant parere minoribus, et quae
Imberbes didicere, senes perdenda fateri. 85
    Iam Saliare Numae carmen qui laudat et illud,
Quod mecum ignorat, solus volt scire videri,
Ingeniis non ille favet plauditque sepultis,
Nostra sed impugnat, nos nostraque lividus odit.
Quod si tam Graiis novitas invisa fuisset 90
Quam nobis, quid nunc esset vetus ?　Aut quid haberet,
Quod legeret tereretque viritim publicus usus ?
Ut primum positis nugari Graecia bellis
Coepit et in vitium fortuna labier aequa,
Nunc athletarum studiis, nunc arsit equorum, 95
Marmoris aut eboris fabros aut aeris amavit,
Suspendit picta voltum mentemque tabella,
Nunc tibicinibus, nunc est gavisa tragoedis ;
Sub nutrice puella velut si luderet infans,
Quod cupide petiit, mature plena reliquit. 100
Quid placet aut odio est, quod non mutabile credas ?
Hoc paces habuere bonae ventique secundi.
    Romae dulce diu fuit et sollemne reclusa
Mane domo vigilare, clienti promere iura,
Cautos nominibus rectis expendere nummos, 105
Maiores audire, minori dicere per quae
Crescere res posset, minui damnosa libido.
Mutavit mentem populus levis et calet uno
Scribendi studio ; pueri patresque severi
Fronde comas vincti cenant et carmina dictant. 110
Ipse ego, qui nullos me adfirmo scribere versus,
Invenior Parthis mendacior, et prius orto
Sole vigil calamum et chartas et scrinia posco.
Navem agere ignarus navis timet, habrotonum aegro
Non audet nisi qui didicit dare, quod medicorum est 115
Promittunt medici, tractant fabrilia fabri ;
Scribimus indocti doctique poemata passim.

Hic error tamen et levis haec insania quantas
Virtutes habeat, sic collige.   Vatis avarus
Non temere est animus; versus amat, hoc studet unum   120
Detrimenta, fugas servorum, incendia ridet,
Non fraudem socio puerove incogitat ullam
Pupillo; vivit siliquis et pane secundo;
Militiae quamquam piger et malus, utilis urbi,
Si das hoc, parvis quoque rebus magna iuvari.   125
Os tenerum pueri balbumque poeta figurat,
Torquet ab obscaenis iam nunc sermonibus aurem,
Mox etiam pectus praeceptis format amicis,
Asperitatis et invidiae corrector et irae,
Recte facta refert, orientia tempora notis   130
Instruit exemplis, inopem solatur et aegrum.
Castis cum pueris ignara puella mariti
Disceret unde preces, vatem ni Musa dedisset ?
Poscit opem chorus et praesentia numina sentit,
Caelestis implorat aquas docta prece blandus,   135
Avertit morbos, metuenda pericula pellit,
Impetrat et pacem et locupletem frugibus annum.
Carmine di superi placantur, carmine Manes.
  Agricolae prisci, fortes parvoque beati,
Condita post frumenta levantes tempore festo   140
Corpus et ipsum animum spe finis dura ferentem,
Cum sociis operum, pueris et coniuge fida,
Tellurem porco, Silvanum lacte piabant,
Floribus et vino Genium memorem brevis aevi.
Fescennina per hunc invecta licentia morem   145
Versibus alternis opprobria rustica fudit,
Libertasque recurrentis accepta per annos
Lusit amabiliter, donec iam saevus apertam
In rabiem coepit verti iocus et per honestas
Ire domos impune minax.   Doluere cruento   150
Dente lacessiti; fuit intactis quoque cura

Condicione super communi, quin etiam lex
Poenaque lata, malo quae nollet carmine quemquam
Describi.   Vertere modum formidine fustis
Ad bene dicendum delectandumque redacti.   155
    Graecia capta ferum victorem cepit, et artis
Intulit agresti Latio.   Sic horridus ille
Defluxit numerus Saturnius, et grave virus
Munditiae pepulere; sed in longum tamen aevum
Manserunt hodieque manent vestigia ruris.   160
Serus enim Graecis admovit acumina chartis,
Et post Punica bella quietus quaerere coepit,
Quid Sophocles et Thespis et Aeschylos utile ferrent.
Temptavit quoque rem si digne vertere posset,
Et placuit sibi, natura sublimis et acer;   165
Nam spirat tragicum satis et feliciter audet,
Sed turpem putat inscite metuitque lituram.
Creditur, ex medio quia res arcessit, habere
Sudoris minimum, sed habet comoedia tanto
Plus oneris quanto veniae minus.   Adspice Plautus   170
Quo pacto partis tutetur amantis ephebi,
Ut patris attenti, lenonis ut insidiosi,
Quantus sit Dossennus edacibus in parasitis,
Quam non adstricto percurrat pulpita socco;
Gestit enim nummum in loculos demittere, post hoc   175
Securus cadat an recto stet fabula talo.
    Quem tulit ad scaenam ventoso Gloria curru,
Exanimat lentus spectator, sedulus inflat;
Sic leve sic parvum est, animum quod laudis avarum
Subruit aut reficit.   Valeat res ludicra, si me   180
Palma negata macrum, donata reducit opimum.
Saepe etiam audacem fugat hoc terretque poetam,
Quod numero plures, virtute et honore minores,
Indocti stolidique et depugnare parati,
Si discordet eques, media inter carmina poscunt   185

Aut ursum aut pugiles; his nam plebecula gaudet.
Verum equitis quoque iam migravit ab aure voluptas
Omnis ad incertos oculos et gaudia vana.
Quattuor aut pluris aulaea premuntur in horas,
Dum fugiunt equitum turmae peditumque catervae;   190
Mox trahitur manibus regum fortuna retortis,
Esseda festinant, pilenta, petorrita, naves,
Captivum portatur ebur, captiva Corinthus.
Si foret in terris, rideret Democritus, seu
Diversum confusa genus panthera camelo   195
Sive elephas albus volgi converteret ora;
Spectaret populum ludis attentius ipsis,
Ut sibi praebentem nimio spectacula plura;
Scriptores autem narrare putaret asello
Fabellam surdo.   Nam quae pervincere voces   200
Evaluere sonum, referunt quem nostra theatra?
Garganum mugire putes nemus aut mare Tuscum,
Tanto cum strepitu ludi spectantur et artes
Divitiaeque peregrinae, quibus oblitus actor
Cum stetit in scaena, concurrit dextera laevae.   205
'Dixit adhuc aliquid?'   'Nil sane.'   'Quid placet ergo?'
'Lana Tarentino violas imitata veneno.'

   Ac ne forte putes me, quae facere ipse recusem,
Cum recte tractent alii, laudare maligne;
Ille per extentum funem mihi posse videtur   210
Ire poeta, meum qui pectus inaniter angit,
Inritat, mulcet, falsis terroribus implet,
Ut magus, et modo me Thebis, modo ponit Athenis.

   Verum age et his, qui se lectori credere malunt
Quam spectatoris fastidia ferre superbi,   215
Curam redde brevem, si munus Apolline dignum
Vis complere libris et vatibus addere calcar,
Ut studio maiore petant Helicona virentem.
Multa quidem nobis facimus mala saepe poetae —

Ut vineta egomet caedam mea — cum tibi librum 220
Sollicito damus aut fesso; cum laedimur, unum
Si quis amicorum est ausus reprehendere versum;
Cum loca iam recitata revolvimus inrevocati;
Cum lamentamur non apparere labores
Nostros et tenui deducta poemata filo; 225
Cum speramus eo rem venturam, ut simul atque
Carmina rescieris nos fingere, commodus ultro
Arcessas et egere vetes et scribere cogas.

Sed tamen est operae pretium cognoscere, qualis
Aedituos habeat belli spectata domique 230
Virtus, indigno non committenda poetae.
Gratus Alexandro regi Magno fuit ille
Choerilus, incultis qui versibus et male natis
Rettulit acceptos, regale nomisma, Philippos.
Sed veluti tractata notam labemque remittunt 235
Atramenta, fere scriptores carmine foedo
Splendida facta linunt. Idem rex ille, poema
Qui tam ridiculum tam care prodigus emit,
Edicto vetuit, ne quis se praeter Apellen
Pingeret, aut alius Lysippo duceret aera 240
Fortis Alexandri voltum simulantia. Quod si
Iudicium subtile videndis artibus illud
Ad libros et ad haec Musarum dona vocares,
Boeotum in crasso iurares aëre natum.

At neque dedecorant tua de se iudicia atque 245
Munera quae multa dantis cum laude tulerunt
Dilecti tibi Vergilius Variusque poetae,
Nec magis expressi voltus per aënea signa,
Quam per vatis opus mores animique virorum
Clarorum adparent.
                    Nec sermones ego mallem 250
Repentis per humum quam res componere gestas
Terrarumque situs et flumina dicere et arces

Montibus impositas et barbara regna, tuisque
Auspiciis totum confecta duella per orbem,
Claustraque custodem pacis cohibentia Ianum,   255
Et formidatam Parthis te principe Romam,
Si quantum cuperem possem quoque ; sed neque parvum
Carmen maiestas recipit tua, nec meus audet
Rem temptare pudor quam vires ferre recusent.
Sedulitas autem stulte quem diligit, urget ;   260
Praecipue cum se numeris commendat et arte :
Discit enim citius meminitque libentius illud
Quod quis deridet, quam quod probat et veneratur.
Nil moror officium quod me gravat, ac neque ficto
In peius voltu proponi cereus usquam   265
Nec prave factis decorari versibus opto,
Ne rubeam pingui donatus munere et una
Cum scriptore meo capsa porrectus operta
Deferar in vicum vendentem tus et odores
Et piper et quicquid chartis amicitur ineptis.   270

II.

A RENUNCIATION OF LYRIC POETRY.

1. Occasion of the Epistle : In this letter to Julius Florus, to
whom i. 3 is also addressed, Horace expresses at greater length the
same general sentiments as in i. 1.   He intends to devote himself to
philosophy and to write only in the field represented by the *Sermones*
and *Epistulae*.

2. Outline :

1. Horace reminds his friend, that while he promised to write to
   him, he expressly said that he was not a good correspon-
   dent.   He is therefore no more liable to blame than a
   slave-dealer would be, who had sold a slave with the
   admission that he had once played truant, 1–24 ;
2. He accounts for his failure to send Florus some verses by
   saying that he has renounced poetry :

a) He no longer feels the necessity of writing verse. The story of the veteran of Lucullus, 24–54 ;

b) He is too old for such youthful folly, 55–57 ;

c) He cannot please everybody ; his readers are like guests at a banquet, who all call for something different, 58–64 ;

d) It is impossible to write amid the distractions of the city :

    1) He has many visits to pay and duties to attend to in widely separated parts of the town, 65–70 ;

    2) The noises and dangers in the streets prevent quiet thought, 70–76 ;

    3) Poets need seclusion. Even in quiet Athens one cannot always write acceptably ; how much less in Rome, 77–86 ;

e) To succeed one must form an alliance for mutual admiration, 87–101 ;

f) Careful and conscientious work is not appreciated, 102–125 ;

g) To write poetry in such times one would need to be blind to his surroundings, like the madman of Argos, 126–140 ;

3. Horace therefore proposes to devote himself to philosophy, as a more profitable study and one more appropriate to his time of life, 141–145 ;

a) If one were suffering from disease, he would consult a physician. One ought to be equally anxious to be cured of false views of life, 146–154 ;

b) Riches cannot make a man wise or permanently happy. Death finally makes all men equal, 155–179 ;

c) True happiness consists in following the golden mean, avoiding both avarice and extravagance, and in indifference to material blessings, 180–204 ;

d) It is not enough to be free from one fault ; one must renounce them all. And when a man has sufficiently enjoyed life, he must be ready to withdraw from it like a satisfied guest, 205–216.

3. Time: Between 20 and 17 B.C.

Flore, bono claroque fidelis amice Neroni,
Si quis forte velit puerum tibi vendere natum
Tibure vel Gabiis, et tecum sic agat: 'Hic et
Candidus et talos a vertice pulcher ad imos
Fiet eritque tuus nummorum milibus octo,   5

Verna ministeriis ad nutus aptus erilis
Litterulis Graecis imbutus, idoneus arti
Cuilibet, argilla quidvis imitaberis uda;
Quin etiam canet indoctum sed dulce bibenti.
Multa fidem promissa levant, ubi plenius aequo   10
Laudat venalis qui volt extrudere merces.
Res urget me nulla; meo sum pauper in aere.
Nemo hoc mangonum faceret tibi; non temere a me
Quivis ferret idem.   Semel hic cessavit et, ut fit,
In scalis latuit metuens pendentis habenae;'   15
Des nummos, excepta nihil te si fuga laedat;
Ille ferat pretium poenae securus opinor.
Prudens emisti vitiosum, dicta tibi est lex;
Insequeris tamen hunc et lite moraris iniqua?
Dixi me pigrum proficiscenti tibi, dixi   20
Talibus officiis prope mancum, ne mea saevus
Iurgares ad te quod epistula nulla rediret.
Quid tum profeci, mecum facientia iura
Si tamen attemptas?
                Quereris super hoc etiam, quod
Exspectata tibi non mittam carmina mendax.   25
Luculli miles collecta viatica multis
Aerumnis, lassus dum noctu stertit, ad assem
Perdiderat; post hoc vemens lupus et sibi et hosti
Iratus pariter, ieiunis dentibus acer,
Praesidium regale loco deiecit, ut aiunt,   30
Summe munito et multarum divite rerum.
Clarus ob id factum, donis ornatur honestis,
Accipit et bis dena super sestertia nummum.
Forte sub hoc tempus castellum evertere praetor
Nescio quod cupiens, hortari coepit eundem   35
Verbis, quae timido quoque possent addere mentem
' I bone, quo virtus tua te vocat, i pede fausto,
Grandia laturus meritorum praemia.   Quid stas?'

Post haec ille catus, quantumvis rusticus 'Ibit,
Ibit eo, quo vis, qui zonam perdidit' inquit.   40
  Romae nutriri mihi contigit atque doceri,
Iratus Grais quantum nocuisset Achilles.
Adiecere bonae paulo plus artis Athenae,
Scilicet ut vellem curvo dinoscere rectum
Atque inter silvas Academi quaerere verum.   45
Dura sed emovere loco me tempora grato,
Civilisque rudem belli tulit aestus in arma,
Caesaris Augusti non responsura lacertis.
Unde simul primum me dimisere Philippi,
Decisis humilem pinnis inopemque paterni   50
Et laris et fundi Paupertas impulit, audax
Ut versus facerem.   Sed quod non desit habentem
Quae poterunt umquam satis expurgare cicutae,
Ni melius dormire putem quam scribere versus?
  Singula de nobis anni praedantur euntes: 55
Eripuere iocos, Venerem, convivia, ludum;
Tendunt extorquere poemata; quid faciam vis?
  Denique non omnes eadem mirantur amantque:
Carmine tu gaudes, hic delectatur iambis,
Ille Bioneis sermonibus et sale nigro.   60
Tres mihi convivae prope dissentire videntur,
Poscentes vario multum diversa palato.
Quid dem?   Quid non dem?   Renuis tu, quod iubet alter;
Quod petis, id sane est invisum acidumque duobus.
  Praeter cetera me Romaene poemata censes   65
Scribere posse inter tot curas totque labores?
Hic sponsum vocat, hic auditum scripta, relictis
Omnibus officiis; cubat hic in colle Quirini,
Hic extremo in Aventino, visendus uterque:
Intervalla vides humane commoda.   'Verum   70
Purae sunt plateae, nihil ut meditantibus obstet.'
Festinat calidus mulis gerulisque redemptor,

Torquet nunc lapidem, nunc ingens machina tignum,
Tristia robustis luctantur funera plaustris,
Hac rabiosa fugit canis, hac lutulenta ruit sus: 75
I nunc et versus tecum meditare canoros.
Scriptorum chorus omnis amat nemus et fugit urbem,
Rite cliens Bacchi somno gaudentis et umbra;
Tu me inter strepitus nocturnos atque diurnos
Vis canere et contracta sequi vestigia vatum? 80
Ingenium, sibi quod vacuas desumpsit Athenas
Et studiis annos septem dedit insenuitque
Libris et curis, statua taciturnius exit
Plerumque et risu populum quatit: hic ego rerum
Fluctibus in mediis et tempestatibus urbis 85
Verba lyrae motura sonum conectere digner?
    Frater erat Romae consulti rhetor, ut alter
Alterius sermone meros audiret honores,
Gracchus ut hic illi, foret huic ut Mucius ille.
Qui minus argutos vexat furor iste poetas? 90
Carmina compono, hic elegos.   Mirabile visu
Caelatumque novem Musis opus!   Adspice primum,
Quanto cum fastu, quanto molimine circum
Spectemus vacuam Romanis vatibus aedem;
Mox etiam, si forte vacas, sequere et procul audi, 95
Quid ferat et quare sibi nectat uterque coronam.
Caedimur et totidem plagis consumimus hostem
Lento Samnites ad lumina prima duello.
Discedo Alcaeus puncto illius; ille meo quis?
Quis nisi Callimachus?   Si plus adposcere visus, 100
Fit Mimnermus et optivo cognomine crescit.
    Multa fero, ut placem genus irritabile vatum,
Cum scribo et supplex populi suffragia capto;
Idem, finitis studiis et mente recepta,
Obturem patulas impune legentibus auris. 105
Ridentur mala qui componunt carmina; verum

Gaudent scribentes et se venerantur et ultro,
Si taceas, laudant quicquid scripsere beati.
At qui legitimum cupiet fecisse poema,
Cum tabulis animum censoris sumet honesti.   110
Audebit, quaecumque parum splendoris habebunt
Et sine pondere erunt et honore indigna ferentur,
Verba movere loco, quamvis invita recedant
Et versentur adhuc intra penetralia Vestae;
Obscurata diu populo bonus eruet atque   115
Proferet in lucem speciosa vocabula rerum,
Quae priscis memorata Catonibus atque Cethegis
Nunc situs informis premit et deserta vetustas;
Adsciscet nova, quae genitor produxerit usus.
Vehemens et liquidus puroque simillimus amni   120
Fundet opes Latiumque beabit divite lingua;
Luxuriantia compescet, nimis aspera sano
Levabit cultu, virtute carentia tollet,
Ludentis speciem dabit et torquebitur, ut qui
Nunc Satyrum, nunc agrestem Cyclopa movetur.   125
    Praetulerim scriptor delirus inersque videri,
Dum mea delectent mala me vel denique fallant,
Quam sapere et ringi? Fuit haud ignobilis Argis,
Qui se credebat miros audire tragoedos
In vacuo laetus sessor plausorque theatro,   130
Cetera qui vitae servaret munia recto
More, bonus sane vicinus, amabilis hospes,
Comis in uxorem, posset qui ignoscere servis
Et signo laeso non insanire lagoenae,
Posset qui rupem et puteum vitare patentem.   135
Hic ubi cognatorum opibus curisque refectus
Expulit elleboro morbum bilemque meraco,
Et redit ad sese 'Pol, me occidistis, amici,
Non servastis' ait, 'cui sic extorta voluptas
Et demptus per vim mentis gratissimus error.'   140

Nimirum sapere est abiectis utile nugis,
Et tempestivum pueris concedere ludum,
Ac non verba sequi fidibus modulanda Latinis,
Sed verae numerosque modosque ediscere vitae.
Quocirca mecum loquor haec tacitusque recordor: 145
Si tibi nulla sitim finiret copia lymphae,
Narrares medicis; quod, quanto plura parasti,
Tanto plura cupis, nulline faterier audes?
Si volnus tibi monstrata radice vel herba
Non fieret levius, fugeres radice vel herba   150
Proficiente nihil curarier: audieras, cui
Rem di donarent, illi decedere pravam
Stultitiam; et, cum sis nihilo sapientior, ex quo
Plenior es, tamen uteris monitoribus isdem?
At si divitiae prudentem reddere possent,   155
Si cupidum timidumque minus te, nempe ruberes,
Viveret in terris te si quis avarior uno.
Si proprium est, quod quis libra mercatus et aere est,
Quaedam, si credis consultis, mancipat usus;
Qui te pascit ager, tuus est, et vilicus Orbi,   160
Cum segetes occat tibi mox frumenta daturas,
Te dominum sentit. Das nummos, accipis uvam,
Pullos, ova, cadum temeti. Nempe modo isto
Paulatim mercaris agrum, fortasse trecentis
Aut etiam supra nummorum milibus emptum.   165
Quid refert, vivas numerato nuper an olim?
Emptor Aricini quondam Veientis et arvi
Emptum cenat holus, quamvis aliter putat; emptis
Sub noctem gelidam lignis calefactat aënum;
Sed vocat usque suum, qua populus adsita certis   170
Limitibus vicina refugit iurgia; tamquam
Sit proprium quicquam, puncto quod mobilis horae
Nunc prece, nunc pretio, nunc vi, nunc morte suprema
Permutet dominos et cedat in altera iura.

Sic quia perpetuus nulli datur usus, et heres   **175**
Heredem alterius velut unda supervenit undam,
Quid vici prosunt aut horrea?   Quidve Calabris
Saltibus adiecti Lucani, si metit Orcus
Grandia cum parvis, non exorabilis auro?

   Gemmas, marmor, ebur, Tyrrhena sigilla, tabellas,   **180**
Argentum, vestes Gaetulo murice tinctas
Sunt qui non habeant, est qui non curat habere.
Cur alter fratrum cessare et ludere et ungui
Praeferat Herodis palmetis pinguibus, alter
Dives et importunus ad umbram lucis ab ortu   **185**
Silvestrem flammis et ferro mitiget agrum,
Scit Genius, natale comes qui temperat astrum,
Naturae deus humanae, mortalis in unum
Quodque caput, voltu mutabilis, albus et ater.
Utar et ex modico quantum res poscet acervo   **190**
Tollam nec metuam, quid de me iudicet heres,
Quod non plura datis invenerit; et tamen idem
Scire volam, quantum simplex hilarisque nepoti
Discrepet et quantum discordet parcus avaro.
Distat enim, spargas tua prodigus, an neque sumptum   **195**
Invitus facias neque plura parare labores,
Ac potius, puer ut festis Quinquatribus olim,
Exiguo gratoque fruaris tempore raptim.
Pauperies immunda tamen procul absit; ego utrum
Nave ferar magna an parva, ferar unus et idem.   **200**
Non agimur tumidis velis Aquilone secundo:
Non tamen adversis aetatem ducimus Austris,
Viribus, ingenio, specie, virtute, loco, re
Extremi primorum, extremis usque priores.

   Non es avarus: abi.   Quid?   Cetera iam simul isto   **205**
Cum vitio fugere?   Caret tibi pectus inani
Ambitione?   Caret mortis formidine et ira?
Somnia, terrores magicos, miracula, sagas,

Nocturnos lemures portentaque Thessala rides ?
Natalis grate numeras ? ignoscis amicis ?   210
Lenior et melior fis accedente senecta ?
Quid te exempta iuvat spinis de pluribus una ?
Vivere si recte nescis, decede peritis.
　Lusisti satis, edisti satis atque bibisti :
Tempus abire tibi est, ne potum largius aequo   215
Rideat et pulset lasciva decentius aetas.

III.

ON THE ART OF POETRY.[1]

ADDRESSED TO THE PISONES.

1. Outline :

I. General rules for poetic composition :
　1. The subject matter :
　　a) The work must have unity, and must not combine discord-
　　　ant elements, 1–13 ;
　　b) Unnecessary digressions must not be introduced merely for
　　　decorative effect, 14–23 ;
　2. The expression :
　　a) Must be uniform in tone ; care must be taken in avoiding
　　　one extreme not to go to the other, 24–31 ;
　　b) All parts of the poem must be equally finished, 32–37 ;
　　c) The arrangement and choice of words :
　　　1) Both depend on choosing a subject within one's
　　　　powers, 38–41 ;
　　　2) A good arrangement consists in saying each thing
　　　　in its proper place, 42–45 ;
　　　3) To secure fitting language :
　　　　(*a*) New words should be employed only when it is
　　　　　necessary, and their meaning should be made
　　　　　clear by the arrangement of the context, 46–51 ;
　　　　(*b*) They may best be drawn from Greek sources.
　　　　　This license, allowed the ancient poets, will
　　　　　not be refused to the moderns, 52–59 ;

---

[1] This Epistle was at an early period, but not by Horace, given the
special title *De Arte Poetica Liber*, and is usually so cited.

(c) Language is a living thing, and words are born and die. The language of one generation must give place to that of another, 60–72 ;

3. **The metre** must be chosen to suit the subject. Each kind of composition has its appropriate verse-form, 73–85 ;

4. The style, too, must suit the subject :
    a) Broad general distinctions must be observed ; the tragic style must differ from the comic, 86–92 ;
    b) In the same work the style must be varied to suit different conditions, 93–98 ;
    c) Since a poem must appeal to the emotions as well as to the intellect, the language of the characters must be suited to their circumstances. Age, sex, and nationality must be duly regarded, 99–118 ;
        1) The poet must follow tradition in the representation of stock characters. If he invents new ones, they must be consistent throughout, 119–127 ;
        2) On the whole it is better to use old material, but it should be handled in an original way, 128–135 ;
        3) For the sake of unity, and to keep up the interest, the introduction must be simple and unpretentious. Homer is a good model, 136–152 ;

II. Special rules for dramatic poetry :
    1. The characters must be carefully drawn. Different periods of life must be represented with their proper characteristics and impulses, 153–178 ;
    2. The dramatic proprieties must be observed. Actions not fit for representation should merely be described, 179–188 ;
    3. The number of actors, the use of the *deus ex machina*, and the division into acts must conform to tradition, 189–192 ;
    4. The chorus must be closely connected with the action of the play ; it must favor the righteous cause ; it must be the hero's confidant, 193–201 ;
    5. The music must be appropriate and subordinate to the dramatic action. Its present development is an extravagant one, 202–219.
    6. The purpose and nature of the satyr drama must be remembered :
        a) Its action must not fall to the level of extravaganza, but must preserve something of the dignity of tragedy, 220–233 ;

    b) Its language, too, should be carefully chosen. It must differ from that of tragedy, without descending to that of the streets, 234–250 ;

   7. The versification must be carefully studied :

    a) The senarius is a skilful combination of iambs and spondees, and must be handled properly, 251–258 ;

    b) The early Roman poets were careless, because the ears of their audience were dull, 258–264 ;

    c) Greek models should be studied and followed, 265–274 ;

        1) The Greeks invented and developed tragedy ; and also the old comedy, which came to an end through excessive freedom of speech, 275–284 ;

        2) Our forefathers followed them and also invented new dramas based on Roman life ; only want of care prevented them from surpassing their teachers, 285–294 ;

III. The poet and his work : Some people think that mere externals make a poet. Hence Horace prefers to exercise the function of critic, 295–308 :

   1. The material :

    a) The first essential is true wisdom, and a knowledge of human character, 309–322 ;

    b) We must follow the Greeks with their high ideals. Roman life is too practical, 323–332 ;

   2. Its proper presentation :

    a) The poet must please or teach, or both, 333–334 :

        1) The didactic parts should be brief, 335–337 ;

        2) The parts designed to please should be credible, 338–340 ;

        3) A combination of amusement with instruction is the best, 341–346 ;

    b) The critic should use judgment. He should view the work as a whole and overlook slight defects. The same faults must not be often repeated, 347–365 ;

   3. The poet's ideals (addressed to the elder Piso):

    a) The poet must have gifts which rise above the ordinary, 366–373 ;

    b) It is better not to write at all than to fall short of the highest standard, 374–384 ;

    c) The poet should subject his work to competent criticism, 385–390 ;

    d) He should remember that poetry is of divine origin, and played an important part in civilizing the race, 391–399 ;

     e) Later it roused to war, and voiced the oracles, 400–407 ;

     f) A combination of natural ability and hard work make the poet, 408–418 ;

     g) He must seek impartial criticism from those capable of expressing a frank opinion, 419–452 ;

     h) A man who refuses to submit his work to criticism, and regards himself as divine, is a dangerous madman, who should be shunned, 453–476.

2. Time: 16 B.C.

Humano capiti cervicem pictor equinam
Iungere si velit et varias inducere plumas
Undique conlatis membris, ut turpiter atrum
Desinat in piscem mulier formosa superne;
Spectatum admissi risum teneatis, amici?   **5**
Credite, Pisones, isti tabulae fore librum
Persimilem, cuius, velut aegri somnia, vanae
Fingentur species, ut nec pes nec caput uni
Reddatur formae. 'Pictoribus atque poetis
Quidlibet audendi semper fuit aequa potestas.'   **10**
Scimus, et hanc veniam petimusque damusque vicissim;
Sed non ut placidis coeant immitia, non ut
Serpentes avibus geminentur, tigribus agni.
   Inceptis gravibus plerumque et magna professis
Purpureus, late qui splendeat, unus et alter   **15**
Adsuitur pannus, cum lucus et ara Dianae
Et properantis aquae per amoenos ambitus agros
Aut flumen Rhenum aut pluvius describitur arcus.
Sed nunc non erat his locus. Et fortasse cupressum
Scis simulare: quid hoc, si fractis enatat exspes   **20**
Navibus, aere dato qui pingitur? Amphora coepit
Institui; currente rota cur urceus exit?
Denique sit quidvis, simplex dumtaxat et unum.
   Maxima pars vatum, pater et iuvenes patre digni,
Decipimur specie recti. Brevis esse laboro,   **25**

Obscurus fio ; sectantem levia nervi
Deficiunt animique ; professus grandia turget ;
Serpit humi tutus nimium timidusque procellae ;
Qui variare cupit rem prodigialiter unam,
Delphinum silvis adpingit, fluctibus aprum.   30
In vitium ducit culpae fuga, si caret arte.

     Aemilium circa ludum faber imus et unguis
Exprimet et mollis imitabitur aere capillos,
Infelix operis summa, quia ponere totum
Nesciet.   Hunc ego me, si quid componere curem,   35
Non magis esse velim, quam naso vivere pravo
Spectandum nigris oculis nigroque capillo.

     Sumite materiam vestris, qui scribitis, aequam
Viribus et versate diu quid ferre recusent,
Quid valeant umeri.   Cui lecta potenter erit res,   40
Nec facundia deseret hunc nec lucidus ordo.

     Ordinis haec virtus erit et Venus, aut ego fallor,
Ut iam nunc dicat iam nunc debentia dici,
Pleraque differat et praesens in tempus omittat ;
Hoc amet, hoc spernat promissi carminis auctor.   45

     In verbis etiam tenuis cautusque serendis
Dixeris egregie, notum si callida verbum
Reddiderit iunctura novum.   Si forte necesse est
Indiciis monstrare recentibus abdita rerum,
Fingere cinctutis non exaudita Cethegis   50
Continget dabiturque licentia sumpta pudenter.

     Et nova fictaque nuper habebunt verba fidem, si
Graeco fonte cadent parce detorta.   Quid autem
Caecilio Plautoque dabit Romanus, ademptum
Vergilio Varioque ?   Ego cur, adquirere pauca   55
Si possum, invideor, cum lingua Catonis et Enni
Sermonem patrium ditaverit et nova rerum
Nomina protulerit ?   Licuit semperque licebit
Signatum praesente nota producere nomen.

Ut silvae foliis pronos mutantur in annos,   60
Prima cadunt, ita verborum vetus interit aetas,
Et iuvenum ritu florent modo nata vigentque.
Debemur morti nos nostraque.   Sive receptus
Terra Neptunus classes Aquilonibus arcet,
Regis opus, sterilisve palus diu aptaque remis   65
Vicinas urbes alit et grave sentit aratrum,
Seu cursum mutavit iniquum frugibus amnis,
Doctus iter melius; mortalia facta peribunt,
Nedum sermonum stet honos et gratia vivax.
Multa renascentur quae iam cecidere, cadentque   70
Quae nunc sunt in honore vocabula, si volet usus,
Quem penes arbitrium est et ius et norma loquendi.
Res gestae regumque ducumque et tristia bella
Quo scribi possent numero, monstravit Homerus.
Versibus impariter iunctis querimonia primum,   75
Post etiam inclusa est voti sententia compos;
Quis tamen exiguos elegos emiserit auctor,
Grammatici certant et adhuc sub iudice lis est.
Archilochum proprio rabies armavit iambo:
Hunc socci cepere pedem grandesque coturni,   80
Alternis aptum sermonibus et popularis
Vincentem strepitus et natum rebus agendis.
Musa dedit fidibus divos puerosque deorum
Et pugilem victorem et equum certamine primum
Et iuvenum curas et libera vina referre.   85
Descriptas servare vices operumque colores,
Cur ego si nequeo ignoroque, poeta salutor?
Cur nescire pudens prave quam discere malo?
Versibus exponi tragicis res comica non volt;
Indignatur item privatis ac prope socco   90
Dignis carminibus narrari cena Thyestae.
Singula quaeque locum teneant sortita decentem.
Interdum tamen et vocem comoedia tollit,

Iratusque Chremes tumido delitigat ore;
Et tragicus plerumque dolet sermone pedestri　　　　　　95
Telephus et Peleus, cum pauper et exsul uterque
Proicit ampullas et sesquipedalia verba,
Si curat cor spectantis tetigisse querella.

　　Non satis est pulchra esse poemata; dulcia sunto
Et quocumque volent animum auditoris agunto.　　　　100
Ut ridentibus arrident, ita flentibus adsunt
Humani voltus: si vis me flere, dolendum est
Primum ipsi tibi: tunc tua me infortunia laedent,
Telephe vel Peleu; male si mandata loqueris,
Aut dormitabo aut ridebo.　Tristia maestum　　　　105
Voltum verba decent, iratum plena minarum,
Ludentem lasciva, severum seria dictu.
Format enim natura prius nos intus ad omnem
Fortunarum habitum; iuvat aut impellit ad iram,
Aut ad humum maerore gravi deducit et angit;　　　110
Post effert animi motus interprete lingua.
Si dicentis erunt fortunis absona dicta,
Romani tollent equites peditesque cachinnum.
Intererit multum divusne loquatur an heros,
Maturusne senex an adhuc florente iuventa　　　　115
Fervidus, et matrona potens an sedula nutrix,
Mercatorne vagus cultorne virentis agelli,
Colchus an Assyrius, Thebis nutritus an Argis.

　　Aut famam sequere aut sibi convenientia finge.
Scriptor honoratum si forte reponis Achillem,　　　120
Impiger, iracundus, inexorabilis, acer
Iura neget sibi nata, nihil non adroget armis.
Sit Medea ferox invictaque, flebilis Ino,
Perfidus Ixion, Io vaga, tristis Orestes.
Si quid inexpertum scaenae committis et audes　　　125
Personam formare novam, servetur ad imum,
Qualis ab incepto processerit, et sibi constet.

Difficile est proprie communia dicere; tuque
Rectius Iliacum carmen deducis in actus,
Quam si proferres ignota indictaque primus.   130
Publica materies privati iuris erit, si
Non circa vilem patulumque moraberis orbem,
Nec verbum verbo curabis reddere fidus
Interpres, nec desilies imitator in artum,
Unde pedem proferre pudor vetet aut operis lex.   135
    Nec sic incipies, ut scriptor cyclicus olim:
'Fortunam Priami cantabo et nobile bellum.'
Quid dignum tanto feret hic promissor hiatu?
Parturient montes, nascetur ridiculus mus.
Quanto rectius hic, qui nil molitur inepte: 140
'Dic mihi, Musa, virum, captae post tempora Troiae
Qui mores hominum multorum vidit et urbes.'
Non fumum ex fulgore, sed ex fumo dare lucem
Cogitat, ut speciosa dehinc miracula promat,
Antiphaten Scyllamque et cum Cyclope Charybdim;   145
Nec reditum Diomedis ab interitu Meleagri,
Nec gemino bellum Troianum orditur ab ovo;
Semper ad eventum festinat et in medias res
Non secus ac notas auditorem rapit, et quae
Desperat tractata nitescere posse, relinquit,   150
Atque ita mentitur, sic veris falsa remiscet,
Primo ne medium, medio ne discrepet imum.
    Tu quid ego et populus mecum desideret audi,
Si plosoris eges aulaea manentis et usque
Sessuri, donec cantor 'vos plaudite' dicat;   155
Aetatis cuiusque notandi sunt tibi mores,
Mobilibusque decor naturis dandus et annis.
Reddere qui voces iam scit puer et pede certo
Signat humum, gestit paribus conludere et iram
Colligit ac ponit temere et mutatur in horas.   160
Imberbis iuvenis tandem custode remoto

Gaudet equis canibusque et aprici gramine campi,
Cereus in vitium flecti, monitoribus asper,
Utilium tardus provisor, prodigus aeris,
Sublimis cupidusque et amata relinquere pernix.   165
Conversis studiis aetas animusque virilis
Quaerit opes et amicitias, inservit honori,
Commisisse cavet quod mox mutare laboret.
Multa senem circumveniunt incommoda, vel quod
Quaerit et inventis miser abstinet ac timet uti,   170
Vel quod res omnis timide gelideque ministrat,
Dilator, spe longus, iners, avidusque futuri,
Difficilis, querulus, laudator temporis acti
Se puero, castigator censorque minorum.
Multa ferunt anni venientes commoda secum,   175
Multa recedentes adimunt.   Ne forte seniles
Mandentur iuveni partes pueroque viriles,
Semper in adiunctis aevoque morabimur aptis.
   Aut agitur res in scaenis aut acta refertur.
Segnius inritant animos demissa per aurem   180
Quam quae sunt oculis subiecta fidelibus et quae
Ipse sibi tradit spectator; non tamen intus
Digna geri promes in scaenam multaque tolles
Ex oculis, quae mox narret facundia praesens.
Ne pueros coram populo Medea trucidet,   185
Aut humana palam cóquat exta nefarius Atreus,
Aut in avem Procne vertatur, Cadmus in anguem.
Quodcumque ostendis mihi sic, incredulus odi.
   Neve minor neu sit quinto productior actu
Fabula, quae posci volt et spectanda reponi;   190
Nec deus intersit, nisi dignus vindice nodus
Inciderit; nec quarta loqui persona laboret.
   Actoris partis chorus officiumque virile
Defendat, neu quid medios intercinat actus
Quod non proposito conducat et haereat apte.   195

Ille bonis faveatque et consilietur amice,
Et regat iratos et amet pacare timentis:
Ille dapes laudet mensae brevis, ille salubrem
Iustitiam legesque et apertis otia portis;
Ille tegat commissa, deosque precetur et oret   200
Ut redeat miseris, abeat fortuna superbis.

Tibia non, ut nunc, orichalco vincta tubaeque
Aemula, sed tenuis simplexque foramine pauco
Adspirare et adesse choris erat utilis atque
Nondum spissa nimis complere sedilia flatu;   205
Quo sane populus numerabilis, utpote parvus,
Et frugi castusque verecundusque coibat.
Postquam coepit agros extendere victor, et urbis
Latior amplecti murus, vinoque diurno
Placari Genius festis impune diebus;   210
Accessit numerisque modisque licentia maior.
Indoctus quid enim saperet liberque laborum
Rusticus urbano confusus, turpis honesto?
Sic priscae motumque et luxuriem addidit arti
Tibicen traxitque vagus per pulpita vestem;   215
Sic etiam fidibus voces crevere severis,
Et tulit eloquium insolitum facundia praeceps,
Utiliumque sagax rerum et divina futuri
Sortilegis non discrepuit sententia Delphis.

Carmine qui tragico vilem certavit ob hircum,   220
Mox etiam agrestis Satyros nudavit et asper
Incolumi gravitate iocum temptavit, eo quod
Inlecebris erat et grata novitate morandus
Spectator functusque sacris et potus et exlex.
Verum ita risores, ita commendare dicacis   225
Conveniet Satyros, ita vertere seria ludo,
Ne quicumque deus, quicumque adhibebitur heros,
Regali conspectus in auro nuper et ostro,
Migret in obscuras humili sermone tabernas,

Aut, dum vitat humum, nubes et inania captet.   230
Effutire levis indigna tragoedia versus,
Ut festis matrona moveri iussa diebus,
Intererit Satyris paullum pudibunda protervis.

  Non ego inornata et dominantia nomina solum
Verbaque, Pisones, Satyrorum scriptor amabo,   235
Nec sic enitar tragico differre colori,
Ut nihil intersit, Davusne loquatur et audax
Pythias, emuncto lucrata Simone talentum,
An custos famulusque dei Silenus alumni.
Ex noto fictum carmen sequar, ut sibi quivis   240
Speret idem, sudet multum frustraque laboret
Ausus idem: tantum series iuncturaque pollet,
Tantum de medio sumptis accedit honoris.
Silvis deducti caveant me iudice Fauni,
Ne velut innati triviis ac paene forenses   245
Aut nimium teneris iuvenentur versibus umquam,
Aut immunda crepent ignominiosaque dicta;
Offenduntur enim, quibus est equus et pater et res,
Nec, si quid fricti ciceris probat et nucis emptor,
Aequis accipiunt animis donantve corona.   250

  Syllaba longa brevi subiecta vocatur iambus,
Pes citus; unde etiam trimetris adcrescere iussit
Nomen iambeis, cum senos redderet ictus
Primus ad extremum similis sibi.   Non ita pridem,
Tardior ut paulo graviorque veniret ad auris,   255
Spondeos stabilis in iura paterna recepit
Commodus et patiens, non ut de sede secunda
Cederet aut quarta socialiter.   Hic et in Acci
Nobilibus trimetris apparet rarus, et Enni
In scaenam missos cum magno pondere versus   260
Aut operae celeris nimium curaque carentis
Aut ignoratae premit artis crimine turpi.
Non quivis videt immodulata poemata iudex,

Et data Romanis venia est indigna poetis.
Idcircone vager scribamque licenter ?   An omnis   265
Visuros peccata putem mea, tutus et intra
Spem veniae cautus ? Vitavi denique culpam,
Non laudem merui.   Vos exemplaria Graeca
Nocturna versate manu, versate diurna.
At vestri proavi Plautinos et numeros et   270
Laudavere sales, nimium patienter utrumque,
Ne dicam stulte, mirati, si modo ego et vos
Scimus inurbanum lepido seponere dicto,
Legitimumque sonum digitis callemus et aure.
   Ignotum tragicae genus invenisse Camenae   275
Dicitur et plaustris vexisse poemata Thespis
Quae canerent agerentque peruncti faecibus ora.
Post hunc personae pallaeque repertor honestae
Aeschylus et modicis instravit pulpita tignis
Et docuit magnumque loqui nitique cothurno.   280
Successit vetus his comoedia, non sine multa
Laude; sed in vitium libertas excidit et vim
Dignam lege regi.   Lex est accepta chorusque
Turpiter obticuit sublato iure nocendi.
Nil intemptatum nostri liquere poetae;   285
Nec minimum meruere decus vestigia Graeca
Ausi deserere et celebrare domestica facta,
Vel qui praetextas vel qui docuere togatas.
Nec virtute foret clarisve potentius armis,
Quam lingua Latium, si non offenderet unum   290
Quemque poetarum limae labor et mora.   Vos, o
Pompilius sanguis, carmen reprehendite quod non
Multa dies et multa litura coercuit atque
Perfectum deciens non castigavit ad unguem.
   Ingenium misera quia fortunatius arte   295
Credit et excludit sanos Helicone poetas
Democritus, bona pars non unguis ponere curat,

Non barbam, secreta petit loca, balnea vitat.
Nanciscetur enim pretium nomenque poetae,
Si tribus Anticyris caput insanabile numquam   300
Tonsori Licino commiserit.   O ego laevus,
Qui purgor bilem sub verni temporis horam!
Non alius faceret meliora poemata: verum
Nil tanti est.   Ergo fungar vice cotis, acutum
Reddere quae ferrum valet, exsors ipsa secandi;   305
Munus et officium, nil scribens ipse, docebo,
Unde parentur opes, quid alat formetque poetam,
Quid deceat, quid non, quo virtus, quo ferat error.
    Scribendi recte sapere est et principium et fons:
Rem tibi Socraticae poterunt ostendere chartae,   310
Verbaque provisam rem non invita sequentur.
Qui didicit patriae quid debeat et quid amicis,
Quo sit amore parens, quo frater amandus et hospes,
Quod sit conscripti, quod iudicis officium, quae
Partes in bellum missi ducis; ille profecto   315
Reddere personae scit convenientia cuique.
Respicere exemplar vitae morumque iubebo
Doctum imitatorem et vivas hinc ducere voces.
Interdum speciosa locis morataque recte
Fabula nullius Veneris, sine pondere et arte,   320
Valdius oblectat populum meliusque moratur,
Quam versus inopes rerum nugaeque canorae.
    Grais ingenium, Grais dedit ore rotundo
Musa loqui, praeter laudem nullius avaris.
Romani pueri longis rationibus assem   325
Discunt in partis centum diducere.   'Dicat
Filius Albini: si de quincunce remota est
Uncia, quid superat?   Poteras dixisse.'   'Triens.'   'Eu!
Rem poteris servare tuam.   Redit uncia, quid fit?'
'Semis.'   At haec animos aerugo et cura peculi   330
Cum semel imbuerit, speramus carmina fingi

Posse linenda cedro et levi servanda cupresso?
  Aut prodesse volunt, aut delectare poetae,
Aut simul et iucunda et idonea dicere vitae.
Quicquid praecipies, esto brevis, ut cito dicta   335
Percipiant animi dociles teneantque fideles:
Omne supervacuum pleno de pectore manat.
Ficta voluptatis causa sint proxima veris.
Ne quodcumque velit poscat sibi fabula credi,
Neu pransae Lamiae vivum puerum extrahat alvo.   340
Centuriae seniorum agitant expertia frugis,
Celsi praetereunt austera poemata Ramnes:
Omne tulit punctum, qui miscuit utile dulci,
Lectorem delectando pariterque monendo.
Hic meret aera liber Sosiis, hic et mare transit   345
Et longum noto scriptori prorogat aevum.
  Sunt delicta tamen quibus ignovisse velimus;
Nam neque chorda sonum reddit, quem volt manus et mens,
Poscentique gravem persaepe remittit acutum;
Nec semper feriet, quodcumque minabitur, arcus.   350
Verum ubi plura nitent in carmine, non ego paucis
Offendar maculis, quas aut incuria fudit
Aut humana parum cavit natura.   Quid ergo est?
Ut scriptor si peccat idem librarius usque,
Quamvis est monitus, venia caret, et citharoedus   355
Ridetur, chorda qui semper oberrat eadem;
Sic mihi, qui multum cessat, fit Choerilus ille,
Quem bis terque bonum cum risu miror; et idem
Indignor quandoque bonus dormitat Homerus.
Verum operi longo fas est obrepere somnum.   360
Ut pictura poesis: erit quae, si propius stes,
Te capiat magis, et quaedam si longius abstes.
Haec amat obscurum; volet haec sub luce videri,
Iudicis argutum quae non formidat acumen;
Haec placuit semel, haec deciens repetita placebit.   365

O maior iuvenum, quamvis et voce paterna
Fingeris ad rectum et per te sapis, hoc tibi dictum
Tolle memor, certis medium et tolerabile rebus
Recte concedi. Consultus iuris et actor
Causarum mediocris abest virtute diserti   370
Messallae, nec scit quantum Cascellius Aulus,
Sed tamen in pretio est; mediocribus esse poetis
Non homines, non di, non concessere columnae.

   Ut gratas inter mensas symphonia discors
Et crassum unguentum et Sardo cum melle papaver   375
Offendunt, poterat duci quia cena sine istis;
Sic animis natum inventumque poema iuvandis,
Si paulum summo decessit, vergit ad imum.
Ludere qui nescit, campestribus abstinet armis,
Indoctusque pilae discive trochive quiescit,   380
Ne spissae risum tollant impune coronae:
Qui nescit versus tamen audet fingere. Quidni?
Liber et ingenuus, praesertim census equestrem
Summam nummorum, vitioque remotus ab omni.

   Tu nihil invita dices faciesve Minerva,   385
Id tibi iudicium est, ea mens; si quid tamen olim
Scripseris, in Maeci descendat iudicis auris
Et patris et nostras, nonumque prematur in annum,
Membranis intus positis; delere licebit,
Quod non edideris; nescit vox missa reverti.   390
   Silvestris homines sacer interpresque deorum
Caedibus et victu foedo deterruit Orpheus,
Dictus ob hoc lenire tigris rabidosque leones.
Dictus et Amphion, Thebanae conditor urbis,
Saxa movere sono testudinis et prece blanda   395
Ducere quo vellet. Fuit haec sapientia quondam,
Publica privatis secernere, sacra profanis,
Concubitu prohibere vago, dare iura maritis,
Oppida moliri, leges incidere ligno.

Sic honor et nomen divinis vatibus atque   400
Carminibus venit.   Post hos insignis Homerus
Tyrtaeusque mares animos in Martia bella
Versibus exacuit; dictae per carmina sortes,
Et vitae monstrata via est; et gratia regum
Pieriis temptata modis; ludusque repertus,   405
Et longorum operum finis: ne forte pudori
Sit tibi Musa lyrae sollers et cantor Apollo.

    Natura fieret laudabile carmen an arte,
Quaesitum est: ego nec studium sine divite vena,
Nec rude quid prosit video ingenium; alterius sic   410
Altera poscit opem res et coniurat amice.
Qui studet optatam cursu contingere metam,
Multa tulit fecitque puer, sudavit et alsit,
Abstinuit Venere et vino; qui Pythia cantat
Tibicen, didicit prius extimuitque magistrum.   415
Nunc satis est dixisse: 'Ego mira poemata pango;
Occupet extremum scabies; mihi turpe relinqui est,
Et quod non didici sane nescire fateri.'

    Ut praeco, ad merces turbam qui cogit emendas,
Adsentatores iubet ad lucrum ire poeta   420
Dives agris, dives positis in faenore nummis.
Si vero est, unctum qui recte ponere possit
Et spondere levi pro paupere et eripere atris
Litibus implicitum, mirabor si sciet inter
Noscere mendacem verumque beatus amicum.   425
Tu seu donaris seu quid donare voles cui,
Nolito ad versus tibi factos ducere plenum
Laetitiae; clamabit enim 'Pulchre! bene! recte!'
Pallescet super his, etiam stillabit amicis
Ex oculis rorem, saliet, tundet pede terram   430
Ut qui conducti plorant in funere dicunt
Et faciunt prope plura dolentibus ex animo, sic
Derisor vero plus laudatore movetur.

Reges dicuntur multis urgere culullis
Et torquere mero, quem perspexisse laborant,   435
An sit amicitia dignus; si carmina condes,
Numquam te fallent animi sub volpe latentes.
Quintilio si quid recitares, 'Corrige, sodes,
Hoc' aiebat 'et hoc.'   Melius te posse negares,
Bis terque expertum frustra; delere iubebat   440
Et male tornatos incudi reddere versus.
Si defendere delictum quam vertere malles,
Nullum ultra verbum aut operam insumebat inanem,
Quin sine rivali teque et tua solus amares.
Vir bonus et prudens versus reprehendet inertis,   445
Culpabit duros, incomptis adlinet atrum
Transverso calamo signum, ambitiosa recidet
Ornamenta, parum claris lucem dare coget,
Arguet ambigue dictum, mutanda notabit,
Fiet Aristarchus; non dicet: 'Cur ego amicum   450
Offendam in nugis?'   Hae nugae seria ducent
In mala derisum semel exceptumque sinistre.
   Ut mala quem scabies aut morbus regius urget
Aut fanaticus error et iracunda Diana,
Vesanum tetigisse timent fugiuntque poetam,   455
Qui sapiunt; agitant pueri incautique sequuntur.
Hic dum sublimis versus ructatur et errat,
Si veluti merulis intentus decidet auceps
In puteum foveamve, licet 'Succurrite' longum
Clamet 'Io cives,' non sit qui tollere curet.   460
Si curet quis opem ferre et demittere funem,
'Qui scis, an prudens huc se deiecerit atque
Servari nolit?' dicam, Siculique poetae
Narrabo interitum.   Deus immortalis haberi
Dum cupit Empedocles, ardentem frigidus Aetnam   465
Insiluit.   Sit ius liceatque perire poetis:
Invitum qui servat, idem facit occidenti.

Nec semel hoc fecit, nêc si retractus erit, iam
Fiet homo et ponet famosae mortis amorem.
Nec satis apparet, cur versus factitet; utrum
Minxerit in patrios cineres, an triste bidental
Moverit incestus.   Certe furit, ac velut ursus,
Obiectos caveae valuit si frangere clatros,
Indoctum doctumque fugat recitator acerbus;
Quem vero arripuit, tenet occiditque legendo,   475
Non missura cutem, nisi plena cruoris, hirudo.

NOTES.

SERMONES — BOOK I.

SERMO I.

The Title: the manuscripts are practically unanimous for *Sermonum liber primus* and *Sermonum liber secundus*. Strict Latinity would require *liber prior* and *liber alter*. On *Sermonum*, see Introd. § 24.

1. qui fit, Maecenas : *how does it happen, Maecenas ?* These words serve as a dedication of the first book of *Sermones* to Horace's friend and patron, Maecenas ; see Introd. § 4. *Qui* is an adverb from the *i*-stem of the interrogative pronoun ; with *qui* and *quo*, *cf. quibus* and *quorum*. See Introd. § 48. *b*. **quam . . . sortem . . . illa** = *illa sorte . . . quam*, a common form of expression in Latin. **sortem** : *lot, condition in life*, either as the result of *fors* or *ratio*.

2. ratio dederit . . . fors obiecerit : *his own choice has given him, or chance has thrown in his way ; cf.* Cic. *ad Att.* xiv. 13. 3, *sed haec fors viderit, ea quae talibus in rebus plus quam ratio potest*. *Dederit* and *obiecerit* are subjunctive by attraction, the relative clause forming an essential part of the consecutive clause *ut . . . vivat*.

3. laudet : *but each man envies ; sc. quisque*, implied in *nemo ; cf.* Cic. *de Orat.* iii. 14. 52, *nemo extulit eum verbis . . . sed contempsit eum*. *Laudet* means 'to praise as happy,' and so 'to envy' ; *cf.* Greek μακαρίζω. Note the asyndeton. **diversa** : *opposite, i.e.* differing widely from his own. **sequentis** : *those who follow*. Note that this idea, expressed in Greek by the article and the participle, is expressed in Latin by the participle alone ; *eos sequentis* would have a different meaning. See note on *quaesitis*, line 38 below.

4. mercatores : *traders ;* the reference is to men who sail in their own ships to foreign ports, *i.e.* wholesale traders, as opposed to *caupones ; cf. Odes*, i. 1. 16. After the general statement of his subject

163

in lines 1–3, Horace presents it more vividly by the selection of specific types. In reading this line, be careful to give the spondees in the first four feet their full quantitative value, otherwise the rhythm is wholly lost. **gravis annis :** a descriptive epithet. Horace has in mind a soldier who has lost the vigor and enthusiasm of youth, but is not yet incapacitated for service. In his walks about the city (see i. 6. 111 f.) he must often have seen such men and heard their complaints.

5. multo . . . labore : note the separation of the adjective and the substantive, — a very common order in Latin. **iam :** *at last, i.e.* after years of service. **membra :** object of *fractus,* which is used in a middle sense. See Introd. § 38. *c.*

6. contra : *on the other hand,* a common expression in the *Serm.* and *Epist. ; cf.* i. 2. 4 ; i. 2. 30 ; i. 6. 12 ; *etc.* **iactantibus :** note the tense. It is in the midst of the storm that the trader envies the soldier. **Austris :** the reference is of course to winds in general, but Horace, as usual, gives vividness to his picture by selecting a specific example. *Auster,* the burning *sirocco,* is often used of a stormy wind ; *cf. Odes,* iii. 3. 4 ; iii. 27. 22 ; iv. 14. 21; *etc.*

7. quid enim? *why so?* a colloquial expression. *Cf.* Porph. *ad loc., quasi interpellante affectu hoc dicitur, et est etiam consuetudinis nostrae.* In Cicero, *quid enim* introduces a point that might be advanced in opposition to an argument, and is always followed by a question ; *e.g. Tusc. Disp.* iv. 4. 8, *quid enim? metusne conturbet?* **concurritur :** impersonal. **horae momento :** *in a short time; cf. puncto mobilis horae, Epist.* ii. 2. 172. In these expressions, *horae* does not have its literal meaning of 'an hour,' but is practically synonymous with *temporis,* as in Livy xxxv. 11. 13, *momento temporis castra relicta erant.* The same thing is probably true of Plin. *N. H.* vii. 172, *Maecenati triennio supremo nullo horae momento contigit somnus,* where of course we have hyperbole.

8. cita mors : contrasted with the trader's end after a long struggle with the gale; *cf.* Porph. *ad loc., quasi diu navem iactantibus austris hoc dicitur.*

9. laudat : for the meaning, see note on line 3 above. **iuris legumque peritus :** the reference is not to the professional lawyer (*causidicus, patronus*), but to the city gentleman skilled in legal lore (*iuris consultus*). His clients called on him early in the morning, at the time of the *salutatio; cf. Epist.* ii. 1. 103–104. The early rising which these services made necessary would appear to Horace a special hardship ; *cf.* i. 6. 122 ; ii. 3. 3.

10. sub galli cantum : *just before cock-crow.* The anxious client arrives betimes.   **ubi** : note the position of the word, a common order in Latin.   **ostia pulsat** : *knocks at the door. Cf. Odes,* i. 4. 13, *Pallida mors aequo pulsat pede pauperum tabernas, Regumque turris.*

11. ille : does not refer to the *consultor,* who comes of his own accord, but with the city gentleman is contrasted a countryman (*agricola,* line 9; *rusticus,* line 17) who, because he has given bail to appear in court on a certain day (*datis vadibus*), is obliged to come to the city against his will (*extractus*) ; *cf.* i. 9. 36.

12. solos, *etc. :* note the spondees in the first four feet, and see note on line 4.   **clamat** : *cries out.* The countryman is evidently visiting the city for the first time, and is amazed at its beauty and magnificence.

13. cetera de genere hoc : *other instances of the kind.* A common expression in Lucretius, of whom there are many reminiscences in Horace. *Cf., e.g.,* Lucr. v. 164, *Cetera de genere hoc adfingere et addere, Memmi, Desiperest.* **adeo sunt multa** : parenthetical, instead of *adeo sunt multa ut . . . valeant.* A common Latin usage. **loquacem** : *i.e.* even so loquacious a fellow as Fabius. Note the emphatic position of the adjective.

14. Fabium : Porph. says *Q.(uod) Fabius Maximus Narbonensis, equestri loco natus, Pompeianas partes secutus, aliquot libros ad Stoicam philosophiam pertinentes conscripsit.* Since such a note might be constructed from the hint given in the text, it is doubtful whether much weight ought to be assigned to this and similar utterances of Porphyrio. **valent** : *are enough to.*   **ne te morer** : *not to delay you, i.e.* to make a long story short ; a parenthetical final clause.

15. quo rem deducam : *to what conclusion I am coming;* more lit., ' to what end I will spin the thread of my discourse.'   **si quis deus** : Horace, in his usual manner, has a specific god in mind, namely, Jupiter, as appears below. See notes on *mercatores,* line 4, and *Austris,* line 6 above.   **en ego . . . iam faciam quod voltis** : *lo! I will forthwith do what you wish.* The god appears to grant the wishes of the dissatisfied men. The scene is sketched vividly, as it might be acted on the stage. The god is thought of as appearing between the pairs of men whose lots in life are to be exchanged.

16. qui modo miles : *sc. eras.* The ellipsis, which is not consciously present to the mind, is characteristic of the colloquial language.

17. hinc vos, vos hinc . . . discedite: *i.e.* go your several ways. Note the chiasmus.

18. mutatis . . . partibus: *with your rôles* (in the drama of life) *changed.* **heia**: *well!* an exclamation of impatience, as the men hesitate to accept the opportunity offered them.

19. nolint: *sc. mutare partes*, the apodosis to *dicat* in line 15. **licet**: *sc. eis*, to the case of which *beatis* is attracted.

20. causae: genitive of the whole with *quid.* **merito**: note the emphatic position. Grammatically *merito* modifies *iratus;* in sense it refers both to the anger and to the mode of expressing it. **quin**: *why . . . not*, the original meaning (*cf. qui*, line 1). It introduces the indirect deliberatives *inflet . . . dicat.* **illis**: the dative is governed both by *buccas inflet* and *iratus* (see note on *merito* above), an example of the ἀπὸ κοινοῦ construction. **ambas . . . buccas inflet**: a comic representation of anger, such as Horace had doubtless seen in some mime, or farce. *Bucca* (French *bouche*) is the colloquial word, which eventually displaced the classical *os. Cf.* Cic. *ad Att.* i. 12. 4, *si rem nullam habebis, quod in buccam venerit scribito.* See Introd. § 55. *a.*

22. facilem: *easy-going, good natured.*

23. praeterea: taking up the subject again with *ille gravem . . .* in line 28. A common expression in Lucretius (*cf. cetera de genere hoc*, line 13, and the note) ; *e.g.* ii. 757, *Praeterea si nulla coloris principiis est Reddita natura. . . . ˙ut qui iocularia*: sc. *percurrit : like one who rattles off jokes, i.e.* like a writer of farces. *Cf.* Liv. vii. 2. 5, *imitari deinde eos iuventus simul inconditis inter se iocularia fundentes versibus coepere.* On the ellipsis, see note on i. 1. 16.

24. quamquam: *and yet.*

25. olim: *sometimes; olim*, from *ol-* + the instrumental ending *-im*, means *at that time (i.e.* any time except the present), hence *formerly, hereafter*, or *sometimes.* **dant crustula**: *cf.* Quint. i. 1. 26, *non excludo autem, id quod est notum irritandae ad discendum infantiae gratia eburneas etiam litterarum formas in lusum offerre;* Hieron. *Epist.* 12, *interim modo litterarum elementa cognoscat, iungat syllabas . . . atque ut voce tinnula ista meditetur, proponantur ei crustula, mulsa praemia.*

26. elementa prima: *their letters.* **velint . . . discere**: *may wish to learn, i.e.* may regard it as a pleasure to learn.

27. sed tamen: *but yet, i.e. quamquam nihil vetat ridentem dicere verum*, implied in *quamquam . . . quid vetat ?* **quaeramus**

seria : *i.e. let us consider the matter seriously.*   *Seria* is the neuter plural of the adjective used as a substantive, object of *quaeramus.* See Introd. § 49. *b.*

28. ille gravem duro, *etc. :* the same examples as in lines 4–14, except that here, since avarice is to be named as the cause of discontent, the *perfidus caupo* (see note on *mercatores*, line 4) is substituted for the *iuris consultus*, whose services were given without compensation.   See above, line 9.   Note the juxtaposition of *gravem* and *duro*, emphasizing the difficulty of the labor. *Cf. Odes*, i. 1. 11.

29. hic: opposed to *ille* in the preceding line.   **nautae =** *mercatores; cf.* Tibull. i. 3. 39, *Nec vagus ignotis repetens compendia terris Presserat externa navita merce ratem.*

30. currunt: a common expression in such a connection.   *Cf. Epist.* i. 1. 45, and Virg. *Aen.* iii. 191, *vastum cava trabe currimus aequor,* cited by Porphyrio.   **hac mente** : *with this idea.* Note the emphatic position of the phrase.

31. senes: *when they are old men.*   **tuta** : contrasted with the dangers of military service or of a seafaring life.

32. sint congesta: the subjunctive shows that the *cum*-clause is part of the indirect discourse introduced by *hac mente.*   **cibaria** : *i.e.* enough to live on ; the word is used of the rations of slaves or of soldiers, and implies the bare necessities of life.

33. parvola : *tiny*, diminutive of *parvus.* The use of diminutives is characteristic of the colloquial language, but here *parvola* is used for the sake of contrast. See note on *magni laboris* below, and Introd. § 55. *e.* **exemplo est** : *sc. eis, that is their model, i.e.* the example they cite in self-justification ; *exemplo* is the dative of purpose, for which the poets, especially Propertius and Ovid, sometimes use the predicate nominative or accusative ; *e.g.* Prop. i. 22. 6. *Sic mihi praecipue, pulvis Etrusca, dolor.*   **magni . . . laboris** : *magni* is contrasted with *parvola*, ' that tiny type of giant industry ' (Conington). *Cf.* line 56 below. The genitive of quality modifies *formica* directly, instead of the usual *formica, animal magni laboris; cf. Odes*, i. 36. 13 ; Liv. iv. 41. 12, *exactae iam aetatis Capitolinus.*

36. quae = *at ea.*   **simul** = *simul ac*, as frequently ; *cf.* line 67 below.   **inversum contristat Aquarius annum** : in January the sun is in Aquarius, and the year has completed its circle ; hence *inversum, brought to an end.*   *Contristat* is appropriately used of the rainy Roman winter ; *cf.* Porph. *ad loc., maxime sole in Aquario constituto tempestates horrendae et frigora ingentia solent esse.*

The adjective *tristis* is a frequent epithet of *imber* and the like ; *cf.*
Odes, i. 3. 14, *tristis Hyadas*.

38. quaesitis = *acquisitis*, modifies *illis, the store that it has got
together*. Notice the difference in meaning between *illis quaesitis*
and *sequentis* in line 2 ; see the note. The use of the simple for the
compound verb is colloquial and poetic.   **sapiens**: *like a true philosopher ;* note the position of the word. *Sapiens* is the Latin equivalent of the Greek *philosophus*. It is used as a substantive ; see note
on line 27 above.   **cum** : adversative, *whereas*.

39. demoveat : potential subjunctive.

40. dum ne : a colloquial expression, instead of the usual *dummodo ne*.   **alter** : note that the word is *alter*, not *alius ;* hence
THE *other man, your rival*. The avaricious man is willing to endure
any hardship or encounter any danger, provided he can keep his
rival from outstripping him in the race for riches.

41. quid iuvat . . . te : *what pleasure can it give you ?*

42. furtim . . . timidum : these words vividly portray the anxiety
which comes with increase of riches.   **deponere** : the usual word
for intrusting money to some one's care ; here used ironically.

43. quod = *at id ; cf. quae* in line 36. The miser tries to justify
his conduct.   **vilem . . . assem**: *a paltry farthing*. The *as* was
the unit of the Roman coinage, originally a pound of copper. It was
gradually reduced until its weight was but half an ounce and its value
less than a cent. It was used proverbially of a small sum ; *cf.*
Epist. ii. 2. 27, *viatica ad assem perdiderat.*   •

44. at ni id fit : *i.e. nisi comminuas*.   **pulchri** : genitive of the
whole ; *cf. causae*, line 20 above.   **constructus acervus** : the poet
has in mind the figure of the ant ; *cf. acervus quem struit*, line 34.

45. milia frumenti : *sc. medimnum*, genitive plural. *Cf.* Lucil.
486 L., *Milia dum centum frumenti tollis medimnum, Vini mille
cadum*.   **triverit** : jussive subjunctive with concessive force ; *cf.* i.
3. 15.   **area** : *threshing-floor*, a paved surface near the field, on
which the sheaves were spread. The grain was then trodden out by
oxen, or threshed out by the *tribulum* or by flails. *Cf.* Varro, *De Re
Rustica*, i. 52, *id* (*tribulum*) *fit e tabula lapidibus aut ferro asperata,
quae cum imposito auriga aut pondere gravi trahitur iumentis iunctis,
discutit e spica grana*. Such threshing-floors may be seen to-day in
Italy and Greece.

46. hoc : *on this account ; cf.* i. 3. 93.

47. reticulum : *the bag* (English *reticule*) in which bread for the use of the troop of slaves was carried. *Cf.* Juv. xii. 60, *Mox cum reticulis et pane et ventre lagonae Aspice sumendas in tempestate secures.*   **venalis** : *slaves;* strictly, slaves offered for sale, who are here represented as being driven in a gang to the slave-market. Such a sight must have been a common one in Rome, and furnishes an apt illustration. The rich man has the burden of his wealth to carry, but can do no more than satisfy his actual needs. *Venalis* is a substantive formed by the ellipsis of *servos.* See note on line 27 above.   **inter** : governs *venalis.* The anastrophe of dissyllabic prepositions is common in Horace.

48. forte vehas : *you should happen to carry.* Horace is fond of conditions of this type.   **accipias . . . portarit** : note the tenses, *you would receive no more* at the halt for dinner, *than he who carried nothing* on the march.

49. quid referat : *what difference would it make ?* apodosis to the protasis implied in *viventi.*   **intra naturae finis viventi** : *to one who lives within the bounds which nature sets, i.e.* if you live according to nature's laws. The dative (*viventi*), which is rare with *refert,* is a dative of reference ; *cf.* Tac. *Ann.* xv. 65, *non referre dedecori, si citharoedus demoveretur et tragoedus succederet,* where Nipperdey proposes to read *dedecoris;* Plaut. *Truc.* 394, *quoi rei te adsimulare retulit ?* The usual construction is the genitive, or *ad* with the accusative.

50. iugera : *acres.* The *iugerum* was strictly about two-thirds of an acre, containing 28,800 square feet, while the acre contains 43,560.   **centum an mille** : either amount would be too great for one *intra naturae finis viventi.*

51. at suave est : an attempt at self-justification by the avaricious man.

52. parvo : *sc. acervo.* See note on line 27 above.   **tantundem** : *just as much* as the rich man, who required no more than the poor man to satisfy his actual needs.   **haurire relinquas** : *allow us to take.*

53. cumeris : *chests* or *bins* of pottery or wicker-work (*cf. Epist.* i. 7.30) contrasted with the granaries of the rich man. Ablative of comparison with *plus.*

54. liquidi : *i.e. aquae,* to be taken with *urna. Urna* is the *jar* in which water was drawn and carried, while *cyatho* is the *ladle* for dipping it out ; they are doubtless to be regarded as *measures.*

55. mallem : *I should prefer.* The form of the apodosis contrary

to fact, since the man is thought of as standing by the little brook
(note *hoc*) and wishing that he might draw from the great river.

56. fonticulo: *brooklet.* The diminutive is here used in its
literal sense and contrasted with *magno.* See note on line 33 above.
eo: ablative of cause, *thus it happens.*

57. plenior . . . iusto: *greater than is right. Iusto* is the
neuter of the adjective used substantively.

58. cum ripa simul: *bank and all.* **Aufidus acer**: as usual,
Horace uses a specific example (see note on *Austris*, line 6 above), and
naturally chooses the river near his home. With the epithet *acer, cf.
Odes,* iii. 30. 10 ; iv. 9. 2 ; iv. 14. 25.

59. qui . . . is: *the man who;* for *is . . . qui* (see note on *quam
sortem . . . illa,* line 1 above).   **tantuli**: genitive with *eget.* See
B. 212. 1.   **eget . . . est opus**: *desires only so much as is actually
necessary.*   **limo turbatam**: the poet is thinking of the Aufidus
when swollen by the spring freshets, at which time only could it
properly be called *magnum flumen.*

61. bona pars = *magna pars.* Porph. says : *bona nunc pro
magna dictum, ut saepe Ennius et alii veteres. Cf. Odes,* iv. 2. 46.
The expression is not found in the fragments of Ennius which have
come down to us, but is found in Ter. *Eun.* 123, *Nam hic quoque
bonam magnamque partem ad te attulit;* Cic. *De Orat.* ii. 3. 14,
bonam partem sermonis in hunc diem esse dilatam.   **cupidine**:
always masculine in Horace.   **falso**: *blind, i.e.* misleading.

62. quia tanti quantum habeas sis: *because you are rated by
the amount of your possessions. Cf.* Lucil. Inc. 23 M., *Quantum
habeas, tantum ipse sies tantique habearis. Tanti* is genitive of
value, used predicately with *sis. Habeas* and *sis* are subjunctive because of the indefinite second person singular.

63. illi: *such a man as that,* the individual suggested by *bona
pars.* The usual construction with *facio* in this sense is the instrumental ablative. The dative occurs also in Cic. *pro Caec.* 11. 30, *quid
huic tu homini facias ?*   **libenter**: *of his own free will.* Note the
emphatic position.

64. quatenus: *as long as, i.e.* since. *Quatenus* always has this
meaning in Horace. It is found first in Lucr. ii. 927, *Quatenus in
pullos animalis vertier ova Cernimus alituum.* Lucr. is followed by
Horace and Ovid, but the usage is not found in prose before Val.
Max.   **id facit**: *i.e. miser est.*   **quidam . . . Athenis**: *a man
at Athens,* a colloquial form of expression.

65. **populi voces** : *popular opinion.*

66. sibilat : a means of expressing disapproval in the theatre, as *plaudo* expressed the reverse. Both words are used metaphorically.

68. Tantalus : the stories of the crime and punishment of Tantalus are variously told. This is the Homeric version, which we might expect Horace to follow. Our English verb to *tantalize* is derived from Tantalus. Note that, as usual, Horace identifies the person addressed and the one with whom he is compared, instead of saying *sicut Tantalus, captas. Cf.* lines 32–33 above.   **captat** : note the intensive verb.

69. quid rides ? *what are you laughing at ?* A rhetorical device. The poet anticipates a derisive laugh at his hackneyed story.

70. saccis : there is evidently a pun on *saccis* and *sacris* (at the end of line 71). Such plays on words are common in comedy, to which satire, especially in its dialogues, is closely allied, since both represent the language of everyday life.

71. indormis inhians : *you fall asleep, gloating over; i.e.* he sits so long in contemplation of his wealth, that sleep overcomes him. **et** : *and yet,* adversative.   **tamquam** : modifies *sacris.*

72. cogeris : the verb has the force of the middle voice, *force yourself.*   **pictis tamquam gaudere tabellis** : *enjoy them as if they were pictures, i.e.* through the sight alone. A painting of a pile of money-bags would in reality be just as useful.

73. quo valeat nummus : *what money is for.*

74. panis . . . holus, vini sextarius : the bare necessaries of life, since wine was regarded as an essential article of food, and not as a luxury. The *sextarius* was .54 of a litre, *i.e.* about a pint.   **ematur** : jussive subjunctive.

75. quis . . . doleat natura negatis : *i.e.* the comforts, but not the luxuries of life ; things whose loss would really be felt. *Negatis* has a conditional force. On the form *quis* (ablative), *cf.* note on *qui,* line 1.

76. an : here, as often, with an ironical force, introducing a *reductio ad absurdum.*   **vigilare** : in apposition with *hoc* in line 78.

77. incendia : fires were of frequent occurrence in ancient Rome, and were greatly dreaded.   **servos** : another source of constant menace. *Cf.* Fest. p. 348, *quot servi, tot hostes, in proverbio est ;* Sen. *Epist.* 47. 5, *deinde eiusdem arrogantiae proverbium iactatur : totidem hostes esse quam servos.* The same dangers are spoken of together in *Epist.* ii. 1. 121.

78. ne te compilent fugientes : *lest they rob you, and take to
their heels.*   The slaves run away, and rob their master before leaving
the house.

79. optarim : potential subjunctive.   **bonorum** : genitive with
pauperrimus, an extension of the construction with adjectives of
plenty and want ; *cf. Odes,* iii. 30. 11 ; *Serm.* ii. 3. 142 ; and see
Introd. § 40. *a.* After *pauperrimus, bonorum,* which is reserved to the
end of the sentence, comes in the nature of a surprise, a common
device in Horace ; note the emphatic position of *horum.*

80. frigore : *a chill* of fever, a common affection in the malarial
district in which Rome was situated.   *Cf. frigida quartana,* ii. 3. 290.

81. casus : *misfortune,* with the double idea of ' chance ' or
' accident,' and ' danger.'   Cf. ii. 5. 49, *si quis casus puerum egerit
Orco.*   **lecto te adfixit** : *has confined you to your bed.*   **qui
adsideat** : *some one to sit by your side ;* the subjunctive has a final
force.

83. gnatis : in the *Sermones,* the spelling of the substantive is
gnatus (*gnata*), while that of the participle is *natus.*   *Cf.* i. 3. 43 ; i.
5. 53 ; ii. 3. 203.   In the *Odes,* both are spelled without the *g.*   *Cf.*
ii. 18. 28 ; iii. 5. 42 ; iv. 4. 55.

85. pueri atque puellae : *of both sexes,* a stereotyped expression.   *Cf.* ii. 3. 130, *Insanum te omnes pueri clamentque puellae.*

86. tu : emphatic personal pronoun, contrasted with *nemo.*
argento : dative governed by *post-ponas,* which is divided by tmesis.
For the tmesis, *cf.* i. 3. 92 ; i. 6. 58.

87. si nemo praestet : a subjunctive protasis with the apodosis
in the indicative (*miraris*).   **merearis** : subjunctive by attraction.

88. an si : see note on *an* in line 76.   **nullo labore** : *sc. tuo,
with no effort on your part.*   **cognatos . . . amicos** : corresponding respectively to *uxor* and *filius* and *vicini, noti,* lines 84 and 85
above.

90. infelix : *fruitlessly,* applied not only to plants (*infelix lolium,*
Virg. *Georg.* i. 154), but to men as well ; *cf. Ars Poet.* 34, *infelix operis
summa.*   **asellum** : the diminutive does not here, as in line 56,
refer merely to size, but, as often, has a notion of contempt, *a sorry ass.*

91. in Campo : *sc. Martio, i.e.* on the race-course.

92. denique : *in short,* summing up the discourse and bringing it
to a close.   **plus** : *a superfluity,* more than enough for your actual
needs

94. parto : *sc. eo,* antecedent of *quod ;* ablative absolute.   **quod**

avebas: with reference to *cum habeas plus*, and to *congesta cibaria*, line 31.   **facias**: *meet with the fate of.*

95. dives: followed by an explanatory consecutive clause, though not modified by an adverb, — not an uncommon construction in the Satires. See i. 7. 13 ; ii. 7. 10 ; *Epist.* i. 16. 12 ; and *cf. ita sordidus, ut* in line 96.

96. ut metiretur nummos: a proverbial expression for great wealth.   *Cf.* Petron. 37, *Fortunata appellatur, quae nummos modio metitur.*

97. servo : the singular may possibly imply that Ummidius had but one slave (*than his slave*), which would vividly portray his meanness.   *Cf.*, however, *Epist.* i. 16. 63, *qui melior servo avarus,* 'how much better is the miser than a slave.'   **ad usque supremum tempus**: *sc. vitae, up to his very last moment.*

99. at : *but in fact.*   He fell a victim not to *penuria victus*, but to the *liberta*.   **liberta** : freed slaves were called *liberti* (*-ae*) with reference to their former masters, *libertini* with reference to their position in the community.

100. divisit medium : *cut in two.*   **Tyndaridarum** : *of Tyndareus' children,* referring to Clytemnestra, who slew her husband Agamemnon with an axe.   On the identification of the *liberta* with Clytemnestra, see note on *Tantalus*, line 68 above.

101. Naevius . . . Nomentanus: the latter was a well-known spendthrift, often mentioned by Horace ; *e.g.* i. 8. 11 ; ii. 1. 22 ; ii. 3. 175 and 224.   The former may possibly be the same as the *simplex Naevius* of ii. 2. 68.

102. pugnantia . . . frontibus adversis : like rams or bulls ; *cf. Virg. Aen.* xii. 716 f., *cum duo conversis inimica in proelia tauri Frontibus incurrunt;* Lucr. vi. 117, *concurrere nubes Frontibus adversis. Frontibus adversis* is purely decorative.   **componere** : *to couple; cf. Sen. de Vit. Beat.* 7. 1, *diversa in eandem copulam coniciantur.*

104. vappam: *a good-for-nothing,* lit. *vapid wine.   Cf.* Plin. *N.H.* 14. 125, *vappae accipit nomen probrosum etiam hominum, cum degeneravit animus.*   **nebulonem** : a colloquial word, occurring also in Lucil. 391 L., *Publius Parus mihi* [*tubitanus*] *quaestor Hibera In terra fuit, lucifugus, nebulo id genus sane.*   It is connected with *nebula, cloud, mist.*

105. Tanain . . . socerumque Viselli : these two men illustrated extremes of some sort.   *Tanain* is in form a Greek accusative.

107. quos ultra citraque : note the anastrophe, and *cf.* line 47 above.   **nequit consistere rectum** : *one cannot be right*, lit. *right cannot exist.*

108. illuc, unde abii, redeo : *i.e.* to the beginning of the Satire. **qui** : *cf. qui fit* in line 1.   *Qui* is used very often by Horace in direct questions, but only here in an indirect question. *Cf.*, however, Lucr. iv. 633, *Nunc aliis alius qui sit cibus unicus aptus Expediam;* iv. 887, *nunc qui fiat . . . dicam.*   **ut avarus** : *on account of avarice, inasmuch as he is avaricious.* The *ut* is explanatory; *cf.* ii. 2. 111, *ut sapiens; Odes*, iii. 5. 42, *ut capitis minor.* Avarice has been found to be the cause of the universal discontent, and is now for the first time directly stated as such.

110. aliena capella : *another's goat.* *Cf.* Ovid, *Ars Amat.* i. 349, *Fertilior seges est alienis semper in agris, Vicinumque pecus grandius uber habet.*

111. tabescat : *cf. Epist.* i. 2. 57, *invidus alterius macrescit rebus opimis.*

112. hunc atque hunc : *one man after the other.* The double meaning of *superare* suggests the following figure.   Note that Horace, in his usual manner, identifies the miser and the charioteer; see note on *Tantalus*, line 68 above.

113. sic : modifying *festinanti* and not correlative with the following *ut.*   **obstat** : *bars his way.*

114. carceribus : *the stalls* from which the chariots started ; also called *claustra; cf. Epist.* i. 14. 9, *amat spatiis obstantia rumpere claustra.*   **missos** : the technical word for the start of a race. *Cf.* Enn. *Ann.* 89, *quam mox emittat pictis ex faucibus currus.* With the whole passage, *cf.* Virg. *Georg.* i. 512, —

> *At cum carceribus sese effudere quadrigae,*
> *Addunt in spatia et frustra retinacula tendens*
> *Fertur equis auriga, neque audit currus habenas.*

115. suos : *sc. equos*, object of *vincentibus.*   **illum praeteritum** : *i.e. aurigam quem praeteriit.*

116. temnens = *contemnens*, a somewhat rare use of the word, and one which is confined to poetry.   See note on *quaesitis*, line 38 above.   **extremos inter euntem** = *quasi inter extremos eat* or *ut inter extremos euntem.*

117. inde fit : *that is why it happens*, the answer to *qui fit* in line 1.   **raro** : a modified statement ; *cf. nemo* in line 1.

119. cedat uti conviva satur : *cf.* Lucr. iii. 938, *Cur non ut*

plenus vitae conviva recedis, Aequo animoque capis securam, stulte,
quietem ?   *Cedat* is subjunctive in a clause of characteristic.

120. Crispini : a Stoic and a versifier, whom Horace satirizes also
in i. 3. 139 ; i. 4. 14 ; and ii. 7. 45. In the second of the passages
named, as is implied here, he is described as an unduly prolific writer.
scrinia : cylindrical boxes, usually of beech-wood, for holding rolls of
manuscript.   **lippi** : this affection, which seems to have been a
common one at Rome, is often the subject of jests. So by Horace,
although he suffered from it himself ; see i. 5. 30 and 49.

121. verbum non amplius addam : a pleonastic expression ; cf.
Lucr. iii. 941, *cur amplius addere quaeris ?*

SERMO III.

1. vitium : this word, from *viere*, 'bend,' 'twist,' and cognate
with *vitis*, 'vine,' designates primarily a straying or deviation from the
norma, or conventional standard ; *cf.* English *wrong*, from Old English
wringan ('bend,' 'twist'), English *wring*. Hence it is applied, not
only to faults, but also to eccentricities of conduct.

2. inducant animum : for *inducant in animum*, *make up their*
mind.   **rogati, iniussi** : note the chiastic order and the resulting
emphasis.

3. Sardus : in the emphatic position, as a term of contempt ; *cf.*
Cic. *ad Fam.* vii. 24, *Sardos venales, alium alio nequiorem.*

4. ille : *the notorious*.   **hoc** : *sc. vitium*.   **Caesar** : the reference
is to Octavian, *i.e.* C. Julius Caesar Octavianus, afterward Augustus.
posset : note the tense, *was in a position to compel him ;* subjunctive
in a characteristic clause.

5. peteret : a future condition transferred to past time.   **patris** :
i.e. his adoptive father, Julius Caesar.

6. collibuisset : in the same construction as *peteret*. The verb is
used only in the tenses from the perfect stem.   **ab ovo usque ad**
mala : a proverbial expression, meaning from the beginning to the end
of a dinner. Eggs formed a part of the *gustatio*, the appetizers which
introduced the *cena* (see ii. 8 and the Outline); while apples and
other fruits were served with the *mensa secunda*, or dessert. Music
was a common form of entertainment at the close of a dinner, but
Tigellius, if the fancy seized him, would sing from beginning to end.

7. io Bacchae : apparently the beginning of a dithyramb.   **modo**
summa voce . . . ima : *i.e.* now in a deep bass voice, now in a

shrill falsetto. The *summa chorda*, which was the longest, had the deepest tone, the *ima* the highest. The terms were reversed when applied to the voice, as we see from Quint. xi. 3. 42, *ima vim non habet, summa rumpi periclitatur.* Horace seems to use the terms suited to the tetrachord, but to apply them to the voice.

8. chordis : probably instrumental ablative.

9. aequale : *consistent; cf.* line 19.   **velut qui . . . hostem** : a combination of *currebat velut fugiens hostem* and *currebat velut is currit qui fugit hostem.*

10. persaepe : *sc. incedebat,* implied in *currebat.* With the whole passage, *cf.* Sall. *Cat.* 15 (of Catiline), *citus modo, modo tardus incessus.*

11. sacra ferret : *i.e.* with slow and stately tread ; *cf.* Ovid, *Amor.* iii. 13. 27, *More patrum sancto velatae vestibus albis Condita supposito vertice sacra ferunt.*   **ducentos** : *hundreds of;* the choice of *ducentos* to represent an indefinite large number is perhaps affected by the alliteration *ducentos . . . decem.* See Introd. § 50.

12. decem servos : a small number for a man of his station. **reges atque tetrarchas** : the cognate accusative, or accusative of the inner object, in its extended form. See Introd. § 38. *b. Cf.* Cic. *ad Att.* ix. 2. 3, *Postumus Curtius venit, nihil nisi classes loquens et exercitus.* Tetrarch was a general title for a petty Oriental prince.

13. omnia magna : in apposition with *reges atque tetrarchas; magna* is in predicate relation to *omnia,* — *all things big.*   **mensa tripes** : *i.e.* an old-fashioned table. Cf. Plin. *N.H.* xxxiv. 14, *nam triclinia aerata abacosque et monopodia Cn. Manlium Asia devicta primum invexisse triumpho suo, quem duxit anno urbis DLXVII, L. Piso auctor est.*

14. concha : *i.e.* a shell, instead of the silver salt-cellar which was sometimes the adornment even of a humble table. Cf. *Odes,* ii. 16. 14.   **salis puri** : *i.e. of plain salt,* not flavored with other condiments ; *cf.* Plin. *N.H.* xxxi. 37, *servandis carnibus aptior (sal) acer et siccus, ut Megaricus. Conditur etiam odoribus additis et pulmentari vicem implet.*

15. quamvis crassa : *however coarse it may be.*   **deciens centena** : *sc. milia sestertium* (genitive plural), about $50,000. **dedisses** : jussive subjunctive with conditional force, *if you had given.*

17. erat : apodosis to the condition contrary to fact ; *erat* is used instead of *fuisset* for vividness.

18. mane : here a substantive, a use mainly confined to poetry

and to post-Augustan prose.   **nil fuit umquam** : *there never was
anything.*   With the use of the neuter, *cf.* i. 6. 55, *dixere quid essem;
Odes,* i. 12. 17.   Introd. § 43. *b.*

19. sic impar sibi : *so inconsistent; cf.* line 9, *nil aequale homini
fuit illi.*   **nunc** : *at this point.*   **dicat** : *may say;* genuine
potential subjunctive, without an implied apodosis.   See B. 280. 1.
quid tu ? *how about yourself ?*   *sc. facis,* and note the emphatic *tu.*

20. immo : *oh, yes.* *Immo* contradicts or corrects a preceding statement, and has therefore the general meaning ' yes ' after a negative
and ' no ' after an affirmative sentence.   **minora** : this word comes in
the nature of a rhetorical surprise, since from the form of the sentence
we should expect *maiora* or *magna.*   See note on *bonorum,* i. 1. 79.

21. Maenius : a typical figure in the satires of Lucilius.

22. ut ignotum : *i.e.* as if we did not know you.   **dare verba** :
deceive, give words instead of the reality ; a common expression in
comedy.   *Cf.* Plaut. *Capt.* 651, *verba mihi data esse video, etc.*

23. egomet mi : note the strong emphasis on the first personal
pronoun.

24. stultus et improbus : note the emphatic position.   **notari** :
for the infinitive with *dignus,* see Introd. § 46. *a.*

25. pervideas . . . inunctis : *look upon your own faults like a
purblind man with anointed eyes.* *Mala* is a stronger expression than
vitia; cf. the ' beam ' and the ' mote ' of scripture.

26. in : *in the case of.*   **acutum** : accusative of the inner object ;
see note on line 12 above.   For a similar phrase, see Lucr. iv. 802,
acute cernere; for a similar construction, i. 8. 41.

27. aquila : *cf. Il.* xvii. 673,—

> Ὣς ἄρα φωνήσας ἀπέβη ξανθὸς Μενέλαος,
> πάντοσε παπταίνων ὥστ' αἰετός, ὅν ῥά τέ φασιν
> ὀξύτατον δέρκεσθαι ὑπουρανίων πετεηνῶν.

serpens Epidaurius : the serpent was regarded by the Greeks as
keen-sighted, whence the name δράκων (from δέρκομαι, δρακεῖν).   The
symbol of Asklepios, whose principal shrine was at Epidaurus, was a
serpent.   When the temple to Asklepios (Aesculapius) was built on
the island in the Tiber, a serpent was brought to it from Epidaurus,
as the representative of the god.

28. vitia . . . tua : both the faults referred to in lines 29–32 are
mentioned by Horace as characteristic of himself.   *Cf. Epist.* i. 20.
25 and i. 1. 94–96.

29. acutis naribus : *keen criticism. Cf.* i. 4. 8, and the opposite
expression, *naris obesae,* in *Epod.* 12. 3.

30. possit : potential subjunctive, like *dicat,* in line 19.

31. rusticius tonso : *his hair is cut in a somewhat countrified
style, and. Cf. Epist.* i. 1. 94. *Tonso* is dative of reference, nearly
equivalent to a possessive genitive.   **toga defluit** : *i.e.* his toga does
not fall about him in carefully arranged folds, but *hangs carelessly.
Cf. Epist.* i. 1. 96.   **male laxus . . . haeret** : *his shoe is too loose,
and will hardly stay on his foot. Male* appears to modify both *laxus*
and *haeret* ἀπὸ κοινοῦ; *cf. illis,* i. 1. 20. For the meaning of *haeret,
cf. Odes,* i. 17. 27 ; iii. 24. 55; *Serm.* i. 10. 49. With the whole passage,
cf. Quint. xi. 3. 137, *et toga et calceus et capillus tam nimia cura
quam neglegentia sunt reprehendenda.*

32. ut melior vir : *sc. sit,* a result clause without an introductory
adverb (see note on i. 1. 95) and with the verb omitted.

34. te ipsum : note the emphasis, expressed both by the words
and their position.

35. concute : *i.e.* give yourself a thorough shaking.   **vitiorum** :
genitive of the whole with *qua ; = qua vitia.*   **inseverit** : subjunctive
in an indirect question, governed by the idea of asking implied in *concute.* The figure is changed to one derived from agriculture, thus
making a mixed metaphor.   **olim** : see note on i. 1. 25.

36. consuetudo : *inseverit* does duty as the verb both of *natura*
and of *consuetudo.* With the latter we should rather expect *insueverit (cf.* i. 4. 105). The similarity of sound between *insueverit* and
inseverit may very likely have determined the choice of the latter
word.

37. filix : the *fern,* called by Virg. *Georg.* ii. 189, *curvis invisa
aratris.* Such weeds were often destroyed by fire. See Plin. *N. H.*
xviii. 300, *sunt qui accendant in arvo et stipulas, magno Vergili
praeconio ; summa autem eius ratio ut herbarum semen exurant.*

38. illuc praevertamur : *let us rather turn to this point.*   **amatorem . . . caecum** : note the emphatic position of the adjective at
the end of its sentence.

39. turpia : *ugly defects, blemishes.* The adjective is used as a
substantive.

40. Balbinum : otherwise unknown. The cognomen is a common
one ; it may have been selected for a doting lover on account of its
resemblance to *balbutire* and *balbus.* See note on line 48 below.

41. vellem : *I could wish,* apodosis of an unfulfilled condition.

42. nomen . . . honestum: whereas as a matter of fact such blindness to one another's faults on the part of friends is stigmatized as flattery.

43. ac pater ut gnati: *sc. vitia non fastidit.*

44. si quod sit vitium = *vitium, si quod sit.*

45. paetum: this word, as well as *pullus, varus,* and *scaurus,* was in actual use as a proper name in distinguished Roman families; all had their origin in personal peculiarities. *Paetus* and *strabo* are thus distinguished by Porph.: *strabo detortis qui est oculis, paetus leniter declinatis.* To be *paetus* was regarded as a mark of beauty, and the term is applied to Venus, *e.g.* by Petron. 68, *quod strabonus est non curo, sicut Venus spectat.* Lines 44–49 seem to be suggested by Lucr. iv. 1160–1169, on the blindness of lovers to the defects of their sweethearts; *cf.* lines 38–39 above.   There is also a parallel passage in Ovid, *Ars Amat.* ii. 657 ff., while the opposite attitude is described in the *Rem. Amor.* 327 ff.   **pullum**: *cf.* Fest. p. 316, *antiqui puerum quem quis amabat pullum eius dicebant.*   **male parvus**: *i.e.* small to the point of deformity, *dwarfed, stunted;* cf. *male laxus,* line 31 above.

47. Sisyphus: Porph. says: *Sisyphus M. Antoni III viri pumilio fuisse dicitur, intra bipedalem staturam, ingenio tamen vivax.*   **varum . . . scaurum**: Porph. thus distinguishes these two defects: *vari appellantur introrsum retortis pedibus: scauri sunt qui extantes talos habent.*

48. balbutit: *fondly calls;* the word really means 'stammer,' or 'lisp,' and is used of ' baby-talk.'   *Cf.* Tibull. ii. 5. 94, *balbaque cum puero dicere verba senem.*

49. parcius: *rather stingily;* the comparatives in this line and in the two following denote a moderate degree of the respective faults. **ineptus**: the positive is used instead of the comparative, because of the meaning of the word, since the fault does not admit degrees. *Cf.* Cic. *de Orat.* ii. 4, 17, *qui in aliquo genere aut inconcinnus aut multus est, is esse ineptus dicitur.*   See i. 6. 16.   The comparative and superlative of the word are rare, but both are used by Quintilian.

50. concinnus: *i.e. commodus,* agreeable.   *Cf.* Plaut. *Mil.* 1024, *age ut tibi maxume concinnumst.*   **amicis**: may be taken both with *videatur* and with *concinnus,* ἀπὸ κοινοῦ.

52. liber: *outspoken.*   **simplex**: *frank, candid.*

53. caldior: the syncopated form of *calidior.* The shorter form, due to a more rapid pronunciation, belongs in general to the colloquial

language. In the Augustan poets the frequent use of the shorter form
is doubtless often due to metrical requirements.

55. invertimus : *i.e.* regard them as faults. In a somewhat similar
sense in *Odes*, iii. 5. 7, *pro curia inversique mores!*

56. incrustare : *befoul*, properly of the deposit left by wine in an
unwashed vessel ; here used figuratively of slander.

57. demissus : *spiritless*, here used in an uncomplimentary sense.
Cf., however, Cic. *de Orat.* ii. 43. 182, *ea omnia, quae proborum, de-
missorum, non acrium, non pertinacium, non litigiosorum, non acer-
borum sunt, valde benevolentiam conciliant.*

58. tardo . . . pingui : *tardo* is here used in a complimentary, or
at least in a neutral, sense ; *pingui*, with depreciatory force. *Cf.*
pingue ingenium, ii. 6. 14.

61. vigent crimina : *i.e.* slander is believed.

62. fictum : *a dissembler*, from *fingere*, 'make up.' *Cf.* English
' fiction.'

63. simplicior quis et est : *et* serves as a connective with the
preceding sentence. Note the order, which is not uncommon in
poetry.

64. libenter obtulerim : *have freely shown myself. Obtulerim* is
subjunctive in a clause of characteristic. The parenthetical clause,
qualem . . . obtulerim, refers only to *simplicior*, not to what
follows.

66. communi sensu : *tact ; cf.* Sen. *Benef.* i. 12. 3, *nemo tam stultus
est, ut monendus sit, ne cui gladiatores aut venationem iam munere
edito mittat, et vestimenta aestiva bruma . . .; sit in beneficio sensus
communis. Tempus, locum observet.*

68. nemo : emphasized by its position, between *vitiis* and *sine*.
Note the anastrophe.

69. urgetur : *loaded down*, as if one carried them in a bag on his
back. *Cf.* ii. 3. 299, and the note ; Catull. 22. 20, *Suus cuique attri-
butus est error, Sed non videmus manticae quod in tergo est.* **amicus
dulcis** : *a kindly friend. Cf.* Cic. *de Amic.* 24. 90, *scitum est illud
Catonis, melius de quibusdam acerbos inimicos mereri quam eos
amicos, qui dulces videantur.*

71. inclinet : like the beam of the balance. *Cf. in trutina . . .*
eadem, line 72.

72. hac lege : *on this condition.*

74. illius : scanned _ ᴗ ᴗ .

76. quatenus : *since*, ' as long as.' See note on i. 1. 64.   **excidi** :

sc. nequit, implied in *nequeunt. Cf.* Lucr. iii. 310, *nec radicitus evelli mala posse putandumst.*

77. stultis : according to the Stoics, vices were the result of *stultitia.*

80. tollere : *to remove* from the table. *Cf.* ii. 8. 10.

81. ligurrierit: *cf.* ii. 4. 79, *dum furta ligurrit.* Subjunctive as part of the condition.

82. Labeone : Porph. says : *M. Antistius Labeo praetorius, iuris etiam peritus, memor libertatis, in qua natus erat, multa contumaciter adversus Caesarem dixisse et fecisse dicitur, propter quod nunc Horatius adulans Augusto insanum eum dicit.*

83. furiosius : implying a more violent madness than *insanus. Cf.* Cic. *Tusc. Disp.* iii. 5. 11, *hanc enim insaniam, quae iuncta stultitia patet latius, a furore disiungimus . . . itaque non est scriptum (in duodecim tabulis) si insanus, sed si furiosus escit.* Here the word is used with ironical exaggeration.

85. insuavis : the opposite of *dulcis,* line 69. **acerbus :** *nay, even harsh,* a stronger expression than *insuavis.*

86. Rusonem : Porph. says : *Octavius Ruso acerbus faenerator fuisse traditur, idem historiarum scriptor.* See note on *Fabium,* i. 1. 14. **debitor aeris :** *the debtor,* in which meaning *debitor* alone is frequent and classical.

87. Kalendae : the monthly interest was due on the Kalends, hence the epithet *tristes,* from the point of view of the debtor. The word is one of a very few in which the letter *k* is retained in classical Latin, doubtless on account of its occurrence in legal formulas.

88. mercedem : *the interest,* in distinction from the principal, *nummos.* **unde unde extricat :** *gets together somehow or other. Unde unde* has the force of *undecumque* (*cf.* Lucr. vi. 1017). The expression occurs only here in classical Latin, unless it be read in Catull. 67. 27, and is probably colloquial. **amaras . . . historias audit :** *i.e.* the creditor forces his unhappy debtor to listen to the reading of his works.

89. porrecto iugulo : as if awaiting the stroke of the executioner's axe. **captivus ut :** *like a prisoner;* explanatory *ut; cf.* i. 1. 108, *ut avarus.*

90. catillum . . . tritum : *i.e.* a rare old bowl. *Cf.* ii. 3. 21, *Quo vafer ille pedes lavisset Sisyphus aere;* and Mart. viii. 6. 9, *Hi duo longaevo censentur Nestore fundi : Pollice de Pylio trita columba nitet.*

92. ante : temporal in sense, modifying *sustulit.*

95. fide: a form of the dative, found in early Latin and in poetry; originally a locative. See B. *App.* 174.   **sponsum negarit**: *should disown his bond.*

96. quis: dative.   **paria . . . peccata**: this was the view of the Stoics. *Cf.* Cic. *Mur.* 29. 61, *omnia peccata esse paria, omne delictum scelus esse nefarium.*   *Fere* qualifies the statement somewhat.

97. sensus moresque: *cf.* Cic. *de Fin.* iv. 19. 55, *recte facta omnia aequalia, omnia peccata paria. Quae cum magnifice primo dici viderentur, considerata minus probabantur ; sensus enim cuiusque et natura rerum atque ipsa veritas clamabat quodam modo non posse adduci, ut inter eas res, quas Zeno exaequaret, nihil interesset.*

99 f. are evidently modelled on Lucr. v. 780 ff.

99. primis: *primeval.*   **animalia**: *creatures*, living things, not yet worthy the name of men.

100. glandem: used generally for food, as the chief article of diet of primitive man.   *Cf.* Lucr. v. 939, *glandiferas inter curabant corpora quercus.*   **cubilia**: *cf.* Lucr. v. 969 ff., *Silvestria membra Nuda dabant terrae, nocturno tempore capti, Circum se foliis ac frondibus involventes.*

101. unguibus: *cf.* Lucr. v. 1283 ff., *Arma antiqua manus ungues dentesque fuerunt, Et lapides et item silvarum fragmina rami . . . Posterius ferri vis est aerisque reperta.*   **porro**: *in due course.*

102. post: here used as an adverb = *postea. Cf. ante*, line 92 above.

103. verba . . . nominaque: *i.e.* verbs and nouns, the two great divisions of language, here used for language itself.   **voces . . . notarent**: *i.e.* give articulate form to their cries (*voces*) and express their feelings ; zeugma. *Notarent* is final subjunctive. *Cf.* Lucr. v. 1087, *varii sensus animalia cogunt Muta tamen cum sint, varias emittere voces.*

105. oppida . . . munire: *cf.* Lucr. v. 1108, *condere coeperunt urbis.*   **ponere leges**: *to make laws;* a somewhat unusual expression, corresponding to the Greek θέσθαι νόμους. *Cf.* Cic. *Verr.* 2. 5. 11. 28, *iste . . . illis legibus, quae in poculis ponebantur, diligenter obtemperabat.*

106. ne: final.

111. fateare necesse est: a favorite expression with Lucr., *e.g.* i. 399, *esse in rebus inane tamen fateare necessest.*

112. evolvere: *unroll*, like a scroll.   **mundi**: *the world*, mankind; the earliest known instance of this use of the word.

113. nec natura potest: *i.e.* men cannot by nature. With the sentiment, *cf.* Sen. *Epist.* 97. 15, *illic dissentiamus cum Epicuro, ubi dicit nihil iustum esse natura.*

114. diversis: *from the opposite, i.e.* evil.   *Cf.* i. 1. 3, *diversa sequentis*, and the note.

115. vincet: *prove.*   **tantundem idemque**: referring respectively to quantity and quality.

116 f. *Cf.* Gell. xi. 18. 3, (Draco) *furem cuiusmodicumque furti supplicio capitis poeniendum esse et alia pleraque nimis severe censuit sanxitque.*

117. divum: with the genitive ending *-um*, which was displaced for the most part in *o*-stems by the ending *-orum* (after the analogy of the pronominal ending *-arum* of the *a*-stems). It was retained in some words, and is frequently found in *deum* and *divum.* **legerit**: *stolen*, lit. *gathered; cf.* English 'sacrilegious.'

118. aequas: *equitable, just.*

119. scutica: *a leather thong*, a milder instrument than the scourge (*flagellum*), which was set with knobs of bone or metal, to tear the flesh.

120. ut: we should expect *ne.* Apparently we have a kind of anacoluthon, as if *verisimile non est* or something similar were going to follow.   **ferula**: *the cane*, used in punishing refractory children and schoolboys.   *Cf.* Mart. x. 62. 10, *ferulaeque tristes, sceptra paedagogorum.*

121. pares res . . . latrociniis: a combination of two constructions, *esse paria furta latrociniis* and *esse pares res furta et latrocinia. Cf.* note on line 9, *velut qui . . . hostem.*

122. magnis: governed by *simile*, brachylogy for *falce simili ei* (*falci*) *qua magna.*

124. si dives, *etc.:* a common expression; *cf. Epist.* i. 1. 107 ; Cic. *Mur.* 29. 61 ; *solos sapientes esse . . . si servitutem serviant, reges*, etc.

126. cur optas quod habes? *i.e. regnum*, with reference to 123–124.   **pater Chrysippus**: so called as one of the heads of the Stoic school; *cf. Ennius pater, Epist.* i. 19. 7, as the father of Roman poetry.

127. crepidas: high Greek shoes, as contrasted with *soleae*, *sandals.*

128. nec: *nor even.*   **sutor est sapiens**: in the same way the *sapiens* is potentially, not actually, king.

129. ut . . . tacet: a localized version of Diog. vii. 125, πάντα
εὖ ποιεῖν τὸν σοφόν, ὡς καὶ πάντα φαμὲν τὰ αὐλήματα εὖ αὐλεῖν τὸν
'Ισμηνίαν. Note the indicative with *quamvis*, and see Introd. § 45. *b*.

130. modulator: *musician*, a broader term than *cantor*. **Alfenus**: apparently a barber of the day, who abandoned his trade and
became a lawyer. **vafer**: this term is often applied to the law and
to lawyers; *cf.* ii. 2. 131, *vafri inscitia iuris.*

136. rumperis: *you burst*, with anger or with 'barking.' Note
the passive used with the force of the middle. **latras**: *bark*, applied humorously to the Cynics, whose name was derived from κύων,
dog. **magnorum maxime regum**: ironical; *great potentate
though you are.* Note the alliteration.

137. ne longum faciam: *in short; cf.* i. 1. 120. **dum . . .
rex ibis**: *while you go, king that you are. Dum* with the future is
rare. It expresses time contemporaneous and coextensive with
vivam. **quadrante**: a fourth of an *as*, about a quarter of a
cent.

138. stipator . . . sectabitur: *i.e.* your only body-guard is. *Cf.*
Varr. *L. L.* vii. 52, *qui circum latera erant regi . . . postea a stipa-
tione stipatores appellarunt.*

139. Crispinus: *cf.* i. 1. 120. **et**: correlative with -*que* in line
141. This combination is rather rare, though it occurs in Cicero. *Cf.*
Enn. *Ann.* 199 V., *Hos et ego in pugna vici victusque sum ab isdem;*
Cic. *de Fin.* v. 22. 64, *quis est quin intellegat et eos . . . fuisse . . .
nosque . . . duci.*

140. stultus: *through folly*, an appositive adjective. *Cf.* line 77
for the force of the word.

SERMO IV.

1. Eupolis . . . poetae: the three greatest of the writers of the
Old Comedy, corresponding to Aeschylus, Sophocles, and Euripides in
Tragedy. *Cf.* Quint. x. 1. 66, *plures eius auctores, Aristophanes ta-
men et Eupolis Cratinusque praecipui. Tragoedias primus in lucem
Aeschylus protulit . . . sed longe clarius inlustraverunt hoc opus
Sophocles atque Euripides.* Of Eupolis (died about 411 B.C.) and
Cratinus (died about 422) only scanty fragments have come down to
us; of Aristophanes (444–388) we have eleven plays, of which two,
the *Ecclesiazusae* and the *Plutus*, belong to the Middle Comedy.

2. alii . . virorum est: for *alii viri, quorum, etc., cf.* i. 1. 1

The reference is to the less famous representatives of the Old Comedy, such as Crates, Phrynichus, *etc.*

3. describi: *i.e.* held up for censure ; *cf. Epist.* ii. 1. 154. On the construction, see note on *notari*, i. 3. 24.   **malus ac fur**: *cf. malos fures*, i. 1. 77.

4. foret = *esset*. This form of the verb is rare in Cicero and is not found in Caesar. It is frequent in Plautus and Terence, and may be archaic or colloquial. Its use was originally confined to conditions contrary to fact and to expressions having a future force.   **alioqui**: *in other respects;* a colloquial word, apparently first used in literature by Horace (Lucr. iii. 414 is doubtful; see Lachmann's note), again in i. 6. 66. It occurs frequently in Pliny's letters.

5. famosus: used in a bad sense, *notorious, infamous.*   **libertate**: *freedom* of speech, a characteristic of the Old Comedy, before it was restrained by law ; *cf.* Quint. x. 1. 65, *antiqua comoedia . . . facundissimae libertatis est et in insectandis vitiis praecipua; Ars Poet.* 281 ff.

6. hinc . . . pendet: *i.e.* takes these as his model. *Cf. Epist.* i. 1. 105, *de te pendentis amici.*   **Lucilius**: see Introd. § 20.

7. mutatis . . . pedibus: *i.e.* using the dactylic hexameter, in which most of the Satires of Lucilius were written, instead of the iambic trimeter of Attic Comedy.

8. emunctae . . . naris: *keen-scented*, in discovering the weaknesses of others. *Cf.* i. 3. 29 ; ii. 2. 89 ; and the opposite expression, *naris obesae*, in *Epod.* 12. 3.   **durus componere**: *harsh in the composition.* For the construction of *componere*, see Introd. § 46. *a.*

9. hoc: *in this* (*i.e.* the following) *respect.*

10. ut magnum: *i.e.* as if it were a great thing. Explanatory *ut*; *cf.* i. 1. 108.   **stans pede in uno**: *i.e.* easily, without effort, apparently proverbial. *Cf.* the reverse expression in Quint. xii. 9. 18, *in his actionibus omni, ut agricolae dicunt, pede standum est.*

11. flueret lutulentus: *i.e.* like a stream swollen and turbid from the spring freshets, whose water was not fit to use until it had been allowed to stand for a while and settle.   **tollere**: *blot out. Cf.* i. 10. 50, *fluere hunc lutulentum, saepe ferentem Plura quidem tollenda relinquendis.*   **velles**: subjunctive in a clause of characteristic, *that you wished.*

12. garrulus: *a wordy fellow;* returning to Lucilius after the digression in lines 9–11. *Cf. sermo merus* in line 48. The style is colloquial.

13. ut multum: *i.e.* as to the amount of his work, ' as to its being much.'   **nil moror**: *I don't care a bit for that,* a colloquial expression.

14. Crispinus : see note on i. 1. 120.   **minimo**: *sc. pignore, at long odds, i.e.* offering a large wager against a small one, the opposite of our form of expression. *Cf.* Catull. 44. 4, *quovis Sabinum pignore esse contendunt;* Virg. *Ecl.* 3. 31, *tu dic, mecum quo pignore certes.* **provocat**: *challenges, sc. contendere,* and *cf.* note on *minimo* above.

15. accipe iam : the repeated imperative shows the impatience of Crispinus, who counts on an easy victory.

16. custodes : *umpires,* to see that there was a fair contest, without cheating or misrepresentation.

17. di bene fecerunt: *i.e.* the gods be thanked.   **quodque**: hyperbaton ; -*que* really connects *inopis* and *pusilli; cf.* i. 6. 43 ; i. 8. 2 ; ii. 3. 139, *etc.*

18. loquentis : *i.e.* so that I speak ; *loquentis* agrees with *animi,* a loose form of expression characteristic of colloquial speech.

20. molliat: subjunctive on account of the idea of expectation or anticipation ; the personal and impersonal ideas are blended, since the person and the thing are identified with each other. See note on *Tantalus,* i. 1. 68.

21. beatus: *sc. est.*   **Fannius** : a parasite of Hermogenes Tigellius ; *cf.* i. 10. 80.   **ultro . . . imagine**: Fannius, without being asked to do so (*ultro*), proffers his books to be read ; *cf. Epist.* i. 12. 23, *si quid petet, ultro defer.* The idea seems to be that Fannius forces his works on a reluctant public, but is happy to have them read under any circumstances. The books are kept in *capsae,* or cylindrical boxes for holding manuscript rolls, and are ornamented with the author's portrait (*imagine*).

22. cum : *whereas;* adversative *cum; cf.* i. 1. 38.

23. volgo recitare : *i.e.* to give a public reading to invited guests, a custom said to have been inaugurated by Asinius Pollio. *Cf.* Sen. *Contr.* 4, Praef. 2, (Asinius Pollio) *primus omnium Romanorum advocatis hominibus scripta sua recitavit.* That Horace read his poems, by request, to his intimate friends, is seen from line 73.   **timentis** : agrees with the genitive implied in *mea* in line 22.

24. genus hoc : *i.e. scripta hoc genus,* satire.   **pluris** : *many,* the logical subject of *sunt,* attracted to the case of *quos.* On the indicative *iuvat* see Introd. § 45. *c.*

26. ab avaritia : *on account of avarice.*   **laborat** : *suffers; is troubled.*

27. capit: *fascinates, i.e.* catches his fancy.

28. argenti splendor . . . aere: *cf. Epist.* i. 6. 17. In *aere*, the reference is doubtless to Corinthian bronzes, which were highly prized. *Cf.* Plin. *Epist.* iii. 6 ; iii. 1. 9.   **stupet**: *has a craze for; cf.* Plin. *Epist.* iii. 1. 9, *sunt in usu et Corinthia, quibus delectatur nec adficitur.*

29. mutat merces: *carries cargoes;* the regular expression; *cf.* Virg. *Ecl.* 4. 38, *nec nautica pinus mutabit merces.*   **surgente a sole ad eum** : *i.e.* from the far east to the west.

30. vespertina . . . regio: *sc. caeli, the west, i.e.* Italy. *Cf.* Lucan, vii. 17, *vespere pacato.*   **quin** : for *quin etiam, nay more.*

32. ampliet ut: *that he may not increase,* depending on *metuens,* with the usual meaning of *ut* after a verb of fearing.

33. versus . . . poetas : used in a general sense. On account of the severity of satirists, they fear and hate all poets.

34. faenum . . . in cornu: at Rome, dangerous cattle were marked this way when driven through the streets. For the comparison of the satirist with an ugly bull, *cf. Epod.* 6. 11, *cave, cave : namque in malos asperrimus Parata tollo cornua.*

35. sibi : dative of advantage, so-called ; *at his witticisms.*

36. chartis inleverit: *scribbled on his paper,* a contemptuous expression.

37. furno: *the* (public) *bakery.*   **lacu**: *the water-tank,* for the general use of the people. *Cf.* Plin. *N. H.* xxxvi. 121, *Agrippa in aedilitate . . . lacus DCC fecit.*

38. pueros et anus: *slaves and old women,* who were notorious sources of gossip.

39. primum : introduces the reply to *odere poetas* in line 33 ; the second point is introduced by *nunc illud quaeram,* in line 64.   **dederim**: potential subjunctive. The perfect in this case does not differ in force from the present.

40. concludere versum: *to write verse;* for *verba pedibus claudendo versum efficere.* The expression for ‘ prose ’ is *oratio soluta,* as opposed to *pedibus claudere.*

41. dixeris : *you would not say.* The apodosis of the protasis implied in *concludere versum.*

42. sermoni propiora : *more like ordinary conversation.* *Cf.* Auct. ad Her. iii. 13. 23, *sermo est oratio remissa et finitima cotidianae locutioni.*

43. ingenium : *intellectual gifts,* not ‘ genius,’ which is rare. **mens divinior** : *inspiration,* ‘ the divine afflatus.’   **os magna sona-**

turum: *the power of lofty expression; magna* is accusative of the inner object.

45. comoedia . . . necne poema esset: *cf.* Cic. *Orat.* 20. 67, *video visum esse nonnullis, Platonis et Democriti locutionem, etsi absit a versu, tamen, quod incitatius feratur et clarissimis verborum luminibus utatur, potius poema putandum quam comicorum poetarum.*

46. acer spiritus ac vis: *fiery inspiration and vigor.*

47. pede certo: *the regular rhythm.*

48. sermo merus: *it being in fact plain prose,* in apposition with *comoedia* in line 45; *cf. garrulus,* line 12 above.   **at**: introduces the words of a defender of comedy as poetry; *cf. Ars Poet.* 93 f. The scene which follows is from an unknown *palliata,* or comedy based on Greek life.   **ardens**: *sc. irā.*

49. meretrice . . . amica: ablative of cause; *cf.* Plaut. *Merc.* 443, *sanus non est ex amore;* 447, *insanior ex amore.*

50. filius . . . recuset: a common incident in comedy.

51. ambulet: *sc. in publico.* Such revels were common enough; the disgrace consisted in carrying them on publicly in broad daylight.

52. Pomponius: otherwise unknown. Evidently a notorious young prodigal.   **istis**: *i.e.* those to which you refer, *quae pater ardens effundit.*

54. puris . . . verbis: *unadorned language; sine figuris et magno sono,* Ps-Acron.

55. quem si dissolvas: *i.e.* of such a sort that if you should write it in prose order. *Dissolvas* means to free from the trammels of metre; see note on line 40.

56. personatus . . . pater: *the father in the play, i.e.* the actor wearing the mask of a father. Masks seem to have been worn by comic actors soon after the time of Terence. The figure of the mask and the color of the hair differed according to the character impersonated. In earlier times the characters were distinguished by their wigs and their dress.   **his**: dative of separation with *eripias.* In good prose we should have *his rebus,* since the form *his* is ambiguous as regards its gender. See Introd. § 49. *b.* **ego quae nunc**: *sc. scribo,* implied in *scripsit.*

58. tempora certa modosque: *i.e.* the rhythm and metre; *cf. pede certo,* line 47. The features which gave satire the outward form of poetry were the metre, the caesura, and the poetic word order, not the language.

60. solvas = *dissolvas;* see line 55.   **postquam . . . refregit**

from Ennius, *Annales*, 270 V., evidently alluding to the opening of
the temple of Janus. *Cf.* Virg. *Aen.* vii. 607, *belli ferratos rumpit
Saturnia postes*. If this verse of Ennius should be written in prose
order, the language would still be that of poetry.

63. alias : this promise was kept many years later by the publication of the *Ars Poetica*.   **iustum . . . poema :** *i.e.* real poetry ;
sc. quaeram and *satura*, implied in *hoc genus scribendi* in line 5.

65. Sulcius . . . et Caprius : these two men belonged to the
class which made a business of bringing criminals to justice for the
sake of the reward. Though less objectionable than the *delatores* of
later times, they were held in disrepute ; *cf.* Cic. *Brut.* 34. 130, *M.
Brutus, in quo magnum fuit, Brute, dedecus generi vestro . . . magi-
stratus non petivit, sed fuit accusator vehemens et molestus ; De
Off.* ii. 14. 50, *duri hominis vel potius vix hominis videtur periculum capitis inferre multis.*

66. rauci male : *very hoarse,* or with unpleasantly hoarse voices,
from constant and vehement pleading in court. *Cf. male laxus,*
i. 3. 31.   **libellis :** *indictments, i.e.* note-books containing their
accusations.

69. ut sis tu : *suppose you are,* concessive *ut : cf.* Ter. *Hec.* 296,
ut taceam, quoivis facile scitu est quam fuerim miser. Note the emphatic *tu.*

70. sim : potential subjunctive.   **Capri neque Sulci :** *sc. similis.*

71. taberna : *book-stall.*   **habeat :** optative subjunctive.
pila : one of the pillars which separated the arcade in which the
book-stall was located from the street. On these were hung lists of
the books for sale within. *Cf. Ars Poet.* 373 ; Mart. i. 117. 10 : —

> Contra Caesaris est forum taberna.
> Scriptis postibus hinc et inde totis
> Omnes ut cito perlegas poetas.

A prominent firm of booksellers at Rome was that of the Sosii,
Epist. i. 20. 2.   **meos :** emphatic, contrasting Horace's *libelli* with
those of Sulcius and Caprius.   **libellos :** *humble works.* The
diminutive is chosen for the sake of a play on the double meaning
of *libelli ; cf.* line 66.

72. quis : dative. See note on *qui,* i. 1. 1.   **quis . . . insudet :**
the subjunctive has a final force, *for the hands of the vulgar to soil.*
Hermogenis Tigelli : the *optimus modulator* of i. 3. 129 ; not the
same as the Tigellius of i. 3. 3. The transposition of the *nomen* and

cognomen is rare in classical prose, but very common in later Latin. It never occurs where all three names are given ; cf. *Odes*, ii. 2. 3 ; *Serm*. i. 6. 12 ; i. 7. 1.

73. amicis : *i.e.* not *volgo ;* cf. line 23 and the note.   **idque coactus** : *and that only on compulsion.*

75. lavantes : *i.e.* in the public baths.   *Cf.* Petron. 92, *dum lavor, paene vapulavi, quia conatus sum circa solium sedentibus carmen recitare.*

77. illud : referring to the following *num . . . faciant.*   **sensu** : *sc. communi*, and *cf.* i. 3. 66.

78. alieno : *unseasonable.*   **laedere gaudes** : the reply of the imaginary opponent.   *Cf.* Lucil. 913 L., *Gaudes, cum de me ista foris sermonibus differs, Et male dicendo in multis sermonibus differs.*

79. hoc : accusative, referring to *laedere.*   **studio** : *purposely. Cf.* Cic. *Rosc. Am.* 91, *ut omnes intellegant me non studio accusare, sed officio defendere.*   **pravus** : predicate adjective = *cum pravus sis.*   **petitum** : the participle, — *where have you found this charge to make against me ?*

80. quis : *any one ;* for *aliquis*, on account of the implied *num.* **denique** : *in short, i.e.* not to go over a list of all the possible sources of the criticism.   •

81. cum quibus : Horace does not use *cum* in the enclitic position with relatives ; *cf. Odes*, ii. 7. 6.   **absentem** : *behind his back*, lit. *in his absence.*   **rodit** : *backbites, slanders.*

82. qui non defendit : *cf.* lines 94–103. The final syllable of *defendit* is here long. This is not a reminiscence of an original long quantity, but is doubtless due to the analogy of such cases. *Cf. figit, Odes*, iii. 24. 5 ; *agit, Serm.* ii. 3. 260 ; and see Introd. § 57. *d.*

84. commissa tacere : *keep a secret ; cf. Epist.* i. 18. 70, *nec retinent patulae commissa fideliter aures.*

85. niger : *black-hearted*, a scoundrel, in contrast with *animae candidae ; cf.* i. 5. 41. *Cf.* Cic. *Caec.* 10. 27, *Phormio, nec minus niger nec minus confidens quam ille Terentianus.*   **hunc . . . caveto** : a parody of an oracular utterance ; *cf.* Liv. xxv. 12. 5, *amnem, Tro-iugena, fuge Cannam.*

86. videas : *you can see ;* an example of the relatively rare ' can '-potential ; see Introd. § 45. *d.*   **quaternos** : *i.e.* four on each of the three couches. Ordinarily three was the maximum number ; *cf.* ii. 8, Outline.

87. aspergere : *slander*, lit. *besprinkle ;* used in the same figurative sense by Auct. ad Her. iv. 49. 62, *circum inspectans huc et illuc, sī quem reperiat cui aliquid mali . . . lingua aspergere possit.*

88. qui praebet aquam: *i.e.* the host (*convivator*, ii. 8. 73) who had water passed around among his guests at the beginning of the dinner; *cf.* Petr. 31, *tandem discubuimus, pueris Alexandrinis aquam in manus nivatam infundentibus;* or used of the hot and cold water furnished for mixing with the wine; *cf.* Juv. v. 63, *quando rogatus adest calidae gelidaeque minister ?*   **hunc**: *sc. aspergere amat.*

89. aperit . . . Liber: *cf. Odes,* iii. 21. 13 ff.   **praecordia**: regarded as the seat of the feelings.   We should say 'heart.'

90. liber: *frank; cf. libertate,* line 5.

91. nigris: *cf. niger,* line 85.

92. pastillos: accusative of the inner object.   The word is a diminutive, cognate with *panis.*   For the meaning, *cf.* Mart. i. 87. 1, *Ne gravis hesterno fragres, Fescennia, vino, Pastillos Cosmi luxuriosa voras.*

94. Capitolini: Porph. says: *Petillius Capitulinus cum Capitoli curam ageret, coronae subreptae de Capitulio causam dixit absolutusque a Caesare est.*   It is known that Petillius Capitolinus was accused of theft and acquitted in spite of strong evidence against him.   The charge mentioned by Porph. may well have been invented to account for the name Capitolinus, since the crime was a proverbial one; *cf.* Plaut. *Trin.* 83, *Nam nunc ego si te surrupuisse suspicer Iovi coronam de capite ex Capitolio; Men.* 941, *at ego te sacram coronam surrupuisse Iovi scio.*

96. me . . . amicoque: a hypermetric verse.   Horace has but one other in his hexameters (i. 6. 102).   Such lines occur several times in the *Odes* (*e.g.* iv. 2. 22) and are not uncommon in Virgil, especially with lines ending in *-que.*

98. in urbe: instead of being in exile.

100. nigrae: with reference to line 85.   **sucus lolliginis**: *cf.* Plin. *N. H.* ix. 84, (*saepiae*) *ubi sensere se adprehendi, effuso atramento, quod pro sanguine his est, infuscata aqua absconduntur.*

101. aerugo: *malice,* lit. *verdigris.   Cf.* Mart. x. 33. 5, *viridi tinctos aerugine versus.*   **quod** = *at id ; cf. quae,* i. 1. 36.

102. prius: *before that, i.e.* he will not even think such things, much less write them down.   **ut si quid**: *i.e. ut promitto, si quid.*

104. hoc mihi iuris: *this privilege,* which is my right; *iuris* is genitive of the whole, governed by *hoc.*

105. dabis: future with the force of an imperative.   **in-**

suevit : with a double accusative, after the analogy of verbs of teaching. *Cf. adsuescere* with the accusative and the ablative of association (or the dative), ii. 2. 109.   **hoc** : *i.e. liberius dicere.*

106. ut fugerem : depends on *notando.*   **vitiorum quaeque** : may be taken both with *fugerem* and *notando*, ἀπὸ κοινοῦ. *Cf. illis*, i. 1. 20.

109. ut male . . . vivat : *how wretchedly young Albius lives*, in a material, not in a moral, sense. The reference is perhaps the same as in line 28.

110. Baius : a Roman gentile name, known from inscriptions. Nothing further is known about the individual mentioned here. **documentum** : *lesson* (*cf. docere*) ; in apposition with the preceding *ut*-clause ; *cf. sermo merus*, line 48.

112. Scetani : otherwise unknown.

115. sapiens : *your philosopher;* see note on i. 1. 38.

116. causas reddet : *will explain.*

118. custodis : *i.e.* a *paedagogus.* See i. 6. 81, *Ipse mihi custos incorruptissimus omnis Circum doctores aderat.*   **vitam** : *health.*

120. nabis sine cortice : a proverbial expression ; *cf.* Plaut. *Aul.* 595, *Quasi pueri qui nare discunt scirpea induitur ratis, qui laborent minus, facilius ut nent et moveant manus.*

121. formabat : *moulded*, a very common metaphor ; *cf. Epist.* ii. 1. 128 ; ii. 2. 8 ; Cic. *Arch.* 3. 4, *ut primum ex pueris excessit Archias atque ab eis artibus quibus aetas puerilis ad humanitatem informari solet.*   **iubebat** : *sc. aliquid*, since Horace does not use an *ut*-clause with *iubere ; ut facerem quid* depends on the verb of saying implied with *habes auctorem.* The apodosis to *sive iubebat* is not *obiciebat*, but the verb of saying understood in line 122. The style is strongly colloquial.

122. quo : *in accordance with which.*

123. iudicibus selectis : the list of those from whom jurors were selected, recorded in the *album iudicum.* At this time senators, *equites*, and *tribuni aerarii* were eligible for such service. On their qualifications, see Cic. *Cluent.* 43. 121, *praetores urbani, qui iurati debent optimum quemque in lectos iudices referre.*

126. avidos : *gluttons;* the adjective is used substantively. **vicinum funus** : *i.e. vicini funus; cf. aliena opprobria*, line 128.

127. sibi parcere : *i.e.* look out for their health, by refraining from over-eating ; *cf. Epist.* i. 7. 11, *Ad mare descendet vates tuus et sibi parcet.*

128. aliena = *aliis obiecta.*

129. ex hoc : *sc. more patris, on account of this early training.*
sanus ab illis : *sc. vitiis, free from those faults.*

130. perniciem : *danger* to life and health ; *cf.* line 118.   **quis**
ignoscas : *sc. vitiis, pardonable faults.* See i. 3. 20 and 140 ; i. 6. 65.
Quis is dative ; *cf.* line 72 above. The subjunctive is a potential
characterizing clause, being parallel with the adjective *mediocribus.*

131. istinc : *i.e. ex istis vitiis.*

132. abstulerit: used absolutely ; *cf. aufers,* ii. 3. 127 ; *aufer,*
ii. 3. 236.   **liber** : *outspoken, frank ; cf.* line 90.

133. consilium proprium : *communion with myself.*   **lectulus** :
' *my own little bed,*' where he lay and reflected, or perhaps a couch for
studying (*lectus lucubratorius*). Note the force of the diminutive ; *cf.*
Cic. *Cat.* i. 4. 9 ; Ov. *Trist.* i. 11. 37 : —

> ' Non haec in nostris, ut quondam, scribimus hortis,
>   Nec, consuete, meum, lectule, corpus habes.'

134. porticus : the colonnades were favorite resorts, especially in
bad weather, or in the heat of the day.   This was particularly true of
the *porticus* adjoining Pompey's theatre ; *cf.* Catull. 55. 3 f. : —

> ' Te campo quaesivimus minore,
>   Te in circo, te in omnibus libellis
>   Te in templo summi Iovis sacrato.
>   In Magni simul ambulatione
>   Femellas omnes, amice, prendi.'

desum mihi : *neglect myself ; cf.* i. 9. 56. ii. 1. 17. He tries to correct his faults by meditating on them, as well as on those of others.

135. dulcis . . . occurram : *i.e.* be agreeable to the friends
whom I meet.

136. quidam : *so and so.*   **non belle** : *sc. fecit.*

137. olim : *ever.* See note on i. 1. 25.

138. compressis . . . labris: a sign of earnest thought. *Cf.*
Pers. iii. 82, *exporrecto trutinantur verba labello.*

139. inludo chartis : *I amuse myself by putting my thoughts on
paper, cf.* i. 10. 37, *haec ego ludo.*   **mediocribus illis** : see line 130
above.

140. concedere : *cf.* line 143, and note the play on the two meanings of the word.

143. Iudaei : Jews were numerous in Rome in Horace's day and very active in making converts. *Cf.* Cic. *Flacc.* 28. 66, *scis, quanta sit* (*Iudaeorum*) *manus, quanta concordia, quantum valeant in contionibus.*

SERMO V.

1. magna . . . Roma : the adjective emphasizes the contrast between Rome and the little village with its *hospitium modicum.* **Aricia** : sixteen miles[1] southeast of Rome, on the lower slope of the Alban Hills. It was about three miles from the celebrated temple and grove of Diana, on the *lacus Nemorensis.* See Macaulay, *Lake Regillus,* 171 ff. : —

> ' From the still glassy lake that sleeps
>   Beneath Aricia's trees —
> Those trees in whose dim shadow
> The ghastly priest doth reign,
> The priest who slew the slayer,
> And shall himself be slain.'

2. hospitio modico : *a modest inn;* cf. Cic. *de Sen.* 23. 84, *ex vita ita discedo tamquam ex hospitio, non tamquam ex domo.* To judge from the references in literature, and from the ruins of inns found at Pompeii, they were never very attractive; *cf. Epist.* i. 11. 11, *neque qui Capua Romam petit imbre lutoque Aspersus volet in caupona vivere.* The well-to-do traveller usually had friends with whom he could stop. **Heliodorus** : unknown, except for this reference of Horace.

3. Graecorum . . . doctissimus : an exaggerated expression characteristic of the mock-heroic style which Horace adopts in several parts of this satire (see notes on lines 9, 20, 51, 73), a form of wit common in modern times. **inde** : *next.* **Forum Appi** : twenty-seven miles beyond Aricia, at the beginning of the Pomptine marshes. A canal led from there to the spring and grove of Feronia, about sixteen miles away.

4. differtum : *crowded,* lit. *stuffed,* apparently a colloquial word, used in a humorous sense; *cf. Epist.* i. 6. 59, *differtum forum;* Caes. *B. C.* iii. 32. 4, *erat plena lictorum et imperiorum provincia, differta praefectis atque exactoribus.* **nautis** : *boatmen,* not 'sailors.' **malignis** : *grasping, extortionate,* contrasted with *benignus* in the sense of *generous; cf.* i. 1. 29, *perfidus caupo.*

---

[1] All the distances are given in Roman miles, = 4854 feet.

5. hoc iter : *i.e.* the forty-three miles from Rome to Forum Appi. **ignavi :** *since we were inclined to take things easily.* For the adjective with causal force, *cf.* i. 3. 85, *acerbus odisti ;* i. 4. 79, *pravus facis.*   **altius . . . praecinctis :** *for more rapid travellers,* evidently a general expression, though derived originally from travel on foot ; *cf.* Petr. 19 ; Sen. *Epist.* 33. 2 (*alte cinctos*); *etc.* When a Roman wished to walk rapidly, he would naturally gird his tunic high, to leave the legs free.   **ac :** *than.* Horace is the first to use *atque* (*ac*) in this sense after a comparative without a preceding negative (Cic. *ad Att.* xiii. 3, is doubtful). The usage is apparently colloquial. It occurs frequently in the *Sermones, e.g.* i. 6. 130 ; i. 10. 59 ; *etc.*

6. unum : *sc. iter, a single day's journey.*   **minus est gravis :** because the road was paved with large blocks of stone, which would cause a carriage, if driven rapidly, to jolt badly. It is difficult to see how this expression can refer to any other mode of travelling, though there is no mention of mules or carriages, as in other parts of the Satire.   **Appia :** used as a substantive, with ellipsis of *via ; cf. Epod.* 4. 14, *Appiam mannis terit.*

7. hic : *here, i.e.* at Forum Appi.   **aquam :** Porph. says, *hodieque Foro Appi viatores propter aquam, quae ibi deterrima est, manere vitant.* The meaning doubtless is that the water was too bad to drink, even when mixed with wine.

8. indico bellum : *declare war against ;* a humorous metaphor. Since the reference is clearly to the water of Forum Appi, the meaning is that Horace took no dinner, or perhaps ate lightly, because he did not venture to risk drinking the water.

9. comites : *i.e.* his fellow-travellers.   **iam nox,** *etc. :* epic diction, used humorously ; see note on *Graecorum . . . doctissimus,* line 3.

10. signa : *i.e.* the constellations ; *cf. Odes,* ii. 8. 10, *taciturna noctis signa.*

11. pueri : the slaves of the travellers.

12. ingerere : historical infinitive, not common in Horace ; *cf.* i. 9. 9 ; *Epist.* i. 7. 67.   **huc appelle . . . satis est :** apparently not a dialogue, but the words of the *pueri,* those of the boatmen being omitted.   **trecentos :** used of an indefinite large number ; *cf. Odes,* ii. 14. 5 ; iii. 4. 79. See Introd. § 50.

13. aes : *the money, i.e.* the fare (*naulum*).   **ligatur :** apparently = *navigio adligatur.*

15. somnos : *sleep ;* for the plural *cf. Odes,* i. 25. 3 ; ii. 16. 15; *Epod.* 5. 96.   **ut :** *while.*

16. prolutus : *soaked. Cf.* Virg. *Aen.* i. 739, *ille impiger hausü
Spumantem pateram et pleno se proluit auro.*   **vappa** : see note on
i. 1. 104.   **viator** : Porph. understood this word to refer collectively
to all the passengers. It seems more probable that it refers to one of
them.

18. pastum : supine.   **retinacula** : *the traces,* by means of
which the mule towed the boat.

19. saxo : instrumental ablative.

20. iamque ... aderat ... cum ... sentimus : a good example of '*cum inversum*' ; B. 288, 2. Here, too, we have a parody
of the heroic style ; see note on line 3.

21. donec : *and then.* **cerebrosus** : *hot-tempered ; cf.* i. 9. 11,
O te, Bolane, cerebri felicem !   **prosilit** : *i.e.* jumps out of the boat.
unus = *quidam,* a unique use of the word.

22. saligno fuste : *a willow cudgel,* doubtless from one of the
trees growing along the bank of the canal.

23. dolat : *belabors,* a colloquial expression. The word is usually
used of hewing timber, and occurs only here in this sense.   **quarta
vix hora** : *i.e.* it was fully ten o'clock. The Roman *hora* was one-
twelfth of the period from sunrise to sunset, and hence differed in
length at various seasons of the year. Its greatest duration was
seventy-five and one-half minutes ; its least, forty-two and one-half.
exponimur : *we are landed ; cf.* Virg. *Aen.* vi. 416, *virum informi
limo glaucaque exponit in ulva.*

24. lavimus : poetic and ante-classical form for *lavamus. Cf.
Odes,* ii. 13. 18.   **Feronia** : an ancient Italian goddess, identified
with Juno, and hence called Juno Feronia. Her temple was three
miles north of Terracina.

25. pransi ; *after having breakfasted.*   **repimus** : *crawl,* making slow progress on account of the steep road. The travellers were
in no haste, since they were to wait for Maecenas and his party at
Anxur.

26. Anxur : the old Volscian name for Terracina. Anxur, however, was at the top of the hill, while the Roman city lay at its
base.

27. venturus erat : probably from a conference with Octavian,
held perhaps at Lanuvium, a favorite resort of his. *Cf.* Suet. *Aug.*
72, *ex secessibus praecipue frequentavit maritima insulasque Campaniae, aut proxima urbi oppida, Lanuvium, Praeneste, Tibur.*

28. Cocceius : L. Cocceius Nerva, *consul suffectus* in 39 B.C., who assisted in making the treaty of Brundisium in 40 B.C. M. Cocceius Nerva, who may have been a brother of Lucius, was great-grandfather of the emperor Nerva.

29. aversos . . . componere amicos : *to bring together friends who were estranged.* The reference is to the reconciliation of Octavian and Antony by the treaty of Brundisium in 40 B.C. See Introd. to the Satire. **soliti** : because they had already done it once.

30. lippus : see note on i. 1. 120.

31. interea : *i.e.* while Horace was attending to his eyes.

32. Capito Fonteius : consul in 33 B.C. He was a friend and partisan of Antony, whom he afterwards accompanied to Syria, whence he was sent on a mission to Cleopatra. On the transposition of the *nomen* and *cognomen*, see note on i. 4. 72. **ad unguem factus homo** : *a polished gentleman.* Porph. says : *translatio a marmorariis qui iuncturas marmorum tum demum perfectas dicunt, si unguis superductus non offendat. Unde iam quaecumque perfectissima esse volumus significare, ad unguem facta dicimus. Cf. Ars Poet.* 294, *castigavit ad unguem.*

33. Antoni . . . amicus : *a bosom friend of Antony. Sc. sit,* and *cf.* Nepos, *Epam.* 2. 1, *eruditus sic ut nemo Thebanus magis ; Cic. de Fin.* i. 4. 11, *scripta multa sunt, sic ut plura nemini e nostris.*

34. Fundos : about twelve miles from Anxur. **Aufidio . . . praetore** : *in the praetorship of Aufidius Luscus,* a satirical expression, as if the vain 'praetor' were as important as a Roman consul. The chief magistrates of the *municipia* had various titles, of which the most common was *duoviri.* According to *C. I. L.* i. 1187 f., the chief magistrates at Fundi were three aediles. *Praetore* may be used for metrical reasons ; Horace frequently uses *praetor* as a typical designation for a magistrate, and twice employs the word in a general sense ; see *Serm.* i. 7. 18 ; *Epist.* ii. 2. 34.

35. scribae : *clerk,* the humble office from which Aufidius had risen. *Cf.* Suet. *Vesp.* 3 (of Vespasian's father-in-law), *nec quicquam amplius quam quaestorio scriba (genitus).*

36. praetextam . . . clavum : the *toga praetexta,* the broad purple stripe on the tunic (*latus clavus*), and the torches borne before him, were rightful *insignia* of Aufidius. He is ridiculed for the display of them which his vanity led him to make. **prunae . . . vatillum** : a pan of coals for lighting the torches (see previous note). Although it was broad daylight, Aufidius paraded this with his other *insignia.*

37. Mamurrarum . . . urbe : Formiae, about thirteen miles from Fundi. Mamurra was a friend of Julius Caesar, and had acquired great wealth in Gaul. Catull. 41. 4 calls him *decoctor Formianus*, 'the bankrupt of Formiae.' *Formiae* does not fit into dactylic verse ; hence the paraphrase. *Cf.* line 87 below.

38. Murena : L. Licinius Terentius Varro Murena, afterwards brother-in-law of Maecenas ; *cf. Odes*, ii. 10. He and Capito evidently had villas on the shore at Formiae, which was a favorite resort. *Cf.* Mart. x. 30. 1, *O temperatae dulce Formiae litus.*

40. Plotius . . . Varius : M. Plotius Tucca and L. Varius, who edited the *Aeneid* after Vi gil's death. On the latter, *cf. Odes*, i. 6 ; *Serm.* i. 6. 55.   **Sinuessae** : eighteen miles from Formiae.

41. animae : *souls.*   **qualis neque candidiores terra tulit** : *the fairest earth ever produced.* The expression *qualis candidiores* seems to be a combination of *quibus candidiores* and *quales candidissimas.* For similar combinations, *cf.* i. 3. 9 and 121.

42. quis : dative.

44. contulerim : potential subjunctive. The tense does not differ in force from the present ; *cf. dederim*, i. 4. 39.   **sanus** : *while I am in my senses; quam diu sana mente sum*, Porph. *Sanus* serves as the protasis of *contulerim.*

45. Campano ponti : a bridge over the Savo, not far from the Campanian frontier.   **villula** : a post-house, for the reception of travellers on public business.

46. parochi : it was their duty to supply those who put up at the *villula* with the necessaries of life, here expressed typically by *ligna salemque.* *Cf.* Cic. *ad Att.* v. 16. 3, *scito non modo nos faenum, aut quod lege Julia dari solet, non accipere, sed ne ligna quidem; nec praeter quattuor lectos et tectum quemquam accipere quidquam.*

47. Capuae : as the distance was short (about seventeen miles), the travellers arrived betimes (*tempore*), and Maecenas had time for a game of ball before the *cena.* The modern Capua is three miles nearer to Rome than the ancient city.

48. lusum : *sc. pila*, and *cf.* note on line 49.

49. pila : instrumental ablative ; see B. 218. 7.   **lippis** ; referring to Horace ; *cf.* line 30 above. That his condition was not always so bad is shown by the description of his habits in i. 6. 123 ff. **crudis** : *dyspeptics*, referring to Virgil. Donatus (p. 59 R.) says : (*Vergilius*) *plerumque a stomacho et a faucibus ac dolore capitis laborabat.* Horace's care of himself is in accordance with the directions of Celsus, i. 2 : *qui parum (concoxit) requiescere debet, et si mane surgendi necessitas fuerit redormire ; qui non concoxit, ex toto conquiescere ac neque exercitationi neque negotiis credere.*

50. Coccei: see line 32 above.   **plenissima** : *well-stocked. Cf.* Juv. viii. 100, *plena domus tunc omnis.*

51. super: *i.e.* it was situated on the hills above the town. **Caudi** : in Samnium, twenty-one miles east of Capua. It was the scene of the inglorious defeat of the Romans by the Samnites in 321 B.C.   **nunc mihi** : the account of the contest between the two buffoons is given in the mock-heroic style, opening with an invocation to the muse ; *cf.* lines 3 and 9 above.

52. Sarmenti : Sarmentus probably belonged to the suite of Maecenas. Quint. vi. 3. 58 gives a specimen of his wit : *Sarmentus seu P. Blessius Iulium, hominem nigrum et macrum et pandum, ‘fibulam ferream’ dixit.*   **Cicirrus** : *the game-cock*, probably a local wit. The *cognomen* is Oscan, and is perhaps onomatopoetic, representing the crowing of a cock.

54. ⋆clarum genus : ironical, since the Oscan-speaking Italiotes were despised by the Romans, as the descendants of an inferior race. *Osci* is nominative plural, predicate to *genus.*

55. domina exstat : *i.e.* he had been a slave (*filius nullius*) and had no lineage.

56. equi feri : *the unicorn*, described as follows by Plin. *N. H.* viii. 76 : *asperrimam feram monocerotem, reliquo corpore equo similem, capite cervo, pedibus elephanto, cauda apro, mugitu gravi, uno cornu nigro media fronte cubitorum duorum eminente.* Messius is likened to this monster, on account of his size and ugliness, as well as on account of the scar mentioned in line 60. For a similar comparison, *cf.* Lucil. 82 L., *Broncus Bovillanus, dente adverso eminulo hic est, Rhinoceros velut Aethiopus.*

58. accipio : *I admit it.*   **caput movet** : playfully imitating the unicorn.   **cornu exsecto** : ablative of quality, used predicatively. He had had a wen cut from his forehead. The Comm. Cruq. says : *hoc enim quasi a natura Campanis fere omnibus inest, ut capitis temporibus magnae verrucae innascantur, in modum cornuum, quos cum incidi faciunt, cicatrices in fronte manent, quasi notae exsectorum cornuum.*

60. sic mutilus : *i.e.* dehorned though you are.   **at** : *and in fact ; cf.* i. 3. 27. The contrast is between the actual state of affairs and the joke of Sarmentus, which exaggerated it.

61. laevi oris: *the left side of his face.* A use of the adjective similar to that in *summus mons*, 'the top of the mountain,' *etc.*

62. in faciem : *on his personal appearance.*

63. pastorem . . . Cyclopa: accusative of the inner object; *cf.* Vell. Paterc. ii. 73, *Plancus . . . cum Glaucum saltasset in convivio;* Juv. vi. 63, *Ledam molli saltante Bathyllo.* See Introd. § 38. *b.* The dance was pantomimic, doubtless representing the wooing of Galatea by the Cyclops, Polyphemus.

64. larva . . . coturnis, *i.e.* he was big and ugly enough to play the part without any paraphernalia. *Coturnis* is the regular spelling in the Mss. of Horace.   **esse** : infinitive in indirect discourse ; the verb of saying is implied in *rogabat.*

65. donasset . . . catenam : a joke on the former servitude of Sarmentus. Slaves when manumitted made an offering to the *lares*, or household gods ; so a runaway slave from the chain-gang might facetiously be supposed to make an offering of his chain. As a matter of fact, Sarmentus had been regularly manumitted.

66. ex voto : *in accordance with his vow.* Thank-offerings were usually symbolic, consisting of the implements of one's trade or profession, a representation of a part of the body which had been cured of disease, or something equally appropriate. *Cf. Odes*, i. 5. 15; iii. 26. 4 ; *Epist.* i. 1. 5.   *Ex voto* has become in English the technical term for such offerings.

68. una libra : slaves received four or five pounds of meal a day as rations. A little fellow like Sarmentus needed but one, and could have sold the rest, and thus soon have earned money enough to purchase his freedom.

69. sic tamque : the terms are not quite synonymous ; *slender as he was and so puny.*

70. prorsus : *very, exceedingly*, modifying *iucunde.*

71. recta : with ellipsis of *via.*   **Beneventum** : about twelve miles from Caudium. It was originally called Maleventum, from the Greek Μαλό-ϝεντα, 'apple town,' and the name was changed for the sake of the omen, since people associated the name with *male*, 'badly.' See Plin. *N. H.* iii. 105, *cetera intus in secunda regione Hirpinorum colonia una Beneventum auspicatius mutato nomine, quae quondam appellata Maleventum.*   **sedulus hospes**: *the attentive host.* Since the travellers stopped at an inn, apparently neither Maecenas nor any member of the company had an intimate friend in the neighborhood. See note on line 2.

72. arsit: *had his house burned up.* · *Cf.* Virg. *Aen.* ii. 311, *proximus ardet Ucalegon;* Juv. iii. 201, *Ultimus ardebit, quem tegula sola tuetur.* Kiessling sees in the involved word order a representation of the confusion of the scene.

73. vaga . . . veterem . . . Volcano: the alliteration and the metonymy (*Volcano* for *igni*) are marks of the mock-heroic style ; see note on line 3 above.   **dilapso**: *falling out* of the stove (see note on line 81). The wood, which the *sedulus hospes* had caused to be piled on too lavishly, fell out, and the fire ran up the side of the room to the roof.

75. avidos: *hungry;* in a different sense in i. 4. 126, *avidos vicinum funus ut aegros exanimat.*   **timentis**: *frightened,* either for fear of punishment, or at the fire, or both.

76. velle: *trying.*   **videres**: *you could see;* an example of the relatively rare 'could'-potential. Cf. *videas,* i. 4. 86 and the note. Here the action of the verb is transferred to the past.

77. ex illo: *sc. tempore, after that, next.* Cf. Prop. ii. 29. 42, *Ex illo felix nox mihi nulla fuit.*   **notos**: *familiar,* because they were near Horace's birthplace.

78. mihi: with *ostentare.*   **Atabulus**: a local name for the *sirocco,* a hot wind from the south. *Cf.* Sen. *Nat. Quaest.* v. 17. 5, *Atabulus Apuliam infestat;* Gell. ii. 22. 25, *sunt alii plurifariam venti commenticii et suae quisque regionis indigenae, ut est Horatianus quoque ille 'atabulus.'*

79. erepsemus = *erepsissemus,* perhaps a contracted form. See Lindsay, *Lat. Lang.* p. 464. The word is used of slow travelling, like *repimus* in line 25 above.   **Trivici**: an obscure village not mentioned elsewhere. *Villa* seems to be used here in the sense of *a little village,* as in Apul. *Met.* viii. 17, *villae vero, quam tunc forte praeteribamus, coloni.* The word may, however, have its usual meaning, in which case *Trivici* would be governed by *vicina* as in Lucan, ix. 432, *ora Sub nimio proiecta die, vicina perusti Aetheris.*

80. lacrimoso fumo: *tearful smoke, i.e.* smoke that brought tears to the eyes.

81. cum foliis: *leaves and all.*   **camino**: *stove.* The word usually means *forge,* but is also applied to an open stove ; *cf. Epist.* i. 11. 19 ; by metonymy = *fire; Serm.* ii. 3. 321.

86. quattuor . . . viginti et milia: *twenty-four miles.* Note the position of *et,* a bold hyperbaton.   **rapimur**: used of rapid travel ; the opposite of *repere,* lines 25 and 79.   **raedis**: *carriages,* large and heavy, with four wheels. *Cf.* Juv. iii. 10, *Dum tota domus raeda componitur una.* The word, like some others connected with horses and carriages (*e.g. petorritum, esseda, mannus*), is not a native Latin one. The Romans themselves believed it to be Gallic ; *cf.* Quint. i. 5. 57, *plurima Gallica evaluerunt ut ' raeda' ac 'petorritum,' quorum altero tamen Cicero, altero Horatius utitur.* That we have here the first mention of carriages, does not of necessity imply that any part of the journey was made on foot, which would be very unusual for men of the station of Maecenas and his party.

87. mansuri: *intending to put up.* Horace uses the future participle very freely, to denote intention, destiny, purpose, and similar ideas. See Introd. § 47.   **oppidulo** : what the name of this village was is uncertain. Some believe it to have been *Equus Tuticus*, as Porph. suggests ; others *Asculum*, either of which would be impossible in hexameter verse in the locative. Porph. suggests that Horace is here imitating Lucil. 254 L., *servorum est festus dies hic, Quem planè hexametro versu non dicere possis.* Lucilius may have followed Archestratus, 48. 3, Ribb., ἰχθύος αὐξηθέντος ὃν ἐν μέτρῳ οὐ θέμις εἰπεῖν. *Cf.* line 37 ; Ovid, *ex Pont.* iv. 12. 1–17.   **non est** : *it is not possible,* a colloquial usage ; *cf.* ii. 5. 103 ; *Epist.* i. 1. 32.

88. perfacile est : *sc. dicere,* from the preceding clause. By zeugma the word here has the meaning *describe.*   **vēnit** : *is actually sold ;* note the emphatic position. Observe the *ē.*   **vilissima rerum** : *the least valuable of all things.*

89. ultra : *farther on, i.e.* to Canusium.

90. callidus : *experienced, knowing.*   **soleat** : the original long quantity of the final syllable is preserved. See Introd. § 57. *d.*

91. lapidosus : *gritty,* from the friable nature of the mill-stones, a characteristic which the bread of Canusium is said to retain to-day. **aquae non ditior urna** : *not a pitcherful richer in water.* *Aquae* is genitive with *ditior* after the analogy of adjectives of plenty, and *urna* is ablative of degree of difference.

92. Diomede : he is said to have founded Beneventum and Equus Tuticus as well. Virgil also connects Diomedes with Apulia. See *Aen.* viii. 9, *Mittitur et magni Venulus Diomedis ad urbem* (referring to Argyripa).

93. flentibus . . . amicis : dative of separation. See B. 188, 2, *d.*   **hic** : *at this point, here.* He probably returned to Rome.

94. Rubos : twenty-four miles from Canusium.   **utpote . . . carpentes** : *since we were making,* explanatory of *fessi.* *Utpote* is

more commonly used with a relative, but *cf.* i. 4. 24, and ii. 4. 9.
With the whole passage, *cf.* Lucil. 87 L., *Praeterea omne iter est hoc
labosum atque lutosum.*

96. postera tempestas: *the weather next day*, for *postridie tempestas.*

97. Bari: Barium was twenty-three miles farther on, on the coast;
hence the epithet *piscosi.*   **Gnatia**: the colloquial form of *Egnatia*,
thirty-seven miles from Barium.   **lymphis . . . exstructa**: *built
under the anger of the water-nymphs*, a facetious way of saying that
the water was bad, a kind of parody of the familiar *dis iratis; cf.* ii.
3. 8, *iratis natus paries dis atque poetis.*

98. risusque iocosque: *food for laughter and jests.*

99. flamma sine: note the anastrophe; see note on *inter*, i. 1.
47.   **tura liquescere**: *that the incense melts.*

100. cupit: *sc. ea = Gnatia.* This miracle, which was probably
due to some volcanic phenomenon, was a feature of the town; *cf.*
Plin. *N.H.* ii. 240, *reperitur apud auctores . . . in Sallentino oppido
Egnatia, imposito ligno in saxum quoddam ibi sacrum, protinus
flammam exsistere.*   **Iudaeus Apella**: the Jews were regarded
by the Romans as especially superstitious. Apella is a common
name for slaves and freedmen, occurring frequently in inscriptions.

101. didici: from Epicurus and his disciple Lucretius. *Cf.*
Lucr. v. 82, *Nam bene qui didicere deos securum agere aevom;*
ii. 646 : —

> ' Omnis enim per se divom natura necessest
> Immortali aevo summa cum pace fruatur,
> Semota ab nostris rebus seiunctaque longe.'

And Tennyson, *Lotus Eaters*, 110, "On the hills like gods together,
careless of mankind."

102. natura: *i.e.* the creative power of the universe. *Cf.* Lucr. i.
630, *rerum natura creatrix.*

103. tristis: *in their anger.* Such portents were commonly
regarded as manifestations of the wrath of the gods.

104. Brundisium: the modern Brindisi, thirty-nine miles from
Gnatia, or, according to others, forty-four. Brindisi has in modern
times become an important town for the same reason which led to its
prominence in antiquity, *i.e.* because it is the most convenient point
of departure from Italy to the Orient and to Egypt.

SERMO VI.

1. non : modifies *suspendis*, in line 5 ; note the emphatic position.
quia : belongs more to the colloquial language than *quod*. *Quia*
is much more frequent than *quod* in early Latin, and from Tacitus
on ; Horace uses the former only twice in the *Odes*, but frequently in
the *Sermones* and *Epistles*.   **Lydorum** : the Lydians are said by
Herod. i. 94, to have settled in Etruria. See also Tac. *Ann.* iv. 55 :
Sardiani decretum Etruriae recitavere ut consanguinei: nam Tyrrhe-
num Lydumque Atye rege genitos ob multitudinem divisisse gentem;
Lydum patriis in terris resedisse, Tyrrheno datum novas ut conderet
sedes; et ducum e nominibus indita vocabula illis per Asiam, his in
Italia. The real origin of the Etruscans is one of the unsolved problems of ethnology. *Lydorum* depends on both *quidquid* and *nemo*,
ἀπὸ κοινοῦ ; *cf. illis*, i. 1. 20.

2. generosior : *of nobler birth*. Note the derivation of the word.
For its application to Maecenas, *cf. Odes*, i. 1. 1.

3. maternus : among the Etruscans, pedigrees were traced on the
mother's side. Horace may or may not have had this in mind. Probably he merely means to say that both branches of Maecenas's family
were distinguished.

4. olim : referring to the time of *fuit*. See note on i. 1. 25.
legionibus : this word, strictly used of Roman troops alone, is here
used in the general sense of forces, as in Plaut. *Amph.* 217, *contra*
Teloboae legiones educunt suas; Sall. *Cat.* 53, *sciebam saepe numero*
parva manu cum magnis legionibus hostium contendisse; and elsewhere.   **imperitarent** : this frequentative or intensive of *impero*
is not found in Caesar or Cicero and is rare in pre-Augustan Latin.
Horace has it four times (*cf. Odes*, i. 15. 25 ; *Serm.* ii. 3. 189 ; ii. 7.
81), apparently with the same meaning as *impero*. The frequent
use of such forms is characteristic of colloquial Latin.   *Cf.* also Lucr.
iii. 1027, *Inde alii multi reges rerumque potentes Occiderunt, magnis*
qui gentibus imperitarunt.

5. naso suspendis adunco : *turn up your nose at; cf.* ii. 8. 64,
suspendens omnia naso. Pers. i. 40, *rides, ait, et nimis uncis naribus*
indulges.

6. ignotos = *ignobiles.*   **libertino** : see note on *liberta*, i. 1.
99. That Horace was not ashamed of his parentage is shown by
the repetition of the phrase *libertino patre natum* in lines 45 and 46.
Cf. Epist. i. 20. 20.

7. cum . . . negas: the explicative use of *cum, in saying that it makes no difference.*

8. ingenuus : *free-born.* Maecenas apparently would not associate with slaves and freedmen. The same thing was true of Augustus ; see Suet. *Aug.* 74, *Valerius Messalla tradit neminem umquam libertinorum adhibitum ab eo* (*i.e.* Augustus) *cenae, excepto Mena, sed asserto in ingenuitatem.*   **persuades hoc tibi vere**: *you are convinced, and rightly.*

9. Tulli : referring to Servius Tullius, who, according to the tradition, was the son of an unknown father and a slave. *Cf.* Liv. iv. 3. 12, *Servium Tullium . . . captiva Corniculana natum, patre nullo matre serva, ingenio virtute regnum tenuisse;* Juv. viii. 259, *Ancilla natus trabeam et diadema Quirini Et fasces meruit, regum ultimus ille bonorum.* With *ante potestatem Tulli, cf. vixere fortes ante Agamemnona, Odes,* iv. 9. 25.   **ignobile regnum** : the adjective is used only with reference to the parentage of Tullius ; *cf.* the passage from Juv. cited in the last note. Translate accordingly.

10. nullis maioribus : *cf.* the passage from Livy, cited in the note on *Tulli,* line 9. A slave was legally *filius nullius.*

11. vixisse : instead of *fuisse,* a common use in Horace ; cf. line 70 below ; i. 4. 98.   **honoribus** : in its technical sense of *public offices.*

12. contra, adverb, *on the other hand.*   **Laevinum** : this particular member of the family is otherwise unknown.   Porph. says : *hic P. Valerius adeo foedis et proiectis in omnem turpitudinem moribus vixit, ut provehi non potuerit ultra quaestoriam dignitatem.*   **Valeri genus** = *Valeri progenies, a descendant of the Valerii.   Cf. Odes,* i. 3. 27, *audax Iapeti genus.*   **unde** = *a quo ; cf. unde generatur, Odes,* i. 12. 17. Horace uses *ab* and the ablative with *fugio* only in *Serm.* i. 1. 68. See note on ii. 3. 4.   **Superbus Tarquinius** : on the transposition of the *nomen* and *cognomen,* see the note on *Serm.* i. 4. 72. Here the order is doubtless influenced by the meaning of the *cognomen.*

14. non umquam . . . licuisse : *was never valued at more than a single penny. Pluris,* genitive of value, is governed by *licuisse,* and *assis* by *pretio.*   **notante** : ablative absolute with *populo. Notante* has a technical force, being the term used of the official rebukes of the censors. For the meaning of *noto, cf.* i. 3. 24 ; i. 4. 5 ; i. 4. 106 ; *etc.*

15. quo : in sense, object of *nosti,* but attracted to the case of *populo.*   **stultus** : *in its folly,* opposed to *sanus.* The idea is emphasized by *ineptus,* line 16.

16. famae servit : *is a slave to mere renown, i.e.* rates highly men of noble birth, regardless of their personal character.   **ineptus** : note the emphatic position, and the chiastic arrangement of the sentence *qui . . . ineptus.*

17. stupet in : *is dazzled by. Stupet* is constructed with *in* and the ablative, *cf.* also Virg. *Aen.* x. 446, *stupet in Turno ;* with the ablative alone, *cf.* i. 4. 28 ; with the accusative, *cf.* Juv. iv. 119, *nemo magis rhombum stupuit.*   **titulis et imaginibus** : *i.e.* the *wax masks* of a long line of ancestors, hung in the hall of the man of high birth, with the *inscriptions* recounting their offices and exploits.

18. nos : *people like us, i.e.* men of education and discretion. The reference is to both Horace and Maecenas, since *a volgo longe longeque remotos* would seem arrogant and out of place, if applied to Horace alone.   **longe longeque** : note the emphasis given by the repetition of the word, which is more effective than *longissime* would have been.

19. esto : *let us suppose a case.*   **Laevino** : *a Laevinus, i.e.* a man like Laevinus.   **mallet** : a paratactic condition contrary to fact ; *if the people preferred,* as in fact they did not.

20. Decio . . . novo : *a Decius of obscure birth,* another type ; *cf. Laevino* in line 19. P. Decius Mus, who devoted himself to death in the battle of Mt. Vesuvius (340 b.c.), to save his country, was the first curule magistrate in his family and hence a *novus homo.*

21. Appius : since the personages named in the passage are *types,* it seems most natural to think of the famous Appius Claudius Caecus. **si** : *since, i.e.* if I were not, as in fact I am not. The mood of *essem* is assimilated to that of *mallet* and *moveret.*

22. vel merito : *sc. facerent, they would be quite right ;* the apodosis to *mallet* and *moveret* is implied in *vel merito.* The thought is that men like Horace ought to be content with their proper sphere in life, and not aspire to positions to which they are not eligible.   **quoniam . . . quiessem** : alluding to the fable of the Ass in the Lion's Skin ; *cf.* ii. 1. 64. Allusions to the fables of Aesop are frequent in Horace. The mood of *quiessem* is assimilated to that of *facerent.*

23. sed : *i.e.* as a matter of fact, the majority of people cannot open their eyes to the truth, but struggle to acquire office.   **Gloria** : *Ambition,* personified. *Cf. Epist.* ii. 1. 177, *Quem tulit ad scaenam ventoso Gloria curru.*   **curru** : ablative of association ; *cf. chordis, Odes,* iv. 9. 4 ; *litore,* ii. 3. 205 ; and see Introd. § 41. *b.*

24. ignotos : *cf.* line 6 above. **generosis** : *cf.* note on line 1 above. **quo tibi . . . sumere** : *what does it profit you to take up?* The infinitive takes the place of a noun in the exclamatory accusative ; *cf. quo mihi fortunam, Epist.* i. 5. 12. See Lane, *Lat. Gr.* 1150 ; G. 343. 1. **Tilli** : the Comm. Cruq. says : *Tillius hic senatu motus est a Caesare quasi Pompeianus; occiso vero Caesare recepit latum iterum clavum, id est senatoriam dignitatem, et tribunus militum factus est.* In the same way Sallust was removed from the senate and afterwards recovered his seat.

25. tribuno : dative, assimilated to the case of *tibi.*

26. privato : serves as the protasis to *esset,* in a condition contrary to fact.

27. ut : *as soon as.* **insanus** : because to Horace it seems madness to desire such things. **nigris . . . pellibus** : senators wore a black or purple shoe, fastened by four black thongs passed about the calf of the leg. These thongs (*corrigiae*) are here called *pelles,* perhaps slightingly. **medium** : *up to the middle.*

28. latum . . . clavum : see note on i. 5. 36.

29. continuo : *immediately.* **quis homo hic** : *who is this fellow ?*

30. aegrotet : used figuratively, as in ii. 3. 307. **Barrus** : a fop of the day ; according to Porph., a man of abandoned character as well. Subject of *aegrotet,* implied in *aegrotat.* **haberi** : depends on *cupiat.*

31. eat . . . iniciat : part of the apodosis of the conditional sentence introduced by *si qui.*

32. singula : his various marks of beauty. An adjective used as a substantive.

34. promittit, *etc. :* apparently referring in a general way to the oath taken by magistrates on assuming their office.

36. ignota matre : *a low-born mother. Cf.* lines 6, 24, 96.

37. curare et quaerere : *cf. cura quaerendi,* line 32.

38. Syri, Damae . . . Dionysi : typical names of slaves. *Syrus,* originally ethnic, 'the Syrian,' is found as the name of one of the *dramatis personae* in Terence's *Heauton* and *Adelphoe ;* again in Horace in *Serm.* ii. 6. 44. *Dama* is a favorite name with Horace, occurring also *Serm.* ii. 5. 18 and 101 ; ii. 7. 54. *Dionysius* occurs only here.

39. deicere : scanned $\_ \cup \cup$, as in Lucr. iii. 877; Virg. *Ecl.* 3. 96. **saxo** : *sc. Tarpeio.* To condemn a criminal to be hurled from the

Tarpeian rock was one of the extraordinary powers of a tribune. *Cf.* Vell. Pater. ii. 24, *Publius Laenas tribunus plebei Sextum Lucilium, qui priore anno tribunus plebei fuerat, saxo Tarpeio deiecit.* **Cadmo** : an executioner or jailer of the period.

40. Novius : *Newman* (*cf. novus*) one of the numerous names in Horace which are selected on account of their appropriateness to the situation. The fact that it is a common Roman *nomen* does not in any way militate against this view. **gradu post me uno** : used metaphorically, but with an allusion to the assignments of the seats in the theatre according to rank.

41. Paulus et Messalla : *cognomina* of the old and aristocratic Aemilian and Valerian families ; hence selected as types of men of family, by way of contrast with Novius.

42. plostra : the colloquial form for *plaustra*. **ducenta** : used indefinitely of a large number. See Introd. § 50.

43. concurrant . . . sonabit : with this mixed form of the conditional sentence, *cf. Odes*, iii. 3. 7–8. **magna** : to be taken with *funera*. **sonabit quod** : *i.e.* will shout loudly enough to ; the relative clause stands to *sonabit* in the relation of an accusative of the inner object.

45. ad me redeo : with reference to line 6. *Cf.* Lucil. 1092 L., *nunc ad te redeo, Ut quae res me impendet rogetur.*

46. rodunt : *cf. Odes*, iv. 3. 16 ; *Serm.* i. 4. 81. **libertino patre natum** : the repetition of the phrase mimics his detractors. *Cf. Odes*, i. 13. 1 and 2 ; i. 35. 15 ; iv. 2. 49 and 50.

47. sim : like *pareret* in line 48, gives the reason of his critics. **convictor** : *intimate friend; cf.* i. 4. 96.

48. tribuno : in the army of Brutus. See Introd. § 3.

49. hoc : referring to the friendship of Maecenas. To this Horace had a right, whereas in the office of military tribune he was out of his proper sphere. **forsit** : this form, for *fors sit*, occurs only here. It is doubtless colloquial. **honorem** : *i.e.* the office of *tribunus militum. Honorem* is the direct object of *invideat*, while *mihi* is the indirect object ; so *te* in line 50, with *amicum* in apposition.

51. cautum : agrees with *te; = cum cautus sis.* **prava ambitione procul** : equivalent to an adjective in appositive relation to *dignos. Cf.* Ovid, *Metam.* i. 20, *frigida pugnabant calidis . . . sine pondere habentia pondus.*

52. felicem : in the emphatic position ; it implies chance or good luck.

53. possim : potential subjunctive.   **hoc** : *on this account; cf.* i. 1. 46.   **casu . . . sortitus** : these words, like *felicem*, imply mere chance. With *sortitus* supply *sim*.

54. nulla . . . fors : *for it was no chance.* Note the emphasis given by the word order.   **olim** : *some time ago.* See note on i. 1. 25.

55. Varius : see note on i. 5. 40.   **quid essem** : *what sort of a man I was.* Cf. Ovid, *Heroid*, 12. 31, *tunc coepi scire quid esses;* and for the use of the neuter referring to a person, *cf. nil,* i. 3. 18.

56. singultim : *brokenly*, the result of *infans pudor*.

57. infans : here has its literal meaning of *speechless, tongue-tied*, caused by *pudor*. *Cf. Odes,* i. 4. 3, *pallida mors.*   **pudor . . . profari** : note the alliteration, and the *singultim* effect produced by the repetition of the *p*.

58. non ego : *i.e.* Horace did not pretend to be the son of a wealthy provincial. Emphasis is given by the anaphora *non . . . non.*

59. Satureiano = *Tarentino*, since *Satureia* was an ancient name for Tarentum. The adjective belongs in sense rather with *rura* than with *caballo*, with which it agrees grammatically ; *cf. Odes,* iii. 6. 38, *Sabellis ligonibus.*   **caballo** : *nag; caballus* is a colloquial word, which became French *cheval*, Italian *cavallo; cf.* English *chivalry*. See note on *buccas,* i. 1. 21. The claim that he *rode* over an ancestral estate (*rura*) would imply that Horace's father was a rich landed proprietor. The adjective *Satureiano* is used on the same principle which actuated the use of *Austris* for *ventis*, in i. 1. 6 ; see note.

60. quod eram : a relative clause; *cf. quid essem* (indirect question) in line 55, and the note.

63. turpi . . . honestum : these adjectives, which are used as substantives, may be either masculine or neuter ; they are probably the latter.

64. patre . . . puro : note the alliteration. The ablatives modify *secernis*.

65. atqui : *yet after all.* Though Horace does not owe his advancement directly to his parentage, he does so indirectly, because of his early training.   **vitiis** : for the derivation and meaning, see note on i. 3. 1. Note the contrast with *recta*.   **mea** : the hyperbaton serves to emphasize *paucis*.

66. mendosa : *cf.* Ovid, *Amores,* ii. 4. 1, *non ego mendosos ausim defendere mores.*

68. sordis : *niggardliness*, as shown by a neglect of the elegancies

of life.   **mala lŭstra**: *evil communications.   Cf.* Paul. p. 120,
(Lustra) *significant lacunas lutosas quae sunt in silvis aprorum
cubilia; a qua similitudine hi qui in locis abditis et sordidis ventri et
desidiae operam dant dicuntur in lustris vitam agere.   Lūstra* would
have a different meaning.

71. pauper: with concessive force.   **macro . . . agello**: a
small farm near Venusia ; *cf. Odes,* iii. 4. 9 ff.   It was confiscated
after the battle of Philippi.

72. Flavi ludum: a school at Venusia.   **magni . . . magnis**:
note the ironical repetition of the adjective, which doubtless contains
the double idea of 'tall' and 'great.'   Big, burly men were selected
as centurions, since they had to chastise unruly soldiers.   Hence they
are referred to as types of bodily strength by Cic. *De Sen.* 10. 33.
Venusia was the seat of one of Sulla's military colonies, in which the
centurions would form the aristocracy of the place.   They and their
sons looked down on Horace, the freedman's child.

74. loculos tabulamque: objects of *suspensi,* which is used in a
middle sense. Cf. *membra,* i. 1. 5.   *Loculi,* which in this sense is
always plural, means *a satchel,* and is apparently synonymous with
capsa; cf. Juv. **x.** 116, *Quisquis adhuc uno parcam colit asse Miner-
vam, Quem sequitur custos angustae vernula capsae.*   The *tabula* was
a tablet, for writing or figuring upon.   The centurions' sons carried
these themselves, instead of having slaves for the purpose, as Juvenal's
schoolboy had, and as Horace had when in Rome.

75. octonos . . . aeris: *sc. asses* or *nummos, their eight asses* (a
month), ten or twelve cents.   The pay of schoolmasters in ancient
Rome was very small, and their lot generally an unhappy one ; this
must have been still more so in the small provincial towns.   *Octonos*
is doubtless not to be taken literally, but as a general term for a small
number.   **Idibus**: interest was due on the Kalends or Ides ; see i.
3. 87 ; *Epod.* 2. 69.   Teachers' salaries appear to have been paid at
the same dates.

76. puerum: *when I was still a boy.*   **ausus**: *sc. est; had the
assurance,* in spite of his humble position and the example of the
'great' centurions.

77. artis: *i.e. artis quibus aetas puerilis ad humanitatem informari solet,* Cic. *Arch.* 3. 4.   Horace's father wished to give him the
education of a gentleman.   **doceat**: causative, *has . . . taught.*

78. servos: *i.e. capsarii,* to carry his books and tablets ; *cf.* line
74 and the note.

79. in magno ut populo : *as was usual in a large city*, where all schoolboys had such attendants.   **avita ex re** : *from an hereditary estate.* Horace, as the son of a freedman, had no *avus.*

80. crederet : subjunctive in an apodosis contrary to fact ; the tense, as compared with *vidisset,* is due to the meaning of the word, since the action of *crederet* might continue into the present.

81. custos : *i.e.* Horace's father acted as his son's *paedagogus;* *cf.* the passage from Juv. cited in the note on line 74.

82. circum . . . aderat : *i.e.* he went around to.   **pudicum** (*sc. me*) : to be taken with *servavit,* while *ab omni . . . facto* is governed by *pudicum.*   **doctores** : of these only Orbilius is mentioned by name ; see *Epist.* ii. 1. 71.

85. sibi . . . vitio . . . verteret : *criticise him ; vitio* is dative of purpose. Note the alliteration.   **olim** : *some day.*

86. praeco : *auctioneer.*   **coactor** : *collector,* of taxes.   *Cf.* Suet. *Vit. Hor. : patre, ut ipse tradit, libertino et exactionum coactore; ut vero creditum est, salsamentario.* There seems to be no reason why Horace should misrepresent his father's calling ; hence the idea that he was a *salsamentarius,* a dealer in salt fish, was undoubtedly erroneous.

87. hoc . . . maior : *the greater.*   **nunc** : *as it is, i.e.* as matters have turned out.

89. paeniteat : potential subjunctive, *I would never regret.* **sanum** : *i.e.* so long as I am in my senses ; *cf.* i. 5. 44.

90. dolo . . . suo : a legal expression, equivalent to *culpa sua.*

92. defendam : against the charge of having a freedman for a father ; *cf.* line 46 above.   **istis** : *such people,* referring, with a contemptuous force, to the individuals implied in *magna pars ;* dative with *discrepat.* Brachylogy for *voci et rationi istorum.*

93. et vox et ratio : *my words and even my thoughts.*   **si** **natura iuberet** : *i.e.* if it were a law of nature, as it is not.

94. a certis annis : *after a given age.*   **remeare** : *i.e. iterum meare, to live over again,* governing *aevum.*

95. ad fastum : *to suit his pride.*   **quoscumque** : a general relative, *any parents whatsoever.*

96. honestos : *dignified by;* note the derivation of the word.

97. fascibus et sellis : *sc. curulibus* with *sellis ;* the *insignia* of the curule magistrates, the former of the consuls and praetors, the latter of the consuls, praetors, curule aediles, and censors.

98. fortasse tuo : *sc. iudicio.* Porph. says : *hoc ad Maecena-*

tem recte dicitur, qui abhorrens senatoriam dignitatem, in equestris honoris gradu se continuit. Fortasse is purely rhetorical, since Horace had no real doubt about Maecenas's opinion.

99. nollem : the subjunctive represents the reason as in the mind of Maecenas.   **onus . . . molestum** : because, as is explained in the following lines, he would have to increase his property to the senatorial rating, and to assume greater state in all the relations of life. **haud umquam** : *cf. non umquam,* line 14.

101. salutandi : referring to receiving calls, as well as to making them.   *Cf.* Cic. *ad Fam.* ix. 20. 3, *mane salutamus domi ;* Hieron. *Epist.* 43, *pudet dicere frequentiam salutandi, qua aut ipsi quotidie ad alios pergimus aut ad nos venientes ceteros expectamus.*   **ducendus et** : hyperbaton for *et ducendus.*   **unus et alter** : we should say *one or two.*

102. uti ne : a fuller form of expression for simple *ne,* a regular classical usage.   **peregreve** : a hypermetric verse ; *cf.* i. 4. 96, and the note.

103. calones : *grooms.*   **caballi** : see note on line 59.

104. ducenda : *must be taken with me,* when making a journey. *Cf. ducendus,* line 101.   **petorrita** : see note on *redis,* i. 5. 96.   Fest. p. 206 says : *petorritum et Gallicum vehiculum esse et nomen eius dictum esse existimant a numero IV rotarum ; alii Osce, quod hi quoque petora quattuor vocant.*   The numeral also had the form *petora* in Gallic, while the last part of the word is cognate with German *Rad,* 'wheel.'   **curto** : *humble.*

105. mulo : ablative of means, like *ire pedibus.*   **vel . . . usque Tarentum** : *all the way to Tarentum ; i.e.* to the end of the peninsula.

106. mantica : *portmanteau, a hand-bag* (*cf. manus*).   He travelled without a baggage train, carrying his scanty luggage on his own mule.   **ulceret** : *galls.*   **armos** : nearly always in classical Latin used of the shoulders of an animal, as *dorsum* is of the back (*cf. umeros* and *tergum*).   Horace evidently rode well forward, to make room for his baggage.   **eques** : *rider,* used in a general sense, doubtless humorously.

107. sordis : *cf.* line 78.   **Tilli** : *cf.* line 24.

108. Tiburte via : the road to Tibur, twenty miles northeast of Rome.   A praetor would be expected to travel in state, with a large retinue of slaves.   On the number of slaves, see notes on i. 3. 11, and on line 116 below.   Note also *praetor* used typically of a high magistrate ; see note on i. 5. 34.

109. lasanum portantes, *etc.: i.e.* carrying their own supplies, 'boarding themselves,' instead of putting up at inns.

110. hoc: *in this respect.*

111. milibus atque aliis: parallel with *hoc, and in thousands of others. Mille* is used indefinitely of a large number. See Introd. § 50 ; and for *aliis,* an adjective used as a substantive in an oblique case with ambiguous gender, see note on *his,* i. 4. 56.

112. solus: *cf.* i. 9. 10, where Horace is represented as attended by a single slave.   **quanti holus ac far:** *sc. stet,* although no ellipsis is consciously present to the writer's mind ; *cf.* our English expression, ' How much ? ' *Quanti* is genitive of value. Horace, as an observer of the various phases of human life, strolls about the *forum holitorium* and other public places. See Introd. § 31.

113. fallacem circum: the Circus Maximus, with its porticoes and the arches under the rows of seats, was a resort for hucksters, astrologers, and similar characters. *Cf.* Cic. *de Div.* i. 58. 132, *de circo astrologos;* Juv. vi. 582, *Si mediocris erit, spatium lustrabit utrimque Metarum et sortes ducet frontemque manumque Praebebit vati crebrum poppysma roganti.*   **vespertinum:** *in the evening,* when the day's business was done, and the forum was filled with idlers and loungers.

114. adsisto divinis: *i.e.* he stands beside the fortune-tellers, and listens to their predictions to the common people.   Horace's own opinion of such matters is shown by *Odes,* i. 11.   **inde:** *from there.*

115. lagani: a kind of pancake.

116. pueris: probably instrumental ablative, since the slaves were regarded merely as part of the *instrumenta cenae. Cf. tonsore, Epist.* i. 1. 94.   **lapis albus:** Porph. says: *marmoream Delphicam significat, quae scilicet pretii magni non est.* The *Delphica* (*sc. mensa*) was a small three-legged table, so-called from its resemblance to the Delphic tripod, for holding the mixing-bowl and wine-cups. The rich man would have a table of costly wood or of some variegated marble.

117. pocula duo: drinking-cups were usually made in pairs. *Cf.* Cic. *Verr.* ii. 2. 19. 47, *scyphorum paria complura;* Virg. *Ecl.* iii. 36 ff. and 44 ff.   **echinus:** an unknown utensil in the shape of a sea-urchin, possibly a salt-cellar. Porph. says, *vitream ampullam intellegere debemus;* the Comm. Cruq., *vas salis;* the pseudo-Acron, *vas aeneum in quo calices lavantur.*

118. cum patera guttus: *an oil-flask and saucer.* Or perhaps the *guttus* was a wine-flask, for pouring libations into the *patera.* **Campana supellex:** of cheap Campanian bronze, instead of silver

Cf. ii. 3. 144.   Porph. says : *Campanam supellectilem vilem intellegi vult, quia Capuae hodie aenea vasa studiosius fabricari dicuntur.*

120. Marsya : statues of Silenus or of Marsyas were erected in the market-places of many free towns of Italy, as a symbol of liberty. One stood in the Roman Forum, near the praetor's tribunal.   Horace implies that the uplifted hand of the figure or the expression of its face indicated its disgust at the appearance of the younger Novius, prob- ably a usurer who had his stand among the neighboring *tabernae argen- tariae.* The story of Marsyas was a favorite subject in plastic art and in painting.

122. quartam : *sc. horam*, *i.e.* three hours after sunrise.   See note on i. 5. 23.   **iaceo** : not necessarily sleeping (*cf. Epist.* ii. 1. 112), but reading or meditating.   *Cf.* Pliny's account of his early morning work, in *Epist.* ix. 36.   **vagor** : *stroll about, cf.* line 113 above ; i. 9. 17.   **ego** : emphatic, contrasting his habits with the life of the rich senator.   **lecto** : ablative absolute with the implied ante- cedent of *quod.   Cf.* i. 1. 94.

123. unguor olivo : preparatory to exercise.   *Cf. Odes*, i. 8. 8. *Unguor* is perhaps used in a middle sense.

124. Natta : a miserly fellow, otherwise unknown, who anointed his body with oil fit only for burning in lamps.

125. ast : archaic form of *at*, used also in *Epod.* 15. 24, and fre- quently by Virgil.   **fessum** : by ball playing.

126. fugio : *I leave.*   **lusum trigonem** : *the game of ball which I have finished playing ;* note the perfect participle.   The *trigo* was a game in which the players stood at the apices of a triangle and passed the ball from one to the other.   The skill consisted in catching and throwing the ball with either hand.

127. pransus : the *prandium*, the first substantial meal of the day, the modern European *déjeuner à la fourchette*, was taken at about noon.   **quantum** : has for its antecedent the object (under- stood) of *pransus*.

128. domesticus otior : *idle about at home.   Otior* is a word formed humorously after the analogy of *negotior*. Except here, it occurs only in Cic. *Off.* iii. 14. 58, *Canius . . . cum se Syracusas otiandi, ut ipse dicere solebat, non negotiandi causa contulisset.* Porph. says : *verbum finxit (Horatius).*

130. victurum : *destined to live.*   See note on *mansuri*, i. 5. 87.

131. quaestor : the lowest of the offices which gave admission to the senate.   The person whose grandfather and father had been *quaestor* would thus be in the lowest class of the *nobiles*, but would have all the annoyances and burdens accompanying the rank.   **atque** : connects *avus* and *pater*.   **fuisset** : *ac si* is followed by the pluperfect subjunctive, instead of the usual perfect after a primary tense, to emphasize the idea of non-reality.

SERMO VII.

1. Proscripti Regis Rupili : Porph. says : *P. Rupilius cognomine Rex, Praenestinus, post exilium, in quod damnatus profugerat, militavit in Africa sub Attio Varo.   Deinde cum praeturam gereret, proscriptus a triumviris confugit ad Brutum et inter comites habitus est.*

2. hybrida : *half-breed, i.e.* half Italian and half Greek.   **Persius** : obviously a banker of Clazomenae.

3. lippis et tonsoribus : the physicians' booths and the barber-shops were favorite lounging places where gossip was retailed.   *Cf.* Plaut. *Amph.* 1013, *In medicinis, in tonstrinis, apud omnes aedis sacras Sum defessus quaeritando.*   The disease of sore eyes was so common at Rome that the physicians' booths would always contain a crowd of such sufferers.   See note on i. 5. 30.

4. dives : *since he was a rich man ;* note the emphatic position of the adjective.

5. etiam : *sc. habebat, was involved in.*

6. durus homo : *an ugly customer*, a hard man to manage. **odio** : *hatefulness.*   **qui posset** : a clause of characteristic, parallel with the adjective *durus.*

7. confidens : in a bad sense, ' *cheeky.*'   *Cf.* Cic. *Tusc. Disp.* iii. 7. 14, *qui fortis est, idem est fidens, quoniam confidens mala consuetudine loquendi in vitio ponitur.*   **tumidus** : *boastful ; cf. Odes*, iv. 3. 8, *regum tumidas minas.*

8. Sisennas, Barros : *i.e.* men like Sisenna and Barrus, who are otherwise unknown, but were evidently celebrated for their vituperative powers.   **equis praecurreret albis** : *i.e.* far outstripped, a proverbial expression.   White horses were regarded as the swiftest. Thus the horses of Rhesus were white (Virg. *Aen.* i. 472 ; *cf.* xii. 83 ff.).   A similar proverbial use is found in Plaut. *Asin.* 278, *Nam si huic occasioni tempus sese supterduxerit, Numquam edepol quadrigis albis indipiscet postea.*

9. ad Regem redeo : *I return to Rex*, the subject of the story. The usual expression after a digression ; *cf.* i. 1. 108 ; i. 6. 45.   **post-**

quam . . . convenit : *when no agreement was reached.* The main
verb is *pugnat*, in line 19 ; *convenit* is impersonal.

10. hoc . . . molesti . . . quo fortes . . . incidit : *i.e.* all men
who are at variance are hard to deal with, in proportion to their valor.
Hoc is correlative to *quo*, with about the same force as if *molesti* and
fortes were comparatives.   **iure** : *rightly, naturally.*

11. adversum bellum : the adjective, which is somewhat redundant, has the same general force as in i. 1. 103, *adversis frontibus;*
it suggests a hand-to-hand fight.

12. animosum : a common epithet of Achilles ; *cf.* Ovid, *Heroid.*
viii. 1, *Pyrrhus Achillides animosus imagine patris.*   **atque** : for
the position of the word, *cf. atque* in i. 6. 131.

13. capitalis : *deadly, i.e.* affecting the life (*caput*).   **ut divideret** : a consecutive clause without an introductory demonstrative
adverb ; *cf.* i. 1. 95, *dives, ut metiretur nummos.*   **ultima mors** :
i.e. death alone.

15. vexet : *embroils; cf. Epist.* i. 3. 33, *vos seu calidus sanguis
seu rerum inscitia vexat.*   **inertis** : *cowards.*

16. Diomedi cum . . . Glauco : see *Iliad*, vi. 119 ff. The incident had become proverbial ; *cf.* Plin. *Epist.* v. 2, *epistulas ingratas ac
ne illam quidem sollertiam Diomedis in permutando munere imitantes*
(note *illam*).

17. pigrior : Horace seems to have the *duos inertis* in mind, since
the reason of Glaucus for declining to fight was not cowardice.
ultro : *into the bargain.*

18. praetore : the word is used in a general sense. Brutus and Cassius had seized the province of Asia, and the former was holding court
at Clazomenae. For a somewhat similar use of the word, *cf.* i. 5. 34.

19. Rupili et Persi : appositive genitive with *par.*   **par** : *the
pair*, a term used of gladiators. Horace is fond of metaphors derived
from gladiators ; see note on i. 1. 103.

20. compositum : *sc. par sit;* in this sense *par* is neuter. The
ellipsis of the subjunctive copula is colloquial usage.   **cum Bitho
Bacchius** : two gladiators of the time. The phrase is appositive to
par understood ; *i.e.* the pair Bithus and Bacchius ; see note on line 19.

21. procurrunt : like gladiators into a conflict.

22. Persius exponit causam : Persius, as the plaintiff, speaks first.
ridetur : the subject, as well as that of the following *laudat*, is Persius.

23. conventu : *the court*, a collective noun in the ablative of
agency.   **cohortem** : *his staff*, the *comites* of Brutus ; *cf. Epist.* i.

8. 14, *Ut placeat iuveni percontare atque cohorti* (of the staff of Tiberius).

25. canem : *the dog-star* (Sirius), a constellation of evil repute, contrasted with *stellas salubres.* On the general subject of the influence of the constellations, see *Odes*, ii. 17. 17–25.   **illum** : *he, i.e. Rex.*

27. fertur . . . securis : *i.e.* in the midst of the primeval forest on the mountain tops, one of the few really poetical expressions in the *Sermones.* Its introduction heightens the comic effect by contrast. For the general principle, see note on i. 5. 3.

28. Praenestinus : *i.e. Rex.* See note on line 1.   **salso . . . fluenti** : *against him with his torrent of bitter wit.* The two adjectives, connected by *-que*, modify *ei* understood, referring to Persius.

29. expressa : *wrung from, i.e.* by the taunt. The word governs *arbusto.*   **arbusto**, *the vineyard*, in which the vine-dresser is at work.   The passer-by calls out ' cuckoo,' an intimation that the cuckoo, the harbinger of spring, has come, and that the vine-dresser is late in his work. The latter replies with such a flood of vituperation that the wayfarer is silenced and put to flight. *Cf.* Plin. *N.H.* xviii. 249, *exprobrationem foedam putantium vites per imitationem cantus alitis temporariae quem cuculum vocant. Arbustum* is for *arbos-(e)tum*, and really refers to the trees on which the vines were trained. *Cf. Odes*, ii. 15. 4.

30. vindemiator : *a vine-dresser*, with whom *Rex* is, in Horace's usual manner, not only compared, but identified. See note on *Tantalus*, i. 1. 68. The word is here scanned with four syllables, *i* before *a* being treated as a semi-vowel.

31. cuculum : probably not the name of the bird, but an imitation of its note ; *cf.* the passage from Pliny cited in the note on *arbusto*, line 29.

32. Graecus : Persius, whose finer wit is contrasted with the coarse *Italo aceto.*   **aceto** : *abuse, satire ;* used metaphorically, but in not exactly the same sense by Plaut. *Pseud.* 739, *ecquid is homo habet aceti ; Bacch.* 405, *nunc experior sitne aceto tibi cor acre in pectore.*

34. consueris : subjunctive in a characteristic clause with accessory causal force. Persius humorously implies that it runs in Brutus's family to kill kings.

35. Regem : Cicero records a similar pun of his on the name of Q. Marcius Rex, in *ad Att.* i. 16. 10, ' *quo usque*,' *inquit,* ' *hunc regem feremus ?* ' ' *Regem appellas*,' *inquam,* ' *cum Rex tui nullam men-*

tionem fecerit?' Ille autem Regis hereditatem spe devoraret.
operum . . . tuorum : genitive of the whole, instead of *hoc tuum
opus est.* With the form of expression, *cf. Odes,* iii. 13. 13, *Fies nobilium tu quoque fontium.*

SERMO VIII.

1. **inutile lignum** : fig-wood seems to have been used for making
wooden statues. Pliny, *N.H.* xvi. 209, does not agree with Horace as
to its value ; he says : *levissimae ex his (ficus, salix, tilia, betulla,
sabucus, populus) ficus et salix ideoque utilissimae. Omnes autem
ad cistas quaeque flexili crate constent habiles. Habent et candorem,
rigorem et in sculpturis facilitatem.* It split easily under the influence
of heat ; *cf.* ii. 5. 29, *seu rubra Canicula findet infantes statuas.*

2. **faceretne** : the *-ne* connects *scamnum* and *Priapum ; cf. Odes,*
i. 30. 6, *solutis Gratiae zonis properentque Nymphae.*   **Priapum** :
the worship of this god originated in Lampsacus ; *cf. Hellespontiaci* in
the passage from Virgil cited on line 4. His statues were placed in
gardens as the symbol of fertility, and served at the same time as
scarecrows.

3. **deum. Deus** : this juxtaposition, and the consequent emphasis,
heighten the comic effect.

4. **dextra** : the god usually held a sickle in his right hand.   *Cf.*
Virg. *Georg.* iv. 110, *Et custos furum atque avium cum falce saligna,
Hellespontiaci servet tutela Priapi.*

5. **ast** : see note on i. 6. 125.   **harundo** : to give motion to the
figure, and an appearance of life, a reed was stuck into the top of its
head, which waved in the wind.

7. **novis . . . hortis** : *the newly made gardens ;* see Introd. to
this Satire. *Cf.* Prop. iv. 8. 1, *Disce, quid Esquilias hac nocte fugarit
aquosas, Cum vicina novis turba cucurrit agris.*

8. **angustis eiecta . . . cellis** : *i.e.* cast out of the narrow cells
which served as their bed-rooms. *Cf.* Cic. *Phil.* ii. 27, 67, *conchyliatis
Cn. Pompei peristromatis servorum in cellis lectos stratos videres.*

9. **conservus** : probably collective. The slaves of a household
often formed burial associations. *Cf. C.I.L.* vi. 10262, *collegium quod
est in domo Sergiae Paullinae ; etc., etc.*   **portanda locabat** : *made
a contract for carrying. Cf. Odes,* ii. 18. 18, *Tu secanda marmora
Locas sub ipsum funus.*

10. **hoc** : *here,* lit. *this,* in agreement with *sepulcrum.*   **miseras**

plebi : *i.e.* free citizens of small means, who could not afford private tombs, but belonged to burial societies. Pantolabus and Nomentanus are cited as types of this class ; *cf.* ii. 1. 22.

12. cippus : the boundary stone, with an inscription defining the limits of the burial place, which had a frontage of 1000 feet and a depth of 300. Porph. says: *eleganter Pantolabo et Nomentano, qui bona sua comederant, lata monimenta praestare nunc dicitur, scilicet quia privata habere non poterant.*

13. heredes . . . sequeretur : *i.e.* with the injunction that the monument (and the lot) should not descend to the heirs of the person or persons who gave it to the society. Stipulative subjunctive ; see Introd. § 45. *c.* The usual form of the inscription, which is of very frequent occurrence, is *hoc monumentum heredes non sequetur*, generally indicated by the initials H·M·H·N·S·

14. Esquiliis habitare salubribus : *to find the Esquiline a healthful dwelling-place.* Note the emphatic position of the adjective.

15. aggere : *the embankment*, which took the place of the wall of Servius Tullius in the northeastern part of the city, where the natural slope did not admit a wall. Portions of the outer retaining wall of the *agger* still exist *in situ*, and parts of the *murus* are found elsewhere. *Cf.* Juv. vi. 588, *Plebeium in circo positum est et in aggere fatum ;* viii. 43, and Mayor's note. **modo**: *but now, a short time ago.* **tristes**: *gloomily.*

17. cum: *while*, referring back to *nunc licet*, as the tenses show. Although the Esquiline had been improved, and its worst features eliminated, the tombs were allowed to stand, and the place was therefore infested by sorcerers whose charms were sought in graveyards. **ferae**: a substantive formed by the ellipsis of *bestiae*. See note on *venalis*, i. 1. 47. **suëtae**: scanned with three syllables ; *cf. insuevit.* i. 4. 105 ; *consueris*, i. 7. 34 ; and for a parallel to *suetae*, Lucr. i. 60, *appellare suemus.*

18. curae . . . labori : final datives.

19. carminibus atque venenis : *spells and potions.* The former were in metrical form. **versant** : *practise on.*

21. vaga luna : a conventional epithet ; *cf.* Virg. *Aen.* i. 742, *hic canit errantem lunam.*

22. protulit os : *cf.* Virg. *Aen.* viii. 591, *Qualis ubi oceani perfusus Lucifer unda . . . Extulit os sacrum caelo tenebrasque resolvit.* **ossa legant** : a conventional expression ; *cf.* Prop. ii. 24. 50, *vix venit extremo quae legat ossa die.* Objects connected with death were sup-

posed to have especial efficacy in magic rites.   *Cf. Epod.* 5. 17, *iubet
sepulcris caprificos erutas.*

23. vidi egomet: these words suggest a parody of the heroic
style, as was observed by the Comm. Cruq.   *Cf.* Virg. *Aen.* iii. 623,
Vidi egomet, duo de numero cum corpora nostro . . . , and see note
on i. 5. 3.   **nigra**: black was associated with death and with the
deities of the underworld ; see line 27 below.   With the whole description, *cf.* Ovid, *Met.* vii. 182, *vestes induta recinctas, Nuda pedem, nudos
umeris infusa capillos.*

24. Canidia: *cf. Epod.* 5 and 17.   The scholiasts say that hèr
real name was Gratidia, and that the name Canidia, which Horace
applies to her, was derived from *canities* (gray hair).   She is said
to have been an *unguentaria* of Naples, with whom Horace had once
been in love.   Note that the quantity and the number of the syllables
in *Canidia* and *Gratidia* agree.   Thus Terentia is called Licymnia in
Odes, ii. 12. 23, where see Bennett's note.

25. maiore: probably referring to age.   **ululantem**: this word
is usually used of the cries of women as distinguished from the shouts
of men ; and frequently of chants and incantations.   *Cf.* Plin. *Epist.*
vi. 20, *audires ululatus feminarum, infantum quiritatus, clamores virorum;* Ovid. *Met.* vii. 190, *ternis ululatibus ora solvit* (Medea); xiv.
405.   **utrasque**: *the pair.*   The plural of *uterque* is used of groups,
and also of individuals who are associated closely together, as col-
leagues or the like.   *Cf.* Caes. *B.G.* i. 53, *utraeque (Ariovisti uxores)
in ea fuga perierunt.*

26. scalpere terram: the digging of a trench was a regular
feature of rites involving the deities of the underworld.   *Cf. Odyss.*
xi. 36 ff.   In such work iron must not be used ; hence *unguibus.*

27. pullam: black victims were regular in such rites.   *Pullus*
(cognate with Greek πελλός and Latin *palleo*) is frequently used of
mourning, the dead, *etc.,* but not invariably ; *cf. Odes,* i. 25. 18 ; Ovid,
Am. ii. 4. 41, *Seu pendent nivea pulli cervice capilli : Leda fuit nigra
conspicienda coma.*   **mordicus**: adverb, *with their teeth.*

28. confusus: *i.e.* they poured the blood into the ditch *together*
(hence *con-*), each from the part of the lamb which she held.   **inde**:
from it, i.e. the ditch.

29. animas: in apposition with *manes.*

30. et = *etiam, also.*   On this rite, *cf.* Virg. *Ecl.* viii. 80 ff.; Ovid,
Heroid. vi. 91, *Devovet absentis simulacraque cerea fingit, Et miserum
tenuis in iecur urget acus.*

31. inferiorem : contrasted with *maior*.

32. servilibus modis : *i.e.* in torture, which was applied only to slaves.   **ut quae . . . peritura** : *sc. esset.* A clause of characteristic.   The ellipsis of the subjunctive copula is colloquial usage.

33. altera : Canidia, as the leader (*cf.* lines 24–25) calls on Hecate, the queen of magic rites.   *Cf.* Virg. *Aen.* vi. 247, *voce vocans Hecaten Caeloque Ereboque potentem.*

34. serpentis : present because of their connection with the furies and their general evil repute ; *cf.*, however, i. 3. 27.

35. infernas canes : regular attendants on Hecate.   *Cf.* Virg. *Aen.* vi. 257, *visaeque canes ululare per umbram Adventante dea.* Note the gender.   **rubentem** : the deep red of the setting moon is described as a blush of shame, as it hides its face behind the tombs.

40. alterna loquentes : *i.e.* answering her questions.

41. umbrae : *the ghosts* (*manes* in line 29) which they had conjured up by their incantations.   **triste et acutum** : accusative of the inner object.   *Cf. sonabit quod*, i. 6. 43, and the note.   The shades spoke with a thin, squeaking voice.   *Cf.* Virg. *Aen.* vi. 493, *pars tollere vocem exiguam;* Shakespeare, *Hamlet*, i. 1, "The sheeted dead Did squeak and gibber in the Roman streets."

42. lupi barbam : *cf.* Plin. *N.H.* xxviii. 157, *veneficiis rostrum lupi resistere inveteratum aiunt, ob idque villarum portis praefigunt.* **variae** : *spotted.*   With the whole passage, *cf.* Shakespeare, *Macbeth*, iv. 1.

43. cerea : scanned as a dissyllable ; *cf. ostrea*, ii. 2. 21, and *aureo* in Virg. *Aen.* x. 116, *solio tum Iuppiter aureo Surgit, caelicolae medium quem ad limina ducunt.*   The ablative is causal, — the fire blazed higher as the waxen image melted and flowed into it.

44. non inultus : because he frightened the witches as much as they had frightened him ; for, as they are engaged in their rites, the wooden statue splits with a loud explosion.   See note on line 1.

48. dentes : *false teeth.*   See the passage from Porph. cited in the next note.   **caliendrum** : *wig,* apparently a high head-dress of hair. Porph. says: *iocatur in has, quasi altera dentibus adpositis uti solita sit, altera quod glabra fuerit caliendrum, id est galericum, habere consuesset.*

49. incantata . . . vincula : *enchanted love-knots.*   *Cf.* Virg. *Ecl.* viii. 73, *Terna tibi haec primum triplici diversa colore Licia circumdo.*

50. videres : *you could see;* see note on i. 5. 76.

SERMO IX.

1. ibam forte: *I chanced to be strolling*.   **Via Sacra**: the
Sacra Via, as it was usually called, ran from the Esquiline, through
the Forum, to the foot of the Capitoline Hill, where it joined the *clivus
Capitolinus*. *Cf. Odes*, iv. 2. 35, *quandoque trahet feroces Per sacrum
clivum merita decorus Fronde Sygambros*.   **sicut . . . mos**: referring to *meditans*.

2. nescio quid . . . nugarum: *some trifle or other*, perhaps a
composition ; *cf. Epist*. i. 19. 42 ; ii. 2. 141 ; Catull. i. 4, *namque tu
solebas Meas esse aliquid putare nugas*. Porph. says: *sic verecunde
poetae nugas et lusus solent appellare versiculos suos*. The word is,
however, common in Horace in a general sense. *Cf*. ii. 6. 43, *vellet
. . . cui concedere nugas hoc genus*.   **totus in illis**: *wholly ab-
sorbed in them*. *Cf. Epist*. i. 1. 11, *omnis in hoc sum*.

3. accurrit: *rushes up*. This word and *arrepta manu* vividly
picture the man's offensive familiarity.   **quidam**: *a fellow*.
Horace does not name him, and the whole incident may be fictitious.

4. quid agis: *how are you ?* This was a common and familiar
greeting. *Cf*. Mart. ii. 67, *Occurris quocumque loco mihi, Postume,
clamas Protinus, et prima est haec tua vox 'quid agis ?'*   **dulcissime rerum**: *my dear fellow*, a still more familiar greeting. *Cf*. Ovid,
Ars Amat. i. 213, *pulcherrime rerum; Heroid*. iv. 125.

5. suaviter: *sc. ago, very well*. Horace replies politely and thereby
loses his opportunity of ridding himself of the man at once. Of course
there is no conscious ellipsis.   **ut nunc est**: *at present*.   **cupio
. . . quae vis**: a conventional form of address. *Cf*. Plaut. *Pers.*
766, *omnia quae tu vis, ea cupio*.

6. adsectaretur: *would join me ;* the imperfect has a conative
force.   **numquid vis**: a hint that he does not care to prolong the
interview, since the formula ' there's nothing I can do for you, I'm
sure ' (note *num*) was one of leave-taking, something like ' that's all,
isn't it ? '

7. noris nos: *yes, make my acquaintance*. *Noris* is perfect
subjunctive, as in the parallel passage in Plaut. *Mil*. 575, *numquid
nunc aliud me vis ? Ne me noveris; cf. Capt*. 191, *numquid vis ?
Venias temperi*.   **docti**: *a man of parts ; doctus* is used especially
of literary ability (*cf. Epist*. i. 19. 1, *docte Maecenas* ; Tibull. iii. 6.
41, *docte Catulle*). In this case, however, other accomplishments are
included, as we see from line 22.   **pluris . . . eris**: *I shall like you*

the better for that. Tʰe weakness of making this amiable rejoinder seals Horace's fate.

8. misere : *dreadfully,* a colloquial use of the word common in comedy, and doubtless in the language of every-day life.

9. ire . . . consistere . . . dicere : the historical infinitives well express Horace's efforts to escape from his tormentor.

10. puero : *my slave, a pedisequus,* or page.   **ad imos . . . talos** : *to my very heels, i.e.* from head to foot ; the full expression, which is a very common one, occurs in *Epist.* ii. 2. 4, *talos a vertice pulcher ad imos.*

11. Bolane : evidently a man noted for his short temper, other-wise unknown.   **cerebri felicem** : *happy in thy hot temper.* *Cerebri* is genitive with *felicem,* an extension of the regular genitive with adjectives, doubtless stimulated by the genitive of specification in Greek; see Introd. § 40. *a.* For the meaning, *cf. cerebrosus,* i. 5. 21.

12. tacitus : *i.e. to myself.*   **quidlibet . . . garriret** : *chat-tered on all sorts of subjects.* *Quidlibet* is accusative of the inner object; *cf.* i. 10. 41 *garrire libellos* ; ii. 6. 77, *Cervius garrit aniles ex re fabellas.*

13. vicos : *the streets.*

14. nil respondebam : *continued to make no reply,* imperfect of continued action. The imperfect indicative with *ut* is rare. **misere cupis** : *you're dreadfully anxious.* *Cf.* line 8.

16. persequar : *I'll stick to you.*   **hinc** : *next, i.e. from here.*

17. circumagi : *to be taken out of your way.*   **quendam** : *a man.*   **non tibi notum** : a hint that it would be better for the bore not to go with him.

18. cubat : *is sick abed.* *Cf.* ii. 3. 289, *pueri menses iam quinque cubantis ; Epist.* ii. 2. 68, *cubat hic in colle Quirini.*   **Caesaris hor-tos** : on the Janiculum near the Tiber. They were left by Julius Caesar to the people of Rome. Shakespeare, *Julius Caesar,* iii. 2, wrongly places them ' on this side Tiber.'

19. nil habeo quod agam : *I've nothing to do,* entirely forgetting the engagement referred to in line 36.   **usque** = *usque eo,* even as far as that, *i.e. I'll go all the way with you.*

20. demitto auriculas : a proverbial expression; *cf.* in English the opposite, ' prick up one's ears.' The diminutive (*cf.* French *oreille*) is colloquial.   **iniquae mentis asellus** : *a stubborn ass.* On the diminutive, see the preceding note.

21. dorso : instrumental ablative ; *cf.* Virg. *Aen.* ii. 708, *ipse subibo* *umeris.*   For the use of the word, see note on *armos*, i. 6. 106.   Perhaps also ablative of comparison with *gravius*, ἀπὸ κοινοῦ.   **subiīt** : the original long quantity of the final syllable is preserved for metrical reasons. . *Cf.* i. 4. 82, and the note.   **incipit ille** : after having frustrated Horace's efforts to get rid of him, the bore begins his monologue.

22. si bene me novi : a colloquial expression : *cf. Epist.* i. 18, 1, *si bene te novi.*   **Viscum** : an intimate friend of Horace and of Maecenas.   See i. 10. 83, and ii. 8. 20.

23. Varium : see note on i. 5. 4.   **quis scribere pluris** : how poor a recommendation to Horace's favor this was is seen from i. 4. 14 ff.

24. membra movere mollius : *dance more gracefully.*   This accomplishment, too, was not highly esteemed.   *Cf.* ii. 1. 24, and Cic. *Murena*, 6. 13, *nemo fere saltat sobrius, nisi forte insanit, neque in solitudine, neque in convivio moderato atque honesto.*   Note the alliteration.

25. Hermogenes : see i. 4. 72.

26. locus : *a good place.*

27. quis : dative.   See note on i. 1. 1.

28. composui : *laid them to rest;* used properly of collecting the ashes and depositing them in the urn.   *Cf.* Prop. ii. 24. 25, *Tu mea compones et dices ' ossa, Properti, Haec tua sunt; heu, heu tu mihi certus eras.'*

28-34. felices . . . aetas : unquestionably an aside ; so Porph. : *hoc Horatius tacitus apud se dicit.*

29. confice : *finish me, i.e.* give me the death stroke, implying that he talked his relatives to death.   **Sabella** : the Sabellian peoples, especially the Marsi and Paeligni, were notorious for the practice of witchcraft.   *Cf. Epod.* 5. 76 ; 7. 28 ; 17. 29, 60.

30. divina urna : the urn in which the lots were placed and shaken (*mota*) before they were drawn ; hence *divina,* as if the urn itself had magic power.   *Cf. Odes,* ii. 3. 26, *omnium Versatur urna serius ocius Sors exitura;* iii. 1. 16, *Omne capax movet urna nomen.*

31. dira venena : poisoning was very prevalent in Rome.   *Cf.* ii. 1. 48 and 53–56; ii. 3. 131 ; Cic. *pro Cluent.;* and Mayor's long and interesting note on Juv. i. 71.   **hosticus** : a poetic word, here used to give an epic effect to the prophetic utterance.   So also *ensis,* instead of *gladius,* corresponding to English ' falchion,' ' glave.'

32. laterum dolor : *pleurisy.*   **tussis** : *cough, i.e. consumption.* **tarda podagra** : *crippling gout, i.e.* which makes one slow.   *Cf.*

Prop. ii. 1. 59, *Tarda Philoctetae sanavit crura Machaon;* and with
the use of the adjective to denote the effect, *pallida mors, Odes,* i. 4. 13.

33. quando . . . cumque = *aliquando. Cf.* Ovid, *Metam.* vi. 544,
quandocumque mihi poenas dabis. Note the tmesis, and *cf.* i. 1. 86.

35. ventum erat: *we had come.* **Vestae**: with ellipsis of
templum or *aedem;* the same construction occurs in Greek and in
English: *e.g.* he went to St. Paul's. Horace would pass the temple
as he crossed the Forum to the Vicus Tuscus, on his way across the
Tiber. **quarta parte diei praeterita** : *i.e.* it was after the beginning of the fourth hour. Horace was out unusually early ; *cf.* i. 6. 122,
ad quartam iaceo. This was the time for transacting legal business ;
cf. Mart. iv. 8. 2 f., *Exercet raucos tertia causidicos, In quintam
varios extendit Roma labores.*

36. respondere: *i.e.* to appear in court, as he had given bail to
do on that day. **vadato**: probably an impersonal ablative absolute
with causal force, since *respondere* in this sense is used absolutely.

37. fecisset: subjunctive in implied indirect discourse, representing the future perfect *fecerit* (*i.e. responderit* of the law). **perdere litem**: *sc. debebat, to lose his case,* which, in case of his
non-appearance, would be decided against him by default.

38. si me amas : *I pray you.* In this colloquial expression, which
in ordinary conversation doubtless formed a word group with a single
accent, we have a semi-elision (and semi-hiatus) of *me*, with shortening of the *e*, as in Greek. *Cf. Epod.* 5. 100 ; Virg. *Ecl.* viii. 103, *credi-
mus? an qui amant? Aen.* vi. 507, *te, amice, nequivi conspicere.*
ades : *give me your help,* as *advocatus. Cf.* the pseudo-Asconius on
Cic. *Div. in Caecil.* 4. 11, *qui defendit alterum in iudicio aut patronus
dicitur si orator est, aut advocatus si aut ius suggerit aut prae-
sentiam suam commodat amico.* **interea***m* : *hang me; cf. dispeream,* in line 47. The latter is common in comedy, while the former
belongs rather to the *sermo cotidianus* of the more cultivated classes.

39. stare : Horace declines for three reasons : (1) he is not strong
enough to stand in court during the trial ; (2) he has no knowledge of
civil law ; (3) he has other business. That the first reason is not consistent with the third, since his errand involved a long walk across the
Tiber, is of no significance under the circumstances.

40. faciam . . . relinquam : indirect deliberatives ; cf. *inflet . . .
dicat,* i. 1. 20.

41. rem : *my case ; pro lite dixit,* Porph. **sodes** : *pray, please,*
for *si audes, if you will* (from *audeo ; cf. avidus*). A colloquial

expression ; *cf.* Cic. *Orat.* 45, 154, *libenter copulando verba iungebant, ut 'sodes' pro 'si audes,' 'sis' pro 'si vis.'*

42. ut durum: *sc. est. Cf. Odes,* i. 24. 19, *durum : sed levius fit patientia;* Ter. *Phorm.* 238, *illud durum (est).*

43. Maecenas quomodo tecum : *sc. agit: on what terms are you and Maecenas ?* The principal object of the bore is to be presented to Horace's friend and patron. It must be remembered that the ellipsis is not a conscious one, any more than in similar expressions in English.

44. hinc repetit : *sc. sermonem, he begins again.*   **paucorum hominum** : genitive of quality. *Cf.* Ter. *Eun.* 409, *immo sic homost : paucorum hominum. Immo nullorum arbitror.* It seems most natural to assign these words, especially *nemo . . . usus,* to the bore. Porph. attributes them to Horace.   **mentis bene sanae**: *of very sound judgment.*

45. haberes . . . velles : the condition contrary to fact shows that the man knows that Horace is unwilling to grant his request ; *you would have . . . if you were only willing.*

46. secundas : *sc. partes, 'second fiddle.'* The expression is of course used with reference to the drama. *Cf.* Plaut. *Merc.* 276, *metuo ne illaec simiae partis ferat;* Cic. *Brut.* 69. 242, *Q. Arrius, qui fuit M. Crassi quasi secundarum.*

47. hunc hominem : *your humble servant,* also from the language of comedy. *Cf.* Ter. *Heaut.* 356, *tibi erunt parata verba, huic homini verbera.*   **tradere** : *introduce,* the regular word ; *cf. Epist.* i. 9. 3 ; i. 18. 78.

48. ni submosses omnis : *if you would not have cleared the field, i.e. si hunc hominem tradere voluisses.* The bore, after hinting at the advantage which Horace would gain by presenting him to Maecenas, adds, 'why (if you had done so already), you would now have rid yourself of your rivals, and would be supreme in his favor.' On the form, see note on i. 5. 79.   **isto . . . modo** : *as you suppose, i.e.* in trying to supplant one another in Maecenas's favor. Note the force of *isto.*   **illic** : *i.e.* in the circle of Maecenas.

49. purior : *more free from,* governing *malis* in common with *aliena.*

50. inquam : *I assure you; cf. Odes,* ii. 8. 13, *ridet hoc, inquam, Venus ipsa; Serm.* ii. 7. 22 ; ii. 8. 27.

51. hic : *so and so;* this man, for example.

52. magnum : *a splendid state of affairs.* The words imply incre-

dulity.   **atqui sic habet** : *sc. res, yet it's so*, in spite of your dis-
belief.

53. **accendis . . . esse** : *you fire me with still greater desire to
be his friend ; quare cupiam* (for *ut ea re cupiam*) is a relative clause
of result.

54. **velis tantummodo** : *you have only to wish it.* Horace's sense
of humor leads him to encourage the fellow.   **quae . . . expugnabis** : *your merit is such that you will take him by storm.*

56. **difficilis** : predicate adjective.   **aditus primos** : *outposts,*
keeping up the figure of *expugnabis* and *vinci.* For Maecenas's caution
with regard to Horace himself, see i. 6. 61, *abeo : et revocas nono post
mense.*   **haud mihi dero** : the bore takes Horace's words seriously
and begins to lay plans as ill-suited as possible to win the friendship
of a man like Maecenas. For the form of *dero, cf.* ii. 1. 17 ; ii. 2. 98 ;
Epist. i. 12. 24.

58. **exclusus fuero** = *exclusus ero,* a colloquialism.   **tempora** :
favorable opportunities, when Maecenas cannot escape him.   *Cf.*
Virg. *Aen.* iv. 293, *temptaturum aditus et quae mollissima fandi
Tempora.*

59. **deducam** : *escort him,* from his house to the forum. *Cf.* Cic.
de Sen. 18. 63, *haec ipsa sunt honorabilia . . . decedi, assurgi, deduci,
reduci.*   **nil . . . mortalibus** : an example of Horace's humor.
The noble sentiment is ludicrously inappropriate to the circumstances.

60. **haec dum agit** : *i.e.* while he is running on.

61. **Fuscus Aristius** : an intimate friend ; see *Odes,* i. 22 ; *Epist.*
i. 10. Horace hopes to make his escape through Fuscus, but the
latter sees the humor of the situation and has a little amusement at
his friend's expense. On the inversion of the *nomen* and *cognomen,*
see note on i. 4. 72.

62. **qui pulchre nosset** : *who knew him well,* subjunctive of characteristic. The expression is colloquial ; *cf.* Cic. *Fam.* x. 23, *Lepidum
pulcre noram.*   **unde venis et quo tendis** : a common form of
salutation ; *cf.* ii. 4. 1, *unde et quo Catius ?*

63. **rogat et respondet** : *sc. Aristius; we ask each other ;* lit. *he
asks and replies.*   **vellere** : *to pull at his toga.*

64. **pressare** : *to pinch,* intensive of *premere.*   **lentissima** :
unresponsive, because he refuses to take the hint.

65. **male salsus** : *with mischievous wit.* For the metaphorical
use of *salsus, cf.* i. 7. 28, *salso multoque fluenti.*

66. dissimulare : *pretends not to notice. Dissimulare* and *urere*
are historical infinitives ; *cf.* line 9.   **iecur urere bilis** : *cf. Odes,*
i. 13. 3, *fervens difficili bile tumet iecur.* The liver was often regarded
as the seat of the emotions.

67. nesciŏ : the regular quantity in the combination *nescio quis.*

69. tricesima sabbata : perhaps asyndeton for *tricesima et
sabbata,* the thirtieth (of the month), and a holiday. Very likely
no particular festival is referred to, but the term is invented by Fuscus.
There is no reason to suppose that he was acquainted with the *minutiae*
of Jewish rites.   **vin tu** : *you surely do not wish, do you ?* implying
a negative answer, while *vis tu* simply asks a question.

70. oppedere : *insult,* a coarse expression.

71. infirmior : *less strong-minded.*

73. surrexe : infinitive in an exclamation, a construction common
in comedy, but found in Horace only in *Epod.* 8. 1 ; *Serm.* ii. 4. 83 ;
ii. 8. 67. For the form, see note on i. 5. 79. The opposite expression
to *solem nigrum surrexe* occurs in Catull. 8. 3, *fulsere quondam can-
didi mihi soles.*

74. sub cultro : like a victim at the altar.

75. adversarius : the person referred to in line 37. He might
have won his case by default, but apparently preferred to have it settled regularly in court. His appearance at this time adds to the humor
of the situation.

76. licet antestari : *may I call you to witness* the arrest. According to the Twelve Tables, a plaintiff had the right, in case a
person whom he summoned refused to go into court, to seize him,
after first appealing to a witness. The law is quoted by Porph. : *Si in
ius vocat, ni it, antestamino ; igitur en capito* (Holder's text).

77. oppono auriculam : as a warning to remember the summons,
the summoner touched the ear of the witness. *Cf.* Plin. *N.H.* xi. 251,
est in aure ima memoriae locus, quem tangentes antestamur. On
auriculam, see note on *auriculas,* line 20.

78. servavit Apollo : Porph. says, *hoc de illo sensu Homerico
sumpsit, quem et Lucilius in sexto satyrarum repraesentavit sic dicens :
ut discerperet hac ;* τόν δ᾽ ἐξήρπαξεν ᾿Απόλλων.

SERMO X.

The first eight lines are lacking in some of the manuscripts of
Horace, and are without doubt spurious. They must be earlier than

the tenth century, since they appear in some manuscripts of that date, but the exact time of their composition and their authorship are uncertain.

1. teste Catone : the reference is to P. Valerius Cato, whose life is sketched by Suet. *de Gramm.* 11. He seems to have prepared an edition of Lucilius, whose works he read with the grammarian Vettius Philocomus (see Suet. *de Gramm.* 2).

4. melior vir : *an abler man; cf.* ii. 1. 29, *Lucili ritu nostrum melioris utroque.*   **longe subtilior** : this form of comparison (with *longe*) is not found elsewhere in Horace, who uses *multo. Cf. Odes,* ii. 8. 7 ; *Serm.* ii. 8. 89, etc. ; and see note on ii. 5. 73.   **illo** : referring to another editor of Lucilius. The use of *ille* and *illo* of two different persons in the same sentence is an awkward construction.

5. funibus udis : rope's ends, wetted in order to strike a heavier blow.

6. poetis antiquis : Naevius, Ennius, and the other earlier poets, whom the boy was to be trained to defend.

7. grammaticorum . . . doctissimus : in apposition with *puer;* who is referred to is not known.

1. nempe . . . dixi : *true, I did say*, with reference to i. 4. 8. **incomposito** : *rude, unformed; cf. durus componere versus,* i. 4. 8. **currere** : *cf.* i. 4. 11, *cum flueret lutulentus.*

2. tam . . . inepte : modifies the verbal noun *fautor*, which with *est = favet.*

3. idem : *at the same time, he.*   **sale multo . . . defricuit** : *rubbed down the city with plenty of salt; sale* must be taken in its literal sense with *defricuit,* but the whole expression is of course metaphorical; *cf.* i. 9. 65 and the note ; *Epist.* ii. 2. 60, *hic delectatur iambis, Ille Bioneis sermonibus et sale nigro.*

4. charta eadem : *in the same work, i.e.* i. 4. For the meaning of *charta, cf.* i. 5. 104.

5. nec tamen : *yet after all. Cf. Epist.* i. 7. 23, *nec tamen ignorat.*   **hoc tribuens** : *though I pay him this tribute.*   **dederim** : potential subjunctive. See note on i. 4. 39.   **sic** : *in that case*, with conditional force, serving as the protasis of *mirer.*

6. Laberi mimos : the mimes of early times were farces, representing scenes from the life of the common people, usually of a coarse nature; *cf.* Ovid, *Trist.* ii. 497, *Quid si scripsissem mimos obscena iocantes, Qui semper vetiti crimen amoris habet.* They first received

literary treatment at the end of the Republic by Decimus Laberius
and Publilius Syrus. Laberius (105–43 B.C.) belonged to the equestrian order. Caesar, whom he had offended, degraded him by making
him act in one of his own mimes. The prologue of protest which he
wrote for the occasion is preserved by Macrobius, *Saturn.* ii. 7.
Although Laberius and Syrus raised the tone of the mime, their work
was not poetry, according to Horace's standard; see i. 4. 45 ff.

7. rictum : used of the open mouth. It is a classical word, used
by Cic. *Verr.* ii. 4. 43. 94 (of a statue of Hercules), *ut rictum eius ac
mentum paullo sit attritius;* Lucr. vi. 1195, *inhorrescens rictum.*
With the expression *diducere rictum, cf.* Juv. x. 230, *Ipse ad con-
spectum cenae diducere rictum Suetus hiat tantum.*

8. est quaedam . . . virtus: parenthetical, *and yet there is some
merit in this, too; hic* is the adverb = *in hoc.*

9. brevitate : *cf.* Quint. vi. 3. 45, *acutior est illa atque velocior
in urbanitate brevitas.*   **currat sententia** : *the thought may flow
freely.*

10. se impediat verbis : *i.e.* overload (and obscure) itself with
useless verbiage.

11. sermone : *language, discourse.*   **modo tristi, saepe
iocoso** : *cf.* Dryden, *Art of Poetry,* i. 75, " Happy who in his verse
can gently steer From grave to light, from pleasant to severe "; better
known in Pope's imitation, "From grave to gay, from lively to
severe."

12. defendente vicem: *playing the part. Cf. Ars Poet.* 194,
Actoris partes chorus officiumque virile Defendat; and for the meaning of *vicem,* Liv. i. 41. 6, *per speciem alienae fungendae vicis opes
suas firmavit;* Plin. *Epist.* vi. 6. 6, *cuius . . . ego vicem debeo
implere.*   **rhetoris** : here used in its Greek sense = *oratoris.*

13. urbani : *a wit. Cf.* Domitius Marsus ap. Quint. vi. 3. 105,
*urbanus homo erit, cuius multa bene dicta responsaque erunt, et qui
in sermonibus, circulis, conviviis, item in contionibus, omni denique
loco ridicule commodeque dicet.*   **parcentis . . . consulto** : *i.e.*
treating the subject lightly, instead of seriously ; *cf. ridiculum . . .
secat,* below. *Cf. Epist.* i. 9. 9 ; Cic. *de Orat.* ii. 58. 236, *est plane
oratoris movere risum . . . quod tristitiam ac severitatem mitigat et
relaxat odiosasque res saepe, quas argumentis dilui non facile est, ioco
risuque dissolvit.*

15. secat : *decides. Cf. Epist.* i. 16. 42, *quo multae magnaeque
secantur iudice lites.*

16. illi, *etc.* : *cf.* i. 4. 1 f., *Eupolis atque Cratinus Aristophanesque poetae Atque alii quorum comoedia prisca virorum est.*   **viris** : attracted into the relative clause.

17. stabant : *succeeded, held their ground.* *Cf.* Ter. *Hec.* Prol. ii. 6. (14), *In eis, quas primum Caecili didici novas, Partim sum earum exactus, partim vix steti;* Ov. *Fasti,* i. 18, *Ingenium vultu statque caditque tuo.*   **pulcher** : *pretty,* with a contemptuous force.

18. simius : the usual form of this word is *simia,* feminine, or as a term of abuse, masculine; *simius* is rare; *cf.* Vatin. ap. Cic. *ad Fam.* v. 10. 1, *simius, non semissis homo, contra me arma tulit.* Porph. says : *Demetrium modulatorem propter maciem ac paucitatem corporis hoc nomine appellat.* *Cf.* line 90 below.

19. Calvum : of the works of C. Licinius Calvus (82–47 B.C.) only scanty fragments remain. He is mentioned with high praise by Cicero and other ancient writers, and his name is often linked with that of Catullus. Horace's attitude toward these great lyric poets is difficult to understand. It must have been modified, at least as far as Catullus is concerned, in his later years, although we have no evidence of any such change of opinion.   **cantare** : for the construction, *cf. Carm. Saec.* 75–76, *Doctus et Phoebi chorus et Dianae Dicere laudes.*

20. Graeca : the extant fragments of Lucilius contain a great number of Greek words. This recommendation of Lucilius is put into the mouth of a defender, in order to be refuted. With the sentiment, *cf.* Cic. *de Off.* i. 31. 111, *ut sermone eo debemus uti, qui innatus est nobis, ne, ut quidam Graeca verba inculcantes, iure optimo rideamur, sic in actiones omnemque vitam nullam discrepantiam conferre debemus.*

21. seri studiorum : *pedants.* True to the principle just laid down, Horace thus translates the Greek ὀψιμαθεῖς. *Cf.* Gell. xi. 7. 3, *est adeo id vitium serae eruditionis quam Graeci ὀψιμαθίαν appellant, ut quod nunquam didiceris, diu ignoraveris, cum id scire aliquando coeperis, magni facias quo in loco cumque et quacumque in re dicere.* **quine putetis** : apparently a combination of *qui putetis* and *putetisne;* see note on i. 5. 9. The joining of -*ne* to the relative is for the most part archaic. *Cf.* Catull. 64, 180, *an patris auxilium sperem, quemne ipse reliqui,* which is not an exact parallel with the passage in Horace. *Qui* may perhaps be interrogative. *Cf.* ii. 3. 251 and the note.

22. Pitholeonti : an unknown poet, perhaps identical with Pitholaus. *Cf.* Suet. *Caes.* 75, *Pitholai carminibus maledicentissimis laceratam existimationem suam civili animo tulit* (Caesar).

23. at : a further justification of Lucilius's practice ; *cf.* line 20.

concinnus: *blended.*   **lingua . . . utraque**: *i.e.* Greek and Latin; *cf. Odes*, iii. 8. 5, *docte sermones utriusque linguae.* Instrumental ablative, modifying *concinnus*, which has the force of a participle, like *mixtus.*

24. nota: the *vintage-mark* on the amphora, here used for the wine itself; *cf. Odes*, ii. 3. 8, *interiore nota Falerni.* The Falernian was a dry wine, while the Chian was sweet.

25. cum versus facias: *i.e.* is this mixing of Greek and Latin allowable in oratory, as well as in poetry? There is no conscious ellipsis. The subjunctive is due to the indefinite second person singular.   **te ipsum**: emphatic. Horace appeals to his opponent's own better judgment.

26. Petilli: *cf.* i. 4. 94 and the note.

27. patris Latini: *your Latin father*, contrasted with *Canusini bilinguis*, line 30 below, where see the note.

28. Pedius Publicola: probably related to Messalla Corvinus (see below), although not his brother, as the pseudo-Acron says. **exsudet**: *are working out*, with hard labor.

29. Corvinus: M. Valerius Messalla Corvinus (circ. 65 B.C.–4 A.D.), the celebrated orator and the patron of Tibullus.

30. Canusini bilinguis: in Apulia the inhabitants spoke Italic (at first Oscan and later Latin) and Greek. *Cf.* Gell. xvii. 17. 1, *Quintus Ennius tria corda habere sese dicebat, quod loqui Graece et Osce et Latine sciret.*

31. mare citra: referring to the Ionian Sea, which separated Italy from Greece.

33. cum somnia vera: *cf.* Ovid, *Heroid.* xviii. 195, *Namque sub aurora iam dormitante lucerna, Somnia quo cerni tempora vera solent*; Tennyson, *Morte d'Arthur*, 341, —

> "Till on to dawn, when dreams
> Begin to feel the truth and stir of day."

34. in silvam . . . ligna feras: a proverbial expression for fruitless labor, like the English 'carry coals to Newcastle.'   **ac si**: *than if.*

36. turgidus: *bombastic.*   **Alpinus**: Porph. says that the reference is to M. Furius Bibaculus, but this is not certain. Schanz, *Geschichte der römischen Litteratur*, i.[2] p. 117, says that there were three poets of the name of Furius, and that here and in ii. 5. 41 the reference is to Furius Alpinus, a contemporary of Horace.   **iugu-**

lat: *cuts the throat of;* *i.e.* describes his death, doubtless with many bloody details.

37. defingit . . . luteum : *muddies up,* by his poor description. **caput**: probably the *mouth,* rather than the source, of the river. According to some, the head of the river god.   **haec ego ludo** : *I amuse myself with such writing as this;* ludo is used by way of contrast with the ambitious work just described ; *cf. inludo chartis,* i. 4. 139.

38. aede : Porph. says: *in aede Musarum, ubi poetae sua carmina recitent.* The place referred to is uncertain, but the reference is evidently to readings of plays whose authors wished to have them put on the stage.   **sonent**: subjunctive in a relative clause of purpose ; *cf. quis . . . insudet,* i. 4. 72.   **Tarpa** : Sp. Maecius Tarpa was appointed by Pompey, in 55 B.C., to be judge or censor of the plays which were offered for presentation in the latter's new theatre.

39. theatris: apparently the so-called dative of the agent. See Introd. § 39. *b.*

40. meretrice . . . Davo . . . Chremeta: stock characters of Roman comedy.   Ablative absolute in a somewhat loose relation to the rest of the sentence; *cf. Odes,* iii. 1. 31, *Mendaxque fundus, arbore nunc aquas Culpante nunc torrentia agros Sidera, nunc hiemes iniquas.*

41. garrire: *rattle off;* *cf.* i. 9. 13, *cum quidlibet ille garriret.* **libellos** is accusative of the inner object.   **Fundani** : C. Fundanius, unknown except from Horace's references to him ; *cf.* ii. 8. 19.

42. Pollio : see *Odes,* ii. 1.   On the tragedies, *cf.* Virg. *Ecl.* viii. 10, *sola Sophocleo tua carmina digna coturno.*   **regum**: of the heroes of tragedy ; *cf. Odes,* iv. 2. 13, *Seu deos regesque canit, deorum Sanguinem, per quos cecidere iusta Morte Centauri, cecidit tremendae Flamma Chimaerae.*

43. canit : of the stately measure of tragedy, contrasted with the colloquial style of comedy (*garrire*).   **pede ter percusso**: *i.e.* in the iambic trimeter, in which the descriptive and narrative parts of tragedies were composed.

44. Varius: see note on *Serm.* i. 5. 40; *cf. Odes,* i. 6. 1. **ducit** : *spins,* a common term in this connection.   *Cf.* Ovid, *Tristia,* i. 11. 17, *tamen ipse trementi Carmina ducebat qualia cumque manu.* **molle atque facetum** : *tender and playful;* the reference is to the *Eclogues* and the earlier work of Virgil.   Since the *Georgics* and *Aeneid* were not yet published, Quintilian's comment apparently rests on a misunderstanding.   *Cf.* Quint. vi. 3. 20, *facetum quoque non tantum circa ridicula opinor consistere : neque enim d:ceret* **Horatius**

facetum carminis genus natura concessum esse Vergilio. Decoris hanc magis et excultae cuiusdam elegantiae appellationem puto. Ideoque in epistulis Cicero haec Bruti refert verba : ' ne illi sunt pedes faceti ac delicatius ingredienti molles.' Quod convenit cum illo Horatiano : ' molle atque facetum Vergilio.'

45. adnuĕrunt : the original quantity, preserved for metrical convenience ; see Introd. § 58.

46. hoc : *i.e.* Satire.   **Varrone Atacino** : see Introd. § 27.

47. quibusdam aliis : see Introd. § 27.

48. inventore : Lucilius, the inventor of this form of Satire. See Introd. § 20.   **illi** : *from him ;* dative of separation with *detrahere.* **ausim** : an old form used as a perfect subjunctive.

49. haerentem : *cf. Odes,* i. 17. 27, *iniciat manus Et scindat haerentem coronam Crinibus.*

50. at dixi : *but I did say.* Although Horace gives Lucilius the credit due him as the originator of this form of satire, yet he believes that in some respects it is possible to improve on him. *Cf.* i. 4. 11 ff.

51. tollenda relinquendis : *i.e.* the parts which ought to be omitted were often greater in amount than those which deserved to be perpetuated.

52. doctus : *'Sir Critic'* (Conington) ; *i.e.* learned critic that you are ; ironical.   **Homero** : *cf. Ars Poet.* 395 ; Lucil. 305 ff. L., *nemo qui culpat Homerum, Perpetuo culpat, neque, quod dixi ante, poësin : Versum unum culpat, verbum, enthymema, locumve.*

53. comis : *witty,* contrasted with *tragici.* Note the juxtaposition of the two words.   **mutat** : *censures,* for *mutandum esse censet. Cf.* Gellius, xvii. 21. 49, *clariorque tunc in poematis eorum* (Ennius, Pacuvius, Accius, *etc.*) *obtrectandis Lucilius fuit.*   Lucilius and Accius were at variance particularly in their theories of orthography. **Acci** : L. Accius (B.C. 170–94), the greatest of Roman tragic poets.

54. Enni : see Introd. § 18. Servius, on *Aen.* ix. 503, tells us that one line was *At tuba terribili sonitu taratantara dixit ;* and, on *Aen.* xi. 601, that another was *Sparsis hastis longis campus splendet et horret,* where Lucilius sarcastically proposed as an emendation, *horret et alget.*   **gravitate minores** : *as inferior in dignity,* to the requirements of epic poetry.

55. non ut maiore : hyperbaton for *ut non maiore.*   **reprensis** : masculine, *than those whom he has criticised.* See Introd. § 49. *b.* .

56. quid vetat . . . nosmet : *i.e.* Lucilius criticised as his predecessors and contemporaries, why should I not criticise him ?

57. illius : here only in Horace scanned with a long penult, while *illius* occurs eleven times.   **rerum** : *his subject.*

58. factos : *finished.*   *Cf.* Cic. *de Orat.* iii. 48. 184, *oratio quae quidem sit polita atque facta quodam modo.*

59. ac si : *than if; cf.* i. 1. 46 ; i. 6. 130.   **pedibus senis** : *i.e.* in hexameter verse : *cf.* i. 4. 7, *mutatis tantum pedibus numerisque*, and the note.

60. scripsisse : the perfect of instantaneous action. See Introd. § 44. *f.*

62. Cassi : an otherwise unknown poet, confused by Porphyrio with Cassius Parmensis, *Epist.* i. 4. 3, who was alive when the Epistle in question was written.

63. capsis : see note on *loculos*, i. 6. 74.

64. ambustum : here used for *combustum*, as in Tac. *Hist.* v. 12, *magna vis frumenti ambusta.*   **fuerit** : jussive subjunctive with concessive force.   **inquam**: *I say*, repeating the criticism of lines 3 and 53.

65. limatior : *more polished.* The word is derived from *lima* ('file'), and the metaphor is a common one.

66. quam . . . auctor : *auctor* apparently refers to Lucilius himself, with the sense *limatior quam exspectari poterat ab auctore carminis rudis et Graecis intacti.* The Satires of Ennius, to whom *auctor* is referred by some, were of a different kind (see Introd. § 18), and Lucilius is expressly spoken of as the inventor of this kind of composition, in line 48.   **rudis** : *new, untried.* *Cf.* Catull. 64. 11, *rudem Amphitriten.*   **Graecis** : dative of the apparent agent.

67. poetarum seniorum turba : *i.e.* Livius, Plautus, Naevius, etc.

68. si foret . . . dilatus : *if his life had been postponed.* On *foret*, see note on i. 4. 4.

69. detereret : *sc. lima.*   **recideret** : *prune away*, like a gardener with his pruning knife.   **ultra perfectum traheretur** : *i.e.* what was superfluous, *the omission* of which would make the work perfect.

71. scaberet : apparently a vulgar word. *Cf.* Lucil. 296 L., *Scaberat, ut porcus contritis arbore costas*, and 800, *caput scabit.*   **vivos** : *to the quick.* *Cf.* Pers. i. 106, *Nec pluteum caedit nec demorsos sapit ungues;* vi. 162, *crudum . . . unguem abrodens.*

72. stilum vertas : the reverse end of the stylus was flat or round, for erasing what had been written, by smoothing the wax.   **digna**

legi : for the classic *digna quae legantur ;* see note on i. 3. 24 ; *cf.* Cic. *Brut.* 18. 71 (of plays of L. Andronicus), *non dignae sunt quae iterum legantur.*

73. scripturus : *if you intend to write.* See note on *mansuri,* i. 5. 87. **neque** : *and do not,* instead of the regular *neve,* a common usage in poetry ; *cf. Odes,* i. 9. 15.

74. contentus : *and be content;* part of the injunction *vertas . . . labores.* **paucis lectoribus** : *i.e.* such writing would appeal only to the educated classes, not to the general public.

75. vilibus in ludis : *i.e.* to be used as school-books. That this was Horace's fate is probable from the great number of manuscripts in which his works are preserved, and is perhaps indicated by Juv. vii. 226, *Quot stabant pueri cum totus decolor esset Flaccus, et haereret nigro fuligo Maroni;* though the reference is sometimes understood to be to busts of Horace and Virgil. Horace elsewhere anticipates this fate for his works ; see *Epist.* i. 20. 17, *Hoc quoque te manet, ut pueros elementa docentem Occupet extremis in vicis balba senectus.*

76. equitem : used collectively, *the knights,* who occupied the first fourteen rows above the orchestra at the theatre, and are typical of the better class. *Cf. Ars Poet.* 248, *quibus est equus et pater et res.*

77. Arbuscula : a famous actress in the mimes, popular in Cicero's day. *Cf.* Cic. *ad Att.* iv. 15. 6, *quaeris nunc de Arbuscula; valde placuit.*

78. Pantilius : this name occurs in inscriptions, *C. I. L.* ix. 5277, and x. 5925, but is doubtless chosen on account of its meaning. See note on *Novius,* i. 6. 40.

79. Demetrius : apparently the *simius* of line 18.

80. Fannius : *cf.* i. 4. 21. **Hermogenes** : *cf.* i. 4. 72 ; i. 9. 25. **conviva** : *parasite.*

81. Plotius : *cf.* i. 5. 40.

82. Valgius : C. Valgius Rufus, a friend of Horace, to whom *Odes,* ii. 9, is addressed. *Cf. Paneg. Messallae,* 180, *Valgius : aeterno propior non alter Homero.* **Octavius** : not Augustus, whom Horace addresses as Caesar and later as Augustus, but the poet and historian. Virg. (?) *Catalepton* 14, says of him : *Scripta quidem tua nos multum mirabimur et te Raptum et Romanam flebimus historiam.*

83. Fuscus : *cf.* i. 9. 61 ; *Odes,* i. 22 ; *Epist.* i. 10. **Viscorum** : otherwise unknown. A Viscus is mentioned in i. 9. 22, and a Viscus Thurinus in *Serm.* ii. 8. 20.

84. ambitione relegata : *without flattery,* since these are great men, whom Horace might be suspected of trying to propitiate.

85. Messalla : see line 28 above.   **fratre** : L. Gellius Publicola, consul in 36 B.C. He was in the army of Brutus, where Horace may have met him, but afterwards went over to Octavian.

86. Bibule : perhaps referring to L. Calpurnius Bibulus. He also was in the army of Brutus.   **Servi** : perhaps a son of the celebrated jurist Servius Sulpicius. Ovid, *Trist.* ii. 441, speaks of poems of his : *nec sunt minus improba Servi carmina.*   **his** : ablative governed by *simul*, which is here used for the first time as a preposition. **Furni** : C. Furnius, consul in 17 B.C. Suet., p. 289. 28, Roth, says : *Furnii pater et filius clari oratores habentur, quorum filius consularis ante patrem moritur.*

88. prudens : *purposely.*   **haec** : *i.e.* the first book of *Sermones.*

89. arridere : *to please.* *Cf.* Cic. *ad Att.* xiii. 21. 3, *inhibere illud tuum, quod valde mihi arriserat.* In a different sense in *Ars Poet.* 101, *ridentibus arrident.*

90. deterius : *less.*

91. discipularum : *female pupils.*   **cathedras** : *arm-chairs,* used especially by women ; *cf.* Mart. iii. 63. 7, *Inter femineas tota qui luce cathedras Desidet atque aliqua semper in aure sonat.*

92. puer : addressed to an amanuensis.

BOOK II.

SERMO I.

1. sunt quibus, *etc.* : on this criticism, see Introd. § 24.   **satura** : Horace does not use this term in the first book. It occurs again in ii. 6. 17. *Satura* was the Horatian orthography ; see Introd. § 15. **videar** : Horace uses both the indicative and the subjunctive after *est qui* and similar expressions, usually with a slightly different meaning ; see Introd. § 45. *c.*   **acer** : *bitter* in invective.

2. legem : *the proper limit ; sc. operis,* and *cf. Ars Poet.* 135, *pudor vetet aut operis lex.* The word is probably used in a double sense, meaning also ' what is lawful.'   **tendere** : the figure is drawn from the stretching of a bow.   **sine nervis** : *without strength,* a figure from the sinews of the body.

4. mille : of an indefinite large number. See Introd. § 50.   **deduci** : the regular word ; *cf. ducit,* i. 10. 44, and *Epist.* ii. 1. 225, *tenui deducta poemata filo.*   **Trebati** : referring to C. Trebatius

Testa, a famous *iuris consultus*, a friend of Cicero.   Into his hands
Horace puts his case.   The brevity of the answers of Trebatius are
characteristic of the experienced lawyer.

5. quiescas : *that you be quiet;* jussive subjunctive governed by
an implied *praescribo*.   There is no conscious ellipsis.   **ne faciam** :
like *quiescas*, depends on an implied *praescribis*.

6. aio : *yes.*   **peream male** : *hang me; cf. interream,* i. 9. 38,
and the note.

7. optimum erat : *would be best;* the indicative, on account of
the implied idea of obligation ; *cf.* Ovid, *Her.* i. 112, *in patrias artes
erudiendus erat.*   **nequeo dormire** : Horace implies that his writing
is due to sleeplessness.   *Cf.* Plin. *Epist.* vii. 4. 4, *dein cum meridie
dormiturus me recepissem nec obreperet somnus . . . id ipsum quod me
ad scribendum sollicitaverat his versibus exaravi.*   Also *Epist.* ii. 2.
54, *melius dormire quam scribere versus.*   **ter** : the number three
was supposed to have a mystic power in prescriptions, magic rites,
etc. ; *cf. Epist.* i. 1. 37.   **uncti** : a regular preliminary to athletic
exercises ; *cf. Odes,* i. 8. 8.

8. transnanto Tiberim : Trebatius was fond of swimming ; *cf.*
Cic. *ad Fam.* vii. 10. 2 (addressed to Trebatius), *qui neque in Oceano
natare volueris, studiosissimus homo natandi.*

9. irriguum mero : *soaked with* (unmixed) *wine; cf.* Cic. *ad Fam.*
vii. 22 (addressed to Trebatius), *inluseras heri inter scyphos, quod
dixeram . . . itaque etsi domum bene potus seroque redieram, tamen
id caput notavi.*   Also Prop. iii. 17. 13, *Quod si, Bacche, tuis per
fervida tempora donis Accersitus erit somnus in ossa mea.   Mero*
(*sc. vino*) is an adjective used as a substantive.   See note on *venalis,*
i. 1. 47.

10. rapit : *carries you away;* stronger than *capit,* which Bentley
reads.   **aude** : *have the courage* to undertake a loftier theme.

11. Caesaris : he received the title of Augustus a few years later,
on January 17, 27 B.C.   See note on *Octavius,* i. 10. 82.   **res** = *res
gestas.*

12. praemia : *cf.* Lucil. 612, L., *Hunc laborem sumas, laudem
qui tibi ac fructum ferat; Epist.* ii. 2. 38, *grandia laturus meritorum
praemia.*   **laturus** : *and you will receive.*   See note on *mansuri,* i.
5. 87, and Introd. § 47.   **cupidum** : *much as I should like to;* the
adjective has a concessive force.   **pater** : a title of respect, used by
Horace in addressing both men and gods ; *cf.* line 42 below, and *Epist.*
i. 6. 54.   Trebatius was more than twenty years older than Horace.

13. quivis: *every one, any one you like.* While disclaiming the ability to write epic poetry, Horace gives a hint, in the next two lines, of what he could do in that field. **horrentia pilis agmina**: with reference to the Roman legions, which are characterized by their principal weapon, the *pilum.*

14. fracta . . . cuspide: *with their lances broken,* — a sign of defeat and flight. **Gallos**: Octavian carried on several campaigns against the Gallic tribes.

15. equo . . . Parthi: the Parthians were the most formidable enemies of the Romans at this time. Their strength lay principally in their cavalry. *Cf. Odes,* i. 19. 11 ; ii. 13. 17.

16. iustum: *as just (sc. eum)* ; of the civic virtues of Caesar. **poteras**: *cf. erat,* line 7, and the note. **fortem**: *as brave (cf. iustum)* ; of his courage in war ; *cf. Odes,* i. 6. 11 ff.

17. Scipiadam: Scipio Africanus Minor. The patronymic is used, as also by Lucilius, Lucretius, and Virgil, because *Scipiōnem* will not fit into hexameter verse. **sapiens** : *sensible,* in choosing a suitable theme ; *cf. Epist.* ii. 1. 50, *Ennius sapiens.* **haud mihi dero**: *cf.* i. 9. 56, and the note.

18. cum res ipsa feret: *when opportunity offers.* **dextro tempore**: the opposite of *laevo tempore,* ii. 4. 4. **Flacci**: *of a Flaccus,* as an obscure bard ; more modest than *mea.* For the rest of Horace's name, see *Serm.* ii. 6. 37 ; and *Epist.* i. 14. 5.

19. attentam: emphatic.

20. male si palpere: the person and the figure are combined, — *who, like a horse, if you stroke him the wrong way.* *Cf. Epist.* i. 4. 16 (of Horace), *Cum ridere voles Epicuri de grege porcum;* and see note on *Tantalus,* i. 1. 68. **tutus**: *i.e.* to protect himself.

21. tristi : *abusive,* the epithet transferred from the effect to the cause ; *cf.* Lucil. 963, L., *tuis saevis factis et tristibus dictis.*

22. Pantolabum : *cf.* i. 8. 11. A name made up from πᾶν λαβεῖν, ' Catch-all,' *quia a multis pecuniam mutuam erogabat,* Porph. *ad loc.* See note on *Novius,* i. 6. 40. **Nomentanum** : *cf.* i. 1. 102.

23. cum: *whereupon.*

24. quid faciam : *what can I do?* Horace implies that it is his nature to write satire : *cf.* Pers. i. 12, *Quid faciam? sed sum petulanti splene cachinno.* **saltat**: see note on i. 9. 24. **Milonius**: otherwise unknown. **ut semel** : Horace elsewhere has *cum semel; ut semel* belongs to the language of comedy. **icto** : *i.e. vino.*

25. numerusque lucernis (accessit): *i.e.* he sees double ; ap-

parently a proverbial expression. *Cf.* Juv. vi. 304, *cum iam vertigine
tectum Ambulat et geminis exsurgit mensa lucernis;* Petr. 64, *et sane
iam lucernae mihi plures videbantur ardere.*

26. Castor: Castor and Pollux, although twins, had different
tastes.   **ovo . . . eodem**: they were the sons of Leda and the
swan (Jupiter).

27. quot capitum . . . totidem studiorum milia: a common
proverbial saying; *cf.* Ter. *Phorm.* 454, *quot homines, tot sententiae,
etc.*   On the use of *mille (milia)* for an indefinite large number, see
Introd. § 50.

28. pedibus claudere verba: *to write verse; cf.* i. 4. 40; i. 10. 59.

29. melioris: *a better man, i.e.* a greater poet and of higher social
position.   After thus silencing Trebatius by freely admitting his inferi-
ority, Horace gives a brief critique of Lucilius's poetry.

30. fidis . . . sodalibus: Porphyrio says: *Aristoxenis sententia
est.   Ille enim in suis scriptis ostendit Sapphonem et Alcaeum volumina
sua loco sodalium habuisse.*   Southey uses the same expression of his
books: "My never failing friends are they, With whom I converse
night and day."   The word *sodalis* implies a high degree of intimacy,
'comrade,' 'boon companion.'   *Cf.* Cic. *de Sen.* 13. 45.   **arcana**:
i.e. his inmost thoughts, his secrets; *cf. Odes,* i. 18. 16, *arcani fides
prodiga.*   **olim**: *i.e.* in his day; see note on i. 1. 25.

31. si male cesserat . . . si bene: *i.e.* if matters had gone ill or
well.   The expression is used impersonally *(sc. illi)*; *cf.* Ovid, *Met.*
x. 80, *seu quod male cesserat illi.*

33. votiva . . . tabella: sailors who had been saved from ship-
wreck often hung pictures commemorating the event in the appropriate
temple.   *Cf. Odes,* i. 5. 13, *me tabula sacer Votiva paries indicat uvida
Suspendisse potenti Vestimenta maris deo.*   Rescue from other disas-
ters, relief from illness, and the like, were similarly commemorated.

34. senis: probably used without reference to his age, but with regard to his times; so Stat. *Silv.* iv. 9. 20, *Bruti senis,* though Brutus
died at the age of thirty-seven.   **Lucanus an Apulus**: both warlike
races; hence Horace's pugnacious spirit and bent for satire.   **anceps**: probably masculine; *cf.* Liv. xxxi. 12, *incertus infans mascu-
lus an femina esset.*   But it may be neuter, as Porph. regarded it; *cf.*
Liv. xxxi. 41, *clauserant portas, incertum vi an voluntate,* though
anceps (est) as an impersonal expression does not seem to occur.

35. Venusinus . . . colonus: Venusia was formerly a city of
the Hirpini.   It was captured in 294 B.C., and in 291 a colony of

twenty thousand citizens was established there, to protect the road from Tarentum into Samnium.   **sub**: *close up to.*

37. quo ne: apparently the construction is influenced by the implied comparative, *quo Romanus tutior esset.*   **Romano**: *the Roman*, like *Lucanus* and *Apulus* in line 34.

38. quod : *any*, modifying *bellum.*

39. sed : adversative to *sequor hunc;   i.e.* Horace follows Lucilius in writing satire, but, unlike his model, he will use his pen for defensive purposes only ; hence *ultro, unprovoked,* 'without just cause.'

40. quemquam animantem : *any living soul.*

41. quem : referring to *ensis;* for a similar comparison, *cf.* Juv. i. 165, *Ense velut stricto quotiens Lucilius ardens Infremuit, rubet auditor.*

42. tutus : *as long as I am safe.*

43. ut : with the force of *utinam.* With the whole passage, *cf.* Catull. 66. 48, *Iuppiter ut Chalybum omne genus pereat* (following Callimachus, frag. 35 *c*). The Chalybians were famous workers in steel.   **positum** : in a double sense, 'laid down' and 'laid aside.'

44. nec : for *neve; cf. neque,* i. 10. 73, and the note.

45. commorit = *commoverit.*   **melius non tangere** : *cf.* our expression, 'let sleeping dogs lie,' and the motto of Scotland, *nemo me impune lacessit.*

46. insignis . . . urbe : *i.e.* he will be the talk of the town.

47. Cervius : an informer, not otherwise known ; not the same, of course, as the garrulous rustic in ii. 6. 77.   **iratus** : *when he is angered.*   **urnam** = *iudicium;* either the urn from which the names of the jurors who were to serve in the trial were drawn, or that into which their votes for condemnation or acquittal were cast.

48. Albuci : modifies *venenum;* probably an objective genitive, *the poison which killed Albucius.*   **quibus est inimica** : *her enemies*, forming a parallel to *iratus* in the preceding line.   **venenum** : *sc. minitatur.*

49. Turius : evidently a corrupt judge, who threatens to condemn his enemy (an expression like *iratus* or *quibus est inimicus* is implied), if ever he be brought to trial before him. Porph. says that it was before this man as praetor that Verres was tried.

50. ut : *how.*   **quo quisque valet** : *i.e.* with his most powerful weapon.   **suspectos** : *the objects of his distrust;* the participle used as a substantive.

51. natura potens : *a powerful natural instinct.*

52. intus: *from within*, apparently a colloquial use of the word.

53. Scaevae: otherwise unknown.   **vivacem**: *too long-lived;* cf. Juv. xiv. 251, *Iam torquet iuvenem longa et cervina senectus.*

54. sceleris: violence, *i.e.* he will not strangle, but will poison her.   **pia**: *filial;* ironical.

55. ut: *as is the fact that.*   **calce**: we should expect *cornu* (*cf.* line 52) ; the change seems to be made because the wolf has feet, but not horns, although he does not use them as offensive weapons.

56. mala . . . cicuta: contrasted with *pia dextera.*   **vitiato**: *drugged.*   **melle**: here probably for *mulsum*, a mixture of wine and honey.

57. ne longum faciam: *in short*, not to make a long story of it.

58. atris: the color of death.   **circumvolat**: note the present, — *is even now hovering over me.*

60. vitae . . . color: *i.e.* whether bright (*candidus*) or dark (*ater, niger*).   **scribam**: note the position of the word, which would normally follow *color; cf.* ii. 3. 211, *Aiax, cum immeritos occidit, desipit, agnos.*   **ut sis vitalis**: *that you won't be long lived, i.e.* if you follow such a course of actions ; cf. *Iliad*, xviii. 95, ὠκύμορος δή μοι, τέκος, ἔσσεαι, οἷ᾽ ἀγορεύεις.

61. maiorum: *of the great;* equivalent to *potentiorum; cf. Epist.* i. 17. 2, *quo pacto deceat maioribus uti.*

62. frigore: *with a chill*, of the coldness of his patrons ; *cf.* Sen. *Epist.* 122. 11, *Montanus Iulius . . . tolerabilis poeta et amicitia Tiberii notus et frigore.*

64. detrahere et pellem: an allusion to the fable of the Ape (Lucian, *Philopseud.* 5) or the Ass in the Lion's skin (Lucian, *Fugit.* 13).   Cf. i. 6. 22, *quoniam in propria non pelle quiessem;* and *Epist.* i. 16. 45, *Introrsum turpem, speciosum pelle decora.*   **per ora**: sc. *hominum* or *virum; cf.* Sall. *Jug.* 31. 10, *incedunt per ora vestra magnifici*, and the epitaph of Ennius, *volito vivos per ora virum.*

65. cederet: for *incederet*, a colloquial use of the word ; *cf.* Sall. *Jug.* 31. 10, quoted in the preceding note.   **Laelius**: *C. Laelius Sapiens*, consul in 140 B.C. He was a patron of Terence, and the principal speaker in the *Laelius*, or *De Amicitia*, of Cicero.   **qui . . . duxit**: *cf. Odes*, iv. 8. 18. *qui domita nomen ab Africa Lucratus rediit.*

67. ingenio: *wit.*   **offensi**: sc. *sunt*, as with *soliti* in line 74. **Metello**: the reference is to *Q. Caecilius Metellus Macedonicus*, consul in 143 B.C., a political enemy of Scipio ; *cf.* Cic. *de Off.* i. 25. 87, *fuit inter P. Africanum et Q. Metellum sine acerbitate dissensio.*

68. Lupo: *L. Cornelius Lentulus Lupus*, consul in 156 B.C., censor in 147 B.C. He was attacked by Lucilius; *cf*. Pers. i. 114, *secuit Lucilius urbem*, *Te, Lupe, te, Muci, et genuinum fregit in illis*. **atqui**: *and yet*. Lucilius attacked prominent men, as well as the common herd, without offending his patrons.

69. arripuit: *dragged to judgment; cf*. i. 9. 77; ii. 3. 224.   **tributim**: *tribe by tribe*, apparently going through the whole list, as the scholiast on Pers. i. 115 says: *urbem autem ideo dixit secuit, quia tribus omnes triginta quinque laceravit, ex quibus urbs tota constat.* Mention of individual tribes occurs in Lucil. in fragments 1094 and 1095 L., *prima, Papiria tu stolidarum . . . Priverno Oufentina venit fluvioque Oufente.*

70. uni aequus virtuti: ' to virtue only and her friends a friend ' (Pope).

71. quin = *quin etiam, nay more.*   **scaena** : *the stage* of public life, where they had to wear a mask of dignity.

72. virtus Scipiadae : *the valiant Scipio*, a common circumlocution ; *cf. Odes*, iii. 21. 11, *prisci Catonis virtus.* On *Scipiadae*, see note on line 17.   **mitis sapientia Laeli** : *the wise and gentle Laelius ;* see preceding note.

73. nugari . . . et ludere : the Comm. Cruq. says : *Scipio Africanus et Laelius feruntur tam fuisse familiares et amici Lucilio, ut quodam tempore Laelio circum lectos triclinii fugienti Lucilius superveniens, eum obtorta mappa quasi feriturus sequeretur.* Cf. also Cic. *de Orat.* ii. 6. 22.   **discincti** : *i.e. tunicis solutis.* The toga was worn only in the city.

74. decoqueretur : subjunctive of anticipation.

75. censum : *rank*, as determined by the census. Lucilius was an *eques*, and according to Porph. was the grand-uncle of Pompey the Great.

76. cum magnis : *i.e. cum Maecenate.*   **invita** : *even though unwilling.*   **usque** : *i.e.* will always be obliged to admit.

77. fragili . . . solido : neuters ; the reference seems to be to the fable of the Viper and the File ; *cf.* Pers. i. 114, quoted above on line 68.

78. nisi quid tu : after his long monologue, Horace appeals to Trebatius for his view, and resumes the dialogue form.

79. nihil hinc diffindere : *to take no exception to this ;* lit. *to cut off nothing from it,* as we speak of weakening an argument.

80. ut . . . caveas : *(may you) take warning and be on your guard; ut* is equivalent to *utinam*, as in line 43, above.   **negoti** :

trouble, difficulty; genitive of the whole, with *quid;* its position in the sentence gives the word a strong emphasis.

81. sanctarum: *sacred,* as they would be in the eyes of a jurist like Trebatius ; *cf.* ii. 2. 131, *vafri inscitia iuris.*

82. mala condiderit . . . carmina : with reference to the Twelve Tables as quoted by Cicero, *de Rep.* iv. 10. 12, *nostrae duodecim tabulae, cum perpaucas res capite sanxissent, in his hanc quoque sanciendam putaverunt, si quis occentavisset sive carmen condidisset, quod infamiam faceret flagitiumve alteri.* The later law of Sulla was milder ; see Ulpian, *Digest.* xlvii. 10. 5, *si quis librum ad infamiam alicuius pertinentem scripserit, composuerit, ediderit, dolove malo fecerit . . . uti de ea re agere liceret.* On *condiderīt,* see i. 5. 90, and Introd. § 57.

83. esto: *very well!* **mala** : Horace humorously takes *mala,* which in the law means 'abusive,' in the sense of *poor, inferior.*

84. iudice Caesare: *even in Caesar's judgment ;* ablative absolute.

85. latraverit: for *allatraverit,* and so followed by the accusative. *Cf. Epod.* 5. 58 ; *Epist.* i. 2. 66. **integer ipse** : *while he himself is blameless; cf. Odes,* i. 22. 1, *integer vitae.*

86. solventur . . . tabulae : *the indictment will be quashed amid general laughter; solventur = dissolventur.* Porph. says, '*tabulae: pro subsellia,*' in which case the expression would be parallel to Juv. vii. 86, *cum fregit subsellia versu,* and the meaning, that the judges are so carried away by the laughter which follows the poet's witty interpretation of the law, that they dismiss the case.

SERMO II.

1. quae . . . et quanta : *what and how great.* **boni**: *good friends.* Line 16 suggests that the party may have assembled at some villa on the sea-coast. **parvo** : *on a little, i.e. frugally ;* ablative of instrument.

2. nec meus : *cf.* Plato, *Symposium,* 177 *a,* ἡ μέν μοι ἀρχὴ τοῦ λόγου ἐστὶ κατὰ τὴν Εὐριπίδου Μελανίππην · οὐ γὰρ ἐμὸς ὁ μῦθος, ἀλλὰ Φαίδρου τοῦδε ὃν μέλλω λέγειν.

3. abnormis sapiens: *a self-taught philosopher; cf.* Cic. *de Amic.* 5. 18, *numquam ego dicam C. Fabricium, M'. Curium, quos sapientes maiores nostri iudicabant, ad istorum normam fuisse sapientis.* **crassa Minerva**: *plain mother-wit;* ablative of quality ; *cf. Ars*

Poet. 385, *Tu nihil invita dices faciesve Minerva;* Cic. *de Amic.* 5. 19, *pingui Minerva;* Quint. i. 10. 28, *crassiore ut vocant Musa.*

4. nitentis: *glittering*, with silver.

5. stupet: *is dazzled; cf.* i. 6. 17.   **insanis**: *senseless, extravagant; cf.* Cic. *Mil.* 20. 53, *insanas substructiones.*

6. falsis: *cf.* line 30.

7. impransi: *fasting, on an empty stomach.*

9. corruptus: *who has been bribed.* The person who is sitting at a bountiful table is a prejudiced judge of the advantages of frugal living.

10. lassus ab: *ab* has a temporal force, — *tired after riding an unbroken horse.*   **Romana . . . militia**: *Roman field sports; cf. Epist.* i. 2. 67, *militat in silvis catulus;* and, on the contrast between the Greek and the Roman sports, *Odes,* iii. 24. 53 ff.

11. graecari: *to play the Greek, i.e.* to imitate the Greeks.   **pila**: see note on *lusumque trigonem,* i. 6. 126.   Ball playing was a favorite form of exercise among the Romans, and several different kinds of games were played.

12. studio fallente: *i.e.* through the interest in the game, which takes one's mind off the hard labor which is involved.   The phrase modifies *agit.*   After *laborem* we must understand *pila lude,* to make the sentence strictly grammatical, but it need not be expressed in the translation.

13. agit: *attracts.*

14. cum labor, *etc.:* a kind of anacoluthon.   The various forms of exercise enumerated above are summed up, and the thought expressed by the participles *sectatus* and *lassus* is repeated in another form after the parenthetical *vel si Romana ,* . . . *aëra disco.*   **extuderit**: *has knocked out,* a colloquial expression.   **siccus, inanis**: *hungry and thirsty,* corresponding in chiastic order to *sperne cibum* and *ne biberis* below.

15. sperne: *i.e.* disdain, if you can.   **Hymettia . . . Falerno**: Macrobius, *Saturnalia,* vii. 12, says that the best *mulsum* was made of new Hymettian honey and old Falernian wine.

16. ne biberis: a form of prohibition not confined to poetry; *cf. Odes,* i. 11. 1, *tu ne quaesieris,* and Cic. *Tusc.* i. 98.   **foris est promus**: *the steward is out,* so that nothing can be got from the pantry.   *Promus* is the noun of agency, cognate with *promere.*   **atrum . . . hiemat**: *is dark and stormy.*   Cf. Virg. *Aen.* v. 11, *inhorruit unda tenebris.*

17. cum sale panis: a proverbial expression; *cf.* Plin. *N. H.*

xxxi: 89, *Varro etiam pulmentarii vice usos veteres (sale) auctor est, et salem cum pane esitasse eos proverbio apparet.*

18. latrantem: *clamoring.*   **leniet**: *stay*; *cf.* ii. 8. 5, *Quae prima iratum ventrem placaverit esca.*   **unde aut qui partum**: *sc. hoc*, *i.e.* that you are satisfied with bread and salt.

20. in te ipso: the answer to *unde* in line 18.   **pulmentaria**: *cf.* Varro, *L. L.* v. 108, *quod edebant cum pulte ab eo pulmentum, ut Plautus: hinc pulmentarium dictum.* Hence *pulmentarium* means, like the Greek ὄψον, anything eaten with bread, a relish. For a special sense of the word, see line 34 below.

21. pinguem: *i.e.* bloated.   **album**: *pale; cf. Odes*, ii. 2. 15, *albo corpore*, of the effects of dropsy.   **ostrea**: considered a great delicacy. The finest came from the Lucrine Lake; *cf. Epod.* 2. 49.

22. scarus: a fish highly prized by the Romans ; *cf. Epod.* 2. 50. **lagois**: perhaps the Alpine grouse. See Plin. *N. H.* x. 133, *sicut Alpium pyrrhocorax luteo rostro niger, et praecipua sapore lagopus.*

23. eripiam: a strong *prohibebo* (*cf. extuderit* in line 14) and hence followed by *quin*.   **quin**: note the position of the word. See Introd. § 53. *g*.   **posito pavone**: *when a peacock is set before you,*—a great luxury. *Posito = anteposito; cf.* line 106 below.

24. tergere: as we say, to 'tickle.'

25. corruptus: *i.e.* prejudiced; *cf.* line 9.   **vanis rerum** = *vanis rebus; cf.* ii. 8. 83, *fictis rerum; Epist.* i. 17. 21, *vilia rerum* and Prop. iii. 9. 7, *omnia rerum. Rerum* is genitive of the whole. **vēneat . . . pandat**: the subjunctive implies the excuse of the glutton for his preference, *because, as you say.*

26. pandat spectacula = *pandenda cauda exhibeat spectaculum; cf. Odes*, i. 33. 16, *Hadriae curvantis Calabros sinus ;* Plin. *N. H.* x. 43, *(pavo) gemmantis expandit colores. Spectacula* is a kind of accusative of the inner object ; see Introd. § 38. *b*.

27. tamquam . . . quicquam: *as if that had anything to do with the matter.*   **ista**: with a contemptuous force, *that plumage which you think so handsome.*

28. cocto: *sc. pavoni.*   **num adest**: the syllable ending in -*m* is scanned short, instead of being elided, as happens sometimes in Lucilius, Terence, and other early poets. Horace may have taken the expression directly from Lucilius, as Palmer suggests. *Cf. si mĕ amas*, i. 9. 38.   **honor**: *adornment, beauty*, as in *Epod.* 11. 6, *hic tertius December . . . silvis honorem decutit.*

29. carne: note the emphatic position of this word and of *nil,*

quamvis distat: for the indicative with *quamvis,* see Introd. § 45. *b.*
nil: *not a whit,* adverbial accusative.   **magis . . . te petere**:
think of your preferring; infinitive in an exclamation; see Introd.
§ 46. *b.*

30. esto: *very well, i.e.* let that pass without further comment.

31. unde datum sentis: *whence is it given you to tell* (by the
taste)? *Cf.* i. 4. 79, *unde petitum hoc in me iacis;* and Pers. v. 124,
unde datum hoc sumis?   **lupus . . . Tiberinus**: the *lupi* (a kind
of bass or pike) caught in the Tiber were preferred to those caught in
the sea; and of the former those were regarded as especially choice
which were caught near the island in the Tiber. *Cf.* Columella, *R. R.*
viii. 16. 4, *docta et erudita palata fastidire docuit (Marcius Philippus)
fluvialem lupum, nisi quem Tiberis adverso torrente defatigasset;*
Lucil. 1181 L., *Illum sumina ducebant atque altilium lanx, hunc pon-
tes Tiberinus duo inter captus catillo.*   **alto**: *the deep;* the adjective used as a substantive; *sc. mari.*

32. hiet: *gapes;* of the dead fish with its open mouth.   **iactatus**: *tossed* by the swirling current; *cf.* the passage from Columella,
quoted in the note on line 31.   **amnis . . . Tusci**: *the Tiber,* which
rises in Etruria; *cf. Odes,* iii. 7. 28, *nec quisquam citus aeque Tusco
denatat alveo.*

33. sub: note the asyndeton.   **trilibrem mullum**: the mullet
was a small fish; hence the epicure prized especially those of unusual
size. *Cf.* Plin. *N. H.* ix. 63, *(mullus) magnitudo modica, binasque
libras ponderis raro admodum exsuperat.*   Seneca, *Epist.* 95. 42, speaks
of one which was said to have weighed four and a half pounds; and
Juvenal, iv. 15, tells how one of six pounds sold for 6000 sesterces
($300).

34. singula . . . pulmenta: *portions;* see note on *pulmentaria,*
line 20 above, and the citation from Varro.   The meaning of *pulmenta*
(= *pulmentaria*) here does not differ in reality from its usual one,
since the portions of the choice fish serve as a relish for the rest of the
banquet.

35. ducit: *attracts; cf.* ii. 7. 102, *ducor libo fumante.*   **video**:
parenthetical, instead of *video speciem te ducere.*   **quo pertinet
ergo**: *what then is the object?*

36. illis: refers to *lupos,* for though they were mentioned last,
Horace is speaking especially of mullets.

38. raro: modifies *ieiunus.*   **volgaria**: *common foods;* the
adjective is used as a substantive.

39. magnum : *sc. mullum, a big one.*

40. vellem : *I should like* (to see) ; the form of the apodosis contrary to fact, since his wish is not likely to be realized.   **Harpyiis
digna** : *i.e.* deserving to be persecuted by the Harpies ; *cf.* Epod. 12. 1,
mulier nigris dignissima barris.   **at vos** : *but, at any rate,* if we
cannot count upon the Harpies, *do you.*

41. praesentes : *who are with us,* contrasted with the absent
Harpies.   **coquite . . . obsonia** : *cook their dainties for them,*
i.e. taint them.   **quamquam** : *and yet* (it is not necessary for the
South Wind to spoil the food, for).

42. putet : *i.e.* the sated glutton can so little appreciate dainty
dishes, that they might as well be spoiled.   *Cf.* Cic. *Acad.* frag. ii. 8,
quibus etiam alabaster plenus unguenti putere videatur.   **mala copia** : *cloying abundance.*   **quando** : causal, since Horace uses
temporal *quando* only of the future (Kiessling).   The use of temporal
quando seems to have disappeared from the *sermo urbanus* at an
early period.

43. sollicitat : *turns; cf.* Celsus, *Praef., sollicitare stomachum
vomitu.*   **rapula** : a kind of small turnip or radish, which was
pickled and used as an appetizer; *cf.* ii. 8. 8, *acria circum Rapula, lactucae, radices, qualia lassum Pervellunt stomachum.*

44. acidas inulas : the root of the elecampane, pickled in vinegar ; *cf.* ii. 8. 51, *inulas amaras; Plin. N. H.* xviii. 91, *inula per se
stomacho inimicissima, eadem dulcibus mixtis saluberrima . . . aliquando pipere aut thymo variata defectus praecipue stomachi excitat.*

45. epulis regum : (*even) from the feasts of the rich ;* for this
meaning of *reges, cf. Odes,* i. 4. 14, *pauperum tabernas regumque
turres.*   **ovis . . . oleis** : these formed part of the *gustatio; cf.* i.
3. 6, and the note.

46. haud ita pridem : *not so very long ago.*

47. Galloni : *cf.* Lucil. 1002 L., quoted by Cic. *de Fin.* ii. 8. 24: *O
Publi, O gurges, Galloni ; es homo miser, inquit. Cenasti in vita
numquam bene, cum omnia in ista Consumis squilla atque acipensere
cum decumano.*

48. rhombus : a kind of flat-fish, which derived its name from its
shape ; usually identified with the turbot, but perhaps a species of
ray.

49. ciconia : Porph. says : (*Sempronius) Rufus instituisse dicitur
ut ciconiarum pulli manducarentur : isque cum repulsam praeturae
tulisset, tale epigramma meruit : —*

> Ciconiarum Rufus iste conditor
> Licet duobus elegantior Plancis,
> Suffragiorum puncta non tulit septem:
> Ciconiarum populus ultus est mortem.

If this be true, *praetorius* is ironical.

51. **mergos**: *gulls;* *cf.* Ovid, *Met.* xi. 795, *Aequor amat nomenque tenet quia mergitur illo.*   **suavis**: *i.e.* 'good eating.'   **edixerit**: the word is chosen with reference to *praetorius*, as if the would-be praetor had issued an edict to that effect.

52. **pravi**: governed by *docilis; cf. Odes,* iv. 6. 43, *docilis modorum,* and see Introd. § 46. *a.*   **docilis**: *quick to learn,* with reference to *docuit* in line 50.   **Romana iuventus**: this epic phrase, as Orelli suggests, may well have been used ironically, parodying Ennius, *Ann.* 538, *Optuma cum pulcris animis Romana iuventus; cf.* Virg. *Aen.* i. 467, *Troiana iuventus.*

53. **sordidus**, *etc. :* while recommending frugal living, Ofellus would not approve of stinginess.   **a . . . victu**: for the construction, *cf. Odes,* iii. 19. 1, *Quantum distet ab Inacho Codrus.* Horace also uses the simple ablative in *Epist.* i. 7. 48, and the dative in *Odes,* iv. 9. 29.   **distabit**: a kind of gnomic use of the future; *i.e.* 'it will be found to differ'; *cf.* Plaut. *Most.* 1041, *qui homo timidus erit, in rebus dubiis nauci non erit.*

54. **vitaveris . . . detorseris**: the future perfect in the protasis (*vitaveris*) is the regular use, to indicate the fulfilment of the condition as prior to that of the conclusion ; *detorseris* has the force of a simple future, a usage common in colloquial language ; *cf.* Caes. *B. G.* iv. 25, *ego certe meum officium rei publicae praestitero,* where Caesar is quoting the words of a common soldier.

55. **pravum detorseris**: see note on *vitium,* i. 3. 1.   **Avidienus**: a notorious miser of the day.

56. **Canis**: on account of his bad temper and dirty habits; *cf. Epist.* i. 2. 26, *canis immundis.*   **ex vero dictum**: *rightly applied.*

57. **quinquennis**: *five years old; i.e.* kept so long as to be spoiled.   **ēst**: from *edo.*   **corna**: cornel berries, which grew wild and therefore cost nothing ; according to Columella, vii. 9, they were used as food for swine ; *cf. Epist.* i. 16. 9, where their association with *pruna* seems to imply that Horace himself did not disdain them.

58. **nisi mutatum**: *until it has turned, i.e.* soured.   **defundere**: *pour out* from the *amphora* into cups for drinking.

59. cuius odorem olei: *i.e. oleum cuius odorem; olei* is in sense the object of *instillat*, but is attracted to the case of the relative ; *cf.* Virg. *Aen.* i. 573, *urbem quam statuo vestra est.*   **licebit**: *although ;* the present *licet* became a conjunction, but the verb was used originally in other tenses as well with the same general force. *Cf.* Cic. *Verr.* ii. 5. 5. 11, *exspectate facinus quamvultis improbum,* for the usual *quamvis.*

60. repotia: *wedding breakfasts; repotia postridie nuptias apud novum maritum cenatur, quia quasi reficitur potatio,* Fest. p. 388.

61. albatus: *in full dress,* lit. *clad in* (*a*) *white* (*toga*). *Cf.* Cic. *Vatin.* 12. 30, *quis umquam cenarit atratus?* and *ibid.* 13. 31 (of a funeral feast), *cum ipse epuli dominus albatus esset.*   **cornu ipse bilibri**: he poured the oil with his own hand from the large horn in which it was kept, being too mean to buy a flask (*gutta*) for use at the table, and fearing that his guests might help themselves too liberally. He was sparing of his oil and free with his vinegar, while to make a good salad he should have followed the reverse practice. Since he did not drink his wine until it had turned sour, he had an abundance of vinegar (see line 58 above).

63. igitur : *well then;* after showing the evils of extravagance and of stinginess, Horace advises a middle course. The post-positive position of *igitur* is the classical usage, and is invariably found in Horace.   **horum utrum**: *i.e.* the extravagant (gluttonous) man, or the miser.

64. aiunt : *the saying is; i.e.* it was a well-known proverb; *cf.* Plaut. *Cas.* 971, *hac lupi, hac canes.* An English parallel is, ' between the devil and the deep sea.'

65. mundus erit, qua : *i.e.* he will be elegant to the extent of not giving offence by meanness ; *cf.* i. 2. 123, *munda hactenus ut neque longa Nec magis alba velit . . . videri,* to which this seems to be the corresponding relative construction in a somewhat condensed form. With the sentiment, *cf.* Cic. *de Off.* i. 36, 130, *adhibenda praeterea munditia est non odiosa neque exquisita nimis, tantum quae fugiat agrestem et inhumanam neglegentiam.*

66. cultus: genitive with *miser; cf. cerebri felicem,* i. 9. 11, and see Introd. § 40. *a.*   **miser**: ' pitiful,' *i.e.* despicable. *Cf.* ii. 8. 18, *divitias miseras.* He will not be open to censure in either direction as regards his mode of life.   **hic** : *such a man.*

67. Albuci : identified by Porphyrio with the person mentioned in ii. 1. 48, *qui, ob cupiditatem nimia·n habendi alienam uxorem, suam* *veneno necavit ;* but this is probably a mere guess on his part.   **dum munia didit** : *i.e.* while assigning them their duties as waiters at the table.

68. saevus erit : *i.e.* punish them beforehand for mistakes which they might make, as Cato is said to have done.   **simplex** : *easy-going*, and hence careless.   **unctam . . . praebebit aquam** : *i.e.* give his guests greasy water to wash their hands in before dinner ; *cf.* i. 4. 88, and the note.

70. nunc : after showing the difference between extravagant and frugal living, the poet comes back to his subject as stated in line 1. **quae quantaque** : *what great advantages ; cf.* line 1.

71. valeas : potential subjunctive with an implied protasis, *si tenui victu utaris.*   **variae res** : *a mixed diet.*

72. ut : *how.*   **memor** : serves as the protasis of *credas ; if you should call to mind.*

73. simplex : *when eaten alone,* contrasted with *variae res.*   **tibi sederit** : *agreed with you, i.e.* digested quietly, contrasted with *stomacho tumultum fert* in line 75.   The subjunctive is due to the idea of indirect discourse implied in *memor.*   *Tibi* is dative of interest **simul** = *simul ac,* as frequently.

74. miscueris : future perfect.   For the long *i, cf.* ii. 5. 101 ; *Odes,* iv. 7. 20 and 21 ; and see Introd. § 57.

76. pituita : scanned in three syllables, the *u* being treated as a semi-vowel.

77. cena dubia : *cf.* Ter. *Phorm.* 342, *cena dubia apponitur. Quid istuc verbist? Ubi tu dubites quid sumas potissimum.*   The expression had doubtless become proverbial, like *Epist.* i. 19. 41, *hinc illae lacrimae.*   **quin** · for *quin etiam, moreover.*   **corpus . . . animum** : not only is the body affected by gluttony, but the mind as well.

78. vitiis : *excesses ;* see note on i. 3. 1.

79. divinae . . . aurae : the soul was conceived by many of the Greek philosophers to be a part of the divine essence.

80. alter : *the other, i.e.* the temperate man, contrasted with the glutton, whose characteristics are sketched in the preceding lines. **dicto citius** : apparently a colloquial expression ; *cf.* Cic. *Phil.* ii. 33. 82, *omnia sunt citius facta quam dixi.* It modifies *sopori . . . dedit* and *curata.* The temperate man eats a light supper and falls asleep at once.   **curata** : used, as often, of refreshing the body by food ; *curare membra* is a variation of the common expression *curare corpus.*

81. vegetus : *fresh, lively*, contrasted with line 77 f. ; *cf.* Liv.
xxii. 47. 10, *fessi cum recentibus ac vegetis pugnabant.*

82. tamen : *i.e.* notwithstanding his usual frugality.   **melius** :
more generous fare; the adjective is used as a substantive.
transcurrere : *change*, a metaphorical use of the word.   **quondam** : *at times; quondam* has the same meanings as *olim;* see note
on i. 1. 25.

84. tenuatum : *sc. laboribus* or *morbo*. Not by poor living, for
frugal living has been shown to be wholesome. The temperate man
will allow himself a more luxurious diet when he actually needs it.
ubique accedent anni : *i.e.* when he grows old.

86. tibi : in the emphatic position ; *but in your case;* dative of
reference or advantage. With the general sentiment, *cf.* Celsus, i. 1,
cavendum ne in secunda valetudine adversae praesidia consumantur.
quidnam : emphatic interrogative, *what on earth ?*

87. praesumis : *anticipate;* i.e. *take before* it is necessary.   **mollitiem** : *indulgence.*

88. valetudo : here, as often, means *ill-health.*   **tarda senectus** : *enfeebling old age*, a conventional epithet; *cf.* Tibull. ii. 2. 19,
dum tarda senectus Inducat rugas. For a similar use of *tarda, cf.
tarda podagra*, i. 9. 32, and see Introd. § 49. *a.*

89. rancidum : *high;* Comm. Cruq., *leviter tantum putentem.*
non quia : *not because*, introducing the statement of a fact, and
hence followed by the indicative.

90. quod . . . consumeret : a substantive clause, explaining
hac mente; subjunctive because it represents the thought of the *antiqui.*

91. commodius : *more fittingly.*   **vitiatum . . . integrum** : *sc.
eum, i.e. aprum.*

93. heroas : as if such customs belonged only to the Golden Age.
tellus . . . prima : *cf. primis terris*, i. 3. 99.

94. das aliquid famae : the introduction to another argument for
frugal living, — that one has a better reputation.   **carmine gratior** :
cf. Plin. *Epist.* vii. 21, *est enim, ut Xenophon ait, ἥδιστον ἄκουσμα
ἔπαινος* (Xen. *Hier.* 1. 14).

95. grandes . . . grande : the same adjective is used purposely.
Note the emphatic position of *grande.*

96. damno : *ruin*, in a financial sense.

97. patruum : the uncle was proverbial for severity ; *cf.* Cic. *Cael.*
25, *patruus pertristis; Odes*, iii. 12. 3 ; *Serm.* ii. 3. 88.   **vicinos** :

sc. iratos.   **iniquum** : *hateful ; cf.* the opposite expression in *Epist.*
i. 18. 101, *quid te tibi reddat amicum.*

99. as, laquei pretium : a familiar expression in comedy and
probably in the colloquial language ; *cf.* Plaut. *Pseud.* 88, *quid de
drachma facere vis? Restim volo mihi emere. Quamobrem? Qui
me faciam pensilem ;* and our familiar expressions, ' go hang yourself,'
' I'll be hanged,' and the like.   **iure** : note the emphatic position.
inquit : *sc. quispiam,* a return to the dialogue form. *Cf. inquit,* i. 4.
79.   **Trausius** : otherwise unknown. He had evidently ruined
himself by extravagant living.   **istis** : *such* (as you have just
uttered).

100. vectigalia : *income,* used commonly of the revenues of a
state, but sometimes of individuals ; *cf. Odes,* iii. 16. 40, *Contracto
melius parva cupidine Vectigalia porrigam ;* Cic. *ad Att.* xii. 19. 1,
equidem iam nil egeo vectigalibus et parvo contentus esse possum. In
the singular, Cic. *Parad.* vi. 3. 49, *non intellegunt homines quam
magnum vectigal sit parsimonia.*

101. amplas : *great enough for ; cf.* Lucr. v. 944, *pabula . . .
miseris mortalibus ampla.*

102. quod superat : *the surplus ;* a substantive clause, object of
insumere.   **melius** : *a better object ;* the adjective is used as a substantive, as in line 82.   **quo insumere possis** : on which you can
spend ; *quo* is the adverb = *in quod. Cf.* i. 1. 73, *quo valeat nummus.*

103. indignus : *i.e.* contrary to his deserts ; *sc. qui egeat,* and *cf.*
Cic. *Tusc. Disp.* iv. 20. 46, *hominum indignorum calamitates.*

105. emetiris : *bestow,* lit. *measure out ; cf.* Cic. *Brut.* 4. 16, *ego
autem voluntatem tibi emetiar.*

106. uni nimirum . . . : *i.e.* of course you will be an exception
to the general rule, that riches have wings.   **recte . . . erunt** : the
use of the adverb with *esse* is colloquial ; see Introd. § 51. *a.*

107. risus : *laughing-stock ; cf.* ii. 5, 37, *iocus.*   **uterne** : since
uter is interrogative, *-ne* is redundant ; *cf.* ii. 3. 295, *quone.*

108. casus dubios : *i.e.* the changes of fortune ; *dubios* is almost
equivalent to *adversos ; cf. Odes,* iv. 9. 36, *et secundis Temporibus dubi-
isque rectus.*

109. adsuerit : transitive ; *cf.* i. 4. 105, *insuevit.*   **superbum** :
pampered.

111. in pace . . . aptarit idonea bello : *cf.* our proverbial expression, ' in time of peace prepare for war.'   **ut sapiens** : *cf. ut
avarus,* i. 1. 108.

112. quo . . . credas: Horace gives a practical example to illustrate his theory.   **his**: *these precepts*.   **puer . . . parvus . . . novi**: evidently Ofellus lived near Venusia.

113. integris: with a long penult; *cf. integrum*, line 92.   **latius**: *more lavishly; cf.* Juv. xiv. 234, *indulgere sibi latius*. *Latius* is the opposite of *anguste; cf.* Caes. *B.C.* iii. 16, *ad rem frumentariam expediendam qua anguste utebatur;* and for the adjective, *angustam pauperiem, Odes*, iii. 2. 1.

114. videas: for the 'can'-potential, see note on i. 4. 86.   **metato**: *confiscated, forfeited*, since the lands which were allotted to the soldiers were first surveyed, or 'measured'; *cf.* Prop. iv. 1. 130, *Abstulit excultas pertica tristis opes. Metatus*, though from a deponent verb, is often used with passive force.

115. fortem mercede colonum: *a sturdy hired man*. Umbrenus (see 134) seems to have left the farm in the hands of Ofellus, paying him a sum of money for working it; *mercede* is ablative of price, though the use of such an ablative modifying a substantive is extremely rare.

116. non . . . temere: *not without some special reason;* two reasons are mentioned in lines 118–119.   **luce profesta**: *a working day; profesta* is opposed to *sacra* in *Odes*, iv. 15. 25, *et profestis lucibus et sacris*.

118. longum post tempus: guests were rare in the country.

119. operum: genitive with *vacuo*, a Grecism. See Introd. § 40. *b*. **vacuo**: *when I was not busy* (dative agreeing with *mihi*), hence *gratus*, 'welcome.'   **per imbrem**: which was the only time when he and his neighbors had leisure to pay visits.

120. bene erat: *sc. nobis*, 'we made merry'; *cf. recte erunt*, line 106, and see Introd. § 51. *a*.   **urbe**: *Roma*.

121. pensilis uva: *raisins, i.e.* grapes, *hung up* and dried; *cf.* Plin. *N.H.* xiv. 16, *durant aliae per hiemes, pensili concamerate nodo*. **secundas mensas**: *dessert*, the second course, consisting usually of fruit and the like; *cf.* i. 3. 5, and the note.

122. duplice ficu: *i.e.* figs split in two and dried.

123. post hoc . . . magistra: *i.e.* no formal *magister* or *arbiter bibendi* was appointed (see *Odes*, ii. 7. 25), but certain delinquencies were punished by a forfeit, hence *culpa magistra*, 'with a fault acting as mistress of the feast.'   **potare**: predicate to *ludus erat;* see Introd. § 46. *d*.

124. venerata: *besought by prayer; cf. Carm. Saec.* 49; *Serm.*

ii. 6. 8.   For the passive use of the participle, see on line 114, above.
ita . . . surgeret: the correlative clause is understood : *ita . . . surgas, ut tibi hunc vinum fundo*, or the like.   *Surgeret* represents *surgas*
transferred to past time and made dependent on *venerata;* it is subjunctive in a substantive clause developed from the optative.

125. explicuit . . . frontis: *cf. Odes*, iii. 29. 16 (*mundae pauperum cenae) sollicitam explicuere frontem.*

126. novos: *i.e.* in addition to the one which had already
occurred.

127. hinc: *i.e.* from such a mode of life as has just been described.   **parcius . . . nituistis**: of good condition of body ; *i.e.*
how much less well-fed have you appeared.

128. pueri : here equivalent to *gnati; cf.* line 15.   **ut** : *since.*
incola : *tenant*, used instead of *dominus*, for the reason given in the
next line.

129. propriae : *i.e.* to hold it as his own, *permanently ; cf.* Lucil.
477 L., *Cetera contemnit et in usura omnia ponit Non magna : proprium vero nil neminem habere.*

130. statuit : *has settled*, with the idea of permanency.

131. nequities : *incapacity, shiftlessness.*   **vafri . . . iuris ·**
i.e. to be understood only by the *vafer* (*homo*); *cf. ius anceps,* ii. 5.
34.   Note the different idea of the jurist Trebatius, ii. 1. 81, *sanctarum
inscitia legum.*

132. postremum : masculine adjective agreeing with *illum, at
the end of his life ;* or adverb ; *cf.* Cic. *de Orat.* iii. 2. 6, *in quo (vesti-
gio) ille postremum institisset.*   **certe** : *at any rate ; i.e.* if neither
incompetency nor ignorance of legal trickery does.

134. nulli : dative of the possessor, with *erit.*   **proprius** : *permanently,* like *propriae* in line 129.

135. vivite fortes, *etc.:* with the sentiment, *cf.* Virg. *Aen.* vi. 95,
Tu ne cede malis, sed contra audentior ito ; i. 207, *Durate et vosmet
rebus servate secundis.*

SERMO III.

1. sic raro scribis: for a similar use of *sic, cf.* Cic. *de Sen.* 8. 26,
*quas quidem (i.e. Graecas litteras) sic avide arripui . . . ut ea ipsa
mihi nota essent, quibus me nunc exemplis uti videtis.* On *scribis,* see
Introd. § 57.

2. membranam : *parchment,* on which books were sometimes
written ; sometimes *charta,* ' papyrus,' was used ; *cf.* i. 5. 104, *Brun-*

disium longae finis chartaeque viaeque est.   **retexens** : *undoing,*
lit. *unweaving ;* for the force of *re-,* cf. *Odes,* i. 28. 11, *refigere ; Epist.*
i. 7. 9, *resignare.*

3. **benignus** : *given to ;* on *vini somnique,* see Introd. § 40. *a.*

4. **dignum sermone** : *worth mentioning.*   **quid fiet** : *i.e.* what
will you produce ?   **at** : *but after all.*   There is some hope that he
will accomplish something.   **ipsis Saturnalibus** : *just at the Saturnalia,* a time of general holiday, hence the fact that the poet has with-
drawn to the country is an indication that he proposes to do some
serious work.   Cf. Plin. *Epist.* ii. 17. 24, *in hanc ego diaetam cum me
recepi, abesse mihi etiam a villa mea videor, magnamque eius volupta-
tem praecipue Saturnalibus capio, cum reliqua pars tecti licentia dierum festisque clamoribus personat : nam nec ipse meorum lusibus nec
illi studiis meis obstrepunt.*   The Saturnalia, at first celebrated on the
17th of December, were, in the last century of the Republican period,
extended to seven days.   Augustus limited the holiday to three days,
so far as legal business was concerned.

5. **huc** : *i.e.* to his Sabine farm, given him by Maecenas about
33 B.C.   **sobrius** : when every one else was drinking; note the
emphatic position.   Cf. Juv. vii. 96, *vinum toto nescire Decembri.*

6. **dignum promissis** : cf. *Epist.* ii. 1. 53 (*Ennius*) *leviter curare
videtur, Quo promissa cadant; Ars Poet.* 138, *Quid dignum tanto
feret hic promissor hiatu.*   **nil est** : *i.e.* nothing comes of the effort.

7. **culpantur frustra calami** : cf. Pers. iii. 12, *Tunc queritur,
crassus calamo quod pendeat umor, Nigra quod infusa vanescat sepia
lympha, Dilutas queritur geminet quod fistula guttas.*   **immeritus** :
cf. *indignus,* ii. 2. 103, *Cur eget indignus quisquam, te divite.*   **laborat . . . paries** : *i.e.* it is pounded by the poet in his desperation.

8. **iratis natus dis** : a common expression, here jestingly ampli-
fied by *atque poetis ;* cf. i. 5. 97 ; Ter. *Andr.* 664, *nescio, nisi mi deos
fuisse iratos, qui auscultaverim ;* Juv. x. 129, *Dis ille adversis genitus
fatoque sinistro.*

9. **atqui voltus erat** : *sc. tibi ; yet you had the look* (when you
left the city).   **minantis** : humorously used in the sense of *promis-
ing, boasting that you would do ;* cf. *Epist.* i. 8. 3, *multa et pulchra
minantem.*

10. **vacuum** : *sc. te ; at leisure.*   **tepido** : *warm,* contrasted
with the less easily heated city houses.   **villula** : *your own little
villa ;* note the force of the diminutive, and cf. *lectulus,* i. 4. 133, with
the note.

11. quorsum pertinuit : *what was the use?*   *Cf.* ii. 2. 35, *quo pertinet ergo Proceros odisse lupos.*   **Platona** : from the connection the reference is probably to the writer of comedy (428–389 B.C.) who forms a connecting link between the Old and the Middle Comedy. Otherwise Horace's well-known tastes would lead us to think of the philosopher.   We get here interesting light on Horace's method of work.   **Menandro** : ablative of association.   See Introd. § 41. *b.*

13. virtute relicta : *i.e.* by ceasing to satirize vice.

14. contemnere : as well as hated.   **improba** : *froward*, because she tempts men to idleness, as the Sirens tempted Odysseus and his companions.

15. quicquid parasti : *i.e.* the reputation which you had acquired.

16. ponendum : *given up;* the simple verb for the compound *deponendum.*   **di te . . . donent** : a formula used to express wishes for good or evil ; *cf.* Catull. 28. 14, *At vobis mala multa di deaeque Dent;* Plaut. *Pseud.* 271, *di te deaeque ament.   Tonsore*, which is withheld until the end of the sentence, takes the place of such a wish, παρὰ προσδοκίαν ; *cf. bonorum*, i. 1. 79 ; *minora*, i. 3. 20.

17. unde : *how?*

18. Ianum ad medium : *i.e.* in the quarter called *ad Ianum medium*, or simply *Ianus* (cf. *Epist.* i. 1. 54), extending along the north side of the Forum, from the Comitium to the Temple of Antoninus and Faustina.   It was so called from an arch (*Ianus medius*), which probably stood near the basilica Aemilia.   It was frequented by moneylenders, bankers, and the like, whence the term *ad Ianum medium* was typical, like our ' on Wall Street.'   *Cf.* Cic. *de Off.* ii. 24. 87, *de quaerenda, de conlocanda pecunia, etiam de utenda, commodius a quibusdam optimis viris ad Ianum medium sedentibus quam ab ullis philosophis ulla in schola disputatur.*

19. fracta est : *wrecked*, a not uncommon metaphor ; *cf.* Cic. *pro Sull.* 14. 41, *patrimonio naufragus.*

20. quaerere : *investigate ;* as a judge and buyer of antiquities.

21. quo . . . aere : used humorously for ancient Corinthian bronzes. Similarly, i. 3. 91, *catillum Evandri manibus tritum deiecit.*   Corinthian bronzes were highly prized ; *cf.* i. 4. 28, *stupet Albius aere*, and the note.

22. sculptum . . . fusum : used respectively of marble and bronze. **durius** : *too rudely, stiffly*, contrasted with *mollius ; cf.* Virg. *Aen.* vi. 847, *Excudent alii spirantia mollius aera ;* and somewhat similarly, *Ars Poet.* 33, *mollis imitabitur aere capillos.*

23. callidus : *shrewdly, i.e. cum lucro; cf.* line 25.   **ponebam** :
paid for, invested in; cf. i. 2. 13, *positis in faenore nummis; Epod.* 2.
70, *Omnem redegit Idibus pecuniam, Quaerit Kalendis ponere.*

24. mercarier : the archaic form of the present passive infinitive,
common in comedy and perhaps in the language of everyday life.
See Introd. § 35. *a.*   **unus** : *I alone.*

25. Mercuriale : the favorite of Mercury, as the god of trade; see
Odes, i. 2. 41, and the note; *Odes,* ii. 17. 29.   *Mercuriale* instead of
Mercurialis, through attraction to *cognomen.*

26. compita : *the street-corners,* where auctions were held; *cf.*
Cic. *de Leg. Agr.* 1. 3. 7, *at hoc etiam nequissimi homines consumptis
patrimoniis faciunt, ut in atriis auctionariis potius quam in triviis
aut in compitis auctionentur.*

27. morbi : genitive of separation in imitation of the Greek construction ; *cf. Odes,* i. 22. 1, *sceleris purus,* and see Introd. § 40. *b.*
Purgo is sometimes constructed with the ablative of separation, or
with the ablative with *ab.*

28. mire : modifying *emovit; it is remarkable how, etc.*   **novus** :
sc. morbus.

29. lateris dolore : *cf.* i. 9. 32, *laterum dolor.*

30. ut . . . cum : *as is the case when.*   **hic** : *for example.*

31. dum ne : *sc. facias; i.e.* provided you don't attack me.   **esto
ut libet** : *i.e.* have any craze you like.   **o bone** : *my good fellow;* a
somewhat patronizing expression ; *cf.* ii. 6. 51 and 95 ; *Epist.* ii. 2. 37.

32. stulti prope omnes : *sc. sunt;* the statement is softened by
prope; cf. i. 3. 96, *quis paria esse fere placuit peccata.*

33. Stertinius : mentioned also in *Epist.* i. 12. 20 ; otherwise unknown.   **crepat** : *prattles, prates,* a contemptuous term.   **unde** :
for *a quo,* to be taken with *docilis* in approximately the sense of *doctus;*
cf. Odes, iii. 11. 1, *te docilis magistro;* Auct. ad Her. iii. 4. 7, *lauda-
bile aut ab idoneis hominibus aut omnibus civibus.*

34. tempore quo : *at the time when.*

35. solatus : *i.e.* for the loss of his fortune.   **sapientem pascere barbam** : *to grow a philosophic beard;* ironical, as if that were
the only thing needful in order to become a philosopher ; *cf.* Plin.
Epist. i. 22. 6, *ex istis qui sapientiae studium habitu corporis prae-
ferunt.*

36. Fabricio . . . ponte : the bridge connecting the island in the
Tiber with the left bank.   It was built of stone by Fabricius in 62 B.C.,
and is still standing, with the inscription recording its construction.

37. male re gesta : with reference to line 18 above.   **vellem** :
I was on the point of.   **operto . . . capite** : as usual when about
to die ; *cf.* Liv. iv. 12. 11, *multi ex plebe spe amissa . . . capitibus
obvolutis se in Tiberim praecipitaverunt ;* Suet. *Jul.* 82, *utque (Caesar)
animadvertit undique se strictis pugionibus peti, toga caput obvolvit.*

38. dexter : *on my right,* hence with good omen.   **cavĕ** : with
short *e,* as frequently.   **faxis** : an archaic form, used instead of
feceris ; really an aorist optative, *fac-s-i-s ; cf. ausim,* i. 10. 48.

39. malus : *false.*

40. insanos . . . inter : *i.e.* among people who are as mad as
yourself.   Note the anastrophe, common with dissyllabic prepositions.

41. primum : introducing a discourse on the subject in the regular
philosophic manner.   **quid sit furere** : *what madness is ; furere* is
the subject of *sit.*

42. nil verbi : equivalent to *nullum verbum ; verbi* is genitive of
the whole ; *cf. vanis rerum,* ii. 2. 25, and the note.   **pereas quin** :
to prevent you from dying, governed by the idea of preventing implied
in *nil verbi addam.*

44. caecum agit : *drives blindly on ; caecum* modifies *quem.*
Chrysippi porticus : the στοά at Athens, where the Stoics taught ;
Chrysippus was once the head of the School ; see note on 1. 3. 126.
grex : *i.e.* his followers, disciples ; *cf. Epist.* i. 4. 16, *Epicuri de
grege porcum.*

45. autumat : *declare,* an archaic word.   **populos** : *whole
nations ;* note the plural.   **formula** : *definition.*

46. sapiente : *the philosopher.* See Introd. § 35. *c.*   **tenet** :
embraces.   **nunc** : introducing the second head of the discourse ;
cf. primum, line 41.

48. insano : attracted to the case of *tibi,* as often in such
expressions.

49. palantis : used proleptically with *pellit.*

50. unus . . . partibus : *i.e.* one mistake, that of leaving the
path, but in different directions.

53. caudam trahat ; *i.e.* is himself an object of ridicule ; Porph.
says : *solent enim pueri deridentes nescientibus a tergo caudam suspen-
dere, ut velut pecus caudam trahant.*

54. nihilum : the earlier and fuller form of *nihil = nĕ hilum,*
not a whit.   **timentis** : *which fears,* equivalent to a relative clause.

55. in campo : *i.e.* on a level, unbroken plain.

56. varum : *i.e. diversum,* constructed with the dative, *cf.* i. 4. 48, *differt sermoni; Epist.* i. 18. 3, *meretrici dispar;* and the usage common in England, 'different to.'

57. clamet : jussive subjunctive with concessive force.   **amica** : best taken as an adjective modifying *mater.*

58. honesta : *honored.*

59. serva : *look out!* a colloquial expression, common in comedy.

61. Ilionam edormit : slept through the part of Ilione, in Pacuvius's play of the same name.   While personating the sleeping Ilione, the drunken actor went to sleep and so missed his cue, which was *mater, te appello. Ilionam* is accusative of the inner object in its freer form ; *cf.* i. 5. 63, and the note ; Introd. § 38. *b.*   **Catienis mille ducentis** : *i.e.* the entire audience took the cue from the mouth of Catienus, who was playing Deiphobus, and shouted it to the sleeping actor, but in vain.   *Mille ducentis* is used indefinitely of a large number.   See Introd. § 50.

62. huic . . . errori : *i.e.* the genuine madness just described.

63. similem : *sc. errorem,* accusative of the inner object with *sanire; cf. Ilionam,* line 61, and the note.

64. insanit : *has a craze for ; cf.* i. 4. 28, *stupet Albius aere.*

65. integer mentis : for the construction, *cf. Odes,* i. 22. 1, *integer vitae.*   **esto** : *i.e.* suppose (for the moment) he is ; let us look into the matter ; cf. i. 6. 19.

66. reddas : the jussive force of *accipe* is carried into the relative clause.

67. magis excors : comparative, *still more mad* (than an *insanus*). *Ex-cors,* because the heart was regarded as the seat of the mind ; *cf.* Juv. vii. 159, *quod laeva in parte mamillae Nil salit Arcadico iuveni.*

68. reiecta praeda : with the force of a condition, parallel with *si acceperis* in the line above.   **praesens** : *propitious.*   Mercury was the god of thieves as well as of traders ; *cf.* line 25 above.

69. scribe : *enter,* in your account book ; addressed to the creditor ; a technical term ; *cf.* Cic. *Rosc. Com.* 1. 2, *quemadmodum turpe est scribere quod non debeatur, sic improbum est non referre quod debeas.*   **decem** : *ten drafts; decem, centum,* and *milia* form a climax.   **a Nerio** : *i.e.* to be paid by Nerius.   *A Nerio* is not ablative of the agent, but *scribe aliquid ab aliquo* is a technical term ; *cf.* Plaut. *Trin.* 182, *a me argentum dedi ; Curc.* 618, *pro istac rem solvi ab trapezita meo;* Cic. *Verr.* ii. 3. 76. 177, *hinc ab aerario pecuniam numerari.*   **non est satis** : paratactic construction with conditional force ; *if that is not enough, add, etc.*   **Cicutae** : a money-lender, mentioned again in line 175, but otherwise unknown. The name may well be a made-up one, from *cicuta* ' hemlock.' See Introd. § 32.

70. nodosi : *crafty;* skilful in binding his debtor ; *cf.* Juv. viii. 50, *Qui iuris nodos et legum aenigmata solvat.*   **catenas** : with the same metaphor as in *nodosi.*

71. tamen : *yet ; i.e.* though you take all these precautions to secure payment.   **Proteus** : so called on account of his skill in extricating himself from toils ; see *Epist.* i. 1. 90 ; Virg. *Geor.* iv. 387 f. ; *Odyss.* iv. 456 f.

72. malis ridentem alienis : *i.e.* laughing at his creditor's expense, or perhaps laughing loudly. Undoubtedly with reference to *Odyss.* xx. 347, μνηστῆρσι δὲ Παλλὰς ᾿Αθήνη ἄσβεστον γέλω ὦρσε, παρέπλαγξεν δὲ νόημα. Οἵδ' ἤδη γναθμοῖσι γελοίων ἀλλοτρίοισιν. The reference in the Homeric passage is to forced, unnatural laughter. Horace may have misunderstood the meaning, or he may use the term humorously without regard to its original force. *Cf.* Valerius Flaccus, viii. 164 (of Medea), *alieno gaudia vultu semper erant.*

74. male rem gerere : *to waste one's property* through mismanagement ; *cf.* Cic. *de Sen.* 7. 22, *quemadmodum nostro more male rem gerentibus patribus bonis interdici solet.*   **contra** : *sc. facere ; the reverse.*

75. putidius : more ' addled.'   **Perelli** : the name of the creditor.

76. dictantis : *i.e.* bidding you write an agreement to pay what you cannot pay ; with a play on the words *scribere* (implied) and *rescribere.*   **rescribere** : *repay; cf.* Ter. *Phorm.* 921, *transi sodes ad forum atque illud mihi argentum rursum iube rescribi.*

77. togam . . . componere : that is, to *settle oneself,* to listen to a long discourse.

80. calet : *is in a fever.*   **me** : accusative governed by *propius,* which has the force of a preposition ; *cf.* Cic. *Phil.* vii. 9. 26, *propius urbem.*

81. ordine : to be taken with *doceo; cf.* Plaut. *Mil.* 875, *rem omnem tibi . . . domi demonstravi ordine* (note the similar position of the word).

82. ellebori : regarded as a cure for insanity ; the best came from Anticyra in Phocis. *Cf. Ars Poet.* 300, *tribus Anticyris caput insanabile.*   **avaris** : since avarice is the principal cause of discontent and foolish conduct, see i. 1.

83. nescio an : *I rather think.*   **omnem Anticȳram** : *i.e.* all the hellebore in the world. See note on line 82 above.   **ratio** : *a fair calculation.*

84. Staberi : otherwise unknown.　　　**summam** : *i.e.* the amount which had been left them. So Trimalchio (Petr. 71) wishes cut on his tomb : *pius, fortis, fidelis, ex parvo crevit, sestertium reliquit tre-centies, nec umquam philosophum audivit.*

85. fecissent : implied indirect discourse, representing the future perfect used by the testator ; *ni fecisset* depends on *damnati dare.*

86. paria : *cf.* i. 7. 19. These were to be exhibited at the funeral games. One hundred pairs was a large, but not an unheard-of, number. **arbitrio Arri** : *i.e.* such as Arrius would order. The reference is to Quintus Arrius, mentioned by Cic. *Vatin.* 13. 31, who gave a dinner at which several thousand guests were present (*cum tot hominum milia accumberent*).

87. frumenti : *sc. et,* which has perhaps been lost from the text ; *also a distribution of grain.* Africa was at this time the granary of Italy ; *cf. Odes,* i. 1. 10, *Quicquid de Libycis verritur areis.*

88. ne sis patruus : *don't play the stern uncle,* and lecture me. On *patruus, cf.* ii. 2. 97 and the note. The words give the thought of Staberius, uttered in anticipation of the protests of his heirs (*hoc pru-dentem . . . vidisse*).

89. hoc : *i.e. sive ego prave, etc.,* above.　　　**prudentem** : *prophetic.* **quid ergo sensit** : *what was his idea?*

91. quoad : occurs only here in Horace, and is very rare in poetry ; scanned as one syllable. See Introd. § 57.

92. acrius : *sc. quam pauperiem.*　　　**ut** : *so much so that ; cf.* i. 1. 95, *dives ut.* Here we have no word which leads up to the result clause.

93. uno quadrante : ablative of measure of difference.　　　**perisset** : standing for the future perfect indicative of Staberius's thought, implied in *videretur.*

95. pulchris divitiis : *cf.* Juv. xiii. 33, *quas habeat veneres aliena pecunia.*

96. parent : *are inferior to.*　　　**construxerit** : with the same metaphor in mind as in *constructus acervus,* i. 1. 44.

97. sapiensne : such short questions were characteristic of the Stoics ; *cf.* Cic. *Parad.* praef. 2, *Cato perfectus . . . Stoicus . . . minutis interrogatiunculis quasi punctis quod proposuit efficit.*　　　**etiam** : *even so, yes ; cf.* Cic. *Acad.* ii. 32, 104, *aut 'etiam' aut 'non' respondere possit.*

98. hoc : *i e.* that he died rich.　　　**paratum** : *won.*

99. magnae laudi : dative of purpose.　　　**quid simile isti** : *sc. fecit; how was the action of Aristippus different ? Isti* has a con-temptuous force.

100. Aristippus: a disciple of Socrates, and founder of the Cyrenaic school. *Cf. Epist.* i. 1. 18, and i. 17. 23. The story is told by Diogenes Laert. ii. 8. 77.

101. irent: note the subjunctive, *because* (in his opinion) *they were going.*

103. nil agit: *has no force.*   **litem quod lite resolvit**: *i.e.* which solves one difficulty by raising another.

104. emptas: *i.e.* as soon as he bought them.

105. musae . . . ulli: *i.e.* any sort of music.

106. non sutor: *though not a shoemaker.*

107. aversus mercaturis: *i.e.* though having a distaste for commerce. *Mercaturis* is dative with *aversus; cf.* line 56 above. The more common construction is *ab* and the ablative, as in Cic. *pro Arch.* 9. 20, *aversus a musis.*   **delirus**: lit. *out of the furrow (de-lira);* hence, out of the straight course, *crazy.*

108. undique: *i.e.* by all.   **merito**: note the emphatic position, *and rightly, too.*   **istis**: with contemptuous force ; *cf. isti* in line 99. For the case, see Introd. § 39. *a.*

110. metuens . . . sacrum: *cf.* i. 1. 71, *tamquam parcere sacris cogeris. Velut* modifies *sacrum;* for the hyperbaton, *cf. tamquam . . . sacris* in the passage just cited.

111. ad: *beside.*

112. illinc: as if *tollere*, or a word of similar meaning, were to follow.

113. esuriens dominus: *i.e. quamvis esuriens et dominus.*

115. positis intus: *i.e.* stored up in his wine-cellar.

116. nihil est: correcting the preceding too modest figure ; *that's nothing.* Both *mille* and *tercentum milibus* are used indefinitely of a large number. See Introd. § 50.

117. acetum: *i.e.* wine which has spoiled (soured), lit. *vinegar; cf.* Plaut. *Rud.* 937, *Sed hic rex cum aceto pransurust Et sale, sine bono pulmento.*   **age**: calling attention to the following condition ; *what if.*   **stramentis**: *straw,* without a coverlet ; *cf.* Plin. *N. H.* xviii. 14, *quies somnusque in stramentis erat.*   **unde-octoginta . . . natus**: *in his seventy-ninth year. Unde-octoginta* is divided between two lines, like *inter-est* in i. 2. 62. The definite year, instead of a general round number, individualizes the case ; *cf.* Juv. vi. 192, *Tune etiam quam sextus et octogesimus annus Pulsat, adhuc Graece?*

118. cui: dative of reference, nearly equivalent to a possessive genitive.   **stragula vestis**: *bed clothing.*

120. paucis: in contrast to line 107.   This is so common that only few people would regard it as madness.   *Nimirum* is of course satirical.

121. iactatur: *is suffering;* lit. '*tossing*' in a fever; *cf.* Cic. *in Cat.* i. 13. 31, *aestu febrique iactantur.*

122. ebibat: *may drink it up,* with special reference to line 115, but applying as well to the other riches, which the heir will sell and consume ; *cf. Odes,* ii. 14. 25, *Absumet heres Caecuba dignior.*   Note the interlocked order of the lines.

123. dis inimice: *hated by the gods; cf. Odes,* i. 26. 1, *musis amicus,* and line 8 above, *iratis dis.*   **ne tibi desit**: *sc. custodis; lest you should yourself be in want; cf.* i. 1. 98, *ne penuria victus opprimeret.*

124. quantulum : diminutive, *what an insignificant bit.*   **enim** : *absurd, for.*   **dierum**: genitive of the whole with *quisque,* instead of *quisque dies.*

125. oleo meliore: the miser economizes in the same way as Avidienus in ii. 2. 55.

126. porrigine: *dandruff.*

127. si . . . satis est: *i.e.* if only the bare necessities of life are needful, — a commonplace of the philosophers, which had become proverbial ; *cf.* Plaut. *Mil.* 749, *Si certumst tibi, Commodulum obsona, ne magno sumptu: mihi quidvis sat est;* Turp. fr. 144 R., *ut philosophi aiunt, isti quibus quidvis sat est.*   **surripis, aufers**: used respectively of secret theft and open robbery.

128. tun: for *tune.*   Emphatic ; *are* you ?

129. tuos: emphatic ; *your own.*   **quos aere pararis**: *for which you have paid money; cf.* Sall. *Jug.* 31. 11, *servi aere parati.*

130. omnes pueri . . . puellae: a proverbial expression for every one (of both sexes); *cf.* i. 1. 85.   Note the irregular position of *que,* not uncommon in poetry.

132. quid enim: *cf.* i. 1. 7.   **neque tu . . . ,** *etc.:* ironical ; with the thought, *cf.* ii. 1. 54 f.

134. an tu reris: *i.e.* did Orestes go mad only after killing his mother ?

135. actum Furiis : *driven mad,* referring to the impulse which led him to commit murder, as well as to the avenging furies which punished the deed.   *Cf.* Virg. *Aen.* iii. 331, *scelerum furiis agitatus Orestes.*

137. quin: *nay; = quin etiam; cf.* i. 4. 30.   **ex quo**: *sc. tempore.*   **male tutae** : *unsafe,* nearly equivalent to *male sanae.*

138. nil sane fecit : *he certainly did nothing.*

141. Furiam : *cf.* Eur. *Orest.* 264, μί' οὖσα τῶν ἐμῶν Ἐρινύων, μέσον μ' ὀχμάζεις. **hunc aliud** : doubtless with reference to a scene from some lost tragedy.   **splendida bilis**: *his wrath ; splendida* is used literally; *cf.* Galen, περὶ Αἰτίων Συμπτωμάτων, ii. 50, μέλαινα χολὴ στιλπνοτέρα αὐτοῦ τοῦ αἵματος ; Pers. iii. 8, *vitrea bilis*.

142. Opimius : probably one of Horace's made-up names, from *opimus ; cf.* i. 6. 40, *Novius*. The effect of the name is heightened by the ironical epithet *pauper ; cf. Odes*, iii. 16. 28, *Magnas inter opes inops*.   **argenti . . . et auri** : genitive with *pauper ; cf.* i. 1. 79, *horum pauperrimus bonorum*.   **positi intus**: *cf.* line 115 above.

143. Veientanum : a very inferior red wine ; *cf.* Pers. v. 147, *Veientanum rubellum, vapida laesum pice*.   **festis diebus . . . profestis** : *cf.* ii. 2. 116.

144. Campana trulla : *cf.* i. 6. 118, and the note ; the *trulla* was a ladle for dipping wine from the *crater ;* Opimius apparently drank from this instead of from a wine-cup.   **vappam** : here used in its literal sense ; *cf.* i. 1. 104, and the note ; i. 5. 16.

145. lethargo : doubtless caused by old age ; *cf. Epist.* i. 8. 10, *veterno*.

147. multum celer atque fidelis : colloquial for *celerrimus atque fidelissimus ; cf.* i. 3. 57 ; ii. 5. 92 ; *etc.*

148. poni: for *apponi ;* the simple verb for a compound is frequent in poetry.

149. pluris : *several people*.

150. ad numerandum: as if the property were going to be divided among the heirs.

151. iam : *presently ; cf. Odes*, i. 4. 16, *iam te premet nox*.

152. vigila : *rouse yourself*.   **hoc age**: *come now !* An expression common in comedy.

153. venae : here means *the blood ; cf.* Ovid, *ex Pont.* iii. 1. 69, *Ad medicum specto venis fugientibus aeger*.

154. ingens : *tremendous*, a purposely strong word.   **fultura** : often used for food ; *cf.* Lucr. ii. 1148, *fulcire cibus (debet)*.

155. tisanarium oryzae : *rice-gruel; tisanarium* from the Greek πτισάνη. *Cf.* Plin. *N. H.* 18. 74 (*Indi*), *maxime oryza gaudent ex qua tisanam conficiunt, quam reliqui mortales ex hordeo*.

156. quanti ergo : *well, how much?*   **octussibus** : *eight asses ;* used of an indefinite small number ; *cf. octonos*, i. 6. 75, and the note.

157. furtis . . . rapinis : because so high a price seems to him robbery.

158. non stultus : to be taken together ; *no fool*.

160. continuo : *forthwith*.

161. cardiacus ; *dyspeptic*, *i.e.* troubled with heartburn.   **Craterum** : a celebrated physician of Cicero's time ; *cf.* Cic. *ad Att.* xii. 14. 4, *de Attica doleo ; credo tamen Cratero.*

162. recte est : *sc. ei.*   A colloquial construction ; see above, *bene erat*, ii. 2. 120, and Introd. § 51. *a.*

163. temptentur : subjunctive, because the reason of Craterus is given.

164. immolet . . . porcum : as a thank offering ; possibly with a reminiscence of the custom referred to in Plaut. *Men.* 292 of sacrificing a pig as a cure for insanity, though of course used somewhat differently here.

166. Anticȳram : to be cured by hellebore ; see line 83 above. *Cf.* Plin. *N. H.* xxv. 52, *Drusum . . . constat hoc medicamento liberatum comitiali morbo in Anticyra insula.   Ibi enim tutissime sumitur.* **barathrone** : *barathro + ne, into a pit;* of throwing away money.

167. paratis : *what you have acquired; cf. Odes,* i. 31. 17, *frui paratis, Latoë, dones.*

169. antiquo censu : *according to the old standard of wealth ; cf. Odes,* ii. 15. 13, *privatus illis census erat brevis.*   Ablative of accordance.   **divisse** : equivalent to *divisisse*, though perhaps a different formation ; *cf. surrexe*, i. 5. 91, and the note.

171. talos nucesque : common playthings ; *cf.* Suet. *Aug.* 83, (*Augustus*) *animi laxandi causa talis ocellatisque nucibus ludebat cum pueris minutis.*

172. sinu laxo : *i.e.* carelessly, in a loose fold of his toga, which served as a pocket.   **ludere** : *sc. eis* (instrumental ablative), *risk them at play.*

173. tristem : *in serious wise.*

174. discors : *of different kinds.*

175. Nomentanum : *cf.* i. 1. 102.   **Cicutam** : *cf.* line 69 above.

176. divos . . . Penatis : *cf. Epist.* i. 7. 94, *per genium, dextramque deosque Penates Obsecro et obtestor.*

178. natura coercet : *sc. quo ; to which nature limits you ; cf.* i. 1. 50, *quid referat intra Naturae finis viventi.*

179. titillet : as we may say, *tickle your fancy.*   **gloria** : *i.e.* a desire for glory.

180. fueritve : note the position of *-ve*, which connects *aedilis* and *praetor*, and see note on line 130 above.

181. praetor : used of the corresponding office in Venusia, *quattuor vir iure dicundo ; cf.* i. 5. 34, and the note.   **intestabilis** : lit. incapable of making a will, or of bearing witness ; here in the general sense of infamous in the eyes of men ; while *sacer* means accursed in the sight of the gods.

182. in cicere, *etc. : i.e.* in largesses of food to the populace ; *cf.* Pers. v. 177, *vigila et cicer ingere large Rixanti populo, nostra ut Floralia possint Aprici meminisse senes.*   **bona . . . perdas** : *waste your substance.*

183. latus . . . spatiere : *cut a swell; cf.* Cic. *Acad.* ii. 127, *erigimur, latiores fieri videmur, humana despicimus.*   **aeneus** : *in bronze,* of a statue ; *cf. Odes,* iv. 1. 20, *te Ponet marmoream sub trabe citrea;* Cic. *Arch.* 9. 22, *in sepulcro Scipionum putatur is (Ennius) esse constitutus ex marmore.*

184. nudus agris, *etc. : cf.* i. 2. 13, *dives agris.*

185. scilicet . . . tu : ironical ; *that* you *forsooth.*   Note the emphasis of *tu* and its position.   **Agrippa** : M. Vipsanius Agrippa was aedile in 33 b.c., when he distinguished himself both by the magnificence of his public works and by the splendor of his games and public exhibitions.

186. astuta . . . leonem : another allusion to the fable of the Ass in the Lion's Skin ; *cf.* i. 6. 22 ; ii. 1. 64.

187 ff. Agamemnon's crime, inspired by ambition, is just as mad as the deed of Ajax. The scene referred to is at the end of the *Ajax* of Sophocles.   **ne quis . . . velit** : modelled on the formula common in the ancient laws, *e.g.* the *Senatus Consultum de Bacchanalibus, C. I. L.* i. 196 ; Lindsay, *Handbook of Latin Inscriptions,* xxxvii. The perfect infinitive is usual in the formula.

188. plebeius : *since I am one of the common people.* The speaker is doubtless conceived of as a philosopher.   **et** : *and besides.*

189. inulto : *unpunished, with impunity ; cf. Odes,* iii. 3. 42, *catulos ferae Celent inultae.*

190. maxime regum, di tibi dent : modelled on *Iliad,* i. 17 f. : —

Ἀτρεῖδαί τε καὶ ἄλλοι ἐϋκνήμιδες Ἀχαιοί,
ὑμῖν μὲν θεοὶ δοῖεν Ὀλύμπια δώματ' ἔχοντες
ἐκπέρσαι Πριάμοιο πόλιν, εὖ δ' οἴκαδ' ἱκέσθαι.

192. consulere : *i.e.* to question you.

193. ab Achille secundus : *next after Achilles, i.e.* second reckoning from Achilles, a common use of *ab;* Plaut. *Pseud.* 597, *septumas aedis a porta.* Ajax was regularly so ranked by the Greek poets.

195. gaudeat : the line is a reminiscence of *Iliad,* i. 255, ἦ κεν γηθήσαι Πρίαμος Πριάμοιό τε παῖδες.   **ut** : *is it that?*   **inhumato** : *sc. illo.*

197. mille ovium : the only case of the use of *mille* (singular) as a substantive in Horace ; the construction is regular in Plautus, and occasionally occurs in Nepos and Cicero ; *e.g.* Nep. *Milt.* 5. 1, *ea (civitas) mille misit militum.*   **insanus . . . dedit** : *went mad and slew.*

199. pro vitula : *like a heifer;* referring to the sacrifice of Iphigenia. Agamemnon, the philosopher says, was no more sane than Ajax.

200. mola . . . salsa : meal and salt were sprinkled on the heads of victims before they were sacrificed.

201. rectum animi servas cursum : *do you keep your senses;* *cf.* Soph. fr. 555, Nauck, εἰς ὀρθὸν φρονεῖς.   **insanus** : *in his madness.* **quid enim** : *why, what?*

202. abstinuit vim : *he withheld violence.* The transitive use of *abstinere* is common in comedy and in Cicero. Horace has the intransitive use with the genitive in *Odes,* iii. 27. 69, *abstineto irarum,* and iv. 9. 37 ; elsewhere the ablative (*e.g. Ars Poet.* 170, 379, 414). Caes. *B. G.* vii. 14 has the intransitive use with *ab* and the ablative, *a mulieribus atque infantibus abstinere;* *cf.* Tac. *Dial.* 40, *se abstinere a;* see Gudeman, *ad loc.*

203. uxore et gnato : Tecmessa and Eurysaces.

204. non ille : strongly emphatic; *cf. Odes,* iv. 9. 51, *non ille timidus perire.*   **ipsum** : *even;* though he was his enemy.

205. verum : *but;* Agamemnon tries to justify himself.   **adverso litore** : ablative of association with *haereo,* as in *Odes,* i. 2. 9, *Piscium et summa genus haesit ulmo.* See Introd. § 41. *b.*

206. prudens : *purposely,* opposed to *insanus.*

207. nempe tuo : *but with your own.*   **non furiosus** : *sc. sum.*

208. alias veris : *different from the true; veris* is ablative ; *cf. Epist.* i. 16. 20, *alium sapiente bonoque.*   **sceleris . . . permixtas** : *cf.* Catull. 64. 405, *malo permixta furore. Tumultu* is ablative of association ; *cf. adverso litore,* line 205 above.

209. commotus : *of unsound mind,* the opposite of *stas animo,* in line 213.

210. stultitia . . . ira : the faults of Agamemnon and Ajax respectively.

211. desipit : note the hyperbaton, and *cf.* ii. 1. 60, *quisquis erit vitae scribam color. Desipit* is emphasized by its position.

212. prudens : *wittingly; cf.* line 206.   **titulos** : *glory*, lit. honorary inscriptions (see note on i. 6. 17), a Roman conception introduced into the Homeric scene.   **inanis** : *cf.* Lucr. iii. 996, *petere imperium quod inane est.*

213. stas animo : *cf. commotus,* line 209.   **tumidum** : *i.e.* with pride ; *cf. Odes,* iv. 3. 8, *regum tumidas minas.*

216. Rufam aut Pusillam : '*golden-hair,*' or '*little darling.*' **forti** : *gallant,* a conventional epithet ; *cf.* ii. 5. 64, *forti nubet procera Corano filia Nasicae.*

217. interdicto : *by an injunction; cf.* Cic. *de Sen.* 7. 22, *ut quem ad modum nostro more male rem gerentibus patribus bonis interdici solet, sic illum . . . a re familiari removerent iudices.*

218. ad sanos abeat tutela propinquos : the words of the Twelve Tables on the subject are preserved by Cic. *de Invent.* ii. 50. 148, *si furiosus escit, agnatum gentiliumque in eo pecuniaque eius potestas esto.*

219. devovet : as Agamemnon did his daughter *pro vitula* (line 199).

220. integer animi : *cf. integer mentis,* line 65 above.   **ne dixeris** : see note on *ne biberis,* ii. 2. 16.   **ergo** : summing up, as in line 158.

222. vitrea : *i.e.* glittering and perishable ; *cf.* Publ. Syr. *Sent.* 171, *Fortuna vitrea est : tum cum splendet frangitur.*

223. circumtonuit : of the noisy rites of the goddess.   **gaudens . . . cruentis** : delighting in deeds of blood.   Bellona was worshipped by fanatics who gashed themselves with knives.

224. nunc : introducing a discussion of the third mark of insanity, luxurious living.   **Nomentanum** : *cf.* line 175 and i. 1. 102.

225. vincet . . . ratio · *cf.* i. 3. 115, *nec vincet ratio hoc.*

226. patrimoni : inheritance, genitive of definition modifying *mille talenta.*

227. edicit : makes proclamation.   Used humorously, as in ii. 2. 51.

228. Tusci . . . vici : a street leading from the Forum toward the Tiber.   It was frequented by all sorts of low characters ; hence *turba impia.*

229. scurris : *parasites,* who make a living by their buffoonery ; *cf.* i. 5. 52, and the note.   **fartor** : probably a sausage-maker.   **Velabro** : a street between the *vicus Tuscus* and the Forum Boarium, fre-

quented by dealers in provisions of all sorts.   See *C. I. L.* vi. 961,
negotiator penoris et vinorum de Velabro.   **macellum** : a general
fish and meat market ; *cf.* Ter. *Eun.* 257, *ad macellum ubi adventa-
mus, Concurrunt laeti mi obviam cuppedinarii omnes, Cetarii, lanii,
coqui, fartores, piscatores.*

231. verba facit : *acts as spokesman.*

234. ocreatus : *in leggings.*   **aprum** : the accusative with *ceno*
is quite frequent in Plautus and in Horace ; otherwise it occurs occasionally only in post-Augustan poetry. See Introd. § 38. *a.*

235. verris : with a net ; *cf.* Sil. Ital. xiv. 262, *seu silvis sectare
feras seu retibus aequor Verrere.*

236. segnis ego : *sc. sum, I am a lazy fellow.*

237. deciens : *sc. centena milia (sestertium)*, and see note on i.
3. 15.

239. Aesopi : a celebrated actor of the time of Cicero. Cicero
uses the same expression, *ad Att.* xi. 15. 3, *filius Aesopi me excruciat.*
Metellae : perhaps the wife of P. Cornelius Lentulus Spinther.

240. deciens solidum : *a whole million;* see note on line 236.
Solidum agrees with *deciens* taken as a sum. The same story is told
of Antony and Cleopatra by Plin. *N. H.* ix. 119 ff.

242. illud idem : *i.e. deciens solidum*, in the form of the pearl.

243. Arri : *cf.* line 86 above.   **nobile** : *ironical.*

244. gemellum : *twins*, agreeing with *par ; cf. Epist.* i. 10. 3,
cetera paene gemelli.

245. impenso : *sc. pretio.* Plin. *N.H.* x. 141, tells us of nightingales
bought for six thousand sesterces (about $300) apiece ; *cf.* also x. 84.

246. quorsum : for *utrovorsum, which way, i.e.* to the side where
the sane men stand, or to the other.   **carbone** : *i.e. ut insani.*
The figure is derived from the connection of white with good luck,
and black with evil ; *cf. Epist.* ii. 2. 189, *vultu mutabilis, albus et
ater.*

247. casas : *toy-houses.* *Cf.* Juv. ix. 61, *rusticus infans Cum
matre et casulis et collusore catello ;* Tib. ii. 1. 24, *Ludet et ex virgis
construet ante casas.*   **plostello** : *a little cart*, diminutive of *plos-
trum*, the colloquial form of *plaustrum.* See Introd. § 55. *b.*

248. par impar : *i.e.* odd or even. The game was played with
nuts ; *cf.* line 171 above.

249. barbatum : *i.e.* a grown-up man.   **amentia verset** : *sc.
eum, i.e.* he would be the victim of madness.

250. ratio evincet : *cf.* line 225 above, and the note.

251. utrumne: the *-ne* is redundant ; *cf. uterne*, ii. 2. 107.   **in pulvere**: *cf. Iliad*, xv. 362 : —

> ὡς ὅτε τις ψάμαθον παῖς ἄγχι θαλάσσης
> ὅστ᾽ ἐπεὶ οὖν ποιήσῃ ἀθύρματα νηπιέῃσιν,
> ἂψ αὖτις συνέχευε ποσὶν καὶ χερσὶν ἀθύρων.

252. ludas opus : *you waste your time.*

254. mutatus : *i.e.* reformed.   **Polemon** : the successor of Xenocrates as head of the old Academy, formerly a dissipated Athenian youth, who was converted to temperance by hearing a discourse of Xenocrates, into whose lecture hall he had burst on returning from a drinking-bout.   **insignia morbi** : *signs of your malady; cf.* Quint. xi. 3. 14, *palliolum sicut fascias, quibus crura vestiuntur, et focalia et aurium ligamenta sola excusare potest valetudo.*

255. cubital : apparently an elbow-cushion ; *cf.* Comm. Cruq., *cubitale pulvillus qui cubito cenantis supponi solebat.*   **potus ille** : *i.e.* Polemon.

256. furtim : *i.e.* when he thought no one was looking.   **coronas** : the garlands which he had worn at the drinking-bout, and still had on.

257. impransi : *sober*, as opposed to *potus* in line 255 ; lit. *fasting.*

259. catelle : *little cub*, a humorous term of endearment ; *cf.* Plaut. *Asin.* 693, *dic igitur med aniticulam, columbulam, catellum.*

260. qui : how ; *cf.* line 108.   **agit** : the original quantity of the *i* was short ; it is used as long after the analogy of verbs which originally had a long final syllable.   See Introd. § 57.

262. nec nunc : with this whole dialogue, *cf.* Ter. *Eun.* 46 ff. The same passage of Terence is also followed by Persius, v. 161–174.

263. finire dolores : *i.e.* by resisting the temptation.

265. servus : referring to Parmeno, Phaedria's slave.   **quae res** : *a thing which*, referring to love.

268. tempestatis . . . ritu mobilia : *i.e.* almost as changeable as the weather.

269. caeca sorte : opposed to *ratione*, line 266.   For the meaning of *sorte*, see i. 1. 1, and the note.

270. reddere certa : *i.e.* to reduce to rule and order.

271. insanire . . . ratione modoque : *to go mad by rule and method.*   Palmer compares Shakespeare, *Hamlet*, ii. 2. 298, "Though this be madness, yet there's method in it."

272. Picenis . . . pomis : the apples of Picenum were highly esteemed; *cf.* ii. 4. 7; Juv. xi. 74, *aemula Picenis et odoris mala recentis.*

273. cameram percusti: if a lover succeeded in snapping an apple-seed so as to hit the ceiling, it was regarded as a sign that his love was returned; *cf.* our Hallowe'en customs. **penes te es**: *i.e* are you in your senses?

274. balba: *lisping*, used of the 'baby talk' of lovers. See note on *Balbinus*, i. 3. 40. **feris**: lit. *strike; cf.* Varro, *ap. Diomedem*, i. 420. 10 K., *(vox) fit vel exilis aurae pulsu vel verberati aeris ictu.*

275. aedificante casas: *cf.* line 247 above. **qui**: *how much?* **cruorem**: of murderous acts inspired by love.

276. ignem gladio scrutare: an example of folly. See Athenaeus, x. 425, 'πῦρ μαχαίρᾳ μὴ σκαλεύειν' ἀντὶ τοῦ τεθυμωμένον ἄνδρα μὴ ἐριδαίνειν· 'πῦρ γὰρ ὁ θυμός, ἡ δ' ἔρις μάχαιρα. **modo**: *i.e.* as lately happened; with reference to the following instance.

277. praecipitat se: *throws himself headlong*, either *in Tiberim* or from some high place. The word is used absolutely, without a conscious ellipsis; *cf.* Livy, xxxiii. 19. 6, *et praecipitasse quosdam non tolerantes famem constabat.*

278. cerritus : *crazy;* apparently connected with Cerrus, a masculine form of Ceres. **commotae mentis** : *cf. commotus*, line 209.

279. absolves: with *crimine* expressed, instead of the genitive of the charge. See B. *App.*, § 327. **sceleris**: genitive of the charge.

280. ex more: *i.e.* as people usually do. **cognata** : kindred, *i.e.* of nearly, but not quite, the same meaning; hence really *different.*

281. libertinus : see note on *liberta*, i. 1. 99. **compita** : *cross-roads*, where the shrines of the *Lares Compitales* were located. **siccus** : *fasting*, which, like *lautis manibus esse*, was required under the circumstances.

283. quid tam magnum : *sc. est quod vos oro; i.e.* what I ask is not so very great a thing. **unum**: repeated for emphasis.

284. dis . . . facile est : a Homeric reminiscence; *cf. Odyss.* v. 25, Τηλέμαχον δὲ σὺ πέμψον ἐπισταμένως, δύνασαι γαρ.

285. nisi litigiosus : *sc. esset, unless he were fond of lawsuits,* for one would surely follow for misrepresentation; *cf.* Varr. *R. R.* ii. 10. 5, *in (servorum) emptione solet stipulatio intercedere sanum eum esse, furtis noxisque solutum; cf.* also *Epist.* ii. 2. 2–19.

286. exciperet: *would except*, from his guarantee. **hoc . . . volgus**: the expression implies that there were many such people.

287. Meneni: an unknown madman.

289. cubantis: *sick abed;* *cf.* i. 9. 18.

290. quartana: *sc. febris, the quartan ague,* occurring every fourth day, according to the Roman method of inclusive reckoning.

291. die . . . ieiunia: Thursday, the day of Jupiter; the reference is to the Jewish rites, to which the anxious mother resorts; *cf.* Juv. vi. 522 (of a superstitious woman), *Hibernum fracta glacie descendat in amnem, Ter matutino Tiberi mergetur, et ipsis Verticibus timidum caput abluet.*

292. levarit: see note on *triverit,* i. 1. 45.

293. ex praecipiti: *from the crisis;* *cf.* Celsus, iii. 18, *praeceps periculum.*

295. quone: *cf. utrumne,* line 251 above; *uterne,* ii. 2. 107.

296. sapientum octavus: *i.e.* an addition to the Seven Wise Men of Greece; *cf.* Juv. ii. 40, *tertius e caelo cecidit Cato.*

297. compellarer: *be abused;* *i.e.* called insane.

298. totidem: *sc. verba, shall hear as much, i.e.* the same.

299. pendentia tergo: *cf.* line 53 above; or perhaps with reference to the two sacks; see note on i. 3. 69; and *cf.* Phaedrus, iv. 10, *Peros imposuit Iuppiter nobis duos: Propriis repletum vitiis post tergum dedit, Alienis ante pectus suspendit gravem.*

300. sic vendas: the regular formula in wishes, usually followed by an *ut*-clause, *e.g. ut dicis qua stultitia . . . putes,* but here, by a kind of anacoluthon, by a direct question; *cf. Odes,* i. 3. 1 f., where jussive subjunctives follow.   **pluris**: *sc. quam emeris;* genitive of price.

301. qua stultitia: *on account of what folly ?*

303. abscisum: *cut off.* Pentheus was torn to pieces by his mother Agave and the other Bacchantes, because he despised the power of Dionysus.

305. liceat: *let it be allowed me, i.e.* without shame.

306. tantum . . . edissere: *only explain.*

308. aedificas: probably on his Sabine Farm.   **longos imitaris**: *you are imitating the great;* the word *longos* is chosen with reference to Horace's short stature; *cf. Epist.* i. 20. 24.

310. corpore maiorem: *too great for his body; corpore* is ablative of comparison.   **Turbonis**: according to Porphyrio, a gladiator of small size but of great courage.

312. verum: *just, reasonable; sc. facere. Cf. Epist.* i. 7. 98, *Metiri se quemque suo modulo ac pede verum est.*

313. tantum dissimilem: *cf.* ii. 5. 92 ; *Epist.* i. 10. 3.

314. absentis ranae : another allusion to the Aesopian fables.
pullis : *the young.*

317. quantane : *cf. quone*, line 295 ; *utrumne*, line 251.

318. num tanto : *sc. magna fuit, not so big as this?*

320. abludit : a ἄπαξ εἰρημένον, equivalent to *abhorret.*

321. oleum . . . camino : a proverbial expression, from the
Greek.

322. sanus : poetic inspiration is regarded as akin to madness ; *cf.*
Ars Poet. 296.

323. horrendam rabiem : one of Horace's besetting sins ; *cf.*
Odes, iii. 9. 23 ; *Epist.* i. 20. 25. As Kiessling remarks, it is a happy
touch that the mention of it here makes the poet finally lose patience,
and break out with *desine.*   **cultum maiorem censu** : *a style of*
living beyond your means ; see note on *censum*, ii. 1. 75.

324. teneas . . . tuis te : *mind your own business*, more literally,
'keep to your own affairs.'   *Tuis* is instrumental ablative ; *cf.* Caes.
B. C. i. 40, *castris se tenebat.*

326. maior . . . insane : *greater — madman!   Insane* has the
same effect as *bonorum*, i. 1. 79 ; *minora*, i. 3. 20 ; where see notes.

SERMO IV.

1. unde et quo : *sc. venit* and *tendit ;* a common formula of
salutation ; *cf.* i. 9. 62.   **Catius** : otherwise unknown. Porphyrio's
identification with a writer on the Epicurean philosophy, mentioned by
Cic. *ad Fam.* xv. 16. 1, and Quint. x. 1. 124, is very improbable.
aventi : *i.e.* though I should like to.

2. ponere signa : *i.e.* commit them to writing.

3. Anyti reum : Socrates. Anytus was the most prominent of
his accusers.

4. peccatum : *my fault.*   **sic** : *i.e.* as I have done ; to be taken
with *interpellarem.*   **laevo** : *unfavorable ; cf.* the opposite *dextro*
tempore, ii. 1. 18.

5. bonus : *i.e.* be a good fellow, and.

6. interciderit : *i.e.* slips your memory.

7. hoc : *i.e.* the power of memory.   **naturae sive artis** : *i.e.*
natural or acquired ; *cf.* Auct. ad Her. iii. 3. 16, *sunt duae memoriae,*
una naturalis, altera artificiosa.

8. quin : *nay.* Catius says that his memory is the result of
training.

9. tenui : equivalent to *subtili*.

10. hominis : *the man*, who invented the system.

11. memor : *from memory*.

12. ovis : as a dinner began with eggs (*cf.* i. 3. 7, note), *bene ab ovis incipit*, as the Comm. Cruq. says.

13. suci : *flavor*.   **magis alba** : *whiter;* with reference, of course, to the inside.

14. ponere : *to serve; cf.* ii. 2. 23, *posito pavone*.   **callosa** : *i.e.* they are firm and.   *Cf.* Plin. *N. H.* x. 145, *quae oblonga sint ova gratioris saporis putat Horatius Flaccus*.

15. suburbano : grown near the city in the well-watered gardens (contrasted with *siccis*) ; *cf.* Plin. *N. H.* xix. 138.   **cole** : *umor fimusque si defuere, maior saporis gratia est; si abundavere, laetior fertilitas*.

16. elutius : *more insipid;* lit. *washed-out*.   **horto** : used for the products of the garden.

17. oppresserit : *i.e.* takes you by surprise.

18. malum : adverb.   **dura** : *tough*.

19. doctus eris : *i.e.* you will do well.

20. pratensibus : *i.e.* which grow in the meadows, opposed to the woods.

22. prandia : *his luncheon*.   The *prandium* was the first substantial meal of the day, taken in the middle of the forenoon.   It corresponded to the French *déjeuner à la fourchette*.

24. mella Falerno : for the *mulsum*, taken at the beginning of the meal ; hence the reason which follows.   See note on ii. 2. 15. *Falerno* is ablative of association ; see Introd. § 41. *b*.

25. vacuis venis : *i.e.* an empty stomach.

29. brevis : *short-leaved*.

30. nascentes . . . lunae : *i.e.* the best shell-fish are taken at the time of the full moon ; *cf.* Lucil. 1062 L., *Luna alit ostrea et inplet echinos, Muribus fibras et pecui addit*.

31. generosae : *i.e.* the best.

34. molle Tarentum : so called on account of the luxury and effeminacy of its people.

35. cenarum . . . artem : the art of giving banquets ; *cf.* Ter. *Andr.* 30, *Quid est, Quod tibi mea ars efficere hoc possit amplius?* The term *ars* was applied not only to professions but to trades ; *e.g. ars coquina, figlina, etc.*

36. exacta : *mastered;* cf. Ovid, *Fasti*, iii. 637, *non habet exactum quid agat, she does not clearly know what to do.*

37. cara . . . mensa : *i.e.* from a dear fish-market. The *mensa* is the slab on which the fish were exposed for sale. **averrere** : *sweep off;* doubtless with some suggestion of the force of *verris*, ii. 3. 235.

38. est : the indicative, instead of the usual subjunctive, an archaic, and perhaps colloquial, usage.

39. in cubitum . . . reponet : *i.e.* will soon (*iam*) eat to repletion and sink back upon his elbow ; cf. *Odes*, i. 27. 6, *impium Lenite clamorem, sodalis, Et cubito remanete presso.*

41. curvat : *bends* by its weight. **inertem** : *insipid.*

42. Cf. Macaulay, *Battle of Lake Regillus*, 185, "From the Laurentian jungle, The wild hog's reedy home."

43. submittit : *supplies.* **non semper edulis** : *i.e.* those taken in the forest are sometimes better.

44. sapiens : *the connoisseur.* **armos** : *the fore-quarters;* cf. ii. 8. 89, *et leporum avolsos, ut multo suavius, armos.*

46. nulli : sc. *palato.* **quaesita** : with concessive force, modifying both *natura* and *aetas.*

47. promit : *produces.*

48. satis : *sc. est ;* the only one out of twenty-four cases in Horace where *est* is omitted in this expression. Kiessling suggests that it is a parody of some proverbial expression in which *est* for *satis est* occurred.

50. securus : *careless, regardless.*

51. Massica : a Campanian wine of the third quality, according to Pliny. Of the Campanian wines in general, he says (*N. H.* xiv. 136), *Campaniae nobilissima exposita sub dio in cadis verberari sole luna, imbre, ventis, aptissimum videtur.*

52. crassi : *roughness.*

53. decedet . . . inimicus : *i.e.* it will have a less strong odor ; will acquire a bouquet. **illa** : *i.e. Massica vina.* Straining through a linen cloth cleared the wine, but took away the flavor as well.

55. Surrentina : a very light Campanian wine suited to invalids ; cf. Plin. *N. H.* xiv. 64, *Tiberius Caesar dicebat consensisse medicos ut nobilitatem Surrentino darent, alioqui esse generosum acetum, C. Caesar, qui successit illi, nobilem vappam.* Mixing it with the lees of Falernian gave it strength and flavor.

56. limum : *sediment.* The wine was clarified with an egg.

57. quatenus: *inasmuch as*, the regular meaning of the word in Horace; *cf.* i. 1. 64.   **volvens aliena**: *i.e.* gathering up foreign substances.

58. marcentem: *jaded*, from excessive drinking.

59. innatat: *i.e.* it does not digest.

60. hillis: sausages, diminutive of *hira*.

61. immorsus: *stimulated;* literally, 'bitten.'   **quin** = *quin etiam; nay . . . even.*

62. fervent adlata: *are brought smoking hot.*

63. duplicis iuris: a particular kind of sauce, made by boiling *simplex ius* and adding the ingredients named in lines 67–69.

64. dulci: *fresh.*

65. muria: *brine*, in which fish were preserved.

66. Byzantia orca: *i.e.* a jar of pickled fish; the Black Sea abounded in tunny fish, of which Byzantium was one of the principal ports of export. *Cf.* the Greek proverb, ἰχθῦς εἰς Ἑλλήσποντον, 'carry fish to the Hellespont,' and see note on i. 10. 34.

67. inferbuit: *has been boiled.*

68. Corycio: Corycus was a mountain in Cilicia, famous for its saffron.   **stetit**: *has stood*, to cool.

69. Venafranae: the best oil came from Venafrum in Samnium; *cf. Odes*, ii. 6. 16.

70. Picenis . . . pomis; *cf.* ii. 3. 272, and the note.   **Tiburtia**: *sc. poma.*

71. nam: used elliptically, like καὶ γάρ in Greek; *and I call your attention to this, for.*   **vennuncula**: *sc. uva.*   **ollis**: *for pots, i.e.* for preserving.

73. hanc: *i.e. uvam.*   **faecem . . . allec**: used as appetizers; *cf.* ii. 8. 9 *qualia lassum Pervellunt stomachum, siser, allec, faecula Coa.*

74. primus . . . invenior: *I am found to be the first.*

75. incretum: from *incernere*, *sift on.*   **puris**: *clean.*

76. milia terna: 3000 sesterces; the sum is used of an indefinite large number. See Introd. § 50.

77. vagos: *roving; i.e.* accustomed to range the seas.   **urgere**: *cramp.*

78. unctis . . . dum furta ligurrit: *i.e.* made greasy because he has taken something from a dish which he was carrying.

80. veteri: old and valuable.   **limus**: *sediment.*   **adhaesit**: perfect of *adhaeresco*, and so equivalent in meaning to *adhaeret.*

81. vilibus: *cheap;* note the emphatic position.

82. neglectis : ablative absolute, with *his* understood.

83. ten: shortened from *tene;* a colloquial form.   **lapides varios** : the reference is to a mosaic pavement, composed of bits of marble of different colors.   **radere** : infinitive in an exclamation ; *cf.* i. 9. 73 ; Introd. § 46. *b.*

84. Tyrias . . . vestis: governed by *circum;* note the anastrophe, which is common with dissyllabic prepositions.   **toralia** : coverings of white linen which were thrown over the purple couches to keep them clean.   The *toralia* could be washed, hence there was no excuse for using soiled ones.

86. haec : *these details*, of neatness.   **tanto reprehendi iustius** : *i.e.* their neglect is more blameworthy than the absence of splendid pavements and Tyrian coverlets would be.

89. auditum : *to hear;* supine.

91. interpres : as a reporter of the teachings of his master. **adde** : *add to this.*   That is, to see the man would enhance the effect of his words.

95. Apparently a parody of Lucr. i. 927, *iuvat integros accedere fontes Atque haurire.*

SERMO V.

1. Tiresia : a famous Theban seer.   He is supposed to continue his conversation with Odysseus at the point where it is concluded in *Odyssey*, xi. 149.   **petenti** : sc. *responsum; cf. Carm. Saec.* 55, *iam Scythae responsa petunt.*

3. quid rides? *cf.* i. 1. 69.   The seer smiles at the greed of Odysseus.   **iamne** : *is it no longer*, when he is assured of his safe return.   **doloso** : *the man of guile,* as if he were referring to a third person ; *doloso* translates the Greek πολύτροπον or πολυμήχανος.   *Cf.* Liv. Andr. *ap. Gell.* xviii. 9. 5, *Virum mihi, Camena, insece versutum.*

4. patriosque penatis : these words introduce a Roman color into the language of Odysseus.

5. nulli . . . mentite : *cf.* Soph. *Oed. Tyr.* 299, ᾧ τἀληθὲς ἐμπέφυκεν ἀνθρώπων μόνῳ.

6. redeam : *am returning;* the future would be expressed by *rediturus sim.*

7. apotheca : *store-house;* often ' wine-vault ' ; Italian, *bottega;* Spanish, *bodega;* French, *boutique.*   **procis** : the suitors of Penelope, who had flocked to Ithaca during the absence of Ulysses.

8. re = *re familiari, money; cf. Epist.* i. 1. 66.   **vilior alga** : a proverbial expression ; *cf. Odes,* iii. 17. 10, *alga inutili;* Virg. *Ecl.* 7. 42, *proiecta vilior alga.* It is especially appropriate as applied to the seafaring Odysseus.

9. quando = *quando quidem.*   **missis ambagibus** : *in plain language.*

10. turdus : the thrush or fieldfare was greatly prized as a delicacy ; *cf. Epist.* i. 15. 40 ; Mart. xiii. 92, *Inter aves turdus, si quid me iudice certum est Inter quadrupedes mattea prima lupus.*

11. privum : *as your own,* like *proprium; cf.* Lucil. 21 L., *Ad cenam adducam et primum hisce abdomina thunni Advenientibus priva dabo cephalaeaque Acharnae.*   **dabitur** : with conditional force, *if a thrush shall be given you;* the paratactic use.   **devolet** : *let it fly away;* appropriately used of a bird.

12. nitet : *flourishes;* of a well-kept property ; *cf.* ii. 2. 127, *quanto aut ego parcius aut vos, O pueri, nituistis.*

13. honores : *cf. Odes,* i. 17. 16, *ruris honorum.*

14. ante Larem : the first fruits were commonly offered to the Lar Familiaris, the guardian spirit of the house.

15. erit : indicative, as in ii. 2. 29, *quamvis distat nil.* See Introd. § 45. *b.*   **sine gente** : as a runaway slave (*fugitivus*), he was *filius nullius.* See note on i. 5. 54.

17. comes exterior : *as his companion walking on his left.* Since weapons were carried in the right hand, the left was the unprotected side ; hence to walk on one's left was a mark of honor ; *cf.* Suet. *Claud.* 24, *et in Capitolium eunti et inde rursus revertenti latus texit (Plautio).*

18. utne : introducing an indignant question ; *what! shall I?* Cf. i. 10. 21, *quine putetis.*   **Damae** : a common slave-name ; *cf.* i. 6. 38. **Troiae** : before Troy.

19. melioribus : dative with a verb of contending ; see Introd. § 39. *a.* Cf. *Epod.* 2. 20, *certantem et uvam purpurae* and Virg. *Ecl.* 5. 8, *tibi certat Amyntas.*   **ergo** : *well then.*

20. fortem . . . animum : a parody of the Homeric τλήμονα. **hoc** : *this disgrace.*

21. maiora tuli : *cf. Odyss.* xx. 18, τέτλαθι δή, κραδίη · καὶ κύντερόν ἄλλο ποτ᾽ ἔτλης.

22. ruam : *rake up;* apparently uniting the meaning of *corruo* and *eruo* ('dig up'); *cf.* Lucil. 901 L, *ruis huc et colligis omnia furtim.*

23. dixi : said impatiently, referring to lines 10–17.   **captes** : the usual word, whence legacy-hunters were called *captatores;* it naturally leads up to the following metaphor.

25. praeroso hamo : *after nibbling the bait* from the end of the hook. Lucian, *Tim.* 18, uses the same metaphor ; *cf.* Mart. vi. 63. 5, *Munera magna quidem misit sed misit in hamo.*

26. artem : *the profession; cf.* Sen. *de Ben.* vi. 38, *qui captandorum testamentorum artem professi sunt ;* see note on ii. 4. 35.

27. foro : *in the forum*, for the prose construction *in foro; cf. mansuri oppidulo*, i. 5. 87.   **res** : *case; cf.* i. 9. 41.   **olim** : *at any time ;* see note on i. 1. 25.

28. improbus : *though he be a scoundrel.*   **ultro** : *actually, i.e.* without just cause, when he ought himself to be arraigned ; *cf.* Liv. i. 5. 3, *latrones . . . ultro accusantes.*

30. priorem = *meliorem.*

32. Quinte : to address one by one's *praenomen* was a sign of familiarity and affection.   **puta** : *for example ; i.e.* supposing that to be his name. The last syllable is short.   **molles** : *sensitive ; cf.* Ter. *Heaut.* 402, *ut patrem tuom vidi esse habitum, diu etiam duras dabit (aures)* ; *mollis* is also used as a general epithet of the ear, in Catull. 25. 2, *mollior . . . imula oricilla ;* Pers. i. 107, *teneras . . . auriculas.*

34. ius anceps : *cf. vafri iuris*, ii. 2. 131.

35. oculos : a general term for what is dearest to a man ; *cf.* our expression, 'the apple of one's eye ' ; Catull. 14. 1, *Ni te plus oculis meis amarem ;* also with the passage in general, *cf.* Plaut. *Pseud.* 510, *eclidito mihi oculum, si dedero.*

36. contemptum . . . pauperet : for *contemnat et pauperet, bring contempt on you and rob you. Paupero* belongs to the language of everyday life ; *cf.* Plaut. fr. *ap. Non.* 157. 7, *quam ego tanta pauperavi per dolum pecunia.*   **cassa nuce** : *an empty nut ;* also colloquial, *cf.* Plaut. *Pseud.* 510, *Ten amatorem esse inventum inanem quasi cassam nucem.*

37. sis iocus : *be a laughing stock ; cf. contemptum*, line 36.

38. pelliculam : *his precious hide.* Note the force of the diminutive. The usual expression is *cutem curare ; cf. Epist.* i. 2. 29 ; i. 4. 15. *Cf.* also Juv. x. 192 (of an old man), *deformem pro cute pellem.* **fi cognitor** : *be his advocate ; cf.* Gaius, iv. 97, *cum enim certis et quasi sollemnibus verbis in locum domini substituatur, cognitor merito domini loco habetur.*

39. persta : *cf.* i. 9. 39.   **seu rubra**, *etc. :* apparently a hit at some verses of Furius Bibaculus (*cf.* i. 10. 36), of which one is known from Quint. viii. 6. 17, *Iuppiter hibernas cana nive conspuat Alpes.* Here *Furius* is substituted for *Iuppiter.* The color of the Dog Star is now a greenish blue, a sign of old age in stars; it was apparently red in ancient times; *cf.* Sen. *Nat. Quaest.* i. 1. 7, *cum in caelo quoque non unus appareat color rerum, sed acrior sit Caniculae rubor, Martis remissior.*

40. infantis: *dumb; cf. Epist.* ii. 2. 83, *statua taciturnius; infans* has its literal meaning, as in i. 6. 57, *infans pudor.*   **pingui tentus omaso**: *stuffed with greasy tripe.*

42. cubito . . . tangens: *nudging his neighbor.*

43. patiens: *sc. laboris*, and *cf.* lines 39–41.

44. thunni: the same metaphor as in line 25.   **cetaria**: either *weirs*, in which the fish were caught (*cf.* Plin. *N. H.* xxxvii. 66 *cetarias*), or the same as *vivaria* (*Epist.* i. 1. 79), in which fish were kept alive until wanted for the table. The word *cetarium* occurs only here.

45. re: *sc. familiari; cf.* line 8 above.

46. sublatus aletur: *shall be taken up and reared.* A sickly child might be exposed for death; it was placed before the father, who took it up if he wished it reared (hence *sublatus*).

47. caelibis: objective genitive. For fear that open devotion to a childless man may be seen through, the will-hunter is advised to pay court also (*praeterea*) to a man with one sickly heir.   **nudet**: *i.e.* deprive you of your prize.   **leniter**: *craftily, slyly*, contrasted with *manifestum*, line 46.   **spem**: *sc. hereditatis.*

48. arrepe officiosus: *work your way by your attentions.* The *ut*-clause is probably best taken with *spem*.   **secundus heres**: *i.e.* heir to the estate in the event of the death of the son; *cf.* Tac. *Ann.* i. 8, *Augusti testamentum Tiberium et Liviam heredes habuit: in spem secundam nepotes pronepotesque, tertio gradu primores civitatis scripserat.*

49. Orco: dative of the goal or end of motion.

50. in vacuum: a legal term.

51. qui . . . cumque: *tmesis;* see Introd. § 53. *o.*   **legendum**: to show that he has been remembered in the will.

53. sic tamen: *but in such a way.*   **limis**: *sc. oculis*: 'out of the tail of your eye'; *cf.* Plaut. *Mil.* 1217, *Aspicito limis, ne ille nos se sentiat videre.* Apparently colloquial.   **prima cera**: the first page of the tablets on which the will was written.   **secundo . . . versu**:

the second line, which generally contained the name of the heir, while
the testator's name appeared in the first.

54. velit : *says;* more lit. ' means.'   **solus** : *sole heir; heres ex
asse.*

55. plerumque : *very often; cf.* i. 10. 15.   **recoctus** : *made
over*, with reference to the story of Medea and Aeson.

56. quinqueviro : a very low official, a sort of policeman.   **corvum** : with reference to the fable of the Fox and the Crow ; *cf.* Phaed.
i. 13.

57. Nasica Corano : an incident of Horace's own day, detailed
below (64 f.), which Tiresias tells in the form of a prophecy.

58. prudens : *purposely.*

59. quicquid . . . non : a parody of divination. It is cited by
Boethius, *Cons.* v. 3, as a *ridiculum vaticinium.*

60. donat : present, because the inspiration is still continued,
although the action of the verb is itself past ; *cf.* Verg. *Aen.* ix. 266,
Cratera antiquum, quem dat Sidonia Dido.

61. tamen : *yet,* or *yes, but.*   **si licet** : *if it be lawful.*

62. iuvenis : Octavian ; born B.C. 63.   **ab alto . . . Aenea** :
cf. Virg. *Aen.* i. 288, *Iulius a magno demissum nomen Iulo;* vi. 500,
genus alto a sanguine Teucri ; alto contains the idea both of antiquity
and nobility.

63. genus : *a scion.* Used also of a single person in *Odes,* i. 3.
27 ; *Serm.* i. 6. 12.   **tellure marique** : a variation of the common
expression *terra marique*, perhaps for mock-heroic effect. See note on
i. 5. 3.

64. forti : *gallant*, apparently a stock epithet for a bridegroom ;
cf. ii. 3. 216, *forti marito ;* here used ironically.

65. metuentis : with the force of *nolentis; cf. Odes,* ii. 2. 7, *penna
metuente solvi.*   **soldum** : *his debts*, strictly the principal ; or perhaps in the sense of pay in full. For the syncopated form, *cf.* i. 3. 53.

66. tabulas : *sc. testamenti ; cf.* line 52.

67. multum : with the force of *saepe ; cf.Odes,* i. 25. 5 ; *Epist.* i.
3. 15 ; *Ars Poet.* 357.

69. legatum : *left as a legacy*, to be paid by the heir to the estate
(*legare ab aliquo*).   **plorare** : governed by the preposition *praeter;*
cf. Cic. *de Fin.* ii. 13. 43, *inter optime valere et gravissime aegrotare
nihil interesse ;* and see Introd. § 46. *d.*

70. ad haec : *besides*, like *praeterea* in line 45.   **mulier dolosa** :
probably a freedwoman mistress ; *cf.* i. 1. 99.

71. **delirum** : *cf.* ii. 3. 107, *delirus et amens Undique dicatur merito.*   **temperet** : *control; cf. Odes*, i. 8. 7, *temperat ora frenis.*

73. **vincit longe** : *it is a far better plan.*   **prius** : *first.*   **ipsum** . . . **caput** : *the citadel, i.e.* the old man himself.

74. **scribet** : paratactic construction for *si scribet.* So *erit. Cf.* Mart. xii. 40, *Mentiris : credo ; recitas mala carmina : laudo.*   **vecors** : of intellectual qualities ; *cf.* ii. 3. 67, *excors.*

76. **facilis** : *compliantly.*   **potiori** : for *utpote potiori, as to your superior.*   **putasne** . . . **poterit** : parataxis, instead of the infinitive in indirect discourse ; *cf.* Plaut. *Rud.* 1269, *Censen hodie despondebit eam mihi, quaeso.*

79. **enim** : *yes indeed, for.*   **donandi parca** : for the construction, *cf. parcus aceti*, ii. 2. 62 ; and in general, *Odyss.* xviii. 275 ff.

81. **sic** : *under such conditions; cf.* i. 10. 5, *nam sic Laberi mimos mirer.*   **tibi** : *your ;* ethical dative.   **quae** : for *at ea ; cf.* i. 1. 36. **uno** : because an old man in love would give more gifts than many young suitors.

83. **canis a corio** : with reference to a Greek proverb, Alciphron iii. 47, οὐδὲ γὰρ κύων σκυτοτραγεῖν μαθοῦσα τῆς τέχνης ἐπιλήσεται ; *cf.* Theocr. 10. 11, χαλεπὸν χορίῳ κύνα γεῦσαι.

84. **me sene** : *when I was an old man, i.e.* still on earth ; a jesting variation of the usual *me iuvene, me puero, etc.*   **improba** : *malicious*, because she enjoyed in advance the discomfiture of the heir. **Thebis** : the home of Tiresias.

85. **ex testamento** : *cf.* Petron. 143, *omnes qui in testamento meo legata habent praeter libertos meos, hac condicione percipient quae dedi, si corpus meum in partes conciderint et astante populo comederint.* **est elata** : the regular term for carrying out a corpse for burial.

87. **si posset** : subjunctive in an indirect question ; *(because she wished to see) if she could.* The ellipsis is colloquial.   **mortua** : *after death.*

89. **operae** : dative, as in i. 9. 56, *haud mihi dero.*   **abundes** : *sc. opera.*

90. **difficilem et morosum** : *cf.* Cic. *de Sen.* 18. 65, *sunt morosi et anxii et iracundi et difficiles senes.*   **garrulus** : *cf.* i. 9. 33.   **ultra** . . . **sileas** : *say nothing but 'yes' and 'no';* more literally, *beyond 'yes' and 'no'; cf. si 'Iane' libentius audis*, ii. 6. 20.

91. **Davus comicus** : *like Davus in the play. Cf personatus pater*, i. 4. 56; and i. 10. 40, *Davo Chremeta eludente*, with the note.

92. **capite obstipo** : *with bowed head; cf.* Pers. iii. 80, *obstipo*

capite et fingentes lumine terram.   **multum** : modifying *similis; cf.*
ii. 3. 147 ; *Epist.* i. 10. 3.

93. grassare : *make your advances;* frequentative of *gradior.*
increbruit : *freshens.*

94. velet : with the hood of the *lacerna* (*cf.* ii. 7. 55), or with a
fold of his *toga.*

95. aurem substringe : *i.e.* gather up your ear with your hand,
so as not to lose a single word.   **loquaci** : if he is inclined to talk.

96. inportunus amat : paratactic ; *if he has an insatiate desire.*
ohe iam : *hold, enough; cf.* i. 5. 12, *ohe, iam satis est.*

97. urge : *ply him* with flattery.

98. infla : *cf.* Cic. *de Domo,* 11. 29, *desinant aliquando me isdem*
inflare verbis.

99. levarit : by his death. *

100. certum : *sharply,* the opposite of *incertum vigilans,* Ovid,
Her. 10. 9.

101. ergo : *so then; cf. Odes,* i. 24. 5, *ergo Quintilium perpetuus*
sopor Urget!   **audieris** : on the long *i,* see note on ii. 2. 74.

102. unde : for the construction, *sc. quaeram,* or a verb of similar
meaning, although there is no conscious ellipsis; cf. ii. 7. 116 ; *Epist.*
i. 5. 12.   **fortem . . . fidelem** : with these adjectives, *cf. spurco* in
line 18.

103. sparge : as one would scatter flowers.   **subinde** : *at once,*
a meaning not found before the Augustan age.   **est** : *you can;*
literally, *it is possible; cf.* i. 5. 87.

105. arbitrio : *cf.* ii. 3. 86, *arbitrio Arri.*   **sine sordibus** :
without meanness ; *cf.* i. 6. 107, *sordes.*

106. vicinia : *the neighbors;* the abstract for the concrete ; *cf.*
Epist. i. 16. 44 ; i. 17. 62.

107. male tussiet : *has a bad cough; i.e.* is in consumption ; *cf.*
tussis, i. 9. 32.

108. ex parte tua : *sc. hereditatis.*   **sit** : *he would like to be.*

109. nummo : *for a song.* It was really a free gift ; but the form
of a sale was gone through.   Cf. Gaius, ii. 252, *olim in usu erat ei, cui*
restituebatur hereditas, nummo uno eam hereditatem dicis causa venire.
and our expression ' in consideration of one dollar,' *etc.*   **addicere** :
a term used of auctioneers, *to knock down.*

110. imperiosa : *imperious;* her command must be obeyed.
trahit : *summons me back* to the shades.   **vive valeque** : a common formula of farewell ; *cf. Epist.* i. 6. 67.

SERMO VI.

1. hoc : referring to what follows, which has reference to his Sabine farm.   **in votis** : *among my prayers.*

2. iugis : *ever-flowing ;* probably to be taken with *aquae; cf. Epist.* i. 15. 16, *iugis aquae.*

3. super his : *above these, i.e.* on the slope of the hill ; *cf.* i. 5. 51, *super Caudi cauponas.*   **foret** : this form is not found in Caesar. Cicero uses it only in his letters to Atticus, always in a future sense ; and *de Rep.* ii. 12. 24. Subjunctive of characteristic.   **auctius** : *more generously.*

4. melius : since it was the gift of his friend Maecenas.   **bene est** : it is well.

5. Maia nate : Mercury, as god of gain ; *cf.* ii. 3. 68.   **propria** : *my own forever; cf. Epist.* i. 17. 5.   **faxis** : the old aorist optative *fac-s-i-s,* used with the force of a perfect subjunctive.

6. ratione mala : *by evil means, i.e.* by dishonesty.   **rem** : *sc. familiarem ; cf.* ii. 3. 18.

7. vitio culpave : *by dissipation* (*cf.* ii. 2. 21, *pinguem vitiis*) *or neglect.*

8. veneror : *pray for; cf.* Cic. *ad Fam.* vi. 7. 2, *qui multa deos venerati sint; Carm. Saec.* 49.   **stultus** : from the philosophical point of view, opposed to *sapiens.*   **si** : introducing a wish ; really a protasis, with the apodosis suppressed. This use is confined for the most part to the Augustan Poets and to Silver Latin.

9. denormat : *spoils the regularity of,* a technical term ; *cf. denormata linea,* Agrimensores, i. 345. 20.

10. urnam argenti : *i.e.* a pot of coins, buried by some one, as in the *Aulularia* of Plautus.   **quae** : *some,* for *aliqua,* on account of *si.* Note the hyperbaton.

11. mercennarius : for *cum mercennarius esset.*

12. illum ipsum : *i.e.* the very field which he had formerly ploughed as a hireling.   **mercatus aravit** : *bought and ploughed.* **amico Hercule** : the story is told by Porphyrio. Hercules was the god who gave gain, especially in the form of hidden treasure, and a tithe of the gain was given to him. *Cf.* Plaut. *Bacch.* 665, *Si frugist, Herculem fecit ex patre: Decumam partem ei dedit, sibi novem abstulit.*

13. gratum : *sc. me.*

14. pingue : agreeing with *pecus* and *ingenium* with a double meaning. So we speak of 'fat-witted' people. *Cf.* ii. 2. 3, *crassa Minerva.*

16. montis : the Sabine Hills.   **in arcem** : *my stronghold*, as situated in the mountains, and as a refuge from the cares of the city.

17. prius : *rather, i.e.* than the delights of country life ; lit. *before ; cf. Odes*, i. 12. 13, *Quid prius dicam solitis parentis Laudibus?*   **saturis** : here used as the general word for this kind of writing, including the *Sermones* and *Epistulae ;* see Introd. § 24 ; and on the orthography, Introd. § 14.   **musa pedestri** : *my prosaic muse; cf. Epist.* ii. 1. 250, *sermones repentis per humum.*

18. mala ambitio : referring to tiresome social duties, the necessity of paying visits and the like ; *cf.* i. 6. 100 ff.   **plumbeus Auster** : the sirocco, an oppressive wind, hence the epithet *plumbeus.*

19. Libitinae : referring to Venus Libitina, in whose temple funeral equipments seem to have been kept.   **quaestus** : *a source of gain,* since the equipments were probably rented, and the proceeds went to the shrine.

20. Matutine pater : an ancient Italian god of the early morning, here identical with Janus, the god of beginnings.   **Iane** : the vocative used in place of the object ; *cf.* Prop. i. 18. 31, *resonent mihi 'Cynthia' silvae ;* see Introd. § 37.

21. unde : for *a quo; cf.* i. 6. 12.   **operum primos vitaeque labores** : *the first labors of their daily life ;* in *operum vitaeque* we have hendiadys.

22. sic dis placitum : *so the gods have willed it, i.e.* that Janus should have this function.

23. Having begun with an invocation to Janus, as god of beginnings, Horace is thus led to speak of the early morning duties at Rome.   **Romae** : *when I am at Rome.*   **sponsorem** : *as a surety, i.e.* to give bail for some friend.   **rapis** : *i.e.* hurry me into court ; *cf.* i. 9. 77, *rapit in ius.*   **Heia** : Horace's thought, represented as an admonition of the god.

24. prior : *sc. te.*   **officio** : *the call of duty.*

25. Aquilo : the cold north wind, the Tramontana.

26. interiore . . . gyro : *a narrower circle,* in which the sun appears to travel in winter.   **trahit** : *drags,* as if the day resisted its curtailing ; *cf.* ii. 5. 110, *me Imperiosa trahit Proserpina.*

27. mi obsit : *would be to my disadvantage,* in case his friend fails to appear in court, and he has to pay the forfeit. Potential subjunctive.   **locuto** : *sc. mihi,* dative of the apparent agent with *luctandum.*

28. luctandum: *i.e.* he had to rush off to some other duty, a morning call or something similar.   **tardis**: *i.e.* people who were going leisurely about their business.

29. quid vis: *what do you mean?*   *Cf.* ii. 5. 53, *quid prima secundo Cera velit versu.*   **improbus**: *a violent, hot-tempered fellow*, whom Horace has jostled in his haste; *cf. Odes*, iii. 9. 22, *improbo Hadria.*

30. precibus: *curses; cf. Epod.* 5. 86, *Thyesteas preces.*   **pulses . . . si recurras**: sarcastic; *of course you would knock over everything in your way, if you should be hurrying back to Maecenas.*

31. ad Maecenatem: said spitefully, and with a touch of envy. **memori mente**: *i.e.* thinking of nothing but him.

32. hoc: *i.e.* to be taunted with his intimacy with Maecenas. **atras**: *dark, gloomy*, because of the use to which it had formerly been put; *cf.* i. 8. 19 ff., and the Outline of i. 8.

33. aliena negotia: *commissions for other people.*

34. secundam: *sc. horam;* about 7 o'clock.

35. orabat: epistolary imperfect.   **sibi adesses**: *i.e.* in court; *cf.* i. 9. 38, *paulum hic ades.*   **Puteal**: *sc. Libonis*, a place in the Forum which had been struck by lightning, and then surrounded by a low wall or curbing, as sacred. The praetor's tribunal was near by.

36. scribae: Horace, as having been a government clerk, is still regarded as a member of the guild.

37. orabant: see note on *orabat*, l. 35 above.   **Quinte**: the praenomen used in familiar address; *cf.* ii. 5. 32, and the note.   **reverti**: *i.e.* to the quaestor's office, in the Forum, which he had just left.

38. imprimat . . . signa: *sign and seal.* Pliny, *N. H.* xxxvii. 10, tells us that Maecenas's seal bore a frog as its device.

39. dixeris: with conditional force; *cf. scribet*, ii. 5. 74.

42. dumtaxat ad hoc: *merely to this extent; taxat* is an old aorist subjunctive of *tango*, and the phrase originally meant 'provided it touches,' or 'reaches to.'   **quem**: *as one whom;* subjunctive of characteristic.   **tollere raeda**: *i.e.* 'give a lift.' For *raeda*, see note on i. 5. 86.

43. iter faciens: *e.g.* on the journey to Brundisium, described in i. 5, or on shorter excursions in the vicinity of Rome.

44. hoc genus: *of this kind;* really in apposition with *nugas.* See Introd. § 38. *c.*   **Thraex**: the Thracians were a class of gladiators, so called on account of their armor, which consisted of a round shield and a short curved sword or dagger. The spelling *Thraex* or *Threx* is

the one found in gladiatorial inscriptions.   **Gallina** : *the Chicken*, a
nickname.   **Syro** : the name of a gladiator, probably a *mirmillo*,
since they were commonly matched against the Thracians.   These
were armed in the Gallic fashion, with heavy armor and a large shield.
Their crest was a fish (μορμίλος), whence the name, *mirmillo*.

45. iam . . . mordent : *are beginning to nip; cf. Hamlet,* i. 4. 1,
" The air bites shrewdly, it is very cold."

46. rimosa . . . aure : *a leaky* (*i.e.* indiscreet) *ear; cf.* Ter.
Eun. 105, *Plenus rimarum sum, hac atque illac perfluo.*   For the op-
posite, see *Odes*, i. 27. 18.   **deponuntur** : often used of secrets ; see
Odes, i. 27. 18, *depone tutis auribus.*

48. noster : *our friend*, meaning himself ; *cf.* i. 9. 47, *hunc hominem;* and see Introd. § 55. *o.*   **spectaverat . . . luserat** : with conditional force ; the subject is *noster.*

49. omnes : *sc. aiunt.*

50. frigidus : *terrifying.*   **per compita** : *around the street cor-
ners*, where the people would be gathered together.

51. consulit : stronger than *interrogat, asks my advice*, consults
me.   **O bone** : *my good fellow.*

52. deos : *the gods*, referring to Maecenas and the court generally.
propius contingis : *associate more intimately with*, come into closer
association with, i.e. than others.

53. numquid . . . audisti : *you haven't heard anything, have
you ?*   **Dacis** : the Dacians had taken the part of Antony, and war
was declared against them in 30 B.C.   In 31 B.C., when the Satire was
written, an invasion was feared.   **ut . . . eris** : how you will persist in making fun ; *cf.* ii. 8. 62, *ut semper gaudes inludere rebus Humanis.*

55. si quicquam : *sc. audivi.*   **militibus promissa . . . praedia** : of an allotment of land to the veterans, which had been promised
by Augustus.   **Triquetra** : *Sicilian*, modifying *tellure*, the island
being so called from its triangular shape.   *Cf.* Lucr. i. 717, *Insula
quem triquetris terrarum gessit in oris.*

57. unum . . . mortalem : *the man of all men.   Cf.* Catull. 22.
10, *unus caprimulgus.*

59. haec inter : in such trifling as this.   With the anastrophe, *cf.*
Epod. 2. 38.   **misero** : *sc. mihi ; for poor me ;* dative of reference.

61. veterum : the writers of earlier days ; *cf.* ii. 3. 11–12.
somno : the mid-day siesta, for which there was not always time in
the city.

62. ducere: *to quaff;* cf. Virg. *Aen.* vi. 714, *Lethaei ad fluminis undam Securos latices et longa oblivia potant.*

63. Pythagorae cognata: Pythagoras forbade the eating of beans, because they were said to contain the souls of the dead. Hence Horace in jest calls them the kindred of Pythagoras.   **simulque**: *and served with it.*

64. satis: *sufficiently,* without oil.   **holuscula**: *cabbage;* note the diminutive, and see Introd. § 55. *e.*

65. cenaeque deum: *feasts fit for the gods.*   **meique**: equivalent to *cum meis; sc. amicis.*

66. Larem: *hearth,* beside which was the altar of the *Lar Familiaris.*   **vernas procacis**: *the saucy house-slaves,* whose forwardness was proverbial; cf. Mart. i. 41. 1, *Urbanus tibi, Caecili, videris. Non es, crede mihi.   Quid ergo ?   Verna.*

67. pasco: cf. Sen. *Epist.* 77. 8, *cena peracta reliquiae circumstantibus dividantur.*   **libatis**: *only partly eaten,* lit. *tasted.*   **prout**: here pronounced in one syllable by synizesis.   See Introd. § 57.

68. inaequalis calices: *i.e.* either *acria* or *modica pocula;* see below, lines 69–70.

69. legibus insanis: such as would be imposed by a *magister bibendi; cf. Odes,* i. 4. 18; *Serm.* ii. 2. 123.   **capit**: *carries, holds, i.e.* is able to stand ; cf. Plaut. *Curc.* 103, *Quantillum sitit ? Modicast, capit quadrantal.*

70. laetius: *i.e.* takes more pleasure in.   **ergo**: *accordingly, i.e.* the conversation corresponds with the nature of the meal.

72. Lepos: a dancer of the day, who appeared in pantomimes.

73. agitamus: *discuss; cf.* i. 4. 138, *haec ego mecum Compressis agito labris.*   **utrumne**: *cf.* ii. 3. 295, and the note.

75. usus rectumne: *self-interest or virtue.*   The former was the doctrine of the Epicureans, the latter that of the Stoics.

76. summumque . . . eius: *i.e.* the *summum bonum.*

77. Cervius: a neighbor of Horace's.   The name may very likely be one of the made-up names, typical of old age.   *Cf.* Juvenal's expression, *cervina senectus,* xiv. 251, which was proverbial.   **haec inter**: *i.e.* during the intervals of this conversation.   Note the anastrophe, common with dissyllabic prepositions, and *cf.* line 59 above. **anilis . . . fabellas**: *old-wives' tales.*   Cervius is a man *abnormis sapiens crassaque Minerva,* like Ofellus in ii. 2, who in place of learned arguments tells plain and simple, but pointed, stories *ex re, i.e. apropos, to the point.*

78. Arelli : some rich and miserly neighbor.   The name is perhaps made from the root of *aridus*.

79. ignarus : *i.e.* foolishly, not knowing that they are *sollicitas*. Note the juxtaposition of *ignarus* and *sollicitas*.   **olim** : *once upon a time*, the regular way of beginning a story.

81. veterem . . . amicum : *i.e.* old friends, guest and host.

82. attentus quaesitis : *i.e.* careful of what he had stored up. **ut tamen** : *i.e.* not so much so that he could not.

83. quid multa : sc. *dicam ; to make a long story short.*

84. sepositi : *set aside*, for special occasions.   **longae** : apparently of the shape of the grain.   The genitive with *nec invidit* is after the analogy of that with verbs of plenty and want.

86. fastidia : *lack of appetite*, the regular term ; *cf.* Plin. *N. H.* viii. 52 (of the lion), *aegritudinem fastidii tantum sentit.*

87. tangentis . . . superbo : the fastidiousness of the guest is vividly pictured.

88. pater . . . domus : *the master of the house;* for obvious reasons used instead of *pater familias ; cf. cenae pater,* ii. 8. 7.

89. ēsset : *ate.*

90. ad hunc : with *inquit*, a construction transferred from verbs implying motion, such as *scribo* and *nuntio*.

91. patientem : *enduring hardship.*

92. vis tu : *won't you*, an exhortation, while *vin tu* (i. 9. 69) is merely interrogative.

93. mihi crede : *take my advice*, trust me.   **terrestria quando** : *etc. :* the Epicurean doctrine.

94. sortita : alloted by fate ; literally, 'having obtained by lot.'

95. quo . . . circa : note the tmesis, and see Introd. § 53. *o.*

96. dum licet : a common Horatian expression ; *cf. Odes,* ii. 11. 16 ; iv. 12. 26 ; *Epist.* i. 11. 20.   **beatus** : *rich and happy; cf. Odes,* i. 4. 14, *beate Sesti.*

97. aevi brevis : genitive of quality ; the expression is the opposite of the adjective *longaevus*.

98. pepulere : *struck*, *i.e.* struck the fancy of, influenced.   **levis** : *light-heartedly, gladly.*

100. nocturni : *by night.*   **iamque tenebat**, *etc. :* a parody of the epic style ; *cf.* i. 5. 3, and the note.

103. canderet : *blazed.*   Characteristic subjunctive.

104. fercula : *courses*, really the trays on which they are served.

105. procul : *near by.*   **hesterna** : *i.e.* from yesterday's feast.

107. veluti succinctus: *i.e.* as if he were a waiter ; *cf.* ii. 8. 10, *puer alte cinctus.*

108. continuatque dapes : *i.e.* serves one course after the other, without intermission.   **nec non:** *and also;* litotes; see Introd. § 53. *k.*   **verniliter:** like a *verna*, whose impudence and greed were proverbial (see note on line 66) ; he cannot resist tasting the dainties himself ; *cf.* ii. 4. 78, *seu puer unctis Tractavit calicem manibus dum furta ligurrit.*   **ipsis . . . officiis:** *i.e.* the duties of a waiter.

110. bonis rebus : ablative modifying *laetum.*

111. agit : *plays the part of.*

112. valvarum strepitus : the clanging of the folding doors, as the servants come in the early morning to clean up the room.

114. Molossis . . . canibus: the Molossian hounds were cele- brated for their great size and watchfulness. *Molossus* is often used as a substantive, with ellipsis of *canis. Cf. Epod.* 6. 5, *Molossus aut fulvus Lacon.*

115. haud . . . est opus : *I don't care for;* lit. *I have no need of;* *cf.* our slang expression, ' I have no use for.'

116. valeas : *good-bye,* in place of the usual *vale.*

SERMO VII.

1. iamdudum ausculto : *I have been listening for a long time*, *i.e.* waiting to be sure that his master was not busy.

2. reformido : *I shrink from so doing,* knowing his master's hot temper.   **Davusne :** *is it Davus?* Horace does not look up, but he thinks he recognizes the voice.   **ita :** *sc. est; yes.*

3. frugi quod sit satis : *honest enough.*

4. ut vitale putes : *i.e.* he is not so good that his master need fear that he will be short-lived ; with reference to the proverb that the good die young. *Cf.* Sen. *Contr.* i. 1. 22 (*Cestius Pius*) *aiebat tam immature magnum ingenium non esse vitale.*   **libertate Decembri :** *i.e.* the freedom allowed at the time of the Saturnalia ; *cf,* ii. 3. 5, and the note.

5. narra : *speak; cf.* ii. 5. 1, *praeter narrata.*

6. gaudet constanter : *persist in taking pleasure.*   **urget pro- positum :** *stick to their purpose.*

7. pars multa : *cf. Odes,* iii. 30. 6, *multa pars mei; Serm.* i. 1. 61, *bona pars hominum,* with the note.   **natat :** *i.e.* drift to and fro with the current; *cf.* Sen. *Epist.* 35. 4, *mutatio voluntatis indicat animum natare.*   **modo . . . interdum** : *cf.* i. 9. 9, *modo ire ocius, interdum consistere;* i. 10. 12, *modo rhetoris atque poetae, interdum urbani.*

8. notatus : *conspicuous*, with some idea of censure; *cf.* i. 6. 14, *notante iudice . . . populo.*

9. tribus anellis : to wear more than a single ring was the mark of a dandy. Isid. *Orig.* xix. 32, mentions the fact that Crassus in his old age wore two rings.   **laeva** : the ring, or rings, were worn on the left hand, because it was used less than the right; *cf. Ateius Capito,* apud Macr. *Saturn.* vii. 13, *hinc factus est ut usus anulorum exemptus dexterae, quae multum negotiorum gerit, in laevam relegaretur.*

10. inaequalis, ut : *i.e.* so inconsistent that; *cf.* i. 1. 95, and the note.   **clavum ut mutaret** : this may possibly mean that he appeared now as a senator with the broad purple stripe, and now as a simple *eques* with the narrow ones; but it seems more likely that it refers to changing his clothes adorned with the laticlave. *Cf.* Mart. v. 79, *Undecies una surrexti, Zoile, cena, Et mutata tibi est synthesis undecies.*

11. conderet : governed by *ut* in line 10.

12. mundior : *i.e.* of the better class.   **honeste** : *i.e.* with self-respect.

13. doctus : the life of a scholar; *cf. Odes,* i. 1. 29, *doctarum frontium.*

14. Vertumnis . . . iniquis : born under the displeasure of all the Vertumni. Vertumnus was the god of the changing seasons; *cf.* Prop. iv. 2. With the expression *Vertumnis iniquis, cf.* i. 5. 97, *Lymphis iratis,* and the note.

15. scurra : *buffoon, parasite; cf.* i. 5. 52, and Plaut. *Trin.* 202, *urbani adsidui cives, quos scurras vocant.*   **iusta** : *well-earned*, by his gluttony.   **cheragra** : *gout in the hand; cf. podagra,* i. 9. 32.

16. contudit articulos : *cf.* Pers. v. 58, *cum lapidosa cheragra Fregerit articulos.*

17. phimum : *dice-box*, the Greek φιμός, from which the *tali* were thrown; *cf. Odes,* i. 4. 18. In this way Volanerius kept up his gambling even after he was crippled.

18. conductum pavit : *hired and kept; cf.* Juv. iii. 141, *quot pascit servos?*

19. levius miser : *bears a lighter load of wretchedness, i.e.* the consistently bad man is happier than one whose whole existence is a

constant wavering between good and evil.　　**ac** : *than*.　　**prior ille** :
i.e. Priscus, spoken of in line 9.

20. contento . . . laxo fune : the figure seems to be that of an
animal tied to a rope which alternately allows him free scope and
brings him up with a jerk.

21. hodie : *now*, used as in the language of every-day life and of
comedy.　　**putida** : ' *rot*,' *stuff*.

22. furcifer : *gallows-bird*, a common epithet of slaves in comedy.
ad te : *sc. tendunt*.　　**laudas . . . plebis** : *cf.* ii. 2. 89–93.

23. idem : *yet you*.

24. si quis deus : *cf.* i. 1. 15.　　**usque** : *every time*.

25. rectius esse : belongs in sense both with *sentis* and with *quod
clamas*.

26. firmus : *with firm purpose*.

27. caeno : with *haeres* and with *evellere*. The figure is a common
one. *Cf.* Ter. *Phorm.* 780, *in eodem luto haesitas ;* Catull. 17. 25, *Et
supinum animum in gravi derelinquere caeno*.

28. absentem : usually applied to the person, but here to the
place ; *cf. Epist.* i. 11. 21, *Romae laudetur Samos absens*.　　**rusticus** :
when you are in the country.

29. levis : *fickle fellow that you are*. With the general sentiment,
cf. Epist. i. 8. 12, *Romae Tiburi amem ventosus. Tibure Romam*.

30. securum : *quiet, i.e.* free from the cares of a formal dinner
party.　　**velut . . . vinctus eas** : *i.e.* like an unwilling slave.

31. amas : *sc. te, you hug yourself ; cf.* Virg. *Aen.* v. 163, *litus ama*.

32. potandum : the *commissatio* at the end was an important
feature of a dinner party.　　**iusserit** : jussive subjunctive with
force of a proviso, *let Maecenas ask you to dinner*.

33. serum sub lumina prima : *i.e.* the invitation is sent at the last
moment, possibly because some guest had excused himself. *Sub
lumina prima* means just at nightfall ; the time would vary according
to the season of the year. With the expression, *cf. sub galli cantum*,
i. 1. 10.

34. oleum : for the lantern with which a slave would escort him
through the streets. The impatient questions show his eagerness to
accept the invitation, and his changeable nature.　　**fert** : the colloquial present with future force ; see Introd. § 44. *a*.

35. blateras : *you bawl out*, a colloquial word. Festus defines it
as " *stulte et percupide loqui*."　　**fugis** : *you tear off*, like a runaway
slave.

36. Mulvius et scurrae : persons who either hoped to be asked to dinner with Horace, or perhaps had actually been asked.   **non referenda** : *i.e.* language that won't bear repeating.   **precati** : *cf. iratis precibus*, ii. 6. 30, and the note.

37. ille : *i.e.* Mulvius.   **dixerit** : future perfect with the force of a future of instantaneous action; *he will say at once; i.e.* he will freely admit.

38. levem : *weak.*   **nasum supinor** : *I throw up my nose*, the better to sniff the savory food. *Nasum* is the object of *supinor* used in a middle sense ; see Introd. § 38. *c.*

39. si quid vis : *if you like; quid* is accusative of extent, lit. ' at all.'

40. ultro : *actually, i.e.* are you to have the assurance to ? See i, 5. 28. and the note.

41. insectere : subjunctive in an indignant question.   **verbis decoris** : *fine words, i.e.* he alleges his duty to his patron, Maecenas.

43. quingentis . . . drachmis : 500 drachmas, or 2000 sesterces, about $100. This was a low price (*cf. Epist.* ii. 2. 5), and shows Davus to be a slave of the lowest class.   **aufer . . . terrere** : *cease to terrify;* the infinitive is used as the object of *aufer;* see Introd. § 46. *d.*

44. stomachum : *cf. Odes*, i. 6. 6, *gravem Pelidae stomachum.* **teneto** : the simple verb for the compound *contineto;* see Introd. § 35. *b.*

45. Crispini : see i. 1. 120, and the note.

68. evasti : paratactic construction for *si evasti; evasti* is another form for *evasisti.*   **credo** : ironical, *of course.*   **doctus** : *i.e.* taught by experience.

69. quaeres : *i.e.* on the contrary, you will seek.   **quando . . . paveas** : another opportunity to be frightened ; the subjunctive has a final force.

71. prava : *perversely.*

73. sapiens : in the sense of *prudens; i.e.* he would be glad to steal silver, but he doesn't dare; and he ironically claims to be *sapiens* on that account.

74. vaga : used proleptically, *i.e. natura prosiliet et vagabitur.*

76. minor : *a slave to; imperiis* is ablative of comparison. **vindicta** : *the rod* which was used in the formal manumission of a slave before the praetor.

77. formidine : *dread* of his master.

78. super: for *insuper, besides.*

79. vicarius: the slave of a slave, bought with his savings (*peculium*), to help him in his work.

80. vester: *i.e.* of you masters. **tibi quid sum ego**: the implication is, either *vicarius* or *conservus.*

82. ut . . . lignum: like a marionette or wooden puppet, by strings worked by some one else.

83. sibi imperiosus: *i.e. qui sibi imperitat; cf.* Stat. *Silv.* ii. 6. 16, *cui triste nihil qui sponte sibique Imperiosus erat,* cited by Bentley.

85. responsare: *defy;* intensive of *respondere.* It is governed by *fortis* in line 86.

86. in se ipso totus: *i.e.* dependent only on himself, and unaffected by external things; *cf. e.g.* Cic. *Paradoxa,* 2. 17, *qui est totus aptus ex sese quique in se uno sua ponit omnia.* **teres atque rotundus**: like a sphere, to which the Stoics compared the *sapiens.*

87. ne . . . morari: *i.e.* that nothing from without may be able to rest on it, on account of its smooth surface.

88. manca: *powerless,* so as to be unable to injure him.

89. his: *these virtues,* of the *sapiens.* For *his = his rebus,* see Introd. § 49. *b.* **quid**: for *aliquid.*

90. te: the second accusative with *poscat.*

91. gelida: *sc. aqua. Cf.* Juv. v. 63, *Quando rogatus adest calidae gelidaeque minister?* For the adjective used as a substantive, see Introd. § 49. *b.*

92. non quis: *you cannot.*

93. dominus: the figure is of *libido,* driving the man as one would a horse, in a chariot.

94. stimulos: *the goad.* **versat**: turns you from your own way to the course he wishes to take.

95. Pausiaca: of Pausias, a famous painter of Sicyon. The man who has a craze for works of art is also a slave. **torpes**: *have a craze for; cf. stupet,* i. 4. 28.

96. Fulvi, *etc.*: names of gladiators. The last is taken from Lucilius, 138 L.

98. rubrica aut carbone: the reference is to posters drawn on the walls with red chalk or with charcoal.

100. nequam et cessator: *a good-for-nothing and an idler,* because he has been sent on some errand, but wastes his time staring at the posters.

101. **veterum**: either masculine, *of the old masters*, or neuter, *of ancient works of art*.   **audis**: *i.e.* are called; *cf.* ii. 6. 20, *si Iane libentius audis.*

102. nil: *good-for-nothing*, like *nequam* or *nihili*.   **libo**: *cake;* they were apparently cooked on the streets in the sight of the passers by.   **tibi**: emphatic; *in your case;* dative of reference.   **ingens**: *tremendous.*

103. virtus . . . responsat: the emphasis is on *virtus* and *animus; is it character and intellect which appreciate; i.e.* is it a sign of character to appreciate ?

105. **enim** : *it is true.*

106. sumi : *i.e. emi.*

107. inamarescunt : *turn sour;* *cf.* ii. 2. 75.

108. inlusi: *taken off their guard* by drunkenness; *cf.* Plaut. *Pseud.* 1251, *(vinum) pedes captat primum, luctator dolosust.*

109. **hic . . . qui puer** : for *hic puer . . . qui.*

110. furtiva: *stolen. Furtiva strigili* is ablative of association; *cf. Odes,* i. 17. 2, *Lucretilem mutat Lycaeo Faunus,* and see Introd. § 41. *b.*

111. gulae parens : the reason for *vendit.*   **idem** : *besides, you.*

112. tecum : *in your own company, alone.*

113. **ponere** : *dispose of,* really *invest,* like a sum of money. **fugitivus et erro** : applied to slaves; *erronem sic definimus, qui non quidem fugit, sed frequenter sine causa vagatur et temporibus in res nugatorias consumptis serius domum redit,* Ulpian, *Dig.* xxi. 1. 17. 14; *Quid sit fugitivus Ofilius sic definit : fugitivus est qui extra domini domum fugae causa, quo se a domino celaret, mansit, id.* xxi. 1. 17. 1.

115. frustra : *to no purpose.*   **comes atra** : *i.e.* Care; *cf. Odes,* iii. 1. 40, *Post equitem sedet atra Cura.*

116. unde mihi lapidem : *sc. reperiam; cf.* ii. 5. 102, and the note; Horace's temper gets the better of him, as at the close of ii. 3.

117. aut insanit, *etc. :* the man is either mad (*cf.* ii. 3. 127 ff.), or writes poetry (*cf.* ii. 3. 321 f.).   **ocius** : *double-quick;* with nearly the force of a superlative.

118. accedes opera nona : *you shall become a ninth laborer;* the singular *opera* in this sense is rare. Apparently Horace had eight slaves (*operae*) on his Sabine Farm — a small number. Sending slaves to the country was a common punishment; *cf.* Plaut. *Most.* 18, *Cis hercle paucas tempestates, Tranio, Augebis ruri numerum, genus ferratile.*

SERMO VIII.

1. `ut` : introducing a direct question, *how;* a colloquial use.   **Nasi-dieni** : scanned in four syllables, the second *i* being pronounced as a semi-vowel.   **beati** : *rich; cf. Odes,* i. 4. 14, *O beate Sesti.*   Here with an underlying ironical force.

2. convivam : *sc. te.*   With the late invitation, *cf.* ii. 7. 32.   **dictus** : *sc. es,* a colloquial use.   **here** : the regular post-Augustan form, while *heri* is the earlier one ; *cf.* Quint. i. 4. 7, *in 'here' neque e plane neque i auditur.*   Augustus himself used the earlier form ; *cf.* Quint. i. 7. 22, *heri ad me venit, quod idem in epistulis Augusti, quas sua manu scripsit aut emendavit, deprehenditur.*

3. de medio . . . die : a *tempestivum convivium,* beginning very early ; for the usual time, see *Epist.* i. 5. 3 ; i. 7. 71.   **ut . . . fuerit melius** : *that I never had a better time; cf. bene erat,* ii. 2. 120.

5. iratum : *cf. latrantem,* ii. 2. 18.

6. in primis : *i.e.* the *gustatio,* consisting of dishes intended to whet the appetite.   The introduction of the boar at this time was a mark of luxury.   *Cf.* Plin. *N. H.* viii. 210, *ad emendationem morum quibus non tota quidem cena sed in principio bini ternique manduntur apri.*   **leni . . . Austro** : *when a mild south wind was blowing; cf.* ii. 2. 41.   Ablative of attendant circumstance.

7. captus : participle, *caught.*   **cenae pater** : *cf. pater domus,* ii. 6. 88.   Great ingenuity is shown in alluding to the host in different ways ; *cf.* lines 16, 23, 36, 43, 58, 73, 75, 93.   **circum** : *i.e.* around the boar.

8. rapula : these and the following articles are regular appetizers ; *cf.* ii. 2. 43.   **lactucae** : *cf.* ii. 4. 59.

9. allec : *brine* in which fish had been kept ; *cf.* ii. 4. 73.   **faecula** : diminutive of *faex; cf.* ii. 4. 73.

10. alte cinctus : *cf.* ii. 6. 107, and the note.   **acernam . . . mensam** : *a maple table,* next in value to the citrus wood, according to Plin. *N. H.* xvi. 66.   One kind was regarded as superior to the citrus ; *cf.* Plin. *N. H.* xvi. 68, *molluscum . . . si magnitudine mensarum caperet haud dubie praeferretur citro.*

11. gausape : *a towel;* the line is modelled on Lucilius 517 L, *Purpureo tersit tunc latas gausape mensas.*

12. sublegit . . . inutile : the *analecta,* a second slave (*cf. puer,* l. 11).   See Martial vii. 20. 17, *Colligere longa turpe nec putat dextra,*

Analecta quidquid et canes reliquerunt. **iaceret . . . posset** : iterative subjunctive. See Introd. § 45. *f.*

13. Attica virgo : *i.e.* a κανηφόρα, alluding to the impressive solemnity of the slave ; *cf.* i. 3. 10, *Saepe (incedebat) velut qui Iunonis sacra ferret.*

14. Hydaspes : *i.e.* an Indian slave from the neighborhood of the river Hydaspes, an unusual luxury at this time. He appears to be named after the river, like Enipeus, *Odes*, iii. 7. 23, and Hebrus, *Odes*, iii. 12. 6.

15. Caecuba : the finest Italian wine ; *cf. Odes*, i. 20. 9.   **Alcon** : another slave.   **maris expers** : *without sea-water*, which was sometimes added to wines ; *cf.* Plin. *N. H.* xiv. 73, *nunc gratia ante omnia est Clazomenio (vino), postquam parcius mari condiunt. Lesbium sponte suae naturae mare sapit ;* Plaut. *Rud.* 588, *quasi vinis Graecis Neptunus nobis suffudit mare.*

17. adpositis : *i.e.* the Caecuban and the Chian.

18. miseras : *pitiful,* as leading to ostentation.   **quis cenantibus una** : *with what fellow-guests.*

19. pulchre fuerit tibi : *you made merry ; cf.* line 4 above, and the note.

20. summus, *etc.* : see the Outline of the Satire, and the diagram.

22. umbras : uninvited persons brought as the parasites of some distinguished guest ; *cf. Epist.* i. 5. 28. Maecenas seems to have had a number of such hangers-on, *e.g.* Sarmentus, i. 5. 52.

23. Porcius : on the significant name, see Introd. § 32.

24. ridiculus . . . absorbere : *i.e.* who made fun by swallowing cakes whole.

25. ad hoc, qui : *cf.* ii. 6. 42, *quem tollere raeda vellet,* and the note.   **si quid** : *i.e.* any elegant or luxurious detail.

26. indice . . . digito : the *forefinger ;* perhaps, as Kiessling suggests, not to be taken literally.

27. nos, inquam : *we, I mean, i.e.* all but Maecenas, the guest of honor.

28. noto : the familiar one ; *sc. suco,* 'flavor.'

29. vel : *for example ; vel,* the old injunctive form of *volo,* has various meanings derived from the idea of 'choosing' or 'selecting' ; *cf.* Epist. i. 5. 15.   **patuit** : *became evident.*

30. ingustata : *without my tasting them ; i.e.* the odor alone revealed the novelty of the dish.

31. melimela . . . delecta : *i.e.* that the red honey apples **were**

gathered by the light of the waning moon ; with the form of expression, *cf.* ii. 2. 31, *lupus . . . hiet.*

32. ipso : *i.e.* Nasidienus.

34. damnose : *i.e.* so as to ruin the host.   **bibimus** : the present with future force. *Cf. fert*, ii. 7. 34, and see Introd. § 44. *a.* **moriemur inulti** : an epic expression ; *cf.* Virg. *Aen.* ii. 670, *numquam omnes hodie moriemur inulti*, and see note on i. 5. 3.

35. vertere : *spreads over ;* lit. *changes ;* historical infinitive.

36. parochi : for the literal meaning of the word, see *Serm.* i. 5. 46. Here it is used for variety (see note on line 7) and with a contemptuous force, implying that Nasidienus is a mere 'purveyor,' lacking the essential qualities of a host.   **acris** : *strong-headed ; cf. acria pocula*, ii. 6. 69.

37. maledicunt liberius : *i.e.* will chaff their host, and make him ridiculous before Maecenas, or will fail to appreciate his banquet. *Cf.* i. 4. 87–89.

39. Allifanis : *sc. vasis*, large drinking-cups, made at Allifae in Samnium. Note the metre, and see note on i. 1. 4, *O fortunati mercatores.*   **vinaria tota** : *whole wine-jars.*

40. secutis : the perfect participle here has the force of a present. **imi convivae lecti** : the parasites, who dared not offend their host and patron.

42. natantis : *i.e.* swimming in the sauce by which the *murena* was surrounded.

43. sub hoc : *thereupon ; cf. Epod.* 5. 83, *Sub haec puer iam non ut ante . . . misit.*

44. post partum : *i.e.* after spawning.   **futura** : *since it would be ;* on the use of the future participle, see Introd. § 47.

45. his : *i.e.* the ingredients which follow.   **prima . . . cella** : *i.e.* the oil first pressed from the olives ; *cf.* Colum. xii. 52. 11, *sint in cella olearia tres labrorum ordines, ut unus primae notae, id est primae pressurae oleum recipiat, alter secundae, tertius tertiae.* **Venafri** : *cf.* ii. 4. 69, and the note.

46. garo : a kind of fish-jelly. The best kind, according to inscriptions of Pompeii, was called *garum-flos*, 'blossom brand.'   **piscis Hiberi** : *Spanish mackerel.*

47. citra mare nato : *i.e. Italo. Cf.* i. 10 31.

48. dum coquitur : the Italian wine is put in while the sauce is cooking, while the Chian is added after it is cooked (*cocto*).

50. quod . . . uvam : *i.e.* the vinegar must be made of Methymnaean (Lesbian) wine which has soured ; lit. *which it, the vinegar, has soured.*

51. primus . . . monstravi : *i.e.* Nasidienus is an original ex-perimenter in the gastronomic art ; *cf.* ii. 2. 50.

52. incoquere : *to cook in, i.e.* to boil in the sauce.   **inlutos** : *unwashed*, the better to retain the flavor of the sea-water.   **Curtil-lus** : another gastronomic artist.

53. ut melius : in a kind of apposition to *echinos; cf. ut suavius* in line 89.   **testa marina** : *i.e.* the sea-urchin.

54. aulaea : *hangings*, used to decorate the walls.   *Cf. Odes*, iii. 29. 15, *sine aulaeis et ostro;* Val. Max. ix. 1. 5, *Attalicis aulaeis contectos parietes.*   These fell with the dust which had accumulated on them during many days.

57. maius : *i.e.* a greater danger, such as an earthquake or some-thing similar.

58. erigimur : *recover ourselves;* the verb is used in a middle sense.   **Rufus** : *i.e.* the host, *Nasidienus Rufus.*

59. quis esset finis : *what would have been the end ? i.e.* of his lamentation.   The imperfect *esset* is used with the force of the plu-perfect.

60. sapiens : *in philosophic wise;* said ironically.   **amicum tolleret** : *raised his friend's spirits.*

62. ut semper gaudes : *how you always delight; cf.* ii. 6. 54.

63. mappa : *with his napkin.*

64. suspendens omnia naso : *always cynical*, a general char-acteristic.   For the expression, *cf.* i. 6. 5, *naso suspendis adunco ignotos.*

65. haec . . . vivendi : *i.e.* 'such is life.'

67. tene . . . torquerier : infinitive of exclamation ; *cf.* i. 9. 72 ; ironical, since Balatro was an *umbra*, and the trouble was not taken for him.

72. agaso : not to be taken literally, but meaning a clumsy slave fit only to serve as a groom or stable-boy.

73. sed convivatoris, *etc. : i.e.* a host's *savoir faire* is shown by his ability to meet accidents, while a dinner which went off smoothly would give no opportunity for its display.   *Cf.* Sen. *Epist.* 85. 34, *tranquillo, at aiunt, quilibet gubernator est.*

75. Nasidienus : he takes this raillery for earnest.   **tibi di . . . dent** : a common formula of blessing or gratitude ; *cf.* Plaut. *Asin.* 44, *Di tibi dent quaequomque optes.*

77. soleas poscit: the sandals were taken off when reclining at table.   Nasidienus calls for his, in order to go out and make arrangements for the continuation of the dinner.   **videres**: *you could see;* *cf. Serm.* i. 5. 76, and see Introd. § 45. *d.*

78. stridere . . . susurros: *i.e.* putting their heads together and exchanging whispers; the whispering is imitated by the alliteration with *s (sigmatismus).*

79. nullos . . . . spectasse: *I would rather have seen it than any play.*

80. quae deinceps risisti: what you found to laugh at next. **Vibidius**, whose empty wine-cup had not been replaced by a full one, asks whether the wine-jar has been broken as well *(quoque).*

83. ridetur: impersonal.   **fictis rerum** : like *vanis rerum*, ii. 2. 25.   The guests exchange jests to cover the real cause of their laughter.   **Balatro secundo**: *with the help of Balatro ; i.e. Balatro fert secundas (cf.* i. 9. 46) to Vibidius.

84. Nasidiene, redis : a parody of the epic manner.   **mutatae frontis** : genitive of quality, predicate to *redis :* with changed countenance, *i.e.* cheered up again.   **ut . . . emendaturus** : *like one who was determined to improve.*   The expression is apparently a proverbial one; *cf.* Ter. *Adelph.* 741, *Illud quod cecidit forte, id arte ut corrigas.*

86. mazonomo : a large dish, originally used for bread ; a Greek word, μαζονόμιον.

87. gruis : the masculine, instead of the usual feminine, and the feminine *anseris* in the next line are apparently intended to indicate the novelty of Nasidienus's dishes.

88. pastum iecur : *i.e.* the liver was artificially fattened, as in the modern *pâté de foie gras.*

90. edit = *edat ;* an archaic form of the present subjunctive, really an optative ; *cf. Epod.* 3. 3.

91. sine clune : intended as a refinement of luxury, though that part of the bird was often regarded as a delicacy ; *cf.* Mart. iii. 60. 7, *Aureus immodicis turtur te clunibus implet.*

92. causas narraret: *i.e.* Nasidienus explains why a male crane is selected, and a white goose, *etc.*

93. ulti : *in revenge.*   They refuse to eat his lauded delicacies.

94. velut : for *velut si.*

95. Canidia : *cf.* i. 8. 24, and the note.   **Afris** : *cf. Odes*, iii. 10. 18, *Nec Mauris animum mitior anguibus.*

EPISTLES — BOOK I.

EPISTLE I.

1. prima dicte, *etc.* : a dedication of the first book of *Epistles* to Maecenas. *Cf. Odes*, i. 1. 1 ; *Serm.* i. 1. 1.   **prima . . . Camena**: with the expression, *cf. Iliad*, ix. 96, Ἀτρείδη κύδιστε, ἄναξ ἀνδρῶν Ἀγάμεμνον, ἐν σοὶ μὲν λήξω, σέο δ' ἄρξομαι. Virg. *Ecl.* viii. 11, *A te principium, tibi desinet ; Odes*, iii. 6. 6.   **Camena** : the Italic name for the goddess of song, the Greek Μοῦσα.

2. spectatum : Horace here likens himself to a gladiator who has earned his discharge by a successful term of service. Instead of saying *me quasi gladiatorem*, he as usual identifies himself with the object of his simile.   **rude** : *the wooden sword*, presented to the discharged gladiator as a symbol of his release from the bloody and deadly contests of the arena.

3. ludo : *the school*, the *ludus gladiatorius*, for the training of gladiators. There is a play on the meaning of *ludus* as applied to some forms of poetry. *Cf.* line 10 below; *Serm.* i. 4. 139, *inludo chartis*.

4. non . . . aetas : *sc. mihi*.   **Veianius** : Porph. says: *Veianius nobilis gladiator post multas palmas, consecratis Herculi Fundano armis suis, in agellum se contulit*, which might have been inferred from the context ; see note on *Fabium, Serm.* i. 1. 14.

5. Herculis ad postem : *i.e.* on one of the columns before the entrance to the temple of Hercules, who would naturally be the patron of gladiators. *Cf. Odes*, i. 5. 13 ff. ; iii. 26. 3 f.   **latet abditus** : *is buried in retirement*.

6. populum . . . exoret : *i.e.* beg for his life, if defeated by an adversary. The unsuccessful combatant was either put to death by the victor, or spared, if the audience desired it. They expressed their wish by turning their thumbs up or down.   **extrema . . . harena** : from the edge of the arena, before the seats of the spectators. *Harena* is the classical orthography ; our word 'arena' comes from the later form without *h*. See B. *App.* § 23.   **totiens** : *i.e.* as often as he was obliged to during his active career. We read in one of the Pompeian *graffiti* of a gladiator who was defeated in his fifty-first contest, and spared (*missus*) by the people. His opponent was fighting for the twenty-sixth time.

7. est qui . . . personet : *some one is always dinning it into*

mihi : dative of reference, with nearly the force of a possessive adjective.   **purgatam** : *attentive*, lit. *cleared*, so as to hear plainly ; an expression parallel with *emunctae naris, Serm.* i. 4. 8, and doubtless colloquial.

8. senescentem . . . equum : *cf.* Enn. *Ann.* ap. Cic. *de Sen.* 5. 14, *Sicut fortis equos, spatio qui saepe supremo Vicit Olumpia, nunc senio confectus quiescit.*   **mature** : *betimes.*

9. peccet . . . ridendus : *i.e.* make a ridiculous failure at the end of his career. The original meaning of *pecco* (**ped-co*) is ' stumble.' **ilia ducat** : *pant with broken wind*, referring to the heaving sides of the animal. For a similar expression, *cf.* Quint. ix. 3. 101, *si quis ducere os exquisitis modis et frontis ac luminum inconstantia trepidare non desinat, rideatur ;* Cic. *Orat.* 25. 86.

10. itaque : *accordingly.*   **ludicra** : *follies* of youth ; *depositis levibus fomentis animi, id est iocis ac versibus,* Porph.

11. quid verum . . . curo : *i.e.* he devotes himself to philosophy. **decens** : *seemly, becoming.*   **omnis in hoc sum** : *cf. Serm.* i. 9. 2, *totus in illis.*

12. condo et compono : *i.e.* he is collecting and arranging a fund of philosophical knowledge for future use, as a steward would store up provisions in a house.   **depromere** : *draw on.*

13. quo duce . . . quo Lare : *i.e.* to what school I attach myself.

14. addictus : *bound*, a legal term used of the insolvent debtor who had been made the slave of his creditor. Cicero uses the word in a similar way of philosophic views, but with an apologetic *quasi*, in *Tusc. Disp.* ii. 2. 5, *qui certis quibusdam destinatisque sententiis quasi addicti et consecrati sunt.* The word was used of the relation of gladiators to their masters, and Horace evidently has his original simile in mind.   **iurare in verba** : since the oath was dictated to the gladiator by his master. The same expression in *Epod.* 15. 4.

15. tempestas : *the weather.* *Cf.* Cic. *Acad.* ii. 3. 8, *ad quamcumque sunt disciplinam quasi tempestate delati, ad eam tamquam ad saxum adhaerescunt.*

16. agilis : *active*, the Greek πρακτικός, in accordance with the views of the Stoics, who recommended an active participation in practical life. *Cf.* Sen. *de Benf.* iv. 2. 2, *virtus . . . ducere debet, imperare, summo loco stare.*   **fio** : the elision of the second of two successive long vowels is not common.   **mersor** : used with middle force. Horace himself took no part in political life, but simply means that he at times inclines toward the Stoics.

17. verae : *true* or *genuine*, as contrasted with the views of other schools, especially of the Epicureans. **rigidus** : *austere*, a conventional epithet. *Cf.* Sen. *Cons. ad Helv.* 12. 4, *Stoicorum rigida et virilis sapientia.* **satelles** : *disciple ; cf.* Tac. *Ann.* xvi. 22, (*Thrasea*) *habet sectatores vel potius satellites, qui nondum contumaciam sententiarum, sed habitum vultumque eius sectantur, rigidi et tristes.*

18. Aristippi : a pupil of Socrates, and founder of the Cyrenaic School of Philosophy based on Hedonism (ἡδονή). See note on line 19. **furtim** : because in his heart he feels the Stoic views to be the more worthy of acceptance. **relabor** : *i.e.* he backslides.

19. et mihi res, *etc. :* Aristippus held that men should enjoy life, without becoming slaves either to pleasure or to duty.

21. opus debentibus : *hirelings* (*operarii*), who were bound to do the day's work for which they were engaged.

22. pupillis : boys who had lost their fathers were under the oversight (*custodia*) of their mothers until their fourteenth year. To these, in their impatience for their freedom, the years seemed to drag.

24. naviter : *with all my might. Navus*, originally *gnavus*, is cognate with *gnarus* and (*g*)*notus ; cf.* German *kennen* and *können*.

25. aeque . . . aeque . . . aeque : the anaphora, instead of *aeque atque* (*ac*), strongly emphasizes the force of *aeque.*

26. neglectum : agreeing with *quod, the neglect of which.*

27. restat : *all that is left is, i.e.* under the circumstances he cannot hope to accomplish more. **ego me ipse** : emphatic. He has learned enough for the guidance of his own life, but not enough to presume to teach others. **elementis** : *general principles.*

28. possis : jussive subjunctive with concessive or conditional force, *suppose you cannot* ; for *non*, see note on *Serm.* ii. 5. 90. **quantum contendere** : *i.e.* see as far ; *quantum* is accusative of extent. **Lynceus** : one of the Argonauts, famed for his sharp sight. He was a Messenian, son of Aphareus, and the brother of Idas. His name was evidently given him on account of his keen-sightedness ; *cf.* English ' lynx-eyed.'

29. idcirco : *for that* (reason), referring to line 28. **lippus inungui** : *i.e.* to use salve for your weak eyes ; *cf. Serm.* i. 5. 30, and the note.

30. desperes : subjunctive because of the indefinite second person and the influence of the neighboring subjunctives. **Glycon** : a famous athlete of the day, whose specialty was the *pancratium*, including

both wrestling and boxing.   His prowess is celebrated in a Greek epigram, *Anth. Pal.* vii. 692 : —

> Γλύκων, τὸ Περγαμηνὸν Ἀσίδι κλέος,
> ὁ παμμάχων κεραυνός, ὁ πλατὺς πόδας,
> ὁ καινὸς Ἄτλας αἴ τ’ ἀνίκατοι χέρες
> ἔρροντι, τὸν δὲ πρόσθεν οὔτ’ ἐν Ἰταλοῖς
> οὔθ’ Ἑλλάδι τρόπωτον οὔτ’ ἐν Ἀσίδι,
> ὁ πάντα νικῶν Ἀΐδης ἀνέτραπεν.

31. cheragra : *cf. Serm.* ii. 7. 15, and the note.

32. est : *sc. aliquid, it is worth something; cf. Serm.* ii. 5. 103.
quadam . . . tenus : *to make some degree of progress; quadam tenus*
is divided by tmesis.   See Introd. § 53. *o*.

33. fervet : *is at fever heat*, a paratactic condition.   **cupidine** :
covetousness.   Cupido is always masculine in Horace.

34. voces : *formulae, charms*, opposed to *verba*, single words.
lenire : *soothe.*   As is seen from this word and those which follow,
Horace's *elementa* are sufficient to help the trouble, not to cure it.

36. tumes : see note on *fervet*, line 33.   **piacula** : *expiations; cf.*
Celsus, *Praef.* 1, *antiquissimo tempore morbi ad iram deorum refere-
bantur.*

37. ter : charms and other formulae of a religious or healing nature
were repeated three times ; *cf. Odes*, iii. 22. 3 ; *Serm.* ii. 1. 7.   **pure** :
referring to the purification which was preliminary to all religious
rites ; *cf. Serm.* ii. 3. 282, *lautis manibus.*   Here, of course, the reference is to mental preparation.

38. amator : the context shows that the word is here used in a bad
sense, as in *Odes*, iii. 4. 79.   Cf. Cic. *Tusc. Disp.* iv. 12. 27, *aliud est
amatorem esse, aliud amantem.*

39. nemo : *i.e.* no one, in short.

40. culturae : *cf.* Cic. *Tusc. Disp.* ii. 5. 13, *cultura animi philosophia est.*

41. prima : probably to be taken in thought with *virtus*, as well
as with *sapientia.   Cf.* Quint. viii. 3. 41, *prima virtus est vitio carere.*

42. caruisse : note the tense ; the first step in wisdom is to have
rid oneself of folly.

43. censum ; *cf. Serm.* ii. 1. 75, and the note.   **repulsam** : the
regular word for defeat at the polls ; *cf. Odes*, iii. 2. 17.   At this time
the elections were still held, although Augustus had the right to
nominate half the candidates, and had the veto power in all cases.   *Cf.*

Suet. *Aug.* 40, *comitiorum pristinum ius reduxit, multiplici poena coercito ambitu.*

44. animi capitisque labore : *i.e.* mental anxiety and danger to life.

45. curris : *cf. Serm.* i. 1. 30, and the note.   **extremos** : *i.e.* dwelling at the ends of the earth.

48. meliori : *i.e.* a wiser man than yourself.

49. pagos et . . . compita : *the villages and cross-roads,* used of a local pugilist.   He would of course be glad to win the prize at Olympia, if he could do it without the severe training which would be necessary.   The Olympic games were still celebrated in Horace's day and continued to be until the end of the fourth century A.D.   *Cf. Odes,* i. 3. 3.

50. magna : in distinction from the insignificant country festivals. *Cf. Serm.* i. 5. 1, *magna Roma.*   **Olympia** : accusative of the inner object, after the analogy of *vincere Olympia.*   See Introd. § 38. *b.*

54. Ianus summus ab imo : *Janus* (quarter) *from top to bottom.* See note on *Serm.* ii. 3. 18.   *Summus ab imo* is equivalent to *a summo ad imum; cf. Ars Poet.* 254, *primus ad extremum similis sibi.*

55. prodocet: *publicly teaches;* note the force of the prefix. **recinunt . . . dictata** : *chant from dictation.*   They repeat the lesson again and again, prompted by the teacher, to fix it in their memory. **senesque**: the old as well as the young are pupils in that school. The figure is made more vivid by the next line, which is repeated from *Serm.* i. 6. 74.

56. loculos : on the construction, see note on *Serm.* i. 6. 74, and Introd. § 38. *c.*

57. mores = *mores probri; cf. Odes,* iii. 24. 35.   **lingua** : *eloquence.*

58. quadringentis: *sc. milibus sestertium* (about $20,000), the equestrian *census.*

59. plebs : *one of the common people.*   **rex eris**, *etc. :* part of a trochaic tetrameter quoted by Isidore, *Origines* viii. 3. 4, *réx eris si récte facies, sí non facies nón eris.*

60. hic : *i.e. recte facere; hic* is attracted to the gender of *murus.* **murus aeneus** : *i.e.* a defence against the ills of life.

61. sibi : of an indefinite subject, *oneself,* instead of *tibi* in direct address.

62. Roscia . . . lex : L. Roscius Otho, when tribune of the people in 68 B.C., passed a law that the fourteen rows of seats at the

theatre just above the orchestra should be assigned to the equites ; *cf.*
Serm. i. 6. 40.   **sodes** : *pray.* The derivation given by Cic. *Orat.*
45. 154, is probably the correct one : *libenter verba iungebant ut*
' *sodes* ' *pro* ' *si audes* ' *;* the meaning of *audes* being *avidus es.*

63. nenia : *ditty*, used of any rhyming formula ; *cf. Epod.* 17. 29,
Sabella pectus increpare carmina, Caputque Marsa dissilire nenia.

64. maribus : *manly.*   **Curiis et . . . Camillis** : types of the
Romans of the good old times.

65. facias : jussive subjunctive, governed by *suadet* understood.
rem : for *rem familiarem ;* notice the emphatic repetition. *Rem*
facias seems to mean practise the art of making money, after the
analogy of *argentariam* (*artem*) *facere* and the like.

67. propius : *i.e.* from nearer the stage ; *cf.* note on line 62.
lacrimosa : *tearful, i.e.* causing tears ; *cf. Serm.* i. 5. 80, *lacrimoso*
fumo.   **Pupi** : a writer of tragedy, otherwise unknown.

68. Fortunae . . . superbae : *cf. Odes*, iii. 29. 50, *Fortuna*
saevo laeta negotio et Ludum insolentem ludere pertinax.   **respon-**
sare : *cf. Serm.* ii. 7. 85, *responsare cupidinibus fortis.*

69. praesens : like a guardian deity ; *cf. Serm.* ii. 3. 68, *praeda*
quam praesens Mercurius fert.   **hortatur et aptat** : *urges and fits*
you.

70. quod si . . . roget : *cf.* line 13 above.

71. porticibus : the colonnades, the lounging places of the populace ; *cf. Serm.* i. 4. 134, and the note.   **iudiciis** : *views.*

72. ipse : *i.e. populus Romanus.*

73. olim : *once upon a time ;* see note on i. 1. 25.   **volpes** : a
familiar fable, referred to also by Lucil. 919–924 L., *leonem Aegrotum*
ac lassum . . . Deducta tum voce leo ' *cur tu ipsa venire Non vis haec ?* '
' *Quid sibi vult, quare fit ut introvorsus et ad te Spectent atque ferant*
vestigia se omnia prorsus ? '

76. belua multorum capitum : a common comparison. The
sentiment is the same as in *Serm.* ii. 1. 27, *quot capitum vivunt, toti-*
dem studiorum.   **nam** : used as an asseverative particle ; *cf.* Plaut.
Most. 368, *quid ego ago nam ?* Ter. *Phorm.* 732, *nam quae haec*
anus est ? Cf. quidnam, etc.

77. conducere publica : *to undertake public contracts*, either for
farming the taxes, or for such services as are mentioned by Juv. iii. 31,
Quis facile est aedem conducere, flumina, portus, Siccandam eluviem,
portandum ad busta cadaver.   **surt qui . . . venentur** : referring
to will-hunters (*captatores*), such as are described in *Serm.* ii. 5.

78. crustis et pomis: *cf. Serm.* ii. 5. 10–17.

79. vivaria : *preserves*, where they may be kept until wanted, like captive animals or like fish in a tank.

80. occulto: *unobserved.*   **verum esto**: *but admit for the sake of argument.*

82. idem : nominative plural.   **durare probantes**: *continue to like.*

83. sinus : of the winding shore of the bay.   **Bais** : the favorite seaside resort of the Romans ; *cf. Odes,* iii. 4. 24, *liquidae Baiae.*
praelucet : *i.e.* is preferable to ; *cf. Odes,* i. 33. 3, *cur tibi iunior Laesa praeniteat fide?*

84. lacus : *sc. Lucrinus,* into which, as well as into the sea, villas were built. *Cf. Odes,* iii. 1. 33–36, *Contracta pisces aequora sentiunt Iactis in altum molibus, etc.*

85. vitiosa : *perverted, morbid;* see note on i. 3. 1.

86. fecerit auspicium: *suggested;* the prompting of *vitiosa libido* is compared with a message from the gods by means of augury.
Teanum : often called *Teanum Sidicinum,* to distinguish it from the Apulian Teanum ; an inland town of Campania and a favorite resort, where the rich man now decides to build a villa.

87. tolletis : future with imperative force.   **lectus genialis** : the couch symbolic of marriage, under the protection of the *genius* of the family. It stood in the *atrium,* for which *aula* is here used.

89. bene esse: *i.e.* that they only enjoy life ; *cf. Serm.* ii. 2. 120, *bene erat (sc. nobis) non piscibus urbe petitis;* and see Introd. § 51. *a.*

90. Protea : *cf. Serm.* ii. 3. 71, and the note.

91. quid pauper: *sc. facit; what of the man who is not rich?*
cenacula: *garrets; cf.* Varro, *L. L.* v. 162, *ubi cenabant, cenaculum vocitabant: posteaquam in superiore parte cenitare coeperunt, superioris domus universa cenacula dicta.* The poor man is as discontented as the rich man, and makes such changes as he can.

92. aeque nauseat : *gets just as seasick.* Apparently a common complaint ; *cf.* Sen. *de Ira,* iii. 37. 3, *num quis se hieme algere miratur? num quis in mari nausiare ?*

94. curatus inaequali tonsore : *by unsymmetric barber trimmed* (Lane). *Cf.* i. 3. 30, *rideri possit eo quod Rusticius tonso toga defluit. Tonsore* is ablative of instrument, instead of *a tonsore; cf. pueris, Serm.* i. 6. 116, and the note.

95. subucula: *under-garment; cf.* Varro, *ap. Nonius,* p. 542, *posteaquam binas tunicas habere coeperunt, instituerunt vocare subuculam* *et indusium.*   **pexae** : *fresh, new;* lit. *combed.* When cloth was prepared by the fullers, the nap was combed up with the *spina fullonia*, and clipped so as to be even.

96. impar : *unevenly, i.e.* with one side higher than the other. Great care was taken, by well-dressed men, in arranging the folds of the toga ; *cf. Serm.* i. 3. 30, cited above on line 94.

97. pugnat secum : is inconsistent ; with the metaphor, *cf. Serm.* i. 1. 102, *pergis pugnantia secum Frontibus adversis componere,* and the note.

98. Note the chiastic arrangement of the line.

99. aestuat : *ebbs and flows,* like the tide of the sea.   **disconvenit** : *is out of harmony.*   Cf. i. 14. 18, *eo disconvenit inter Meque et te,* the only other place where the word is found in classical Latin.

100. mutat quadrata rotundis : probably a proverbial expression. For the construction, *cf. Serm.* ii. 7. 110, *qui puer uvam Furtiva mutat strigili,* and the note.

101. insanire . . . sollemnia : *i.e.* that I am no more mad than the greater part of mankind. *Sollemnia* is accusative of the inner object, after the analogy of *insanire sollemnem insaniam.*

102. curatoris a praetore dati : *a guardian assigned by the praetor ; cf. Serm.* ii. 3. 217.

103. rerum tutela mearum : 'the (self-appointed) protector of my fortunes.' *Cf. Odes,* iv. 14. 43, *o tuiela praesens Italiae.*

104. prave sectum . . . unguem : the Romans gave great attention to the care of their nails ; *cf.* i. 7. 49–50.

105. respicientis : *i.e.* looking to you for counsel.

106. ad summam : *i.e.* to sum up the whole argument.

107. honoratus : *i.e.* is chosen to office.

108. nisi cum, *etc. :* as usual Horace ends his serious discourse with a jest, in this case a play on the double meaning of *sanus,* 'sane ' and ' sound ' (in health).   **pituita** : scanned in three syllables.

EPISTLE II.

1. Maxime : the cognomen precedes, as in *Serm.* 1. 6. 12 ; see note. Who is referred to, is uncertain.

2. declamas : *are declaiming, i.e.* studying oratory.   **Praeneste** : a favorite resort of Horace ; *cf. Odes,* iii. 4. 23.   Locative ablative.

3. quid sit pulchrum . . . quid non : a summary of ethical principles.

4. planius : *more clearly.*   **Chrysippus** : *cf. Serm.* i. 3. 126, and the note.   **Crantore** : the head of the Academic School. He and Chrysippus are mentioned as typical of philosophers in general.

5. crediderim : *have come to think ; = sentiam.*   **distinet** : *distracts ; i.e.* unless you have something else to think of.

7. barbariae : applied after the Greek usage to Phrygia ; *cf. Odes,* ii. 4. 9, *Barbarae postquam cecidere turmae Thessalo victore.* **lento** : *lingering,* of the ten-year siege.   **duello** : the archaic form of *bello.*

8. stultorum : used in the philosophic sense.   **aestus** : *the fitful passions;* the metaphor is the same as in *sententia aestuat,* i. 1. 99.

9. Antenor : *cf. Iliad,* vii. 347 f. ; Liv. i. 1. 1, (*Aeneas Antenorque*) *pacis reddendaeque Helenae semper auctores fuerunt.*   **censet . . . praecidere** : advises cutting away, like a diseased limb. For the construction, *cf.* Liv. xliii. 5. 8, *munera mitti legatis censuerunt, etc.*

10. quid Paris : *sc. facit; cf. quid pauper,* i. 1. 91.   **ut . . . regnet** : probably stipulative subjunctive (see Introd. 45. *e*) ; *i.e.* Paris says that he cannot be forced to give up Helen, even on the promise of securing safety and happiness.

11. Nestor : *cf. Iliad,* i. 247 ff.

12. inter . . . et inter : for the repetition of the preposition, *cf. Serm.* i. 7. 11, *inter Hectora . . . atque inter Achillem.*

13. hunc : *i.e.* Agamemnon.

14. quicquid . . . Achivi : *i.e.* whatever folly the kings commit is visited on the Greeks as a whole. *Quicquid* is an accusative of the inner object ; *cf. insanire sollemnia,* i. 1. 101.

16. peccatur : impersonal, governed by the ablatives in the preceding line.

17. rursus : again, *i.e.* on the other hand ; *cf. Serm.* i. 3. 28, *at tibi contra Evenit, inquirant vitia ut tua rursus et illi.*

19. domitor Troiae : Odysseus was the real conqueror of the city. This line and the next two are a translation of the beginning of the *Odyssey. Cf. Ars Poet.* 141–143.

23. Sirenum voces : the Sirens were beautiful maidens, who, by their sweet singing, lured to destruction those who passed near their isle. When Odysseus sailed by, he stopped the ears of his companions with wax, and had them bind him to the mast, so that he might hear the songs without danger. *Cf. Odyss.* xii. 39 ff.   **Circae pocula** : Circe, who dwelt in the island of Aeaea, was famous for her skill in the magic arts. When Odysseus was driven to Aeaea, some of his companions wandered to Circe's palace, and drinking the drugged wine which she set before them, were changed into swine. *Cf. Odyss.* x. 136 ff.

24. stultus cupidusque : *foolishly and greedily*, in distinction from Odysseus himself, who did not drink until he had received an antidote from Hermes.

25. turpis : with the double meaning of *hideous*, like a beast, and *degraded*.　　**excors** : *unreasoning, foolish; cf. Serm.* ii. 3. 67, *an magis excors, Reiecta praeda quam praesens Mercurius fert.*

26. canis : the dog with the Greeks and Romans was a symbol of uncleanness, and *canis* is often used as a term of reproach ; *e.g. Epod.* 6. 1.

27. numerus : *mere ciphers*, of no value alone, but swelling the sum total of humanity.　　**fruges consumere nati** : a translation of an Homeric phrase, *Iliad*, vi. 142, βροτῶν, οἳ ἀρούρης καρπὸν ἔδουσιν.

28. sponsi : for *proci, suitors.*　　**Alcinoi . . . iuventus** : Alcinous was king of the Phaeacians, a mythical people, who led a life of peace and perfect happiness in the island of Scheria, with which Corcyra was afterward identified. *Cf. Odyss.* viii. 248 ff.　　**nebulones** : with the force of an adjective modifying *sponsi*.

29. cute curanda : of a life of idleness, like *pelliculam curare, Serm.* ii. 5. 38.　　**operata** : *busy*, used sarcastically.

30. pulchrum : *noble, fine*, with sarcastic reference to *pulchrum* in line 3.

31. cessatum . . . curam : *to lull care to rest; cessatum* is the supine modifying *ducere*.

32. de nocte : *before daylight. Cf.* Ter. *Adelph.* 840, *rus cras cum filio Cum primo luci ibo hinc. De nocte censeo.*

33. expergisceris : present with future force, *won't you get up ?* **atqui** : *and yet*, implying that a negative answer was expected to the preceding question.

34. noles : *sc. currere.*　　**curres hydropicus** : *i.e.* you will have to take exercise for your health. *Cf.* Celsus, iii. 21, *hydropicis multum ambulandum, currendum aliquid est.*

35. posces : from a slave. *Cf.* ii. 1. 112, *et prius orto Sole vigil calamum et chartas et scrinia posco.*

36. intendes animum : *i.e.* employ your mind. The same metaphor as in *tendere opus*, ii. 1. 2.

37. vigil : *sleepless.*　　**nam cur** : equivalent to *cur nam, Why in* *the world ?* *Nam* has asseverative force, as in i. 1. 76. *Cf.* Plaut. *Aul.* 43, *nam cur me verberas ?*

39. ēst = *edit* from *edo.*   **in annum** : *for a year*, with somewhat the same force as in i. 18. 109, *provisae frugis in annum copia.*

40. dimidium . . . habet : *well begun is half done;* the proverb is an old one; *cf.* Plat. *de Legg.* 6. 753 e, ἀρχὴ γὰρ λέγεται μὲν ἡμισὺ παντὸς ἐν ταῖς παροιμίαις ἔργου.   **sapere aude** : *dare to be wise;* cf. Virg. *Aen.* viii. 364, *aude, hospes, contemnere opes.*

42. rusticus : *i.e.* is like the clown who. *Cf.* note on *spectatum,* i. 1. 2. The reference is doubtless to some familiar story, but it is not otherwise known to us.

43. labitur . . . aevum : the abundance of dactyls and the repetition of the liquid *l* are appropriate to the flowing stream.

44. argentum : *money;* cf. *Serm.* i. 1. 86, *cum tu argento post omnia ponis.*   **beata** : *rich;* cf. *dotata coniunx, Odes,* iii. 24. 19 ; and for the meaning of *beata, Odes,* i. 29. 1, *beatis gazis.*

45. pacantur : *are subdued, i.e.* we enlarge our estates by clearing the woods and tilling the soil. *Cf.* Virg. *Aen.* vi. 803, *Alcides . . . Erymanthi pacarit nemora.*

46. contingit : present of continued action ; *cf.* i. 4. 10, *cui Gratia, fama, valetudo contingat abunde;* i. 15. 44.

48. deduxit : the gnomic perfect ; *never has, and hence never will.* See Introd. § 44. *d.*

50. comportatis : *accumulated*, with reference to *acervus* in line 47.   **bene uti** : *i.e.* to enjoy.   **cogitat** : *thinks to*, in the sense of 'expects to.'

51. sic . . . ut : *i.e.* as little as.

52. pictae tabulae : *pictures. Tabulae* alone is often used with that meaning, with ellipsis of *pictae;* e.g. Ars Poet. 6, *isti tabulae fore librum persimilem.*   **fomenta** : *applications* of hot water, which would be agreeable to a well person, but give no pleasure to one sick with gout.

54. sincerum : *clean.* The comparison of the soul with a vase is found in Plato, *Protag.* 314 *b.*

56. certum finem : *i.e.* set as a fixed limit to your desires the amount which is sufficient for your needs.   **voto** : dative of the indirect object.

57. alterius : note the word ; *his rival;* see note on *alter, Serm.* i. 1. 40. With the general sentiment, *cf. Serm.* i. 1. 110.

58. Siculi . . . tyranni : their cruelty, especially that of Dionysius and Phalaris, was proverbial ; *cf.* Cic. *Verr.* ii. 5. 56. 145, *non Dionysius ille nec Phalaris, tulit enim illa quondam insula (Sicilia) multos et crudelis tyrannos.*

59. moderabitur : *restrain.* Horace dwells longer on the defect of *ira,* as his own besetting sin. *Cf. Serm.* ii. 3. 323.

60. dolor . . . et mens : *his angry feelings,* hendiadys.

61. odio . . . inulto : dative, *for his unsatisfied vengeance.*

62. ira furor brevis : proverbial ; *cf.* Sen. *de Ira,* i. 1. 2, *quidam itaque ex sapientibus viris iram dixerunt brevem insaniam.*

63. tu : note the postponement of the subject to the second part of the sentence ; *cf. Serm.* i. 6. 122.

64. fingit : *trains, moulds* to his will. **tenera . . . cervice** : *i.e.* when it is still young. **magister** : *the trainer.* *Cf.* Varr. *Sat. Men.* 559, *nam ut ecus qui ad vehendum est natus, tamen hic traditur magistro.*

65. viam : accusative of the inner object. See Introd. § 38.*b.* **qua monstrat eques** : *where his rider shows the way.* **venaticus** : *i.e.* trained for the chase.

66. cervinam pellem : *i.e.* the puppies were trained for the chase by being taught to bark at a stuffed stag. **aula** : *courtyard;* for *atrium ; cf.* i. 1. 87, *lectus genialis est in aula.*

67. nunc . . . puer : *now, when still young.*

68. melioribus : masculine, as in i. 1. 48.

69. quo semel . . . testa diu : *cf.* "You may break, you may shatter the vase, if you will, The scent of the roses will cling to it still."

70. strenuus : *i.e.* in your enthusiasm. Horace advocates the golden mean, even in the pursuit of virtue.

71. insto : *press after.*

EPISTLE III.

1. quibus terrarum . . . oris : *cf.* Virg. *Aen.* i. 331, *quibus orbis in oris. Oris* implies remote lands. **militet** : *is serving,* here used of the commander of the expedition.

2. Claudius : his full name was *Tiberius Claudius Nero.* **privignus** : *stepson;* Tiberius was the son of Tiberius Claudius Nero and Livia, the wife of Augustus. He was adopted by Augustus in 3 A.D., after the death of Gaius and Lucius Caesar. **scire laboro** : *cf. nosse laboro, Serm.* ii. 8. 19.

3. Thraca : a poetical and earlier form of *Thracia,* used according

to Servius (on *Aen.* xii. 335) by Cicero, *de Rep.* ii. 4.   In Horace
again in *Epist.* i. 16. 13.   In this and the two following lines successive
stages of the journey to Armenia are mentioned.   **nivali compede
vinctus** : a general epithet of the proverbially cold Hebrus.

4. freta . . . currentia : the Hellespont, which has a strong west-
ward current.   **vicinas . . . turris** : at Sestos and Abydos.   The
width is less than a mile at the narrowest point.

6. studiosa : *learned.*   **cohors** : *suite,* attendants on the commander, with or without special appointments.   So Catullus accompanied Memmius to Bithynia.   **operum** : to be joined with *quid;*
genitive of the whole.   **curo** : equivalent to *scire laboro,* line 2.

7. sumit : *cf. Odes,* i. 12. 2, *sumis celebrare; Ars Poet.* 38, *sumite
materiam vestris . . . aequam viribus.*

8. bella et paces : *i.e.* his deeds in war and in peace ; *cf. Serm.*
ii. 1. 10–17.   **longum in aevum** : *cf. Odes,* iv. 14. 3, *virtutes in
aevum . . . aeternet.*

9. quid : *sc. sumit* or *struit.*   **Titius** : otherwise unknown.
Romana venturus in ora : *i.e.* to be talked of, to become famous ;
cf. Ennius, *ap.* Cic. *Tusc. Disp.* i. 15. 34, *volito vivos per ora virum.*

10. Pindarici fontis : the spring at which Pindar drank ; on the
difficulty of imitating Pindar, *cf. Odes,* iv. 2 ; hence *non expalluit.*
Faustus : object of *expalluit; cf. Odes,* iii. 27. 25 ff., *Europe . . . sca-
tentem beluis pontum palluit.*

11. lacus et rivos apertos : *tanks* (*cf. Serm.* i. 4. 37) *and
streams,* in distinction from *Pindarici fontis.*   For the general idea,
cf. Quint. x. 1. 109, *non enim pluvias, ut ait Pindarus, aquas colligit
(Cicero), sed vivo gurgite exundat.*

12. ut : *how ; cf. Serm.* ii. 8. 1, *ut Nasidieni iuvit te cena ?*   **fidibusne Latinis . . . modos** : *cf. Odes,* iii. 30. 13, *princeps Aeolium
carmen ad Italos Deduxisse modos.*

13. Thebanos : *i.e.* Pindaric.   **auspice Musa** : *with the favor
of the Muse.*

14. desaevit : *rant,* as the personages of tragedy do ; *cf. Serm.*
i. 10, 36, *Turgidus Alpinus iugulat dum Memnona.*   **ampullatur** :
of the bombastic language of tragedy ; *cf. Ars Poet.* 97, *Telephus et
Peleus . . . Proicit ampullas et sesquipedalia verba.*   The word seems
to be coined by Horace, after the Greek ληκυθίζω.

15. mihi : *my friend,* a good example of the so-called ethical
dative.   **Celsus** : apparently referring to Celsus Albinovanus, to
whom *Epist.* i. 8 is addressed.

16. privatas . . . opes : *material of his own*, instead of borrowing from earlier writers, whose works were already in the public library. *Cf. Ars Poet.* 131, *Publica materies privati iuris erit, si. . . .*

17. Palatinus . . . Apollo : referring to the public library founded by Octavian in 28 B.C., in the temple of Apollo on the Palatine Hill.

19. cornicula : the reference is to the well-known fable of the Jack-daw (here the crow) which dressed itself in borrowed plumage. The diminutive expresses humorous compassion, *the poor little crow.*

20. furtivis : *stolen ; cf. Serm.* ii. 7. 110.   **audes** : *venture on.*

21. quae . . . circumvolitas : *cf. Odes,* iv. 2. 27 f., *apis Matinae more modoque Grata carpentis thyma per laborem Plurimum.* **agilis** : *busy ; cf.* i. 1. 16, *nunc agilis fio.*

22. hirtum : *rough*, like a neglected field. For the use of *turpiter, cf. Odes,* iii. 11, 35, *splendide mendax ; Ars Poet.* 3, *turpiter atrum.*

23. linguam . . . acuis : metaphorically of the work of the pleader.   **civica iura respondere** : *i.e.* act as *iure consultus ;* see note on *Serm.* i. 1. 9. The technical term is *ius civile respondere.*

25. hederae : applying strictly only to *condis . . . carmen. Cf. Odes,* i. 1. 29, *doctarum hederae praemia fontium.*

26. curarum : appositive genitive, *i.e.* cares which, like cold compresses, diminish your ardor.

27. caelestis : *heaven-born.*

29. nobis . . . cari : *i.e.* with self-respect.

30. sit tibi curae quantae conveniat : *is as dear to you as he ought to be ; curae* is the dative of purpose.

31. Munatius : probably the son of Lucius Munatius Plancus, to whom *Odes* i. 7 is addressed.   **male sarta . . . coit** : like a wound which has been sewed up, but does not heal.

33. rerum inscitia : *i.e.* ignorance of the world.

34. feros : *high-spirited.*

36. pascitur . . . votiva : *cf. Odes,* iv. 2. 54, *Me tener solvet vitulus, relicta Matre qui largis iuvenescit herbis In mea vota.*

EPISTLE IV.

1. Albi : Albius Tibullus, the elegiac poet (54–19 B.C.), an intimate friend of Horace. *Odes* i. 33 is also addressed to him.   **sermonum** : referring to Horace's work, the *Sermones.*   **candide** : *fair, impartial*, not necessarily implying a favorable judgment. Evidently the

Sermones had met some criticism to which the term could not, in Horace's opinion, be applied.

2. Pedana : Pedum was an ancient town between Tibur and Praeneste. It had apparently ceased to exist in Horace's time, though the name was still applied to the district. Tibullus seems to have had a villa in the neighborhood.

3. scribere : *sc. dicam te.*   **Cassi Parmensi** : so called to distinguish him from C. Cassius Longinus. He also was one of the conspirators against the life of Caesar and a fellow-soldier of Horace in the army of Brutus.   **opuscula** : literary *works.* Cassius tried many kinds of composition. The diminutive is used by Horace of his lyrics in i. 19. 35.

4. tacitum : *i.e.* in silent thought.   **reptare** : *strolling.* Of slow progress, like *repere* in *Serm.* i. 5. 25, *milia tum . . . tria repimus.*

5. curantem : *meditating on.*

6. non eras : *you were never;* the action continues into the present ; see Introd. § 44. *b.*   **pectore** : *soul.*

7. dederunt : scanned with a short penultimate *e,* the ancient quantity. See Introd. § 57.   **artem fruendi** : *i.e.* the power of enjoying the bounty of the gods.

8. nutricula : *a fond nurse;* note the diminutive.

9. sapere et fari : *i.e.* to think and to speak wisely.

10. gratia : *powerful friends,* the abstract for the concrete, with reference to his relations with Messalla and his circle ; see note on *Serm.* i. 10. 85.

11. mundus victus : *i.e.* the means of living decently; *cf. Serm.* ii. 2. 65, *Mundus erit qua non offendat sordibus, atque In neutram partem cultus miser.*

12. inter, *etc. : i.e.* amid the changing fortunes of life.

13. omnem crede : *i.e.* believe after the dawn of each day that it is your last.

14. superveniet : *sc. vitae.* With the thought, *cf. Odes,* i. 9. 13 ff., *Quid sit futurum cras, fuge quaerere et, Quem Fors dierum cumque dabit, lucro Appone.*

15. me pinguem : the Epistle closes with a jest ; *cf. Serm.* i. 1. 120, *etc.* On Horace's personal appearance, *cf.* Suet. *Vit. Hor. habitu corporis brevis fuit atque obesus.*   **bene curata cute** : *cf.* i. 2. 29, *in cute curando,* and the note.

16. porcum : identifying the person with that with which he is compared. See note on *Serm.* ii. 1. 20.

EPISTLE V.

1. Archiacis: *i.e.* probably made by a carpenter called Archias. Porph. says: *Archias breves lectos fecit.* In any case, cheap unpretentious furniture is meant. For the arrangement of the couches, see Outline of *Serm.* ii. 8. **recumbere**: *cf. Odes*, iii. 3. 11, *Quos inter Augustus recumbens*, a frequent use of the word.

2. modica: with reference to quality; *cf. Serm.* i. 5. 2, *hospitio modico.* **holus omne**: *i.e.* a meal consisting of nothing but vegetables; *holus* is object of *cenare;* see Introd. § 38. *a.*

3. supremo sole: *just as the sun is setting;* the opposite of *primo sole; cf.* Ovid, *Met.* ix. 93, *primo feriente cacumina sole.* The late hour is also characteristic of a modest repast; *cf. Serm.* ii. 8. 3, *de medio potare die*, and the note.

4. iterum Tauro: *sc. consule, in the second consulship of* (T. Statilius) *Taurus.* The date is 26 B.C.; his colleague was Augustus. **diffusa**: *i.e.* drawn off from the jar (*dolium*) and sealed up in *amphorae.* **palustris Minturnas**: situated on the marshy land about the mouth of the Liris. Falernian and Massic wine came from the same neighborhood.

5. Petrinum: a mountain, according to the Comm. Cruq. Porph. says: *Petrinus vicus olim et locus in agro Falerno.*

6. arcesse: *sc. me, invite me;* if Torquatus is not satisfied with Horace's wine, he must do the entertaining himself; *cf.* Plautus, *Amph.* 951, *Blepharonem arcessat qui nobiscum prandeat.* **vel imperium fer**: *i.e.* leave the matter to me; put up with my directions as host and master of the feast; on *dominus* for host, see *Serm.* ii. 8. 93.

7. splendet: *i.e.* have been cleaned in honor of your visit. The wall about the hearth and the pictures of the Lares became blackened with soot, which had to be cleaned off from time to time. **tibi**: *in your honor;* dative of reference.

8. levis spes: *i.e.* hopes about trifling matters. **certamina divitiarum**: *the struggle for wealth*, not of course in a bad sense.

9. Moschi: Porph. says: *Moschus hic Pergamenus fuit rhetor notissimus. Reus veneficii fuit, cuius causam ex primis tunc oratores egerunt, Torquatus hic, de quo nunc dicit, cuius extat oratio, et Asinius Pollio.* **nato Caesare**: to whom this refers is uncertain, probably to Augustus; see note on *aestivam noctem*, line 11.

10. veniam somnumque: *an excuse for sleep;* hendiadys.

11. aestivam noctem: The birthday of Augustus fell on September

23, but the term *aestivam noctem* may be used generally of the hot season. Some think that the reference is to Julius Caesar, whose birthday was on July 12, but Horace uses Caesar of Augustus thirty-two times, and of Julius Caesar only twice (*Odes* i. 2. 44 ; *Serm.* i. 9. 18), and in both cases the meaning is made evident by the context. *Caesare* without further definition would naturally refer to Augustus. **tendere**: *prolong.* *Cf.* Virg. *Aen.* i. 748, *vario noctem sermone trahebat Infelix Dido.*

12. fortunam: for the construction, *cf. unde mihi lapidem, Serm.* ii. 7. 116, and see note.

13. ob heredis curam: with the thought, *cf. Odes,* iv. 7. 19, *Cuncta manus avidas fugient heredis, amico Quae dederis animo;* Pers. vi. 33, *cenam funeris heres Negleget iratus, quod rem curtaveris.*

14. adsidet: *is next door to,* apparently with reference to the seats in the theatres, *etc.* **flores**: the regular accompaniment of a banquet or a drinking bout ; *cf. Odes,* iii. 19. 21, *Parcentes ego dexteras Odi: sparge rosas.*

15. vel: *if you like;* the old injunctive form of *velle.*

16. ebrietas: *wine;* the English ' drunkenness' is not an equivalent here. **dissignat**: *open;* lit. *unseal.* **operta recludit**: *cf. Serm.* i. 4. 89, *Condita cum verax aperit praecordia Liber.*

17. spes . . . ratas: *i.e.* it makes one hopeful and confident. *Cf.* Sen. *de Ira,* i. 13. 3, *ebrietas facit protervos et audaces.* **ad proelia trudit inertem**: *cf.* Sen. *de Ira,* i. 13. 3, *multi meliores ad ferrum fuere male sobrii.*

18. addocet artis: *i.e.* teaches new arts.

19. fecundi: in a double sense, *full* and *inspiring.*

20. contracta . . . in paupertate: *in the chains of poverty.* **solutum**: *free.*

21. haec: *the following duties.* **idoneus . . . et non invitus**: *i.e.* I am both able and willing. **imperor**: *I charge myself;* the verb is used in a middle sense.

22. toral: *cf. Serm.* ii. 4. 84, and the note.

23. conruget naris: *make you turn up your nose; cf.* Pers. iii. 86, *multumque torosa iuventus Ingeminat tremulos naso crispante cachinnos.* **ne non . . . ostendat tibi te**: *i.e.* that you may be able to see your face in the polished metal.

25. foras eliminet: *carry across the threshold* of the dining-room.

26. Butram, *etc.:* persons otherwise unknown.

27. potior puella: *i.e.* a girl whose society he prefers to ours.

28. umbris: *cf. Serm.* ii. 8. 22, and the note. Torquatus may bring a friend or two if he likes.

29. sed . . . caprae: *i.e.* he must not bring too many *umbrae*. *Caprae = hirci; cf. Epod.* 12. 5, *gravis hirsutis cubet hircus in alis.*

31. postico falle: *i.e.* slip out the back door, and escape the client who is lying in wait for you in the atrium. *Postico* is ablative of the way by which.

EPISTLE VI.

1. nil admirari: *i.e.* to be indifferent to material things.

3. hunc: *yonder*, with a gesture. **decedentia . . . momentis**: *the seasons moving in regular courses.*

4. formidine: *i.e.* superstitious fear.

5. imbuti: *touched, affected.* **quid**: introducing the question, which is afterward repeated by *quomodo* with a change of construction. Cic. *Rosc. Am.* 17. 49, *quid censes ipsum Sex. Roscium, quo studio et qua intellegentia esse in rusticis rebus.*

6. maris: to be taken with *munera*, referring to the pearls for which the Red Sea and the Persian Gulf were famous.

7. ludicra: in apposition with *plausus* and *dona; i.e.* such worthless trifles as office and popular favor. **dona**: *i.e. honores* (office). *Quiritis* is used collectively.

8. ore: *expression*, by which emotions would be denoted in the mimes.

9. his adversa: *the opposite of these, i.e.* poverty and defeat at the polls. **miratur**: *i.e.* rates them too high, the opposite of *nil admirari*, a philosophic indifference.

10. pavor: *excitement; cf.* Virg. *Aen.* v. 137, *exsultantiaque haurit Corda pavor pulsans laudumque arrecta cupido.*

11. simul: for *simul ac; cf. Serm.* i. 1. 36. **exterret**: *startles. Cf.* Virg. *Aen.* xi. 806, *fugit ante omnes exterritus Arruns Laetitia mixtoque metu.*

12. quid ad rem: *sc. interest.*

13. spe: *expectation.*

14. animoque et corpore: equivalent to *sensu et ore*, line 8.

16. ultra quam satis est: *i.e.* without moderation.

17. i nunc: *i.e.* if you can, after what has been said. **aera**: *bronzes;* see note on *aere, Serm.* i. 4. 28. **artis**: *works of art.*

18. suspice: *admire;* the opposite of *despice.*

19. loquentem: *as you speak* (as an orator), a rare use of the word; *cf.* Cic. *Orat.* 32. 113, *non idem loqui esse quod dicere.*

20. navus: *busy; cf. naviter,* i. 1. 24.   **forum**: as the seat of trade.

21. dotalibus: *gained by marriage,* not by his own industry.

22. Mutus: otherwise unknown.   **indignum**: *a shame,* in apposition with the following clause.   **sit**: the subjunctive is due to the idea that the criticism comes from others.

24. in apricum: *i.e.* into the light of the sun; for the usual *in apertum.*

26. porticus Agrippae: a portico near the Pantheon, built by Agrippa and adorned with paintings representing the expedition of the Argonauts. It is mentioned here as one of the most popular lounging places in Rome.   **via Appi** = *via Appia;* the most famous and fashionable of the Roman roads. *Cf. Serm.* i. 5. 6, and the note.

27. ire tamen restat, *etc.: i.e.* you must one day die. *Cf. Odes,* iv. 7. 14, *ubi decidimus, Quo pater Aeneas, quo dives Tullus et Ancus.*

28. si latus, *etc.:* one should study the way of living happily, just as one would try to look out for one's bodily health. *Cf.* i. 2. 38, *Nam cur Quae laedunt oculos festinas demere, si quid Est animum, differs curandi tempus in annum ?*

31. hoc age: *give your attention to this; cf. Serm.* ii. 3. 152. **verba**: *a mere name; cf.* i. 17. 41, *virtus nomen inane est.*   **putas**: *i.e. if* you think, a paratactic condition.

32. lucum ligna: *sc. esse ; i.e.* that a sacred grove is but so much fire-wood. The expression has a proverbial ring.   **cave . . . alter**: *see to it that no one reaches port before you;* with the expression, *cf. Odes,* i. 14. 2, *fortiter occupa Portum;* and with the thought, Pers. v. 136, *Tolle recens primus piper e sitiente camelo.*

33. Cibyratica: *of Cibyra,* a commercial city of Phrygia, not far from the Lycian frontier.   **Bithyna**: Bithynia was important commercially, especially in the lines of timber and marble ; *cf. Odes,* iii. 7. 3, *Thyna merce beatum.*

34. rotundentur: *be rounded off.* The expression is colloquial ; *cf.* etr. 76, *uno cursu centies sestertium corrotundavi.*

35. quadret: of a fourth thousand, with reference to the four sides of a square.

36. scilicet: *of course ;* ironical.

38. bene nummatum: a colloquial expression, like our 'well-

heeled.'   **Suadela**: the goddess of persuasion. The rich man will
be eloquent and successful in love.

39. aeris : *i.e.* ready money.   **Cappadocum rex** : Ariobar-
zanes, of whom Cic. *ad Att.* vi. 1. 3, says : *nullum aerarium, nullum
vectigal habet.*

40. fuerīs : with ī, the original quantity of the perfect subjunctive,
originally an aorist optative. See note on *miscuerīs*, *Serm.* ii. 2. 74.
hic : *i.e.* like him.   **chlamydes** : to be used for a chorus of warriors.

43. milia quinque : the point is that Lucullus was a genuine rich
man, for he did not know how much he possessed.

44. tolleret : *he might take*, representing the imperative or an
equivalent jussive subjunctive in the direct form.

45. exilis : *poor ; cf. Odes*, i. 4. 17, *domus exilis Plutonia.*   **ubi
non . . . supersunt** : *where there are not many superfluous things.*
et : note the hyperbaton.

46. fallunt : *i.e.* are forgotten by.   **prosunt furibus** : *i.e.* they
can be stolen without being noticed.

47. The language of line 2 repeated with ironical force.

48. hoc . . . opus : *i.e. rem facere.*

49. species : *state.*   **gratia** : *cf.* i. 4. 10.

50. qui dictet nomina : *i.e.* a *nomenclator*, whose business it
was to inform his master of the names of people whom he did not
know, but wished to address by name. Final subjunctive.   **laevum** :
the slave walked on the left of his master ; *cf. Serm.* ii. 5. 17, and
the note.

51. pondera : the reference may be to *stepping-stones* in the streets,
such as are seen at Pompeii, and are called *pondera* in inscriptions ;
some understand the word to mean *weights* on the counter of a shop.

52. multum valet : *has great influence.*   **Fabia, Velina** : *sc.
tribu.*

53. curule . . . ebur : the *sella curulis.*

54. frater, pater : *cf.* Ps.-Quint. *Decl.* 321, *quotiens blandiri volumus his qui esse amici videntur, nulla adulatio procedere ultra hoc
nomen potest, quam ut fratres vocemus.* On *pater*, see *Serm.* ii. 1. 12.

55. adopta : *adopt him*, by the use of the term *pater* or *frater.*
Cf. Spart. *Jul.* 4. 1, *unumquemque, ut erat aetas, vel patrem vel filium
vel parentem affatus blandissime est.*

56. si . . . vivit : *i.e.* if the pleasures of the table are the greatest
happiness.   **lucet** : *day has come ; it is sunrise* ; *i.e.* it is time to be
up and doing.

57. piscemur, venemur: *let us fish and hunt* — in the market.

58. Gargilius: a common name, but the individual here referred to is otherwise unknown.

59. differtum forum populumque: for *forum differtum populo.* On *differtum*, see note on *Serm.* i. 5. 3.

60. e multis: *i.e.* of the long train of mules which he had taken with him.

61. crudi: *i.e.* with our last meal still undigested. *Cf.* Juv. i. 142, *cum tu deponis amictum Turgidus et crudum pavonem in balnea portas.*

62. Caerite cera digni: *i.e.* deserving to lose their citizenship. *Cf.* Gell. xvi. 13. 17, *primos municipes sine suffragii iure Caerites esse factos accepimus . . . pro sacris bello Gallico receptis custoditisque. Hinc 'tabulae Caerites' appellatae versa vice, in quas censores referri iubebant, quos notae causa suffragiis privabant.*

63. remigium: *the crew*, contemptuous for *socii;* the abstract for the concrete. The reference is to the slaying of the cattle of Helios, *Odyss.* xiii. 313 ff.

65. Mimnermus: an elegiac poet of Colophon, a contemporary of Solon (circ. 600 B.C.).   **sine amore**, *etc.*: a fragment of Mimnermus, expressing this sentiment, has come down to us.

67. vive, vale: *cf. Serm.* ii. 5. 110, *vive valeque.* Horace closes abruptly, as he often does.   **istis**: *i.e.* than what has been told you.

68. candidus imperti: *i.e.* be a good fellow and tell me.

EPISTLE VII.

1. quinque dies: a general term for a few days ; *cf. Serm.* i. 3. 16, *quinque diebus nil erat in loculis.* See Introd. § 50.   **rure**: the form used by Horace ; *ruri* is the earlier form of the locative. See note on *here, Serm.* ii. 8. 2.

2. Sextilem: the sixth month counting from March, which was originally the beginning of the year ; the name August was given to it in 8 B.C., in honor of Augustus.   **mendax**: *cf.* ii. 2. 25, *Expectata tibi non mittam carmina mendax.*

3. sanum recteque valentem: practically synonymous ; *sound and in good health.*

4. quam . . . das aegro: *which you give me when I am sick.* **aegrotare**: instead of the usual *ne aegrotem.*

5. dum: *as long as.*   **ficus prima**: the fig ripened in early

September, the unhealthiest month at Rome. *Cf. Odes*, iii. 23. 8, *Pomifero grave tempus anno.*

6. dissignatorem : *the undertaker*, who arranged (*dissigno*) for funerals.   **decorat** : Horace regularly uses a singular verb with a compound subject. See Introd. § 43. *a*.   **lictoribus atris** : in grand funerals lictors clad in black and carrying the *fasces* marched in the procession. They wore the masks of such ancestors of the deceased as had filled curule offices. See note on *imaginibus, Serm.* i. 6. 17. The lictors are spoken of as ornaments of the *dissignator*, the leader in the procession.

7. pueris : dative of interest. *Cf.* Mart. x. 62. 12, *aestate pueri si valent, satis discunt.*   **matercula** : *fond mother; cf. nutricula*, i. 4. 8.

8. officiosa sedulitas : *i.e.* conscientiousness in performing cere-monial duties, such as paying morning calls, listening to recitations, and the like. *Cf.* ii. 2. 67, *Hic sponsum vocat, hic auditum scripta relictis Omnibus officiis.*   **opella** : *petty business;* the force of the diminutive. At this season, when people of importance were for the most part out of town, the legal business would be of that character. The word occurs also in Lucr. i. 1114, *pernosces parva perdoctus opella.*

9. testamenta resignat : *i.e.* causes death. The will was sealed and deposited in some safe place, and was unsealed only at the death of the maker.

10. bruma : *the winter ;* lit. the winter solstice, the shortest day (* *breu-ma* > *bruma, sc. dies*). The idea is that if the cold weather is early and severe, Horace will go to the shore.

11. sibi parcet : *i.e.* will take care of his health.

12. contractus : *huddled-up,* a self-explanatory word.

13. cum Zephyris . . . et hirundine prima : the harbingers of spring ; *cf. Odes*, iv. 7. 9, *frigora mitescunt Zephyris ;* Ovid, *Fasti*, ii. 853, *Fallimur, an veris praenuntia venit hirundo?*

14. quo more : *i.e.* showing that he gave him what he himself could not use.   **Calaber** : the name seems to be used merely to localize the story, though possibly, as Kiessling suggests, it may be a reminiscence of Horace's youth.

15. sodes : see note on *Serm.* i. 9. 41.

16. tolle : *take with you*, in distinction from *vescere*.   **benigne** : *sc. facis ; you're very kind.* A polite form of refusal.

17. non invisa : *i.e.* your children will be glad if you take them some as a gift.

18. tam teneor, *etc.: i.e.* I am as much obliged as if I took all I could carry.

20. prodigus et stultus : *i.e.* only a wasteful fool.

21. haec seges . . . tulit: *i.e.* such seed bears ingratitude. *Tulit* is the gnomic perfect ; see Introd. § 44. *d.*

22. ait esse paratus : a Greek construction for the regular *ait se esse paratum.*

23. quid distent aera lupinis : *i.e.* he knows the true value of things ; the seeds of the lupine (*lupinis*), a kind of vetch, were used as money (*aera*) on the stage ; *cf.* Plaut. *Poen.* 597, *aurumst profecto hic, spectatores, comicum : Macerato hoc pingues fiunt auro in barbaria boves.*

24. pro: *in proportion to.*   **merentis** : *my benefactor ; eius qui meret ut memet dignum praestem* (Kiessling).

25. quod si : *i.e.* if you require constant personal attendance on my part.   **reddes** : the future as an imperative ; so below in line 27 ; see Introd. § 44. *c.*

26. latus: *chest.*   **nigros . . . capillos**: *cf.* i. 20. 24. Horace's forehead had broadened from loss of hair. On a narrow forehead as a mark of beauty, *cf. Odes,* i. 33. 5, *insignem tenui fronte Lycorida.*

27. dulce loqui: *cf. Odes,* i. 22. 23, *Lalagen . . . dulce loquentem.* The infinitive is used as a noun, object of *redde ;* see Introd. § 46. *d.*

28. Cinarae : mentioned by Horace also in *Odes* iv. 1. 4 ; iv. 13. 21 ; *Epist.* i. 14. 33. He seems to have had a real attachment for her.

29. volpecula : the manuscript reading. Bentley's conjecture, *nitedula,* is brilliant but unnecessary. The diminutive is colloquial usage. See Introd. § 55. *e.*

30. cumeram : *cf. Serm.* i. 1. 53, and the note.   **pasta** : with middle force.

32. mustela : *the weasel,* 'mouse-catcher.'   **procul** : *near by,* modifying an implied participle.

33. cavum : *i.e.* the hole by which it had entered the bin.

34. compellor : *am called to account.*   **hac imagine** : *i.e.* by this simile.   **resigno** : *give back* ; used of paying back something given as a gift or loan ; *cf. Odes,* iii. 29. 54, *resigno quae dedit* (*Fortuna*).

35. somnum plebis : *cf. Odes,* iii. 1. 21, *Somnus agrestium Lenis virorum non humiles domos fastidit.* Horace means to say that he practises what he preaches, and does not praise frugal living when his own stomach is full of dainties.

36. Arabum : their wealth was proverbial. *Cf. Odes*, iii. **24. 1,**
intactis opulentior Thesauris Arabum.

37. verecundum: *sc. me* ; *my modesty.*

38. audisti : *you have been addressed as.* *Cf. Serm.* ii. **6, 20,**
Matutine pater seu Iane libentius audis ; and the idiom *bene audire a,*
e.g. Cic. *de Fin.* iii. 17. 57, *bene audire a parentibus.*   **verbo** : ablative of degree of difference.

39. reponere : equivalent to *resignare ; cf.* line 34 above.

40. Telemachus : when declining a gift of three horses from **Mene**
laus ; see *Odyss.* iv. 601 ff. Horace's words in lines 41–43 are a paraphrase of the passage.   **patientis** : a translation of the Greek πολύ-
τλας. **Ulixi** : genitive, instead of the regular but less common *Ulixis.*

43. tibi : with *apta* and *relinquam,* ἀπὸ κοινοῦ. See Introd. § 42.

44. regia Roma : as mistress of the world. *Cf. Odes*, iv. 14. 44,
tutela praesens Italiae dominaeque Romae.

45. vacuum : *quiet, peaceful.* *Cf.* ii. 2. 81, *vacuas Athenas.* The
meaning ' free from care ' (*cf. Odes*, i. 32. 1) is transferred from persons to places.   **imbelle** : *peaceful.*

46. Philippus : L. Marcius Philippus, consul in 91 B.C., distin-
guished for his energy (hence *strenuus*) and wit. He was an able
orator. *Cf.* Cic. *Brut.* 47. 173, *duobus summis, Crasso et Antonio,*
L. Philippus proximus accedebat, sed longo intervallo tamen proximus.
He is classed with Lucullus and Hortensius, as regards luxury, by
Varro, *R. R.* iii. 3. 10, *quis enim propter nobilitatem ignorat piscinas*
Philippi, Hortensi, Lucullorum?

47. officiis : see note on *officiosa sedulitas,* line 8 above.   **octa-**
vam circiter horam : *i.e.* at about two o'clock. The exact time
differed according to the season ; see note on *Serm.* i. 5. 23. Business
was usually over with the fifth hour; *cf.* Mart. iv. 8, *In quintam*
varios extendit Roma labores : Sexta quies lassis, septima finis erit.

48. Carinas : a fashionable quarter in Rome, where Quintus
Cicero, Pompey, and other distinguished Romans had their houses.
It was on the western slope of the Esquiline, about where the church
of S. Pietro in Vincoli now stands. It was not far from the Forum,
but the approach was steep and Philippus was old.

49. ut aiunt : *cf.* i. 6. 40.

50. adrasum : *who had been shaved.*   **umbra** : here in the
sense of *shop* or *booth.*

51. proprios : that service was usually done by the barber
leniter : *quietly.*

52. **non laeve**: *skilfully ;* litotes.   **iussa . . . accipiebat**: *i.e.* he was his regular *pedisequus*.

53. **abi, quaere**: a paratactic arrangement not uncommon with the imperative.   **unde domo**: *i.e.* what his home is ; *domo* is ablative of the place from which.

54. **quo patre quove patrono**: *i.e.* whether he is freeborn or not ; if not, he had no father according to law, and the name of his *patronus* is wanted.

55. **Volteium Menam** : the name shows that he was a freedman. When a slave became free, he adopted the gentile name of his former master, keeping his own name, which was usually of Greek origin, as a cognomen.

56. **praeconem**: *an auctioneer*, as is shown by line 65.   The word *praeco* has various meanings, as applied to trades.   **sine crimine**: *i.e.* with an unblemished record.

57. **properare**: this and the following infinitives depend on *notum*.   **loco**: *on occasion, i.e.* at the proper time.   Locative ablative with temporal force ; *cf. Odes*, iv. 12. 28, *dulce est desipere in loco*.   **cessare**: *i.e.* to take recreation ; *cf.* ii. 2. 183, *cur alter fratrum cessare . . . praeferat*.   **uti**: *sc. quaesitis*.

58. **parvis**: *humble*.   **lare certo**: *i.e.* a home of his own.

59. **ludis**: the theatrical performances and games of the circus. **post decisa negotia Campo**: *i.e.* athletic exercises in the Campus Martius after business hours.   *Cf. Odes*, i. 8. 4 ff.

60. **libet**: *sc. mihi*.

61. **non sane**: a strong negative.   **credere . . . mirari**: historical infinitives.

62. **benigne**: *cf.* line 16, and the note.

63. **neget**: subjunctive in an indignant question.   **improbus**: *the impudent wretch.*

64. **neglegit aut horret**: *i.e.* he has the assurance to scorn the invitation or he is afraid to accept.   **mane** : *the next morning*.

65. **tunicato**: the mark of the poorer people ; *cf.* Tac. *Dial.* 7, *vulgus imperitum et tunicatus hic populus*.   **popello**: the diminutive implies contempt.   **scruta**: second-hand articles; *cf.* Lucil. 1062, *d*, L., *Quidni? et scruta quidem ut vendat scrutarius laudat, Praefractam strigilem, soleam improbus dimidiatam*.

66. **occupat**: *i.e.* he greets him first.   *Cf. Serm.* i. 9. 6, *'num quid vis ?' occupo*.   For the etiquette in such a case, *cf.* Mart. iii. 95. 1 ff. : —

> *Numquam dices have, sed reddis, Naevole, semper,*
> *Quod prior et corvus dicere saepe solet.*
> *Cur hoc expectas a me, rogo, Naevole, dicas:*
> *Nam puto nec melior, Naevole, nec prior es.*

67. excusare: *pleads as his excuse*, for not accepting the invitation. Historical infinitive.   **mercennaria vincla**: *i.e.* the necessity for following his trade.

68. quod non . . . venisset: *i.e.* had not made an early morning call, to return thanks for the invitation. Subjunctive on account of the implied indirect discourse ; so *providisset*.

69. providisset: *had not seen* (and greeted) *him first*, as was due the superior from the inferior ; see note on line 66.   **sic . . . si**: *on condition that.*

70. ut libet: *if you please.*

71. i: *go ahead!*   **rem**: *cf.* i. 1. 65, and the note.

72. dicenda tacenda: *i.e.* he spoke freely and without restraint. *Cf.* Enn. *ap.* Gell. xii. 4. 4, *cui . . . cuncta malaque et bona dictu evomeret.*

74. occultum: *hidden*, by the bait ; *cf. opertum hamum*, i. 16. 51.

75. mane cliens: *i.e.* appearing regularly to make his morning call.   **certus conviva**: a regular guest at the *cena*. *Cf. lare certo*, line 58.

76. rura : accusative of the goal, like *rus;* the plural is not often so used.   **indictis . . . Latinis**: *sc. feriis.* They were held on a day which was not fixed, but was appointed and announced each year ; hence *indictis.* They were celebrated on the Alban Mount in honor of Jupiter Latiaris at the end of April or the beginning of May, and were the occasion of a *iustitium*, or suspension of legal business. Hence Philippus had nothing to detain him in the city.

77. impositus mannis: *i.e.* in a carriage drawn by *manni*, or Celtic horses.

78. videt: *i.e.* the change in Volteius.

79. dum . . . quaerit: may be translated by a present participle. **requiem**: recreation, *i.e. amusement.* The form *requietem* is sometimes used.

80. septem . . . sestertia: 7000 sesterces (about $350).

82. ultra quam satis est: *i.e.* with too many details.

83. nitido: referring to his dress and bodily condition ; *cf. Serm.* ii. 2. 128, *nituisti.* Here the contrast is between the elegant townsman and the rustic farmer.

84. crepat mera: *talks of nothing but. Sulcos* and *vineta* are accusative of the inner object; *cf. Serm.* i. 3. 13, *reges atque tetrarchas, Omnia magna loquens,* and see Introd. § 38. *b.*   **ulmos**: on which to grow vines, as is the custom still in Italy ; *cf.* i. 16. 3, *amicta vitibus ulmo.*

85. immoritur studiis : *i.e.* he nearly kills himself with work. *Studiis* is dative ; *cf.* Quint. ix. 3. 72, *qui se immoriturum legationi dixerat.*

86. morbo . . . capellae: goats are especially liable to sickness. *Cf.* Varro, *R. R.* ii. 3. 5, *capras sanas sanus nemo promittit; nunquam enim sine febri sunt.*

87. mentita seges: *sc. est,* and for the personification, *cf. Odes,* iii. 1. 30, *fundus mendax.*   **enectus**: the word chosen (it usually means killed by violence) seems to indicate that he worked his ox to death.

88. media de nocte: *i.e.* without waiting for daylight; *arripuit* further points to a sudden resolution.   **caballum**: *cf. Serm.* i. 6. 59, and the note.

90. scabrum intonsumque: *unkempt and unshaven,* a contrast to his appearance as described in line 50.

91. durus attentusque: *cf. Serm.* ii. 6. 82, *asper et attentus quaesitis.*

92. pol: *by Pollux,* an expression common in Plautus ; *cf.* ii. 2. 138.

93. ponere: for *imponere ; cf. Serm.* i. 3. 42, *isti Errori nomen virtus posuisset honestum* ; and see Introd. § 35. *b.*

94. quod : *wherefore.*   **genium** : your guardian spirit ; *cf.* Ter. *Andr.* 289, *Quod ego per hanc te dextram oro et genium tuom.*

96. qui semel, *etc.* : the moral of the story.

98. modulo ac pede : *foot-rule.*   **verum est** : *it is right ; cf. Serm.* ii. 3. 312.

EPISTLE VIII.

1. Celso . . . Albinovano: the cognomen precedes the gentile name, as in i. 2. 1.   **gaudere et bene rem gerere**: *i.e.* greeting and best wishes. *Cf.* Plaut. *Trin.* 772, *salutem ei nuntiet verbis patris: Illum bene gerere rem et valere et vivere.*

2. rogata : *sc. a me ; at my request.*   **comiti**: *a member of the staff; cf.* i. 3. 6, and the note.   **scribae** : a private secretary, not an official *scriba.*   **Neronis**: *i.e.* Tiberius ; *cf.* i. 3. 2, and the note.

3. quaeret : *sc. Albinovanus.*   **minantem** : *boasting that he* *would do*, a poetical use of the word; *cf. Serm.* ii. 3. 9, *Atqui vultus erat multa et praeclara minantis.*

4. haud quia: colloquial and post-Augustan for *non quo.*   **grando . . . vitis**: a common disaster; *cf. Odes*, iii. 1. 29, *verberatae grandine vineae.*

5. momorderit: used of cold in *Serm.* ii. 6. 45, *Matutina parum cautos iam frigora mordent.*

6. longinquis . . . agris: in summer cattle were sent to the plains of Lucania to pasture. *Cf. Epod.* 1. 27, *pecusve Calabris ante sidus fervidum Lucana mutat pascuis.*

10. cur . . . properent: a rhetorical question in the indirect form, equivalent in force to a causal clause.   **arcere**: for *prohibere; cf.* i. 1. 31, *Nodosa corpus nolis prohibere cheragra.*

11. sequar . . . credam: depending on *quia*, line 7.

12. ventosus: *fickle as the wind.* With the general thought, *cf. Serm.* ii. 7. 28, *Romae rus optas, absentem rusticus urbem Tollis ad astra levis.*   **Tibur**: according to Suetonius (*Vit. Horat.*), Horace had an estate at Tibur : *vixit plurimum in secessu ruris sui Sabini aut Tiburtini, domusque eius ostenditur circa Tiburti luculum. Cf.* also i. 6. 45, *sed vacuum placet Tibur.*

13. quo pacto rem gerat et se: *i.e.* how he succeeds and fares.

14. iuveni: *i.e.* Tiberius, who was at this time twenty-three years old.

15. gaudere: to express your pleasure, *i.e.* to congratulate him. **subinde**: *then; i.e.* afterward; not necessarily immediately, but when the occasion offered.

16. auriculis: *his dear ears;* note the force of the diminutive.

EPISTLE IX.

1. Septimius: doubtless the friend addressed in *Odes* ii. 6. **Claudi**: Tiberius Claudius Nero.   **nimirum**: *of course;* ironical. **unus**: *i.e.* better than any one else; *cf. Serm.* ii. 3. 24, *domos mercarier unus Cum lucro noram.*

3. scilicet: *forsooth*, emphasizing *prece cogit.*   **tradere**: *introduce; cf. Serm.* i. 9. 47, *hunc hominem velles si tradere.*

4. dignum: *as worthy.*   **honesta**: the neuter is more general than the masculine would have been, *everything honorable.*   **Neronis**: *of a Nero, i.e.* of a man of Nero's character.

5. fungi: *sc. me.*

6. valdius : *better; cf. Ars Poet.* 320, *fabula nullius veneris . . . valdius oblectat populum.* This shorter (colloquial) form is much less common than *validius.*

8. mea finxisse minora : *i.e.* pretended my influence was less than it really was.

9. commodus : *obliging.*

10. maioris . . . culpae : *i.e.* that suggested in lines 8–9.

11. frontis urbanae : *i.e.* the assurance of the man of the world, as contrasted with *pudor rusticus.*   **descendi** : *I have had recourse. Cf.* Virg. *Aen.* v. 782, *preces descendere in omnes.*   **praemia** : *privileges. Cf. Serm.* i. 5. 35, *insani praemia scribae.*

13. scribe tui gregis : *enroll in your company.* For this use of the genitive of the whole, *cf. Odes,* iii. 13. 13, *Fies nobilium tu quoque fontium. Grex* is here synonymous with the *cohors* of i. 3. 6 ; *Serm.* i. 7. 23. For a similar use of the word, *cf.* i. 4. 16, *Epicuri de grege porcum.*   **fortem bonumque** : a conventional phrase ; *cf. Serm.* ii. 5. 64, *forti Corano ; Odes,* iv. 4. 29, *Fortes creantur fortibus et bonis.*

EPISTLE X.

1. iubemus : the so-called 'plural of modesty.'

2. amatores : referring to Horace alone, but plural on account of *iubemus.*

3. dissimiles : the genuine plural, agreeing with *nos,* subject of *adnuimus.*   **cetera** : accusative of specification.   **gemelli** : diminutive of affection.

4. negat : parenthetical with a change of construction. As to their dislikes they agree perfectly, but in their likes there is the one difference, which is the subject of the Epistle.

5. noti : *well-acquainted.*

7. circumlita : the word is used because the moss is thought of as giving color to the stones, as paint would.

8. quid quaeris : *in short,* a common phrase in Cicero's letters, in force very much like *quid multa.*   **vivo** : *I really live,* contrasted with mere existing.   **regno** : *am king.*   **ista** : the demonstrative pronoun of the second person, looking forward to *effertis* and also with a touch of contempt.

9. rumore secundo : *with shouts of approval,* a common expression ; a sort of poetic formula. *Cf.* Enn. *Ann.* 260, *Mox auferre domos populi rumore secundo.*

10. liba recuso : the priest's slave was fed so much on sacrificial cakes, that he became tired of them. As usual Horace identifies himself with the object of his comparison.

11. pane : ablative with *egeo; cf. Odes*, i. 22. 2. Horace uses the genitive in *Serm.* i. 1. 59 ; i. 4. 118, *etc.* **iam** : modifying *potiore, which has come to be preferable.*

12. naturae convenienter : *in harmony with nature; cf. Serm.* i. 1. 50. *Naturae* illustrates the use of the dative with adverbs derived from verbs or adjectives which govern the dative ; *cf. cui non conveniet*, line 42 below.

13. ponendaeque domo : dative of the gerundive, expressing purpose. *Domui* is the more common form of the dative, but appears seldom in poetry.

15. plus tepeant hiemes : not that the winter was less severe in the country, but the country house was kept warm and comfortable. *Cf. Serm.* ii. 3. 10, *tepido villula tecto.*

16. leniat . . . leonis : *i.e.* where the summer is cooler. The sun enters the constellation of the Lion July 23d, and at about the same time the Dog-star rises. The Lion is represented as roused to fury by the heat of the sun.

18. divellat : *interrupts*, instead of the more usual *abrumpat.*

19. Libycis . . . lapillis : referring to mosaic pavements. The Numidian marble was a favorite one. The pavements were, of course, made of bits of marble of different colors and kinds, but Horace, as usual, takes a special example. The pavements were often sprinkled with perfumes, but even then did not smell so sweet as the grass.

20. vicis : *the streets, cf. Serm.* i. 9. 13, *cum ille . . . vicos, urbem laudaret.* **plumbum** : the lead pipes in which the water was carried from the reservoirs to the tanks (*lacus*).

21. trepidat : *cf. Odes,* ii. 3. 12, *quid obliquo laborat Lympha fugax trepidare cursum.*

22. nempe : *why!* **varias** : *i.e.* of variegated marbles, such as the Phrygian. **nutritur silva** : even in the city one tries to counterfeit the beauties of nature ; *cf. Odes,* iii. 10. 5, *nemus Inter pulchra satum tecta.*

23. longos prospicit agros : an example is the house of Maecenas ; *cf. Odes,* iii. 29. 5 ff.

24. expelles : paratactic use of the future, with conditional force. For the expression, *cf.* Catull. 105, *Mentula conatur Pipleum scandere montem : Musae furcillis praecipitem eiciunt.*

25. mala . . . fastidia: *perverse contempt.*

26. Sidonio . . . ostro: the genuine costly Phoenician purple, known variously as Sidonian and Tyrian. Dative with *contendere*. **contendere**: *to compare*, so as to distinguish the real from the imitation.

27. Aquinatem . . . fucum: a kind of lichen from which a purple dye was extracted. The business seems to have been carried on at Aquinum, but we have no other mention of it.

28. propiusve medullis: *closer to his heart; i.e.* which will more nearly affect his interests.

29. vero distinguere falsum: in moral questions, contrasted with the material one just mentioned; *vero* is ablative of separation.

30. plus nimio: *excessively*, *far too much*. *Cf. Odes*, i. 18. 15, *tollens vacuom plus nimio Gloria verticem.*

31. quatient: *cf. Odes*, iii. 3. 4, *mente quatit solida;* and with the general sentiment, *Odes*, ii. 10. **mirabere**: with the sentiment, *cf.* that of i. 6.

33. reges: *the rich*, as is clear from *paupere tecto. Cf. Serm.* i. 2. 86. **praecurrere**: as in a race; *cf. Serm.* i. 7. 8, *Barros ut equis praecurreret albis.*

34. cervus equum: according to Aristotle, *Rhet.* ii. 20, this fable was invented by Stesichorus, to warn the people of Himera against putting themselves in the power of Phalaris.

35. minor: *the loser, i.e.* the horse.

36. opes: *help*, strictly 'material resources'; *cf.* Cic. *ad Att.* ix. 16, *(Caesar) iam 'opes' meas, non ut superioribus litteris 'opem' expectat.*

39. veritus: *through fear of.* **metallis**: *riches*, lit. *mines*, which were one of the principal sources of wealth to the Romans.

40. improbus: *i.e.* as he richly deserves.

41. aeternum: *for ever;* accusative of the inner object with *serviet. Cf.* Virg. *Aen.* vi. 617, *sedet aeternumque sedebit Infelix Theseus.* **nesciet**: future, looking forward to the time of *serviet*.

42. cui non conveniet, *etc.*: the sentence is condensed, the thought being: a man whose property is not suited to his condition in life will be like a man with a badly fitting shoe, which will trip him up if it is too large, and gall him if it is too tight. **olim**: *cf. Serm.* i. 1. 25, and the note.

44. laetus: *if you are contented and happy;* a condensed expression for *si laetus sorte tua vives, vives sapienter.*

45. nec dimittes: *and do not let me go;* the future in a mild command.   **incastigatum** : a word coined by Horace.

46. cessare : *i.e.* to take a proper amount of rest and recreation. *Cf.* i. 7. 57.

47. imperat aut servit: *is either master or slave*; *cf.* Sen. *de Vita Beat.* 26. 1. *divitiae enim apud sapientem virum in servitute sunt, apud stultum in imperio.*

48. digna: *i.e.* which ought by right.   **sequi funem** : the metaphor is from leading an animal ; *cf. Serm.* ii. 7. 20, *Qui iam contento iam laxo fune laborat. Tortum* seems to mean strong, well twisted, and so is not altogether colorless.

49. dictabam : the epistolary imperfect ; as Horace began his letter somewhat after the conventional manner, so he closes.   **putre** : *crumbling.*   **Vacunae** : a Sabine goddess, whose name, of uncertain meaning, Horace connects, seriously or humorously, with *vaco vacuus, etc.*

50. non simul esses: *that you were not with me*, a colloquial expression ; *cf.* Cic. *ad Att.* vi. 2. 8, *scribis morderi te interdum, quod non simul sis.* The subjunctive represents Horace's thought when he wrote the letter, viewed from the time when the letter was received.

EPISTLE XI.

1. quid tibi visa: *sc. est, how did you like ?* For the neuter *quid, cf. Serm.* i. 6. 55, *dixere quid essem.*   **Bullati**: otherwise unknown.   **nota** : *famous;* Lesbos was especially noted as the home of Alcaeus and Sappho.

2. concinna : *trim*, of the elegance of the buildings and the regularity of the city.   **regia** : *capital, royal abode.*

3. maiora minorave fama : *i.e.* did they come up to your expectations ?

4. cunctane . . . sordent ? *i.e.* are they all inferior ?   **prae** : *in comparison with.*

5. venit in votum : *i.e.* would you wish to live in. *Cf. Serm.* ii. 6. 1, *hoc erat in votis.*

6. Lebedum : a small town on the coast between Smyrna and Colophon. The point is, do you find any place, however insignificant, attractive after the discomforts of travel ?   **odio maris atque viarum** : *cf. Odes*, ii. 6. 7, *Sit modus lasso maris et viarum.*

7. Gabiis . . . Fidenis: these two towns, important places in

early times, had, with Ulubrae (line 30 below), become typical examples of deserted cities. *Cf.* Juv. x. 99 ff., *Huius, qui trahitur, praetextam*
sumere mavis, An Fidenarum Gabiorumque esse potestas Et de men-
sura ius dicere, vasa minora Frangere pannosus vacuis aedilis Ulubris.

8. vellem: *I should be glad; cf. Serm.* i. 1. 55.

9. et: note the hyperbaton.

10. Neptunum . . . spectare: *cf.* Lucr. ii. 1 f. *Suave, mari magno*
turbantibus aequora ventis, E terra magnum alterius spectare laborem.

11. Capua Romam: by the Appian Way; *cf. Serm.* i. 5. 6.

12. in caupona vivere: although an inn may be a delightful
haven of rest under the circumstances, he would not wish to spend his
whole life in one.

13. frigus collegit: *has been thoroughly chilled.* **furnos**: *cf.*
Serm. i. 4. 37, and the note. A man who was cold might well take
refuge in a public bakery or in a bath, but would not be contented to
remain there forever.

14. plene: *to the full.*

16. trans Aegaeum . . . vendas: *i.e.* the merchant does not
sell his ship and remain on the other side of the Aegean because he
has had a stormy passage.

17. incolumi: *a healthy man;* dative governed by *facit; cf. Serm.*
i. 1. 63. **Rhodos et Mytilene**: *cf. Odes,* i. 7. 1. **facit quod**:
are what; lit. *do to him what.*

18. paenula: a rough heavy *cloak,* worn in cold or rainy weather.
The Eastern resorts are as little suited to a man in sound health as
such a cloak would be in the heat of summer. **campestre**: *sc.*
velamentum, a leather apron worn when exercising in the Campus;
cf. Aug. *Civ. Dei,* xiv. 17, *campestria Latinum verbum est, sed ex eo*
dictum, quod iuvenes, qui exercebantur in Campo, pudenda operiebant.
This, Horace says, would be an inappropriate dress in cold weather.

19. Tiberis: *i.e.* swimming in the Tiber, a favorite form of exercise; *cf. Serm.* ii. 1. 8. **caminus**: whence our word 'chimney,' a
kind of stove; *cf. Serm.* i. 5. 81.

20. dum licet, *etc.*: *while one may and while fortune smiles; i.e.*
as long as one is *incolumis* (*cf.* line 17).

21. absens: *i.e.* from a distance. Note the emphatic position of
this word and of *Romae.*

23. in annum: *cf.* i. 2. 39, *differs curandi tempus in annum ?*

24. vixisse . . . dicas: *cf. vivo,* i. 10. 8, and the note.

26. arbiter: *which commands,* as we speak of a place commanding a fine view; with the general sense, *cf. Odes*, i. 3. 15, *arbiter Hadriae*.

.28. strenua inertia: oxymoron; *cf.* Plin. *Epist.* ix. 6. 4, *otiosissimae occupationes*.   **navibus atque quadrigis**: *i.e.* by travel on land and sea. Perhaps, as Kiessling suggests, there is in *quadrigis* a reference to the metaphor in *Serm.* i. 1. 112.

29. hic: *at home.*

30. Ulubris: an obscure village in the Pomptine Marshes. See note on *Gabiis . . . Fidenis*, line 7.

EPISTLE XII.

2. recte frueris: *i.e.* if you know how to enjoy them to the full. *Cf.* i. 6. 29, *recte vivere.*   **non est ut**: *it is not possible that; cf. Odes*, iii. 1. 9. *est, ut viro vir latius ordinet Arbusta sulcis.*

3. ab Iove: the only case of *ab* before a consonant in the *Serm.* and *Epist.*   **tolle**: *away with. Cf. Odes*, ii. 5. 9, *tolle cupidem immitis uvae.*

7. in medio positorum: *what is at hand;* the genitive is governed by *abstemius;* a Greek construction; see Introd. § 40. *b.*

8. urtica: *nettle;* used as food.   **ut**: *though.*

9. liquidus Fortunae rivus: the Pactolus, which had become proverbial. *Cf. Epod.* 15. 19, *Sis pecore et multa dives tellure licebit Tibique Pactolus fluat.*

10. vel quia: *i.e.* you will live economically from a natural love of it, or because you think it right.   **nescit** = *nequit.*

12. Democriti: Democritus of Abdera, a contemporary of Socrates, called 'the laughing philosopher.' Cicero says of him (*de Fin.* v. 29. 87), *certe ut quam minime a cogitationibus abduceretur, patrimonium neglexit, agros deseruit incultos.*

13. peregre est: *is abroad.*

14. inter: *in the midst of; cf.* i. 4. 12, *Inter spem curamque, timores inter et iras.*   **scabiem**: *cf.* Cic. *de Leg.* i. 17. 47, *quae natura bona sunt, quia dulcedine hac et scabie carent, non cernunt satis.*

15. nil parvum sapias: *i.e.* you follow no petty philosophy; *parvum* is accusative of the inner object.   **adhuc**: so far.   **sublimia**: celestial themes, such as are mentioned below.

16. compescant: *control; cf. Odes*, i. 16. 22, *compesce mentem.* **temperet**: *cf. Odes*, i. 12. 15, *Qui mare ac terras variisque mundum Temperat horis.*

17. stellae : *the planets.*   **sponte sua iussaene** : *i.e.* whether they are endowed with intelligence, and control themselves, or are ruled by mechanical laws.

18. quid premat, *etc.* : of the phases of the moon ; *obscurum* is used proleptically with *premat, buries in darkness* ; *cf.* Virg. *Aen.* iv. 80, *post ubi digressi, lumenque obscura vicissim Luna premit.*

19. quid velit et possit : *i.e.* its meaning and power.   **concordia discors** : *the discordant harmony,* an oxymoron. Manilius, i. 141, speaks of it as *discordia concors.*

20. Empedocles : a native of Agrigentum, who lived about 450 B.C. He believed that all things had their origin and their end in the influence of love and hate on the four elements, — earth, air, water, and fire.   **Stertinium acumen** : *cf. virtus Scipiadae, Serm.* ii. i. 72, and the note. Stertinius is mentioned as a type of the Stoics ; *cf. Serm.* ii. 3. 33 and 296.

21. piscis seu porrum : *i.e.* costly or simple fare ; *cf. Serm.* ii. 2. 120, *piscibus urbe petitis.*   **trucidas** : with reference to the Pythagorean belief that animals and some vegetables contained the souls of human beings ; *cf. Serm.* ii. 6. 64, *faba Pythagorae cognata.*

22. utere : *i.e.* make friends with.   **Pompeio Grospho** : *cf. Odes,* ii. 16.   **ultro** : *freely,* more lit. *without being asked.*

23. verum : *right ; cf.* i. 7. 98.

24. amicorum : appositional genitive. The idea seems to be that one can secure friends at a small outlay when those who are to be won by favors are good men ; for their desires and demands will be small.

25. ignores . . . loco res : note the rhyme (probably accidental).

26. Cantaber : the Cantabrians were conquered by Agrippa in 19 B.C.

27. Armenius : Armenia submitted to Tiberius without resistance, after the king Artaxias had been murdered by his subjects. **Phraates** : he restored to the Romans the standards which had been taken from Crassus, and sought their friendship in 20 B.C.

28. genibus minor : *i.e.* humbled and on his knees, as he is represented in coins commemorative of the event.

EPISTLE XIII.

1. saepe diuque : *repeatedly and at length.*

2. reddes : future with imperative force.   **signata** : *i.e.* packed in a *scrinium* (*cf. Serm.* i. 1. 120) and sealed.   **Vini** : otherwise unknown.

3. denique : *finally;* *i.e.* even if everything else is favorable, it is to be given only if Augustus asks for it.

4. studio nostri : *through your interest in me.*   **pecces** : probably used in the same sense as in i. 1. 9.   **odium . . . importes** *i.e.* make the gift unwelcome.

5. sedulus : *cf. Serm.* i. 5. 71.   **opera vehemente** : *i.e.* by too great enthusiasm.

6. uret : *galls.*

7. quo perferre iuberis : *your destination;* sc. *ibi* modifying *impingas.*

9. vertas in risum : *i.e.* are laughed at as rightly named. **fabula** : *the talk of the town; cf. Epod.* 11. 8, *heu me, per Urbem . . . fabula quanta fui.*

10. uteris : the future has the force of an imperative.   **lamas** : *bogs;* from the stem *lac-* (of *lacus*) + -*ma.*

11. victor propositi : *i.e.* having accomplished your purpose.

12. sic : looks forward to the following purpose clauses introduced by *ne.*

14. Pyrria : *Pyrria nomen est ancillae in quadam fabula Titinii, quae furata lanae glomos ita gestavit ut deprehensa sit,* Comm. Cruq.

15. tribulis : a member of the same tribe as his host, and so invited for political reasons. The reference is to a humble guest who comes on foot, carrying his sandals and cap under his arm, since he had neither slave nor litter (*lectica*).

16. volgo : *i.e.* to anybody and everybody.

17. quae possint : a clause of characteristic; he is not to boast of the excellence of the poems which he is carrying.

18. oratus : *i.e.* although many people earnestly beg you to stop and tell them your errand.   **nitere porro** : *push on.*

19. cave : with short final *e,* as was usual in comedy and doubtless in the language of every day.   **mandataque frangas** : *and break what has been entrusted to you,* as if he were a beast of burden and the poems were fragile ware.

EPISTLE XIV.

1. vilice : the steward or overseer of the slaves on a country estate. His duties and qualifications are described at length by Cato, *de Agr.* 5.   **silvarum** : *cf. Serm.* ii. 6. 3, *paulum silvae super his foret.*   **mihi me reddentis** : *i.e.* that makes me myself again.

2. habitatum : with concessive force, *though it is occupied by* **focis** : *households ;* lit. *hearths.*

3. Variam : a small town on the Anio, eight miles from Tibur ; it was the nearest market town.   **patres** : *i.e. patres familias,* who went to Varia to market, and for the local political meetings.

4. certemus : *let us decide,* as of a wager.   **spinas** : *thorns,* used metaphorically of moral failings.

5. res : *his property, i.e.* the estate.

6. Lamiae : subjective genitive. For the name, see *Odes,* iii. 17. **moratur** : for the indicative with *quamvis,* see Introd. § 45. *b.*

7. fratrem . . . de fratre : the repetition emphasizes the persistence of the laments ; *cf. Odes,* i. 13. 1, *cum tu, Lydia, Telephi . . . Telephi.*

8. insolabiliter : a word coined by Horace. The spondaic rhythm suits the thought.   **istuc** : *to where you are, i.e.* to his country residence.

9. amat : *longs to; cf. Odes,* iii. 9. 24, *tecum vivere amem.* **spatiis** : *the course ;* a metaphor from the races.

10. viventem : general ; *he who lives.*

11. *Cf. Serm.* i. 1. 1 ff.

12. causatur : *blames ;* lit. gives as the cause of his discontent.

13. qui se non effugit : *cf.* i. 11. 27, *Caelum non animum mutant qui trans mare currunt.*

14. mediastinus : *when you were a drudge ;* the term is used of a slave who had no fixed duties, but was liable to be called on to do any kind of work ; *i.e.* he was *in medio.*   **tacita prece** : *i.e.* as something too good to be prayed for openly.

15. ludos et balnea : the chief attractions of the city for the common people.

17. quandocumque : *i.e.* only when it is absolutely necessary.

18. eo : *in that respect.*   **disconvenit** : *cf.* i. 1. 99, *vitae disconvenit toto ordine,* and the note.

19. tesqua : according to the Comm. Cruq., the word is Sabine. Except for its use here and in Lucan vi. 41, it is archaic.

20. mecum qui sentit : *i.e.* I and people like me.

21. uncta : *greasy.*   **popina** : a word of Sabine origin ; the corresponding Latin form would be *coquina.*

23. angulus iste : the contemptuous term applied by the *vilicus* to Horace's estate.   **piper et tus** : the products of Arabia and India, which of course could not be grown at all in Italy.   **ocius** : *rather than,* lit. *sooner than.*

24. **vicina . . . taberna** : Horace's villa was three or four miles from the nearest road.

25. **meretrix tibicina** : like the *copa* of Virgil's poem of that name.

26. **strepitum** : *cf. Odes*, iv. 3. 17, *testudinis aureae dulcem strepitum.* **terrae gravis** : *i.e.* treading heavily on the earth. *Cf. Odes* iii. 18. 15, *Gaudet invisam pepulisse fossor Ter pede terram.* **et tamen urges** : and yet, though you have no amusements, you have to struggle with the neglected fields ; *cf.* Tibull. i. 9. 8, *Et durum terrae rusticus urguet opus.*

28. **strictis frondibus** : used for fodder. *Cf.* Cato, *de Agr.* 30, *bubus frondem ulmeam, populneam, querneam, ficulneam, usque dum habebis, dato.*

29. **rivus** : the Digentia.

30. **multa mole** : *with many a dam.*

31. **quid . . . dividat** : *i.e.* what makes the difference between us.

32. **tenues** : *fine*, of fine material. **nitidi** : *cf. Odes*, ii. 7. 7, *coronatus nitentes Malobathro Syrio capillos.*

33. **immunem** : *though with empty hands.* **Cinarae** : see note on i. 7. 28.

34. **bibulum** : governed by *scis*. **liquidi** : *clear.* **media de luce** : *cf. Serm.* ii. 8. 3, *de medio potare die.*

35. **cena brevis** : *i.e.* a dinner of few courses begun at the usual time instead of *media de luce*. **somnus in herba** : instead of the *comissatio*, or symposium.

36. **nec lusisse . . . sed non incidere** : *i.e.* he is not ashamed of having enjoyed the pleasures of youth, but he would be ashamed not to be able to cut them short at the proper time.

38. **limat** : lit. *files*, and so like *mordet* in *Odes*, iv. 3. 16. *Oculo . . . limat* makes a play on the expression *limis oculis, Serm.* ii. 5. 53, where see note.

39. **rident** : that is, they laugh good-naturedly at Horace's attempts at farm work.

40. **diaria** : *daily rations*, instead of the abundance of the country.

41. **horum** : *i.e. servorum urbanorum.*

42. **calo** : *the stable boy*, who comes with Horace from the city, where his duties are doubtless those of a *mediastinus* (*cf.* line 14).

43. **piger** : to be taken with *bos*, although it makes an awkward caesura ; *because of his laziness*, supposing the horse to have an easier life.

44. censebo : *I should advise*, approaching the potential subjunctive in its force.   **exerceat** : *should practice;* jussive subjunctive
dependent on *censebo*.

EPISTLE XV.

1. Veliae : a town in Lucania, twenty-four miles south of Paestum,
noted for its excellent climate.   **caelum** : *the weather*.   **Vala** :
C. Numonius Vala, a friend of Horace's, living in the vicinity of Velia
and Salernum.   The name occurs in inscriptions of that region.
Salernum : a town in Campania, twenty-three miles north of Paestum,
still noted for its beauty.

2. quorum hominum : *i.e.* what sort of people there are there,
whether they are friendly and hospitable.   A genitive of quality.
qualis via : *what sort of road there is*.   The *via Popillia* led from
Capua to Salernum, but then turned off toward Rhegium, so that there
was no regular Roman road leading to Velia.   **Baias** : see note on
i. 1. 83.

3. Musa Antonius : a freedman and physician of Augustus, who
had cured him of a serious illness, in 23 B.C., by the cold water treatment.   See Suet. *Aug.* 81, *quia calida fomenta non proderant, frigidis
curari coactus auctore Antonio Musa*.   On the inversion of the names,
see *Superbus, Serm.* i. 6. 12, and the note.   **supervacuas** : *useless*,
because he prescribed the cold water treatment, and Baiae was noted
for its hot baths.   **illis . . . invisum** : *i.e.* Horace is unpopular at
Baiae, because he does not use the local baths.

4. cum : *now that*.

5. murteta : *myrtle groves* near Baiae, in which there were hot
baths, mentioned by Celsus, ii. 17 and iii. 2.

6. dicta : *which are said to*.   **cessantem** : lingering, *i.e.*
'chronic.'

7. sulpura : *i.e.* sulphur baths.   **vicus gemit** : *the town (i.e.*
Baiae) *laments*.

8. supponere fontibus : as in a shower bath.

9. Clusinis : at Clusium in Etruria.   The cold baths there are not
elsewhere mentioned.   **Gabios** : *cf.* Juv. vii. 3, *cum celebres notique poetae Balneolum Gabiis, Romae conducere furnos Temptarent*.

10. deversoria nota : *sc. equo ; the familiar inns*, where the road
turned off toward Baiae.

12. laeva stomachosus habena : *with an angry pull on the left* *rein*, as the horse tries to turn off to the right: *habena* is ablative of instrument, 'showing his anger with the left rein.'

13. equi . . . in ore: *i.e.* the horse is guided by the bit and not by words.

14. Horace renews the questions which he interrupted by the digression beginning with line 2, and asks about the supply of bread and water.

15. collectos: *i.e.* in cisterns.

16. iugis aquae: *running water; cf. Serm.* ii. 6. 2.   **nihil moror**: *I don't care at all for. Cf.* Plaut. *Trin.* 297, *Nil ego istos moror faeceos mores.*

17. quidvis: *anything*, not referring to wine alone.   **perferre**: *put up with.*

18. ad mare cum veni: *i.e.* when I mingle with the fashionable world at a seaside resort.

19. cum spe divite: *cf.* i. 5. 17, *(ebrietas) spes iubet esse ratas.*

21. Lucanae: with reference to Velia.   **iuvenem**: *i.e.* as if I were a young man.

The questions are renewed after another digression, which artistically breaks the monotony of a series of inquiries.

22. lepores: highly esteemed as food; *cf.* Mart. xiii. 92, *Inter quadrupedes mattea prima lepus.*   **apros**: the Lucanian boars were famous. *Cf. Serm.* ii. 8. 6.

23. echinos: *sea-urchins. Cf. Serm.* ii. 4. 33, *Miseno oriuntur echini.* The sea-urchin is a favorite article of food with the Greeks of to-day.

24. Phaeax: *i.e.* 'well groomed' like a Phaeacian; *cf.* i. 2. 28, *Alcinoique In cute curanda plus aequo operata iuventus.*

25. accredere: the preposition seems to have intensive force, *fully believe.*

26. Maenius: *cf. Serm.* i. 3. 21.

27. fortiter: with sarcastic force.   **urbanus**: *cf.* i. 9. 11, *frontis urbanae praemia; urbanus* is to be taken with *scurra; cf.* Plaut. *Most.* 15, *Tu urbanus vero scurra, deliciae popli, Rus mihi tu obiectas ?*

28. vagus: explained by the following relative clause. He was not a *certus conviva* (*cf.* i. 7. 75) at some great man's house.   **praesepe**: *cf.* Plaut. *Curc.* 227, *Tormento non retineri potuit ferreo, Quin reciperet se huc esum ad praesepem suam.*

29. impransus: *on an empty stomach*, the *prandium* being the first substantial meal of the day; *cf. Serm.* ii. 2. 7, *impransi mecum disquirite.*

civem . . . hoste: a proverbial expression. *Cf.* Plaut. *Trin.* 102, *Hostisne an civis comedis parvi pendere.*

30. fingere saevus: a common use of the infinitive in Horace. See Introd. § 46. *a.*

31. pernicies et tempestas: for a similar comparison, *cf.* Plaut. *Capt.* 911, *Clades calamitasque intemperies modo in nostram advenit domum.*   **barathrum**: as we might say, *bottomless pit.*

32. quicquid quaesierat: *i.e.* all his earnings.

33. nequitiae: *his wicked wit,* which called forth applause or inspired fear.   **nil . . . abstulerat**: *i.e.* when he had failed to get dainties or the means of purchasing them, he ate coarse food with avidity.

34. patinas: *whole platefuls.* Accusative object of *cenabat;* see Introd. § 38. *a.*   **omasi**: *tripe,* a coarse food.

35. agninae: a substantive with ellipsis of *carnis. Cf.* Plaut. *Aul.* 373, *Capt.* 849.   **tribus ursis**: so with us the bear is proverbial for his appetite ; *cf.* the expression, ' hungry as a bear.' **quod satis esset** : *enough for. Quod* refers loosely to *patinas,* without taking its gender and number. *Esset* is subjunctive in a clause of characteristic.

36. scilicet ut: *so as to be able to say.*   **lamna**: the syncopated form is perhaps colloquial ; see note on *caldior,* i. 3. 53. *Cf. Odes* ii. 2. 5, *inimice lamnae.*

37. correctus Bestius: *i.e.* reformed to the standard of Bestius ; more lit., ' corrected so as to become a Bestius.' Bestius is referred to by Persius, vi. 37, *Bestius urguet doctores Graios.* He is perhaps taken, like Maenius, from Lucilius ; at any rate, it is obvious that he criticised the luxurious living of his time to such an extent as to become proverbial.

38. quicquid . . . praedae maioris: *i.e.* whenever he had made a richer haul than usual.

39. verterat in fumum et cinerem: *i.e.* after he had lost his property ; a common metaphor. Note the pluperfect with *ubi,* to represent the action as completed in the past.

41. turdo: a luxury ; *cf. Serm.* ii. 2. 74 ; ii. 5. 10.   **volva**: the sow's *matrix,* considered a great delicacy by the Romans.

42. nimirum: *you see.*   **hic**: *that sort of a man. Cf.* i. 6. 40, *ne fueris hic tu.*

43. satis . . . fortis: *i.e.* in putting up with ordinary living.

44. unctius: *richer. Cf.* Mart. v. 44. 7, *unctior cena.*

46. fundata: *solidly invested. Cf.* Cic. *Rab. Post.* i. 1. 1, *quod*

fortunas suas, fundatas praesertim atque optime constitutas, potestati
regiae libidinique commiserat.

EPISTLE XVI.

1. ne perconteris: that you may not ask, depending on *scribetur*
in line 4.　　**Quincti**: who he was, is unknown.　Kiessling points out
that the epithet *optimus* is used sparingly by Horace.　He applies it
to his father (*Serm.* i. 4. 105), to Maecenas (*Serm.* 1. 5. 27), to Virgil
(*Serm.* i. 6. 54), and to Aristius Fuscus (*Serm.* i. 10. 82), while he
calls Trebatius *pater optime* (*Serm.* ii. 1. 12).　Hence Quinctius must
have stood high in his list of friends.

2. arvo: land ploughed for grain, and hence equivalent here to
grain.

3. pratis: *pasture lands*, hence referring to cattle ; *cf. arvo*, line 2
above.

4. forma: *aspect*, as determined by the kind of crops.　　**situs**:
its situation.　　**loquaciter**: *i.e.* in full detail, implying that the subject is one on which Horace loves to talk.

5. continui montes: *sc. sint;* it would be an uninterrupted
mass of hilly ground but for the valley.　　**ni dissocientur**: *if they*
(the mountains) *were not divided.*　A condition contrary to fact with
the present subjunctive ; an archaic usage.

6. sed ut: *i.e.* the valley is shaded, except that the rising sun
shines on its right slope and the setting sun on its left.

8. quid si: *i.e.* what would you say to the following in addition to
what I have already told you ?

10. fruge : *i.e. glandibus.*

11. Tarentum : famous for its beauty and admired by Horace ;
cf. Odes, ii. 6. 13 f.

12. fons : possibly the *fons Bandusiae* of *Odes*, iii. 13.　　**rivo** :
the Digentia ; *cf.* i. 14. 29 f.　　**idoneus** : *i.e.* large enough to.

13. Hebrus : proverbially cold ; *cf.* i. 3. 3, and the note.　　**ambiat** :
flows through in winding course ; cf. Ars Poet. 17, *properantis aquae*
per amoenos ambitus agros.

14. capiti . . . alvo : *cf.* i. 15. 8.

15. dulces . . . amoenae : respectively subjective and objective,
dear and *charming.*

16. incolumem : *in good health; cf.* i. 11. 17.　　**Septembribus**
horis : the unhealthful season in the city ; *cf.* i. 7. 5, and the note.

17. quod audis : *what you are said to be;* cf. i. 7. 38, and the note.

18. iactamus . . . omnis Roma : *all of us Romans have been extolling.* For the construction, cf. *Odes,* iv. 2. 50, *Non semel dicemus, io Triumphe, Civitas omnis;* i. 10. 1.

19. vereor, *etc. : i.e.* I fear that you may care more for reputation than for real worth.

20. alium sapiente : the ablative of comparison with *alius;* cf. ii. 1. 240, *alius Lysippo.*

22. febrem : *the quartan ague* (*quartana,* Serm. ii. 3. 290), which was intermittent, and, according to Celsus, iii. 3, *incipiunt fere ab horrore . . . ubi totum corpus intremit.* **sub tempus edendi** : *at meal time;* for the force of *sub,* cf. *Serm.* i. 1. 10.

23. unctis : since the ancients ate for the most part with their fingers, this epithet has not the grotesque effect that it would have if translated literally into English. As Doederlein says, it is practically the same as ' with knife and fork in hand.'

24. stultorum incurata : note the emphatic position of both words. **pudor malus** : *false shame;* cf. ii. 3. 39.

25. tibi : dative of the apparent agent with *pugnata.*

26. vacuas : *attentive,* to the flattery. *Cf.* Lucr. i. 50, *vacuas auris animumque . . . adhibe veram ad rationem.*

27-29. According to the Comm. Cruq., these lines are from a panegyric of Augustus by L. Varius.

28. servet in ambiguo : *i.e.* may he not reveal.

30. pateris : *allow yourself.*

31. respondesne : *-ne* here apparently has the force of *nonne;* cf. *Epod.* 4. 7, *videsne . . . ut ora vertat huc et huc euntium Liberrima indignatio?* **tuo nomine** : *i.e.* accepting the compliment. **nempe** : the reply of Quinctius to Horace's insinuation, ' *Why, of course.*'

32. ac tu : *and so do you,* as well as I.

33. qui : *i.e. populus;* cf. line 21.

34. detulerit fascis indigno : cf. *Serm.* i. 6. 15, *populo, qui stultus honores Saepe dat indignis.*

35. tristis recedo : cf. *Lucr.* iii. 997, *semper victus tristisque recedit.*

36. idem : *i.e. populus.* **furem** : *sc. me esse.*

37. laqueo . . . paternum : as a type of the height of wickedness; cf. *Odes,* ii. 13. 4, *Illum et parentis crediderim sui Fregisse cervicem.*

38. colores : *i.e.* from pale to red and back again ; hence the plural.

40. mendosum : the opposite of *emendatus* in line 30. **medi-candum** : *i.e.* in a moral sense.

41. qui . . . servat : *i.e.* the law-abiding citizen.

42. quo . . . iudice : *i.e.* as one of the *iudices selecti;* see *Serm.* i. 4. 123, and the note. **secantur** : *are decided;* lit. ' cut off.' An unusual meaning of the word ; *cf. Serm.* i. 10. 15.

43. sponsore : *surety.* **tenentur** : with *res* means *secured,* with *causae, won;* zeugma.

44. sed videt : his private life does not correspond with his repu-tation as a public man.

45. introrsum turpem . . . decora : see *Serm.* ii. 1. 64, and the note.

46. Mere negative virtue amounts to little.

47. loris non ureris : *cf. Epod.* 4. 3, *Hibericis peruste funibus latus; Serm.* ii. 7. 58, *uri virgis.*

48. cruce : crucifixion was a common punishment for slaves.

49. Sabellus : apparently for the first person, *a plain, honest Sabine like myself;* so called on account of his estate in the Sabine country.

50. cautus enim metuit . . . lupus : yet he cannot be called *bonus et frugi.*

51. miluus : perhaps a kind of flying fish, ' kite-fish' ; Plin. *N. H.* ix. 82, *volat hirundo, sane perquam similis volucri hirundini, item miluus.* Or perhaps, as the connection with *accipiter* suggests, the bird itself. Birds are sometimes caught with hook and line.

52. oderunt : contrasted with an implied *metuunt.* Note the em-phatic position of *oderunt* and *virtutis amore; it is from love of virtue that the good cannot bear to do wrong.*

53. tu : emphatic ; contrasted with *boni.* **formidine poenae** : contrasted with *virtutis amore.*

54. sit : jussive subjunctive with conditional force.

55. unum : sc. *modium.*

56. Iamnum . . . non facinus : *i.e.* in his master's eyes, though morally it is the same thing. **pacto . . . isto** : *in that case, i.e.* according to your standard. Note the force of *isto.*

57. vir bonus : such a one as is described in lines 41 f.

59. clare, clare : with the order and repetition, *cf.* line 14 above. He prays loudly, but mutters his real wishes.

60. metuens audiri : for the construction, *cf.* i. 7. 4. **Laverna** : a goddess of thieves.

61. iusto sanctoque : attracted to the case of *mihi*, understood.
videri : emphatic, *to* SEEM.

63. qui : *how?*

64. in triviis fixum : probably simply lying on the ground in the dust and mud.

66. mihi : *in my eyes;* dative of the person judging. B. 188. 2. *b.*

67. perdidit arma : the height of disgrace was to be a ῥιψάσπις, as Horace humorously describes himself as having been at Philippi ; *cf. Odes*, ii. 7. 10.

69. possis : the indefinite second person, addressed to people in general.   **captivum** : *i.e.* such a man is really a slave, and may have his uses.

70. durus : *cf.* i. 7. 91, *durus, Voltei, nimis attentusque videris Esse mihi.* The man is really working for his own interests, but he benefits the public more than he does himself.

72. annonae prosit : *i.e.* bring down the price of grain, — as we say, ' relieve the market,' — by importing large quantities.   **penus** : *cf.* Cic. *Nat. Deor.* ii. 27. 68, *est enim omne quo vescuntur homines penus.*

73. Pentheu : a paraphrase of Euripides, *Bacchae*, 492–498, where Dionysus, disguised as a Lydian priest, defies Pentheus, king of Thebes, who had attempted to prevent the introduction of the Bacchic worship.

79. ultima linea : *i.e.* the line which marks the finish of the race.

EPISTLE XVII.

1. consulis : on *quamvis* with the indicative, see Introd. § 45. *b.*

2. quo tandem pacto : *how, pray;* transferred to the indirect form.   **maioribus** : *great men. Cf. Serm.* ii. 1. 61, *maiorum amicus.*   **uti** : *to treat, i.e.* in one's association with them.

3. docendus adhuc : *i.e.* who has not himself learned the full lesson.   **amiculus** : *a humble friend*, the force of the diminutive.

4. caecus iter monstrare : a proverbial saying, somewhat like ours of the blind leading the blind.

5. et nos : *even I;* so-called ' plural of modesty.'   **fecisse** : perfect infinitive emphasizing the accomplishment of the act. *Cf.* i. 18. 59 ; *Serm.* i. 2. 28 ; ii. 3. 187 ; *Ars Poet.* 98 ; and see Introd. § 44. *f.*

6. primam in horam : while the attendant on the great would have to be up before sunrise, to be on time with his morning call. *Cf.* Mart. iv. 8. 1, *Prima salutantes atque altera conterit hora.*

7. pulvis . . . strepitus . . . caupona : on journeys which the client sometimes made with his patron ; *cf. Serm.* ii. 6. 42.

8. Ferentinum : probably a small village near the *Aqua* Ferentina, the outlet of the Lacus Nemorensis. It is mentioned as a type of an obscure town; *cf.* i. 11. 8, *Gabiis desertior atque Fidenis vicus,* and the note.   **iubebo** : for the tense, see note on *censebo,* i. 14. 44.

10. natus moriensque fefellit : *i.e.* who was born and died in obscurity; *cf.* Ovid, *Trist.* iii. 4. 25, *Crede mihi : bene qui latuit, bene vixit.*

12. te tractare : *cf. Serm.* ii. 2. 85, *Tractari mollius aetas Imbecilla volet.*   **siccus** : the opposite of *unctum ; cf.* i. 15. 44. *ubi quid melius contingit et unctius.*

13. holus : object of *pranderet ; cf.* ii. 3. 245 ; Introd. § 38. *a.*

14. Aristippus : *cf.* i. 1. 18. The speaker is Diogenes, and the story is told by Diog. Laert. ii. 68.

15. notat : *censures ; cf. Serm.* i. 4. 5.

16. doce, vel iunior audi : *i.e.* either tell me which of these two philosophers you think is right (and why), or, as you are a younger man than I, listen to my reason for preferring the view of Aristippus.

18. eludebat : *parried.*   **mordacem** : with a play on the derivation and literal meaning of *cynicum,* from the Greek κύων, ' dog.'

19. scurror : *I play the buffoon.*

20. splendidius : *nobler.*   **equus . . . rex** : depending on *officium facio.* The expression is proverbial in Greek.

21. verum dante minor : but thereby admit yourself to be the inferior of the one who gives them.

22. fers te : *i.e.* you represent yourself as.   **nullius** : probably neuter. *Cf. Ars Poet.* 324, *praeter laudem nullius avaris.* See Introd. § 49. *b.*

23. Aristippum decuit : *i.e.* he could adapt himself to anything. **color** : with the same sense as in *Serm.* ii. 1. 60, *quisquis erit vitae, scribam, color.*   **status et res** : *position and circumstances.*

24. temptantem maiora : *i.e.* aiming high.   **aequum** : *contented; cf. Odes,* iii. 29. 33, *quod adest memento Componere aequus.*

25. duplici panno : *with its double coat of rags,* referring to the dress of the Cynics. *Cf.* Juv. iii. 115, *facinus maioris abollae,* and Mayor's note.   **patientia** : the chief characteristic of the Stoics. *Cf.* line 13.

27. alter : *Aristippus.*   **exspectabit** : *wait for* ; *i.e.* he will appear in public just as he is.

29. personam feret . . . utramque : *i.e.* will play either part, that of the rich man of the world or the poor philosopher. The *persona* was strictly the mask ; *cf. personatus pater, Serm.* i. 4. 56.

30. Mileti textam : woven at Miletus, which was celebrated for its fine wool; *cf.* Virg. *Georg.* iii. 306, *quamvis Milesia magno Vellera mutentur Tyrias incocta rubores.*   **peius . . . vitabit** : *cf. Odes,* iv. 9. 50, *peius leto flagitium timet.*

33. res gerere : a career of action. The infinitive is the subject of *attingit.*

34. attingit solium Iovis : not only figurative, but with reference to the end of the triumphal procession before the statue of Jupiter in his temple on the Capitoline Hill.   **caelestia temptat** : *cf. Odes,* i. 1. 6, *Terrarum dominos evehit ad deos;* iii. 2. 21, *Virtus recludens immeritis mori Caelum.*

35. principibus . . . viris : *i.e.* such as are referred to in lines 33, 34.

36. non cuivis . . . Corinthum : a proverbial expression from the Greek.

37. sedit : *i.e.* sits inactive and makes no attempt to succeed. Gnomic perfect, as is also *timuit* ; see Introd. § 44. *d.*

38. fecitne : *ne* has the force of *nonne ; cf.* i. 16. 31.

39. hic : *in this; i.e.* in the answer to the preceding question. **quod quaerimus** : *i.e.* the object of the whole discussion.

40. animis . . . corpore : ablative of comparison with *maius.* **maius** : *too great for.*

41. subit : *takes it up; cf. Serm.* 1. 9. 21, *cum gravius dorso subiit onus.*

42. experiens : *enterprising.*

44. ferent : *will receive,* as gifts.   **sumas pudenter** : *modestly accept,* contrasted with *rapias.* Cf. *Ars Poet.* 51, *licentia sumpta pudenter.*

45. caput : *the main point.*   **erat** : at the time when you attached yourself to a patron. The action continues into the present; *cf. eras,* i. 4. 6 ; Introd. § 44. *b.*

46. indotata . . . soror : on the feelings of the Romans on this subject, see Plaut. *Trin.* 689 f., *ne mihi hanc famam differant, Me germanam meam sororem in concubinatum tibi, si sine dote dem, dedisse magis quam in matrimonium.*

47. nec pascere firmus : *i.e.* does not yield enough for their needs. For the construction of the infinitive, see Introd. § 46. *a.*

48. clamat ' victum date ' : *i.e.* he is no better than a common beggar.　　**succinit alter :** *a rival* (beggar) *chimes in.*

49. et mihi : *me too !* sc. *date victum.*　　**quadra :** a round loaf marked off into four parts by lines across the top, so that it could easily be broken.　*Cf.* pseudo-Virg. *Moret.* 47, *Levat opus palmisque suum dilatat in orbem Et notat impressis aequo discrimine quadris.*

50. tacitus pasci : the reference does not seem to be to the familiar fable of the Fox and the Crow, but, as Porph. says, to the habits of crows in general : *nam corvus cum accedit ad cibum strepitu vocis alias aves arcessit, unde fit ut solus pasci non possit.*

52. Brundisium . . . aut Surrentum : *i.e.* on a business or a pleasure trip.　*Surrentum,* the modern Sorrento, was noted in ancient times, as it is to-day, for its beauty and for its delightful climate.

55. refert : *repeats.*　　**acumina :** *the clever tricks.*　　**catellam :** apparently the diminutive of *catena,* not of *catulus.*　One is reminded of the modern actress and her stolen diamonds.

59. planum : *an impostor,* who pretends to have broken his leg. A Greek word, πλάνος, from πλάνομαι ; lit. ' *tramp,*' *vagabond.*

60. per Osirim : the worship of the Egyptian god Osiris gained a footing in Rome as early as the time of Sulla (about 80 B.C.), and a temple of Isis and Osiris was built by the Triumvirs after Caesar's death, in 44 B.C.

62. quaere peregrinum : implying that it is an old trick in that town.　Note the assonance (imitating the *vicinia rauca*), caused by the repetition of *r* and *c* in these and the following words.

EPISTLE XVIII.

1. liberrime : *independent.*

2. amicum : object of *professus,* the concrete for the abstract ; *cf. Odes,* i. 35. 22, *nec comitem abnegat.*

4. discolor : the dress of the matron was the white *stola,* while the courtesan was obliged to wear a dark *toga ; discolor* sometimes means merely *different,* but the choice of the word was doubtless influenced by the fact referred to.　　**scurrae :** dative with a verb meaning ' differ from ' ; see Introd. § 39. *a.*

5. huic vitio : *i.e.* that implied in *scurrantis* and *scurra.*

6. inconcinna : *cf.* i. 17. 29, *Personamque feret non inconcinnus utramque.*

7. tonsa cute, dentibus atris: *i.e.* by ostentatious disregard of personal appearance: *tonsa cute* means with the hair closely clipped, instead of being properly trimmed.

9. medium: *cf. Odes*, ii. 10. 5 ff.

10. alter: *the one, i.e.* the *scurra*.   **imi lecti**: on the lowest couch, which was occupied by the host (see Outline of *Serm*. ii. 8), and the *scurrae*.

11. derisor: *cf. Serm.* i. 4. 87 ff.

12. iterat voces: *sc. divitis.* He repeats his remarks, so that they may not by any chance be lost to the company; *cf.* the conduct of Nomentanus in *Serm*. ii. 8.   **verba cadentia tollit**: he takes up words which fall from his patron's lips and makes them prominent; see previous note.

13. puerum . . . reddere: a schoolboy repeating what had been dictated to him by his master.

14. partis tractare secundas: *cf. Serm.* i. 9. 46. The actors who played the *secundas partes* in the mimes seem to have imitated the action of the principal actors. *Cf.* Suet. *Caligula*, 57, *cum in Laureolo mimo, in quo actor proripiens se ruina sanguinem vomit, plures secundarum certatim experimentum artis darent, cruore scaena abundavit.*

15. rixatur: the man who prides himself on his independence refuses to agree to anything and argues noisily and rudely about trifles. **lana caprina**: proverbial expression for a matter of no importance.

16. nugis: ablative of instrument with *armatus*.   **ut non . . . prima fides**: exclamatory *ut*, *the idea that my opinion should not settle the matter!*

17. vere: with *placet*.

18. pretium . . . sordet: for the meaning of *sordet*, *cf.* i. 11. 4. A second life would be poor compensation for not expressing my opinion. Perhaps a burlesque of *Iliad*, ix. 444 ff.

19. Castor an Docilis: gladiators (*cf. Serm.* ii. 6. 44) or actors (*cf. Serm.* ii. 6. 72).

20. Minuci . . . via: *cf.* Cic. *ad Att.* ix. 6. 1. It seems to have been the road between Beneventum and Brundisium, which Horace took on his journey to Brundisium.

21. damnosa: *ruinous; cf.* ii. 1. 107, *damnosa libido*.   **praeceps**: because it may send one headlong to ruin.

22. gloria: *ostentation*.

23. argenti: *money; cf.* i. 2. 44.   **importuna**: *insatiate;* to be taken with *sitis. Cf.* Virg. *Aen.* iii. 57, *auri sacra fames*.

24. fuga: *i.e.* dread of; *cf.* i. 1. 46, *pauperiem fugiens.*

25. decem: used as a round number. See Introd. § 50.   **instructior**: *better equipped;* used ironically.

26. regit: *i.e.* tries to guide him.

28. prope vera: *i.e.* what is nearly true; *cf.* i. 6. 1, *prope res una.* **contendere**: *i.e. mecum certare,* line 30.

29. patiuntur: *i.e.* are enough for.

30. arta . . . toga: in distinction from the flowing one, which was at this time regarded as a mark of luxury. *Cf. Epod.* 4. 8; *Epist.* i. 19. 13.

31. Eutrapelus: P. Volumnius Eutrapelus, who received his cognomen on account of his wit (εὐτραπελία). See Cic. *ad Fam.* vii. 32 and 33. Nepos, *Att.* 9. 4.

32. beatus enim iam: *for now rich,* in his own opinion.

33. sumet: the future represents the thought of Eutrapelus as he makes the gift.

34. in lucem: *cf.* i. 17. 6.

35. officium: his duty, perhaps with reference to the *salutatio,* or perhaps used in a general sense.   **nummos alienos**: a variation of the common *aes alienum.*   **pascet**: *i.e.* will fatten, make great. **ad imum**: *worst of all;* the last stage in his downward career.

36. Thraex: a gladiator; see note on *Serm.* ii. 6. 44.   **holitoris**: *a market gardener.*

37. arcanum . . . scrutaberis: *i.e.* don't be too inquisitive about his private affairs. The future is equivalent to an imperative.   **illius**: *i.e.* the *dives amicus,* line 24.

38. commissum teges: *cf. Serm.* i. 4. 84.   **vino tortus**: *cf. Odes,* iii. 21. 13, and *Ars Poet.* 435.   **ira**: *i.e.* caused by some slight put upon him by his patron, which might lead him to revenge himself by betraying secrets.

39. aliena: *i.e.* the patron's.

40. venari: since *poemata panges* suits the taste of Lollius, it is probable that *venari* is not a chance example, but that his unknown patron was fond of the chase; *cf.* line 45 below.   **panges**: *cf.* Lucr. i. 25, (*versibus*) *quos ego de rerum natura pangere conor;* iv. 8.

41. gratia . . . dissiluit: *i.e.* the bond of affection was broken. The story of the two brothers who disagreed about the value of music is told in the *Antiope* of Euripides, and was familiar to the Romans through the *Antiopa* of Pacuvius. It is referred to by Cic. *de Orat.* ii. 37. 155; *de Inv.* i. 50. 94; *de Rep.* i. 18. 30.

42. suspecta: as effeminate. **severo**: *by the austere brother*, *i.e.* Zethus ; dative of the agent with *suspecta*.

46. Aetolis: doubtless suggested by the hunt of the Calydonian boar. Such literary epithets, which were suggestive to the cultivated reader, are common in the Augustan poets. (See Sellar, *Roman Poets of the Augustan Age*, *Virgil*, p. 235.) **onerata iumenta**: with this scene, *cf.* i. 6. 58 ff.

47. inhumanae: *unsocial*. The opposite of the geniality implied in *humani nil a me alienum puto*, Ter. *Heaut.* 77. **senium**: *moroseness*, which was sometimes characteristic of old age ; *cf. Cic. de Sen.* 18. 65, *at sunt morosi et anxii et iracundi et difficiles senes*.

48. pariter: *as well as your patron*. **pulmenta**: *cf. Serm.* ii. 2. 20.

49. sollemne: *customary, habitual. Cf. Serm.* ii. 2. 10. **opus**: in apposition with the preceding clause ; *cf. sermo merus, Serm.* i. 4. 48. **famae**: *cf. Serm.* ii. 2. 94 f.; i. 4. 118.

52. speciosius: adverb ; *in better form*, than you.

53. coronae: *the ring* of spectators. *Cf. Ars Poet.* 381.

54. proelia campestria: the athletic games in the Campus Martius. See *Odes*, i. 8. 5 ff. **saevam . . . militiam**: three years of military service formed a regular part of the career of a young man in the position of Lollius.

55. Cantabrica bella: the campaign against the Cantabrians, under the lead of Augustus himself, in 27–25 B.C. *Cf. Odes*, iii. 8. 22 ; iv. 14. 41.

56. refigit: *is taking down* (in 20 B.C.). *Cf. Odes*, iv. 15. 6 ff. ; and for the meaning of *refigit*, *Odes*, i. 28. 11.

57. si quid abest: *i.e.* he is extending the Roman sway over the whole world. **adiudicat**: a technical term, used of the *iudex* who *assigned* a piece of land to one of two claimants.

58. ne . . . absis: parenthetical purpose, like *ut ita dicam*, and the like ; *not to shirk*, you do take part in your patron's amusements, even though they are not in accordance with your tastes. **inexcusabilis** = *inexcusatus. Cf. flebilis, Odes*, i. 24. 9.

59. extra numerum modumque: *unseemly*, lit. *out of time and tune*.

60. curas: for the indicative with *quamvis*, see Introd. § 45. *b*. **nugaris**: by leading a sham battle, as described below. For the general meaning of the word, *cf. Serm.* ii. 1. 73.

61. Actia: in prose, and usually in poetry, the form *Actiaca* is used. *Cf.* Virg. *Aen.* viii. 675.

62. pueros: *slaves*, or perhaps free-born children from the neighborhood.   **hostili more**: *i.e.* in realistic fashion.

63. lacus: some lake on or near his estates.

64. velox: *swift;* with reference to the wings with which Victory is represented in art.   **coronet**: the anticipated result of the contest; hence the subjunctive.

65. suis studiis: returning to the thought in lines 39–40.

66. utroque pollice: enthusiastically.   In the arena the gladiator was approved *pollice presso*, the opposite being *pollicem vertere*. **tuum . . . ludum**: *i.e. tua studia.*

67. ut moneam: see note on line 58 above.

68. quid de quoque: Porph. says: *tria dixit: quid dicas, de quo dicas, cui dicas.*   If so, *de quoque* is equivalent to *et de quo.*

69. percontatorem: *the gossip;* lit. 'the man who asks questions.'

70. patulae: in a double sense, *wide open*, to hear everything, and *rimosae*, see *Serm.* ii. 6. 46.

71. irrevocabile: *cf. Ars Poet.* 390.

72. non . . . ulla: *nulla.* On *non* with the volitive subjunctive, see *Serm.* ii. 5. 90, note.   **iecur ulceret**: *i.e.* do not fall in love with them.   For *iecur* as the seat of the emotions, see *Odes*, i. 13. 4, etc.

74. pueri . . . puellae: appositive genitive with *munere.*

75. parvo: *of little value*, but which the patron will regard as imposing a heavy obligation.   **beet**: *i.e. beatum faciat; beo* was nearly obsolete in Horace's time.   The word is in general rare and confined to poetry.   **incommodus**: *churlishly;* the opposite of *commodus, Odes*, iv. 8. 1.   **angat**: *i.e.* by refusing the gift.

76. qualem commendes: *i.e.* what sort of people you introduce to him, and thus become responsible for.

78. quondam: *sometimes.*   **tradimus**: *introduce; cf.* i. 9. 47.

79. sua culpa: emphatic, *his own fault.*   **deceptus**: *i.e.* since you have been deceived.

80. penitus notum: *i.e.* a man whom you thoroughly know. **crimina**: (false) *accusations, calumny*, opposed to *sua culpa* in line 79.

82. Theonino: Theon was evidently a proverbial calumniator. The Comm. Cruq. says: *Luthienus Theon libertinus dicacitatis amari-*

tudine praeter ceteros ita patronum suum exasperavit, ut domo eius summoveretur et quaternario legato iuberetur restem sibi palumque emere.   **circumroditur**: *cf. Odes*, iv. 3. 16.   **ecquid . . . sentis**: *do you not perceive ?*

84. paries . . . ardet: on the common occurrence of fires at Rome, see note on *Serm.* i. 1. 77.

87. in alto: with ellipsis of *mari, on the deep.*

88. hoc age: *i.e.* give your mind to this; see note on *Serm.* ii. 3. 152.

90. agilem: *cf.* i. 1. 16.   **navum**: *cf.* i. 1. 24.

91. This line is regarded by many as an interpolation from i. 14. 34.

93. formidare tepores: *i.e.* abstain for your health's sake, to avoid the heating effect of the wine.

94. nubem: a common metaphor in English as well.   **plerumque**: *often; cf. Serm.* ii. 5. 55.

95. obscuri: *crafty, ' dark.'*

96. inter cuncta: *amid all the business of life.*   **leges et percontabere**: future with the force of a mild imperative.   **doctos**: *i.e.* the philosophers.

97. traducere . . . aevum: a variation of the expression *traducere vitam.*

98. semper: with *agitet; i.e.* whether there is any escape. **inops**: because it can never be satisfied, and the only escape is in getting rid of it.

99. rerum mediocriter utilium: the expression is qualified by *mediocriter,* because it does not include the *summum bonum,* virtue.

100. virtutem . . . donet: *i.e.* whether virtue can be learned or is inborn.

101. tibi reddat amicum: the opposite in Plaut. *Bacch.* 417, *Iam aderit tempus, quom sese etiam ipse oderit.*

102. pure tranquillet: *sc. te ; gives you genuine peace.*   **honos**: *i.e.* a successful political career.   **lucellum**: *cf. Serm.* ii. 5. 82.

103. secretum iter: *i.e.* a life of retirement.   **fallentis**: *cf.* i. 17. 10.

104. reficit: *restores me to health ; i.e.* the cold baths ; *cf.* i. 15. 4.

105. Mandela: the district adjacent to the modern Cantalupo di Bardella, on the hills above the confluence of the Digentia and the Anio, a short distance from Horace's estate.   **pagus**: used for the inhabitants of the district ; *cf. Odes,* iii. 18. 12.

106. sentire: *sc. me.*

107. etiam minus: *cf. Epod.* i. 31 ; *Serm.* ii. 6. 3.   **ut vivam** :
on the understanding that I am to live; stipulative subjunctive ; see
Introd. § 45. *e.*   **mihi** : *for myself,* without social or political
demands on my time. So-called 'dative of advantage.'

109. in annum : *i.e.* until the next harvest ; *cf.* Pers. vi. 25, *Messe
tenus propria vive, et granaria, fas est, Emole.   Quid metuas?   Occa ;
et seges altera in herba est.*

110. neu fluitem : *cf.* his advice to Tibullus, i. 4. 12 ff.

111. sed : a correction of the preceding wish, since such a state of
mind depends on oneself.   **ponit** : *sets before one; cf. Serm.* ii. 2.
23, *etc.*

EPISTLE XIX.

1. docte : and hence presumably familiar with the works of
Cratinus ; *cf. Odes,* iii. 8. 5.   **Cratino** : *cf. Serm.* i. 4. 1.   He
was famous for his conviviality.   An epigram of his, which Horace
seems to have in mind, is preserved in the *Anthologia Palatina,* xiii.
29, (ἀοιδὸς) ὕδωρ δὲ πίνων οὐδὲν ἂν τέκοι σοφόν.

3. potoribus : dative of apparent agent, as in *Serm.* i. 10. 16.
See Introd. § 39. *b.*   **ut** : *ever since.*

4. adscripsit : *enrolled among; cf. Odes,* iii. 3. 35.

6. laudibus vini : *cf., e.g., Iliad,* vi. 261, ἀνδρὶ δὲ κεκμηῶτι μένος
μέγα οἶνος ἀέξει.   Ablative of cause.   **vinosus** : *fond of wine, a wine-
bibber;* sc. *fuisse.*

7. pater : a title of honor ; see note on *Serm.* i. 3. 126.   Ennius
is called the father of Roman poetry ; he says of himself, *Sat.* 8, *numquam poetor nisi si podager.*

8. prosiluit : like the warriors he described ; *cf. desaevit,* i. 3. 14.
Forum puteaľque Libonis : *i.e.* a business life.   The *puteal Libonis*
was a place in the Forum, which had been struck by lightning and
surrounded with a low circular wall.   It was between the temples of
Castor and Vesta, and the stalls of the money-changers were close by.
See *Serm.* ii. 6. 35.

9. siccis : *cf. Odes,* i. 18. 3.   **cantare** : the infinitive, object of
adimam.   See Introd. § 46. *d.*   **severis** : especially water-drinkers ;
cf. Catull. 27. 5, *hinc abite, lymphae, Vini pernicies (i.e.* 'water, which
only spoils wine'), *et ad severos Migrate.*   Dative of separation.

10. edixi : *i.e.* passed this law ; see note on ii. 2. 51.

11. nocturno . . . diurno : *cf. Ars Poet.* 269.   Instead of *certare* *diurno*, which the hearer would expect, Horace substitutes *putere*, a common rhetorical device. *Cf. minora, Serm.* i. 3. 20.

13. exiguae togae : *cf.* i. 18. 30, and the note.   **textore :** ablative of instrument ; *cf. tonsore*, i. 1. 94.   **Catonem :** probably *Cato Uticensis;* see *Odes*, i. 12. 35.

15. Iarbitam : Porph. says : *hic Iarbutha (sic) Maurus regio genere fuit ortus, qui dum Timaginem imitatus post convivium et inter pocula declamantem, propter insolentiam faciendi quod conabatur, ipse diruptus est.*   **Timagenis :** Timagenes was a rhetorician of Alexandria, who was brought to Rome as a prisoner by A. Gabinius in 55 B.C. His various fortunes are given by Sen. *Contr.* x. 5. 22, *ex captivo cocus, ex coco lecticarius, ex lecticario usque in intimam amicitiam Caesaris felix.*

16. urbanus : *witty.*

17. vitiis : ablative of respect with *imitabile.*

18. pallerem : *if I were pale;* protasis contrary to fact.   **biberent :** *they would drink;* i.e. the imitators, who have been implied, but not yet directly mentioned.   **exsangue :** of the effect, like *pallida mors, Odes*, i. 4. 13. See Plin. *N. H.* xx. 160, *omne cuminum pallorem bibentibus gignit.*

19. servum : used as an adjective, as in Ovid, *Fast.* vi. 558, *serva manus.*

20. bilem : *cf. Serm.* i. 9. 66 ; ii. 3. 141.

21. libera : opposed to *servum pecus.*   **per vacuum . . . princeps :** *i.e.* a leader in a new field; *cf. Odes*, iii. 30. 11–14.

22. aliena : *sc. vestigia.*

23. Parios iambos : *i.e.* the iambics of Archilochus, of Paros, who was the first to make extensive use of that metre. The reference is to the *Epodes.*

24. numeros animosque : *the rhythm and spirit.*

25. non res et agentia verba : *not the subject-matter and the words which pursued.*   **Lycamben :** a citizen of Paros, who refused to give his daughter in marriage to Archilochus ; the latter thereupon lampooned him in such bitter language that he hanged himself and his daughter.

26. foliis : *cf. Odes*, i. 1. 29.   **brevioribus :** *scantier.*

27. artem : *the technique.*

28. temperat : *moulds.*   **Archilochi . . . pede :** *by the measure of Archilochus.*   **mascula :** *i.e.* strong and worthy to rank with men.

29. ordine : *arrangement*, probably with reference to the strophes.

30. socerum : like Lycambes.   **atris** : *abusive; cf. Epod.* 6. 15 ; *Serm.* i. 4. 85.

31. sponsae : with reference to Nebule, the daughter of Lycambes ; see note on line 25.   **famoso** : *cf. Serm.* ii. 1. 68.

32. hunc : Alcaeus.   *Cf. Odes,* iii. 30. 13 f.

33. immemorata : *i.e.* words not spoken before ; *cf. Odes,* iii. 1. 2, *carmina non prius audita.*

34. ingenuis : *gentle, noble ; i.e.* such people as are mentioned in *Serm.* i. 10. 81–90.

35. opuscula : *cf.* i. 4. 3.

36. premat : equivalent to *deprimat, disparages; cf. Ars Poet.* 262.

37. ventosae : *fickle as the wind ; cf.* i. 8. 12.   **suffragia venor** : the figure is from the elections, but the reference is undoubtedly to the *recitationes; cf. Serm.* i. 10. 38.

38. tritae : *worn out ; cf.* Pers. i. 54, *Scis comitem horridulum trita donare lacerna.*

39-40. Horace listens to the works only of *nobilium scriptorum, i.e.* writers of real merit, and does not himself recite his own poems, except as stated in *Serm.* i. 4. 73.

39. ultor : *i.e.* he gets even by reading his works to them in turn. The expression is of course used jocosely.

40. grammaticas ambire tribus : like a politician canvassing for votes.   **pulpita** : the *reader's desk*, passing from the figure to the reality.

41. hinc illae lacrimae : this expression, from Ter. *Andria*, 126, had become proverbial.   **theatris** : *i.e.* halls hired or lent for recitations.   *Cf. Serm.* i. 10. 38.

42. nugis : *trifles*, a modest estimate of his *opuscula ; cf. Serm.* i. 9. 2.

43. rides : *i.e.* you are joking ; *cf. Serm.* ii. 6. 54.   **ait** : *sc. quidam.*   **Iovis** : *i.e.* Augustus.

44. manare : used with transitive force.

45. tibi pulcher : *cf.* Cic. *Tusc. Disp.* v. 22. 63, (of poets), *in hoc enim genere nescio quo pacto magis quam in aliis sum cuique pulchrum est. Tibi* is dative of the person judging. B. 188, II. *b.*   **naribus uti** : *i.e.* to turn up my nose at them ; *cf. Serm.* i. 6. 5.

46. acuto . . . ungui : *cf.* Cic. *Tusc. Disp.* v. 27. 77, *adulescentium greges Lacedaemone vidimus ipsi incredibili contentione certantis, pugnis, calcibus, unguibus, morsu denique.*

47. iste locus: *i.e.* the place chosen by the opponent (note *iste*' for the contest, as if of gladiators.   **diludia**: occurs only here Porph. explains it as *intermissionem ludorum vel dilationem*.

48. ludus: with the double meaning of *play* and *sport*.   **genuit** gnomic perfect; see Introd. § 44. *d.*

EPISTLE XX.

1. Vertumnum: *Vertumnus deus est praesens vertendarum rerum, hoc est emendarum ac vendendarum, qui in vico Turario sacellum habuit*, Porph. His statue stood near the book-stalls in the Vicus Tuscus (*cf. Serm.* ii. 3. 228).   **Ianum**: *cf.* i. 1. 54. The place designated by *Vertumnum Ianumque* was also of bad repute. Hence the verb *prostes* in line 2, with a double meaning.

2. scilicet: sarcastic.   **Sosiorum**: *Sosii illo tempore fratres erant bibliopolae celeberrimi*, Porph. *Cf. Ars Poet.* 345, *hic meret aera liber Sosiis.*   **pumice**: the ends of the roll which formed the book were smoothed with pumice: *cf.* Catull. 1. 1, *Cui dono lepidum novum libellum Arida modo pumice expolitum ?*

3. clavis et sigilla: the keys and seals with which the *scrinia* or *armarii* were closed. The figure by which the book is compared with the handsome slave is kept up throughout.

4. paucis: *cf. Serm.* i. 4. 73.   **communia**: *cf.* Sen. *Contr.* i. 2. 5, *meretrix vocata es, in communi loco stetisti.*

5. non ita: *i.e.* not to desire publicity.   **fuge**: *i.e.* hasten to go your way, before I change my mind.   **descendere**: the regular word for going down to the Forum from the hills about it, but doubtless with the secondary meaning of descending to a lower life.

6. emisso: when you have once gone forth; *cf.* i. 18. 71.   **quid egi**: the lament of the book.

7. quid volui: *cf.* Virg. *Ecl.* ii. 58, *quid volui misero mihi ?*

8. in breve cogi: with reference to the book, means to roll up and put away.   **plenus**: *sated; cf.* ii. 1. 100.

9. augur: *the prophet, i.e.* Horace himself.

10. deserat: subjunctive because of the idea of anticipation. **aetas**: *your youthful beauty. Cf.* Afranius, *ap.* Non. 2. 2, *Aetas et corpus tenerum et morigeratio, Haec sunt venena formosarum mulierum.*

11. manibus sordescere: *cf. Serm.* i. 4. 72.

12. tineas: *cf. Serm.* ii. 3. 119.   **inertis**: in its literal sense of *in-ars, vandal;* see Cic. *de Fin.* ii. 34. 115, *artes, quibus qui carebant 'inertes' a maioribus nominabantur;* Juv. iii. 207, *divina opici rodebant carmina mures.*

13. fugies . . . aut vinctus mitteris : *i.e.* run away of your own accord, or be sent by the book-seller. *Vinctus, bound* (of the slave) or *tied in a bundle* (of the books). **Uticam . . . Ilerdam :** used of the provinces generally, where a book which had lost its popularity at Rome might find a sale for a time.

14. monitor : referring to Horace, like *augur* in line 9.

15. qui . . . iratus : *i.e.* the donkey driver lost his temper at his stubborn animal, which he could not keep from the edge of a cliff, and pushed him off.

16. invitum servare : *cf. Ars Poet.* 467.

17. pueros elementa docentem : *i.e.* used as a school-book. Double accusative with *docentem.*

18. extremis in vicis : *i.e.* in the suburbs, in inferior schools.

19. sol tepidus : *i.e.* toward evening, when the sun is no longer hot, and more people are in the streets.

20. libertino natum patre : *cf. Serm.* i. 6. 46.   **in tenui re :** *cf. Serm.* i. 6. 58 f.

21. nido : ablative of comparison with *maiores; too great for the nest. Cf. Serm.* ii. 3. 310, *corpore maiorem.*   **loqueris :** future with the force of an imperative.

22. ut . . . addas : *i.e.* the more obscure his origin, the greater credit does he deserve for what he has accomplished.

24. corporis exigui : *of short stature;* genitive of description. *Cf. Serm.* ii. 3. 309.   **praecanum :** probably prematurely gray, though *prae-* may be intensive, as it often is in composition.   **solibus aptum :** *i.e.* fond of lounging in the sun.

25. irasci celerem : *cf. Serm.* ii. 3. 323.

27. Decembris : according to Suetonius, Horace was born on the sixth day before the Ides (December 8).

28. quo . . . anno : *i.e.* 21 B.C.   **dixit :** *nominated.* Lollius was elected without a colleague, since the other consulship was intended for Augustus. When Augustus declined the position, Lollius named Lepidus as his colleague. *Dixit* has little Ms. authority as compared with *duxit,* but is the technical term.

BOOK II.

EPISTLE I.

1. solus: a slight exaggeration, since Augustus had the support of Agrippa, with whom he had shared the proconsular authority since 23 B.C., and the tribunician power since 18 B.C. Agrippa had spent most of the time in the East.

2. moribus: Augustus made a great effort to improve the morals of the people. *Cf. Odes*, iv. 15. 9 ff.

3. in publica commoda: *against the public weal.*

4. morer tua tempora: *waste your time. Cf. te morer, Serm.* i. 1. 14.

5. Romulus . . . Pollux: all deified only after death, while Augustus receives divine honors during his earthly life.

6. deorum in templa: *i.e.* into the abode of the gods. *Cf.* Ennius, *Ann.* i. 66 V, *unus erit quem tu tolles in caerula caeli Templa.*

7. colunt: by zeugma, *inhabit . . . care for.*

8. agros adsignant: *cf. Serm.* i. 3. 105.

9. ploravere: *had to lament.* **respondere**: *correspond; cf. Serm.* ii. 8. 66.

11. notaque . . . portenta: *the storied monsters,* overcome by Hercules in the course of his twelve labors. **fatali**: *imposed on him by fate; cf. Odes,* iii. 3. 19, *fatalis iudex.*

12. invidiam: *i.e.* the jealousy of Juno. **domari**: as if it too were one of the *portenta.* **supremo fine**: *i.e.* only by death; *cf. Serm.* i. 7. 23, *ultima mors.*

13. urit: *i.e.* dazzles and pains; *cf.* i. 10. 43; i. 13. 6. **artis**: *virtues; cf. Odes,* iii. 3. 9, *hac arte.*

14. exstinctus amabitur: *cf. Odes,* iii. 24. 31, *Virtutem incolumem odimus, Sublatam ex oculis quaerimus, invidi.*

15. praesenti: *while still among us,* in distinction from Hercules and the heroes mentioned in line 5. **maturos**: *timely.*

16. iurandas: *i.e.* at which oaths are to be taken. *Cf.* Suet. *Aug.* 52, *templa . . . in nulla provincia nisi communi suo Romaeque nomine recepit. Nam in urbe quidem pertinacissime abstinuit hoc honore.*

19. nostris ducibus: *e.g.* Romulus. **Grais**: *sc. ducibus; e.g.* Castor, Pollux, and Heracles.

20. cetera : *i.e. in other respects ;* in literary matters.   Accusative object of *aestimat*.

21. terris semota : *cf.* line 14 above.

22. fastidit et odit : *cf.* Tac. *Dial.* 23, *rhetorum nostrorum commentarios fastidiunt oderunt, Calvi mirantur.*

23. veterum : neuter, like *cetera, semota, defuncta*.   **tabulas** : the laws of the Twelve Tables, which exerted an important literary influence and were used as school-books in early times.

24. bis quinque viri : the decemvirs.

25. Gabiis : dependent on the following *cum*, which, in Horace's usual manner, is expressed only with the second of the two words which it governs.   **aequata** : *made on equal terms.*

26. pontificum libros : *i.e.* the books containing the directions for the ritual, and the annals of the pontiffs (*annales pontificum, annales maximi*).   **volumina vatum** : such as the Sibylline books and the proverbs and saws assigned to the Marcii.

27. Albano . . . monte : the Alban Mount, with its shrine of Juppiter Latiaris and its sacred associations, is thought of as the abode of the Muses, like Helicon in Greece.   **Musas . . . locutas** : *cf.* Quint. x. 1. 99, *licet Varro Musas, Aeli Stilonis sententia, Plautino dicat sermone locuturas fuisse, si Latine loqui vellent.*

29. pensantur eadem trutina : *cf. Serm.* i. 3. 72.   The idea is that if the same rule is applied to the Romans, that the oldest are the best, there is nothing to be said.

30. non est quod : *there is no reason why.*

31. intra . . . extra : adverbs.   **olea** : governed by the following *in ; cf.* the position of *Gabiis*, line 25 above.   The thought is ' olives haven't stones, nuts haven't shells ' ; fruits differ in their characteristics, and so do the Greeks and Romans.

32. venimus . . . fortunae : we have conquered the Greeks ; therefore, if we argue as suggested, we surpass them in other respects as well.

34. dies : *time.*

35. quotus annus : *which year in order*, the answer being in an ordinal number.

36. decidit : *cf. Odes*, iv. 7. 14.

38. excludat . . . finis : *let there be a limit, to prevent disputes*, like a boundary-stone in a field.

39. probus : *sterling, classic.*

41. referendus erit : *is he to be counted ?*

43. iste : the man you mention ; the reply of the opponent.   **ho-neste** : *with honor, i.e.* he will not disgrace his company.

45. utor permisso : I take advantage of the admission, *i.e.* he proceeds, after the manner of argument called *sorites*, gradually to reach a limit where his opponent will cease to admit that the term *veteres* applies.

46. unum : *sc. annum.*

47. cadat elusus : *is foiled and loses his case ;* the subjunctive, because of the idea of anticipation.   **ruentis acervi** : the heap, Greek σωρός, from which the style of argument derives its name ; see line 45 above.

48. redit in fastos : *trusts to the calendar.*

49. Libitina : the goddess of death ; *cf. Odes,* iii. 30. 7 ; *Serm.* ii. 6. 19.

50. sapiens : so called because of his philosophical poem, the *Epicharmus.*   **fortis** : because in his *Annals* he sang the *fortia facta patrum.*   **alter Homerus** : Ennius says that Homer appeared to him in a dream and told him that his soul had passed into a peacock, and then into Ennius's body.

51. leviter curare : *i.e. securus esse,* Porph.

52. somnia Pythgorea : see note on *alter Homerus,* line 50.   The dream of Ennius is called 'Pythagorean,' because such transmigrations of souls were a prominent feature of Pythagoras's philosophy.

53. Naevius : see Introd. § 17.   **in manibus** : *i.e.* is still read. **non** : equivalent to *nonne* ; *cf. Odes,* iii. 20. 1.

54. paene recens : *i.e.* almost as if he were a modern writer.

56. Pacuvius : see Introd. § 18.   **docti . . . alti** : *cf.* Quint. x. 1. 97, *virium Accio plus tribuitur, Pacuvium videri doctiorem, qui esse docti affectant, volunt.*   **Accius** : see note on *Serm.* i. 10. 53.

57. Afrani : Lucius Afranius, born in 154 B.C., a writer of *togatae,* or comedies based on Roman life ; hence the expression *Afrani toga.* A few fragments of his works have come down to us.   **Menandro** : 'the star of the new comedy,' an Athenian, who lived from 342–291 B.C.   Only fragments of his works have been preserved.

58. properare : of the vivacity and rapid action of his comedies. **Epicharmi** : a famous writer of the so-called Sicilian comedy, which was developed from the Doric farce.   He was born in Cos in 540 B.C., but went as a boy to Sicilian Megara and thence to Syracuse, where he lived until his death in 450 B.C.

59. Caecilius : a Roman comic writer, a native of Insubrian Gaul, who lived from 219–166 B.C.   Only a few fragments of his works have survived, but he was ranked high by the ancients.   **Terentius** : the well-known writer of comedy (185–159 B.C.).

60. ediscit : with reference to the epic poets first mentioned.   *Cf.* Cic. *Tusc. Disp.* ii. 11. 27, *poetae ita . . . dulces, ut non legantur modo, sed etiam ediscantur.*   **arto** : *i.e.* too small for the large audiences.

62. Livi : *i.e.* Livius Andronicus, whose first play was produced in 240 B.C.

63. est ubi : *i.e.* sometimes.

64. ita : *to such a degree.*

66. pleraque : *much ;* the more common meaning of the word after Cicero.

67. ignave : *carelessly*, with too little art ; *sc. dicere.*

68. mecum facit : *i.e.* it agrees with me.   **Iove . . . aequo** : *propitio, si quidem Iove irato fit ut errent homines ac delirent,* Porph.   *Cf. Serm.* ii. 3. 8, *iratis dis.*   There may be a complimentary reference to Augustus ; *cf.* i. 19. 43.

69. Livi : Livius Andronicus.

70. plagosum : apparently not elsewhere used in the active sense.   See Introd. § 1.

71. Orbilium : one of Horace's teachers at Rome.   **dictare** : *dictated*, to be learned by heart, the usual method of instruction ; *cf.* i. 1. 55 ; i. 18. 13 ; *Serm.* i. 10. 75.   **videri** : *i.e.* to their admirers.

72. exactis : *perfect works.*

74. concinnior : *better turned.*   **unus et alter** : *one or two.*

75. ducit : *carries with it.*

76. quicquam : *anything*, used instead of *aliquid*, because of the negative implied in *indignor =non probo, ferre non possum*, or the like.   **crasse** : *coarsely, roughly ; cf. Serm.* ii. 2. 3.

77. nuper : *sc. compositum sit.*

78. antiquis : either neuter or masculine.   See Introd. § 49. *b.*

79. crocum floresque : *i.e.* the stage, which was perfumed with saffron-water.   *Cf.* Lucr. ii. 416, *cum scaena croco Cilici perfusa recens est ;* Prop. iv. 1. 16, *pulpita sollemnes non oluere crocos.*   There is no other reference to flowers on the stage.   Porph. takes *flores* as referring to a play of Atta's : *in fabula quae inscribitur Matertera ita florum genera enumerat, ut sine dubio reprehendendus sit ob nimiam loquacitatem.*   The general meaning seems to be : 'if I express a doubt whether the plays of Atta ought still to be produced.'   **Atta** :

a writer of *togatae*, contemporary with Afranius (see line 57). He died in 77 B.C.

81. patres: *the older men.*

82. Aesopus . . . Roscius: two actors of the Ciceronian epoch, of whom the former was a great tragic actor, while the latter excelled in comedy; hence the adjectives, *gravis*, 'dignified,' and *doctus*, 'clever.'

84. parere minoribus: *i.e.* to follow the taste of the younger generation.

85. imberbes: *in their youth.*　　**senes**: *in their old age.*

86. Saliare . . . carmen: the hymns of the Salii, a priesthood said by Livy (i. 20) to have been instituted by Numa, are preserved in a few fragments. They were almost unintelligible in later times. *Cf.* Quint. i. 6. 40, *Saliorum carmina vix sacerdotibus suis satis intellecta.*

87. quod mecum ignorat: *i.e.* of which he knows as little as I.

89. nostra . . . nos nostraque: emphatic. His conduct is due not to admiration of the past, but to envy of his contemporaries. **lividus**: *cf. Serm.* i. 4. 93.

92. tereret: *wear out, thumb.*　　**viritim**: *individually.*　　**publicus usus**: *the general public;* abstract for concrete.

93. positis . . . bellis: probably referring to the Persian wars, which were followed by great literary activity at Athens.　　**nugari**: *to amuse herself,* in distinction from the stern business of war.

94. in vitium: from the Roman point of view, which regarded all such pursuits as unworthy of serious attention.　　**fortuna . . . aequa**: *since fortune was kind.*　　**labier**: *to drift.* On the archaic form, see Introd. § 35. *a.*

95. athletarum: with reference to the great national games. **equorum**: for the chariot races.

96. fabros: *workers in.*

97. suspendit . . . voltum mentemque: *fixed eyes and mind on. Cf.* i. 6. 14.

98. tibicinibus: music in general.

99. sub nutrice: *at its nurse's feet.*　　**puella**: the feminine, because the comparison is with *Graecia.*

100. quod . . . petiit . . . reliquit: *cf. Ars Poet.* 160.　　**plena**: *cf.* i. 20. 8.

102. paces: the plural, because the reference is to *periods* of peace.

103. diu : in contrast with the early development of the arts in Greece. **sollemne** : *customary.* **reclusa . . . domo vigilare** *to be up early with open house;* to receive calls of clients ; *cf. Serm.* i. 1. 10.

104. promere iura : in early times, until the publication of the Twelve Tables, knowledge of the law was confined to the patricians.

105. cautos nominibus rectis : *secured by good names, i.e.* those of responsible debtors. With the meaning of *nominibus, cf. Serm.* i. 2. 16.

106. maiores audire : *i.e.* to receive instruction and counsel from older men. **per quae . . . posset** : to be taken both with *audire* and *dicere.*

107. damnosa libido : *cf.* i. 18. 21.

108. calet : *is fired.*

110. fronde : *i.e.* with the ivy sacred to poets ; *cf. Odes,* i. 1. 29. **comas** : accusative governed by *vincti,* which has a middle force. See Introd. § 38. *c.* **dictant** : *i.e.* to an amanuensis (*notarius*). *Cf. Serm.* i. 10. 92.

111. qui . . . versus ; *cf.* i. 1. 10.

112. Parthis mendacior : a proverbial expression ; *cf.* Livy, xxi. 4. 9, *perfidia plus quam Punica;* a common opinion of a powerful enemy. **prius orto sole vigil** : *cf. Serm.* i. 6. 122. The Romans frequently composed before getting up in the morning.

114. habrotonum : a bitter herb, apparently a kind of wormwood. *Cf.* Lucr. iv. 125 (Munro's note). It is mentioned by Plin. *N. H.* xxi. 160 as a medicine. Porphyrio's comment is, *quod minore periculo etiam indoctus miscere potest et dare,* which makes the comparison all the stronger.

115. medicorum . . . medici : the repetition makes the state-ment the more emphatic.

116. promittunt : almost = *profitentur.*

117. indocti doctique : *skilled and unskilled, i.e.* even without special preparation, in contrast with lines 114–116.

118. error : *i.e.* this departure from the life described in lines 103–107.

119. sic collige : *cf. Serm.* ii. 1. 51. **avarus** : *cf.* Ovid, *Ars Amat.* iii. 541, *Nec nos ambitio nec amor nos tangit habendi.*

120. non temere : *i.e.* is not apt to be.

121. fugas servorum, incendia : *cf. Serm.* i. 1. 76 f.

122. fraudem socio : *cf. Odes,* iii. 24. 59 f.

123. vivit . . . secundo : *i.e.* he is not luxurious. *Pane secundo* (ablative of instrument) refers to coarse bread called *panis secundarius*. *Cf*. Suet. *Aug*. 76, *cibi . . . minimi erat (Augustus) atque vulgaris fere. Secundarium panem . . . appetebat*.

124. militiae : locative or genitive (see Introd. § 40. *a*).

125. si das : *if you admit*.   **parvis rebus** : such as are enumerated in the following lines.

126. figurat : *moulds*, since reading was taught from the works of the poets.

127. obscaenis : such as he heard from his nurse and the *paedagogus; cf*. Tac. *Dial*. 29.   **iam nunc** : *i.e.* even now, in early childhood, when his mind is *tener*.

128. mox etiam : *i.e.* when his mind is ready for such instruction.

130. orientia tempora : *the rising generation ;* abstract for concrete.   **notis . . . exemplis** : *familiar examples*, drawn from the history of great and good men.

131. aegrum : *sick at heart*.

132. cum pueris puella : with reference to the chorus in the *Carm. Saec. ;* see *Carm. Saec.*

134. praesentia : *propitious*.

135. caelestis . . . aquas : *cf. Carm. Saec*. 31 f.   **docta** : *i.e.* taught it by the poet.   **blandus** : *persuasive ; cf. Odes*, iv. 1. 8.

138. Manes : *i.e. di Manes*, in distinction from *di superi. Cf*. Virg. *Aen*. xii. 646, *vos o mihi manes, Este boni, quoniam superis aversa voluntas*.

139. agricolae prisci : the development of dramatic poetry from the harvest festival.   **fortes** : *cf. Serm*. ii. 2. 115.   **parvo beati** : Virg. *Georg*. ii. 472, *patiens operum exiguoque adsueta iuventus*.

141. spe finis : *i.e.* by the hope of rest at the end of the year's toil.

142. pueris et coniuge : who helped him in his work, before the days of slaves. *Cf. Serm*. ii. 2. 115.

143. Tellurem : *the earth*, mentioned by Varro, *R. R*. i. 1. 5, as one of the gods of the farmer.   **porco** : *a sow ; cf*. Cato, *de Agr*. 134, *priusquam messim facies, porcam praecidaneam hoc modo fieri (i.e.* 'sacrificed') *oportet. Cereri porco femina. Porco* is an epicene noun.   **Silvanum** : a rustic god of the fields and woods, and protector of boundaries ; *cf. Epod*. 2. 22.

144. Genium : *cf*. i. 7. 94.   **memorem brevis aevi** : because the life of the genius is identified with that of man ; logically *memorem* belongs with the subject.

145. Fescennina licentia: the earliest form of the drama, a sort of rude banter. See Paul. *Fest.* p. 60, *Fescennini versus, qui canebantur in nuptiis, ex urbe Fescennia dicuntur allati, sive ideo dicti quia fascinum putabantur arcere.* Very likely, as has been suggested, the derivation of the word is from *fascinum*, but its form is due to the influence of the word *Fescennia*, with which it was connected by popular etymology. The Fescennine verses survived in classical times in wedding songs and in the songs of the soldiers during triumphs. *Cf.* Livy, vii. 2.

147. accepta: *handed down.*

148. amabiliter: *in a friendly way*, *i.e.* without ill-feeling. **iam saevus**: *sc. factus, finally becoming savage*, contrasted with *amabiliter.*

149. coepit: in classical prose the passive of *coepit* is commonly used with a passive infinitive.

150. impune: because not yet restricted by law. **cruento**: *which drew blood.*

151. intactis quoque: *even those who were not assailed; cf. Serm.* ii. 1. 23, *cum sibi quisque timet, quamquam est intactus.*

152. super: with the force of *de.* Found in early Latin and Livy; in Cicero only in the *Letters.* **lex poenaque**: first in the Twelve Tables, with a capital penalty ; *cf.* Cic. *de Rep.* iv. 10. 12. Also in the *Lex Cornelia* of 81 B.C.

153. malo: *abusive; cf. Serm.* ii. 1. 82. **nollet**: almost = *vetaret.*

154. describi: *cf. Serm.* i. 4. 3. **vertere modum**: *cf.* our colloquial expression, 'changed their tune.' **fustis**: death was inflicted in early times by *fustuarium, beating to death.* *Cf.* Livy, v. 6. 14, *fustuarium meretur qui signa relinquit aut praesidio decedit.*

156. Graecia capta: the first Roman writer, Livius Andronicus, was a Greek captive from Tarentum, and the influence of Greek models on the Roman literature was very great. Greece was not actually conquered by Rome until 146 B.C., but the dates must not be pressed.

157. horridus: *rude, uncouth.*

158. defluxit: *passed out of use.* **numerus Saturnius**: the native Roman metre, occurring seldom except in the earliest poetry, *e.g.* the *Punic War* of Naevius. Whether it was based on quantity or on accent is a disputed point. **grave virus**: 'noisome venom.'

160. vestigia ruris: *traces of rustic rudeness; cf. agresti Latio,* line 157.

161. serus: *sc. ferus victor*, from line 156.   **acumina**: it is implied that the Romans had the ability to succeed in literature, but did
not apply themselves to it until late.

162. post . . . quietus: *i.e.* having a period of peace after the
second Punic war.

163. Sophocles . . . Thespis . . . Aeschylus: representing the
growth of the Greek tragic drama, Thespis being its reputed founder.
As a matter of fact, the Romans adapted the plays of Euripides more
than those of Aeschylus and Sophocles. The name *Eurīpĭdēs* will not
fit into hexameter verse in the nominative.

164. rem: *i.e.* the subject-matter.   **vertere** : *translate*.   **posset**: an indirect question, introduced by *si ; cf. posset, Serm.* ii. 5. 87.

165. placuit sibi : *i.e.* was satisfied with the result.   **sublimis
et acer**: the lofty and vigorous character of the early Romans fitted
them for the writing and appreciation of tragedy. It soon lost its
popularity, however.

166. spirat tragicum : *has tragic inspiration ; cf. Odes,* ii. 16. 38 ;
Serm. i. 4. 46. *Tragicum* is accusative of the inner object. See Introd. § 38. *b*.   **satis** : perhaps modifies *feliciter audet : i.e.* the early
tragic writers were measurably successful in innovations in language ;
so especially Ennius and Pacuvius.

167. turpem : because it seems too mechanical.   **metuit**: on account of the labor involved. With the whole passage, *cf. Ars Poet.*
289 ff.

168. ex medio : *i.e.* from every-day life.

170. oneris : *i.e.* the labor of revision and of careful writing.
veniae : *indulgence*, since the common people can see weaknesses
in plays which depict their own life.

171. quo pacto : *i.e.* how carelessly.   **ephebi** : *a youth ;* really
a Greek word meaning a young man between 18 and 20 years of age.

172. attenti : *cf.* i. 7. 91 ; *Serm.* ii. 6. 82. These are stock characters in the comedies of Plautus ; *cf. Serm.* i. 10. 40.

173. quantus Dossennus: *what a Dossennus he (Plautus) is.
Dossennus* was a stock character, the buffoon or clown, in the *fabulae
Atellanae*, an early Italian (Oscan) form of the drama. See Livy,
vii. 2. 11–12.

174. quam non adstricto . . . socco: *with what a loose sock.*

175. gestit . . . demittere: that is, he aims only at making money
without regard to artistic work ; hardly a fair criticism of Plautus.

176. securus: *indifferent ; cf. leviter curare*, line 51.   **cadat**

. . . **talo**: *i.e.* fails or succeeds. The plays were sold outright, and their success or failure was a matter of unconcern to the author from the pecuniary point of view; *recto talo, squarely,* is an expression borrowed from the Greek.

177. quem tulit . . . Gloria: *i.e.* the poet who writes plays for fame and not for money. **ventoso curru**: *in her wind-wafted chariot.* *Cf. Serm.* i. 6. 23. *Ventoso* suggests the fickleness of popular favor; *cf.* i. 19. 37.

178. exanimat: *kills with anxiety.* **lentus**: *cold. Cf. Odes,* iii. 19. 28; iv. 13. 6.

180. valeat: *good-by to.* **res ludicra**: *i.e.* comedy.

181. reducit: *brings me home,* from the theatre. *Cf. Odes,* iv. 2. 17.

182. audacem . . . poetam: *i.e.* the poet who is bold enough to try to write artistically and elegantly.

184. depugnare: *to fight the matter out, i.e.* to have their way by force against the more cultured part of the audience.

185. eques: *the knights,* the more cultivated part of the specta-tors. *Cf. Serm.* i. 10. 76. **poscunt . . . pugiles**: a similar thing actually happened to Terence. *Cf. Hec. Prol.* 1. 1–5; 2. 25–34.

186. pugiles: *cf.* Suet. *Aug.* 45, (*Augustus*) *spectavit studiossisime pugiles et maxime Latinos.* **plebecula**: *the dear people;* note the force of the diminutive.

187. migravit ab aure: *i.e.* they no longer take pleasure in the language and rhythm of the plays, but look for spectacular features. The Romans were fond of realistic effects and of extravagant display ; see Cic. *ad Fam.* vii. 1.

188. incertos: *roving,* because they are not fixed as the ear is by the rhythm.

189. premuntur: *are kept down, i.e.* a play goes on for many hours with spectacular effects of all kinds. In the ancient theatre the curtain was lowered at the beginning of a performance and raised at its close.

190. fugiunt: *fly across the stage.*

191. regum fortuna: for *reges fortunati,* kings once favored by fortune; *cf. Catonis virtus, Odes,* iii. 21. 11. **manibus retortis**: *cf. Odes,* iii. 5. 22.

192. pilenta: two-wheeled covered carriages, used by women, in which the priestesses and vestals rode in the triumphal procession. **petorrita**: *cf. Serm.* i. 6. 104. **naves**: probably the beaks of ships (*rostra*), though ships themselves may have been carried in the processions. *Cf.* Prop. ii. 1. 33, *regum auratis circumdata colla catenis, Actiaque in Sacra currere rostra via.*

193. captiva Corinthus : *i.e.* the spoils of Corinth. Sometimes paintings of cities were carried in the triumph, as well as those of other features of the victory. *Cf.* Cic. *Pis.* 25. 60, *quid tandem habet iste currus? quid vincti ante currum duces? quid simulacra oppidorum? quid aurum? quid argentum?*

195. diversum . . . camelo : *the camelopard* or *giraffe*. *Cf.* Plin. *N. H.* viii. 69, *camelopardalis dictatoris Caesaris Circensibus ludis primum visa Romae* (in 46 B.C.). For the construction of *genus*, see Introd. § 38. c.

197. spectaret : *sc. Democritus.*

198. nimio . . . plura : *cf.* i. 10. 30.

199. scriptores : *i.e.* the authors of the plays.   **narrare asello surdo** : a proverbial expression.

200. voces : of actors.   **pervincere** : *overcome, rise above;* Ars Poet. 82.

201. evaluere : a use of the perfect parallel to that of the gnomic perfect, *have been able to,* and so *are able to, will be able to.*

202. Garganum . . . nemus : *cf. Odes,* ii. 9. 7.   **mugire** : *cf. Odes,* iii. 10. 6.

203. artes : works of art, carried in the processions described in line 191 f. For this meaning of *artes, cf.* i. 6. 17.

204. oblitus : note the quantity of the *i.* The idea is that of being overloaded with excessive adornment.

205. concurrit . . . laevae : *i.e.* in applause.   **dextera . . . laevae** : *sc. manus . . . manui,* and see Introd. § 49. b.

206. dixit . . . aliquid? the words of one spectator to another, on hearing the applause.   **sane** : emphasizes *nil; cf.* i. 7. 61.

207. lana : *i.e.* the actor's dress.   **Tarentino . . . veneno** : Tarentine dye, considered second only to the Tyrian purple ; *cf.* Plin. *N. H.* ix. 137.

208. ne . . . putes : Horace disclaims any prejudice against dramatic poetry as such. A parenthetical final clause.

209. maligne : *grudgingly, in niggardly wise; cf. Odes,* i. 28. 23.

210. per extentum . . . ire : proverbial for anything difficult.

211. inaniter : *with illusions, i.e.* by a mere representation of the reality. *Cf.* Virg. *Aen.* i. 464, *animum pictura pascit inani.*

213. ut magus, et : *and like a magician.* Note the hyperbaton.

214. et his : *to these as well ; i.e.* the writers of other than dramatic literature.   **lectori** : of book-poetry, contrasted with *spectatoris.*

216. redde : *give* (as their due).   *Cf. Odes*, ii. 7. 17, *etc.* **munus . . . dignum** : the library in the temple of Apollo on the Palatine.   *Cf.* i. 3. 17.

218. Helicona : a mountain in southwestern Boeotia, regarded as the abode of the Muses.

219. multa . . . facimus : *i.e.* we are in part to blame, since we submit our works to you at unfavorable times.   *Cf.* Martial, x. 19. 12 ff.

220. vineta . . . caedam : apparently a proverbial expression for injuring oneself.   *Cf.* Tibull. i. 2. 100, *quid messis uris acerba tuas? Caedam* therefore means *cut down, destroy.*

221. cum laedimur, *etc.* : *i.e.* when we are too sensitive to criticism.

223. cum loca . . . revolvimus : *i.e.* when we repeat passages which we consider fine, without being asked to do so (*inrevocati*).

224. non apparere labores : that our labor is not appreciated.

225. tenui deducta filo : a common metaphor.   *Cf., e.g., Serm.* i. 10. 44.

226. cum speramus, *etc.* : when we hope for immediate recognition.

227. ultro : *i.e.* making the advances.

229. operae pretium : *worth while ; cf. Serm.* i. 2. 37.

230. aedituos : *the temple-keepers*, who showed shrines to visitors, and pointed out their beauties.   Poets are represented metaphorically as performing this service for *virtus.*

233. Choerilus : an epic poet of Iasos who followed Alexander into Asia and wrote of his deeds.   **versibus** : dative ; the money was set down to the credit of his verses, as if to a person.   **male natis** : *misbegotten.*

234. rettulit acceptos : *entered* (in his account book) *as received.* **Philippos** : gold coins worth about $4.00; so-called because they bore an image of Philip of Macedon ; *cf.* the French *Louis, Louis d'or ;* English, *sovereign.*

235. remittunt : *leave, i.e.* cause.   *Cf. Serm.* ii. 4. 69 ; *Ars Poet.* 349.

236. fere : *as a rule.*

237. linunt : *besmear,* the word being due to the preceding comparison.   *Cf.,* however, *oblitus,* line 204.

239. edicto vetuit : *cf.* Plin. *N. H.* vii. 125, *idem hic imperatot edixit nequis ipsum alius quam Apelles pingeret, quam Pyrgoteles scal-*

peret, quam Lysippus ex aere duceret. Cf. also Cic. *ad Fam.* v. 2.
Apellen : the most famous of Greek painters, an Ionian by birth.
Many stories are told of the realism of his pictures.

240. alius Lysippo : *other than Lysippus;* ablative of comparison ; *cf.* i. 16. 20. Lysippus was one of the most noted Greek sculptors,
a native of Sicyon. See Plin. *N. H.* xxxiv. 63, *nobilitatur Lysippus et
temulenta tibicine et canibus ac venatione. Fecit et Alexandrum Magnum multis operibus a pueritia eius ortus.* See note on line 241 below.
aera : *bronze statues.*

241. voltum simulantia : *cf.* Prop. iii. 9. 9, *Gloria Lysippi est
animosa effingere signa.*

242. iudicium subtile : *cf. Serm.* ii. 7. 101.   Plin. *N. H.* xxxv.
85, however, says : *Alexandro Magno frequenter in officinam venti-
tanti . . . imperite multa disserenti (Apelles) silentium comiter sua-
debat, rideri eum dicens a pueris, qui colores tererent.*   **artibus** :
works of art ; *cf.* line 203 above.

243. ad libros . . . et dona : *i.e.* to literary works in distinction
from painting and statuary.

244. Boeotum : genitive plural.   The Boeotians were proverbial
in ancient times for stupidity, and the characteristic was attributed to
the heavy air of their moist, swampy country.   *Cf.* Cic. *de Fato*, 4. 7,
*Athenis tenue caelum, ex quo etiam acutiores putantur Attici ; cras-
sum Thebis, itaque pingues Thebani.*

246. munera : Virgil is said to have received 1,000,000 sesterces
for the lines on Marcellus in *Aen.* vi. 862 ff., and Varius the same sum
for his tragedy *Thyestes.*

247. Varius : see note on *Serm.* i. 5. 40.

248. expressi : *depicted; cf.* Cic. *Arch.* 6. 14, *quam multas nobis
imagines fortissimorum virorum expressas scriptores Graeci et Latini
reliquerunt.*

250. sermones : referring both to the *Sermones* and to the
Epistles ; see Introd. § 24.

251. repentis per humum : *cf. Serm.* ii. 6. 17, *musa pedestri.*
res . . . gestas : *i.e.* an epic poem dealing with the exploits of
Augustus.

252. terrarumque situs, *etc. : i.e.* the descriptions of the scenes
of the epic.

254. duella : the archaic form of *bella.*   In this passage, as in
Serm. ii. 1. 13 f., Horace gives an idea of what he might have done in
the epic line.

255. claustraque . . . Ianum: referring to the closing of the temple of Janus ; *cf. Odes*, iv. 15. 9.

256. Parthis: one of the deeds of which Augustus was most proud, which the poets of the Augustan age constantly refer to, was the recovery of the standards lost by Crassus at Carrhae in 53 B.C.

257. parvum : *humble*.

258. recipit: *admit*.

259. vires ferre recusent : *cf. Ars Poet*. 39.

260. stulte: emphatic, modifying *diligit; who foolishly attempts devotion beyond his powers*.   **urget**: *i.e. vires ferre recusant*, and it crushes him.

261. numeris et arte: *i.e.* in poetry.   **commendat**: *recommends; cf.* i. 18. 7.

262. discit: *sc. aliquis*, implied in *quis* below. The idea is that one remembers faults more easily than one does merits. *Cf.* Cic. *de Orat*. i. 28. 129, *nihil est enim tam insigne nec tam ad diuturnitatem memoriae stabile quam id, in quo aliquid offenderis*.

264. nil moror : *I care nothing; cf.* i. 15. 16.   **officium quod me gravat**: *cf. sedulitas . . . urget*, line 260.

265. proponi cereus : *i.e.* to have waxen images of himself offered for sale.

267. pingui : *stupid; cf. Serm*. ii. 6. 14.

268. cum scriptore meo : *i.e.* both the poet and his subject are consigned to oblivion.   **porrectus** : like a corpse on the bier.

269. vicum : the *Vicus Tuscus;* see note on *Serm*. ii. 3. 228.

270. amicitur : unsalable poems were used for wrapping paper ; *cf.* Catull. 95. 7, *Volusi annales Paduam morientur ad ipsam Et laxas scombris saepe dabunt tunicas*.

EPISTLE II.

1. Flore: *cf.* i. 3. 1.   **amice** : as a member of the *cohors amicorum; cf.* i. 3. 6.   **Neroni** : *i.e. Tiberius; cf.* i. 3. 2.

2. puerum . . . natum Tibure vel Gabiis : *i.e. a verna* of Italian birth, regarded as more valuable than the foreign slaves.

3. agat : *deal, treat*, of the seller recommending his goods.

5. fiet eritque : the double term is characteristic of legal forms, such as bills of sale and the like.   **nummorum . . . octo**: *8000* sesterces (about $400), an average price for a slave of the kind.

6. ministeriis : dative with *aptus*.

7. litterulis : a contemptuous expression natural in the mouth of the slave dealer.   **imbutus :** *with a smattering of.* Cf. Tac. *Dial.* 19, *elementis studiorum etsi non instructus, at certe imbutus.*   **idoneus arti cuilibet :** *i.e.* capable of being taught any accomplishment. He could be made a reader or an amanuensis, or the like.

8. argilla . . . uda : *i.e.* he is still impressionable and capable of being moulded to any form one might desire.

9. indoctum sed dulce : *i.e.* in a sweet but untrained voice. **bibenti :** *i.e.* his singing would be acceptable at a *comissatio* or symposium, where his hearers would be less critical.

10. multa, *etc.: i.e.* too many promises are suspicious, and give the impression that the seller is anxious to get rid of a worthless article. **levant** = *leviorem faciunt.*

11. extrudere : *to get off his hands;* see Introd. § 55. *a.*

12. res . . . nulla : *i.e.* I am under no necessity.   **meo . . . aere :** *i.e.* in humble circumstances, but out of debt. *Meum aes* is the opposite of *aes alienum.* Cf. Cic. *Verr.* ii. 4. 6. 11, *hominem . . . non modo in aere alieno nullo, sed in suis nummis multis esse.*

13. hoc . . . faceret : *i.e.* would treat you so fairly.   **non temere :** *not without special reason; i.e.* I would not do this for every one.

14. semel : emphatic ; *just once.*   **cessavit :** see note on *cessator, Serm.* ii. 7. 100.

15. in scalis : *under the stairs.* Cf. Cic. *Mil.* 15. 40 (*cum Clodius*) *se . . . fugiens in scalarum tenebras abdidisset.*   **pendentis habenae :** *i.e.* the thong (*lorum*), hung up in a conspicuous place as a warning.

16. excepta : the regular word for an exception or provision in a bargain ; *cf. Serm.* ii. 3. 286.   **des :** the apodosis of *si velit . . . agat,* in lines 2–3.

17. poenae securus : *without fear of penalty,* since he had expressly mentioned the slave's fault.   On the case of *poenae,* see Introd. § 40. *a.*

18. prudens : *wittingly, with your eyes open.*   **lex :** *the conditions* of the sale.

19. moraris : *i.e.* consume his time.

20. dixi, *etc. :* the application of the example.

21. mancum : *crippled,* a stronger word than *pigrum.*   **talibus officiis :** *i.e.* letter writing ; dative of purpose with *mancum.*   **mea :** with *epistula,* a bold hyperbaton.

23. mecum facientia iura : *the law which is on my side ;* since he had warned his friend, as the slave dealer had the purchaser.

24. super hoc : *hoc* seems to be accusative, since the expression *super haec* is of frequent occurrence.

26. Luculli miles : Horace illustrates the situation by an anecdote. **viatica** : strictly, *travelling expenses; cf.* i. 17. 54. Here it means *savings* from his pay, from booty, *etc.*

27. ad assem : *to a penny ; i.e.* wholly.

28. vemens lupus : in apposition with the subject of *deiecit*, the person being identified, as frequently in Horace, with the thing with which he is compared. The comparison of soldiers with wolves is a common one. *Vemens* is probably a contracted form for *vehemens.*

30. praesidium : *garrison.* **deiecit** : the technical word.

31. rerum : genitive with *divite.* See Introd. § 40. *a.*

32. donis honestis : *gifts of honor*, such as *coronae aureae, hastae purae, phalerae, torques, armillae.*

33. bis dena sestertia : *20,000 sesterces* (about $1000), probably his share from the sale of the booty. **nummum** : not commonly used after *sestertia*, to which it is frequently equivalent. Here it means *in cash.*

34. praetor : *general*, the original meaning of the word.

35. nesciŏ : the regular quantity in the combination *nescio quis, etc.*

36. mentem : here meaning *courage*, like *animus. Cf.* i. 2. 60. **timido quoque** : *even to a coward.*

37. pede fausto : *i.e.* and good luck go with you, an assurance of the ease of the undertaking, as well as a wish. Ablative of attendant circumstance.

38. laturus : *and you will receive.* See Introd. § 47. **quid stas ?** *cf. Serm.* i. 1. 19.

39. ibit, ibit : ironically repeating the *i . . . i* of line 37.

40. zonam : money-belt. Apparently not like those of modern times, but with a purse (*crumena*) hanging from them. *Cf.*, however, C. Gracch. ap. Gell. xv. 12. 4, *zonas . . . plenas argenti.*

41. contigit : *it has been my good fortune; cf.* i. 2. 46. **doceri . . . Achilles** : *i.e.* to study Greek and read the *Iliad*, which was used as a text-book. *Cf.* Plin. *Epist.* ii. 14. 2, *in foro pueros a centum-viralibus causis auspicari ut ab Homero in scholis.*

43. Athenae : Horace, like many young men of his day, went to Athens to complete his education. See Introd. § 2.

44. ut vellem . . . dinoscere: of the study of philosophy. **curvo**: used somewhat humorously for *wrong*, as deflected from the straight path. The same idea is found in *pravum* and *vitium*. See note on *Serm.* i. 3. 1.

45. silvas Academi: *i.e.* the Academy, a grove in the suburbs of Athens, where Plato had his school. Academus, from whom the grove derived its name, was an Athenian hero, often identified with Cadmus.

47. aestus: *the tide; cf. Odes*, ii. 7. 15–16.

48. non responsura: *i.e.* fated not to be a match for.

49. unde: *i.e. ex aestu belli civilis.*   **simul primum**: a rare combination ; *cf. simul ac* and *cum primum.*

50. decisis . . . pinnis: *with clipped wings*, to be taken with *humilem* (*laid low*), as the position shows.   **paterni laris et fundi**: genitive with *inopem*. His father's estate was evidently confiscated.

51. audax: with the subject of *facerem*, *that I should venture to make verses.*

52. quod non desit: *i.e. quod satis sit*, object of *habentem.* **habentem**: *sc. me.*

53. expurgare: *cure*, of the disease of writing.   **cicutae**: regarded as a cure for madness.

55. singula: *one thing after another.*   **anni . . . euntes**: *the years as they pass.*

56. ludum: of amusements in general.

57. extorquere: implying resistance on Horace's part.

58. denique, etc.: *finally* tastes differ, and he cannot please every one.

59. carmine: *lyric poetry*, such as the *Odes*.   **iambis**: such as the *Epodes; cf. Epod.* 14. 7.

60. Bioneis: Bion the Borysthenite was a Scythian philosopher, who lived about 250 B.C. He was notorious for his wit and cynicism. The reference is to the *Sermones*.   **sale nigro**: *caustic wit. Cf. Serm.* ii. 4. 74, where *sal nigrum* is used of a coarse strong salt. Doubtless, however, *nigro* is used with something of a figurative meaning, as in *Serm.* i. 4. 85 and 100.

61. tres convivae: a small number of guests, but all of different tastes.   **prope**: ironical.

62. multum diversa: *widely different things. Cf.* i. 10. 3.

64. acidum: used especially of wine.

65. praeter cetera: *above all.*

67. sponsum: supine. *Cf. Serm.* ii. 6. 23. **auditum scripta**: *i.e.* to a recitation of his works.

68. omnibus officiis: *i.e.* all other business. **cubat**: *lies sick;* cf. *Serm.* i. 9. 18.

70. humane commoda: *reasonably convenient,* ironical. *Humane* is used to intensify *commodum,* like *misere.* **verum**: a suggestion that the case is not so bad after all.

71. purae: *clear, free from obstruction.* **meditantibus**: *i.e.* he can compose as he goes. *Cf. Serm.* i. 9. 2.

72. festinat: emphatic; nay, the contractor rushes on in hot haste. **mulis gerulisque**: instrumental ablative.

73. torquet: *swings.* **machina**: *a derrick* or *crane.*

74. tristia funera: cf. *Serm.* i. 6. 42 f. **robustis**: *heavy,* made strong for carrying great loads.

75. hac: sc. *via; hac . . . hac* is poetic and rare; see Introd. § 48. *a;* cf. Virg. *Aen.* i. 467 f.

76. i nunc: *go now,* if you can. *Cf.* i. 6. 17.

77. scriptorum = *poetarum;* cf. ii. 1. 36. **urbem**: *the city,* used in a general sense.

78. rite: *regularly,* for all time. **cliens Bacchi**: cf. i. 19. 4.

80. contracta vestigia: *i.e.* the narrow path; for *contracta,* cf. *contractus* in i. 7. 12.

81. ingenium: *a mind, i.e.* a man of intellect. The idea is that not even in Athens can one give himself entirely to study and literary pursuits without making himself ridiculous; much less is it possible at Rome. **vacuas**: *quiet;* cf. i. 7. 45. **desumpsit**: *has chosen* as a home.

82. insenuit: *has grown gray.*

83. curis: *meditation, study.* **statua taciturnius**: a proverbial expression; *cf. Serm.* ii. 5. 40.

84. hic: *here, i.e.* in Rome.

86. motura: *designed to rouse, i.e.* suited for lyric poetry. **conectere**: *to weave.* **digner**: *am I to think fit?*

87. ut alter: of such a sort that they praised each other. For the form of the result clause, *cf.* i. 16. 12.

88. meros honores: *nothing but praise.*

89. Gracchus: probably C. Gracchus, who was the greatest orator of his time. As Tiberius Gracchus was also a celebrated orator, Horace may use the name without special regard to either. **illi**: *in his eyes;* dative of the person judging. **Mucius**: there were three

celebrated jurists named Mucius Scaevola. Here, too, Horace may use
the name generally, or he may have the eldest in mind as contemporary with the Gracchi.

90. qui minus: how much the less.

91. hic: *another*, very probably Propertius, who calls himself the
Roman Callimachus (Prop. iv. 1. 64 ; *cf.* line 100 below).   **mirabile
. . . opus**: in apposition with *carmina* and *elegos*, and representing
the praise bestowed by the two poets on each other.

92. novem Musis: *i.e.* all the muses must have taken part in its
production.

93. molimine: conscious effort.   **circum spectemus**: tmesis ;
cf. Serm. i. 2. 62–63 ; ii. 3. 117–118 ; Introd. § 53. *o.*

94. vacuam . . . aedem: apparently referring to the `bibliotheca
Latina` in the temple of Apollo on the Palatine.

95. mox etiam: their books are received into the Palatine Library,
and later they recite their works in public.   **sequere**: to the hall
where the recitation was given, perhaps also in the same temple.

96. coronam: the prize of victory ; *cf. Odes,* i. 26. 8.

97. caedimur . . . hostem: like gladiators in combat.

98. Samnites: heavy armed gladiators, originally from Campania ;
cf. Liv. ix. 40. 17.   **ad lumina prima**: *i.e.* until evening, when the
lights were lit.   **duello**: originally a combat between two, and perhaps here used on account of its original signification.

99. discedo: *I come off* from the contest.   **Alcaeus**: *an
Alcaeus, i.e.* the equal of Alcaeus ; *cf. Odes,* ii. 13. 26.   **puncto**:
vote.   **meo**: *sc. puncto.*

100. Callimachus: the most brilliant of the Alexandrian school
of Greek poets, a native of Cyrene. His elegies were imitated by
Catullus, Ovid, and Propertius.   **si plus . . . visus**: *i.e.* if this does
not satisfy him.   **adposcere**: an archaic word found only here and
in Ter. *Heaut.* 838.

101. Mimnermus: flourished 640–600 B.C., by some regarded as a
greater elegiac poet than Callimachus.   **optivo** = *adoptivo*, since the
name was not his by birth, but by adoption.

102. multa fero: *I endure a great deal.*

103. suffragia capto: *cf.* i. 19. 37.

104. mente recepta: since writing poetry is looked on as a
species of madness ; *cf.* line 90 above.

105. obturem: apodosis to the protasis implied in *finitis . .
recepta.*   **impune**: with *obturem.*

106. verum : *yet*.

107. scribentes : *i.e.* in the act of writing.   **ultro** : *of their own accord*, explained by *si taceas*.

108. beati : with *laudant*, *i.e.* happy in their self-conceit.

109. legitimum : *i.e.* corresponding to the rules of art ; *cf. Ars Poet.* 274.

110. cum tabulis : *i.e.* when he takes his tablets in hand to write. **honesti** : *conscientious*.

111. audebit : *he will have the courage*.

113. movere loco : *expel*, as the censor removes unworthy members from the senate.

114. intra penetralia Vestae : *within the shrine of Vesta*.

115. populo : with *eruet*.   **bonus** : *kindly*.

117. Catonibus atque Cethegis : *i.e.* men like Cato (the censor) and Cethegus (consul in 204 B.C.), types of the olden time.

118. situs : *neglect, rust*.   **informis** : of the effect produced, *disfiguring, ugly*.   **deserta** : *abandoned*.

119. adsciscet nova : *sc. verba*, as the censor enrolls new members in the senate.   **genitor** : *as father*.   **usus** : *usage*.

120. vehemens : *powerful*.

121. beabit : *bless, enrich*.   *Cf. Ars Poet.* 57 ; and on the word, i. 18. 75.

122. luxuriantia : *sc. verba, excessive*, likened to a vine which grows too rank.   **aspera** : *rough*.   **sano** : *well-regulated*. He will not polish his work so much as to take away its strength.

123. virtute carentia : *i.e. ignava* ; *cf.* ii. 1. 67.   **tollet** : *elevate*, *i.e.* improve their tone.

124. ludentis : *of one at play*, *i.e.* without effort.   **torquebitur** : *will use all his efforts ; exert himself to the utmost ; torquebitur* has a middle force.

125. Satyrum . . . Cyclopa : accusative of the inner object ; *cf. Serm.* i. 5. 63.   **movetur** : *dances*, passive with the force of the middle.

126. praetulerim : *I should prefer*, rather than to take all this trouble. Potential subjunctive.   **delirus** : see note on *Serm.* ii. 3. 107.

127. denique : *at least*.

128. ringi : *to be vexed*, lit. to show one's teeth like an angry dog. *Cf.* Ter. *Phorm.* 341, *Dum tibi fit quod placeat, ille ringitur*, on which Donatus's comment is : *ringi est stomachari tacitum : est enim translatio a canibus latraturis*.   **haud ignobilis** : *sc. quidam*, a well-known man, *i.e.* the story is a familiar one.   **Argis** : *at Argos*, the

Latin form of the word ; cf. Varro, Ling. Lat. ix. 50, Graecanice hoc Argos, Latine Argi.

130. sessor plausorque : i.e. regularly sitting and applauding.

131. servaret : characteristic subjunctive ; in other respects a man who. Cf. credebat in line 129. Vitae munia is explained in the following lines.

133. ignoscere servis : cf. Serm. i. 3. 80 f.

134. signo laeso : i.e. has stolen a jar of wine. The jars were closed and sealed.

135. rupem . . . vitare : cf. Serm. ii. 3. 56 f. **puteum . . . patentem** : an open well, i.e. with the cover off.

136. opibus : very nearly = ope.

137. elleboro : regarded as a remedy for madness ; cf. Serm. ii. 3. 82. **bilem** : supposed to cause insanity ; cf. Plaut. Amph. 720, atra bili percita est.

138. Pol : cf. i. 7. 93, and the note.

141. nimirum sapere, etc. : finally, the proper occupation for a man of Horace's time of life is the study of philosophy ; cf. i. 1. **nugis** : cf. ludicra, i. 1. 10, and Serm. i. 9. 2.

142. pueris : governed both by tempestivum and by concedere, ἀπὸ κοινοῖ ; see Introd. § 42.

143. sequi : follow after, i.e. try to find.

144. numerosque modosque : cf. i. 18. 59.

145. recordor : i.e. he recalls to his mind the precepts which he has learned from his teachers.

146. sitim : i.e. if you had dropsy ; cf. Odes, ii. 2. 13.

147. quanto . . . cupis : avarice, a vice which Horace is constantly satirizing, is likened to a dropsy of the mind.

148. nulline . . . audes : i.e. would you be ashamed to confess your trouble and have it treated ? Cf. i. 16. 24.

149. monstrata : i.e. prescribed.

150. fugeres . . . curarier : you would refuse to be treated ; with the construction, cf. Odes, i. 9. 13. On the form curarier, see Introd. § 35. a.

151. audieras : from the people who believed it ; cf. i. 1. 53 f.

152. donarent : a general statement, put into a past tense after audieras. **decedere** : the technical expression for being cured of a disease ; cf. Lucr. ii. 34, Nec calidae citius decedunt corpore febres.

153. ex quo : 'from the time when ' ; i.e. since you became richer

154. plenior : richer ; cf. Odes, ii. 12. 24.

156. nempe : *surely.*

158. libra . . . et aere : the usual way of conveying property at Rome was by a symbolic sale, in which a balance, held by a third party, was struck by the recipient with a copper coin.

159. consultis : for *iuris consultis ; cf.* line 87 above.   **mancipat** : *makes your property ;* strictly this term can be used only of the process described in the note to line 158, but it is here used figuratively.   **usus** : *possession,* which if long enough continued gave a legal title.

160. qui te pascit ager : *i.e.* the field which grows the grain on which you live is yours, whether you own it or another.   **Orbi** : otherwise unknown ; doubtless a rich neighbor of the poet.

161. daturas : *which are to give you;* see Introd. § 47.

163. temeti : an old word for wine.   **modo isto** : since the elision of the last syllable of an iambic word before an accented syllable is very rare, probably *isto* is to be pronounced *sto,* according to the popular usage. The form is read in Cicero's Letters and may have been the original reading here.

164. trecentis . . . milibus : *300,000 sesterces* (about $15,000).

166. nuper an olim : *i.e.* some time ago (by buying the estate) or from time to time, as you buy provisions.

167. emptor quondam : for *qui quondam emit.*   **Aricini Veientis et arvi** : *of an estate at Aricia or Veii.*

168. emptum : emphatic, *boughten.* So *emptis. Cf. Epod.* ii. 48, *dapes inemptas.*

169. sub noctem : *at nightfall.*

170. usque . . . qua . . . iurgia : *as far as where the line of poplars avoids quarrels with the neighbors by the fixed boundary which it makes;* i.e. the owner plants a line of poplars and by thus fixing his boundary line avoids the possibility of dispute. This estate he calls his, though, as has been shown, it is only so in a certain sense. The poplars are said to avoid quarrels since they free the owner from them. *Limitibus* is ablative of instrument.

172. puncto . . . mobilis horae : *in a short time;* see note on *horae momento, Serm.* i. 1. 7.

173. prece : that is as a gift.   **pretio** : *by sale.*   **vi** : for example, by confiscation.   **morte suprema** : *by death, which ends all.*

176. alterius : *sc. heredis ;* a succession of heirs.   **velut . . . undam** : as wave follows wave. *Cf.* Ovid, *Met.* xv. 181, *ut unda im-*

*pellitur unda.   Urgeturque eadem veniente urgetque priorem Tempora
sic fugiunt pariter.*

177. vici : *great estates.*   **Calabris** : . . **Lucani** : referring to
possessions in cattle. The herds were pastured in Apulia and Calabria in winter, and driven to the hills of Lucania and Samnium in the
summer. *Cf. Epod.* 1. 27.

178. Orcus : the comparison of death with a reaper is a familiar
one.

179. non exorabilis auro : *cf. Odes,* ii. 18. 34 ff.

180. sigilla : small statuettes of bronze. *Cf.* Plin. *N. H.* xxxiv.
34, *signa quoque Tuscanica per terras dispersa quin in Etruria facti-
tata sint non est dubium.*

181. argentum : *plate; cf.* i. 6. 17.   **Gaetulo** : the Gaetulian
purple was famous.

182. est qui non curat : there is one who does not care, namely,
the poet himself. Note the indicative, contrasted with the subjunctive
after an indefinite antecedent. See Introd. § 45. c.

183. alter fratrum : such differences of temperament in brothers
was a favorite subject in comedy ; so in the *Adelphi* of Terence.
cessare : *cf.* i. 7. 57.   **ungui** : to be anointed with oil, for a banquet
or revel ; *cf. Odes,* ii. 11. 17.

184. Herodis : Herod the Great, king of Judaea, 39–4 b.c.   **palmetis** : used here as a synonym for great riches, since the yield in
dates from such a grove would be great.

185. importunus : *insatiate; cf. Serm.* ii. 5. 96.   **ad umbram
lucis** : *i.e.* until nightfall.

186. mitiget : *subdues; cf. pacantur,* i. 2. 45 ; the wild land is
subdued like an enemy with fire and steel.

187. Genius : *cf.* ii. 1. 144.   **natale astrum** : *his natal star ;
cf. Odes,* ii. 17. 21. For Horace's views on astrology, *cf. Odes,* i. 11 ;
Serm. i. 6. 114.   **temperat** : *controls.*

188. deus . . . mortalis : *i.e.* a god as regards its nature and its
power, but mortal as regards the individual ; see note on i. 7. 94.

189. voltu mutabilis : *i.e.* representing men of different character.   **albus et ater** : applying to fortune (*cf. Odes,* i. 12. 27) and to
character ; *cf.* Cic. *Phil.* ii. 16. 41, *qui albus aterne fuerit ignoras ;*
Catull. 93. 2, *Nec scire utrum sis albus an ater homo.*

190. utar : used absolutely, as in i. 7. 57.   **ex modico acervo** :
the opposite of *Serm.* i. 1. 51.   **res** : *circumstances.*

192. datis : *i.e.* than what was actually left him.

193. scire volam: I shall wish to know the difference between good living and extravagance, and between frugality and parsimony, and regulate my life accordingly. **simplex**: *frank, open.*

197. ac potius: *or rather.* **Quinquatribus**: the festival of Minerva, from March 19 to March 23. It was observed as a school holiday, since Minerva was the goddess of wisdom and learning.

198. raptim: *i.e.* crowding as much enjoyment as possible into the short time.

199. utrum . . . an: as if *nihil distat* preceded.

201. tumidis velis: *i.e.* my sails are not swollen by too favorable a wind (*cf. Odes,* ii. 10. 23), nor yet are they wholly unfavorable.

202. aetatem ducimus: *cf. Epod.* 17. 63.

203. specie: *appearances.*

204. usque: *always.*

205. non es: with concessive force. **abi**: *good, go in peace;* a colloquial expression; *verbum vel sibi vel alteri blandientis,* Donatus on Ter. *Ad.* 765. **cetera**: *sc. vitia* from *vitio.* **inani**: *cf.* ii. 1. 211.

207. ira: to be taken like *formidine* with *mortis; cf.* Lucr. iii. 1045, *Tu vero dubitabis et indignabere obire?*

208. somnia: *i.e.* a superstitious belief in dreams.

209. nocturnos lemures: *umbras vagantes hominum ante diem mortuorum et ideo metuendas,* Porph. *ad loc.* **Thessala**: the Thessalian witches and witchcraft were famous; *cf. Epod.* 5. 45; *Odes,* i. 27. 21.

210. natalis . . . numeras: *i.e.* do you enjoy each year as it passes? **ignoscis amicis**: *cf. Serm.* i. 3. 25 f.; i. 3. 84 f.

212. exempta . . . una: *sc. spina.* **spinis**: *cf.* i. 14. 4.

213. decede peritis: *make way for those who do. Peritis* is dative; *cf. Odes,* ii. 6. 15.

215. abire: as from a banquet; *cf. Serm.* i. 1. 119. **largius aequo**: *more plentifully than is proper.*

216. pulset: *drive you forth.* **lasciva decentius**: *in which merry-making is more seemly.*

EPISTLE III.

1. humano capiti, *etc.*: Horace forcibly illustrates the necessity of unity by describing an absurd composition in the pictorial art. **humano . . . equinam**: the contrast is heightened by the chiastic order.

2. velit: *should take it into his head.*   **inducere**: the regular word for 'laying on' color.

3. membris: probably dative with *inducere*.   **undique**: *i.e.* from all sorts of animals.   **turpiter atrum**: to be taken together (*ugly black*), contrasted with *formosa superne*.

5. spectatum: supine.   **amici**: even though you were friends of the painter.

6. Pisones: according to Porphyrio, the Epistle is addressed to L. Calpurnius Piso, consul in 15 B.C., and *praefectus urbis* under Tiberius. His two sons are included in the term *Pisones*.   **librum**: a poem of any kind. *Cf.* ii. 1. 220.

7. vanae . . . species: *fancies.* There is no criticism in the term itself, except in so far as it is qualified by the following *ut*-clause.

9. reddatur: *is suited to, corresponds to.*   **pictoribus**, *etc.*: a reply to Horace's words.

10. aequa: *equal, like, i.e.* both for painters and poets.

11. petimus damusque: we ask it as poets and grant it to painters.

12. sed . . . non ut: *but not on the understanding that; i.e.* there are limits.   **coeant**: *cf.* i. 5. 25. Stipulative subjunctive; see Introd. § 45. *e.*

13. geminentur: *i.e.* united in one form.

14. inceptis: *beginnings.*   **plerumque** = *saepe; cf. Serm.* ii. 5. 55.

15. purpureus . . . pannus: the reference does not seem to be to the purple stripe on the tunic or toga, but rather to a patchwork effect.   **splendeat**: subjunctive of purpose.

16. lucus et ara, *etc.*: these incongruous details are doubtless real examples taken from poets of the day, but they cannot be identified.

17. ambitus: *the winding course.*

18. Rhenum: the adjective, instead of the substantive *Rhenus; cf. Odes*, i. 10. 15.

19. sed: with an implied ellipsis; *very good, but.*   **cupressum . . . simulare**: apparently proverbial; *cf.* Porph. *ad loc., hoc proverbium est in malum pictorem qui nesciebat aliud bene pingere quam cupressum. Ab hoc naufragus quidam petiit ut periculum suum exprimeret. Ille interrogavit, num ex cupresso vellet aliquid adicere. Quod proverbium Graecis in usu est.*

20. si enatat: *i.e.* if you are painting an *ex voto* (see note on *Serm.* i. 5. 66.) for a man who has been shipwrecked. *Cf. Odes*, i. 5. 13; *Serm.* ii. 1. 33.

21. aere dato : *i.e.* he has paid his money, and has a right to expect a good piece of work.

22. rota : the potter's wheel.   urceus : *a pitcher*. The potter plans an *amphora* and produces a small jug.   *Cf.* line 139 below.

23. denique : *in short*, summing up the bearing of the preceding examples.   dumtaxat : *provided it be*. See note on *Serm.* ii. 6. 42.

24. vatum : *of us poets*, on account of *decipimur*.

25. specie : *idea, notion; i.e.* our own idea, which is often wrong.

26. levia : *smoothness, polish.*   nervi : *strength.*

27. grandia : *a lofty style; cf.* Quint. x. 2. 16, *plerumque (imitatores) declinant in peius et proxima virtutibus vitia comprehendunt fiuntque pro grandibus tumidi.*

28. procellae : perhaps used in the same sense as in *Odes*, ii. 10. 1 f., in which case there is a mixture of metaphors, or, as in iv. 2. 25, of the dangers which attend a high flight.

29. rem . . . unam : *a simple subject*.   prodigialiter : *i.e.* by introducing marvels.   The word seems to be coined by Horace.

31. caret : the subject is the same as that of *appingit.*

32. Aemilium . . . ludum : Porph. says : *Aemilii Lepidi ludus gladiatorius fuit, quid nunc Polycleti balineum est.*   imus : *i.e.* the most obscure.

33. exprimet : *cf.* ii. 1. 248.   mollis : *i.e.* with lifelike effect.

34. infelix operis summa : *unsuccessful in his work as a whole.* ponere : *to represent; cf. Odes*, iv. 8. 8.

35. hunc : *i.e.* a man like that ; *cf.* i. 6. 40, *ne fueris hic tu;* Introd. § 48. *a.*

36. pravo : *crooked.*

37. spectandum : *worth looking at, an object of admiration.* nigris . . . capillo : regarded as a mark of beauty ; *cf. Odes*, i. 32. 11.

38. materiam : *a subject.*   qui scribitis : *all ye who write;* not addressed to the Pisones.

39. versate : *consider;* perhaps with the idea of trying the weight before raising it to the shoulders.

40. potenter : *according to his powers;* κατὰ τὸ δυνατόν, Porph.

41. facundia : *the power of expression.*   lucidus ordo : *clear arrangement.*

42. ordinis : stands first in the sentence, as the subject of the discussion ; *so far as arrangement is concerned.*   Venus : *charm.* aut ego fallor : *unless I am mistaken.*

43. ut iam nunc . . . dici: *i.e.* to say each thing in its proper place.   **iam nunc**: *just now.*

44. pleraque: *many things.*

45. promissi: *i.e.* one which has been long promised.

46. in verbis . . . serendis: in the choice of words.

47. callida . . . novum: *i.e.* to use common words in such connections as to give an impression of novelty.

48. si forte necesse est: new words may be coined in moderation and with circumspection, to express new ideas which cannot be expressed in words yet in use.   So especially Lucretius, and Cicero in his philosophical works.

49. indiciis: *signs.*   **abdita rerum**: *abstruse thoughts; rerum* is genitive of the whole ; see Introd. § 40. *c.*

50. cinctutis: *kilted,* an example of a new word.   The *cinctus* or *campestre* was a loin-cloth which in early times was worn under the toga instead of the tunic.   See i. 11. 18.   **Cethegis**: typical of the olden time ; *cf.* ii. 2. 117.

51. continget: *sc. tibi; you will be allowed.*   **sumpta pudenter**: *if used with moderation.*

52. fidem: *acceptance, credit.*

53. Graeco . . . detorta: not borrowed words (*cf. Serm.* i. 10. 20), but words formed after the analogy of the Greek.   **quid autem**: *i.e.* why should the privilege of coining new words be allowed the early poets and denied to their successors ?

55. Vergilio: Virgil was criticised for his use of Greek words. **adquirere pauca**: contrasted with *ditaverit,* line 57.

56. invideor: for *mihi invidetur ;* perhaps colloquial, or after the analogy of the Greek φθονοῦμαι. *Cf. imperor,* i. 5. 21.

59. signatum: *stamped,* like a coin.   **praesente nota**: *the current device,* or mint-mark.

60. foliis: ablative of specification.   *Cf. mutati voluntate,* Cic. *ad Fam.* v. 21. 1.   **pronos in annos**: *in annos* is from year to year ; *cf. in horas,* line 160 below ; *Serm.* ii. 7. 10 ; *Odes,* ii. 13. 14. *Pronos* gives the idea of rapid change ; *cf. Odes,* iv. 6. 39.   With the simile, *cf. Iliad,* vi. 146 f.

61. prima cadunt: a clause coördinate with *mutantur ;* there is an ellipsis in thought of something like *nova succrescunt.*

63. debemur: *i.e.* in consequence of a natural law.   **nostraque**: *and our works.*   **receptus . . . aratrum**: the reference probably is to the works planned by Julius Caesar and interrupted by his death.

They are described as they would be if actually completed. These undertakings became proverbial for difficult tasks; *cf.* Quint. iii. 8. 16, *an siccari palus Pomptina, an portus fieri Ostiae possit.*

64. arcet: *protects;* *cf.* Cic. in *Cat.* i. 13. 33, *tu, Juppiter, hunc a tuis aris ceterisque templis arcebis*, which (sometimes with the simple ablative in place of the abl. with *ab*) is the usual prose construction.

65. regis opus: *i.e.* a work like those of the Babylonian and Egyptian kings, or like those attributed to the early Roman kings. **sterilis**: *unproductive, barren.*   **palus diu**: the reference is to the Pomptine Marshes. The final syllable of *diu* is shortened before the following vowel; *cf. si mě amas, Serm.* i. 9. 38; Introd. § 57. *a.*

67. iniquum frugibus: on account of the floods; see *Odes*, i. 2.

68. facta: *deeds*, more general than *opera*, which it includes. **peribunt**: *are doomed to perish;* with the same general force as the future participle.

69. nedum: *much less.* From *nedum existimes honorem stare*, with ellipsis of the subjunctive and attraction of the infinitive into its mood and tense.   **sermonum**: *words*, in distinction from *facta.* **stet . . . vivax**: *endure and live.*

70. multa renascentur: archaic words are common in the poets, and were used to excess by the archaistic school of writers, in the time of Hadrian and the Antonines (117–180 A.D.).

71. usus: *cf.* ii. 2. 119.

72. arbitrium . . . ius . . . norma: *arbitrium quod statuimus nulla causa allata, ius facultas quam ceteri ultro agnoscunt; norma regula a nobis praescripta cui ceteri obtemperant (Orelli).*

73. res gestae . . . bella: the themes of epic poetry.

74. quo . . . numero: the hexameter, which doubtless existed before Homer.

75. versibus impariter iunctis: the elegiac distich, consisting of alternate lines of dactylic hexameter and pentameter. *Impariter* is one of Horace's new words.   **querimonia**: *i.e. dirges*, apparently the earliest use to which the metre was put, though its sphere was afterwards greatly extended.

76. voti sententia compos : *i.e.* the songs of successful lovers.

77. tamen: though the use of the metre is certain, its inventor is a matter of dispute. It is attributed to Archilochus, Mimnermus, and Callinus by different authorities.   **exiguos**: *slight*, as compared with the heroic hexameter.

79. proprio: *his own.* The iambic poetry was the special vehicle of invective, and Archilochus is believed to have been the inventor of this type.   **rabies**: *cf.* i. 19. 30 f.

80. socci: *comedy;* see note on ii. 1. 174.   **cepere**: *adopted;* *i.e.* later.   **coturni**: *tragedy;* really the buskin, or high boot, worn by the tragic actor, to add to his height and dignity. *Cf. Odes,* ii. 1. 12.   On the orthography of the word, see *Serm.* i. 5. 64.

81. alternis . . . sermonibus: *dialogue.*   **popularis strepitus**: the natural hum of a large audience.

82. natum rebus agendis: *i.e.* like the hexameter (*cf.* line 73), suited for describing action.

83. fidibus : *to the lyre, i.e.* to lyric poetry.   **pueros deorum** : *kings and heroes; cf. Odes,* iv. 2.   The reference is to hymns.

84. pugilem . . . primum: odes celebrating victories in the games, such as Pindar's.   For *equum, cf. Odes,* iv. 2. 17 f.

85. iuvenum curas: *i.e.* love songs.   **libera** : *which frees from care.*

86. descriptas . . . vices: the lines which have been drawn, as just described.   **colores**: *style, tone; cf. Serm.* ii. 1. 60.

88. pudens prave : to be taken together, *from false shame; cf. pudor malus,* i. 16. 24.

89. versibus . . . tragicis: *i.e.* in the style and metre of tragedy.

90. indignatur : a stronger *non vult.*   **privatis** : *i.e.* suited to everyday life.

91. cena Thyestae : a typical instance of a tragic subject.

92. singula quaeque : *each subject,* a summing-up of the preceding lines.   **sortita** : see note on *Serm.* ii. 6. 94.

93. et: *even.*   **vocem . . . tollit** : *cf. Serm.* i. 4. 48 ff.

94. delitigat: probably with reference to *Heaut.* 1035 f. Chremes is a common name in comedy.   In *delitigat, de-* has an intensive force, as in *deproeliari, desaevire;* the word is a coinage of Horace's.

95. plerumque : *often; cf.* line 14 above.   **sermone pedestri** : *cf. Odes,* ii. 12. 9 ; *Serm.* ii. 6. 17 ; Quint. x. 1. 81, *multum enim supra prosam orationem, quam pedestrem Graeci vocant (Plato) surgit.*

96. Telephus : the hero of tragedies by Aeschylus, Sophocles, Euripides, Agathon, Ennius, and Accius.   **Peleus** : the hero of tragedies of Sophocles and Euripides.

97. proicit : *throws aside;* for *abicit,* as in *Serm.* ii. 3. 100 ; ii. 7. 53.   **ampullas** : *cf.* i. 3. 14, and the note.   **sesquipedalia verba** : of the grandiloquent style of tragedy, perhaps with special reference to the polysyllabic compounds of the early Roman tragic poets.

98. curat: *sc. tragicus.*

99. pulchra: *beautiful*, in an artistic sense.   **dulcia sunto**: *they must have feeling; dulcia* is used of the language of simple pathos, as distinguished from the *sesquipedalia verba.*

104. male: with *mandata*, words poorly assigned, *i.e.* not suited to your position, since Horace is speaking rather of the language of the tragedy than the delivery of the actor; *cf. fortunis absona*, line 112 below.

106. voltum: *character, part*, as indicated by the mask.

108. format: *adapts, i.e.* we are capable of sympathizing with every phase of fortune.

109. iuvat: *makes us glad.*

111. motus: *emotions.*   **interprete lingua**: *through the medium of the tongue.*

112. fortunis absona: *i.e. male mandata; cf.* line 104.

113. equites peditesque: *i.e.* the whole audience, high and low alike; *pedites* seems to be used humorously, for the sake of contrast with *equites.*   **cachinnum**: used of derisive laughter, or jeers.

114. divusne . . . an heros: a finer distinction than that above, based on a difference in character, not in station.

115. maturusne senex: *cf. Odes*, iv. 4. 55. The distinction is here between differences of temperament, due to differences in age.

116. potens: *noble, great; cf. Odes*, ii. 18. 12 ; *Epod.* 2. 8.

119. famam: *tradition*, which prescribed conventional types.

120. honoratum: apparently *restored to honor*, in distinction from his situation at the beginning of the *Iliad.*   **reponis**: lit. *represent again*, since he had once been described by Homer.

122. nihil non: *everything;* litotes.   **armis**: dative, contrasted with *iura.*

123. Medea: the daughter of Aeëtes, king of Colchis, celebrated for her skill in the magic arts. She fled with Jason to Greece, and when deserted by him, murdered their two children and her rival. Her story is the subject of one of the tragedies of Euripides. In the case of Medea and the other characters of the tragedy here mentioned, Horace names their most striking characteristics.   **invicta**: *unyielding.*   **Ino**: the daughter of Cadmus and wife of Athamas. In endeavoring to escape from her husband, who had gone mad, she threw herself from a cliff, near Corinth, into the sea. The mother and child were rescued by a dolphin.

124. Ixion: notorious for his treachery, first to his father-in-law

Deïoneus, whose death he caused, and then to Zeus, who had taken pity on him and purified him from his guilt.   **Io**: the daughter of Inachus. She incurred the jealousy of Juno, who changed her into a heifer. Juno then sent a gad-fly which pursued her over land and sea.   **Orestes**: see *Serm.* ii. 3. 133 ; ii. 3. 137.

125. inexpertum : *i.e.* a new character.

126. servetur . . . constet: *i.e.* let it be *sibi convenientem ; cf.* line 119.

128. proprie communia dicere: *i.e.* to give individuality to common types of character.

129. deducis : the present indicative contrasted with the imperfect subjunctive *proferres*, seems to imply that Piso was writing a tragedy based on the story of the *Iliad.* The thought is that it is better to take the familiar characters of myth and song, and show one's originality in handling them, than to attempt to create new types of character ; *i.e.* to make new characters who shall be *ferox invictaque, flebilis, etc. ;* see lines 123–124.

131. publica materies: *i.e.* the common stock of legends and myths.   **privati iuris** : *i.e.* you can make it your own by handling it in an original manner.

132. vilem . . . orbem : *i.e.* the beaten track.

133. verbum verbo . . . reddere: *i.e.* simply translate your original, as the early Roman poets did.

134. desilies . . . in artum: *i.e.* rashly get into a tight place ; *desilies* implies recklessness.

135. pudor : *i.e.* respect for your original.   **operis lex** : *the law of composition.*

136. scriptor cyclicus: one of the so-called cyclic writers, who wrote on subjects connected with the Trojan War and the expedition of the Seven against Thebes.

137. fortunam . . . bellum : contrasted with the simple and unostentatious beginning of the *Iliad.*

138. hiatu: lit. *the opening of the mouth, i.e.* of such a high-sounding introduction.

139. parturient . . . mus: a Greek proverb.

141–142. A paraphrase of *Odyss.* i. 1–3.

143. fumum . . . lucem : the contrast between a fire which blazes up quickly and then smokes, and one which begins with smoke and afterwards burns brightly.

144. speciosa . . . miracula : *i.e.* his beautiful and marvellous tale.

146. reditum . . . Meleagri: the reference is doubtless to some cyclic writer, who sang of the return of Diomedes from Troy, and began his story with the death of Meleager, the uncle of Diomedes.

147. gemino ab ovo: *i.e.* with the birth of Helen, the daughter of Leda and the Swan ; *cf. Serm.* ii. 1. 26.

148. semper . . . festinat: *i.e.* without undue digression. **in medias res**: so Virgil begins in the middle of his story, and the *Iliad* in the tenth year of the Trojan war.

150. tractata nitescere posse: *i.e.* of being able to treat brilliantly.

151. ita . . . sic: *with this object in view*, explained by the following purpose clause. **mentitur**: *i.e.* invents.

152. primo . . . imum: *i.e.* so that it is consistent throughout.

153. et populus mecum: *and the people as well.*

154. aulaea: *i.e.* the raising of the curtain at the end of the performance. See note on ii. 1. 189.

155. cantor: probably the slave who stood near the flute-player and sang the lyric parts of a comedy, while the actor made the appropriate gestures.

157. decor: *i.e.* its fitting representation. **naturis et annis**: *i.e.* the change in temperament at different periods in life.

158. reddere voces: *i.e.* to talk, to reply in words.

160. iram colligit: a common expression in poetry ; *cf.* Ovid, *Metam.* i. 234, *colligit os rabiem.* **in horas**: *from hour to hour.*

161. tandem: *at last*, indicating his impatient desire for freedom from restraint.

162. equis canibusque: *horses and hounds. Cf.* Ter. *Andr.* 55, *Quod plerique omnes faciunt adulescentuli, Ut animum ad aliquod studium adiungant, aut equos Alere aut canes ad venandum.* **campi**: *i.e.* the Campus Martius.

163. flecti: the infinitive depends on *cereus, as easily moulded as wax.* See Introd. § 46. *a.*

164. utilium . . . provisor: *i.e* slow in learning what is best for him.

165. amata: *what has pleased him.* **relinquere pernix**: *i.e.* he changes his fancies quickly ; *cf.* ii. 1. 100.

166. conversis studiis: *with a change of taste ;* the desires of the mature man are directly the opposite of those of the youth.

167. inservit honori: *i.e.* he devotes himself to securing political preferment.

168. **commisisse**: the perfect infinitive pictures the act as completed. See Introd. § 44. *f.*

169. **incommoda**: *disagreeable circumstances*, explained by the *quod* clauses which follow.

170. **inventis**: *i.e.* the wealth which he has acquired ; opposed to *prodigus aeris*, line 164.

171. **gelide**: opposed to the *ardor* which is characteristic of the youth.

172. **spe longus**: *i.e.* clinging to his hopes, and not pushing on to their speedy fulfilment.   **avidus futuri**: *i.e.* eager for a long life, in which to carry out his plans.

173. **difficilis**: *ill-natured;* cf. *Serm.* ii. 5. 90, and the note.

174. **minorum**: *of his juniors;* cf. ii. 1. 84.

175. **venientes . . . recedentes**: the years up to the prime of life are referred to as "coming," those after as "going."

176. **seniles . . . viriles**: note the rhyme; *cf. ignores . . . loco res*, i. 12. 25.

178. **aevo**: to be taken both with *adiunctis* and *aptis*. On the position *of -que*, cf. *Serm.* i. 4. 115.

179. **scaenis**: the plural, because it is a general direction.

180. **segnius**: *i.e.* are slower to.

182. **ipse sibi tradit**: contrasted with *acta refertur.*

183. **digna geri**: *cf. Serm.* i. 3. 24.

184. **facundia praesens**: *i.e.* the eloquence of an actor on the stage, who is supposed to have witnessed the deed.

185. **ne . . . trucidet**: this is in accordance with the action in the *Medea* of Euripides, while in the *Medea* of Seneca, which was not intended for representation on the stage, the children are killed *coram populo.*

188. **sic**: *i.e.* before my eyes on the stage.   **incredulus**: *i.e.* the miracle is less easily believed if actually represented than if described. **odi**: *I dislike.*

189. **quinto . . . actu**: the division of the Greek dramas into acts seems to have been the work of the Alexandrians ; the plays of Plautus and Terence were first divided into acts by the editors of the sixteenth century, who, however, followed rules laid down by the Roman grammarians.

191. **nec**: instead of *neve;* cf. *Serm.* i. 10. 73.   **deus**: the reference is, of course, to the *deus ex machina*, introduced to bring the action to a successful *dénouement.* The device seems to have been abused by unskilful or indolent writers; hence **Horace's** injunction.

192. quarta . . . persona: the number of actors who *simultaneously* took part in the action of the Greek tragedies was gradually increased from one to three. The same actor might personate two characters who did not appear together, and additional *mutae personae* were sometimes introduced. The same was true in general of the old comedy, but not of the new.   **laboret**: *struggle*, contrary to the rules of the art.

193. actoris partis: *i.e.* the chorus should take part in the action of the play through its leader, and by representing something connected with the action, an army, a group of suppliants, *etc.* On account of the arrangement of the Roman theatre, the chorus stood upon the stage, and was thus even more closely connected with the actors than in the Greek drama.   **officium virile**: *its full duty; cf.* Cic. *Verr.* ii. 4. 81, *est aliqua mea pars virilis, quod eius civitatis sum, quam ille claram reddidit.* With *partes defendat, cf. Serm.* i. 10. 12. The function of the chorus was in general to interpret the action to the audience and to comment on its ethical bearing.

194. actus: governed by *inter* in composition.

195. proposito: *the theme, the plot.*

196-201. Note the combination of polysyndeton and asyndetic anaphora in this description of the duties of the chorus.

196. bonis faveat: the chorus usually pleaded the cause of right and justice.   **consilietur**: *give counsel;* lit. *consult for the interest of.*

197. pacare timentis: *to soothe those who fear.*

198. mensae brevis: *cf. cena brevis*, i. 14. 35.

199. apertis otia portis: *cf. Odes*, iii. 5. 23. *Apertis portis* seems to be ablative of quality.

200. tegat commissa: *keep secrets,* as the confidant of the actors. *Cf. Odes*, iii. 2. 25 ff.

201. fortuna: *i.e.* good fortune ; *cf. Serm.* ii. 6. 49.

202. tibia: Horace now considers the musical part of the drama, and sketches the development of the *tibia.*   **orichalco**: a kind of copper (Plin. *N.H.* xxxiv. 2), called by the Greeks ὀρείχαλκος. It was connected by popular etymology with *aurum*, and hence often spelled *aurichalcum.*

203. tenuis: with reference to the sound.   **simplex**: *i.e.* not double, as in later times.   **foramine pauco**: *with few holes. Pau* *cus* in the singular is comparatively rare, and seems to belong to the *sermo plebeius.*

204. adspirare et adesse : *to accompany and support.*   **erat utilis** : *was used to. Cf. flebilis* for *fletus, Odes,* i. 24. 9.

206. quo: *to which,* referring to *sedilia.*   **numerabilis** : *easily counted ;* a word coined by Horace. The Greek εὐαρίθμητος.

207. frugi verecundus : and so content with simple music.

208. postquam : with the growth of the state and the increase of luxury, the taste for more elaborate music was developed.   **urbis** : general.

209. latior : *of wider extent.*   **vino diurno** : a mark of luxury ; *cf. Odes,* i. 1. 20 ; *Serm.* ii. 8. 3.

210. placari Genius: *cf.* ii. 1. 144.   **impune** : *i.e.* without reproach.

211. numerisque modisque: *cf.* ii. 2. 144.

212. saperet: *cf.* ii. 1. 68 ; subjunctive in a dubitative question transferred to the past.   **laborum**: for the construction, *cf. Odes,* iii. 17. 16 ; see Introd. § 40. *b.*

213. turpis honesto : the lower classes were not yet separated from the senators and knights.

214. sic: *consequently.*   **motumque et luxuriem** : 'movement of limb and splendid dress' (Bryce).

215. vagus : *moving about,* instead of standing in one place as formerly.   **traxit vestem** : *i.e.* he was clad in a long flowing robe.

216. voces : *notes.* New strings were added to the original number.   **severis** : *grave ;* contrasted with the *tibia.*

217. eloquium : *language.* The language of the chorus was affected by the change in the music.   **praeceps** : *headlong, impetuous.*

219. sententia : *i.e.* its style was wild and obscure, like that of the Delphic oracle ; *sortilegis* is used in a general sense, not literally.

220. qui : *i.e.* the early tragic actor. The derivation of *tragoedia* from τράγος ᾠδή was generally accepted in ancient times, although the name is now believed to have arisen from the dress and appearance of the actors.

221. nudavit : *i.e.* the chorus laid aside their robes and appeared as satyrs, lightly clad in skins.   **asper** : *i.e.* rudely.

222. incolumi gravitate : *i.e.* the dignity of the gods and heroes was not sacrificed ; *cf.* lines 225–233.

223. morandus : *kept in his place, interested.*

224. functusque sacris : a banquet always accompanied the sacrifices, and free drinking was a feature of the Dionysiac festival.

225. ita : *with this in mind,* explained by the following purpose clauses.

226. vertere seria ludo : *i.e.* to pass from the gravity of tragedy to the gayety of the satyr-drama.

228. nuper : *previously,* not necessarily in the immediately preceding tragedy.

229. tabernas : *hovels;* the meaning is to represent the lower classes, with language to match.

230. aut . . . captet : *i.e.* in aiming to avoid commonplace language, become bombastic.

231. indigna : *not deigning.*

232. festis . . . diebus: on the *Hilaria* matrons danced. *Cf.* also *Odes*, ii. 12. 17. Dancing, except on religious festivals, was regarded as disreputable.

233. paullum pudibunda : *for a time only and with proper modesty;* note the alliteration.

234. dominantia : *current, common, i.e.* not figurative or in any way peculiar or noteworthy; a translation of the Greek κύρια. **nomina verbaque** : *cf. Serm.* i. 3. 103.

235. Satyrorum scriptor : *i.e.* if I write satyr-dramas.

236. differre: for the dative with this verb, *cf. Serm.* i. 4. 48.

237. Davus . . . Pythias . . . Simone : characters of Roman comedy.

238. emuncto : a coarse expression, taken from comedy ; *cf.* Ter. *Phorm.* 682, *emunxi argento senes.*

239. Silenus : an old satyr, the companion of Bacchus ; a common character in the satyr-drama. His language should differ from that of the slaves. *Cf.* Virg. *Ecl.* vi. 31 ff.

240. carmen : *a poetic style; cf.* Quint. x. 7. 19, *cum hanc facilitatem (extemporalem) non in prosa modo multi sunt consecuti, sed etiam in carmine.* **ex noto** : from familiar materials.

242. series : *cf.* line 46, *in verbis serendis.* **iunctura** : *cf.* lines 47–48.

243. de medio sumptis : *cf.* Cic. *Orat.* 49. 163, *verba . . . legenda sunt potissimum bene sonantia, sed ea non ut poetae exquisita ad sonum, sed sumpta de medio.* **honoris** : *adornment; cf. Odes,* ii. 19. 14.

244. deducti : *brought upon the stage.*   **Fauni** : used as synony-mous with *Satyri.*

245. innati triviis . . . forenses : *i.e.* natives of the city ; there seems to be no contrast intended between *innati triviis* and *forenses.*

246. teneris : *too refined, decadent,* contrasted with the coarse vigor of the country. Both extremes are to be avoided.   **iuvenen-tur** : apparently a new coinage of Horace ; a translation of the Greek νεανιεύεσθαι, which means 'to act like a youth,' and hence 'to act wil-fully or wantonly.'

247. immunda : *obscenities.*   **crepent** : *blurt out.* *Cf.* i. 7. 84.

248. quibus est equus et pater et res : *i.e.* the knights.   *Cf. Serm.* i. 10. 76.

249. fricti ciceris . . . emptor : the common people.   *Cf. Serm.* ii. 3. 182.

250. aequis . . . animis : *with favor.*   **donantve corona** : *award you a crown,* as in Greece ; here used figuratively.

251. syllaba . . . iambus : Horace begins his treatment of the metre with a definition of the iambus.

252. pes citus : *cf. Odes,* i. 16. 24, *celeres iambos.*   **unde** : *for which reason.*   **trimetris . . . nomen** : *the name 'trimeter'* ; *trimetris* is attracted to the case of *iambeis.*   **adcrescere** : (gradually) *to become attached.*   **iussit** : *sc. pes.*

253. cum : *although.*   **senos . . . ictus** : *six beats.*   It was called 'trimeter' as consisting of three dipodies of two feet each.

254. primus ad extremum similis : *i.e.* all the feet were iambic. **non ita pridem** : *not so very long before,* referring not to Horace's own day, but to the time of *iussit* or to the early days of the iambic trimeter.   Kiessling compares Cic. *Brut.* 10. 41, *Themistocles . . . fuit regnante iam Graecia, nostra autem civitate non ita pridem dominatu regio liberata.*

256. stabilis : *stately,* contrasted with the *pes citus.*   **paterna** : *hereditary.*

257. non ut : *not, however, to the extent that.*   **secunda . . . aut quarta** : the iambus also retained its place in the last foot.

258. socialiter : *in full partnership,* a word coined by Horace. **hic** : *i.e. iambus.*

259. nobilibus : *well-known, familiar.*

260. Note the metre of the line, which imitates the peculiarity which it describes.

262. premit : *sc. iambus,* which, through its absence, brings the charge. For the meaning of *premit*, *cf.* Liv. iii. 13. 1, *premebat reum praeter volgatam invidiam crimen unum.*

263. non quivis . . . iudex: not every one is competent to judge good poetry, hence the early Roman audiences were tolerant. Cicero, however, says of a later time, *de Orat.* iii. 50. 196, *at in his (numeris et modis), si paulum modo offensum est, theatra tota reclamant.* On the metre, see Introd. § 56.

264. indigna: *unworthy of them, i.e.* which they ought not to have needed.   **poetis:** dative ; but it may be taken with *indigna* as well, ἀπὸ κοινοῦ; see Introd. § 42.

265. idcirco: *therefore,* because indulgence has been given to others.   **vager:** *roam unrestrained; cf. vaga, Serm.* ii. 7. 74. **an:** *or rather.*   **omnis visuros:** shall I think that every one will see my faults, and therefore avoid criticism ?

266. intra spem veniae: *i.e.* not going so far as to be beyond pardon.

267. vitavi denique culpam: in that case I have only avoided blame, not deserved praise ; *i.e.* such self-restraint is no more than ought to be expected.

269. nocturna . . . diurna: *i.e.* read them night and day. *Cf.* i. 19. 11, and the note.

270. Plautinos . . . numeros: *cf.* ii. 1. 170 ff.

271. nimium patienter: *with too much indulgence.*

273. inurbanum: *coarse.*   **lepido:** *witty.*

274. digitis: the fingers were used for counting the feet ; *cf.* Quint. ix. 4. 51, *tempora etiam animo metiuntur et pedum et digitorum ictu intervalla signant quibusdam modis.*

276. plaustris: Horace appears to have confused the beginnings of comedy and those of tragedy ; for while Thespis was the inventor of tragedy, the rest of the description is appropriate only to comedy.

277. peruncti faecibus ora: this practice, which was confined to comedy, seems to have had the same purpose as the mask, — to disguise the actor.

278. repertor: Aeschylus was credited with the invention of many theatrical properties, some of which were doubtless in use before his time.   **honestae:** *decorative, beautiful; cf. honor,* line 243 above.

279. pulpita: *a stage,* which was at first temporary and of moderate size (*modicis tignis*).

280. magnum loqui: *to adopt a lofty style.* *Magnum* is accusative of the inner object.

281. successit: although the origin of comedy seems to have been as early as that of tragedy, its development was slower, and the statement of the poet is true of the old comedy.   **his**: *i.e.* Thespis and Aeschylus.

282. libertas: *freedom of speech; cf. Serm.* i. 4. 1 ff.   **excidit**: *descended.*

283. est accepta: *sc. a comoedia.*

284. turpiter: with *obticuit;* the disgrace consisted in the fact that it had been necessary to restrain them by law.

285. nil intemptatum: *i.e.* the Roman poets tried their hand at all the branches of Greek drama.

287. domestica facta : *i.e.* episodes in their national history and life.

288. praetextas: tragedies based on Roman myth and history, in which many of the characters were clad in the *toga praetexta.* We should expect the term *praetextatae,* corresponding to *togatae,* but *praetextae* is the usual form.   **togatas**: comedies representing scenes from Roman daily life, in which the principal personages wore the *toga.*

290. unum quemque : some critics believe that in this tmesis Horace is illustrating the carelessness which he censures, but *cf.* ii. 2. 188.

291. limae labor : *cf. Serm.* i. 10. 65.

292. Pompilius sanguis : the Calpurnii, the *gens* of the Pisones, claimed descent from Numa, through his son Calpus.   For the nominative instead of the vocative, *cf. Odes,* i. 2. 43.

293. multa dies : *long time;* note the gender of *dies.*   **coercuit**: *pruned; cf.* Cic. *de Sen.* 15. 52, *quam (vitem) serpentem multiplici lapsu et erratico ferro amputans coercet ars agricolarum.*

294. perfectum : *to perfection,* agreeing with *quod.*   **castigavit ad unguem**: a figure drawn from the sculptor's art ; see note on *Serm.* i. 5. 32.

295. ingenium : *talent, natural ability.*   **misera** : *pitiful,* because of the mechanical labor it involves.

296. excludit sanos . . . poetas: *cf.* Cic. *de Div.* i. 37. 80, *negat sine furore Democritus quemquam poetam magnum esse posse.*

297. bona pars: *i.e.* most poets ; *cf. Odes,* iv. 2. 46 ; *Serm.* i. 1. 61.   **unguis ponere**: *i.e.* they affect negligence in their personal appearance ; there is perhaps a reference to *ad unguem* in line 294.

299. nanciscetur : the subject is ' one,' implied in *bona pars.*

300. tribus Anticyris : see note on *Serm.* ii. 3. 83 ; although there were three towns of this name, *tribus* is very likely used in a general sense; see Introd. § 50.

301. Licino: a barber of the day, otherwise unknown. The statement of Ps-Acron and the Comm. Cruq., who identify him with a wealthy Licinius, procurator of Gaul under Augustus, has little probability. **O ego laevus**: *what a fool I am!*

302. bilem: accusative with *purgor*, which is used in a middle sense. **horam**: *season*.

303. faceret: *sc. si purgarer bilem.*

304. nil tanti est: *it is by no means worth while.* **fungar vice cotis**: *i.e.* I will teach others to write. The expression goes back to Isocrates.

305. valet = *potest*.

306. munus et officium: *function and duty; sc. scriptoris.*

307. opes: *material*.

308. virtus: *literary ability*.

309. recte: to be taken with *scribendi; cf. Serm.* i. 4. 13. **sapere**: *good sense;* a reply to the thought in line 296.

310. rem: *your subject, material.* **Socraticae . . . chartae**: *i.e.* the writings of Plato, Xenophon, and the later pupils of Socrates.

311. verba . . . sequentur: *cf.* the proverb attributed to Cato, *rem tene, verba sequentur;* Cic. *De Orat.* iii. 31. 125, *rerum enim copia verborum copiam gignit.*

312. quid debeat: *what one owes.*

314. conscripti: *sc. patris, a senator.* **iudicis**: *cf. Serm.* i. 4. 123, and the note.

315. partes: *the rôle.*

317. exemplar: *model; cf.* i. 2. 18.

318. doctum imitatorem: *i.e.* the well-trained delineator of character.

319. speciosa locis: *i.e.* with brilliant passages, although as a whole not artistic or strong. **morata recte**: *i.e.* true to life; with the characters correctly drawn.

321. valdius: the colloquial form; see note on *Serm.* i. 3. 53.

322. inopes rerum: *i.e.* without ideas. For the case of *rerum*, see Introd. § 40. *a.* **nugae canorae**: *i.e.* with polished and musical versification, but with commonplace subject-matter.

323. Grais: *i.e.* the superiority of the Greeks in literature is due to their devotion to the arts rather than to commerce. **ore rotundo**: in well-rounded phrases, the Greek στρογγύλῳ.

324. praeter laudem . . . avaris : contrasted by anticipation with the avarice of the Romans and their greed for gain.

326. dicat, *etc. :* picturing a recitation at school.

327. Albini : a usurer of the day, according to Ps-Acron.

328. poteras : the imperfect seems to express impatience, *you might have told me by this time.* See Introd. § 44. *b.*

330. aerugo : *disease,* lit. *verdigris ; cf. Serm.* i. 4. 101. **peculi** : lit. the savings of a slave, thus stigmatizing such parsimony as sordid and unworthy of a freeman.

332. linenda cedro : the unwritten sides of valuable manuscripts were smeared with oil of cedar, to keep off moths ; hence the phrase means *worth keeping. Cf.* Pers. i. 42, *cedro digna locutus.* **cupresso** : according to the Comm. Cruq., book-boxes of cypress wood were used to protect manuscripts from worms.

335. esto brevis : *cf. Serm.* i. 10. 9 f.

336. dociles . . . fideles : predicate adjectives.

337. omne supervacuum . . . manat : *i.e.* everything that is more than enough to be intelligible is lost, just as liquid which is poured into a full vessel flows off.

338. voluptatis causa : *i.e. ut delectent.* **proxima veris** : *i.e.* such as might be imagined as actually taking place ; *credible.*

339. ne : parenthetical final particle, *I say this that . . . not.* **fabula** : *a play.*

340. Lamiae : a queen of Libya, who was loved by Zeus. Hera destroyed her offspring, whereupon she became an ogress and fed upon children.

341. centuriae seniorum : *i.e.* the older men. According to the Servian constitution, those in each class who were over forty-five years old. **expertia frugis** : *i.e.* without any moral.

342. Ramnes : the young nobles. The *Ramnes* were one of the three original centuries of *equites,* consisting of young men of good family.

343. omne tulit punctum : that is, he pleases and wins the approval of everybody. On *punctum,* see ii. 2. 99. *Tulit* is gnomic perfect ; see Introd. § 44. *d.*

345. Sosiis : a well-known publishing firm of the day ; see i. 20. 2. **mare transit** : *i.e.* it is popular abroad as well as at home. *Cf.* the opposite idea in i. 20. 13.

346. longum : proleptic, *to a distant day.*

347. sunt delicta . . . velimus : *i.e.* there are some faults which we cannot avoid, for which we would ask indulgence.   **ignovisse**: the perfect infinitive has nearly, if not quite, the force of the present. This use is especially common with *volo* and *nolo*, doubtless through the analogy of the usage in laws; *cf. Serm.* ii. 3. 187, and Introd. § 44. *f.*

348. chorda : *the string*, of a lyre.

350. minabitur : *sc. ferire.*

351. plura nitent : there are more brilliant passages, *i.e.* they are in the majority.

352. incuria : the national failing mentioned in line 291.

353. humana parum cavit natura : blemishes such as are referred to in lines 347 f.   **quid ergo est** : *how is it then, i.e.* what faults are pardonable and what are not ?

354. ut : *as.*   **scriptor . . . librarius** : *a copyist.*   **peccat idem** : *makes the same mistake.*

357. multum cessat : *is often negligent.*   **fit Choerilus ille** : *is like our friend Choerilus; cf.* ii. 1. 232. *Ille* means strictly 'the well-known,' or something equivalent.

358. bis terque bonum : *if he is good two or three times;* for the use of *-que* in this expression, *cf. unus et alter*, ii. 1. 74.

359. indignor : *I am vexed*, because I expect perfection ; this is inconsistent with lines 351–352.

360. verum : *but yet.*

361. ut pictura poesis : *i.e.* poetry should be judged like a painting.   *Cf.* Auct. ad Her. iv. 28. 39, *poema loquens pictura, pictura tacitum poema debet esse.*

362. abstes : a rare word, not elsewhere found in this sense. *Cf.* Plaut. *Trin.* 264, *Mille modis amor ignorandust, procul adhibendust, atque abstandus.*

363. amat obscurum : *needs a dim light.*

364. iudicis : *critic.*

365. A picture which is to be exhibited once needs a different treatment from one which is to be seen again and again.

366. O maior iuvenum : addressed to the elder of the two Pisos, who may have shown a tendency to do careless work.

368. tolle : *take to heart; cf.* i. 18. 12.   **certis rebus** : *particular things,* such as are mentioned in the following lines.

370. abest virtute : *may not have the ability.*

371. Messallae : see note on *Serm.* i. 10. 29.   **Cascellius Aulus** : a distinguished lawyer of the Ciceronian epoch.

372. mediocribus: attracted to the case of *poetis*.

373. columnae: the pillars in front of the book-shops (*cf. pilae*, *Serm.* i. 4. 71) on which the names of the books which were for sale were posted. The meaning is that such a poet's works will not sell.

374. symphonia: *the music* which often formed a feature of a banquet. *Symphonia discors* is an oxymoron.

375. crassum: *thick*, *i.e.* not well mixed.   **Sardo melle**: the Sardinian honey was bitter. Porph. says: *Corsicum et Sardum mel pessimi saporis est.*   **papaver**: *cf.* Plin. *N. H.* xix. 168, *papaver candidum, cuius semen tostum in secunda mensa cum melle apud antiquos dabatur.*

376. duci: *carried on*, like *vitam ducere*, not parallel with *producimus*, *Serm.* i. 5. 70.

377. natum inventumque: *natum* of the inspiration which suggests the poem; *inventum* of the artistic details.

378. summo decessit: *has fallen short of perfection.*

379. campestribus armis: of the military sports in the Campus Martius; *cf.* i. 18. 54.

380. indoctus: followed by the genitive, after the analogy of *imperitus, etc.*   **pilae discive**: *cf. Serm.* ii. 2. 11.   **trochi**: *cf. Odes*, iii. 24. 57.

381. spissae: *cf.* line 205 and i. 19. 41.   **impune**: *rightly, without criticism.*   **coronae**: *cf.* i. 18. 53.

382. fingere: with *nescit* and *audet.*   **quidni**: ironical.

383. liber: opposed to *servus.*   **ingenuus**: opposed to *libertinus*; *cf. Serm.* i. 6. 8.   **census**: participle, *rated at;* the construction with the ablative is more frequent; the accusative occurs in Cic. *Flacc.* 32. 80, the only other example before Gellius.   **equestrem summam**: *cf.* i. 1. 58, and the note.

385. tu: addressed to the elder of the Pisos; *cf.* v. 366.   **invita . . . Minerva**: *cf.* Cic. *de Off.* i. 31. 110, *nihil dicet invita Minerva, ut aiunt, id est adversante et repugnante natura.*

386. olim: *ever.*

387. Maeci: *i.e.* Maecius Tarpa; see note on *Serm.* i. 10. 38.

388. nonumque in annum: perhaps with reference to the *Smyrna* of C. Helvidius Cinna. *Cf.* Catull. 95. 1, *Zmyrna mei Cinnae nonam post denique messem Quam coepta est nonamque edita post hiemem.* The numeral is indefinite; see Introd. § 50.

389. membranis intus positis: *i.e.* the poem is to be finished and then laid away for nine years. On *membranis*, see *Serm.* ii. 3. 2.

390. nescit . . . reverti: *cf.* i. 18. 71.

391. silvestris homines: *i.e.* primitive men.   **sacer**: *cf. Odes*, iv. 9. 28, *vate sacro*.

392. victu foedo: *cf. Serm.* i. 3. 100, *glandem*.

393. lenire tigris: *cf. Odes*, iii. 11. 13.

394. Amphion: son of Zeus and Antiope and brother of Zethus. He played so skilfully on the lyre given him by Hermes, that the stones moved into place of their own accord and formed the walls of Thebes ; *cf. Odes*, iii. 11. 2.

395. prece blanda: the words of his songs distinguished from the music of the lyre.

396. sapientia: predicate.

398. concubitu . . . vago: *cf. Serm.* i. 3. 109.   **iura**: *i.e.* regulating inheritance, *etc.*

399. ligno: the laws of Solon were cut on tablets of wood called ἄξονες.

400. honor et nomen: *honor and reputation*, a common combination in Latin.

401. hos: Orpheus and Amphion, and the other *divini vates*. **Homerus**: *sc. fuit.*

402. Tyrtaeus: an elegiac poet whose poems were an inspiration to the Spartans during the second Messenian war (685–668 B.C.).   He appears to have been born at Aphidnae in Attica ; but the story that he was a lame schoolmaster, whom the Athenians sent to the Lacedaemonians when the latter had been commanded by the oracle to apply to Athens for help, is doubtless an invention of later times.   **mares**: *cf.* i. 1. 64.

403. sortes: *the oracles*, such as that at Delphi, were given in metrical form.

404. vitae . . . via: by the gnomic and didactic poets, Hesiod, Solon, Theognis, *etc.*   **gratia regum . . . temptata**: referring to the lyric poets, Pindar, Simonides, Bacchylides, and the like, who had kings as their patrons.

405. Pieriis: the Muses, so-called from their birthplace, Pieria, a district in southeastern Macedonia, near Mount Olympus ; *cf. Odes*, iv. 3. 18.   **ludus**: dramatic festivals, originally celebrated at the end of the harvest, hence *longorum operum finis* (406).

406. ne . . . sit: (I say this) *that you may not be ashamed.*

408. natura . . . an arte: *i.e.* whether poets are born or made. The question is often discussed.

409. vena: *cf. Odes*, ii. 18. 10.

410. rude: *untrained.*　　**sic:** *to such a degree,* or *so true is it that.*

411. coniurat amice: *forms a friendly alliance.*

412. metam: *goal,* used in a different sense from that in *Odes,* i. 1. 4.

414. Pythia cantat: *plays at the Pythian games; cf. coronari Olympia,* i. 1. 50.

416. nunc: *nowadays.*

417. occupet extremum scabies: like our expression, 'the devil take the hindmost.' Porph. says: *hoc ex lusu puerorum sustulit, qui ludentes solent dicere: 'quisque ad me novissimus venerit, habeat scabiem.'* The last clause is rearranged by Lucian Mueller to form a trochaic tetrameter: *habeat scabiem quisquis ad me venerit novissimus.*

418. sane: *at all,* with *nescire.*

419. praeco: *an auctioneer.*

420. ad lucrum: *i.e.* to gain something from him.

421. Repeated from *Serm.* i. 2. 13.

422. vero: *but.*　　**unctum:** *cf.* i. 15. 44.　　**ponere:** *serve; cf. Serm.* ii. 2. 23. For the use of the simple verb for the compound, see Introd. § 35. *b.*

423. levi: *irresponsible,* who, on account of his *levitas,* has got into debt.　　**atris:** *gloomy, harassing; cf. atrae curae, Odes,* iv. 11. 35.

425. beatus: *wealthy as he is; cf.* ii. 2. 108.

426. donaris: future perfect.

427. tibi: dative of the apparent agent with *factos.*　　**plenum laetitiae** : because he has received the gift or counts on receiving it.

429. super his: *at these, i.e.* at verses intended to cause terror. **amicis:** *sympathetic.*

430. saliet : *i.e.* he will leap from his seat in admiration. **tundet pede terram:** stamp in indignation or delight at some scene.

431. conducti : *hired mourners* sang dirges at the Roman funerals. *Cf.* Lucil. 808, L., *mercede quae conductae flent alieno in funere, Praeficae multo et capillos scindunt et clamant magis.*

433. derisor : his real character, although he flatters his patron. *Cf.* i. 18. 11.

435. torquere mero : *cf. Odes,* iii. 21. 13; *Serm.* i. 4. 89; i. 18. 38. **laborent:** subjunctive in indirect discourse.

436. an : implying an affirmative answer.

437. sub volpe : with reference to the fable of the Fox and the Crow.

438. Quintilio : referring to Quintilius Varus, whose death in 23 B.C. Horace laments in *Odes*, i. 24. He is cited as an example of a true friend and a sincere critic.   **recitares** : iterative subjunctive ; see B. 302. 3. *a*.   **sodes** : *cf*. i. 1. 62.

439. aiebat : *he used to say*.   **negares** : protasis without an introductory word (*cf. Serm.* ii. 3. 57), or perhaps dependent on *si* in line 438.

441. tornatos : *turned*. The *tornus* was used in bronze working. If the work was a failure, the object was placed on the anvil and hammered into a mass, in order to make a new attempt.

442. vertere : *change, reform*.   **malles** : see note on *negares*, line 439.

444. quin : *to prevent you from*.   **sine rivali** : *cf*. Cic. *ad Quint. Frat*. iii. 8. 4, *o di, quam ineptus, quam se ipsum amans sine rivali*.

445. vir bonus et prudens : like Quintilius, line 438.   **inertis** : *weak*.

446. duros : *harsh ; cf. Serm*. i. 4. 8.   **incomptis** : *lacking elegance*.

447. transverso calamo : drawing the stilus across (through) them.   **ambitiosa** : *pretentious*.

448. parum claris : *obscure*, not expressing the thought clearly.

449. arguet : *censure*.

450. Aristarchus : *an Aristarchus*, referring to the famous Alexandrine critic (circ. 156 B.C.), especially noted for his work on the text of Homer. His name had become proverbial as that of a keen, but not necessarily severe critic.

451. hae nugae : *i.e.* these so-called trifles.   **seria** : *serious*.

452. semel : *once for all*, *i.e.* when he reads his poems in public, the judgment is unfavorable and final.

453. morbus regius : *the jaundice*, so called, according to Celsus (iii. 24), on account of the costly remedies necessary for its cure. It was not contagious, but the patient was probably avoided on account of his bad temper.

454. fanaticus : strictly applied to the mad devotees of the Cappadocian goddess identified with Bellona. *Cf. Serm.* ii. 3. 223.   **iracunda Diana** : *the wrath of Diana ;* the cause of the *fanaticus error*. *Diana* here stands for *luna*, which was supposed to cause '*lunacy*.' With the expression, *cf. lymphis iratis, Serm.* i. 5. 97.

455. tetigisse: the infinitive is used as **the object of** *timent*, instead of a clause with *ne*. The perfect has nearly the force of the present, but may denote the effect of having touched him. See Introd. § 44. *f*.

456. agitant: *plague;* cf. *Serm.* i. 3. 133.　　**incauti**: *careless people;* the madman was likely to turn and attack his tormentors.

457. sublimis: *with his head in the air*, and his thoughts above all earthly affairs.　　**errat**: *i.e.* wanders from the road.

459. in puteum: Thales is said to have fallen into a well while contemplating the stars as he walked. See Plato, *Theaet.* 174 A. **longum**: *so as to be heard at a distance; longum* is accusative of the inner object.

460. sit: *there would be.*

462. qui scis an: *how do you know that . . . not*, with *an* for *an non*, an expression from the colloquial language.　　**prudens**: *on purpose.*

463. Siculi poetae: Empedocles, whose act is described in the next line. See note on i. 12. 20.

464. deus immortalis haberi: according to the story, he wished the manner of his death to be unknown, that it might be thought that he had been enrolled among the gods ; but one of his bronze sandals was cast up by the volcano, and the truth thus discovered.

465. frigidus: *in cold blood. Frigidus* is contrasted by a grim jest with *ardentem.*

467. idem facit occidenti: *does the same as kill him;* a Greek construction. With the thought, *cf.* Sen. *Phoen.* 100, *occidere est vetare cupientem mori.* This is the only spondaic verse in the *Sermones* and *Epistles.*

468. iam: *at once. Cf. Odes,* i. 4. 16.

469. homo: as if he had wished to appear a god like Empedocles. **famosae**: *notorious.*

470. cur versus factitet: *i.e.* why he has been visited with this ˉˉenzy.

471. bidental: when a place was struck by lightning, sheep (*bidentes*) were sacrificed, and the place was surrounded by a low wall or curb.

474. indoctum doctumque: *i.e.* he makes no distinction of persons.

476. hirudo: *like a leech.* As often, Horace identifies the person with the thing with which the person is compared ; see Introd. § 53. *q.*